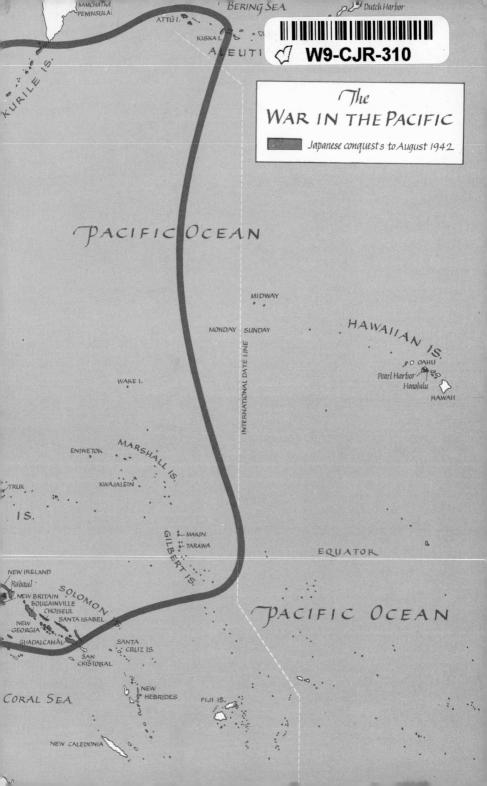

The
WAR IN THE PACIFIC
Japanese conquests to August 1942

The Rising Sun

VOLUME 2

VOLUME 2

the Rising Sun

The Decline and Fall of the Japanese Empire

1936-1945

JOHN TOLAND

RANDOM HOUSE / NEW YORK

Pictorial Layout: Wladisaw Finne

PART FIVE

The Gathering Forces

18

Of Mice and Men

1.

If 1943 was the Year of the Sheep in Japan, it was the year of the conference to the Allies, with sites ranging from Casablanca to Cairo and from Quebec to Teheran. Before the agonizing battle of Guadalcanal ended, Roosevelt and Churchill had made plans to meet their partner, Stalin, at Casablanca. It seemed the perfect setting for a momentous convocation, the name itself synonymous with mystery and intrigue, but what should have been the first memorable Big Three conference of the war began with a disappointment. A suspicious Stalin politely refused to attend, on the grounds that he was too busy holding back Hitler's legions.

And there was even pressure by American Secret Service agents to keep Roosevelt from the conference. They objected to his presence in an active war theater replete with German spies and saboteurs. But the danger itself must have appealed to the President; he had often remarked how he enjoyed escaping, if only for a few days, from the dreary politics of Washington.

Both Roosevelt and Churchill stayed at the Anfa Hotel, a modern building four miles outside the city, atop a hill, surrounded by tropical gardens and luxurious private villas, a visual paradise with bougainvillea and begonia in bloom and the brilliant blue of the Mediterranean as a background. The entire hotel area was fenced in by barbed wire and protected by an army of military police. Squads of security agents lurked around the grounds, and most of the Moroccan servants had been replaced by GI's and Tommies.

The American military leaders—the Joint Chiefs of Staff—held preliminary discussions at the hotel on January 13. Unexpected triumphs had come in the past two months on both sides of the world, and it was time to take another look at global strategy and make long-range plans for victory in Europe and the Far East. The British wanted a limited war in the Pacific; only after Hitler was defeated should full attention be turned to the Far East. The American Chiefs, spurred by the thorny Admiral King, felt that the British underestimated the Japanese, and decided to call for both offensive and defensive operations in the Pacific and Burma.

The next day they met with their British counterparts. From the first, King took the offensive; only 15 percent of Allied resources was going into the Pacific and this was far too little to keep the Japanese from consolidating their initial victories.

The British Chief of Staff, Sir Alan Brooke, with his habitual air of barely concealed irritation, replied that the Japanese were definitely on the defensive. Moreover, the situation in the West was now so favorable that victory was possible before the end of the year—but not if forces and matériel had to be diverted to places like Burma.

King retorted that Japan was still powerful, and if the Burma campaign was not pressed Chiang Kai-shek might pull out of the war. Seizure of the Philippines would probably have to wait for the defeat of Hitler, but the prompt capture of Truk and the Marianas was mandatory.

King's rugged eloquence had little effect on the British. They had come to Casablanca determined to have their own way, and moreover, had arrived elaborately prepared to get it. Anchored a few miles away was a 6,000-ton liner, their staff headquarters and communications center. It also contained "technical mechanism for presenting every quantative calculation that might be called for."

In private King urged his compatriots to be firm, and at a meeting of the Combined Chiefs on January 17 Marshall threatened the British: if the Pacific did not get 30 percent of Allied resources it "would necessitate the United States regretfully withdrawing from the commitments in the European theater." The British, somewhat shaken, countered by suggesting that operations in the Far East be limited in 1943 to the seizure of Rabaul and Burma.

King would not give up on the Marianas. There were already enough forces in the area for a campaign and it would be a waste of manpower to let them sit idle. Besides, the operation wouldn't drain off any resources intended for Europe.

The British reaction was lukewarm. Nothing should be undertaken in the Pacific that might weaken the attack on Germany. King's response was icy; it was up to the Americans alone to decide where and when to attack in the Pacific.

His words left no doubt that the Pacific was closest to the hearts of Americans. The names Pearl Harbor, Bataan and Guadalcanal stirred them more than Rome, Paris and Berlin. A reasonable compromise, taking into account this national pride (and shame) would have to be worked out.

Brooke was dejected. He feared that nothing the British could ever say would have "much effect in weaning King away from the Pacific." The war in Europe was "just a nuisance that kept him from waging his Pacific War undisturbed." At lunch he despairingly told Sir John Dill, "It is no use, we shall never get agreement with them."

The objective Dill had often acted as a buffer between Brooke and the Americans since Christmas 1941, when he became the British representative in Washington of the Combined Chiefs of Staff. "You have already got agreement on most of the points," he placated the general. "It only remains to settle the rest."

"I won't budge an inch," Brooke said.

"Of course you will," Dill coaxed him with a smile. "You know you have to reach an agreement or else put the whole thing up to the Prime Minister and the President. And you know as well as I do the mess that *they* would make of it."

By evening the planners for both sides had worked out an agreement outlining the Allied objectives for 1943 in such general terms that both Brooke and King were satisfied. It stated that "operations in the Pacific shall continue with the object of maintaining pressure on Japan" (which pleased King) but that such operations should not excessively drain resources from Europe (which pleased Brooke). However, it was the American Chiefs of Staff who would decide whether they were a drain. When Harry Hopkins read the agreement he wrote Dill: "I think this is a *very* good paper and damn good plan—so I am feeling much better."

Both Churchill and Roosevelt accepted it almost without question. Churchill was high in his praise of the Combined Chiefs and said, "There never has been, in all of the interallied conferences I have known, anything like the prolonged professional examination of the whole scene of the world war in its military, its armament production and its economic aspects."

But the differences had merely been masked by compromise; it was a bandage over a deep wound.

On the last day of the conference Prime Minister and President, basking in the hot African sun, chatted in generalities with the reporters about the course of the war. Then, without preliminaries, Roosevelt made an announcement. "The elimination of German, Japanese and Italian war power," he said deliberately and thoughtfully, "means the unconditional surrender of Germany, Italy and Japan."

It was a bombshell to everyone but Churchill, who had heard Roosevelt utter the phrase the previous day at a private luncheon attended by Hopkins and Elliott Roosevelt. Churchill had first frowned, then he broke into a grin and said, "Perfect! And I can just see how Goebbels and the rest of 'em'll squeal!"*

But it was soon apparent that Hitler and Tojo had been handed an invaluable piece of propaganda to incite their people to resist to the end. Moreover, many in the Allied camp, particularly the military, were disturbed by the pronouncement. Admiral William O. Leahy, for example, reasoned that now the enemy had to be destroyed; diplomacy had been abandoned and the Allies were set on the rigid course of unlimited war.

* Churchill later wrote Robert Sherwood that he had not heard Roosevelt use the phrase until the press conference and that he himself wouldn't have used those words. Still later, however, he admitted in a statement to Parliament that the words *had* been mentioned previously, "probably in informal talk, I think at mealtimes."

2.

In the Pacific, Lieutenant General Hitoshi Imamura decided to use the lull after Guadalcanal to his advantage and reinforce the garrison at Lae, now the capital of New Guinea, with 6,400 troops. This strategic town, some 150 miles west of Buna on the north coast, was important to the defense of Rabaul itself. At midnight, on the last day of February, a convoy of eight transports and eight destroyers under Rear Admiral Masatomi Kimura left Rabaul on a counterclockwise course around New Britain into what would soon be called the Bismarck Sea. As the ships plowed through stormy waters the next afternoon, a B-24 sighted them. The following day they were found again and attacked by twenty-nine heavy bombers. One transport was sunk and two others set afire, but the convoy continued on course.

The U. S. Fifth Air Force (formerly the Allied Air Force) in New Guinea, however, was stronger than the Japanese knew. There were at the time 207 bombers and 127 fighters in the area and General George Kenney had drastically modified his bombers as part of a revolutionary attack technique against surface vessels. The noses of B-25's had been stripped and outfitted with eight .50-caliber machine guns for strafing from as low as 200 feet. The pilots could also get down almost to sea level and release their bombs just before reaching the target. The bombs, which would either hit the ship or skip into its side, were equipped with five-second delay fuses, allowing the attackers to be at a safe distance before the explosions. Kenney had been waiting for the proper time to try out this skip bombing and Kimura's convoy was the perfect opportunity.

At ten o'clock in the morning on March 3, eighteen B-17 Flying Fortresses and twenty medium bombers made a conventional run on the transports from 7,000 feet, followed by eighteen Australian Beaufighters strafing the line of ships. Kimura was undeterred. Then a dozen B-25 skip bombers swooped in a few yards above the waves. The Japanese captains assumed they were torpedo bombers and had begun to turn their ships away when the multiple machine guns in the noses of the B-25's sprayed the troops crowded on the decks. It was slaughter. At the last minute bombs tumbled down from masthead level. Almost half the bombs, seventeen of them, found their mark.

A dozen more planes came in low. These were light bombers, but instead of launching torpedoes they, too, "skipped" their bombs and raked the decks with machine guns in their noses as they hurdled over the transports. Their bombing score was better, eleven out of twenty. Every ship was hit in the first few minutes, and either sunk or badly damaged. One destroyer went down and three others were left crippled.

The attack continued through the afternoon. The damaged ships were finished off, and the survivors in rafts and lifeboats ruthlessly strafed. The attackers were in no mood to fight a gentleman's war. They had heard too many stories from Australians whose buddies had been bayoneted after capture and left to perish with placards reading: "It took them a long time to die."*

The debacle, together with the sinking of four freighters and a tanker by American submarines, discouraged Imamura from sending further reinforcements to New Guinea by convoy. He could not afford to let that island become another Guadalcanal.

Allied troops were already moving in force toward Lae; from there they could leap across the strait between New Guinea and New Britain and launch a ground assault on Rabaul itself. MacArthur's ambitious plan necessitated an additional eighteen hundred planes and five fresh divisions.

His request called for a major reassessment of priorities, and representatives of each of the Pacific commands were summoned to Washington to participate in the Pacific Military Conference. Inevitably it revived the continuing debate over theater priorities. The Army Air Force representative did not support MacArthur;

---

* Admiral Morison wrote: "It was a grisly task, but a military necessity since Japanese soldiers do not surrender and, within swimming distance of shore, they could not be allowed to land and join the Lae garrison. . . . Several hundred swam ashore, and for a month there was open season on Nips in Papua; the natives had the time of their lives tracking them down as in the old head-hunting days." Japanese survivors of this massacre still resent reading American stories castigating their aviators for shooting Americans in parachutes while regarding the strafing of helpless Japanese as a "military necessity." Both instances, in their eyes, were military necessities.

he claimed that the Casablanca agreement gave the bombing offensive against Germany first priority. The Navy just as vigorously called for seizure of Rabaul as well as "adequate forces" to keep the Japanese on the defensive.

Unanimity was impossible and the problem was brought to the Joint Chiefs. Here the debate resumed, with Admiral King predictably championing the Pacific and General Arnold's deputy refusing to let up on the air raids over Germany. Each used the vague Casablanca decisions to support his argument. But settlement had to be reached and it was eventually agreed to limit the drive on Rabaul but prepare for the "ultimate seizure of the Bismarck Archipelago."

MacArthur accepted the compromise with uncharacteristic equanimity and set his planners to work on Operation Cartwheel. It was a complicated, yard-by-yard offensive involving thirteen separate phases. It would begin about the middle of June and conclude in December with a combined Army-Navy assault on Rabaul.

New Guinea was a point of contention at Imperial Headquarters as well. The Army wanted to defend it in force; it would make an excellent stage for massive ground operations. To the Navy, the Solomons were far more important. Its islands had many more air bases than New Guinea, and if Bougainville fell, Rabaul—and Truk itself, headquarters of Combined Fleet—would be endangered. The Army insisted that New Guinea was more significant; if it was lost, the Philippines and Java would be cut off. Strategic logic was on the side of the Navy, and it had already been proved how costly it was to send convoys to New Guinea. But the more skillful Army advocates prevailed. On March 25 Admiral Yamamoto and General Imamura each received a directive giving priority to New Guinea.

For both Americans and Japanese it was a time for planning and preparation rather than combat; in the lull each side strengthened bases and brought up reinforcements. The Imperial Navy had lost the argument, but it was Admiral Yamamoto who was ordered to deliver the first strikes against the enemy. His task was to destroy Allied air and sea power in the entire area, and he devised I-Go (Operation I), which would first concentrate on the Solomons, then New Guinea.

Early in April he moved to Rabaul with Ugaki, Kuroshima,

Watanabe, and other key members of his staff, to take personal charge of the offensive. On April 7 Guadalcanal was hit with the greatest air concentration since Pearl Harbor—224 fighters and bombers. The pilots returned, as usual, with enthusiastic reports, and as usual, little damage had been done. One destroyer and two smaller ships had been sunk, and seven Marine fighter planes shot down.

Yamamoto then turned his attention to New Guinea and launched three big strikes within four days at Oro Bay, Port Moresby and Milne Bay. Pilots reported that 175 planes had been destroyed and one cruiser, two destroyers and twenty-five transports sunk. No more than five Allied planes had been eliminated, one transport and one merchantman sent to the bottom and another beached, but the reports led Yamamoto to believe that the aims of I-Go had been achieved.

Before returning to Truk, he scheduled a one-day inspection tour of defenses in the Solomons. His first stop would be Ballale, a small island off southern Bougainville, for a brief visit with troops from General Maruyama's division who were recuperating from their ordeal on Guadalcanal. He wanted to thank them in person for their sacrifices.

General Imamura had misgivings about the tour and told Yamamoto of his own narrow escape from an American fighter plane near Bougainville. But Yamamoto was insistent; even the commander of the Eleventh Air Fleet could not dissuade him. Commander Watanabe wrote out the schedule by hand and personally took it to Eighth Fleet headquarters. He wanted the information delivered by courier, but a communications officer said it had to be sent by radio. Watanabe protested; the Americans would pick up the message and perhaps decode it. Impossible, said the communications officer. "This code only went into effect on April first and cannot be broken."

Watanabe's fears were justified. Moments after the message had been transmitted it was intercepted and delivered to Combat Intelligence headquarters at Pearl Harbor. The men in the cellar, who had helped win the Battle of Midway, labored most of the night and by dawn of April 14 had a decoded plain text in Japanese. Lieutenant Colonel Alva Lasswell, a Marine language officer, and his staff filled in the blanks and identified the code symbols for the place names. RR, for example, meant Rabaul, and RXZ was Ballale.

At 8:02 A.M. Commander Edward Layton, the fleet intelligence officer, was admitted to Admiral Nimitz' office. "Our old friend Yamamoto," said Layton and handed over the message. The admiral read that Yamamoto would leave Rabaul at 6 A.M., April 18, in a medium bomber escorted by six fighters, and would arrive at Ballale Island at 8 A.M. He looked up with a smile. "Do we try to get him?"

"He's unique among their people," Layton replied. Yamamoto was idolized by the younger officers, and by the enlisted men as well. "You know the Japanese psychology; it would stun the nation."

"The one thing that concerns me is whether they could find a more effective fleet commander." The answer was that Yamamoto was "head and shoulders" above all other Japanese admirals. "It's down in Halsey's bailiwick," said Nimitz finally. "If there's a way, he'll find it. All right, we'll try it."

Nimitz wrote out a message for Halsey authorizing him to "initiate preliminary planning." The mission was approved by both Secretary of the Navy Frank Knox and the President, and on April 15 Nimitz radioed Halsey final approval with a "good luck and good hunting."

Sunday, April 18, dawned clear and humid. Exactly two years before, Doolittle had bombed Tokyo. Yamamoto, methodical as ever, was ready. His aides had persuaded him to wear green fatigues rather than his more conspicuous dress whites. As he approached his plane, a Mitsubishi bomber, he turned to the naval commander in Rabaul, Vice Admiral Jinichi Kusaka (cousin of Nagumo's chief of staff), and handed him two scrolls to give to the new commander of the Eighth Fleet. They were poems by Emperor Meiji, copied out by Yamamoto.

The admiral's plane left Rabaul at exactly 6 A.M., Tokyo time. With him was his secretary, the fleet medical officer and the staff officer for air. A second Mitsubishi took off with Chief of Staff Ugaki and several other staff officers. Commander Watanabe watched both planes disappear, disappointed that he was not in the party.

The two bombers headed south at 5,000 feet, so close that

Ugaki feared their wings might collide. Six Zero fighters hovered protectively overhead. It was a pleasant, uneventful trip, and soon after Bougainville appeared on the left the planes began to descend for a landing at the Kahili airfield.

From the south, sixteen tightly grouped P-38 Lightning fighters from Henderson Field were approaching Bougainville at 2,000 feet. Their commander, Major John W. Mitchell, looked at his watch. It was 9:34 (an hour later than Tokyo time). They had flown more than six hundred miles over open water, extra fuel tanks strapped onto the wings, on an indirect course with only a compass and an air-speed indicator to guide them—and, incredibly, had reached the interception point at the right moment. Hopefully, Yamamoto's plane would appear in one minute. It should be about three miles to the west. There wasn't a plane in sight.

"Bogey's eleven o'clock." It was one of Mitchell's pilots breaking radio silence in a low voice. "High."

Mitchell counted eight enemy planes. Two were bombers. There should have been one. Could the four Lightnings in the "killer" group knock down both bombers? The leader of this group, Captain Thomas G. Lanphier, Jr., was also counting the Japanese planes. They looked like bursts of antiaircraft fire. He switched to internal fuel, dumping his auxiliary tanks. The Japanese came on, unsuspecting. Two miles from the coast Lanphier noticed silvery belly tanks falling from the Zeros. The ambushers had been discovered. The two Japanese bombers began diving toward the jungle.

Zeros came hurtling at Lanphier and he opened fire.

"Leave the Zeros, Tom," Mitchell called from far above. "Bore in on the bombers. Get the bombers. Damn it all, the bombers!"

Ugaki's plane was barely skimming the jungle. "What happened?" he asked the plane commander, who was bracing himself in the aisle.

"I think there is some operational mistake," he said.

Ugaki looked up and saw a tangle of Zeros and Lightnings. Where was Yamamoto? The other bomber abruptly swung off and disappeared.

Two of Lanphier's planes were already out of action; one pilot couldn't release his belly tanks and his wing man had to stay with him. It was up to Lanphier and his own wing man, Lieutenant Rex T. Barber, to shoot down the two bombers. Lanphier fought his way past three Zeros, kicked his plane over on its back. He caught a glimpse of a bomber below. He plunged down and loosed a long, steady burst. The Mitsubishi's right engine and wing flamed up.

Barber closed in on the other Mitsubishi. He opened fire and could see the bomber shudder. He continued raking the plane, and the top of its tail section disintegrated. Barber hurtled by. He looked back and was sure he saw "debris rising from the jungle." Both he and Lanphier were sure they had shot down the first bomber, Yamamoto's.

Ugaki had seen his commander's plane crash into the jungle. "Look at Yamamoto's plane!" Stunned, he pointed to a pillar of black smoke. "It's over!" His own plane shimmied from a hit in the right wing and plunged toward the sea. The pilot held back on the controls but could not stop the dive. The Mitsubishi careened into the water.

"This is the end of Ugaki!" he told himself as water enfolded him. He didn't try to struggle in the darkness. As in a dream he saw light above and felt himself rising to the surface. He gasped for breath. A wing was burning; everything else had disappeared. He was two hundred yards from shore and began swimming, using breaststrokes. Exhausted, he reached for a floatbox but couldn't hang on and only then realized that his right arm was broken. He clung to the box with his left hand and kicked his way to the shore.

The first Lightnings returning to Henderson Field did barrel rolls and those on the ground knew Yamamoto had been shot down. A message went out to Halsey:

POP GOES THE WEASEL. P-38's LED BY MAJOR JOHN W. MITCHELL USA VISITED KAHILI AREA ABOUT 0930. SHOT DOWN TWO BOMBERS ESCORTED BY ZEROS FLYING CLOSE FORMATION. ONE SHOT BELIEVED TO BE TEST FLIGHT. THREE ZEROS ADDED TO THE SCORE SUM TOTAL SIX. ONE P-38 FAILED RETURN. APRIL 18 SEEMS TO BE OUR DAY.

Halsey read the message the next morning at his regular conference. Admiral Turner "whooped and applauded." "Hold on, Kelly," said Halsey. "What's so good about it? I'd hoped to lead that scoundrel up Pennsylvania Avenue in chains, with the rest of you kicking him where it would do the most good!" He ordered the story withheld from the press. It might reveal to the Japanese that their code had been broken.*

Commander Watanabe, overwhelmed with grief, supervised the cremation of Yamamoto's body. He put the ashes in a small wooden box lined with papaya leaves. At Truk he boarded *Musashi* for the sad trip home. On May 21 the superbattleship arrived in Tokyo Bay and a radio announcer told the nation in a choked voice that Yamamoto had "met gallant death in a war plane."

His ashes were divided and put into two urns for two ceremonies, one in Nagaoka, Yamamoto's birthplace, and the other for a state funeral. The latter took place on June 5—the anniversary of the funeral of Japan's other great naval hero, Admiral Togo. A million citizens lined the streets of Tokyo to watch the cortege. Commander Watanabe, carrying his former chess partner's sword, walked right behind the artillery caisson on which the ashes were mounted. They were interred in Hibiya Park.

Yamamoto's successor, Admiral Mineichi Koga, said, "There was only one Yamamoto and no one can replace him."

The tragic death of their greatest war hero was "an insupportable blow" to the Japanese people. Moreover, it closely followed the grim announcement that the United States had retaken the Aleutian island of Attu. Propagandists attempted to present the death of 2,351 Japanese on that dreary island off Alaska as an inspirational epic that would be "a tremendous stimulant to the fighting spirit of our nation."

But the Emperor himself was deeply distressed. "In the future, please see to it that you have a reasonable chance of success before launching into an operation," he told Army Chief of Staff Sugiyama —and then unburdened himself at length in the presence of his chief aide-de-camp, General Shigeru Hasunuma. "They [the Army and Navy Chiefs of Staff] should have foreseen that such a situation would develop. Instead it took them a week to prepare countermeasures after the enemy landed on May twelfth. They mentioned something about 'heavy fog,' but they should have known about the fog. . . . Are the Navy and the Army really frank with each other? It seems as if one makes an impossible demand, and the other irresponsibly promises to fulfill it. Whatever the two

* Japanese communications officers never suspected their code had been broken. To the end of the war they were convinced it was "unbreakable."

agree upon must be carried out. If they can't accomplish what they promise each other, it's worse than making the promises in the first place. If there is friction between the Army and the Navy, this war cannot be concluded successfully. They must be completely open with each other in planning their operations. . . . If we continue getting involved in such operations it will only help raise enemy morale, as in the case of Guadalcanal. Neutral nations will waver; China will be encouraged, and it will have a serious effect on the nations of the Greater East Asia Sphere. Isn't there any way we can confront the United States forces somewhere and beat them? . . . Sugiyama was saying something to the effect that a Decisive Battle by the Navy should 'finish off' this war, but it is an impossible idea."

The fall of Attu also engendered outspoken criticism of Imperial Headquarters by high-ranking Navy officers. "We should have just pounded Attu and withdrawn from there," Vice Admiral Takijiro Onishi told a civilian friend, Yoshio Kodama—the same Kodama who had plotted with Tsuji to assassinate Prince Konoye. "But we took a foolish liking to the place and poured in too much matériel and unnecessary personnel, making it impossible to leave. There are also many islands like that in the south."

Kodama said he thought Japan's strategy was "too much concerned with outward show."

Onishi was in accord. "Just as the Army and Navy are squabbling over every trivial thing, Air Force headquarters and Fleet Administration headquarters are, as you know, at loggerheads with each other. No matter how often we point out the absolute necessity of strengthening the air force, Fleet Administration headquarters sticks to its old ideas of 'Fleet First' and can only view the overall situation in this light. In the final analysis, unless the Navy itself is driven up against the wall, it won't get around to reforming those things which should be reformed. But when that comes it will already be too late."

Onishi's rancor went beyond the general progress of the war. He felt that Fleet Administration headquarters and its outmoded ideas of "Fleet First" were overriding the more important needs of the air force. His, of course, was a parochial point of view but it reflected the growing rivalry between individual departments, civilian as well as military.

The slow but significant drop in production aggravated the situation. Losses of matériel in battle could no longer be replaced and even the minimum requirements of the Army and Navy could not be met. Not only had commanders of occupied areas failed to develop local natural resources but a mere fraction of what was produced reached the homeland because of Japan's limited merchant marine and America's devastating submarine assaults on the ships taking the long trip north.

This crippling lack of raw materials was compounded by controls that often overlapped and were inconsistent. Economic mobilization in the United States, on the other hand, was accelerating. While the output in Japan under the stimulus of war had risen one-fourth, that in America had gone up about two-thirds, and Japan's manufacturing efficiency was but 35 percent that of her enemy's. More significant, Japan's gross national product (using 1940 as an index basis of 100) had gone up a meager 2 points by the beginning of 1943, while America's had climbed to 136. Moreover, it was a well-planned expansion on all levels. The Japanese had failed to diversify. Their output of munitions had soared —but at the expense of nonmilitary items. The ten years before Pearl Harbor had seen such growth in production that the leaders had assumed they could carry on a major war without any substantial enlargement.

Confronted with reality, they made every effort to raise the general level. Within a few months, the gross national product was on the upswing. Total output showed a marked increase and production of military items climbed higher than ever. The prospect was promising, but was it too late?

Shipping remained the most crucial problem. The carefully allotted budget was upset by the fall of Attu and the secret evacuation of the nearby island of Kiska.* With these two bridgeheads in the Aleutians gone, the Kurile Islands would have to be fortified and manned. All this would divert a vast amount of shipping from the beleaguered areas in the south.

The liaison conference came to grips with this emergency in June, concluding that the Kuriles had to be turned into a fortress

---

* When the Americans stormed in to take Kiska with almost thirty-five thousand troops, they could find nothing but three mongrel dogs. This inspired a GI ballad, "Tales of Kiska," which included these lines:

It took three days before we learnt
That more than dogs there simply weren't.

even though it meant national power would suffer a loss: the production of iron would have to be lowered 250,000 tons, aluminum
6,000 tons and coal 650,000 tons.

"We are facing a grave crisis," Colonel Tanemura wrote in his
"Diary" that night. It was a crisis made more acrimonious by the
debilitating struggle between the Army and the Navy for strategic
materials. Admiral Soemu Toyoda began referring to the Army as
"horse dung." In public he declared that he would rather his daughter married a beggar than an Army man.

The debate on shipping was abruptly overshadowed a few days
later, on June 30, by the announcement that the hiatus in the
Solomons was over. Admiral Halsey had leapfrogged his amphibious force halfway up The Slot to the island of New Georgia, the
key to the central Solomons. The Japanese garrison was on the
alert, and reinforcements soon brought its strength up to five thousand, but the defenders could not repel the Army and Marine divisions that had splashed ashore. It could be no more than a matter
of weeks before the island was overrun. Then there would be little
between the Americans and strategic Bougainville.

The Emperor summoned the Prime Minister. Tojo left the audience shaken by His Majesty's "grave concern" and sent for
the man whose advice he had often relied upon, General Kenryo
Sato. His face a mask, Tojo said, "Ask the General Staffs where
they plan to stop the enemy."

"We will never get an answer," Sato replied. "Neither the Army
nor the Navy can possibly draw up a plan to stop them." Tojo was
silent but his face could no longer hide his distress.

"What happened at the Palace?" Sato asked.

"The Emperor is very worried about all this," Tojo muttered
and lapsed into silence again.

"What exactly did the Emperor say?" Sato prodded him.

The Prime Minister abruptly straightened up from his slouch
and said, "To tell the truth, the Emperor said, 'You keep repeating
that the Imperial Army is invulnerable, yet whenever the enemy
lands you lose the battle. You've never been able to repulse an
enemy landing. Can't you do it *somewhere*? How is this war going
to turn out?'"* He shrugged his shoulders as if to make light of

* In the next few weeks the Emperor expressed his displeasure a number
of times. On August 5 he upbraided Army Chief of Staff Sugiyama for the

what he had just revealed. "Well, he said something to that effect."

But Sato insisted that by uttering such words to his Prime Minister, the Emperor must have concluded that he wouldn't get a direct answer from either the Army or Navy Chief of Staff. "That's probably why he finally put the question to you. And if that's the case, I repeat, it's a grave matter. He must be losing confidence in the military."

Tojo protested that Sato went too far. "What I said now is not exactly the Emperor's words. He didn't express lack of confidence in the military. On the other hand, I do admit he was sorely troubled. I'm going to speak to Sugiyama. You talk to the Operations chief, and then we must come up with some measure. It is extremely urgent. Without saying it's an order of the Emperor, we must insist on a definite strategic plan indicating exactly where we can stem the enemy counteroffensive and where our last defense line should be."

Sato was in agreement and, moreover, added an urgent admonition: "We must also conduct our political strategy with all this in mind."

The central instrument of Japan's political aims was still the Greater East Asia Co-prosperity Sphere, and if Japan was losing the battle of production, she was winning the battle of propaganda throughout a large part of the continent. It was a policy that envisaged an Asia united "in the spirit of universal brotherhood" under the leadership of Japan, with each nation allotted its "proper place" by the Emperor; it would lead to peace and prosperity. Established in November 1938 by the first Konoye government, it had already induced millions of Asians to co-operate in the war against the West.

It had been created by idealists who wanted to free Asia from exploitation by the white man. As with many dreams, it was taken

---

series of defeats in New Guinea and the Solomons. "We can't continue being pushed back inch by inch. Constant setbacks will produce a great effect not only on the enemy but on the third nations. When are you going to wage the Decisive Battle?" "Things have gone wrong for us everywhere," Sugiyama replied. "I am deeply sorry."

Three days later the Navy was the target of His Majesty's displeasure. "What in the world is the Navy doing?" he asked Hasunuma. "Isn't there any way we can get our men to attack the enemy? They are gradually being pushed back and losing their confidence. Couldn't they somehow deal the enemy a heavy blow somewhere?"

over and exploited by realists. First came those who looked upon Southeast Asia with its wealth of natural resources as a solution to economic ills; Japan could not remain a modern state under the humiliating domination of trade by the West. Militarists also saw in its policy the answer to their most pressing need—raw materials for war—and became its most ardent champions. What had gone from idealism to opportunism now developed into an unlikely combination of both. Corrupted as the Co-prosperity Sphere was by the militarists and their nationalist supporters, its call for Pan-Asianism remained relatively undiminished in its appeal to the masses.

Colonialism with its concomitant exploitation had helped raise Asia out of the mire of its past. But by the turn of the century its historical role had been fulfilled and colonialism itself was challenged by the rise of nationalism. Woodrow Wilson's idealistic demand for the self-determination of nations after World War I seemed to apply to Asians as well as Europeans. But the promised democracy never came to the East, where colonies remained colonies; the West had two standards of freedom, one for itself and one for those east of Suez. With each year the gap between East and West widened as the Western masters, particularly the British, offered mere patchwork reforms.

Except for China, a continent that should have been ripe for revolution remained dormant; rebels of each country waited for someone else to revolt first. They no longer looked to democratic leaders; instead, their idols were dictators like Hitler, who had achieved dramatic diplomatic and military victories over England and France. All over Asia the Fascist salute and the worker's clenched fist vied for popularity.

Britain's attempts to win support from Asians in her war against the Axis were met with derision. In 1940 Dr. Ba Maw, who had been educated at Cambridge and became the first premier of Burma, warned his parliament to remember Britain's "idealistic" war aims in World War I. "With the same moral fervour she declared that in fighting Germany she was defending the smaller nationalities; she was making the world safe for democracy; . . . and she had absolutely no territorial ambitions. . . . But what was the result? What happened when the battle and the shouting were done and the victors obtained their victory? The British Empire added to itself roughly a million and a half square miles of new territory as a result of the war. What happened to the doctrine of self-determination? When I, with my usual recklessness, mentioned self-determination before the Joint Select Committee at the time the Committee was hammering out Burma's constitution, the British representatives were amused." But this seditious speech was not amusing to the British and Ba Maw was thrown in jail.

The next year the signing of the Atlantic Charter by Churchill and Roosevelt again brought a glimmer of hope to some Asian political leaders that the West had at last dropped its double standard of freedom. Hadn't it proclaimed "the right of all people to choose the form of government under which they will live"? Churchill soon made it clear, however, that the Charter did not apply to the British colonies—in other words, only to white nations.

The time, therefore, was more than ripe for wide acceptance of Japan's rallying cry for a Pan-Asia. Since the middle of the previous century, her own independence had been a constant reminder that Asians could be free. Admiral Togo's crushing defeat of the Russian fleet in 1905 had marked the emergence of Asia from Western domination and given all Orientals a sense of pride. The fall of Singapore in 1942 gave more dramatic proof that the white man was not invincible. The sight of the British retreating on all fronts was heady to Asians, and much of the continent was about ready to actively ally itself with the victors.

The glaring exception, of course, was China, where hundreds of thousands of Japanese troops were still entangled in a frustrating, endless battle. Most Japanese could not see why Chiang Kai-shek continued to fight. Wasn't it obvious that he was being used as a tool by Churchill and Roosevelt?* There were some liberal Japa-

---

* That the average Japanese saw only the idealism in the Co-prosperity Sphere was indicated by the winning slogans in a contest held by the *Japan Times & Advertiser:*

> "Japanese Action Spells Construction
> Enemy Action Spells Self-Destruction"

> "With Firmness We Fight
> With Kindness We Build"

> "Fight Onward till Asia Is Asia's Own"

> "In the Freedom of the East
> Lies the Peace of the West"

nese, however, who had always opposed Japan's occupation of China. One was Mamoru Shigemitsu, the ambassador to the collaborationist puppet government in Nanking. He was now arguing that the success of the Co-prosperity Sphere depended on a just solution of the China problem. How could Japan call for the end of colonialism while treating a large part of China like a colony? The unequal treaties that existed with Nanking should be abolished and economic aid offered without restrictions.

Tojo, who had fully supported the war in China as a militarist, saw the issue in a different perspective as prime minister, and welcomed Shigemitsu's proposal. There was stubborn resistance from Army leaders, but by the beginning of 1943 Tojo had persuaded them that the best way to get raw materials from China was to adopt the Shigemitsu plan. Arrangements were made to return the Japanese settlements in Soochow, Hankow, Hangchow and Tientsin to the Nanking government, and new treaties were negotiated. Shigemitsu was recalled to Tokyo to become the new foreign minister and in the Diet he urged again and again that *all* of East Asia be freed from military occupation and given political freedom. "For Japan it means the establishment of the 'good neighbor' policy and the improvement of our international relations."

It was Shigemitsu who had initiated this new phase of the crusade, but Tojo who led it. He announced to the Diet that Burma would be recognized as an independent state before the end of the year. In March a Burmese delegation was invited to Tokyo. It was headed by Dr. Ba Maw, who had escaped from jail just before the British evacuated Burma. The Burmese were greeted warmly. Ba Maw was overwhelmed by the surge of patriotic feeling he found on all sides. Japan was "the very vortex of the whole Asian conflict." Tojo, General Sugiyama, Admiral Shimada and Shigemitsu all struck him as true products of the "exploding Asian age, dynamic, daring, full of the new Asian consciousness underlying the concept of the Greater East Asia Co-prosperity Sphere." Tojo, moreover, was showing "astonishing farsightedness" that "positively amounted to political vision" in his determination to give independence to the occupied countries.

3.

In America the Co-prosperity Sphere was almost universally ridiculed as crude propaganda, but the author, Pearl Buck, tried to warn her fellow Americans that the spirit of Pan-Asianism did indeed run deep. She wrote Mrs. Roosevelt, a few days after Pearl Harbor, that there was "in all the Oriental peoples a very deep sense that the white man generally is, or may be, their common enemy, and that in the final analysis it remains always a possibility that the point may come when these peoples, even such present enemies as the Chinese and Japanese, may unite as colored against white. They are not now at that point, but the possibility is always in their minds. It may be best expressed by a remark made lately by a Chinese professor. 'Although the Japanese are our enemies just now, if it came to the ultimate choice, we would rather be a dependency of Japan than of the United States, because at least the Japanese do not consider us an inferior race.' The truth is that these peoples of the Orient, even those now allied with us, are secretly watchful of our behavior toward them as peoples of a different race, and if they fear at all that they will not in the long run be treated as our complete equals, they will go with us only so far as their temporary purposes are served, and then turn against us as a white race historically aggressive against them, at least from their point of view, and historically their exploiters."

She warned that an underground colored solidarity was "growing in the world as these politically awakened Asiatic peoples come to a knowledge of themselves, and unless we are exceedingly wise and careful, the result of this awakening is going to be disastrous to us. . . . We white people are for the most part ignorant or oblivious to the fact that there may develop out of all this struggle an entirely new alignment of peoples according to race and color, but the Asiatic peoples never forget the possibility, and all that they do will be done with the reservations necessary for that new alignment. I have found to my horror that there is such a reservation even in the minds of many of our colored Americans, who though they are naturally and wishfully loyal to our country, have yet because of the stubbornness of race prejudice here been led to believe, from their own experience and the propaganda of Japanese here also, that there is no hope of fairness from the white man, and that the colored peoples must unite and conquer the white man before there can be any way of getting rid of the yoke of race prejudice."*

Mrs. Buck voiced her concern publicly in an article in the *New York Times Magazine,* published a week before Midway.

. . . This Second World War has taken on a new and dangerous aspect most of all because of Japan. Although we may not be willing to know it, it is possible that we are already embarked upon the bitterest and the longest of human wars, the war between the East and the West, and this means the war between the white man and his world and the colored man and his world. . . .

In India it [the racial problem] is the burning question, whose flames leap higher every hour; in Burma it is a raging fire; in Java, yes, and in the Philippines and in China.

The main barrier between East and West today is that the white man is not willing to give up his superiority and the colored man is no longer willing to endure his inferiority. . . . The white man is a century behind the colored man. The white man is still thinking in terms of colonies and colonial government. The colored man knows that colonies and colonial-mindedness are anachronisms. The colonial

---

* Paradoxically, white skin has been a mark of feminine beauty in Japan since earliest times. There is an old proverb: "White skin makes up for seven defects." Early in the Meiji period writers began expressing their admiration for the white skin of Westerners, and in the 1920's Japan's favorite movie stars were Clara Bow, Gloria Swanson and Greta Garbo. This predilection is illustrated in Junichiro Tanizaki's novel *The Love of an Idiot.* He compares a Japanese girl, Naomi, with a Russian woman:

The latter's skin color . . . was so extraordinarily white, an almost ghostly beauty of white skin under which the blood vessels of light violet color were faintly visible like the veining of marble. Compared with this skin, that of Naomi's lacked transparency and glow and was rather dull to the eye.

Expression of this preference for fair skin and Occidental features had to be banned while Japan was proclaiming itself the "champion of the colored nations" in the battle against "whites." But the fact remained that the Japanese did not consider themselves to be "yellow." The women preferred, and still do, to call the color of their skin *komugi-iro* (wheat color); and the word for lighter shades of their own skin was *shiroi* (white). Traditionally, white was always the color of virtue; the hero in the kabuki theater, for example, always wore dazzling white make up, a popular symbol similar to the white hat of the "good" cowboy in American movies.

way of life is over, whether the white man knows it or not, and all that remains is to kick off the shell of the chrysalis. The man of Asia today is not a colonial and he has made up his mind he will never be a colonial again.

. . . In short if the white man does not now save himself by discovering that all men are really born free and equal, he may not be able to save himself at all. For the colored man is going to insist on that human equality and that freedom. . . .

Unfortunately Mrs. Buck's prophetic article had little effect on Washington. No efforts were made to counter charges of American color prejudice by Asians. On the contrary, the government was lending weight to these charges by grossly mistreating American citizens of Japanese ancestry. Immediately after Pearl Harbor, fear overran the West Coast and demands followed that all Japanese, citizens as well as aliens, be evacuated to the interior.

"I don't think it's a sensible thing to do," General John L. De-Witt, commander of the Western Defense Command, told the Provost Marshal General over the phone. "An American citizen, after all, is an American citizen. And while they all may not be loyal, I think we can weed the disloyal out of the loyal and lock them up if necessary."

Secretary of War Henry Stimson concurred, but agitation all along the West Coast grew with each Japanese victory. In California, District Attorney Earl Warren warned that unless the Japanese-Americans were evacuated promptly there might be a repetition of Pearl Harbor. Governor Charles Sprague of Oregon wired the U. S. Attorney General demanding "more thorough action for protection against possible alien activity, particularly by Japanese residing on coast." The mayor of Seattle, Earl Millikin, declared that of the city's estimated 8,000 Japanese, "7,900 probably are above question but the other 100 would burn this town down and let the Japanese planes come in and bring on something that would dwarf Pearl Harbor."

Nor was rising anti-Japanese feeling by any means confined to the Pacific Coast. In a national poll 41 percent believed that "the Japanese people will always want to go to war to make themselves as powerful as possible"; 21 percent considered the Germans militaristic by nature. It was understandable, therefore, that a consummate politician like Roosevelt would heed these voices—it was an election year—and against the advice of J. Edgar Hoover, he ordered the War Department to implement a mass Nisei evacuation. The Supreme Court upheld the legality of the act. At first the intention was to settle the Japanese-Americans in the interior, but residents of the areas selected protested so vehemently that it was considered advisable to place the "prisoners" in government camps.

A similar plan to relocate German and Italian aliens aroused such protest that the government canceled it, explaining that it would affect the nation's economic structure and lower morale among citizens of those nationalities. But there was no one to speak for the Nisei, who were citizens but usually referred to as "aliens" —their skin was a different color. Almost 110,000 loyal Americans, whose sole crime was their ancestry, were uprooted from their homes, which they were forced to sell for a pittance. They were interned behind barbed wire in "relocation centers" along the coast which were little better than concentration camps; many were even deprived of their life savings.*

Elmer Davis, Director of the Office of War Information, protested officially to the President:

. . . Japanese propaganda to the Philippines, Burma, and elsewhere insists that this is a racial war. We can combat this effectively with counter propaganda only if our deeds permit us to tell the truth. More-

---

* These actions are perhaps understandable under the pressure of war hysteria, but the postwar attitude of the government is difficult to equate with democracy. Little indemnity was paid to people who had lost their land and most of their personal possessions through no fault of their own. Damages were estimated at $400,000,000 but only $40,000,000 were paid in reparations—ten cents to the dollar.

The case of some 4,000 depositors in the California branch of the Yokohama Specie Bank is particularly shameful. The government seized all the bank's assets as "enemy property," thus freezing the life savings of these depositors. It took the Office of Alien Property until 1957 to decide to return this money—at the rate of two cents to the dollar. It was such a miserly sum that only 1,600 depositors applied for the refunds. These people appealed the low rates and a court finally ordered the OAP to pay them the rest of their savings. On learning this the other 2,400 depositors asked for their money but were told by the OPA that they had lost title to it, since they had neglected to accept the original 2 percent offer. It was not until October 24, 1966, almost twenty-five years after Pearl Harbor, that the Supreme Court finally agreed to hear their appeal. On April 10, 1967, the Court reversed the decision and remanded the case to the Court of Appeals for the District of Columbia Circuit "for further proceedings consistent with this opinion." At last, on August 1, 1969, the case was settled in favor of the depositors "approximately at the prewar rate without interest."

over, as citizens ourselves who believe deeply in the things for which
we fight, we cannot help but be disturbed by the insistent public misunderstanding of the Nisei; competent authorities, including Naval
Intelligence people, say that fully 85 percent of the Nisei are loyal to
this country and that it *is* possible to distinguish the sheep from the
goats.

But Davis' warning was no more heeded than Pearl Buck's.
Washington remained blind to the effect the Nisei evacuation
might have on the peoples of Asia. Nor was much thought given
to their postwar problems. Asia was solely a battlefield, the importance of which continued to grow in the minds of the Joint
Chiefs of Staff even in the face of persistent British resistance. On
May 8, 1943, Churchill cabled Stalin:

I AM IN MID-ATLANTIC ON MY WAY TO WASHINGTON TO SETTLE
FURTHER EXPLOITATION IN EUROPE AFTER SICILY, AND FUR-
THER TO DEAL WITH THE PROBLEM OF THE INDIAN OCEAN AND
THE OFFENSIVE AGAINST JAPAN THERE.

He was bound for another conference, this one with the Americans alone, which he had personally christened "Trident." Three
days later his ship arrived off Staten Island. The following afternoon at two-thirty he met at the White House with Roosevelt and
military leaders of both countries. He said the British had come to
Trident "adhering to the Casablanca decisions." The African campaign was about over and the invasion of Sicily was imminent. What
should come next? In his opinion, the first objective should be the
defeat of Italy. This "would cause a chill of loneliness over the
German people, and might be the beginning of their dawn." It
would, moreover, dramatically change the situation in the Balkans
and permit the shift of many British battleships and carriers to
the Bay of Bengal or the Pacific.

The time had also come, he said, to "study the long-term plan
for the defeat of Japan." Assuming Germany would be defeated in
1944, the British pledged to "concentrate on the great campaign
against Japan in 1945." In any case, the best solution to the war in
the Far East was to bring Russia in.

Roosevelt replied that a million tons of Japanese shipping had
been sent to the bottom, and if this continued the enemy's field of

operations would be seriously restricted. But for America to keep up this devastating naval offensive, it would be necessary to set up air bases in China; and that country, he warned, might collapse unless more aid was sent at once.

For nine days the conferees worked hard to come to a working agreement. The two military staffs held as many as four meetings a day; on the principal war issues six plenaries alone, attended by Churchill and Roosevelt, took place.

But Brooke, with his low threshold of patience, became more and more irritated at the deliberate Admiral King and his incessant "desire to find every loophole he possibly can to divert strength to the Pacific." Their quarrel broke out into the open on May 21 at a Combined Chiefs meeting when King insisted that "unremitting pressure" on Japan not only be maintained but extended. He wanted an air offensive from China bases within the year, as well as operations in Burma, seizure of the Marshall and Gilbert islands, New Guinea and the Solomons-Bismarck archipelago.

The British were outraged. They also refused to set a firm date for the invasion of Europe across the English Channel. The American argument prevailed, however, and at the final meeting both Roosevelt and Churchill gave approval to a channel invasion on May 1, 1944, and to "unremitting pressure" against Japan, with a face-saving proviso that the Combined Chiefs should review operations "before action is taken."

But disagreement over theater priorities was a difficult one to lay to rest. In less than three months Roosevelt and Churchill met again in Quebec at the Hotel Frontenac. Once more the Americans pressed for a major offensive in Burma and once more Churchill tried to side-step the issue by proposing, instead, a supplementary assault on Sumatra. Roosevelt would not be diverted. Such an attack would lead *away* from Japan. They should concentrate all resources on the Burma Road, which was the shortest route to Tokyo.

The debate unresolved, the Combined Chiefs retired to their own conference room, still ruffled with one another. Those waiting outside in the corridor were startled by pistol shots from inside.

"My God, now they've started shooting!" someone cried out.

It was merely a dramatic experiment. Lord Mountbatten, an avid supporter of using a new kind of ice, Pykrete, to create floating airfields, had fired his pistol into a block of ordinary ice, shattering it, and then at a block of Pykrete. The bullet caromed off, nicking King's trousers.

Mountbatten was unsuccessful in his advocacy of Pykrete, but his military capabilities were recognized and he was given the Southeast Asia Command—which included Burma.

4.

That country, which was now the responsibility of Mountbatten, was about to be granted independence by Japan. A constitution was hastily composed, incorporating both democratic and totalitarian theories. It proclaimed that Burma would be a fully independent and sovereign nation, all of whose powers were derived from the people, while asserting that she would be "ruled over by the *Naingandaw Adipadi,* or Head of State, who shall have sovereign status and power." The official slogan of the new nation was also inspired by Hitler: "One Blood, One Voice, One Leader."

Early in July Dr. Ba Maw, the obvious choice for *Adipadi,* met Tojo in Singapore. The Prime Minister had news he thought would please Ba Maw: the Japanese were turning over to the new nation most of the Shan States—located on Burma's eastern border. Two sections, however, would go to Thailand.

Ba Maw's feelings were mixed. "Neither the Burmese nor the Shans will be completely happy about the dismemberment of the Shan territory and its people." Tojo was apologetic, but Japan had promised the two sections to Thailand as a price for becoming an ally.

"But we have come in with you too," said Ba Maw, "and we also have our claims."

Tojo tried to shrug it off and jokingly promised to "pay off Burma some other way." Ba Maw turned aggressive and spoke accusingly of the arrogant and often arbitrary behavior of the Japanese soldiers in Burma.

Tojo was in Singapore for another reason: to confer with Subhas Chandra Bose, the leader of the militant disobedience campaign in India who, unlike Gandhi and Nehru, believed that force alone could lead to India's freedom. A large man—he towered over Tojo and Ba Maw—Bose was a passionate revolutionary with a charismatic personality and a gift for oratory. He had come to Singapore to recruit the thousands of Indian troops who had surrendered in the Malay campaign. They had already endorsed his crusade—the battle of freedom from Great Britain—and had accepted him as leader of the Indian Independence League in East Asia.

At a mass meeting he addressed the recruits with zeal: "When France declared war on Germany in 1939 and the campaign began, there was but one cry which rose from the lips of the German soldiers—'To Paris, to Paris!' When the brave soldiers of Nippon set out on their march in December 1941, there was but one cry which rose from their lips—'To Singapore, to Singapore!' Comrades, let your battle cry be 'To Delhi, to Delhi!' "

Tojo's promise of independence for Burma materialized on August 1. At ten o'clock General Masakazu Kawabe ordered withdrawal of the Japanese military administration. It was a bright morning with occasional spits of rain, and Rangoon was in a holiday mood. One hour and twenty minutes later, at Government House, Burma was declared to be an independent and sovereign country with Dr. Ba Maw as Head of State, and that afternoon he read a proclamation in Burmese declaring war against the United States and Great Britain. He cautioned his people, however, that there was more to freedom than cheering and celebration. "Many have wept to see this day of liberation which they had almost despaired of seeing within their lifetime," he said. "But we know that there are not only dreams, there are also realities. . . . Now that independence has come to us out of this war, we must defend it in this war. . . . Burma is definitely in the front line in the present war. . . . It is clear we must adopt a front-line policy."

On October 14 the Philippines proclaimed their independence and a week later the Provisional Government of Free India was established, with Chandra Bose as Head of State. The West failed to see the significance of these events. The new governments were puppets of Japan, but through them millions of Asians glimpsed freedom from the white man for the first time. Their enthusiasm reached a culmination when China, Thailand, Manchukuo, the Philippines and Burma sent representatives to Tokyo for the

Greater East Asia Conference early in November.* Chandra Bose attended as an observer.

"We were getting together," Ba Maw wrote, "not so much as separate peoples but as members of a single historical family containing all these peoples." José Laurel, President of the Philippines, who had secretly been charged by Quezon to pretend cooperation with the Japanese, now found Pan-Asianism irresistible. "One billion Orientals, one billion people of Greater East Asia," he proclaimed with eyes glistening, at the formal reception on the eve of the initial meeting, "how could they have been dominated, a great portion of them particularly by England and America?"

The austere setting of the conference room in the Diet Building belied the fervor of the conferees on November 5. Tables, covered with blue wool cloth, were laid out in the shape of a squarish horseshoe, flanked by three dwarf trees. As chairman, Tojo sat at the head of the horseshoe with his delegation. On his right were Burma, Manchukuo and China, and on the left Thailand, the Philippines and India.

"It is an incontrovertible fact," said Tojo in his concise manner, "that the nations of Greater East Asia are bound in every respect by ties of an inseparable relationship. I firmly believe that such being the case, it is their common mission to secure the stability of Greater East Asia and to construct a new order of common prosperity and well-being."

Wang Ching-wei, head of the Nanking government—the first of the puppets—declared: "In the war of Greater East Asia we want victory, in the construction of Greater East Asia we want common prosperity. All the nations of East Asia should love their own countries, love their neighbors and love East Asia. Our motto for China is resurgence of China and defense of East Asia."

Prince Wan Waithayakon of Thailand took the floor, followed by Chang Chung-hui, Prime Minister of Manchukuo, and then Laurel. The Filipino's emotions were evident in his voice as well as through his words. "United together one and all into a compact and solid organization there can no longer be any power

* The Indonesian political leader, Sukarno, was not invited. According to Kenryo Sato, Tojo opposed giving Indonesia independence at this time because Japan's war effort depended on her raw materials, and Indonesia was not "quite ready to handle all that treasure."

that can stop or delay the acquisition by the one billion Orientals of the free and untrammeled right and opportunity of shaping their own destiny. God in His infinite wisdom will not abandon Japan and will not abandon the peoples of Greater East Asia. God will come and descend from Heaven, weep with us, and glorify the courage and bravery of our peoples and enable us to liberate ourselves and make our children and our children's children free, happy and prosperous."

Ba Maw was fittingly saved for the last. "It is impossible to exaggerate the feelings which are born out of an occasion like this," he said fervently. "For years in Burma I dreamed my Asiatic dreams. My Asiatic blood has always called to other Asiatics. In my dreams, both sleeping and waking, I have heard the voice of Asia calling to her children.

"Today . . . I hear Asia's voice calling again, but this time not in a dream . . . I have listened with the greatest emotion to all the speeches delivered around this table. All these speeches have been memorable, moving, and—I may be exaggerating, and if so you must forgive me—I seem to hear in them the same voice of Asia gathering her children together. It is the call of our Asiatic blood. This is not the time to think with our minds; this is the time to think with our blood, and it is this thinking with the blood which has brought me all the way from Burma to Japan. . . .

"Only a very few years back the Asiatic people seemed to have lived in another world, even in different worlds, divided, estranged, and not knowing each other or even caring to know. Asia as a homeland did not exist a few years ago. Asia was not one then, but many, as many as the enemies which kept her divided, large parts of her following like a shadow one or another of these enemy powers.

"In the past, which now seems to be a very long time ago, it was inconceivable that the Asiatic peoples should meet together as we are meeting here today. Well, the impossible has happened. It has happened in a way which outstrips the boldest fantasy or dream of the boldest dreamer among us. . . .

"I say that today's meeting is a great symbolic act. As His Excellency the Chairman has said, we are truly creating a new world based upon justice, equality and reciprocity, upon the great principle of live and let live. From every point of view East Asia is a world in itself. . . . We Asiatics forgot this fact for long centuries and paid heavily for it, for as a result the Asiatics lost Asia. Now that we have once more, thanks to Japan, recaptured this truth and acted upon it, the Asiatics shall certainly recover Asia. In that simple truth lies the whole destiny of Asia. . . .

"We have once more discovered that we are Asiatics, discovered our Asiatic blood, and it is this Asiatic blood which will redeem us and give us back Asia. Let us therefore march ahead to the end of our road, a thousand million East Asiatics marching into a new world where East Asiatics will be forever free, prosperous, and will find at last their abiding home."

This was the voice of awakening Asia, and for Tojo these hours were the most satisfying of his career. He dominated the proceedings subtly, beaming paternally upon the representatives. He saw it as more than a military alliance; he too had been caught up in the Pan-Asian spirit—and his military comrades were troubled.

The following afternoon Chandra Bose climaxed the final session with a speech that rivaled Ba Maw's for emotional pitch. ". . . I do not think that it is an accident that this assembly has been convened in the Land of the Rising Sun. This is not the first time that the world has turned to the East for light and guidance. Attempts to create a new order in this world have been made before and are being made elsewhere, but they have failed. . . .

"For India there is no other path but the path of uncompromising struggle against British imperialism. Even if it were possible for other nations to think of compromising with England, for the Indian people at least it is out of the question. Compromising with Britain means to compromise with slavery, and we are determined not to compromise with slavery any more."

Affected by his own oratory, Bose could not continue. The audience waited, transfixed, until the Indian leader composed himself again. "But we have to pay the price of our liberty. . . . I do not know how many members of our national army will survive the coming war, but that is of no consequence to us. Whether we individually live or die, whether we survive the war and live to see India free or not, what is of consequence is the fact that India shall be free."

Toshi Go of the *Nippon Times* (until recently the *Japan Times & Advertiser*) called the conference a "soul-stirring reunion of blood brothers" and one of the most momentous gatherings in the history of the world.

Here, I felt, all were my brothers, not merely in a figurative sense, but literally as sons of the same Mother Asia. Japanese, Chinese, Thai, Manchukuoan, Filipino, Burmese, Indian—Asiatics all, and, therefore, brothers.

He believed, as did Ba Maw, that no matter how polite individual Westerners were to him personally, they could never really understand what it was to be an Asian.

I too have felt that only Asiatics could really understand and work effectively for the welfare of Asiatics, and I too have longed for the day when all Asiatics would be able to push aside the artificial barriers which Western intruders had set up between us and work together hand in hand for the common well-being of Asia. As I looked upon the Assembly Saturday, I felt that that day had at last come, that the ties of blood had prevailed at last, that as long-lost brothers who had found one another again we were about to restore the fortunes of our one Asiatic family.

As I noted the obvious sincerity and fervor with which all the speakers stressed this realization of oneness, which all of them apparently realized with overwhelming force, the conviction became solidly implanted in me that never again would this unity be broken. Whatever the fortunes of war, whatever the strains future problems may create, whatever the form future world organizations might eventually take, the consciousness of blood brotherhood which this Assembly had crystallized could never be dissolved. The oneness of Asia is a fact so fundamental, so elemental, so natural, and hence so inevitable that once realized, it could never again be lost.

The Joint Declaration, unanimously adopted by the conferees, called for an order of common prosperity and well-being based on justice, respect for each other's independence, sovereignty and traditions, efforts to accelerate economic development on a basis of reciprocity, and an end to all racial discrimination.*

* Tojo's adviser, Kenryo Sato, drafted the original declaration and meant what he wrote. Critics of the draft argued that his strong statement on racial prejudice might backfire, but Sato maintained that oppressive as the Japa-

It was the Pacific version of the Atlantic Charter, a promise of
the dream long held by Asians. Those who came to Tokyo may
have been puppets but, born in servitude, they now felt free and
had jointly proclaimed for the first time a Brave New World for
Asia.

5.

Two weeks later the leader of Asia's largest nation, Chiang Kai-
shek, met with Roosevelt and Churchill in Cairo to determine,
he hoped, an entirely different kind of continent. Churchill did
not welcome Chiang's presence, certain it would increase Roosevelt's interest in the Far East.

Indeed, the China problem was the first item on the agenda—
not, as Churchill and Brooke had hoped, the last. But Churchill,
who had not met Chiang Kai-shek before, was favorably impressed
by the Generalissimo's "calm, reserved and efficient personality."
However, the Prime Minister couldn't seriously regard China as a
great power and resented the attention Roosevelt gave Chiang.
"To the President, China means four hundred million people who
are going to count in the world of tomorrow," Churchill's physician,
Lord Moran, wrote in his diary, "but Winston thinks only of the
colour of their skin; it is when he talks of India or China that you
remember he is a Victorian."

The Chinese delegation left Cairo in a cheerful mood, since
Roosevelt, despite Churchill's objections, had promised an amphibious assault across the Bay of Bengal within the next few
months and, moreover, left the impression he was going to back
up the Generalissimo massively.

The three Allies disagreed not only on military priorities for
China but on the political future of Asia. Each waged a separate

nese sometimes were in their occupational policies, racial discrimination was
never practiced. "Why hesitate to use this article when it is a reality?"

At the League of Nations, the Japanese had previously attempted to insert
a racial-equality paragraph in the resolution endorsing the "principle of
equality of nations." Britain blocked the measure, and Woodrow Wilson,
chairman at the time, ruled it should not be instituted "in view of the serious
objections of some of us." Only Britain and the United States voted against
the resolution.

war for different reasons. Churchill had no thought of dismembering
the British Empire; Chiang Kai-shek was primarily interested in
eliminating the Communists and setting himself up as the sole
leader in his country; and Roosevelt was intent exclusively on bringing about the surrender of Japan as soon as possible.

Roosevelt did realize that Asia could not emerge unchanged
from the war but he could not appreciate, except to a limited degree, the admonition of such Americans as Pearl Buck and Wendell Willkie that Asia was determined to free itself from Western
domination.

On November 27 Churchill and Roosevelt left Cairo separately,
the debate on the Far East still at issue, to fly on to Teheran to
meet Josef Stalin. The Prime Minister was apprehensive as he
was driven slowly through the streets of the Iranian capital and
people began to press up to his car. Assassins with pistols or bombs
would have an easy time, he thought, and it was with great relief
that he finally entered the British legation, a ramshackle structure
very close to the elaborate Soviet embassy.

After the oppressive heat of Cairo, Teheran, lying just below
the Caspian Sea, felt colder than it was. The countryside was
bleak and dusty, studded with mud huts that had not changed for
a thousand years; Teheran itself, though an oasis in the midst of a
vast desolation, struck many of the conferees as an artificial, modern and uninteresting city.

The following morning, a Sunday, the Soviets warned Roosevelt
that Axis agents might be in the city to assassinate him, and offered
to have his headquarters transferred to a building on their own
embassy grounds. Here conferences could be held without risky
travel back and forth through the streets. Harry Hopkins and
Averell Harriman discussed the matter with Churchill's chief of
staff, General Hastings Ismay, and though they agreed it was
probably a Russian trick, they all advised Roosevelt to make the
move.* A heavily guarded caravan of cars left the American lega-

* There *was* a plan to assassinate the Big Three at Teheran. It had been
devised by SS Sturmbannführer (Major) Otto Skorzeny, Hitler's favorite commando—who had recently rescued the imprisoned Mussolini—with the help
of the Führer and Himmler. But Skorzeny could get little specific information
from the lone German agent planted in Teheran by the *Abwehr* (military
intelligence), and informed his superiors that a successful assassination or

tion, followed moments later by a single car carrying the President, Hopkins and Admiral Leahy. The driver, a Secret Service man, took a roundabout way but drove so fast that he beat the decoy presidential caravan to the Russian embassy. It was a welcome diversion to Roosevelt, and he was in an expansive mood when, fifteen minutes later, Stalin called on him. It was their first meeting. "I am glad to see you," Roosevelt said through his interpreter, Charles ("Chip") Bohlen. "I have tried for a long time to bring this about."

Through his own interpreter, M. Pavlov, Stalin apologized for not meeting the President sooner; it was his fault but he had been very busy with military matters. He was a rather slight, low-slung man who appeared stockier than he was because of his square-cut, loose tunic; with his discolored teeth, pockmarked face and yellow eyes, he reminded George Kennan of "an old, battle-scarred tiger."

They talked of Chiang Kai-shek and the Burma offensive. Stalin didn't think much of Chinese soldiers or their leadership; Roosevelt said there was a great need to educate the people of Indochina, Burma, Malaya and the East Indies in self-government. He boasted about America's good record in helping prepare the Filipinos for freedom, confidentially adding that India was a sore point with Winston—and cautioned Stalin not to bring it up.

The Big Three met a few minutes later for the first time at the initial plenary session of the conference. Roosevelt proposed that Stalin "make a few opening remarks."

"No," Pavlov interpreted, "he would rather listen."

Roosevelt welcomed the Russians as "new members of the family circle"; the Big Three meetings would be friendly and frank and the co-operation of the three nations would outlast the war by generations. "He beamed on all around the table and looked very much like the kind, rich uncle paying a visit to his poorer relatives," Churchill's interpreter, A. H. Birse, recalled.

---

kidnap operation was impossible. According to *Hitler's Plot to Kill the Big Three*, by Laslo Havas (published in 1969), half a dozen Germans were subsequently parachuted into Iran but were killed before they could carry out their mission, largely through the efforts of a double agent, Ernst Merser, and an adventurous American, Peter Ferguson. In 1970 Skorzeny wrote that he had never heard of this operation. "I honestly doubt," he added, "that the action ever took place."

The Prime Minister had a feverish cold and his throat was so sore that he could barely talk, but his eloquence was unimpaired. The people around the table, he said, "probably represented the greatest concentration of worldly power that had ever been seen in the history of mankind" and that in their hands "lay perhaps the shortening of the war, almost certainly victory, and, beyond any shadow of doubt, the happiness and fortunes of mankind."

Once more Roosevelt turned to Stalin, suggesting that, as host, he would undoubtedly like to say a few words. Stalin conferred briefly with Pavlov, who rose, looked at his notes and said, "I take pleasure in welcoming those present. I think that history will show that this opportunity which we have, and the power which our people have invested in us, can be used to full advantage within the frame of our potential collaboration." Pavlov hesitated and then added with some embarrassment, "Marshal Stalin says, 'Now let's get down to business!' "

Roosevelt reviewed the war in the Pacific, saving his most dramatic announcement to the end for Stalin's benefit: an immense invasion of Normandy, Operation Overlord, had been set for May 1, 1944.

"We Soviets welcome your successes in the Pacific," Stalin replied. "Unfortunately we have not been able to help because we require too many of our troops on the eastern front and are unable to launch any operations against Japan at this time." But once Germany had been defeated, reinforcements could be sent to eastern Siberia. "*Then,*" he said, "by our common front, we shall win." It was the first promise that the Soviets would join in the fight against Japan.

The meeting ended at seven-twenty—they had been at the large round table for three hours and twenty minutes—and the Russians served tea and cakes. The Americans were reassured by Stalin's quiet and unassuming manner, but not so the British. Admiral Leahy, who had regarded him merely as a bandit leader, admitted he was wrong; Stalin was obviously an intelligent man whose approach was direct, agreeable and considerate, if occasionally brutally frank. General Ismay, on the other hand, still felt he was "completely ruthless and devoid of the milk of human kindness," and was thankful he was "neither his enemy nor dependent on his friendship."

"This conference is over when it has only just begun," Brooke told Lord Moran. "Stalin has got the President in his pocket." Churchill, too, was glum, and when Moran asked if anything had gone wrong, he replied curtly, "A bloody lot has gone wrong."

That night at dinner the Big Three talked of many things—of France, Poland, Germany, Hitler—and unconditional surrender. Stalin questioned the wisdom of the vague pronouncement made at Casablanca; leaving it unclarified would unite the German people. "Whereas drawing up specific terms, no matter how harsh, and telling the German people that this is what they have to accept would, in my opinion, hasten the day of German capitulation."

The next day after lunch Stalin again called on Roosevelt and was handed several memoranda. One was a request for establishing bases in Siberia for a thousand American heavy bombers, and another suggested further preliminary co-operation in the war against Japan. Stalin promised to study the requests and summarily closed the subject.

The plenary that afternoon concentrated on Operation Overlord. It was Churchill against Stalin, with Roosevelt mediating, cigarette holder clenched between teeth, and often getting in the last word, even if it was irrelevant. It was bad, Brooke thought, from beginning to end. After listening to the arguments of the last two days, he felt "like entering a lunatic asylum or nursing home."

Stalin peered at Churchill across the vast table and said he wanted to pose a very direct question to the Prime Minister. "Do you really believe in Overlord, or are you stalling on it to make us feel better?"

The reply was pure Churchill. "Provided the conditions previously stated for Overlord are established when the time comes, it will be our stern duty to hurl across the Channel against the Germans every sinew of our strength." On this rolling sentence the session ended.

That evening Stalin, the host at dinner, mercilessly teased Churchill. At first the Prime Minister didn't realize his leg was being pulled. "Fifty thousand Germans must be killed," Stalin said with a straight face. Churchill pushed back his chair and stood up. "I will not be a party to any butchery in cold blood. What happens in hot blood is another thing."

"Fifty thousand must be shot!" Stalin repeated.

Churchill flushed. "I would rather be taken out into the garden here and now and be shot myself than sully my own and my country's honor by such infamy."

Roosevelt tried to smooth Churchill's ruffled feathers. "I have a compromise to propose," he said facetiously. "Not fifty thousand, but only forty-nine thousand should be shot."

Churchill stamped out of the room, with Stalin trailing behind saying it was just a joke. Churchill was persuaded to return to the table but was still suspicious. Stalin, grinning, again began to bait him. "You are pro-German," he said. "The Devil is a Communist, and my friend God a conservative." This time Churchill took it good-naturedly and before the end of the evening Stalin had an arm draped around the Prime Minister's shoulder as if they were fellow revolutionaries.

At midnight Lord Moran went to Churchill's room to see if his services were needed and found the Prime Minister talking to Anthony Eden about the postwar world. "There might be a more bloody war," he was saying in an exhausted voice, eyes closed. "I shall not be there. I shall be asleep. I want to sleep a billion years." He lit a cigar and said he had told Stalin that Britain wanted no new territory. "He rather pressed the point. You see, it would make it easier for Russia if we took something. When I asked what Russia wanted, Stalin said, 'When the time comes we will speak.'"

Churchill's pulse count was one hundred, and Moran warned him it was because of "all the stuff" he drank. "It will soon fall," said Churchill cheerfully but a moment later became gloomier than ever and stared at Moran, eyes popping. "I believe man might destroy man and wipe out civilization. Europe would be desolate and I may be held responsible." He went on in this vein for several minutes, then suddenly asked, "Do you think my strength will last out the war? I fancy sometimes that I am nearly spent."

A night's rest returned the Big Three to the equable relationship of the first day. At lunch Stalin was clearly delighted at Roosevelt's unsolicited suggestion that Russia be granted use of the warm-water port of Dairen in Manchuria. And at dinner Churchill acted as if nothing had happened the night before. Stalin, however, was ill at ease. First he sniffed the cocktails suspiciously and asked Interpreter Birse, who had been placed at his left, what they were made of. Birse's explanation "failed to allay his doubts" and he took whiskey neat. Good, he said, but ordinary vodka was better. He sat uncomfortably on the edge of his chair, dismayed by the array of knives and forks in front of him. "It is a problem which to use," he confided to Birse. "You will have to tell me, and also when I can begin to eat. I am unused to your customs."

Churchill, in a sentimental mood, announced that it was his sixty-ninth birthday party and that, in the Russian manner, anybody could propose a toast at any time. He himself began with a toast to the King, then praised his two comrades in exaggerated terms. He lauded Roosevelt for devoting himself to the weak and helpless and for preventing a revolution in 1933, and declared that the Marshal deserved the title of Stalin the Great.

Stalin's reply diverted the attention of the waiter serving "Persian Lantern," a huge ice cream pudding sitting atop a block of ice with a lighted candle inside. Absently the waiter let the platter tip, and the pudding slid off the ice onto Pavlov's head. With ice cream oozing down his hair and face and onto his shoes, the imperturbable interpreter didn't skip a word: "Mr. Stalin says that the Red Army is worthy of the Soviet people. . . ."

Stalin abruptly turned his sarcasm on the British Chief of Staff. "General Brooke," he said, staring directly at him, "has not been very friendly to the Red Army and has been critical of us. Let him come to Moscow, and I'll show him that Russians aren't bad chaps. It will pay him to be friends."

Brooke rose, locking Stalin's eyes with his own. "I am surprised that you should have found it necessary to raise accusations against me that are entirely unfounded. You will remember that this morning while we were discussing cover plans Mr. Churchill said that 'in war Truth must have an escort of lies.' You will also remember that you yourself told us that in all your great offensives your real intentions were always kept concealed from the outer world. You told us that all your dummy tanks and dummy aeroplanes were always massed on those fronts that were of an immediate interest, while your true intentions were covered by a cloak of complete secrecy. Well, Marshal, you have been misled by dummy tanks and dummy aeroplanes, and you have failed to observe those feelings of true friendship which I have for the Red Army, nor have you seen the feelings of genuine comradeship which I bear towards all its members."

Stalin's face remained inscrutable. He turned to Churchill and said, "I like that man. He rings true. I must have a talk with him afterwards."

It was another tense moment, but it was quickly over and was followed by a succession of toasts. Leahy was bored, but it amused King to see Stalin hopping up from his chair and trotting around the table to clink glasses. After dinner Stalin lingered on as if reluctant to let the evening end. Churchill approached him and, equally expansive, said, "England is becoming a shade pinker."

"That's a sign of good health," Stalin replied. "I want to call Mr. Churchill my friend."

"Call me Winston. I call you Joe behind your back."

"No, I want to call you my friend. I'd like to be allowed to call you my good friend."

Churchill was equal to this: "I drink to the proletarian masses!"

"I drink to the Conservative party," said Stalin.

For the Russians, Teheran was largely successful, since they had achieved what they most wanted, a firm date for the second front. The first meeting between Roosevelt and Stalin had also seemed to point the way to closer co-operation in the future. Although Roosevelt had found the Marshal more tough-minded than he had imagined, he was "get-at-able." As the two men parted, Roosevelt said, "We came here with hope and determination. We leave here friends in fact, in spirit, and in purpose."*

Churchill was "well content" with the military solutions reached at Teheran, but not Brooke. "One thing is quite clear," he wrote in his diary, "the more politicians you put together to settle the prosecution of the war, the longer you postpone its conclusion!"

The round of meetings was still not over. The Americans and British returned to Cairo to iron out their own major problem—

* Six months later Roosevelt told the author Edgar Snow that he had tried his utmost to convince Stalin of America's friendliness and his own good intentions. "In fact the biggest thing I accomplished at Teheran was to get Joe Stalin to see some of my own problems here. I told him, 'You know, I have troubles you don't have at all. You don't have to worry about being re-elected for instance.' . . . I also told him something about our press and how to interpret it. 'Don't get hot under the collar,' I said, 'every time Colonel McCormick or Hearst takes a crack at you. They don't represent me or my Administration and they don't represent the majority of the people.' He seemed relieved to hear that."

whether to concentrate almost everything on Operation Overlord or carry on the powerful offensive Roosevelt had promised Chiang Kai-shek.

King and Leahy led those arguing that the promise to the Chinese should not be broken. What if China dropped out of the war? This would free hundreds of thousands of Japanese troops to fight MacArthur and Nimitz. The British countered that Teheran had changed everything. Stalin's promise to join in the attack on Japan once Germany was beaten made China much less important for final victory.

On the afternoon of December 5, after more than two days of fruitless discussion, the deadlock was dramatically broken. Roosevelt sent a laconic private message to Churchill: BUCCANEER IS OFF. This was the Bay of Bengal operation, the point of contention. Churchill was so delighted that he phoned Ismay and said cryptically, "He that ruleth his spirit is greater than he that taketh a city."

A message, prepared by Roosevelt and Hopkins, and approved by Churchill, was sent to Chiang Kai-shek:

CONFERENCE WITH STALIN INVOLVES US IN COMBINED GRAND OPERATION ON EUROPEAN CONTINENT IN THE LATE SPRING GIVING FAIR PROSPECT OF TERMINATING WAR WITH GERMANY BY END OF SUMMER OF 1944. THESE OPERATIONS IMPOSE SO LARGE A REQUIREMENT OF HEAVY LANDING CRAFT AS TO MAKE IT IMPRACTICABLE TO DEVOTE A SUFFICIENT NUMBER TO THE AMPHIBIOUS OPERATION IN THE BAY OF BENGAL SIMULTANEOUSLY WITH LAUNCHING OF TARZAN [Burma operation] TO INSURE SUCCESS OF OPERATION. . . .

As 1943 drew to an end, so did the time for talk. Men on the battlefield, not at the conference table, would make the next decisions.

19

To the Marianas

1.

After Guadalcanal, world attention was centered on Europe, where the military action was accelerating. With the fall of Sicily, the drive up the boot of Italy and the surrender of that country by Field Marshal Pietro Badoglio, the Allies ruled the Mediterranean. Germany itself was being pounded from the air, at night by British Bomber Command and during the day by the U. S. Eighth Air Force. The Ruhr was practically destroyed and Hamburg had been leveled by a fire storm.

In Russia, Hitler's Sixth Army had been wiped out at Stalingrad in one of the greatest military debacles of history, and with the help of U. S. Lend-Lease and British aid, the Red Army was already storming west. By October 1943 it had recaptured some 300,000 square miles, including Kharkov, Smolensk and Orel to approach the historic gates of Kiev.

On the other side of the world, Operation Cartwheel—the two-pronged drive of MacArthur and Halsey on Rabaul—was proceeding steadily but sluggishly. These were battles of attrition and though the Japanese contested every phase, their supplies were so limited and they had so little shipping and air support that they were unable to stem the inexorable Allied tide.

Halsey's amphibious force had cleared New Georgia by mid-August. Its defense cost so many planes, ships and troops that Imperial Headquarters finally did what men like Kenryo Sato had been urging for months—ordered a cessation of all further reinforcements to the Solomons; the garrisons of each island would have to hold off the Americans as best they could, for as long as possible, and then withdraw by barge and destroyer. Against tactics born of such desperation, Halsey relentlessly continued up The Slot—to Vella Lavella, to Choiseul and finally to Bougainville, where fourteen thousand Marines landed on the first day of November. It was the last stop before Rabaul.

MacArthur was making even slower progress on New Guinea. Checked in his drive up the east coast on the twin garrisons of Salamaua and Lae, which had been sent only 750 reinforcements and an order to "stand fast," he launched a triple attack—one by ground, one by sea and one by air. While Australian and American infantrymen slogged up toward Salamaua, an amphibious force landed on the coast above Lae, and seventeen hundred parachutists, personally observed by MacArthur, dropped to the west. The parachutists and amphibious troops converged; they captured Lae in eleven days and neutralized Salamaua. MacArthur was at last in position to launch his assault across Dampier Strait to New Britain—and Rabaul.

Operation Cartwheel was moving, but its cost in time was more than expected and gave new weight to a decision made at the end of November in Cairo which was obscured by British-American disagreement on priorities: that the main thrust toward Japan should be through the small islands of the central Pacific. It would lead through the Gilbert and Marshall islands to the Carolines, and then up toward Japan itself—and would be commanded by Admiral Nimitz.

MacArthur was informed that Rabaul would be neutralized, not taken, and his drive to Tokyo—by way of New Guinea and the Philippines—would proceed as planned but with reduced priorities. But he would not accept relegation to a secondary role. The Central Route, protested MacArthur, was "time-consuming and expensive in our naval power and shipping" and *his* route could be "supported by land-based aircraft which is utterly essential and will immediately cut the enemy lines from Japan to his conquered territory to the southward."

The Joint Chiefs stood firm. The road through the central Pacific was shorter and would make it easier to isolate Japan from her domain in the south. Protracted land battles involving large forces in New Guinea and the Philippines could be avoided. The key battles would be fought on atolls and small islands which the Japanese would have to defend with limited air and ground power. The U. S. Navy, on the other hand, had superiority in carrier-based air power and could easily support landings.

Nimitiz' drive had begun with two simultaneous landings in the Gilbert Islands, some two thousand miles southwest of Pearl Harbor. On the morning of November 20, two days before Roosevelt and Churchill met Chiang Kai-shek in Cairo, GI's of the 27th Division waded up the beaches of Makin Atoll after a heavy naval barrage. There were fewer than eight hundred defenders, most of them labor troops, but it took the invaders, trained in a World War I style of combat by overage officers, four days to clear the atoll, at a cost of sixty-six dead.

At the same time, 105 miles to the south, men of the 2nd Marine Division began loading into landing craft and amphtracs (amphibious tractors) off Tarawa. The Marines joked and boasted to keep up their courage. "I should have joined the Boy Scouts," said one. "I just want to spit in a dead Jap's face," said a youngster barely old enough to be out of high school. "Just open his mouth and let him have it."

They faced a much more difficult task than the GI's at Makin. Tarawa Atoll was heavily fortified and held by almost five thousand men, more than half of whom were well-trained combat effectives: the Sasebo 7th Special Landing Force of 1,497 troops led by Commander Takeo Sugai, and the 3rd Special Base Force, a naval landing unit of 1,122 men. The atoll commander, Rear Admiral Keijo Shibasaki, claimed that Tarawa could not be taken by a million men in a hundred years and issued orders "to defend to the last man all vital areas and destroy the enemy at the water's edge."

The defense was centered on Betio in the southwest corner of the atoll, a tiny island a few acres smaller than Monaco. Shaped like a bird, its legs a long jetty, it was protected by a wide shelf of coral. The landing would take place on both sides of the jetty, and the Marines would have to storm a four-foot-high sea wall made of green coconut logs and coral; behind it were well-constructed gun emplacements and trenches.

At dawn the Japanese batteries on Betio opened fire at the approaching armada. The Americans retaliated with three thousand tons of shells. After two and a half hours the entire island was blanketed in flames and it seemed impossible that any human being could have survived the bombardment. From a transport *Time* correspondent Robert Sherrod watched a shell splash near an LST (landing ship, tank). Another sent up a geyser just off his own ship's stern. "My God, what wide shooting!" exclaimed Sherrod, who imagined the shells came from American destroyers. "Those boys need some practice." "You don't think that's our own guns doing that shooting, do you?" a Marine major retorted.

By the time the first three assault waves began slogging ashore the Japanese were out of their shelters manning the sea wall. Their steady rifle and machine-gun fire cut down the Marines, covering the beach with dead and dying who could not be removed in the devastating fusillade. The commander of a platoon of medium tanks refused to grind away over the bodies and ordered his men to back out into the sea and make a detour. Four tanks sank out of sight into potholes, their crews trapped inside; the other two were easy targets for 40-mm. guns.

Shortly after noon 5,000 Marines were ashore, but heavy casualties left them disorganized and vulnerable to night attack. Half of Shibasaki's troops were dead by dusk and his communications had been knocked out by naval gunfire. Consequently, few Japanese infiltrated American lines during the night. The following afternoon, after two more battalions landed, the Marines gained control of most of the island. Admiral Shibasaki was killed in his concrete command post, and his successor radioed Tokyo on November 22: OUR WEAPONS HAVE BEEN DESTROYED AND FROM NOW ON EVERYONE IS ATTEMPTING A FINAL CHARGE. . . . MAY JAPAN EXIST FOR TEN THOUSAND YEARS!

It took four more days before the atoll was completely secured. Almost all the 5,000 defenders were dead; only 17 Japanese and 129 Korean laborers were captured. More than a thousand Americans had died for a few acres of coral, but its capture and that of Makin marked Nimitz' first long stride toward Tokyo.

Ahead lay the Marshalls, 32 island groups and 867 reefs covering more than 400,000 square miles. The original plan had been to take the three most strategic atolls simultaneously but Marine General Holland Smith, after the resistance at Tarawa, considered this too dangerous. Admiral Spruance, the overall invasion commander, agreed. But Nimitz countered with a radical idea that dismayed both Smith and Spruance: leapfrog the first two atolls and assault the third, the heart of the Marshalls, Kwajalein. This was the largest coral atoll in the world, some one hundred islets forming a huge lagoon sixty-six miles long and twenty miles wide.

Spruance and Smith feared that a direct attack on Kwajalein would lay them open to air attack from nearby Japanese bases, but Nimitz persisted. On February 1, 1944, the main island of Kwajalein was subjected to the most concentrated bombardment of the Pacific war. Thirty-six thousand shells from naval vessels and field artillery emplaced on an outlying islet thundered down on Kwajalein. Above the trajectory of shells droned formations of Liberators which released their bombs into the holocaust. The effect was so devastating that one observer reported: "The entire island looked as if it had been picked up to 20,000 feet and then dropped."

The leap into the center of the Marshalls came as a complete surprise to the Japanese. There were 8,500 men on the atoll, but most of them were rear-echelon personnel. Only 2,200 were combat-trained; and they had no defense against American armor. Frustrated officers would beat upon the turrets with swords while their men held grenades to the sides of the tanks until they exploded. They were convinced the Americans had a secret weapon, a device that could detect metal in the dark; every time someone left his hiding place he was killed. Word spread to take off helmets and ground bayonets after dusk. They still were killed; the "secret weapon" was concentrated and steady fire power. It was a hopeless battle for the Japanese but they fought almost to the last man, as at Tarawa. It was a week before the entire atoll was secured and it took the lives of 373 Americans.

Against the advice of his own commanders, Nimitz' success at

Kwajalein inspired him to propose yet another bold operation once the Marshalls were secured: a leap of more than twelve hundred miles beyond the Carolines all the way to the Marianas. He envisaged using these islands as a base from which the new B-29 Superfortresses could bomb Japan.

His proposal was attacked from all sides at a joint Army-Navy meeting at Pearl Harbor in January. MacArthur saw it as a further diminution of his own drive to Japan, and his representative, Major General Richard Sutherland, strongly urged that all resources be concentrated instead in the southwest Pacific area. He was supported by Lieutenant General George Kenney, who considered the idea of bombing Japan with Marianas-based B-29's "just a stunt." Even a Navy representative resisted. Rear Admiral Thomas Kinkaid declared that "any talk of the Marianas for a base leaves me cold."

Nimitz was overridden, and emphasis once more shifted to MacArthur's Route to Tokyo. But in Washington, the conclusions of the Pearl Harbor meeting struck Admiral Ernest King "with indignant dismay." He wrote Nimitz: "The idea of rolling up the Japanese along the New Guinea coast, through Halmahera and Mindanao, and up through the Philippines to Luzon, as our major strategic concept, to the exclusion of clearing our Central Pacific line of communications to the Philippines is absurd. Further it is not in accordance with the decisions of the Joint Chiefs of Staff."

Early in February, Sutherland arrived in Washington to advocate MacArthur's case. Without any basis in fact, he told the Joint Chiefs that Nimitz' plans were "relatively weak and slow of progress." MacArthur could be in Mindanao by December if given the resources.

King had no intention of handing over more naval forces to the southwest Pacific theater. With some sarcasm he said that MacArthur had "apparently not accepted" the Cairo decision "and desires a commitment to an advance along a single axis. I do not think that this is a propitious time to change our agreed strategy."

To avoid turning a strategic debate into a personal one, General Marshall suggested that the Joint Strategic Survey Committee study the matter again and report on which route to Japan was preferable. The committee recommendation came back almost immediately: the Central Route should be given priority "with

operations in the Southwest Pacific cooperating with and supporting that effort."

MacArthur's role would have been permanently diminished had
it not been for the fact that his old antagonist, Marshall, too, was
dissatisfied with the committee's conclusions, and after a month's
discussion, the Joint Chiefs emerged with a compromise between
the central Pacific and southwest Pacific concepts of strategy. On
March 12 they issued a directive to Nimitz and MacArthur ordering the former to occupy the Marianas by June 15 and the latter
to invade Mindanao with the support of the Pacific Fleet exactly
five months later.

2.

The new American thrusts had forced Imperial Headquarters
to readjust their defenses. The desperate scramble of the Army
and Navy for appropriations, strategic materials and factories centered on plane production, since both services agreed that the way
to victory lay in the air. They agreed to share equally the 45,000
planes to be produced the following year. But a month later, in
early January 1944, the Navy requested more than their allotment
—26,000 planes.

The Navy's case was persuasive and Tojo acquiesced. "This is
too great a problem to settle so quickly," protested his friend and
adviser, Kenryo Sato. Until this time the Supreme Command had
depended on the Navy to win the Decisive Battle against America
on the seas, but now that dream was over. Henceforth the Army
would have to play the major role, and the small islands that lay
between the advancing Americans and Japan would have to be
the "unsinkable carriers," bases for future land battles. The majority of planes, therefore, would have to go to the service that fought
these battles, the Army.

Tojo realized that his first decision had been prompted by a
desire to keep peace with the Navy. Sato was obviously right and
Tojo told him to inform the Navy of the change in priorities. The
Navy, in turn, refused to accept the reversed decision. On February 10 the battle was openly joined at a meeting of the Chiefs
of Staffs and their advisers at the Palace. Admiral Nagano main-

tained that the crucial battles with the enemy would still take place
at sea. He was challenged by Army Chief of Staff Sugiyama, who
had been promoted to field marshal. "If we gave you all the planes
you want, would this battle turn the tide of war?"

Nagano bristled. "Of course I can't guarantee anything of the
kind! Can *you* guarantee that if we gave you all the planes, you
would turn the tide?"

Distracted by a suggestion from Admiral Oka that they all take
a break for tea, the antagonists calmed down, but the problem remained unsolved until Sato came up with an ingenious if
questionable solution: concentrate production on fighters to the
exclusion of bombers. Then an additional 5,000 planes, a total
of 50,000 for equal distribution, could be manufactured, only
1,000 shy of the Navy's demand for 26,000 planes. To make up
for this deficit, Sato offered 3,500 tons of aluminum. The Navy
accepted.

The tempest was over but not the military problems which had
aggravated it. The American advance through the central Pacific
continued unchecked. On February 17 Nimitz' amphibious force
leapfrogged from Kwajalein to the Eniwetok islands at the western
limit of the Marshalls, by-passing four atolls where the Japanese
had air bases. That same day and the next, American carrier planes
also attacked Truk in the Carolines, the home of Combined Fleet,
destroying seventy planes on the ground and sinking two auxiliary
cruisers, a destroyer, an aircraft ferry, two submarine tenders and
twenty-three merchant ships—200,000 tons of shipping in all.

These successive disasters prompted Sato to give Tojo some
more unsolicited advice: "We should withdraw to the Philippines,
and there gamble on the final decisive battle."

"Is that the opinion of the General Staff?" Tojo asked grimly.

"No, it is my personal opinion."

"Did you consult the General Staff?"

"That's just the point: the General Staff would certainly oppose
such a plan. It's my conviction that we should simply override
the military." And the first thing to do was abandon the Carolines
and the Marianas and fall back to the Philippines.

Tojo got red in the face. "Last year at an imperial conference
we made the Marianas and Carolines our last defense line! Do

you mean to say that six months later we should give them up without a single fight?"

Sato held his ground. There were only seven airfields in that area and they could easily be neutralized by the Americans before any invasion. But in the Philippines there were hundreds of islands that could be used as bases. "This should be the last battlefield of the war, since if that battle is lost, we won't be able to fight another. That's why we should concentrate all our efforts on one last struggle—and then start a peace offensive." By "peace" he meant to settle for any conditions that would let Japan retain her honor.

Tojo interrupted him. "Don't ever again mention the phrase 'peace offensive.' If you or I ever breathed the words 'wa' or 'wahei' [peace] the morale of our troops would deteriorate."

Sato left, encouraged by the Prime Minister's sympathetic reaction, but his counsel helped lead to an unexpected consequence. Later that evening Tojo suggested to Chief of Staff Sugiyama that he resign. In this "critical situation," Tojo explained, it would be best if he himself concurrently held the posts of war minister and chief of staff.

"That would be a violation of our long tradition," Sugiyama protested. One man shouldn't be responsible for both political and military decisions. The catastrophe at Stalingrad, he pointed out, had resulted from Hitler's concentration of power.

"Führer Hitler was an enlisted man," said Tojo. "I am a general." He assured the marshal that he had been giving as much thought to military affairs as political. "You don't have to worry on that score."

"That's easy to say, but when one man handles two jobs and is torn by a conflict of interest between them, to which does he give the greater importance?" Moreover, it would establish a dangerous precedent for the future.

"In such an unprecedented and widespread war as this, we must take every measure even if it means breaking precedent."

Sugiyama was losing his patience. "If you do this, it will be impossible to maintain order in the Army!"

"That won't happen" was the tight-lipped answer. "If anyone complains, we'll replace him. No objections will be allowed."

The following day, February 21, Tojo relieved Sugiyama as Army Chief of Staff and took the post himself; he also replaced Navy Chief of Staff Nagano with Navy Minister Shigetaro Shimada. The four most important military posts in the nation were now concentrated in the hands of two men.

Sato burst into Tojo's office shouting, "Mr. Prime Minister, what you have done is tremendous!" Tojo was already wearing the braid of the chief of staff. Since becoming prime minister he had discovered that the independence of the Supreme Command was a "big factor" in Japan's military reversals. He was obviously pleased by Sato's reaction and permitted himself a brief smile. "If some of the young officers cause any disturbance about this," he said sternly, "I will not let them get away with it." *Gekokujo* would not be tolerated. "Keep an eye on them."

For the next few hours Sato was engrossed in plans for the last decisive battle in the Philippines. He was interrupted by a phone call from Tojo, who spoke in his new role as chief of staff. "I am going to defend the Marianas and Carolines," he announced curtly.

Tojo's arbitrary consolidation of power, which he and Sato regarded as a curb on the autocratic control of the military, was interpreted by others as a dangerous step toward military dictatorship. Prince Chichibu, the eldest of the Emperor's three brothers, did not believe the same man should be prime minister, war minister and chief of staff. Like Sugiyama, he put this question to Tojo: "What will you do when the General Staff and the War Ministry do not agree on the conduct of war?" Tojo angrily replied in writing: "The most important thing before us at this stage is to achieve victory with all our national resources. So I'll thank you to discuss personal affairs after the war is over. . . . As for the current move, it is only natural that there be much criticism and opposition, since the measure is an unprecedented one. Let us leave it to future historians to determine the right or wrong of this step. Actually, the co-operation between the high command and the government is going very well and there is no trouble at all. My conscience would never let me violate the basic principle of the fundamental character of Japan. If you have any questions on this point, I'll be glad to answer them. If I should ever feel that

I am no longer loyal to the Emperor, I will offer my sincere apology and commit hara-kiri in his presence."*

The *jushin* (the former premiers) shared Prince Chichibu's concern. To them, moreover, Tojo's leadership was responsible for Japan's plight. They all wanted Tojo removed as prime minister, and two of their number, Prince Konoye and Admiral Okada, went further—his replacement must be a man who would make immediate peace overtures to the Allies. Konoye tried to enlist Marquis Kido in the cause for peace. The Privy Seal was sympathetic but refused to help; privately he thought it would be precipitous to use his influence on the Emperor.

There were even those in the military working for peace, but for different reasons. The most important was Rear Admiral Sokichi Takagi, a brilliant research expert who had been ordered by Admiral Shimada to conduct a thorough study of the mistakes made in the war as reflected in top-secret files. His analysis of air and shipping losses led him to the inevitable conclusion that Japan could not win the war. Appalled by the extent of the collapse in the Pacific, he saw as the only solution Tojo's dismissal and an immediate quest for peace no matter what the consequences.

Takagi feared that if he submitted this information to Shimada, his own life would be endangered—and the report itself shelved. He met in secret with former Navy Minister Admiral Mitsumasa Yonai and Vice Admiral Shigeyoshi Inoue, both advocates of peace, and told them what he had uncovered. They encouraged him to share his findings with Admiral Okada and others who were in a better position to act. But weeks passed and Tojo still remained in office. Impatient, Takagi assembled half a dozen Navy men he could trust—commanders and captains—and persuaded them that the nation could not survive unless they assassinated Tojo. But how should it be done? Surreptitious inquiries were

* In the Diet the previous year, Tojo had denied that his regime was a dictatorship: "People ofter refer to this as a dictatorial government, but I should like to make the matter clear . . . The man called Tojo is no more than a single humble subject. I am just the same as you. The sole difference is that I have been given the responsibility of being prime minister. To this extent I am different. It is only when I am exposed to the light of His Majesty that I shine. Were it not for this light, I would be no better than a pebble by the roadside. It is because I enjoy the confidence of His Majesty and occupy my present position that I shine. This puts me in a completely different category from those European rulers who are known as dictators."

made to right-wing organizations (experts on assassination). On the basis of their suggestions and personal investigation of Tojo's daily routine, Takagi concluded that an automobile "accident" would ensure success with such a prominent target. The assassins, in three cars, would intercept a Tojo motorcade. One vehicle would crash into Tojo's car, bringing it to a halt; the other two would pull alongside and gun down the Prime Minister with automatic revolvers. The conspirators would all wear uniforms. The others would escape to Formosa in a Navy plane, but Takagi would remain behind and take all the responsibility.*

Ironically, Tojo himself had begun the search for peace. Before the fall of Singapore he had been involved in an attempt to negotiate with the Allies. On February 12, 1942, he was summoned to the Palace and instructed by the Emperor (at Kido's prompting) "not to miss any opportunity to terminate the war." Tojo sent for the German ambassador, General Eugen Ott, and made him promise not to reveal what he would hear to anyone but Ribbentrop and Hitler: Tojo suggested that Germany and Japan secretly approach the Allies with an offer of peace; he would fly to Berlin to represent the empire personally, if Hitler would send a long-range bomber. The reply from Berlin was polite but lukewarm. Hitler could not take the risk of Tojo crashing in a German plane.

---

* Another assassination attempt by an elite group of fifty aviation technocrats had already failed. These young men dealt with the research and production of Army planes. Just before Pearl Harbor they had sent an appeal to Tojo to delay war for twenty years, until Japan would be properly prepared to engage a major power. Tojo listened to their arguments in a private meeting and promised to give them two decades to build up the air force. Consequently, when war came they held Tojo personally responsible. Within six months their fears about the issue of the war were confirmed by technical setbacks: for example, machine tools were losing their precision, and defects in plane design would take years to correct. During the battle for Guadalcanal, Tojo told these technical experts to devise some way to fly planes without gas, suggesting they use "something like air." They laughed aloud until they realized he was serious, then unanimously pledged themselves to a program for peace. They went to Prince Konoye with their demands and later to Tojo himself. The subsequent reprimand incited the fifteen most headstrong to vow to assassinate Tojo. One evening their leader, First Lieutenant Hiroshi Sato, after drinking too much *sake,* quarreled with their commanding officer and blurted out, "A man like Tojo should be killed." *Kempei* investigated the group, but the only one punished was Sato; he was given a week's confinement on a drunk charge. The ringleaders, however, were all sent to the front.

Tojo was discouraged by the German lack of enthusiasm but was not averse to further efforts in the same direction, although he was naïve about how peace might be achieved. On Ambassador Kurusu's return from America later that summer (the Japanese diplomats in Washington were exchanged for Grew and his subordinates), Tojo took him aside at a party given in the diplomat's honor, and in Sugiyama's presence said, "Please arrange to end the war at an early date." Startled by the Prime Minister's "simplicity of mind," Kurusu remarked, "It is easier to start a war than end one."

Japan's fleet and merchant shipping losses were as catastrophic as Takagi's secret report indicated. Most of this tonnage had been sent to the bottom by marauding American submarines and little was being done in the Imperial Navy to counter this, the gravest of all threats to Japan's supply lines.

The unpreparedness on the part of the Navy was the result of a combination of tradition and of reluctance to engage in defensive warfare. British naval officers had helped establish the Imperial Navy, which adopted all things English so readily that the Naval Academy at Etajima became a replica of Dartmouth. Bricks were brought from England, and a lock of Lord Nelson's hair enshrined in Memorial Hall. Imitation extended to the galley, and once a day a Western meal, complete with knives, forks and spoons, was served throughout the Navy. In battle, Japanese captains followed British tradition by going down with their sinking ship. More important, the Japanese inherited the British aversion to wage war on commercial vessels, and their submarines were designed to support the fleet and do battle against enemy warships rather than go after defenseless shipping. But such a policy could succeed only if an enemy shared it. The Germans did not, and when their submarines launched devastating raids on British merchantmen in World War I, the British had been forced to retaliate in kind as well as create an efficient antisubmarine service.

The Japanese did neither. They were still using their outmoded, outsized submarines almost exclusively against enemy warships and had virtually ignored antisubmarine warfare; it had little appeal to young officers just starting their careers who wanted more dashing duty. By the fall of 1941 there were but two full-time officers on the Navy General Staff assigned to "rear-line defense"—which included mining, antiaircraft defense and antisubmarine warfare. Operationally such duty was considered as unimportant as it was undesirable.

A single officer, with the derogatory title of "Staff Officer for Training," was responsible for protecting all shipping along six hundred miles of the Honshu coast, in addition to the vast area between Tokyo Bay and Iwo Jima. Moreover, when hostilities broke out there were no provisions for organizing merchant ships into convoys. Most shipmasters wanted to sail alone, anyway, but within six months American submarines had torpedoed so many solo merchantmen that the First Convoy Escort Fleet was established, with headquarters on Formosa. This emergency unit, comprised mostly of overage naval reserve officers, had eight destroyers with which to cover an extensive area. Combined Fleet was reluctant to release any more ships, out of sympathy for destroyer commanders, who detested the monotonous task of herding transports.

By the end of the first year since Pearl Harbor, U. S. submarines had sunk 139 cargo vessels, 560,000 gross tons in all, and at last Imperial Headquarters realized that the war was being lost through an oversight. At home there were pleas for more gasoline, bauxite and other vital production materials. At the front, commanders were begging for food, ammunition and reinforcements. But there weren't enough merchant ships to satisfy anyone's needs, and every week more were going down. It wasn't until March 1943, however, that the Second Convoy Escort Fleet was organized, with headquarters on Saipan. The total resources of both convoy fleets were still pitiful—sixteen destroyers, five coast defense frigates and five torpedo boats.

These stop-gap measures would have been ineffective in any case, but in the meantime the Americans had markedly raised the quality of their own underwater service. Scores of improved submarines were built and manned by well-trained crews; drastically redesigned torpedoes replaced the early, faulty ones, which had occasionally run in a circle and too often had failed to detonate. Accordingly, in September the Japanese suffered a record 172,082 gross-ton loss. The time for drastic measures was long since past, but none were taken until mid-November when Grand Escort

Command Headquarters was created. Its commander, Admiral Koshiro Oikawa (who had been navy minister at the time Tojo took over two years before), was given four escort carriers and the 901st Naval Air Group. Unfortunately, all four of the big ships needed extensive repairs and the airmen had no training in anti-submarine tactics. The convoys continued to run haphazardly, each escort-ship commander acting as he thought fit. Losses climbed to 265,068 gross tons in November, but still the government was averse to the adoption of a full-fledged convoy system. Commanders at the front needed supplies too urgently, and small groups of from two to five ships would get there faster. These smaller groups, however, remained easy prey, and the heavy losses continued into the first two months of 1944.

There was no alternative. The "big" convoy system (twenty merchant ships, as compared to Allied convoys of seventy in the Atlantic) finally went into operation early in March. At first it appeared to have wrought a miracle. In the first month, losses dropped drastically. But the elation at Imperial Headquarters was ill-founded. The U. S. Navy was also implementing a new system and had recalled numerous submarines for training. They would soon be sent out again to launch "wolf pack" raids.

3.

Admiral Togo's epic victory at Tsushima had left future Japanese admirals with an unenviable heritage: the concept of the Decisive Battle, wherein all issues would be settled at one stroke. Unlike his predecessor, the new commander of Combined Fleet, Admiral Mineichi Koga, was cool and conservative—an efficient, plodding officer governed by logic. Yet he too was obsessed by the dream of a battle which would change the course of the war. Being a pragmatist, he was also aware that chances of success were small, but it was Japan's last hope. On March 8 he issued his battle plan, giving it the name of Operation Z. Once the advancing American fleet broke into the Philippine Sea by way of the Marianas or the Palaus or New Guinea, the Combined Fleet would sally forth in full strength. In his efficient, methodical way, he set about concentrating the bulk of Japan's surface force, and near the end of the month gave orders to transfer his headquarters from the battle-ship *Musashi,* anchored at Palau, to the Philippines.

"Let us go out and die together," he said to his chief of staff, Admiral Shigeru Fukudome, before they flew south. Yamamoto, he added, had died "at exactly the right time" and he "envied him that fact." At nine o'clock on the last day of March they took off separately in two four-engine Kawanishi flying boats and headed due west for the three-hour flight to Mindanao. But before reaching the Philippines, they encountered a storm and Koga's plane disappeared. The fate of Admiral Koga (like that of Amelia Earhart) remains a mystery.* Within a year Combined Fleet had lost two commanders, both while flying near the front.

Fukudome's plane banked to the right to skirt the storm and changed course north toward Manila, but strong headwinds continued to impede the flying boat's progress and by two o'clock in the morning it was almost out of fuel. The pilot sent word back to Fukudome to prepare for an emergency landing. To the left in the moonlight the admiral could see a long narrow island; it looked like Cebu. During their descent the moon abruptly disappeared from sight; below, the sea was lost in blackness. The pilot became disoriented and lost control. Fukudome, an expert flier himself, groped his way forward, still gripping a briefcase which contained a detailed copy of Operation Z and its cipher system. He reached over the pilot's shoulder and yanked back on the controls to try to bring the bulky flying boat out of its dive. But he pulled too far. The Kawanishi stalled. It fell off on one wing and cartwheeled heavily into the sea.

Fukudome felt water engulf him. He accepted death—the war was lost, anyway—but then he surfaced, still instinctively clinging to the briefcase. The water was bright with flames. He and ten others were free of the wreckage, but the admiral, weighted down by the briefcase, could not stay afloat. He clutched at a seat cushion and started kicking toward the dim shoreline of Cebu. Hour after

---

* There are several theories about Koga's death. One is that he was ambushed, like Yamamoto; U. S. Navy planes shot down his plane and the dying Koga was picked up by an American submarine. There are no available American records of such an ambush or the recovery of the Koga plane. It could have crashed on some island, but it seems far more likely that it was lost at sea, victim of the storm.

hour he struggled against the strong current. By dawn he was alone. The others must be far ahead. In the distance Fukudome made out the silhouette of a tall chimney. He recognized the Asano Cement Plant, which was only six miles south of Cebu City, Japanese headquarters for the central Philippines. It was fairly safe territory, even though the island was infested by guerrillas.

He flailed wearily in the water for another hour, close to the limit of his endurance, before he saw several *bancas* (fishing canoes) approaching. He hesitated. Were they guerrillas? He had to chance capture but let the briefcase go. As he was dragged aboard the first *banca,* one of the fishermen—they had seen the flames—caught a glimpse of the slowly sinking briefcase and retrieved it just before it disappeared.

The admiral was taken to Balud along with eight of his comrades; the other two escaped to Japanese headquarters in Cebu City. The captives were delivered to the nearest guerrilla unit, where they told Captain Marcelino Erediano, who had studied at Tokyo Imperial University for a year, that they were unimportant staff officers from Japan on a routine inspection of the area. Erediano, however, noticed that one of them (Fukudome) was treated with considerable deference by the others. Perhaps he was a high-ranking general? Moreover, the papers in the briefcase with their red TOP SECRET markings were of obvious import. A runner was sent with this information to the commander of all Cebu guerrillas, Lieutenant Colonel James Cushing, an American mining engineer, half Irish, half Mexican. Cushing was an ex-boxer—a hard-drinking, impish individualist. He would have preferred sitting out the war in the mountains with his Filipino wife and child, enjoying life, but the people of Cebu had persuaded him that he alone could unify the quarreling groups of guerrillas on the island.

Cushing immediately radioed MacArthur on his little ATR4A that ten Japanese, including a high-ranking officer, had been captured along with a "whole case" of important documents, some of which looked like a cipher system. The message was picked up by Colonel Wendell Fertig, an engineering officer who had become commander of all guerrillas on Mindanao, and he relayed it to Australia. Here it created such a "tremendous stir" that the Navy offered to divert an operational submarine from its duties as soon as possible and send it to Negros, the island just west of Cebu, to pick up the prisoners and the documents.

Fukudome, his leg injured in the crash, had to be carried on a litter. It took over a week to reach Cushing's mountain hideout in Tupas, ten miles west of Cebu City, and by that time the admiral, under incessant questioning by Erediano, "admitted" that he was Admiral Koga and could even speak some English.

Shortly after Fukudome was delivered to Cushing, Japanese troops from Cebu City, alerted by the two men who had escaped, launched an attack on Tupas. Their commander, Lieutenant Colonel Seito Onishi, threatened to burn down villages and execute civilians in reprisal unless the prisoners were promptly released to him. Cushing retreated farther in the mountains and radioed MacArthur that he could get the documents to Negros but doubted he could deliver Admiral Koga and the other prisoners.

MacArthur replied: ENEMY PRISONERS MUST BE HELD AT ALL COSTS.

It was an impossible order. Cushing had twenty-five men, and Onishi's troops were closing in. He sent the documents to Negros with two runners but informed MacArthur that he would be forced to release "Koga" to avoid continued reprisals. The enraged MacArthur relieved Cushing of command and reduced him to the grade of private.

But "Private" Cushing was still in command, and had to negotiate with Onishi without delay. He asked "Koga" to compose a note requesting Colonel Onishi to refrain from further punitive action in exchange for himself and the others. Fukudome signed the note using Koga's name. It was delivered to Onishi by a civilian, who returned with the colonel's written promise to abide by the proposal. Fukudome was again loaded on a litter. Cushing warmly shook his hand; by now they were friends and even Cushing's fierce mastiff, who bristled at the other Japanese, allowed the admiral to pat him. It was only a moment but it was unique in such a relentless war. An unarmed platoon, led by Lieutenant Pedro Villareal, escorted the prisoners down the mountain path to their freedom.

Fukudome's briefcase found its way to MacArthur via submarine. Its contents were among the most significant enemy documents seized during the war, but Jim Cushing was in disgrace and subject, he imagined with some justification, to worse punishment when MacArthur returned to the Philippines.*

Koga was replaced by Admiral Soemu Toyoda, formerly commander at Yokosuka Naval Base. A brilliant man, he was noted for being so meticulous and sarcastic that more than one subordinate had suffered a nervous breakdown. Moreover, he had been ashore since the start of the war and it was imperative to select for him a chief of staff with broad experience at sea at the highest level. The obvious choice was Admiral Ryunosuke Kusaka, Nagumo's former chief of staff, and now serving under his cousin Admiral Junichi Kusaka at Rabaul. Before leaving Rabaul, he was given a farewell party—a banquet consisting of two cans of sea eel, two slices of broiled eggplant mixed in bean paste, weed soup, and rice boiled with barley. General Imamura contributed half a dozen bottles of *sake*.

There was one way to get out of Rabaul—by air—and risk the fate of Yamamoto and Koga. American fighters patrolled overhead almost constantly. For safety, Kusaka's plane took off in the dark, its occupants cheered by a final toast—this time Johnnie Walker Black Label whiskey. At four o'clock the bomber swept low over the harbor, its exhausts lengthened to hide the flames. With dawn their fears of discovery were borne out. A flight of enemy fighters flashed by so close that Kusaka could see the pilots. Inexplicably, the Americans continued on course—without firing a round at Admiral Toyoda's new chief of staff.

The Kusaka plane refueled at Truk and went on to Saipan. Here the admiral held a reunion with Nagumo, who, after Midway and

* Due largely to the efforts of General Courtney Whitney, head of the Allied Intelligence Bureau, Cushing was reinstated. After the war he was awarded a substantial cash bonus for his contributions to victory. It should have been enough money to last Cushing for life in the Islands, but he spent it all in a few months on a series of celebrations that ranged across the Pacific to California. He died in the Philippines twenty years later, beloved by the men who had fought with him, but still a confirmed individualist to the end.

On Cebu there persists the belief that it was Koga who had been held by Cushing, and that he later committed suicide in Manila. The Japanese commander on Cebu, Colonel Onishi, also believed it was Koga he had rescued and that he subsequently committed hara-kiri.

Admiral Fukudome is still alive and spoke of his captivity but was reluctant to go into detail. Most of the information about this event came from Cushing and his comrades.

Guadalcanal, had been reduced to commanding a small area fleet. After Rabaul with its Draconian regime, Kusaka was appalled by the meager defenses on such a strategic island and recommended that much more be done. The next morning Kusaka took off for Iwo Jima, where he inspected the little volcanic island during refueling. It was well fortified but lacked sufficient machine guns and artillery. He promised the island commander—Captain Tsunezo Wachi, the secret agent and assistant naval attaché in Mexico City before Pearl Harbor—that he would send more weapons, and wished him a good fight.

Upon arrival at Combined Fleet shore headquarters outside Tokyo, Kusaka's immediate problem was to determine once again where and how the next major battle should be fought. Like his predecessors, Kusaka was imbued with the idea of the Decisive Battle, and inevitably his plan of operation was similar to Koga's. In March the Navy had been drastically reorganized, and now its main force, Vice Admiral Jisaburo Ozawa's First Mobile Fleet, was anchored at Lingga Roads, off Singapore, close to its fuel supply but far from the critical area of the Philippines. Kusaka recalled an old Chinese proverb: "No matter how strong the bow, an arrow in long flight cannot tear the sheerest cloth." It would be necessary to bring the Mobile Fleet forward "in a hop, skip and a jump." The hop would be to Tawi Tawi, one of the southernmost of the Philippine islands; the skip the center of the Philippines; and the jump to the Palaus or Saipan. Kusaka's plan was hand-carried to Toyoda, who was still at Yokosuka. It was approved, and emerged as A-Go (Operation A).

Kusaka recalled the neglected defenses of Saipan, and since the island's strength was essential to the operation, he hounded Army officials who were responsible. Tojo, annoyed by Kusaka's persistence, wrote him: "I personally guarantee with 'a large seal' the defense of Saipan!" The messenger, a colonel, added that the Army *hoped* the Americans would land at Saipan; they would be wiped out.

By the end of April the technical details of A-Go were resolved and a few days later Admiral Toyoda issued the general orders. The "decisive" battle area would be the Palaus, and if the Americans headed straight for the Marianas, they would have to be "lured" south (to save Mobile Fleet fuel and be closer to land air bases), where "a decisive battle with full strength will be opened at a favorable opportunity." The enemy would be "attacked and destroyed for the most part in a day assault." But first the 540 land-based naval planes of the First Air Fleet would destroy "at least one third of the enemy task-force carrier units."

On May 10 Kusaka's "hop, skip and jump" started; Ozawa's Mobile Fleet pulled out of Lingga Roads and headed for Tawi Tawi.

4.

The next American target was Saipan, the most strategic island of the Marianas; Nimitz would be in command. In the meantime MacArthur had already taken another long step toward *his* objective, the Philippines, by jumping all the way from eastern New Guinea to Hollandia, an important harbor area near the northwest end of the island, in an ambitious amphibious operation that completely surprised the 11,000 defenders. The roar of Allied naval guns sent most of the Japanese flying—90 percent were service troops—and the 52,000 invaders had little trouble in clearing the area. At minimal cost MacArthur had secured an excellent air, naval and logistics base. A week after the Mobile Fleet left Lingga Roads he took another stride toward Tokyo—this one a 120-mile lunge farther west to the Sarmi area, which was served by two excellent airfields, with another under construction. There were 14,000 Japanese on hand, but less than half were combat troops and they were caught as unawares as their comrades in Hollandia. They put up little resistance—two Americans were killed on the first day—and MacArthur had another valuable base.

His next objective was Biak, a small island to the west, strategically located in the mouth of New Guinea's largest bay. Biak was forty-five miles long and twenty miles wide, and had three serviceable airstrips which the Japanese considered important enough to defend with 10,000 men. On May 20 the Americans began a week of bombing, but this failed to alert the Japanese commander to the impending invasion, and the 41st Division landed on the island against almost no opposition. The first waves of GI's came ashore at the wrong place but by noon they had established a strong beachhead.

On the Combined Fleet's new flagship, the cruiser *Oyodo,*

Toyoda's staff was shaken by the "suddenness" of the Biak landing; it had come on the thirty-ninth anniversary of Tsushima. Kusaka, however, saw it as an opportunity. "If we take it back," he said, "that will draw the Pacific Fleet in sufficiently close so that we can have the Decisive Battle near Palau." His reasoning swayed everyone except the intelligence officer, Commander Chikataka Nakajima, who was of the opinion that MacArthur's landing at Biak was secondary and that the main offensive, completely supported by the Pacific Fleet, would be directed at Saipan. But Kusaka prevailed, and almost overnight a hasty plan to reinforce Biak, Operation KON, was devised.

Nakajima was, of course, right. The three divisions that would land at Saipan in nineteen days—on June 15—had finished arduous training and rehearsed co-ordinated landings in Hawaii; and a flotilla of 110 naval transport vessels, together with an entire division of Liberty ships, was assembling to transport them, along with 7,000 corps and garrison troops, the thirty-two hundred miles to the landing area.

The Marianas, a chain of tropical volcanic islands, were discovered by Magellan in 1521. He was so impressed by the native boats and their rigging that he named them the Islands of the Lateen Sails, but to his less poetic crew they were known as the Islands of the Thieves. In the seventeenth century they were officially renamed to honor Mariana of Austria, widow of Philip IV of Spain, but with the years the Spanish influence waned. America seized Guam, the largest of the islands, during the Spanish-American War. A few months later, in 1899, the harried Spaniards sold the rest of their holdings in the Carolines, Marshalls and Marianas to Germany for some $4,000,000. America could have had the islands, but the McKinley Administration thought they weren't worth that much money.

During World War I the Japanese occupied all these islands, and being on the winning side, were afterward given the mandate over them by the League of Nations. In 1935 they built Aslito Airfield at the southern end of Saipan, and a little later constructed a seaplane base on the west coast and a fighter strip at the northern tip. Some Americans accused Japan of using the island as a military and naval base contrary to the League of Nations Covenant, but there was no more than a handful of troops on the island.*

All native children—they were Chamorros—were required to attend a Japanese school for at least six years, and the brightest boys were encouraged to study at a specialized agricultural training school. Sugar cane was the main crop and production increased under the South Sea Development Company. By the time of Pearl Harbor, Saipan had become a little Tokyo; of its more than thirty thousand people, fewer than four thousand were Chamorros. The island was the length of Manhattan but more than twice its width. Between 1,554-foot Mount Tapotchau in the center and Mount Marpi at the northern end stretched a jagged ridge, pocked with thousands of caves and marked by numerous little peaks and escarpments. This rugged area, as well as the cane fields which covered 70 percent of the island's eighty-five square miles, was ideally suited for defensive warfare.

During the first two years of the war Saipan was nothing but a supply and staging area. Even after the fall of Tarawa and Kwajalein the garrison continued to be little more than a token force, and except for construction of scattered pillboxes, almost nothing was done to fortify the island that was Nimitz' next target.

On the morning of February 23, 1944, his carrier-based bombers attacked the island's airfields. Civilians heard the firing of their own antiaircraft guns, but where were the Japanese planes? Daily they had flown so low and in such numbers that it was al-

---

* These American suspicions helped give rise to sensational stories involving the last flight of Amelia Earhart. Miss Earhart and her navigator, Fred Noonan, took off from Lae, New Guinea, on a July morning in 1937, in a twin-engine Lockheed, and disappeared. After the war, rumors persisted that the two had purposely veered off course to spy on military installations on Saipan and had crashed near the seaplane base. They were supposedly imprisoned and then either died of injuries or were executed. Tony Benavente, a police official on Saipan, helped two American officials investigate the case. They interviewed some fifteen men and women (later characterized by Mr. Benavente as "reliable witnesses") who identified the pictures of Earhart and Noonan as "two American prisoners" they had seen in the summer of 1937, and one said he had noticed two blindfolded Caucasians answering descriptions of Earhart and Noonan in the sidecar of a Japanese motorcycle near the seaplane base. A Japanese told him they were American spies who had been picked up offshore.

Nevertheless, there is no conclusive evidence as to the fate of Amelia Earhart, nor is any confirmation on the subject available from official Japanese sources.

most impossible to teach school. Seventy-four Japanese planes from Saipan, Tinian and Guam did get into the air, but they couldn't prevent the enemy from destroying 101 planes on the ground. They did manage to shoot down six Americans, but only seven of the seventy-four returned safely to their bases.

On Saipan, quiet life was gone for good. Schools and plants were closed to allow the civilians to build shelters and help construct another airstrip. With work their spirits rose and they regained confidence. But orders came to repatriate old people, women and children to Japan. On March 3 *Amerika-maru* sailed with seventeen hundred passengers, most of them families of officials of the South Sea Development Company or influential citizens. It never reached the homeland. Three days later torpedoes sent it to the bottom. Troop transports bound for the Marianas were also torpedoed, and survivors, arriving in Saipan dejected and without weapons, brought with them the feeling of doom.

In an attempt to stem the succession of American victories in the central Pacific, Imperial Headquarters reorganized the entire command structure of the region and sent Admiral Nagumo to Saipan to command a newly created Central Pacific Area Fleet. Theoretically Nagumo was supreme commander of all forces in the area, Army as well as Navy, but guidelines from Tokyo were so vague that he was virtually a figurehead.

Late in May the 43rd Division, around which the defense of Saipan would be centered, sailed from Japan in two echelons. The first arrived safely, but the second—a convoy which was carrying more than 7,000 troops—was subjected to a series of submarine attacks, and five of the seven transports were sunk. The other two crammed their decks with survivors and continued on. About 5,500 finally reached Saipan with many badly burned or wounded. Few had equipment or weapons. The division was so disorganized that one staff officer, Major Takashi Hirakushi, reported that it would be six months before it could conduct any kind of defense.

Nor were the positions they would defend yet prepared. Lieutenant General Hideyoshi Obata of the 31st Army, who commanded all ground troops in the Marianas from headquarters in Saipan, officially warned Admiral Nagumo. "Specifically," he wrote, "unless the units are supplied with cement, steel reinforcements for cement, barbed wire, lumber, etc., which cannot be obtained in these islands, no matter how many soldiers there are they can do nothing in regard to fortifications but sit around with their arms folded, and the situation is unbearable." The situation now would not improve. Thousands of tons of building materials had already been sunk in transit and no more was on the way.

Time had also run out on the 31,629 defenders (25,469 Army, 6,160 Navy personnel). A massive armada of American ships—535—was converging on Saipan. They carried 127,571 troops, two thirds of them Marines. At sea on June 7, they received word of another mighty assault. On one ship filled with Marines the loudspeaker voice said, "The invasion of France has started. That is all." There was silence. "Thank God!" someone finally said.

D-Day passed almost unnoticed in Japan. Combined Fleet was preoccupied with Operation KON. The first attempt to reinforce Biak had failed; destroyers and transports were turned back by persistent air attacks. A second attempt by six destroyers was already under way. Near noon of June 8 one of these was sunk by bombers, and the remaining five scuttled back north upon encountering a single American destroyer at midnight.

Admiral Ozawa, commander of the Mobile Fleet, was not as easily intimidated. He radioed Combined Fleet that the airfields of Biak were too valuable to lose and reminded his superiors that another attempt to retake the island "might draw the American Fleet into the anticipated zone of decisive battle and enable us to launch A-Go." Kusaka needed no urging—it was his own plan, after all—and he persuaded Toyoda to let Ozawa make a final endeavor in greater force. KON was strengthened with a light cruiser, six destroyers and the two great battleships, *Musashi* and *Yamato*. On the afternoon of June 10 this redoubtable force left Tawi Tawi for the south.

While Japanese attention was focused on Biak, the Americans were approaching their primary target, Saipan, more than thirteen hundred miles to the northeast. At midday, June 11, they launched a strike of 208 fighters and 8 torpedo bombers against Tinian and Saipan. Ignoring inaccurate antiaircraft fire, they descended on the two islands, which were separated by a narrow channel, strafing and bombing. On Saipan, they left more than a hundred planes smoldering and flames sweeping through the four-foot-high savannah grass on the slopes above Garapan, the largest town on the island.

The whole purpose of Operation KON was suddenly negated. The Marianas were the main target. Combined Fleet suspended KON and ordered its commander to rendezvous with Ozawa in the waters west of Saipan.

Before the two forces met, seven American battleships and eleven destroyers began bombarding Saipan and Tinian. It was June 13, two days before the landing. During the day they expended fifteen thousand 16- and 5-inch shells, but the gun crews had limited experience in shore bombardment, which called for slow, patient adjustment on specific targets, and little damage of military importance was inflicted. Before dawn they were joined by a more practiced fire-support group—eight battleships, six heavy cruisers and five light cruisers. This time the aim was deliberate and accurate.

In Garapan a young volunteer nurse by the name of Shizuko Miura—a tomboy with a round merry face—flinched as the first shells landed. She peered out the window of the first-aid station into the dim light. The Americans were bombarding the town again. As the explosions moved closer she helped transfer those wounded in the earlier shelling to a dugout. With daylight came enemy planes and an even more violent barrage from the ships. It is June 14, Shizuko thought calmly. I have lived for eighteen years and my time to die has come. A shell shook the dugout like an earthquake and knocked her to the ground. She staggered outside. The first-aid station was obliterated. She saw a piece of red metal—it was shrapnel—and, curious, touched it with her finger. It burned her. Planes droned overhead but no one was firing at them. Garapan was aflame. The heat was so intense that she could hardly breathe. She started to make her way through the rubbled streets strewn with bodies.

Offshore two 96-man underwater demolition teams were boldly exploring the reefs south of Garapan. They found no obstacles but their presence helped convince Lieutenant General Yoshitsugu Saito, commander of the 43rd Division, that the invasion was actually at hand and would come on the west coast. He concentrated his troops to meet the attack, shifted his artillery and set up new headquarters on the west coast. Saito was eminently unsuited by nature and training to lead combat troops. He was a stodgy, colorless cavalryman whose previous command had been a horse procurement unit. That his division was chosen as the nucleus of Saipan's defense proved how unimportant the island was considered by Tokyo.

Many of the other troops on Saipan were random units salvaged from sinkings. They were poorly organized, lacked leadership and were without weapons. Admiral Nagumo was the titular head of this haphazard defense force, but he always deferred to General Obata of 31st Army—and *he* was away on an inspection trip of the Palaus, and his chief of staff, Major General Keiji Igeta, was outranked by Saito.

This put the tactical command of the island under the hapless Saito. He was saddled with the philosophy that had governed and depleted the defense against every invasion to date. Tokyo had decreed that as usual, Saipan was to be defended primarily on the beaches, not in depth.

Transports and LST's carrying the 2nd and 4th Marine divisions were drawing close to the west coast of Saipan and would be in position for debarkation the following morning, June 15. On the island they would encounter more than one kind of enemy. As the medical officer of one unit warned: after facing sharks, barracuda, sea snakes, razor-sharp coral, poison fish and giant clams in the surf, they would find worse hazards ashore—leprosy, typhus, filariasis, typhoid and dysentery as well as snakes and giant lizards.

"Sir," one private ventured, "why don't we let the Japs keep the island?"

A more ominous admonition came from a graduate of UCLA, an American girl of Japanese descent who had been visiting a sick aunt in Japan when the war broke out. Nicknamed "Tokyo Rose" by the Americans, she first went on the air as "Ann," short for "announcer," and currently called herself "Orphan Annie, your favorite enemy."

"I've got some swell recordings for you," she was broadcasting, "just in from the States. You'd better enjoy them while you can, because tomorrow at oh-six-hundred you're hitting Saipan . . . and we're ready for you. So, while you're still alive, let's listen to . . ."

The dark ships slowly drew nearer to Saipan, the skies overhead glowing red from burning buildings, grass and woods. Marines on deck could barely make out the formidable silhouette of Mount Tapotchau through the early-morning haze. As the sky lightened, the island—a shadowy purplish land mass—looked like "a great monster rising out of the sea." Charan Kanoa emerged detail by detail; the two divisions would land on a four-mile front centering on the little town. Five miles to the north Garapan, too, took form. There a diversionary force would pretend to land.

Battleships, cruisers and destroyers began the final bombardment at five-thirty. The dug-in defenders along the beaches and on the slopes crouched through the ordeal, prepared to fight to the death. One made a final notation in his diary: "We are waiting with 'Molotov cocktails' and hand grenades ready for the word to rush forward recklessly into the enemy ranks with our swords in our hands. All that worries me is what will happen to Japan after we die."

Twelve minutes later Vice Admiral Richmond Kelly Turner, in command of the Joint Expeditionary Force, issued the order: "Land the Landing Force." Over loudspeakers boomed the chaplains' last prayers and blessings. On *Time* correspondent Robert Sherrod's ship, Chaplain Cunningham was saying, ". . . most of you will return, but some of you will meet the God who made you." A lieutenant colonel named Tompkins turned to Sherrod and remarked, "Perish-the-thought Department!"

Winches lowered boats; hatches were cleared. At seven o'clock the shelling ceased and thirty-four LST's churned up to the line of departure, a little over two miles from shore. The huge bow doors of the bulky vessels yawned open and amphtracs, loaded with Marines, crawled out and began circling in the water like great water bugs. Planes—the first of 155—were already bombing the Charan Kanoa area to keep the beach defenders pinned down; when they left half an hour later the entire shoreline was veiled by clouds of smoke and dust. The bombing was a "thrilling" sight to Sherrod but he wrote in his notebook: "I fear all this smoke and noise does not mean Japs have been killed."

Soon after eight o'clock 719 amphtracs, filled with eight battalions of Marines, started for shore preceded by gunboats and amphibian tanks. Officers passed out chewing gum and warned their

men to be ready to discard their heavy cartridge belts in case they
had to swim for it.

The four-mile-wide flotilla raked to within eight hundred yards
of the shore before a shower of mortar and artillery shells rained
down upon the invaders. Eighteen amphibian tanks clambered
like crabs over the barrier reef. Behind them several amphtracs
were sunk but the rest followed over the reef and into the shallow
blue-green lagoon. Dozens of planes coming in low strafed the
beach while warships pounded shore defenses for the last time
with their 5-inch guns. It was a spectacular sight, organized
bedlam.

The landing plan was original. The tanks were to crawl up on
the beach and cover the amphtracs, which would transport the
troops all the way to high ground. The first wave hit the beach
at eight forty-four, and within twenty minutes, more than eight
thousand Marines had landed. It was soon evident that all the intense preinvasion bombardment had not silenced the Japanese.
Innumerable machine-gun nests and mortar emplacements between the beaches and the ridge opened up a withering fire which
did not stop until their crews were blasted to bits. While it lasted
it was so accurate that most of the amphtracs had to discharge
their load at the edge of the beach. The ones getting through encountered another kind of obstacle: they got bogged down in the
sand or were caught in craters and didn't have the power to climb
out.

The Marines fought their way slowly into Charan Kanoa. It
wasn't made of bamboo and paper as they had imagined, but was
a complex of concrete one- and two-story structures covered with
bougainvillea in bloom. Each was a little fort. At the center of
town they infiltrated past a baseball diamond and grandstand incongruously flanked by a Buddhist temple.

From a flimsy thirty-foot-high observation tower perched on the
slopes behind Garapan, Admiral Nagumo watched the invasion.
He stood transfixed at the sight of the overwhelming number of
ships but turned briefly to Yeoman Noda, who had served as a
clerk under Yamamoto until his death, to note that at least four
of the battleships he had sunk at Pearl Harbor were back in action. His tone indicated as much admiration as concern.

Not far away, a stray American shell plummeted down on

General Saito's staff during an outdoor meeting near the cave that served as his command post. When the smoke cleared, Saito was still sitting unhurt and silent, with his sword stuck in the ground between his spread legs. On both sides men lay sprawled. Half the staff was dead.

But he remained optimistic about the battle itself (although Marines continued to land—twenty thousand during the day—they had suffered two thousand casualties, and only half of the beachhead had been secured) and radioed Tokyo:

AFTER DARK THIS DIVISION WILL LAUNCH A NIGHT ATTACK
IN FORCE AND EXPECT TO ANNIHILATE THE ENEMY AT ONE
SWOOP.

The men who had to plan the night attack were not as confident. With the division scattered and their own casualties mounting, there were only thirty-six tanks and a thousand infantrymen available to "annihilate the enemy at one swoop."

The operation went wrong from the beginning. Saito was to meet the attack force on a hill above Charan Kanoa to send them off personally, but the Americans, attracted by all the movement toward the assembly point, scattered the general's staff with accurate artillery fire. The tankers waited hour after hour for Saito, who had become separated from his staff in the confusion and darkness. After midnight word came that he had been burned to death in a sugar-cane fire. Major Hirakushi, transformed from public relations officer to commander of the infantry, was relieved of that duty and dispatched to recover the general's body while another officer took charge of the assault. He mounted the first tank, but before it had gone half a mile a shell brought it to a standstill. The remaining tanks clanked down the hill without bothering to wait for the infantrymen. At the bottom they blundered into the swamp east of town and most of them became mired down. The tanks that managed to churn free were finally joined by the panting infantrymen. Officers, swords aloft, led the headlong charge. The Japanese burst into the Marine positions with such vigor that it took a cannonade from 5-inch naval guns and intense machine-gun and rifle fire to stop them. They regrouped and charged again and again. Almost seven hundred died and the American lines were still intact.

Major Hirakushi nearly lost his own life in his attempt to find Saito's body. Incendiary shells made an inferno of a cane field he was crossing and only his sword saved him. Using it as a scythe, he cut a path through to safety. Exhausted, he reached the division command post an hour before dawn. A solitary figure was sitting outside the cave, chin on chest. It was General Saito. "Are you all right, Division Commander?" Hirakushi asked. Saito looked up but made no response.

In a cave overlooking Garapan the nurse Shizuko Miura, who had escaped through the burning town the day before, huddled with other civilians. A soldier peered in with word that more Americans were starting to land just below Garapan, and the tank corps located near the town was moving out to stop them. Shizuko scrambled outside. Her elder brother was in one of the tanks. Below, Garapan was still in flames and through the smoky dawn she saw a ship (it was an LST) approach the reef south of town.

"It's starting!" a soldier shouted. Boats—amphtracs—were disgorging from the mother ship. She watched, almost hypnotized, as the strange craft scuttled over the reef. Angry spits of fire winked from woods along the shore. Tanks rolled out of Garapan and started toward the beach.

"My brother!" Shizuko exclaimed.

"Girl, get back in the cave where it's safe," a soldier warned her.

She ignored him and pushed through a crowd of men to get a better look. The tanks were at the pier. Their guns barked, accompanied by the rattling of machine-gun and rifle fire from the woods. Some of the American boats turned back. Two white hospital ships approached the reef. Flames suddenly leaped out of one.

There were flashes from the big warships far beyond the reef. Then came a series of distant rumbles that were drowned out by shattering explosions from Garapan. The air trembled from the concussions. Enemy planes swept in strafing the shore. The firing from the woods ceased. More landing craft were swarming toward the reef. Here they stopped; tiny figures leaped out, and holding guns high above their heads, waded across the wide lagoon toward the dock area. Fifteen minutes later they were scrambling up the piers; their faces seemed to be blackened. The tanks were silent. Her brother and all the other tankers must have been killed.

To the south, across the water, she could make out the silhouette of Tinian, where she had last seen her mother, father and younger sisters. Had that island too been invaded? Were she and her elder sister, who had evacuated Garapan a week earlier, the only ones in the family alive? Unable to make herself go back to the safety of the cave, she stared vacantly at the death and destruction below. She roused herself with a sudden decision: she would volunteer as a nurse at the main field hospital near Mount Donnay on the other side of the island.

She took a last look at smoldering Garapan. Small boats were clustered around the piers and Americans already pushed inland. "Brother, good-bye," she said and started resolutely up the ridge.

"Hey, woman, where do you think you're going?" a soldier called to her from the mouth of the cave. "Enemy planes!" He pointed in the air with his rifle but she hurried on, ignoring the fighters that swooped down.

Once over the ridge the war seemed far away. She passed a long line of civilians waiting for hardtack. A young woman broke away from the group and embraced her—it was her older sister. Shizuko told her about their brother's death and that she was going to Mount Donnay.

"*Bakayaro!*" Her brother-in-law was indignant. "You can't go alone to a place where there are only men! Your parents entrusted you to my care. If something happened to you, how could I apologize to them?"

"The rest of the family is dead!" she burst out. "Do you want to be the only one alive?" These fools had not seen the destruction of Garapan, the corpses littering the streets; they still imagined the soldiers would protect them.

She reached the hospital on the slopes of Mount Donnay as the sun was setting. It was a barren field where a vast gathering of wounded men lay on the ground in rows so close together that she could hardly walk between them. Overcome by the stench, she did not notice a middle-aged captain, a surgeon, surveying her through round, thick glasses. "Women can't do anything here," he scolded. "Besides, this is the Army and we can't permit civilians to remain. Go back down the mountain before it gets too dark."

She told him that her father and mother and younger sisters were dead and that she had seen her brother killed in battle at Garapan. The captain walked away but she followed him, pleading. He stopped to talk with another doctor, a young lieutenant, still ignoring her. Finally he motioned to her. "All right," he said sternly, "from now on you are a nurse." He gave her his Red Cross armband and the lieutenant clapped a helmet on her head. "This is the Army, and never act selfishly," said the captain. There were eleven of them to care for all the wounded—three doctors, seven medics and herself. "Obey your commander's order at all times. Many painful and sad things are going to take place. Don't give up and do your best." She looked down at the armband with such obvious pride that the lieutenant gave a little laugh. "She's young and I'm afraid she may become emotional."

Her first duty was holding a flashlight for the little medical team which worked rapidly down a long line of patients. A medic jerked at a protruding piece of shrapnel in one man's back. The patient groaned, fainted. "It's easier when they pass out," the medic told her and yanked again, without success. The captain, the chief surgeon, came over and cut away flesh with a scalpel. The aide tried a third time. Shizuko's hand shook, and the light wavered. "Steady!" said the surgeon as he pulled out a red-and-black piece of shrapnel as big as a fist. Shizuko felt cold sweat under her arms as the surgeon gave the patient an injection. The medic took a mouthful of water and sprayed it on the man's face.

The next patient was wounded in the left foot. The surgeon handed her a pair of scissors. "Cut off the trousers," he said. She found a blood-soaked bandage underneath, stuck to the wound as if it were glued. She plucked at it, fearing the man might scream if she pulled too hard.

"Don't hesitate, nurse," said the surgeon sharply. "If you're afraid of a wound and feel so much pity that you can't hurt a patient, you're useless. Here." The patient gritted his teeth. The bandage came free under the surgeon's steady pull and she could see shattered bones. Blood flooded out.

The surgeon examined the wound. "The foot won't be of any use now. We should cut it off." He pricked the foot with the scissors. "Do you feel it?"

"No."

"It's to be expected." He turned to Shizuko. "Nurse, cut off the flesh—and no hesitation."

Nauseated, Shizuko began clipping the loose flesh. The soldier trembled with every tentative swish of the blades, and greasy sweat broke out on his forehead. At last she was finished. The surgeon, who had been watching impatiently, turned to a colleague. "Shall we operate?" he wondered and asked the medic how many anesthetic injections were left. There were but three boxes. "We'll treat him later," the surgeon decided. "Cover the wound, nurse. With the same bandage." She replaced the old blood-stained bandage and the patient was carried to one side.

"This time, nurse, do the whole thing by yourself," said the surgeon. What little confidence she had left vanished. She hoped she'd get someone with a slight wound. A new patient was brought in and the stretcher-bearers smiled at her. She gritted her teeth and somehow got the bandage off for the surgeon's inspection. Each time it was easier. Concerned about the young soldier with the wounded foot, she finally got up her courage to remind the surgeon that he was supposed to operate.

"I completely forgot," he said and ordered the patient carried to the "operating table"—the words themselves made Shizuko's heart beat quickly. The stretcher was placed on two boxes while a medic brought out a plate filled with instruments. First the patient was injected in the back. As soon as the anesthetic took effect the surgeon deftly cut flesh from around the bone with a scalpel that glittered in the light. The medic began hacking with a little saw, scattering the bone in a white powderlike substance. The patient groaned in pain.

"Cheer up! It'll be over in a minute," the medic who was holding the flashlight encouraged him.

Moments later—it seemed like an hour to Shizuko—the bone was severed and the surgeon began trimming away thick pulpy flesh. A stream of red spurted out of the stump. The doctor grabbed at the blood vessel with pincers, but it slipped away and he couldn't find it in the uncertain light. Shizuko could see the blue vessel plainly and pushed forward impatiently, "Doctor, I can pick it up."

Without a word he handed her the pincers. Quickly she plucked up the spurting vessel. The surgeon took the pincers while she bound it tightly with hemp yarn.

"All right," said the surgeon. He put in a few stitches, like an expert seamstress, applied some gauze, bandaged the stump and again injected the patient.

"Thank you very much," said the soldier in a voice as faint as a whisper.

The Marines had done little that day except buttress lines in preparation for a drive across the island. Most of their artillery was ashore, and GI's of the 27th Division were landing. General Saito still had hopes of pushing the Americans back into the sea with the help of tanks and men of a naval Special Landing Force. His first objective was an enemy concentration near the Saipan radio station in the suburbs of Garapan. The attack was set for dusk but the orders were so confusing, the communications so poor, and the problems of terrain so difficult that it wasn't until ten hours later that twenty-five tanks and five hundred men funneled down the ravine leading to the radio station.

The Marines, alerted by the squeak and rattle of armor, called for illumination. Ships lobbed star shells overhead, catching the attackers in the open where they were overwhelmed by a deluge of fire from artillery, mortar, bazooka, rifle and machine gun. Tanks burst into fire, silhouetting others which rumbled out of the shadows. Within an hour most of them were either destroyed or abandoned, but the infantry kept fighting until after dawn. It was no use. The Americans were still in place. They would never be driven into the sea.

The failure of the counterattack was ignored by Tokyo. The Army General Staff, in the name of the Emperor, radioed 31st Army:

BECAUSE THE FATE OF THE JAPANESE EMPIRE DEPENDS ON THE RESULT OF YOUR OPERATION, INSPIRE THE SPIRIT OF THE OFFICERS AND MEN AND TO THE VERY END CONTINUE TO DESTROY THE ENEMY GALLANTLY AND PERSISTENTLY, THUS ASSUAGING THE ANXIETY OF OUR EMPEROR.

General Igeta replied:

HAVE RECEIVED YOUR HONORABLE IMPERIAL WORDS AND WE ARE GRATEFUL FOR BOUNDLESS MAGNANIMITY OF THE IM-

PERIAL FAVOR. BY BECOMING THE BULWARK OF THE PACIFIC
WITH 10,000 DEATHS, WE HOPE TO REQUITE THE IMPERIAL
FAVOR.

The Japanese were again committed to a useless fight to the
death.

With dawn Shizuko could see that the hospital area was surrounded by rocky little peaks. It was like a stadium with no protection from air raids. There were at least a thousand wounded
men on the ground, and the little valley resounded with their constant but subdued chorus of agony. If there is a hell, she thought,
this is it.

With two aides holding a large can she went down the lanes
of men doling out water. She put a cup to the lips of an inert corporal. He seemed dead. Another patient shook him. "Yoshida,
it's water! You wanted it so much. Look, Yoshida, it's a nurse
from Japan!" The corporal slowly opened his eyes and groped
for her. She grasped his feeble hand tightly and said, "Soldier, I've
brought you water. Drink." He mumbled. "He's dreaming of
home," his friend explained. The word "home" tightened her
throat; then she remembered the admonition about becoming
emotional.

She bent over another figure. He had nothing on but a loincloth,
and kept his face hidden in his hands. His left eye was black, "as
big as a ping-pong ball." It was covered with squirming maggots.
The other eye had been gouged out by the worms. Her hands
trembled. "Let me treat you, soldier." He remained silent as she
picked out the maggots one by one with pincers and dropped them
into a can. "My brother was in the Army," she said. "He was a
tank man. On June fourth he came to Saipan from Manchuria,
and on the sixteenth, near Garapan, he died fighting the enemy.
That's why I can't see a soldier without thinking of him as my
brother."

"Is that why you came here?" he said in a toneless voice. She
explained why she had become a nurse. Tears flowed out of his
terrible left eye. "Thank you."

She started to speak about her family and he painfully fumbled for something tucked under his loincloth. It was a bloodstained picture of a woman in kimono.

"Is this your wife?" The man—his name was Lieutenant Shinoda —nodded. "She's still young."

He told her that he had joined the Army three days after the wedding. "When I was wounded all I could think of was my wife. I wanted to live for her sake. But I shall die . . ."

Shizuko couldn't speak. She resumed plucking out maggots, removing all but those tenaciously clinging to the center of the eyes. To kill these she soaked two wads of gauze in mercurochrome and placed them over his eyes. She applied a bandage and told him she would return. "Help is surely coming. Hold out until then because your wife is waiting for you."

The next day—it was June 18 and the Marines had cut Saipan in two just below Mount Donnay—Shizuko managed to find him a uniform. She changed his eye bandage but discovered that the mercurochrome had done no good. The gauze itself was alive with maggots. He wanted the picture sent back to his wife when he died.

"You won't die. I will surely cure you. And we've heard that reinforcements are coming. Then you can return to the homeland. Keep up your spirits!" To change the subject she talked about her brother and four sisters. She alone was a tomboy and her mother always told her, "Shizuko, behave like a woman." She told Shinoda how lucky he was to have someone waiting back home and how hard the doctors and medics were working to save men like him.

"Nurse, you're really great," said a lively voice. She looked up at a baby-faced second lieutenant. His right arm was in a sling and he had other wounds, but he was in good spirits. "Cheer up!" he told his dejected companions. "How can you call yourselves soldiers and be so downcast? Reinforcements will come in time!" All at once his eyes glistened and he said as if in a dream, "I have a sister in Hokkaido who is about as old as you. For the past two days I've been admiring you and it made me wonder what my sister was doing."

20

"Seven Lives to Repay Our Country!"

1.

Word of American landings on Saipan brought a swift reaction from Admiral Soemu Toyoda. He radioed Admiral Ozawa to "attack the enemy in the Marianas area and annihilate his fleet." Five minutes later Toyoda sent a second message, which repeated Togo's famous words at Tsushima Bay:

THE RISE AND FALL OF IMPERIAL JAPAN DEPENDS ON
THIS ONE BATTLE. EVERY MAN SHALL DO HIS UTMOST.

As the Mobile Fleet moved closer to the Marianas, Ozawa and his staff completed plans for the battle. The admiral was tall and stocky. A cool, reticent man, he moved and thought with deliberation. Trained in torpedo warfare, he had assiduously studied carrier tactics and was confident he could beat the Americans, even though he was outnumbered 2 to 1 in flattops. His aircraft had longer range and could attack from as far out as three hundred miles, almost a hundred miles beyond American capabilities.

He could also utilize Guam for refueling and rearming in a sort of shuttle operation. Consequently, he could stay out of range of the enemy while attacking; moreover, he would have support from the 500 planes based in the Marianas. Along with his own 473 planes, that should give him as many as Spruance had.

But plans are only as good as the information they are based on and already, unbeknownst to Ozawa, a large portion of the land-based planes had been destroyed by marauding American carrier pilots flying the new Hellcat fighter.* It could outclimb and out-dive the Zero and was heavily armed. The pilot was protected by heavy armor plating behind, and a thick, bulletproof wind shield ahead. "I love this airplane so much," said one Navy pilot, "that if it could cook I'd marry it."

The pilots themselves were better prepared than their predecessors. Each had at least two years' training and over 300 flying hours, whereas their antagonists were faint copies of those who had fought at Pearl Harbor and Midway. They had six months' training at the most and many had logged few hours in the air. And they were called upon to fly a somewhat improved version of the Zero of Pearl Harbor days that was now so outclassed.

On the afternoon of June 18 one of Ozawa's search planes discovered "an enemy force, including an unknown number of carriers" west of Saipan. Forty miles away from this first sighting another search plane reported "unknown number of carriers, plus ten other ships."

This was Spruance's striking power, Task Force 58, commanded by Vice Admiral Marc Mitscher, who had skippered *Hornet* in the Doolittle raid and the Battle of Midway. He was small, taciturn, hard-bitten. Usually he sat at the after end of his flag

---

* On June 4, 1942, a Zero fighter, piloted by Petty Officer Tadayoshi Koga, came in for a forced landing on lonely Akutan Island in the Aleutians. A single enemy machine-gun bullet had severed its pressure-gauge indicator line. Its wheels caught in the tundra and the plane flipped over, breaking Koga's neck. A month later the practically intact Zero was found, and American engineers designed a fighter to send up against it—the F6F Hellcat.

It is interesting, and sad, to note that two years had gone by since Colonel Claire Chennault furnished the War Department with complete details of the Zero, along with suggestions for greater maneuverability of the P-40 against the swift Japanese plane—all of which was filed and forgotten. Many an American pilot's life would surely have been saved in the intervening time, as was later indicated by the Hellcat's superiority over the Zero.

bridge in a steel armchair facing the stern, his bald head covered by a duck-billed lobster-man's hat. His was a formidable aggregation, almost twice the size of the Mobile Fleet: seven big carriers, eight light ones, seven battleships, eight heavy cruisers, thirteen light cruisers and sixty-nine destroyers.

Rear Admiral Sueo Obayashi, commander of the three Japanese carriers nearest Mitscher, was tempted to attack at once. The basic principle of air battle was to strike first. After informing Ozawa, he ordered an immediate assault.

Some of his planes were in the air before a message arrived from Ozawa requesting all ships to retire and prepare for a massive aerial battle the next morning. Obayashi recovered his planes. "Let's do it properly tomorrow," he told his staff, but privately he feared that such a "golden opportunity" would not present itself again.

Mitscher still had no warning that the Mobile Fleet was approaching. He had been cautioned by Spruance not to sortie in search of the enemy—the main assignment of Task Force 58 was to "cover" Saipan—but when direction-finding apparatus detected Ozawa in the area he told his chief of staff, Captain Arleigh Burke, "It might be a hell of a battle for a while, but I think we can win it," and asked permission by voice radio just before midnight to "come to a westerly course at oh-one-thirty in order to commence treatment of the enemy at oh-five-hundred."

Like Mitscher, Spruance wanted to destroy Ozawa's carriers, yet was bound by definite orders to "capture, occupy and defend Saipan, Tinian and Guam." Allowing Mitscher to be lured away from the Marianas, therefore, would be too much of a "gamble"; he remembered, moreover, how Admiral Togo had waited at Tsushima Strait for the Imperial Russian Fleet to come to him ("We had somewhat the same situation"), and he answered: "Change proposed does not appear advisable. . . . End run by other [enemy] carrier groups remains possibility and must not be overlooked."

At four-forty-five on June 19 Ozawa again launched search planes, but it was a cloudy, squally morning and it wasn't until seven-thirty that Task Force 58 was finally discovered southwest of Saipan. On the bridge of the flagship—the newly commissioned

33,000-ton 800-foot-long carrier *Taiho*—there was no doubt that this would be a historic day for the Imperial Navy, perhaps another Tsushima. Before the first wave of seventy-one planes took off, flight leaders reported to the bridge vowing to avenge the shame of Midway.

Twenty-six minutes later the second wave—128 planes—lifted from the decks. A dive-bomber pilot, Warrant Officer Akio Komatsu, noticed a torpedo (it had come from the U. S. submarine *Albacore*) plowing directly at *Taiho*. Without hesitation he rammed his stick to the side and forward, and his bomber arced in a suicide dive at the running torpedo. His plane intercepted it a hundred yards short of the carrier. From the bridge Ozawa and his staff watched as plane and torpedo were both destroyed in one thundering geyser. Then they saw the track of another "fish." The big carrier began a turn but the second torpedo smashed into her starboard side. The damage seemed of slight consequence. What could a single hit do to a ship that was "unsinkable"?

Aboard *Oyodo,* the flagship of the Combined Fleet, which was just weighing anchor at Yokosuka harbor, Vice Admiral Kusaka was not as confident of the day as Ozawa. He had reservations about the Mobile Fleet's long-range attack; it was like a boxer reaching too far out. But he became infected by the optimism around him—the staff gave Ozawa four out of five chances for victory. He started to call his steward to prepare *sake* cups for a celebration, but decided not to tempt fate; he could wait until the first wave had contact with the enemy. Two hours passed without a report. Confidence on the bridge was replaced by uneasiness and then doubt. At last a message arrived: *Taiho* had been "somewhat damaged." Toyoda was silent but the staff exchanged perturbed looks; Kusaka had a sickening premonition that worse news was coming.

At ten o'clock American radar picked up Ozawa's first wave. Mitscher personally sounded the alarm over the radio with a "Hey, Rube!"—the signal for all Hellcats to return to their ships and prepare for battle. By the time the raiders were within seventy-two miles of his flagship, the new *Lexington,* fighters began taking off from her flight deck. The first to see the enemy was Lieutenant Commander C. W. Brewer. He rolled over, and followed by his eleven men, streaked toward the enemy. He blew up a Japanese bomber, blasted the wing off another, then shook off a Zero and set it afire—and moments later gunned down another.

Now Hellcats from three other carriers joined the fight. They viciously ripped into the oncoming Japanese formation, sending at least twenty-five spinning into the sea. The rest pressed on toward the carriers—but encountered a second wave of Hellcats. Sixteen more tumbled down. A single Japanese penetrated the defense line to hit the battleship *South Dakota*.

The second wave was sixty miles from target when a dozen Hellcats from *Essex* swept in on them. Fighters from other carriers quickly closed in and in a few minutes had shot down almost seventy planes. Ozawa's third wave, forty-seven planes, was given the wrong co-ordinates and only twelve were diverted in time to the battle area. Seven of these were shot down. The eighty-four planes of the fourth wave were also misdirected. Six finally reached the carriers but did no damage. The main group, after a futile search for American carriers, jettisoned their bombs and headed for Guam. As they were making their final approach on Orote Field, twenty-seven Hellcats on the prowl hurtled down and destroyed thirty planes—those that landed were so badly shot up that they could not be repaired. In a few hours Ozawa had lost 346 planes while shooting down 15. Japanese naval air power had been crippled, and permanently.

Although not a single American bomb or torpedo had been launched against the Mobile Fleet, it too had been dealt a devastating blow. Just before noon the skipper of the submarine *Cavalla,* Commander Herman J. Kessler, raised his periscope to behold a picture "too good to be true": *Shokaku*—a veteran of Pearl Harbor, Coral Sea and Santa Cruz—was recovering planes. But Kessler couldn't make out what kind of flag she was flying; it might be an American ship. He took another look: *God damn! there was the Rising Sun, big as hell.* He moved in and at 1,000 yards loosed a spread of six torpedoes. Three hit, setting off a series of internal detonations. Flames enveloped the carrier. As her bow settled, water poured through the No. 1 elevator into the hangar. She turned over heavily and sank just after three o'clock.

Taiho, hit by the single torpedo from *Albacore* at the beginning of the battle, had inadvertently become a floating bomb; a damage-control officer had ordered all ventilating ducts opened on the theory that this would clear gasoline fumes. Instead, his action caused the vapors to permeate the ship. Half an hour after *Shokaku* went down, a shuddering explosion wracked *Taiho*. From her bridge the senior staff officer, Captain Toshikazu Ohmae, saw the armored flight deck suddenly "blossom up like Mount Fuji." The hull on the hangar level blew out and the carrier began to settle rapidly.

Ozawa wanted to stay with the ship. He would listen to no one until Ohmae, who had been his close subordinate for years, said, "The battle is still going on and you should remain in command for the final victory." Ozawa silently followed his senior staff officer into a cutter. Fifteen minutes after they had transferred to a cruiser there was a second thunderous detonation. *Taiho* tilted sharply to port and slid into the water stern first.

At Combined Fleet headquarters, aboard *Oyodo,* there was no longer any doubt that A-Go had failed. The staff debated whether the Mobile Fleet should be ordered to fall back at once. Kusaka didn't think the decision should be left up to Ozawa. From personal experience at Midway he knew how difficult it was for a commander to retire on his own from a losing battle. He got Toyoda's approval to dispatch an order to withdraw.

Ozawa had already pulled back to the northwest under cover of darkness to refuel in order to resume the battle the next morning. His opponent, Mitscher, had recovered his planes, and with Spruance's concurrence, started after the Mobile Fleet with three of his four carrier groups. But he headed southwest, the wrong direction, and it wasn't until three-forty the following afternoon that a search plane finally located Ozawa some 275 miles away. Though dusk would fall in a few hours, Mitscher decided to gamble: the target was barely within range of his planes; they would have to strike in the fading light of day; and, finally, try to find their way home in darkness. He turned Task Force 58 into the wind and launched 216 planes. The sun was low as the attackers sighted half a dozen enemy oilers. A few planes peeled off and sank two of these ships while the rest, with orders to concentrate on carriers, fanned out to the northwest.

The clouds above the Mobile Fleet were brilliantly colored in the sunset. Ozawa managed to get seventy-five planes into the air, and these, with the help of antiaircraft fire, knocked down twenty

Americans but the others broke through the screen. Bombers hit Ozawa's new flagship, *Zuikaku* (sister ship of *Shokaku*), the light carrier *Chiyoda,* a battleship and a cruiser, but inflicted no serious damage.

Then four torpedo planes from *Belleau Wood* dropped out of the clouds and swept in low on another carrier, *Hiyo*. They were led by Lieutenant (j.g.) George Brown, who had vowed at takeoff to get a carrier no matter what. His plane was set on fire but he came in relentlessly and dropped his torpedo.

At his machine gun in the stern of *Hiyo,* Chief Petty Officer Mitsukuni Oshita heard the cry "Torpedo coming!" He began to count. At 12 he knew the torpedo had missed, and relaxed. An explosion jarred *Hiyo*. Oshita had counted too fast.

A second torpedo rocked the carrier. Fires spread from deck to deck and all power went off. Dead in the water, she began listing to port and the word went out to abandon ship. At the extreme stern, Oshita and a dozen others heard nothing and refused to leave *Hiyo* without a definite order. The ship settled rapidly. Water gurgled up to Oshita's machine gun and he, along with his comrades, started for the rail.

"Wait!" Their commander, a young ensign, drew his sword threateningly. "Sing 'Umi-Yukaba'!" They hurried through the traditional song, but the ensign continued to restrain them with his sword. "Now sing 'the Naval March,'" he ordered. The cowed men sang until the water reached their knees, then broke past the officer and over the side.

Oshita looked back. Fire belched out of the carrier. Spotlighted in the red glare, the ensign clung to the stern rail, sword in hand, still singing. He disappeared as the great bow reared high, and Oshita had to swim desperately to avoid the suction. "The ship is going down!" someone shouted. Oshita turned around. *Hiyo* was sticking up like the finger of a giant. She plunged out of sight with "a horrible sigh" as if, thought Oshita, she were saying, "This is the end."

The long trip home for Mitscher's fliers had turned into a nightmare. Pilot after pilot reported he was running out of gas. "I'm going in while I've still got power. So long," called one. "Where's somebody? I'm lost," radioed a second. Sending out these men

had been a daring decision and Mitscher now made another. He
ordered the lights on his carriers turned on even though it made
them glaring targets for prowling submarines. "The effect on the
pilots left behind was magnetic," Lieutenant Commander Robert
Winston recalled. "They stood open-mouthed for the sheer audacity of asking the Japs to come and get us. Then a spontaneous
cheer went up. To hell with the Japs around us. Our pilots were
not to be expendable." Fortunately for the Americans, there were
no enemy submarines in the area, and all but thirty-eight of the
returning pilots were saved.

The battle was over. Officially it would be known as the Battle
of the Philippine Sea, but to Americans who were there it would
always be "the Great Marianas Turkey Shoot," a name originated
by Commander Paul Buie of *Lexington*. They had sunk three heavy
carriers and destroyed 92 percent of Ozawa's carrier planes and
72 percent of his float planes, as well as fifty Guam-based aircraft,
a total of 475 or so—at a cost of 2 oilers and 130 planes, including
eighty which had splashed near or crashed on their carriers. But
the victory was marred by acrid criticism of the man who had
engineered it, for not pursuing Ozawa more aggressively. Admiral
J. J. ("Jocko") Clark, commander of four carriers in the battle,
charged that Raymond Spruance had missed "the chance of the
century," and Admiral A. E. Montgomery, who led four other carriers, officially reported that the results "were extremely disappointing to all hands." At naval air headquarters in Pearl Harbor
the common complaint was: "This is what comes of placing a
nonaviator in command over carriers."

Spruance made no excuses. It would have been "much better
and more satisfactory" to have gone after Ozawa's carriers, but
he had done what Nimitz wanted—protected Saipan—and in doing
so forever after changed the course of war in the Pacific.*

The night after the battle Ozawa dictated a letter of resignation
to Admiral Toyoda but the commander in chief of Combined Fleet
refused even to read the letter. "I am more responsible for this

---

* When Admiral King landed at Aslito Field shortly after Saipan was
secured, his first act was to assure Spruance that he had "done exactly the
correct thing with the Fifth Fleet in the Battle of the Philippine Sea, no
matter what anyone else might say, especially since he had to remember that
the Japanese had another fleet ready in the Inland Sea to pounce upon"—
the numerous transports and supply ships that were not yet unloaded.

defeat than Admiral Ozawa," he said, "and I will not accept his resignation."

Admiral Ugaki marked the occasion with another *haiku:*

> *The battle is ended*
> *but the gloomy sky of the rainy season*
> *remains over us.*

2.

The crushing defeat at sea doomed the defenders of Saipan. On the day *Shokaku* and *Taiho* went down, the commander of all American troops on Saipan, Marine General Holland Smith, readied his troops for a final drive up the island. His men had already suffered heavy casualties, particularly from night mortar fire. Marine Captain John A. Magruder watched medics tenderly load corpses into a truck and approached to see if there was anyone he knew. He recognized a youthful, fair-haired replacement and remembered how exuberant he had been upon arrival at the front. A yellow paperback book stuck out of his back pocket—*Our Hearts Were Young and Gay.*

On June 22 two Marine divisions started the offensive to the north while the Army division, the 27th, mopped up the remaining Japanese cut off in the extreme south. The Marine lines were so extended, however, that Smith ordered the 27th Division to take over the center, and the next morning the GI's started up the wooded valley running just east of Mount Tapotchau. It was a narrow gulch not a thousand yards wide, and the remnants of the 136th Regiment of Saito's division looked down on them from cliffs and precipitous hills honeycombed with caves. The GI's, commanded by Major General Ralph Smith, advanced cautiously throughout the day to the annoyance of Holland Smith—his nickname was "Howlin' Mad." He complained to Major General Sanderford Jarman, the senior Army officer on the island, that "if it was not an Army division, and there would be a great cry set up more or less of a political nature," he'd relieve the other Smith on the spot. The leadership of the 27th, he was convinced, stemmed largely "from a gentlemen's club known as the Seventh Regiment, traditionally New York's 'silk stocking' outfit, and likewise a worthy unit, *per se,* with an impeccable reputation for annual balls, banquets and shipshape summer camps."

Ralph Smith acknowledged that his division "was not carrying its full share" and that he was "in no way satisfied with what his regimental commanders had done during the day." He promised Jarman to "personally see to it that the division went forward." Even Smith's presence at the front the following morning did little to move the Army troops up the gorge, which was already known as "Death Valley."

"Howlin' Mad" conferred with Admiral Richmond Turner ("Terrible Turner"), and the two went out to see Spruance on *Indianapolis.* "Ralph Smith has shown that he lacks aggressive spirit," said Smith, "and his division is slowing down our advance. He should be relieved." He suggested that Jarman take over the 27th until another commander was appointed, and Spruance concurred.*

* Even before the battle subsided, Lieutenant General Robert C. Richardson, commanding general of all Army forces in the Pacific Ocean Areas, had appointed an all-Army board to investigate the case. It concluded that Holland Smith had authority to relieve Ralph Smith but that the Marine general "was not fully informed regarding conditions in the zone of the 27th Infantry Division" and the relief of the Army Smith "was not justified by the facts."

In Washington, Marshall's deputy, Major General Thomas T. Handy, while admitting that there was some justification for criticizing the GI's for lack of aggressiveness in Death Valley, reported that "Holland Smith's fitness for this command is open to question" because of prejudice against Army personnel and that "bad blood had developed between the Marines and the Army on Saipan" to a dangerous degree. "In my opinion, it would be desirable that both Smiths be ordered out of the Pacific Ocean Area."

A few days after the battle Richardson inflamed more tempers by flying to Saipan to pass out decorations to Army troops without consulting Nimitz and without approval of Holland Smith. He also reportedly told the Marine commander, "I want you to know you cannot push the Army around the way you have been doing." This was resented not only by Holland Smith but by Spruance and Turner, who vigorously complained to Nimitz of Richardson's "high-handed and irregular actions."

The feud between the two services was taken up by the press. The San Francisco *Examiner,* a Hearst paper, charged that Marine casualties in places like Saipan were excessive, far greater than MacArthur's, and concluded that "the supreme command in the Pacific should, of course, be logically and efficiently entrusted" to him. *Time* and *Life,* Henry Luce's two influential magazines, retaliated with a vigorous defense of Holland Smith, *Time* asserting that "when field commanders hesitate to remove subordinates for fear of interservice contention, battles and lives will be needlessly lost."

But a change of commanders made no perceptible difference, and the progress up Death Valley remained painfully slow. The Marines on the right were also stalled, but the 2nd Marine Division on the left fought its way to the top of Mount Tapotchau where the rest of hilly Saipan stretched out to the north like some quiescent monster.

This rugged terrain was about all that stood between the Americans and victory. By nightfall of June 25 there were less than twelve hundred able-bodied men and three tanks left of all Japanese Army front-line units, and General Igeta of the 31st Army was compelled to radio his commander in Guam that Saipan could not be held.

THE FIGHT ON SAIPAN AS THINGS STAND NOW IS PROGRESSING ONE-SIDEDLY, SINCE ALONG WITH THE TREMENDOUS POWER OF HIS BARRAGES, THE ENEMY HOLDS CONTROL OF SEA AND AIR. IN DAYTIME EVEN THE DEPLOYMENT OF UNITS IS VERY DIFFICULT, AND AT NIGHT THE ENEMY CAN MAKE OUT OUR MOVEMENTS WITH EASE BY USING ILLUMINATION SHELLS. MOREOVER, OUR COMMUNICATIONS ARE BECOMING DISRUPTED, AND LIAISON IS BECOMING INCREASINGLY DIFFICULT. DUE TO OUR SERIOUS LACK OF WEAPONS AND EQUIPMENT, ACTIVITY AND CONTROL ARE HINDERED CONSIDERABLY. MOREOVER, WE ARE MENACED BY BRAZENLY LOW-FLYING PLANES, AND THE ENEMY BLASTS AT US FROM ALL SIDES WITH FIERCE NAVAL AND ARTILLERY CROSS FIRE. AS A RESULT, EVEN IF WE REMOVE UNITS FROM THE FRONT LINES AND SEND THEM TO THE REAR, THEIR FIGHTING STRENGTH IS CUT DOWN EVERY DAY. ALSO, THE ENEMY ATTACKS WITH FIERCE CONCENTRATION OF BOMBS AND ARTILLERY. STEP BY STEP HE COMES TOWARD US AND CONCENTRATES HIS FIRE ON US AS WE WITHDRAW, SO THAT WHEREVER WE GO WE ARE QUICKLY SURROUNDED BY FIRE.

But there would be no surrender.

. . . THE POSITIONS ARE TO BE DEFENDED TO THE BITTER END, AND UNLESS HE HAS OTHER ORDERS, EVERY SOLDIER MUST STAND HIS GROUND.

General Saito's report to Tokyo was more emotional:

> . . . PLEASE APOLOGIZE DEEPLY TO THE EMPEROR THAT WE
> CANNOT DO BETTER THAN WE ARE DOING. . . . THERE IS NO
> HOPE FOR VICTORY IN PLACES WHERE WE DO NOT HAVE CON-
> TROL OF THE AIR AND WE ARE STILL HOPING HERE FOR AERIAL
> REINFORCEMENTS. . . . PRAYING FOR THE GOOD HEALTH OF
> THE EMPEROR, WE ALL CRY "BANZAI!"

3.

For Tojo the collapse of Saipan was a political as well as military reverse—a direct threat to his position as prime minister. His popularity had waned as the war situation worsened. Criticism, most of it covert, came from all sides. Prince Chichibu referred to him as "Emperor Tojo." Signs in some Navy offices read: KILL TOJO AND SHIMADA! OUR IMPERIAL COMBINED FLEET IS NOW POWERLESS. PREPARE AT ONCE TO RE-FORM THE CABINET SO WE CAN SEEK PEACE. Among Army intellectuals he was known as *"Jotohei"* ("superior private," the rank above Pfc.) and his administration was labeled "government-by-privates."

Substance was given to this name-calling by the findings of an investigation just concluded by the Army General Staff's own Conduct of War Section. Its chief, Colonel Sei Matsutani, reported that after an exhaustive study by himself, Colonel Sako Tanemura and a major named Hashimoto, there was "now no hope for Japan to reverse the unfavorable war situation. The state of Germany today is about the same as Japan's and grows gradually worse. It is time for us to end the war."

Matsutani took his report to two influential members on the General Staff. The first admitted the validity of the conclusions but forbade Matsutani to release them. The second, equally impressed, refused to allow the colonel to present his case to the Prime Minister. But Matsutani could not be intimidated and brought his findings to Tojo. The colonel expected Tojo to react violently, but he listened quietly, passively. His "sour" face, however, belied his polite demeanor, and within a week the outspoken Matsutani was transferred to China.*

On Saipan General Saito, following orders from 31st Army, once more moved his headquarters, this time to a small cave a mile north of Mount Tapotchau. On June 28 all the military leaders—Nagumo, Saito and Igeta—held a joint staff meeting. Igeta took charge. Except for the former public relations officer, Major Hirakushi, Saito's staff had few suggestions to offer. They crouched listlessly on their haunches; one or two tried to sleep. Saito and Nagumo sat in silence as Igeta outlined a final line of resistance two thirds of the way up the island. They would dig in, from Tanapag in the west to the opposite coast.

There was little reaction. Wearily Saito said that the proposal sounded "all right" to him, and a Navy commander, speaking for Nagumo, said, "We leave it to the Army." The question remained as to how to do it. The troops were dispersed across the northern half of Saipan; there were few lines of communication. Able-bodied men were selected to contact all units. Major Hirakushi set out for Mount Donnay to assemble the remnants of the 136th Regiment. The only soldiers he could find in the area were at the field hospital. He called out for men of the regiment; no one came forward. He reported back to Saito that he could find no troops to build the eastern section of the final line.

Igeta said nothing.

Shizuko had lost all concept of time. On one of her daily visits to Lieutenant Shinoda, a comrade lying nearby began to berate her: "Why didn't you come and see him last night? Poor Lieutenant

---

* In China, Matsutani replaced an even more outspoken colonel, Tsuji, who had just been shipped out to Burma. (His forthright views on Guadalcanal had undoubtedly made him *persona non grata* in Tokyo.) Matsutani never believed there was any connection between his audience with Tojo and his sudden transfer. He had held the China post two years previously and was well qualified for the job.

On the other hand, Colonel Tanemura, who helped with the controversial report and replaced Matsutani as chief of the section, wrote in his "Imperial Headquarters [Army] Diary" on July 3, 1944: "The reason for his transfer is not clear. However, it is believed that his recent outside activities to bring about termination of the war have somehow reached the ears of his superiors, and roused their rage."

Shinoda called for you all through the night and died just an hour ago."

She crouched beside Shinoda's body. There wasn't a maggot on his face. He looked "pale and beautiful." She picked up the photograph of his round-faced wife.

"Couldn't you hear him calling you?" another soldier said in an accusing voice. She couldn't answer. All through the night she had heard voices continuously calling "Nurse!" but it was like "hearing cicadas singing." It was impossible to answer each call.

Yet—she should have recognized Shinoda's urgent voice. She reported his death to one of the medics, who said. "Poor fellow, he had so many maggots that the other patients kicked him until he found this corner off by himself."

Her routine had become a mélange of horrors: the crude toilet filling up with maggots; the dead bodies that rotted and gave off a ghastly phosphorescence at night; the piteous groans and cries of patients; the air raids; the shells shrieking overhead. She had to forget she was a woman in the presence of men stripped naked; she had to forget she was a human being as she amputated arms and legs with a surgical saw and then sewed up the ragged flesh. There was no more anesthesia for operations, and patients would scream until they fainted. The fortunate ones remained unconscious until the operation was over.

In the past few months Prince Konoye had become the confederate of a score of military as well as civilian leaders—among them General Koji Sakai of the General Staff and Admiral Okada—who were disturbed by the course of the war and Tojo's leadership. General Sakai made a clandestine visit to Konoye's suburban home. "To be on the safe side" the general wore civilian clothes. "If Tojo learns what I am about to tell you, I'm sure he will retaliate," he warned. He wanted to impress Konoye that the war should be ended quickly. "Germany still has defensive power, and while the enemy has to fight in both east and west we should take advantage of the situation and enter into negotiations for peace. It will not be to our advantage to wait until Germany is defeated." Tojo could not possibly negotiate such a peace. A new cabinet must be formed.

General Sakai was one of the few liberals in the Army, and

Konoye wondered if the Army leadership "could be persuaded to follow this policy."

"At present they don't speak openly but they all think as I do," the general replied. Matsutani's report had been circulated secretly and a number of Army leaders wanted the Throne informed of its findings.

And after that, what? Konoye wanted to know. How should the Emperor face Tojo with the matter?

"His Majesty should say, 'Despite all efforts by our Army and Navy, the enemy has succeeded in landing on Saipan. What do you think of future operations, Tojo?' He should then ask how they were to meet the requirements of the Army and Navy regarding munitions, planes, ships and oil; about protecting the population from air raids; and what should be done to repel enemy offensives." General Sakai acknowledged that Tojo could answer these questions in several ways—but hoped they would force him "to resign at once."

4.

On June 30 the GI's finally broke through Death Valley ("No one had any tougher job to do," observed Major General Harry Schmidt, commander of the 4th Marine Division), and the entire three-division front was at last connected.

At the Donnay field hospital, a "dying game" order was received. Medics distributed grenades, one for each eight men. The chief surgeon—the captain—climbed up to a little rise at dusk and shouted that "by order of the high command," the field hospital was transferred to a village on the west coast a mile and a half above Tanapag and four miles from the northern tip of Saipan. The vast arena was silent. "All ambulatory patients will accompany me. But to my great sorrow, I must abandon you comrades who cannot walk. Men, die an honorable death as Japanese soldiers."

Shizuko told the captain, "I'm going to stay and kill myself with my patients!"

"You will join us," he said. "That is an order."

All the soldiers wanted to say good-bye and crowded around her. Even those who couldn't walk crawled nearer. There was no need to draw words from them. There was only one subject—home. Each man tried to tell her something about his family. She promised over and over to tell what had happened if she got back to Japan.

One whose jaw had been shot away got her attention. Slavering, he weakly scrawled "Chiba-ken" in the dirt, and then "Takeda." "I understand," she said. "You come from Chiba prefecture and your name is Takeda."

A young officer, his uniform dyed with blood, forced out a few painful words. "You know . . . the song . . . of Kudanzaka?"

"Yes, I like it very much." It was a haunting song about an aged mother from the country taking her dead son's medal to the Yasukuni Shrine in Kudanzaka. She began to sing:

"From Ueno Station to Kudanzaka
I get impatient, not knowing my way around.
It has taken me all day, leaning on my cane,
To come and see you, my son, at Kudanzaka.

The great torii [gate] *looming up in the sky*
Leads to a magnificent shrine
That enrolls my son among the gods.
Your unworthy mother weeps in her joy.

I was a black hen who gave birth to a hawk.
And such good fortune is more than I deserve.
I wanted to show you your Order of the Golden Kite,
And have come to see you, my son, at Kudanzaka."

She stopped. There was silence except for stifled sobs. "We, too, will go to Yasukuni Shrine!" the young officer exclaimed.

Others joined in: "Let us all go to Yasukuni Shrine together!"

The captain started to lead Shizuko away, along with three hundred patients. Voices followed them: "Thank you, nurse"; "Goodbye, nurse"; "Commander . . . Sergeant . . . nurse . . . thank you all for your kindness."

They reached the end of the field. Shizuko heard a voice cry out, "Good-bye, Mother!" There was a sharp blast—a grenade. She crouched on the ground and flinched as one grenade after another exploded in rapid succession.

The American advance up the island, which had begun so laboriously, was now almost unopposed. It had become, as one Marine put it, a "rabbit hunt." This constant pressure had prevented the Japanese from forming their final defensive line across the island, and by July 5 they had been herded into the northern quarter of Saipan.

Japanese headquarters was now on a ridge facing the west coast, a few hundred yards from the new field hospital. The cave overlooked a gulch, already nicknamed "the Valley of Hell." That afternoon Major Hirakushi left the cave to inspect the front lines. They were nonexistent. The men had already retreated on their own before the American drive. Hirakushi's report was greeted by an incredulous silence. Finally General Igeta said, "Tomorrow morning we will begin assembling all remaining troops in the area for the final attack. Let us end this battle."

That evening the headquarters group ate the last of their food— a single can of crab meat and a small rice ball apiece. Hirakushi had been saving two cigarettes which Prince Kaya gave him in Japan as a memento. They were passed from man to man, smoked until they were too small to hold. Hirakushi asked if Igeta and Saito would participate in the final assault. Admiral Nagumo, who had said almost nothing during the long retreat, answered for them: "We three will commit suicide."

Hirakushi wanted to know what would happen to the thousands of civilians who shared the caves with the soldiers and sailors. "There is no longer any distinction between civilians and troops," Saito replied. "It would be better for them to join in the attack with bamboo spears than be captured.* Write out instructions to that effect."

Three hundred sets of Saito's order were mimeographed, but before they could be distributed a messenger arrived from the naval communications cave located several miles to the north.

---

* Government propaganda in Japan, portraying Americans and British as "devils," was both widespread and effective. One observer noted in his diary: "I rode a train with a volunteer corps the other day. Their leader lectured, 'Churchill and Roosevelt formed what they called the Atlantic Charter and agreed to kill all Japanese. They made a statement they would kill men and women. We won't let them kill us!' It seems the public believes that the enemy are going to remove the testicles of the Japanese so that they won't have children, or that they will be sent to secluded islands."

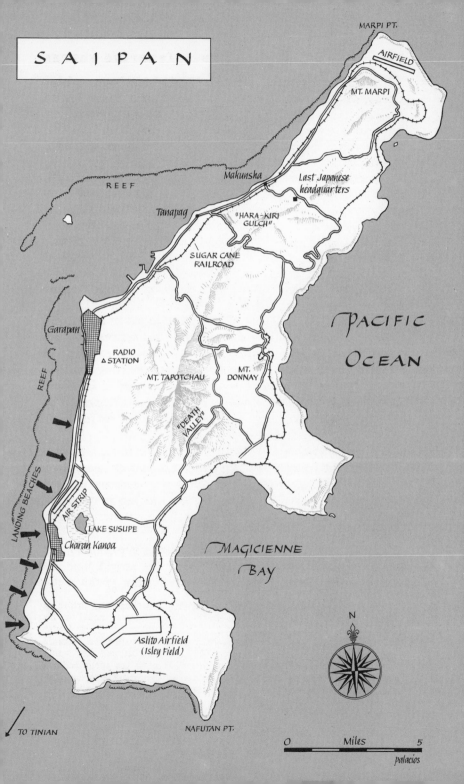

Tokyo ordered the defenders to continue the battle "to gain time"; there was a promise of reinforcements.

The Navy staff officers accepted the order, but the Army would not abandon the last assault. "The arrow has been shot," said one Army man. Another accused the Navy of cowardice. The Navy said it was no time to call names; the Army was disobeying a direct order from Imperial Headquarters.

Nagumo, Igeta and Saito took no part in the argument, which lasted through the night. At dawn, July 6, the shelling and bombing resumed, and a sentry at the mouth of the cave reported that an enemy tank was "peering over" the edge of the cliff above.

Saito, who had been quietly conferring with Nagumo and Igeta, beckoned to Hirakushi. He said the three of them had decided to die at ten o'clock. "Excuse us for going first."

"Do you plan to do it here?"

"Yes, here."

Hirakushi said it would be better to commit suicide privately in a smaller cave nearby. The major left to prepare the new cave while Saito read aloud a farewell message that he wanted conveyed to all Army troops:

". . . Our comrades have fallen one after another. Despite the bitterness of defeat, we pledge, 'Seven lives to repay our country.'
. . . Whether we attack or whether we stay where we are, there is only death. However, in death there is life. We must utilize this opportunity to exalt true Japanese manhood. I will advance with those who remain to deliver still another blow to the American devils, and leave my bones on Saipan as a bulwark of the Pacific.

As it says in the *Senjinkun* [Battle Ethics]: 'I will never suffer the disgrace of being taken alive,' and 'I will offer up the courage of my soul and calmly rejoice in living by the eternal principle.'

Here I pray with you for the eternal life of the Emperor and the welfare of the country and I advance to seek out the enemy.

Follow me."

Hirakushi led the three commanders to the new cave. "What means are you going to use?" he asked.

"We will go through the first step of *seppuku* [cutting open the stomach]," said Saito. "But *seppuku* will take too long, so have an officer stand behind each of us and shoot us in the back of the head." Saito selected Hirakushi. Nagumo requested a naval officer; Igeta didn't express any preference.

Hirakushi returned to the main cave and asked for someone from the Navy to "assist Admiral Nagumo with his suicide." No one answered. Finally a young Army aide said, "Let me do the job." Another Army aide volunteered to shoot Igeta, and the three started back to the suicide cave.

The commanders, all wearing khaki fatigue uniforms, were sitting cross-legged near the mouth of the cave with the diminutive Nagumo in the middle. Hirakushi turned to find some water to wash their faces when he heard a Navy officer call out that his group was heading north alone. Hirakushi started forward to stop them. Behind there were three sharp reports. He spun around. The three commanders were lying sprawled on the ground. Behind the bodies stood the two young aides, smoking pistols in hand. The commanders, impatient, had gone ahead without him.

All Hirakushi could do now was burn the bodies and regimental flags. He rounded up men to help, but other officers stopped him —smoke would attract the enemy. Hirakushi agreed to wait until after midnight, just before launching the last attack. The ordeal of the past few days finally took its toll. He collapsed on the floor of the command cave into deep sleep.

It was dark when he woke up. Soldiers and sailors in nondescript uniforms, and armed with rifles, swords and bamboo spears, were assembling outside. They were haphazardly divided into groups and in the moonlight officers began to shepherd them toward the beach. All along the ridge men were filtering down to the narrow coastal plain. At zero hour they would charge independently toward American positions around Tanapag. To Hirakushi the men looked like "spiritless sheep being led to the slaughter," and the officers "guides to the Gates of Hell." Before he left, the major ordered two men to burn the regimental flags and the bodies of the three commanders, then silently led his group, a dozen men, down the steep slope.

More than three thousand Japanese—including civilians like Shizuko's brother-in-law—emerged onto the coastal plain. They left the slope behind littered with thousands upon thousands of empty *sake* and beer bottles.*

---

* Twenty-five years later they still covered the ridge.

Hirakushi and his men reached the shore at four o'clock in the morning on July 7. He stripped and waded into the tepid water to bathe. Rapt, he stared out at the barrier reef, a ghostly shimmering line in the moonlight. Overhead a thick cloud reminded him of a Japanese mother in quilted kimono carrying a baby on her back. As the cloud pulled apart, he conjured up in the lightening sky images of his mother, his wife, his friends. He shook himself free of this fantasy and returned to shore to dress. It felt good to be clean. He was ready to die.

Distant voices were shouting *"Wah! Wah!"*—a Japanese battle cry. There was a crackle of rifle fire from the ridge. The signal to attack! Without waiting for him, his men took off headlong down the beach toward Tanapag. Pistol in one hand (a Taisho with a clip of six shells) and sword in the other, he started after them. He was enveloped by an explosion and felt as if he were floating right into a huge column of bursting fire. I'm dead, he thought just before the world went black.

At Tanapag the 27th Division had been warned by Holland Smith to expect "an all-out *banzai* attack" along the coast before dawn.* The Japanese swarmed on Tanapag. In the lead half a dozen men held aloft a great red flag, like the vanguard in a dramatic pageant. Behind pressed the fighting troops and then—the most incredible sight of all—hundreds of men with bandaged heads, on crutches, scarcely armed, limping and hobbling.

They swept down the narrow tracks of the sugar-cane railway that skirted the beach and smashed against the 1st and 2nd battalions of the 105th Infantry Regiment like a human tidal wave. It reminded the commander of the 2nd Battalion, Major Edward McCarthy, of a "stampede staged in the old Wild West movies." The Japanese "just kept coming and didn't stop. If you shot one, five more would take his place." They "ran right over" the Americans.

The commander of the 1st Battalion, another Irishman, Lieutenant Colonel William J. O'Brien, stood his ground, an example to his men, a pistol in each hand. Seriously wounded, he fired until his clips were empty, then manned a .50-caliber machine gun until he was killed. The Japanese surged over the two steadfast battal-

* The term *"banzai"* attack was never used by the Japanese.

ions of GI's (the same ones accused of advancing too slowly up Death Valley), killing or wounding more than 650 of them.

To their right another group of raiders funneled through a winding canyon—soon to be known as "Hara-kiri Gulch"—and hit the 3rd Battalion but these troops were too well emplaced above the gulch and could not be dislodged.

Yeoman Noda, who had served both Yamamoto and Nagumo to the end, was with the large group that overran the Americans on the beach. Shrieking and frenzied, this was hardly a military formation. Suddenly Noda felt as if he had been clouted in the hip with a baseball bat—but there was no pain. He staggered, tried to keep moving but fell—he had been hit by a machine-gun slug. American bodies lay on all sides.* Noda picked up a GI canteen and drank deeply. He tried to struggle to his feet but his right shoe was like lead.

Unable to bend forward to unlace the shoe, he found an American bayonet and wrenched a stick from the grasp of a dead Japanese. He tied the bayonet to the stick and laboriously hacked at his shoelaces until he could push off the shoe. He still couldn't stand and decided his trouser legs were holding him back. He cut them off but remained as helpless as ever.

He sank back on the sand, resigned. Now the time has come to die, he told himself. In the light of dawn he saw a pool of blood in the sand. To his amazement—his own blood. A few yards away four wounded Japanese were lying on their backs, smoking calmly, as if it were a beach in Japan.

"We're about to die," one of them observed casually and flipped Noda a pack of Hikaris. Noda stretched out on the sand, smoking the cigarette, his mind a blank. He was roused by the soldier who had given him the cigarettes. "Hey, Navy man," he said, "we are about to die. Will you join us?"

Noda held up a grenade. "I have one."

"Excuse us for preceding you."

Noda huddled to avoid grenade shrapnel and shut his eyes. There was a detonation. He looked up and saw four sprawled bodies. How terrible to die by grenade, he thought and was again attracted by the stream of blood flowing from his own body. He

---

* Sherrod inspected the scene a few hours later. "The whole area seemed to be a mass of dead bodies, stinking guts and brains."

considered a tourniquet but changed his mind. It would be better to bleed to death.

He was growing weaker. *I'm only twenty-seven and why should I die here? Whether I live or die won't bring about Japanese victory.* He began remembering things in the past—his school days, catching *dojo* (mudfish). He fainted. The next thing he heard was the chirping of a bird. The landscape was devastated, not a palm tree or bush. Only bodies and ugly craters of sand. If there was no tree, how could it be a bird? What was happening?

There was a mutter of voices speaking a strange language. He felt a kick in the side. He groaned and two Marine corpsmen loaded him onto a stretcher. He saw medics kicking other bodies, Americans as well as Japanese, and just before passing out again he congratulated himself: *If I hadn't been wakened by that bird I would be dead.*

Ahead in Tanapag, Major McCarthy and his surviving officers and noncoms had finally managed to form a perimeter within the village itself. All morning they were pressed slowly back in a vicious house-to-house battle until a platoon of medium tanks rumbled in. Other reinforcements arrived and by late afternoon only isolated little groups of Japanese were alive. The last attack was over.

Just offshore on a white hospital ship, Major Hirakushi was opening his left eye. All he could see was a clean white wall. *I am alive! I have a second life!* He was naked, covered with a blanket. It took some time before he realized his left hand was handcuffed to the bed and that he had been wounded in the head and shoulder. He was so exhausted that it didn't occur to him until later that he, an officer, had disgraced himself by surviving the last assault. All he could think was: *I am alive! I am alive!*

At the new field hospital in the Valley of Hell, Shizuko had crouched in her foxhole throughout the night. In the waxing daylight she noticed movement on the heights above. Dark faces peered through the undergrowth. They were Negro GI's. In her panic she imagined they were gorillas coming down the incline. So the fantastic rumor was true! Americans were using them in battle.

All around her, wounded men had emerged from their dugouts, and turning north, bowed low toward the Imperial Palace. Suddenly strange, raucous music blared from an amplifier—she had never before heard such noise. Its wild, disturbing rhythm echoed throughout the entire valley (it was American jazz). The unreality of the scene robbed her of the resolve to kill herself.

The chief surgeon ordered her to give herself up by waving a white handkerchief. She hesitated; the Americans would rape her. "Save yourself!" his assistant, the lieutenant, urged her. As she stood paralyzed at the rim of the foxhole, the Negroes charged forward, lobbing grenades and shouting. All Shizuko could see were their teeth and eyes. The chief surgeon put a pistol to his throat and pulled the trigger. The lieutenant slashed his neck three times with a knife and collapsed over Shizuko. Warm blood flowed onto her legs. She picked up a hand grenade. She felt cold. *Now I am going to die.* She tried to cry "Mother" but nothing came out. She pulled the safety pin, rapped the grenade against a rock to activate it and threw herself on top of it.

Shizuko heard voices but could not understand them. Cautiously opening her eyes, she discovered that she was in a house. She tried to rise but a young American officer said in Japanese, "You are wounded—don't move."

Shizuko couldn't believe Japanese was coming out of an enemy. Why hadn't she died? She asked for water but the young captain told her she couldn't have any. He poured something out of a can. She tried to drink it but had to spit it out. It was tomato juice and she couldn't stand the taste. He ordered her to finish it and she did. It wasn't death that terrified her, but the Americans. She asked what had happened to the men in the Valley of Hell.

"All died except you," said the officer, an interpreter. He told her that he had studied at a Japanese university and wanted to help her countrymen. "We believe in humanity, even in war." He assured her that many Japanese civilians had survived and were in an internment camp near Charan Kanoa. She didn't believe him. Everybody knew the American devils tore Japanese prisoners apart with tanks. She blurted out that she feared Americans, especially the black ones.

He laughed. "It was Negroes who saved you."

She pleaded with the captain to let her die with her compatriots, and he got permission to take her by truck to Charan Kanoa. As they drove along the coast road in the bright starlight he told her there were many bodies of civilians in the sea. He asked if she wanted to see them. He ordered the vehicle stopped. With the help of two Negroes he carried her to a cliff. Below, floating bodies clustered the water's edge. One woman had two children lashed to her.

Almost to himself the young officer asked, "Why do Japanese kill themselves like this?" Tears flowed down his cheeks.

Just past midnight they entered Charan Kanoa. To her surprise it was bright with electric lights. Tents sprouted all over. It was a different world. The captain told her this was the camp for Japanese, but she knew it was a trick. She was going to be shot here. Then she saw Japanese children clinging to a wire fence surrounding the tent city. She insisted on getting out, though the captain argued that she should continue to the hospital. "Do you have acquaintances out there? Is that it?"

"There's my mother!" she lied.

She was lifted out of the truck on a stretcher. She insisted on walking and staggered through the gate before she fell. Many friendly hands lifted her up. She was back with her own.

On July 9 at 4:15 P.M., Admiral Turner announced that Saipan was officially secured, and attention turned to neighboring Tinian and Guam. Marines who had once glumly predicted "Golden Gate in '48" were now saying "Home Alive in '45." The battle on Saipan had ended but there remained the onerous and dangerous job of mopping up several thousand stragglers who were hiding in caves. "It means," one cynical Marine commented, "that if you get shot now, you were hit in your own rear areas."

A different but equally difficult task confronted the Americans at the northern tip of the island. There thousands of civilians had gathered and were committing mass suicide rather than surrender. Interpreters and captured Japanese, using public address systems, pleaded with crowds at Marpi Point, which dropped off spectacularly more than a hundred feet to rocky shallows. The fighting was over; safety and food were waiting; the names of those who had already surrendered were read off. Still men threw their children from the cliff and jumped after them; and mothers with babies on their backs would leap into the boiling surf.

There were so many floating bodies that "naval small craft were unable to steer a course without running over them." Lieutenant

Emery Cleaves of the minesweeper *Chief* saw the corpse of a nude woman, drowned while giving birth. "The baby's head had entered this world, but that was all of him." Nearby "a small boy of four or five had drowned with his arm firmly clenched around the neck of a Jap soldier; the two bodies rocked crazily in the waves."

Elsewhere on the island families remained hidden from the new conquerors day after day. The Okuyamas—father, mother and four children—found a cave. On the morning of July 17 they were sunbathing on the ledge overlooking the rugged northeast coast, when a soldier from a nearby cave shouted "Enemy!" and pointed above them to the top of the cliff. Fourteen-year-old Ryoko Okuyama, the eldest child, glanced up at four or five big red-faced Americans in camouflage uniforms. They looked so different from the much smaller Japanese soldiers.

The Japanese fired his rifle and the Americans began dropping grenades. The Okuyamas braced themselves against a depression, kicking them off the ledge, but when the missiles continued to fall, the father—a tailor—herded his family down to the bottom of the cliff to another cave. Inside they found a sergeant, an exhausted correspondent from the *Asahi Shimbun*, and an abandoned newborn baby which cried until Mrs. Okuyama picked it up. As the loud American voices came nearer and the sound of gunfire intensified, the baby began to scream. "Quiet it," the sergeant whispered. "Any way!"

Mrs. Okuyama, an attractive woman of thirty-four, tried to nurse the baby but it kept crying. In desperation she put the hem of her jacket over the baby's mouth, and finally stifled the noise. The baby was dead. The sound of machine-gun fire echoed violently in the cave. The voices were just outside. The sergeant handed Okuyama a grenade, held another himself.

Ryoko looked at her father in farewell. Pale and tense, he nodded slightly. The sergeant removed the safety pin of his grenade, so did Okuyama. "We are all going to a nice place together," the mother told four-year-old Yoshitada, the youngest child. He smiled as if it were a game. The two men struck the grenades simultaneously against rocks at their feet. As the fuses hissed, Ryoko thought in rapid succession: Am I going to be a Buddha? Do human beings really have souls? Is there really another world? She felt the cave shake—the concussion had thrown her against the rock wall. Dazed, she heard her little brother give a feeble groan, and she fainted.

She didn't know how long she had remained unconscious. First she saw a vague brightness of red, and as it came into focus she realized it was the open abdomen of the sergeant who was sitting before her, legs crossed, as if asleep. The huge wound was so neat that it reminded her of the human-body exhibit in biology class. The organs, all in place, were "beautiful."

She herself was covered with blood and raw flesh. Appalled, she moved her arms and legs—no pain. She twisted. Still not much pain. Her nine-year-old brother's shirt was blown off. Pieces of shrapnel were sticking in his bare chest, leaving black, burned spots. He was dead. So were her father, little Yoshitada and her six-year-old sister. The flesh had been blown from her sister's head, revealing a skull the color and texture of a transparent candle. Ryoko had a horrifying feeling of loneliness. She was the only one alive. Then she felt something touch her left shoulder.

"Mother, you are alive!"

"I'm dying" was the calm reply. Her mother's legs were shattered and Ryoko ripped strips from a piece of cloth nearby to make bandages.

"It won't work," Mrs. Okuyama said quietly. "I'm going to die. You can't stop the bleeding with something like that."

"But the blood isn't coming out any more!"

"It has all run out," Mrs. Okuyama said. She stared at the bodies of her family. "I'm glad they had a clean death." She turned to Ryoko. "Only you are alive."

"*Okusan, okusan* [Madame]!" It was the *Asahi* man. His agonized voice was almost inaudible. Mother and daughter were astonished to find that someone else had survived. "Kill me. *Okusan,* please."

"I'm dying too," Mrs. Okuyama told him. "My legs are gone. I can't even move. I can't help you."

He looked up slowly; then, writhing in agony, he slammed his head against a jagged rock. He groaned and tried again and again. Finally he was dead.

"After I die you mustn't stay here," Mrs. Okuyama said to her daughter. With darkness she was to leave. "You must live long and follow the path of righteousness with a strong mind." She had written the same words when Ryoko entered middle school.

Mrs. Okuyama painfully unwound a *furoshiki* from her waist— it was filled with money—and tied it tightly around her daughter. "Soon I'll be dead. My vision is getting blurred. I want to lie down. Will you help me?" All the while there was a soft smile on her face. For the first time Ryoko realized how gentle her mother was. How could she ever have feared her?

"My hearing is fading now. Give me your hands." She grasped Ryoko's hands. "I can't talk any more," she said faintly.

"Mother, don't die!"

Mrs. Okuyama smiled and nodded her head. Her lips moved but no sound issued. She was dead.

Almost 22,000 Japanese civilians—two out of three—perished needlessly. And almost the entire garrison—at least 30,000—died.

For the victors the battle was also the most costly to date in the Pacific. Of the 71,000 Americans who had landed on Saipan, 14,111 were killed, wounded or missing in action—more than double the losses at Guadalcanal—but the main bastion protecting Japan's homeland had been seized, and the enemy's carrier-based striking power had been crippled. Even more important, the low-lands of southern Saipan offered the Americans the first site from which massive B-29 bombing raids could be launched at the heart of the Japanese Empire, Tokyo.

PART SIX

The Decisive Battle

21

"Let No Heart
Be Faint"

1.

Never before had a modern Japanese leader gathered to himself so much power. To the world Tojo's position seemed unassailable but in reality his rule was at the point of collapse. Ever since Midway, Imperial Headquarters had refused to acknowledge the growing power of America* and the diminishing power of Japan. Shipping losses continued to mount as the American submarine campaign intensified. To the north the Aleutian outposts had been abandoned; to the south, the Solomons and New Guinea had been overrun; and in the central Pacific the defense line—the Marshalls, the Gilberts and finally the Marianas —had collapsed.

At home, production levels were still maintained, but at the expense of extraordinary sacrifices by the people. Not only had many civilian enterprises been converted to war production and more women brought into industry, but teen-agers had been added

---

* There were almost a hundred U. S. fleet and escort carriers in the Pacific by late summer of 1944.

to the labor force. Classroom time was reduced to a minimum and school buildings transformed into military supply depots.

A seven-day workweek was established, with the Sundays so cherished by Japanese "abolished." Trains had become crowded to such an extent that a number of infants were suffocated; trips of more than 100 kilometers required a police permit; diners and sleepers were discontinued. The people's aggression turned on the trains when they were late, now a common occurrence; they stole seat covers and broke windows to get in and out. Consumer goods of every description were drastically curtailed. Food was rationed, clothing was at a premium, coffins had to be used over and over, and there was little gas or charcoal for heating homes. Newspapers were reduced in size, and publication of afternoon editions was suspended; about ten thousand amusement places—including geisha houses—were shut down. Life in Japan, in short, had become drab and onerous. "What kind of a Tokyo has this turned out to be!" lamented comedian Roppa Furukawa in his diary. "Ah, it's no fun being alive any more!"

These extreme austerity measures—coupled with the suspicion that the abandonment of territory, culminating with the fall of Saipan, was more serious than the official communiqués indicated —fostered unrest which centered around Tojo, the symbol of war and power.

The most outrageous rumors were accepted and passed on: Tojo was using tobacco, whiskey and other loot from the occupied southern areas to bribe members of the Imperial Household Ministry, the board of chamberlains, the *jushin* and privy councilors; he had even paid off the Emperor's brothers—Chichibu and Takamatsu—with automobiles.*

He was ridiculed—behind his back, naturally—for allowing his

---

* These rumors had no basis in fact, but there was some justification for complaints. Tojo did misappropriate power in his utilization of the *kempeitai* to control dissidents. Known pacifists such as Konoye were under strict surveillance, and many citizens had been jailed and a few tortured to death for espousing Christianity or fomenting political opposition. Seigo Nakano, an avowed Nazi, was arrested after making a public speech against Tojo. Soon after his release he committed hara-kiri under such mysterious circumstances that it was commonly believed *kempei* agents had "persuaded" him to kill himself.

The impression was real and caused widespread public indignation, but the extent of the repression was exaggerated.

wife to make public speeches and radio broadcasts and engage in other active efforts to support the war. She was nicknamed *"To Bi-rei,"* a play on the Japanese version of Madame Chiang Kai-shek's name, *"So Bi-rei."* Following the disaster at Saipan, Mrs. Tojo was inundated by anonymous phone calls asking if her husband had committed suicide yet.

There were some who were not willing to leave such a final action up to the Prime Minister himself. In addition to Admiral Sokichi Takagi, whose group was planning to ambush Tojo by machine gun, rebels in the Army also sought his assassination. A major named Tsunoda, recently transferred from China to Imperial Headquarters—together with Tatsukuma Ushijima, president of the Tokyo chapter of *Toa Renmei* (East Asia Federation)— was planning to throw a special hydrocyanic bomb at Tojo's car as it slowed on a curve in the Imperial Palace grounds near the Iwaida Bridge. The time was set: the third week of July. But the plot was betrayed by the Emperor's youngest brother, Prince Mikasa, to whom a friend of the conspirators had unintentionally revealed the plan. Instead of giving it his blessing ("Such action was tantamount to rebellion against the Throne") he informed a member of Imperial Headquarters. Ushijima and Tsunoda were arrested by the *kempeitai* and sentenced to death, but as had happened so often in the past, they were given a stay of execution.

Confronted with extensive discontent, Tojo sought advice from the man who had proposed him as prime minister and given his official support through the past months of crisis—the Privy Seal. The counsel Tojo received was as unexpected as it was unwelcome. Kido, finally roused to action by the fall of Saipan, was critical of the recent fusion of power: the two top positions in the Cabinet held by Tojo himself, and the dual role of Admiral Shimada (the Navy Minister-cum-Navy Chief of Staff was regarded by other Navy men as Tojo's *kaban-mochi*—briefcase carrier). "Everyone is concerned about this," said Kido, "and the Emperor himself is extremely annoyed."

Profoundly discomposed, Tojo withdrew without saying a word but returned later in the day. He was willing to reshuffle the Cabinet but not to surrender his own posts. Kido greeted this compromise with a coolness that seemed hostile to Tojo. He shot to his feet. "There's no sense in talking to you today!" he exclaimed.

He marched out of Kido's office with a slam of the door, but by the time he reached his official residence he had sobered. He told Kenryo Sato, "If Kido has that attitude, it means the Emperor's confidence in me is lost. Therefore I'm giving up the idea of reforming the Cabinet; instead I will resign."

"It's out of the question to resign at the most critical time of the war!" shouted Sato. All he had to do was replace Shimada with Admiral Yonai; it would appease both the Navy and liberals like Konoye.

But Tojo found it too distasteful to dismiss Shimada, who had supported him so faithfully. Sato quoted the Chinese saying that "in order to attain true justice one should not hesitate to kill one's parents if necessary." "You must 'kill' Shimada no matter how painful it may be. Your obligation to Shimada is a personal matter. You started this war and you cannot give up in the middle of it."

It was what Tojo himself believed. He summoned Shimada and informed him he would have to resign as navy minister. The admiral was gracious. "I who am leaving can do so with lightened shoulders," he said. "You who stay must continue to bear great responsibilities." He wished Tojo a "good fight" in his coming struggle, and as they shook hands the disciplined Tojo broke down.

The next day, July 17, Shimada submitted his resignation but contrary to Sato's prediction, the liberals were not appeased. Neither was Kido, and after prodding from Konoye, he promised that though major political questions were outside his province, he would report to the Throne the consensus of the *jushin*'s recommendations in reference to Tojo.

Exhilarated, Konoye drove to the home of Baron Hiranuma, where he found two other *jushin,* Admiral Okada and Baron Reijiro Wakatsuki. He told them of Kido's surprising offer. "Now I understand what Kido has been trying to do," Admiral Okada remarked.

By six-thirty all the *jushin* had arrived. Conspiracy was in the air, and after months of ineffectual private complaints, they greeted one another with a sense of purpose. "I should like to draw your attention to the fact that even if the Tojo Cabinet is re-formed," Wakatsuki warned, "the people will not support it."

Admiral Yonai revealed that he had just been "earnestly" invited to join the Cabinet as Shimada's replacement. He had refused, but fully expected Tojo to make a personal appeal and if that failed, go to the Throne for backing. "I have already made up my mind not to accept the offer even if that last step is taken."

Not all the *jushin* wanted Tojo's resignation. General Nobuyuki Abe charged that it was "irresponsible to talk exclusively of knocking down the Cabinet. How can we be sure of getting a better one?"

"Whether the Cabinet is overthrown or not or whether the next one is weak or not is not the point," Hiranuma interjected. The country had reached a crisis and a change of cabinets had to be made—and quickly.

"If I were asked, I wouldn't join the Cabinet," said Hirota, the diplomat who had headed the Cabinet after the 2/26 Incident.

They finally worked out a resolution that pleased everyone but Abe. It read:

The minds and hearts of the people must be infused with new life if the empire is to survive the great problems facing it. All of us in the nation must co-operate and work together. A partial reorganization of the Cabinet will be useless. A powerful new cabinet must be formed that will surge forward unswervingly.

Abe wondered if the results of their meeting shouldn't be passed on to Tojo. The answer was unanimous—No. The resolution was hand-carried to Kido's home. The Privy Seal promised to present it to the Emperor the next morning.

In his office Prime Minister Tojo and Kenryo Sato were pondering Yonai's refusal to join the Cabinet. Sato thought the fault lay with the go-between who had represented Tojo. "Your true intentions haven't yet been gotten across to Yonai," he said. "Let me speak for you direct."

Sato changed to civilian clothes and, unrecognized, slipped by newsmen assigned to the admiral's residence. He pushed his way past the maid, who said her master wasn't in, and fell asleep in the waiting room. An hour later he woke up when Yonai returned from the *jushin* meeting.

Sato tried to impress Yonai that it was essential to save the Cabinet in the middle of war; and his acceptance of a portfolio would accomplish this. Tojo's sole desire was to change the tide of battle. "I can see why you object to his cabinet, but that is merely a personal opinion. At this most critical time I beg you to co-operate with the Tojo Cabinet to overcome our problems."

"I am not an expert in politics." Yonai smiled wryly. "You can see that from my own cabinet. I'm an admiral, not a politician. And I'd like to die an admiral. If you want to use me, make me an adviser to the Navy Minister."

From Yonai's tone it was clear that he could not be persuaded. Sato started back to Tojo's office. He had tried but failed, and now his final advice would negate everything he had previously said. It was two o'clock in the morning, but Tojo was still working in his shirt sleeves, smoke from his ever-present cigarette curling up to the lampshade above his head. Tojo looked up.

"Please resign," said Sato.

Tojo let his breath out in a long sigh. "I will see the Emperor in the morning," he said. "Would you please put in writing what led to my resignation."

As Sato sat down and began to write, he knew in his heart that the war was over, and tears dropped onto the paper.

In the morning, July 18, Tojo—skin sallow, eyes lusterless— told his cabinet in a weary voice that he had decided to resign because of the loss of Saipan. He had hesitated so long only because of the "Badoglio" group in Japan.* The responsibility for Japan's defeat, he added caustically, would have to be borne by the *jushin* and others who had forced him out of office. His shoulders sagged. It was the hottest day of the year. "I must ask you all to resign," he said.

The atmosphere was awkward as each man wrote his resignation. It was ironic that exactly four years earlier Tojo had been chosen war minister.

Stony-faced, Tojo delivered the documents to Kido. The Privy Seal asked whom he would like to succeed him. "I won't say whom I want," Tojo replied with sarcasm. "I imagine the *jushin* have already decided who it will be." Then he started down the long corridor to the Emperor's office to make his last report as prime minister.

* He was referring to the Marshal Pietro Badoglio government, which had surrendered Italy unconditionally to the Allies the previous summer.

The *jushin* had not yet selected his successor but were about to. They met this time in the afternoon—and with Kido as the dominating presence—in the West Room of the Palace. Also present were the Grand Chamberlain and President of the Privy Council Yoshimichi Hara.

General Abe, who had always supported Tojo, wanted the Navy —in the person of Yonai—to form the new cabinet.

"I did take part in politics once," the admiral observed. "And I might try again as navy minister, but I can't become prime minister." Military men had "a one-sided education" and this made them unsuited for such a role. "Politics should be left to politicians."

Konoye appreciated Yonai's idealism but they had to consider the matter from a practical point of view. "Politics today cannot be carried on without the Army's participation."

Kido and Konoye had long since privately agreed that there should be an interim cabinet before the imperial family became involved. "The bolstering of home defense," Kido retorted, "the increase of Army strength in the homeland, and that of the military police, force us to choose someone from the Army." Wakatsuki acquiesced and so did Yonai. Moments earlier the latter had warned about the dangers of choosing a military man; now he suggested Count Hisaichi Terauchi, who had been promoted to field marshal the year before.

Konoye was willing to accept Terauchi, but not before he had emphasized two points: "First, why did Tojo fall? Of course, it was partially because many unfavorable things were said about him, but also because the Army, unlike the Navy, interferes with every phase of political as well as economic life." This would have to cease. "Second, the nation nowadays seems to be drifting toward a leftist revolution. Everything points in that direction. Losing the war is a dreadful thing, but a revolution is far more dreadful. Once defeated, we may recover in due time, but a leftist revolution would play havoc with the national essence." He wondered if Terauchi could control the dissident elements.

"He is all right," Kido said, "but since he is so far away from here, at the front, it would be difficult to bring him back. We'd better choose someone else."

For a second time Yonai nominated a military man, General

Yoshijiro Umezu, the commander of the Kwantung Army who had just been recalled to replace Tojo as chief of staff.

"It's not good to remove him so soon from his new post," objected Kido, who privately thought Umezu would be a poor choice.

Konoye suggested a Navy man, the aged Kantaro Suzuki, who had narrowly escaped death in the 2/26 Incident. "I was with him in the Privy Council," Hara said, "and know him well. He will never accept the offer." Hiranuma's motion of Field Marshal Shunroku Hata, commander in chief in China, got a lukewarm reception.

Again Yonai suggested a general, Kuniaki Koiso. "He's a good man, capable and courageous. I knew him well when he was in my cabinet."

"How does he get along with Army men?" Kido asked.

"Not so badly, I believe," General Abe replied. "He's different from Tojo."

"He's first-rate and devoutly religious," Hiranuma commented.

"I have no objections," said Wakatsuki, "although I don't know him."

Okada thought they were making too hasty a choice, and Konoye supported him. This inspired a lengthy and inconclusive dispute, and in the end they were forced to advise the Emperor to choose one of the three Army men—Terauchi, Hata or Koiso. It was already eight o'clock. They had debated for four hours and it was with a sense of relief that they passed on the responsibility to His Majesty.

Marquis Kido reported immediately to the Emperor, with the suggestion that His Majesty query the Army on Terauchi's availability before making a choice. The answer came from Tojo, who by chance was at the Palace for the installation of his successor, General Umezu. Tojo advised against releasing Terauchi from his post at such a critical time. That left only Hata and Koiso, and the Emperor, after considering Kido's presentations, selected the latter.

During the night Prince Konoye began worrying about Koiso. Would he be able to control the leftists and remain independent of the Army? Perhaps there should be co-premiers, one from the Army, one from the Navy. A combination of Koiso and Yonai, for example. And since Yonai himself had recommended Koiso, it was obvious the two would get along.

The next day he discussed it with Baron Hiranuma, who thought it was a splendid idea. And, more important, so did the Privy Seal. But Yonai remained reluctant. Since he had refused Tojo's invitation to join his cabinet, it would be "improper" now to accept a much more prominent position. But why not navy minister? "I'm confident of handling that post. I'm not ashamed to admit that I might prove to be the best possible navy minister."

Konoye was almost as pleased as if Yonai had accepted co-premiership. With Yonai in the Cabinet, strongly supported by Kido and the Emperor, it would amount to the same thing.

General Koiso arrived from Korea the following afternoon. He was taken directly and without explanation to the waiting room adjoining the Imperial Chamber. Nicknamed "the Tiger of Korea" more for his looks than for his military prowess, he had slanted, catlike eyes, a flat nose and thin lips. He liked *sake* parties and was jovial enough to tolerate another nickname—"Champion Bald-head of Japan." He knew there was a good chance he might be named prime minister and had in his pocket a list of close comrades in Korea for cabinet posts, but his expectations diminished sharply at the entrance of Admiral Yonai. Before he could question Yonai, Kido appeared to usher the two into His Majesty's presence. Who should go first? asked the general, and Kido replied, "Koiso." But the Emperor treated both of them exactly alike. He said they would have to co-operate in forming a new cabinet and warned them not to antagonize Russia.

Yonai was as mystified as Koiso and when the audience was over, he asked Marquis Kido which one was prime minister. "Koiso, of course," said the Privy Seal.

What a strange conversation! Koiso thought. He turned to Yonai. "What office are you going to take? Navy minister?"

"That's the only post I'm capable of filling," the admiral replied.

Tojo's forced resignation gave his wife a sense of relief. Now, at least, the daily hazard of assassination was over. (Coincidentally, Tojo's ally Adolf Hitler had just barely escaped death from a bomb explosion.) Her reasoning was correct. Admiral Takagi, for instance, canceled his plan to gun down Tojo, who had now joined the distinguished but purely advisory circle of *jushin*.

2.

Although General MacArthur had been given a target date to invade the Philippines—a preliminary landing at Mindanao to establish airfields, followed three weeks later by a major one at Leyte—the Joint Chiefs had suggested in mid-June that he by-pass the other Philippine islands, including Luzon, and leapfrog all the way from Leyte to Formosa. This would, in effect, eliminate Mac-Arthur's cherished role as Liberator of the Philippines, and his reply was in keeping with his indignation:

. . . THE PHILIPPINES IS AMERICAN TERRITORY WHERE OUR UNSUPPORTED FORCES WERE DESTROYED BY THE ENEMY. PRACTICALLY ALL OF THE 17,000,000 FILIPINOS REMAIN LOYAL TO THE UNITED STATES AND ARE UNDERGOING THE GREATEST PRIVATION AND SUFFERING BECAUSE WE HAVE NOT BEEN ABLE TO SUPPORT OR SUCCOR THEM. WE HAVE A GREAT NATIONAL OBLIGATION TO DISCHARGE.
MOREOVER, IF THE UNITED STATES SHOULD DELIBERATELY BYPASS THE PHILIPPINES, LEAVING OUR PRISONERS, NATION-ALS, AND LOYAL FILIPINOS IN ENEMY HANDS WITHOUT AN EFFORT TO RETRIEVE THEM AT EARLIEST MOMENT, WE WOULD INCUR THE GRAVEST PSYCHOLOGICAL REACTION. WE WOULD ADMIT THE TRUTH OF JAPANESE PROPAGANDA TO THE EFFECT THAT WE HAD ABANDONED THE FILIPINOS AND WOULD NOT SHED AMERICAN BLOOD TO REDEEM THEM; WE WOULD UNDOUBTEDLY INCUR THE OPEN HOSTILITY OF THAT PEOPLE; WE WOULD PROBABLY SUFFER SUCH LOSS OF PRESTIGE AMONG ALL THE PEOPLES OF THE FAR EAST THAT IT WOULD AD-VERSELY AFFECT THE UNITED STATES FOR MANY YEARS. . . .

Marshall replied with a forceful admonition "not to let personal feelings and Philippine politics" overshadow his primary objective, the winning of the war. He asserted that "bypassing" was by no means "synonymous with abandonment." MacArthur, however, was offered the opportunity of reviewing the matter directly with the President. The occasion was to be an unprecedented meeting five weeks hence in Hawaii between Roosevelt, MacArthur and Nimitz. Marshall, Arnold and King were not invited; it was an indication to King that the President, with the Democrats holding their national convention in Chicago, "wished to emphasize his role as Commander in Chief of the Army and Navy."

Roosevelt and his party boarded the heavy cruiser *Baltimore* at San Diego the day after he was nominated for a fourth term. Early in the afternoon of July 26 the cruiser, presidential flag flapping at the main, passed Diamond Head. MacArthur, whose plane had just landed after the long trip from Brisbane, met the President at the pier. The general was still in his winter uniform.

"Douglas," chided Admiral Leahy, a friend for almost forty years, "why don't you wear the right kind of clothes when you come up here to see us?"

"Well, you haven't been where I came from, and it's cold up there in the sky."

The presidential party passed through long lines of soldiers and a cheering crowd to the site of the conference, a palatial private home on Waikiki Beach. There was no longer need to debate priorities of men and matériel, nor was there any question of the success of whatever was to come. After dinner Roosevelt pointed to Mindanao on a map of the Pacific and said, "Douglas, where do we go from here?"

"Leyte, Mr. President, and then Luzon!" MacArthur expounded at length on the advisability of seizing Luzon before invading Formosa. Nimitz made no comment.

The next morning formal talks began in a large living room whose walls were covered with operational maps. Using a long bamboo pointer, MacArthur again urged the occupation of Luzon. This time Nimitz countered, also aided by the pointer, with his own plan for striking directly at Formosa. Roosevelt leaned back in his wheelchair, relishing the lesson in geography. Tactfully he narrowed down the points of disagreement. But his mediation was not necessary. Nimitz, a good listener, finally accepted the validity of MacArthur's argument that national honor and strategy made the liberation of all the Philippines essential before moving on to Formosa.

After lunch MacArthur assured Roosevelt there would be no friction between him and Nimitz. "We see eye to eye, Mr. President," he said. "We understand each other perfectly." Later, as his plane took off for Brisbane, he turned to an aide with a triumphant "We've sold it!"

While the Americans prepared the complex strategy leading up to the Leyte invasion—which was given a definite date, December 20—Imperial Headquarters in Tokyo was attempting to guess their intentions. A "Plan for the Conduct of Future Operations" envisaged attacks on four areas: the Philippines; Formosa and Okinawa; the home islands; and the Kuriles in the north. Though it was given the optimistic name SHO-GO (Operation Victory), it was a plan born of desperation, a series of last-ditch defenses. It was obvious that the Philippines was the next American objective—SHO-1—and it was agreed that this should be made the scene of the Final Decisive Battle both on land and sea.

The question was where and how to meet this challenge and force this confrontation into a genuinely conclusive conflict. It was a problem of geography. The Philippine archipelago, almost 7,100 islands, lay some 500 miles off the mainland of Asia, 230 miles south of Formosa. It extended 1,150 miles from Mindanao due north through the Visayans—the central islands including Cebu and Leyte—to Luzon, the largest and most important island. Only eleven of the islands had an area larger than one thousand square miles and two of these, Mindanao and Luzon, comprised more than two thirds of the total land area. Strategically, however, Leyte—one-thirteenth the size of Mindanao—was equally important. It was in the heart of the archipelago, and its spacious gulf was an invitation to an invasion from the sea.

Southern Army's operations officer wanted to oppose the Americans wherever they landed first—which would be somewhere in the south—before they had a chance to set up bases. But he was overruled by the Army General Staff. It would be impossible to predict exactly where the enemy would first strike. Rather than disperse troops on a number of southern islands, the bulk should be concentrated on Luzon, which had the best roads and could be most easily defended.

The conquest of the Philippines called for combined sea and land operations of a magnitude never before attempted by the United States. MacArthur would lead the assault, but he would have Nimitz' full support. It was the Navy's task to neutralize Japanese air power. The first strike was delivered on September 6 by Vice Admiral Marc Mitscher's Task Force 38. For three days his bombers hit the Palaus, 550 miles due east of Mindanao. Then he shifted the attack to Mindanao itself on September 9 and 10.

These aerial raids spurred Japanese preparations for the defense of the Philippines. In Manila, Field Marshal Terauchi, whose Southern Army was charged with the defense of the vast area from New Guinea to Burma, believed with Tokyo that ground-based planes could sink most of the enemy convoys before they beached. But the local commander of ground troops, Lieutenant General Shigenori Kuroda of the 14th Area Army, argued that the concept was good but you couldn't "fight with concept alone. Words will not sink American ships and that becomes clear when you compare our aircraft with theirs." Japanese air power was negligible and the battle would have to be won on land.

There was even disagreement on how this kind of battle should be fought. "Annihilation at the Beachhead" had been standard operating procedure in all previous invasions. But opposition to this policy was growing. Beach defenses had proved helpless against naval bombardment followed by a determined assault. Imperial Headquarters ordered Terauchi to set up resistance in depth.

The order was passed on to the officer responsible for the defense of Mindanao and the Visayans—Lieutenant General Sosaku Suzuki, who had once been rudely roused out of bed in Malaya by an indignant Colonel Tsuji.* He commanded the 35th Army, the equivalent of a U. S. Army Corps, and had headquarters in Cebu

---

* "It was the Ishihara-Tsuji clique—the personification of *gekokujo*," General Suzuki told a fellow officer, Major Yoshitaka Horie, after leaving Malaya, "that brought the Japanese Army to this deplorable situation. In Malaya, Tsuji's speech and conduct were often insolent; and there was this problem of inhumane treatment of Chinese merchants, so I advised General Yamashita to punish Tsuji severely and then dismiss him. But he feigned ignorance. I tell you, so long as they [Tsuji, Ishihara, and their like] exert influence on the Army, it can only lead to ruin. Extermination of these poisonous insects should take precedence over all other problems."

City. The general was described by his colleagues as a gentle man "of great heart" and "straight as bamboo."

Suzuki not only feared the American invasion would come sooner than his superiors in Tokyo and Manila did (he told his chief of staff to expect a landing about the first of October) but predicted correctly that the enemy would concentrate his attack on Leyte. He placed the 30th Division in northern Mindanao so it could quickly be transferred to Leyte. But immediate events made him doubt his own prophecy. On September 10 a message arrived from a naval observation unit that the enemy was landing near Davao on the south coast of Mindanao. Two hours later another report arrived:

AMERICAN MARINES USING AMPHIBIOUS TANKS HAVE LANDED ON SOUTHERN TIP OF SMALL ISLAND LOCATED ACROSS THE BANKS FROM DAVAO.

Suzuki transferred the 30th Division back to the south of Mindanao and alerted Manila. The Fourth Air Army began ferrying planes from New Guinea to the Philippines while Combined Fleet alerted its forces for SHO-1. But there had been no enemy landing. Observers on a hill overlooking the bay had mistaken choppy waves for landing craft.

"Let this mishap be a lesson," Suzuki told his staff. The next time, he trusted, they would not act so precipitously.

Two days later Mitscher resumed his attacks, which would eventually sweep up through the Philippines all the way to Okinawa. Within forty-eight hours, 2,400 sorties had been launched at the Visayans. The damage was so complete and the American casualty rate so minimal that Admiral Halsey, who commanded Third Fleet (which now included most of the ships in Spruance's old Fifth Fleet), asked himself why the Leyte invasion date should not be advanced. He sat in a corner of the bridge of the battleship *New Jersey* and "thought it over." It was really none of his business and might "upset a great many applecarts, possibly all the way up to Mr. Roosevelt and Mr. Churchill," but it might also "cut months off the war."

Halsey summoned his chief of staff, Robert ("Mick") Carney,

and his secretary, Harold Stassen, and said, "I'm going to stick my neck out. Send an urgent dispatch to CINCPAC." It recommended cancellation of preliminary operations on Yap, Morotai and Mindanao, and seizure of Leyte "at the earliest possible date." Nimitz forwarded the dispatch to Quebec, where Roosevelt and Churchill were again meeting. The boldness of Halsey's suggestion intrigued them, but they needed MacArthur's blessing.

The general was aboard *Nashville* on his way to Morotai, one of the Spice Islands between New Guinea and Mindanao, the next to the last step on his route to the Philippines. *Nashville* was under radio silence, and the decision rested on MacArthur's chief of staff, General Sutherland, who had remained in New Guinea. He knew his chief would welcome an earlier liberation of the Philippines, so, in MacArthur's name, he radioed Quebec that the invasion of Leyte could take place on October 20, two months ahead of schedule.

On September 15 MacArthur's troops landed unopposed on Morotai while Halsey's were meeting stiff resistance on Pelelieu, one of the Palau islands.* Six days later Mitscher continued his

---

* Pelelieu was defended with such determination that it took a statistical average of 1,589 rounds of heavy and light ammunition to kill each Japanese soldier. American casualties were extremely heavy. In one month of bitter combat, 1,121 Marines were killed.

The Marines were feuding with their own Navy and Army in equal proportions. Just before disembarking for the assault, Marines on correspondent Tom Lea's transport left this notice on the ship's bulletin board in the Ship's Officers Wardroom:

A MESSAGE OF THANKS
From: Marines aboard U.S.S. *Repulsive*
To: Officers and Men aboard U.S.S. *Repulsive*

1. It gives us great pleasure at this time to extend our sincere thanks to all members of the crew for their kind and considerate treatment of Marines during this cruise.

2. We non-combatants realize that the brave and stalwart members of the crew are winning the war in the Pacific. You Navy people even go within ten miles of a Japanese island, thereby risking your precious lives. Oh how courageous you are! Oh how our piles bleed for you.

3. Because of your actions during this voyage it is our heartfelt wish that:

a. The U.S.S. *Repulsive* receives a Jap torpedo immediately after debarkation of all troops.

b. The crew of the U.S.S. *Repulsive* is stranded on Beach Orange Three where Marine units which sailed aboard the ship may repay devastating sweeps of the Philippines. Daringly he brought his carriers to within forty miles of the east coast of Luzon to launch four air strikes at the Manila area. The strips at Clark and Nichols fields were plowed up, more than two hundred planes destroyed and the shipping in Manila Bay ravaged. Only fifteen U. S. aircraft were lost and no Japanese plane was able to break through the screen protecting Task Force 38.

3.

Now, even in Tokyo, it was clear that the American invasion of the Philippines was imminent. General Kuroda, who had realistically prophesied that Japanese land-based planes could not thwart American sea power, was relieved of his command on the specious grounds that he was "devoting more time to his golf, reading and personal matters than to the execution of his official duties."

His replacement as commander of all ground troops in the Islands was one of the heroes of the early victories, the conqueror of Singapore. After that campaign, General Tomoyuki Yamashita had been sent to Manchuria to train troops. He was not allowed to stop off in Tokyo. This, explained Imperial Headquarters, was to prevent the Russians from learning of his new assignment, but Yamashita, who had been at odds with Tojo for years, was convinced it was just an excuse to get him out of public sight.

On his way south Yamashita told his operations officer, Major Shigeharu Asaeda, who like his chief was impatient for action, that he feared the Philippine campaign was "going to be another Battle of Minatogawa"—one fought by a commander who knew from the beginning he had no chance of victory. But he hid this pessimism from his new staff, and upon arrival at 14th Area Army headquarters at Fort McKinley near Manila on October 6, told them that the fate of Japan rested on the outcome of the battle. Each officer had a "heavy responsibility" to fight resolutely, daringly

---

in some measure the good fellowship extended by the crew and officers during the trip.

4. In conclusion we Marines wish to say to all you dear, dear boys in the Navy:

"Bugger you, you bloody bastards!"

and with determination to win. "If we all remember this, the Japanese Army must win in the end."

Less than twenty thousand troops—the 16th Division—were garrisoned on the island that was MacArthur's target, Leyte. This unit had landed on the east coast of Luzon on Christmas Eve, 1941, and after participating in the seizure of Manila, fought on Bataan. But the majority of its present complement, including its commander, Lieutenant General Shiro Makino, were replacements who had never before been in battle. In the Japanese Army their reputation was poor; they were mostly draftees from the Kyoto-Osaka region and were "better businessmen than fighters."

Leyte was wedged between two larger islands, Samar directly to the northeast and Mindanao to the south. In shape it resembled a molar with its roots pointing to Mindanao. On the east coast a fertile plain ran along Leyte Gulf for thirty-five miles. No reefs protected its open sandy beaches, making it a perfect site for landing operations. But a few miles inland MacArthur's men would have to cross a complex of swamps, streams and rice paddies which were almost impassable except by road during the rainy season, which had already begun. The rest of the island was mountainous and heavily wooded, equally difficult to attack or defend. It was infested with small bands of guerrillas, who were in conflict with one another as often as with the Japanese. Their principal value to MacArthur was the reliable information they radioed him about General Makino's defenses.

There were almost a million people on the island, all of them —except for 3,076 Chinese, and a sprinkling of Europeans, Americans and Japanese—placid Visayans who lived by farming and fishing. The principal crops were rice, sugar cane, corn and copra.

At Hollandia as well as at Manus, one of the Admiralty islands two hundred miles north of New Guinea, a vast armada—including battleships, cruisers, small carriers, destroyers, transports, tankers, amphibious craft, minesweepers, salvage tugs and floating drydocks—was preparing to set sail for Leyte. The ships were manned by 50,000 sailors, and the transports and amphibious craft carried 165,000 troops of MacArthur's Sixth Army. The invasion of Leyte would be by far the greatest operation in the

Pacific. For the first time all the forces of MacArthur, Nimitz and the overseas bomber commands would be united.

The safe passage of this convoy was still Mitscher's concern and to accomplish this he was to range from the Philippine Sea to the East China Sea and back. Task Force 38, which had already practically eliminated Japanese air power in the Philippines, first steamed a thousand miles north to Okinawa, an island the Japanese considered part of the homeland. Mitscher's 1,396 sorties on October 10 destroyed a hundred planes and considerable shipping, including four cargo vessels, a submarine tender and a dozen torpedo boats.

The admiral swung back south to bomb northern Luzon the following day. Then he reversed course again and just before sunrise on October 12 launched fighters from his four carrier groups at Formosa. Here he met his first serious opposition. Vice Admiral Shigeru Fukudome, commander of the Sixth Base Air Force, sent up 230 fighters to ambush the Americans. Many of his young pilots had learned their combat technology only from films,* but they would probably outnumber the enemy at least 3 to 2.

From his command post Fukudome saw in the distance enemy planes sweep down to his airfields; high above, tiny specks—Zero interceptors—began plummeting toward the Americans. There were flashing explosions and long arching trails of smoke. Fukudome excitedly clapped his hands. "Well done! Well done! A tremendous success!" But the Americans continued to come on in perfect formation. The downed planes were his own. His fighters had been like "so many eggs thrown against the stone wall of the indomitable enemy formation."

Fukudome lost a third of his interceptors in the first strike, and the rest in the second. There was nothing to send up against the third. The Americans resumed their raids the following morning and, unopposed, damaged Formosan air installations more heavily than the previous day. The Japanese retaliated at dusk. Thirty-odd bombers specially designed for night attacks swept out toward

---

* The Toho Motion Picture Company constructed a lake in Setagaya and filled it with six-foot models of U. S. warships. Atop a tower a movie camera on a boom took pictures of the vessels from various angles, simulating different speeds of approach. These films were shown as a substitute for flight training in order to save fuel.

Task Force 38, skimming the waves to avoid radar detection. Three dive bombers eluded interceptors and released their bombs at the carrier *Franklin*. Two bombs went wide, but the third exploded on the deck-edge elevator. Fire broke out on the port quarter but was soon extinguished. The heavy cruiser *Canberra* (named after the Australian cruiser sunk in the Battle of Savo) was not so fortunate. A torpedo slammed into her side, ripping a huge hole. Water cascaded in and she came to a dead stop ninety miles from Formosa.

Halsey, on his flagship *New Jersey*, faced a difficult decision. Should he abandon *Canberra* or risk another ship in an attempt to tow her at 4 knots the thirteen hundred miles to Ulithi Atoll in the Carolines? Halsey characteristically took the chance and ordered another cruiser to draw *Canberra* clear. To divert the Japanese he ordered a third and unscheduled series of raids on Formosa. In the morning Mitscher sent out three sweeps against Formosan airfields while 109 huge Army Air Force B-29's left their bases deep inside China to hit the Takao area. By dusk, over five hundred Japanese planes had been destroyed in the three-day air battle.

But the surviving Japanese pilots, whose vision of battle had come from a lakeful of models on the Toho film lot, reported the biggest victory in Japanese naval history, and as Halsey's fleet withdrew to strike elsewhere, Admiral Toyoda—at the time in Formosa on an inspection trip—saw this action as confirmation of American disaster. He ordered Fukudome to go after the "remnants" of the Third Fleet with every bomber left. The next day, October 15, Fukudome launched three strikes. One group alone found the enemy, and it was repelled. The following afternoon a flight of 107 aircraft caught up with the retreating Americans. Only three penetrated the fighter screen and one hit the light cruiser *Houston* with a torpedo. Over sixty-five hundred tons of water rushed in and she seemed destined to share the fate of the first *Houston*, destroyed off Java, but damage-control parties kept the leaks in check, and like *Canberra*, she was towed away.

Halsey had not lost a single ship in the sweeps extending from Okinawa to Luzon. Facetiously he radioed Nimitz: THE THIRD FLEET'S SUNKEN AND DAMAGED SHIPS HAVE BEEN SALVAGED AND

ARE RETIRING AT HIGH SPEED TOWARD THE ENEMY. He was heading
south to support the coming invasion of Leyte.

In Japan neither Combined Fleet nor Imperial Headquarters
had any reason to doubt the reports of momentous victories by
returning pilots. An official communiqué was issued on October
16 announcing that in the Formosan battle eleven enemy carriers,
two battleships, three cruisers and one destroyer or light cruiser
had been sunk and almost as many others damaged. In addition,
112 planes had been shot down. It was admitted that 312 Japanese aircraft had not yet "returned" but this was small price for
crippling the Third Fleet. The Emperor called for a celebration in
Hibiya Park.

To the south a typhoon raged through the Philippines, but by
dawn of October 17 the storm had subsided. Through a sea
whipped by heavy winds an American attack group—two light
cruisers, four destroyers and eight destroyer transports—followed
three minesweepers into Leyte Gulf. For twenty minutes one of
the cruisers, *Denver,* shelled Suluan, a small island in the mouth
of the gulf. Then the 6th Ranger Infantry Battalion debarked
from the transports in a driving rain to land unopposed. The Rangers were looking for mine charts in a lighthouse but found none.
They disposed of most of the thirty-two-man Japanese garrison,
but not before a lookout sent out a radio warning. He so exaggerated the size of the attack group (he reported that "two battleships, two converted aircraft carriers and six destroyers" lay off
his island) that their presence created a major alert. Admiral
Toyoda, still on Formosa, signaled Admiral Takeo Kurita to bring
his formidable First Striking Force up from Singapore, then ordered
Ozawa's Mobile Fleet to steam out of the Inland Sea (where it
had reorganized after its crushing defeat in the Philippine Sea) and
head south toward the Philippines. He also instructed submarines
to make for the Leyte area and attack the American fleet. Then
he took off for Japan so he could be at Combined Fleet Headquarters once the Decisive Battle started.

But the man in charge of the defense of the Visayans saw the
Suluan alert as yet another false report. At Cebu, General Sosaku
Suzuki remembered the panic when whitecaps off Mindanao were
reported as landing craft. How could the enemy possibly launch

an invasion after suffering a greater naval defeat than at Pearl Harbor? His superiors in Manila were just as skeptical; observation pilots had reported seeing nothing in Leyte Gulf through the clouds and rain.

On Leyte itself, General Makino alone feared it was a genuine invasion and ordered an alert—against the advice of his staff, who argued that the American shipping in the mouth of Leyte Gulf was the remnants of the Formosa battle blown south by the typhoon.

October 18 dawned fair, and the Rangers had no trouble landing on Homonhon, an island next to little Suluan. (One of Makino's staff officers flew over the gulf about this time but saw nothing through the fog.) There were no Japanese, no fortifications. Without opposition ("Here we are with all these goddamn bullets and no Japs!") the Rangers accomplished their mission: the erection of a navigation light to guide the convoy. Fifteen miles to the south, other Rangers were swarming ashore at Dinagat, a much bigger island guarding the lower approaches to the gulf. It, too, was uninhabited, and a second navigation light was set up at the tip end, Desolation Point. The convoy would enter the gulf between these two islands.

By noon the entrance to Leyte had been secured. Two hours later the battleship *Pennsylvania,* along with two cruisers and several destroyers, began to bombard Leyte itself along the gulf. Then underwater teams in landing craft moved in to scout conditions on the beaches. Japanese dug in along the neat rows of coconut trees lining the beach road opened fire, sinking one of the craft. Ignoring the hail of bullets, the other teams went to work and were soon back with a welcome report: the shore was clear of mines and obstacles.

Makino's communications—inadequate to begin with—had been almost completely disrupted by the storm, and he knew none of this. Reassured by the officer who had just flown over the gulf and seen nothing of import, he reported to Suzuki that the American ships sighted earlier in the gulf had probably been looking for refuge from the typhoon.

In Japan this complacency was not shared by Combined Fleet. Just before noon Admiral Toyoda gave the execute to Sho-1, and for the first time his staff revealed to the Army at a combined meeting its detailed plan for an exhaustive battle; the Navy would attack the landing forces in Leyte Gulf with every available ship. This "all-or-nothing" attitude distressed General Kenryo Sato. If the Navy failed, what chance would the Army have in *its* Decisive Battle? "The Combined Fleet belongs not only to the Navy but to the state," Sato pointed out. Its destruction—he used the word "self-destruction"—would leave the homeland open to invasion. "Only the existence of the fleet will make the enemy cautious," he said in a choked voice. "So please, gentlemen, be prudent."

"I am very grateful to know," said Rear Admiral Nakazawa, the Operations Section chief, "that the Combined Fleet is so highly regarded by you Army men." His words were sincere. He pleaded for "a fitting place to die." The Philippines would be the last opportunity. "Please give the Combined Fleet the chance to bloom as flowers of death." His voice faltered. "This is the Navy's earnest request."

Sato could not withstand the tears or the argument. He acceded gracefully. That afternoon the Emperor gave his blessing to Sho-1.

South of the Philippines, scattered over thousands of square miles, the invasion convoy—420 transports and 157 warships—was steaming steadily toward Leyte Gulf. In the van were battleships, cruisers and destroyers of the support and bombardment units, and just before dawn on October 19 they entered the gulf and began shelling the landing beaches. At the same time carrier planes were striking at every air base on the Visayans. They almost completely destroyed the remaining Japanese air power in the area.

The stage was at last set for the appearance of the gigantic invasion convoy. At eleven o'clock that evening it rendezvoused seventeen miles east of Leyte Gulf and steamed slowly toward the opening, marked by the navigation lights on the islands of Dinagat and Homonhon. Protestant and Catholic services were piped over public address systems, and more than one man had the sinking feeling that he was listening to his own last rites. Up ahead could be heard the muted boom of destroyers lobbing shells onto the landing areas.

In eleven hours the GI's would storm those beaches, and they tried to rest in the stuffy holds. Those who could not sleep counted the slow hours in their bunks or came up on deck in search of fresh air. The ships seemed to be barely moving as they glided through the mouth of the gulf. There was little talk; everyone was too engrossed in his own thoughts and fears. On the left loomed an ominous mass, Dinagat Island, dark except at the tip end, Desolation Point, where a white beacon steadily gleamed.

A GI fell overboard. It was reported over the circuit: "Ships astern keep lookout." Rescue seemed hopeless in the swift-running phosphorescent waters, but twenty minutes later a small craft near the end of the formation sighted the soldier and hauled him aboard.

In the first gray light of October 20—MacArthur had designated it A-Day, since D-Day, to the public, meant June 6, 1944—the dim outline of Leyte materialized. The sun rose behind the convoy, illuminating clear skies overhead. In minutes it was uncomfortably hot. The quiet was shattered abruptly as three battleships opened fire. Gray smoke plumes erupted along Violet and Yellow beaches near Dulag. Twelve minutes later a Japanese observation plane appeared. Ack-ack bursts bloomed on all sides, but the little aircraft moved off unharmed.

At about seven o'clock three other battleships joined in the cannonade, their target White and Red beaches to the north, just below Tacloban, the capital. Within an hour the transports began moving sedately over the glassy water to positions seven miles offshore. The battleships ceased fire to allow cruisers, destroyers and gunboats to move in closer and take up the bombardment. The continuous thunder of guns was suddenly exceeded by an awesome *swoosh* as thousands of rockets shot up simultaneously from the little gunboats. Seconds later there was a thunderous clap. The entire shoreline was "a solid sheet of blinding and exploding flame." When the smoke cleared, those on the transports stared incredulous—where there had been lush jungle growth now lay "a barren, tangled, smoking, dust-covered waste."

At nine forty-five—fifteen minutes before H-hour—the landing craft, which had been jockeying for position as if they were in a sulky race, bored in toward the beaches on a twelve-mile front. In the north the 1st Cavalry Division stormed ashore at White Beach. Sharpshooters knocked snipers out of palm trees with carbines and Garands; concrete pillboxes were dynamited and cavalrymen swept onto the coastal highway. To their left the 24th Infantry Division also landed without difficulty—two of their men, one a Filipino, planted the American and Philippine flags on Red Beach—but they ran into nests of resolute Japanese and it took them several hours to reach the road. Farther south the 96th Infantry Division splashed safely ashore at Orange and Blue beaches. Fortunately, most of the artillery located at Catmon Hill, which dominated the region, had been destroyed by the naval bombardment. They pushed inland for almost a mile before they were slowed by marshes and scattered resistance. To their left at the extreme southern end—Violet and Yellow beaches—the 7th Infantry Division, which had seen action at Attu and Kwajalein, encountered the stiffest opposition, but Dulag was captured by noon.

MacArthur watched the landings intently from the bridge of the cruiser *Nashville* until lunch. He reappeared on deck a little before two o'clock, wearing a fresh khaki uniform, sunglasses and marshal's cap. He climbed into a barge loaded with officers and newsmen. It headed for the transport *John Land,* on which Sergio Osmeña, the President of the Philippines since Quezon's death three months earlier, waited along with General Carlos Romulo to be picked up. Romulo hadn't seen MacArthur for two years and eagerly clambered down the rope ladder.

"Carlos, my boy!" MacArthur exclaimed. "Here we are—home!"

Osmeña's affable greeting to MacArthur belied his true feelings. It had taken a personal plea from President Roosevelt to persuade him to return to the Philippines in the shadow of the general. But the exhilaration of the moment overrode personal differences. They were all talking at once. "We're here" was repeated over and over. MacArthur slapped Sutherland on the knee. "Believe it or not," he said with a grin, "we're back."

The barge grounded on Red Beach, some five miles below Tacloban. The ramp flapped down and MacArthur stepped into knee-deep water. He was followed by Osmeña, General George Kenney and the others. The diminutive Romulo, who was wearing new shoes, had difficulty keeping up with MacArthur's long strides.

The shore was encumbered by four damaged landing craft, one still burning, and occasionally the party heard the rattle of machine-gun and rifle fire. Corncob pipe in mouth and armed with an old revolver of his father's which he kept in his back pocket, MacArthur searched a palm grove for the 24th Division commander, Major General Frederick Irving. "This is what I dreamed about," Romulo heard him mutter.

Prone GI's were concentrating fire on something ahead. "Hey, there's General MacArthur," said one.

His buddy didn't even bother to look up. "Oh yeah? And I suppose he's got Eleanor Roosevelt along with him."

After a brief chat with General Irving, MacArthur returned to his party. He motioned to Osmeña, put a hand on his shoulder. "Mr. President, how does it feel to be home?" he asked. They sat down on a fallen tree. "As soon as we take Tacloban I am turning the administration over to you. This may be sooner than we planned, things are going so smoothly."

"I am ready whenever you are, General."

They were interrupted by a Signal Corps officer who extended a hand microphone. The "Voice of Freedom" was back on the air. As MacArthur began to talk, his voice charged with emotion and hands trembling, a few drops of rain fell. "People of the Philippines, I have returned. By the grace of Almighty God our forces stand again on Philippine soil . . . At my side is your President, Sergio Osmeña, worthy successor of that great patriot, Manuel Quezon, with members of his cabinet."

In the background, trucks were noisily grinding across the beach, and planes roared overhead. There was an occasional distant boom from ships offshore shelling inland positions. His voice rising, the general called on the people to rally to him in the spirit of Bataan and Corregidor. "As the lines of battle roll forward to bring you within the zone of operations, rise and strike. . . . For your homes and hearths, strike! For future generations of your sons and daughters, strike! In the name of your sacred dead, strike! Let no heart be faint. Let every arm be steeled. The guidance of divine God points the way. Follow in His name to the Holy Grail of righteous victory!"

Osmeña took the microphone. The liberation of the Islands would be a joint enterprise of the Americans and Filipinos, and he urged the populace to co-operate. "We have the word of America that our country, which has been ravaged by war, will be reconstructed and rehabilitated. Steps have already been taken to this end. With the return of normal conditions, law and order will be fully re-established and democratic processes of constitutional government restored."

Romulo also praised the Americans. "You must continue keeping faith with them. You cannot let America down."

Euphoric, MacArthur wandered around the wet grove talking to GI's until an officer nervously said, "Sir, there are snipers over there," and pointed to nearby trees. MacArthur seemed not to hear. He sat down on a log and stared into the distance, at the land he had sworn to liberate.

A few miles to the north, troopers of the 1st Cavalry had reached the outskirts of Tacloban. They dug in, setting up mortars and machine guns in case of a night attack. Instead they were overwhelmed by the liberated. Filipinos crowded past the sentries. There were old people, young mothers with babies; Robert Shaplen of *The New Yorker* saw an aged, wrinkled-faced woman standing, arms outstretched toward the GI's with a beatific smile on her face. She seemed to be in the middle of a dream, too stunned to believe that she was wide awake.

The Americans had a substantial beachhead in the middle of the Philippines along with more than 100,000 tons of cargo. The cost was minimal—forty-nine GI's had died. Roosevelt radioed his congratulations to MacArthur: YOU HAVE THE NATION'S GRATITUDE AND THE NATION'S PRAYERS FOR SUCCESS AS YOU AND YOUR MEN FIGHT YOUR WAY BACK.

The invaders' losses had been light because the defense system had been shattered by the three-day bombardment. Their forward positions destroyed, their ranks thinned by shelling and strafing, the Japanese had fallen back, often leaderless. Few of the units were in communication with Division headquarters. That night Colonel Kanao Kondo of the 22nd Artillery Regiment accused the commander of the 1st Battalion of retreating without orders. Kondo refused to accept the excuse that almost the entire battalion had been killed or wounded, and their guns destroyed. "Why didn't you die?" he raged and ordered the survivors to fight to the end where they stood.

General Makino had no details of the progress of the fighting.

On the eve of the invasion he had hastily evacuated his headquarters in Tacloban and was heading inland when the Americans came ashore. He had not yet been able to report what little he knew to his superiors.

At Fort McKinley, Yamashita was trying to evaluate the scanty information from Leyte. Just after ten o'clock his new chief of staff, Lieutenant General Akira Muto, arrived from Sumatra, where he had been "exiled" by Tojo. He was without baggage and wore a grimy uniform—during a bombing at an airfield he had leaped into a muddy ditch to save himself.

Yamashita told him of the invasion. "Very interesting" was his remark. "But where is Leyte?" They were joined by Colonel Ichiji Sugita (Yamashita's interpreter at Singapore), who had just flown in from Tokyo with distressing news for both of them: Imperial Headquarters ordered the 14th Area Army to fight the Decisive Battle on Leyte.

The next day, October 21, MacArthur's four divisions continued to press forward against little resistance. Dulag's airfield was overrun; most of Tacloban was liberated, and a special town meeting was scheduled for the following morning to welcome the victors and to recruit native labor for the Philippine Civil Affairs Unit. Filipinos crowded the market place, ignoring occasional bursts of fire in the outskirts. "We had to obey the Japanese to save our necks," said Saturino Gonzales, a member of the Provincial Board. He spoke to the audience but his words were directed to the Americans—in English. "But there was never any doubt, as you know, what our feelings were beneath. I ask you to consider now what the policies of the American government were like before the Japanese came and how they are to be compared to the Japanese administration. You will now understand the famous democratic ways of the United States."

The next speaker held up a can of K ration. The crowd got the point and cheered in English: "Long live the Americans! Lovely Americans!"

An American colonel told the crowd that the Philippines were theirs: "Your Commonwealth Government will be set up under your own president, President Osmeña. We are going to see that you get food and clothing. We want you to be patient. We need labor. You will get paid for the work you do in Philippine currency and with it you will be able to buy the rice and the other products we will bring. But, by God, you'll do it as free men!"

The *New Yorker* man, Shaplen, doubted that the audience understood everything the colonel said, but their enthusiasm was such that the next speaker, an ex-governor of Leyte, pledged that they would work for the Americans "three hundred and sixty-five days a year, and we will work for nothing."

The colonel's protests were overridden by cries of "Lovely Americans! We will work, we will work!"

In Manila, 340 miles to the northwest, Yamashita was making a final attempt to persuade Field Marshal Terauchi to protest Tokyo's order to make Leyte the site of the conclusive land battle of the Philippines. How could reinforcements break through the American air and submarine blockade around the island? Besides, before sufficient troops and supplies reached Leyte the battle would be over. And was it MacArthur's primary target? Perhaps this was merely a feint before the full-scale invasion of Luzon.

But his arguments came to naught; Terauchi never wavered in his belief that the imminent naval-air counterattack would sink the enemy invasion fleet in Leyte Gulf. The marshal (Muto characterized him as being "in extremely high spirits and optimistic") ordered the 14th Area Army "to totally destroy the enemy on Leyte." Reluctantly Yamashita passed on the order to Suzuki, and promised to send substantial infantry reinforcements to Leyte. Naval support could be expected to reach the island "on the twenty-fourth and twenty-fifth of October."

On Leyte, Makino had been forced to split his 16th Division into the Northern and Southern Leyte Defense Forces. His orders were couched in aggressive prose, but privately he hoped his troops would not collapse before help arrived.

By the next day the Tacloban area was secure enough for the invaders to permit the public appearance of the Allied leaders. Early in the afternoon a Filipino brass band roamed the streets of Tacloban in a weapons carrier; a loudspeaker repeated interminably that MacArthur and Osmeña were coming and there would be ceremonies. Led by the band, an impromptu parade formed and by three o'clock a crowd clustered around the steps of the capitol building.

The MacArthur party disembarked at the old wharf from two PT boats, and with the general in the lead, marched to the capitol. From the steps of the building MacArthur formally announced the establishment of the Philippine Civil Government under President Osmeña and promised to liberate the rest of the Islands. It was a short, unemotional speech, but the fiesta crowd cheered every sentence.

A bugler sounded To the Colors as American and Philippine flags were raised simultaneously. MacArthur shook hands with Osmeña and Romulo. "I and my staff will now retire," he said and started back to the wharf.

22

The Battle
of Leyte Gulf

1.

The Mobile Fleet and First Striking Force—the remnants of the Combined Fleet—were approaching the Philippines from the north and west. Vice Admiral Jisaburo Ozawa commanded the Mobile Fleet, whose air power had been shattered in the Marianas and whose remaining planes had proved so ineffectual in the three-day air battle off Formosa. Still, it made a formidable appearance, with the large carrier *Zuikaku,* light carriers *Zuiho, Chitose* and *Chiyoda,* and the battleships *Ise* and *Hyuga,* remodeled into semi-carriers. But it was a hollow striking force. There were only 116 planes distributed among the six ships.

The First Striking Force, coming from Singapore, was under the command of Vice Admiral Takeo Kurita. He came from a family of scholars—his father had compiled a distinguished history of Japan—but he was a man of action. He had skippered five de-stroyers and twice commanded torpedo divisions, then a cruiser division. He had escorted the troops who were to land on Midway, and after participating in the battles around Guadalcanal (including the bombardment of Henderson Field by *Kongo* and *Haruna*), took over the Second Fleet in time to participate in the Battle of the Philippine Sea. His new fleet was strictly a surface force but its fire power was truly redoubtable. It included the two largest and most fearsome battleships in the world, *Musashi* and *Yamato,* as well as five old but serviceable battleships—among them *Haruna,* so often reported sunk, and her sister ship, *Kongo*—eleven heavy cruisers, two light cruisers and nineteen destroyers. The First Striking Force could throw more tons of shells than any fleet afloat.

It arrived at Brunei, Borneo, on October 20 as the Americans were landing on Leyte. Early the next morning Kurita received orders to enter Leyte Gulf at dawn of October 25 and destroy enemy amphibious shipping. Combined Fleet suggested a two-pronged attack: one group would work its way through the confining waters of the Visayans, debouch into the Pacific through San Bernardino Strait, turn south past Samar and enter Leyte Gulf from the east; the other group would break into the gulf from the south through the narrow Surigao Strait between Mindanao and Leyte.

On the long approaches to the battle area, both groups might easily be discovered and ambushed by American submarines and surface units as well as aircraft. Kurita and his staff were willing to accept these perils. What they objected to was the mission as such. They were eager to die in a battle against carriers, but why risk His Majesty's greatest battleships for transports that would already be unloaded? Combined Fleet sympathized with these objections but stood firm. It was too late for any alternative. Kurita, however, was given permission to engage carriers if they came within range.

Kurita decided to bring the major part of his fleet through San Bernardino Strait in order to keep it beyond the range of enemy search planes as long as possible. A detachment of two old battleships and four destroyers under Vice Admiral Teiji Nishimura would take the much shorter southern route. Both groups would enter Leyte Gulf at dawn on the twenty-fifth and converge on the enemy transports and their covering force.

Kurita was resigned to the loss of at least half his ships, but so many of his junior officers openly protested this calculated risk that he abandoned his usual reticence to address his division commanders and their staffs on the deck of the flagship, the heavy cruiser *Atago.* He told them that the war situation was far more critical than they could possibly know. "Would it not be a shame to have the fleet remain intact while our nation perishes? I believe that Imperial Headquarters is giving us a glorious opportunity. You must remember that there are such things as miracles. What man can say that there is no chance for our fleet to turn the tide of war in a Decisive Battle?"

Kurita's words, calm but forceful, were greeted with cries of *"Banzai!"*

At 8 A.M. on October 22, the main body of First Striking Force sortied from Brunei and began steaming northward, followed by the smaller Nishimura detachment, which turned east at the tip of Borneo and headed toward the south entrance to Leyte Gulf, Surigao Strait. The main body continued northeast through the darkness on a zigzag course at 18 knots, skirting the west coast of the long narrow island of Palawan in the 25-mile-wide passage formed by uncharted reefs (aptly called "the Dangerous Ground") and the island itself. In these swift waters near the reefs, two American picket submarines, *Darter* and *Dace,* patrolled the surface side by side. At sixteen minutes past midnight the conning tower of *Darter* reported: "Radar contact, one three one true, thirty thousand yards—contact is doubtful—probably rain cloud."

Rain cloud hell! thought the captain, Commander David McClintock, who was topside. That's the Jap fleet.

The radar operator's report confirmed his guess, and he relayed the information by megaphone to the skipper of *Dace,* Commander Bladen Clagett. "Let's go get them," Clagett called back and both submarines gave chase at flank speed with *Darter* in the lead.

By 4:50 A.M. they had closed the Japanese, and all hands on *Darter* were called to battle stations. At 5:10 she reversed course, submerged. Through the periscope, in the faint light of dawn, McClintock made out a gray mass in the distance. A Japanese column was coming straight at him! He looked to the southeast and saw another column of battleships, cruisers and destroyers several miles away.

The gray vessels bearing down on him grew larger. At 5:25 McClintock identified the lead ship, a heavy cruiser making huge bow waves. It was a beautiful sight and McClintock hoped it was the flagship. All tubes were ready and the range was just under 1,000 yards when the column abruptly zigged to the west, placing the target at a perfect angle. "Fire one!" ordered McClintock. A searchlight on the cruiser signaled. Had she detected the spread of six torpedoes? No, she was holding her course. McClintock took a bearing on the next cruiser.

His first torpedoes were heading for the flagship, *Atago.* On the bridge, Kurita and his chief of staff, Rear Admiral Tomiji Koyanagi, suddenly felt four great tremors in succession. The cruiser began to sink. A destroyer was signaled, and Kurita and his staff swam to it.

On *Dace,* Clagett surveyed the scene through his periscope. "Good Lord," he exclaimed, "it looks like the Fourth of July out there! One is sinking and another is burning. The Japs are firing all over the place. What a show! Stand by for a setup—here they come!" He studied two ships bearing down on him. "Let them pass—they are only cruisers." Behind was a bigger target he mistook for a *Kongo*-class battleship. "Fire one, fire two, fire three, fire four, fire five, fire six," Clagett ordered, and then, "Take her deep, Earl. Let's get the hell out of here!"

They heard the thump of torpedoes striking home and a crackle "like cellophane being crumpled close to our ears." The heavy cruiser *Maya* was breaking up.

Even before Kurita had reached the perilous waters of the central Philippines, he had lost two heavy cruisers, and a third, *Takao,* was in such bad shape that she had to turn back to Borneo. Moreover, his course had been discovered; yet there was nothing to do but continue. At noon he received a message from Combined Fleet which told him what he knew better than anyone else:

IT IS VERY PROBABLE THAT THE ENEMY IS AWARE OF THE FACT THAT WE HAVE CONCENTRATED OUR FORCES . . . HE WILL PROBABLY ACT IN THE FOLLOWING MANNER: (A) CONCENTRATE SUBMARINES IN GREAT STRENGTH IN THE SAN BERNARDINO AND SURIGAO STRAITS AREA. (B) PLAN ATTACKS ON OUR SURFACE FORCES, USING LARGE TYPE PLANES AND TASK FORCES AFTER TOMORROW MORNING. (C) PLAN DECISIVE ACTION BY CONCENTRATING HIS SURFACE STRENGTH IN THE AREA EAST OF SAN BERNARDINO STRAIT AND TACLOBAN WHERE HE HAS HIS TRANSPORT GROUP . . .

AS TO OUR OPERATIONS: (A) EXECUTE OUR ORIGINAL PLAN . . .

2.

By dawn—it was October 24—Kurita was aboard a new flagship, the mighty *Yamato*. His ships were in two circular formations seven miles apart. *Yamato* and her sister ship, *Musashi*, were in the center of the first group, and *Kongo* in the middle of the second. A huge pagodalike tower rose above the deck of *Yamato*. Near the top in the flag bridge was Kurita's headquarters. Just below, in the operations room, his staff was trying to assimilate the fragments of information that were slowly coming in. The First Striking Force went around the southern tip of Mindoro and continued on up into the Sibuyan Sea. The most hazardous part of the trip—a daylight passage following a circumscribed course among numerous islets—not only limited maneuver but was a matchless stalking ground for submarines. But there was no other way to get to San Bernardino Strait, the gateway to the Philippine Sea. Kurita had come to doubt the report that the air engagements off Formosa had crippled American carrier power, but he did not know that Japanese air power in the Philippines had itself been practically annihilated by Halsey and could give him little if any support.

Shortly after 8 A.M. Kurita was again discovered—this time by an American search plane. He radioed Manila for fighter protection. Fewer than a dozen Zeros could be spared and none of these managed to reach the First Striking Force. Every other available land-based plane—180 in all—was sent out to attack Halsey's Third Fleet, which stretched across the Philippine Sea from mid-Luzon to Leyte. Hellcats from Mitscher's Task Force 38 knocked down almost all of the Japanese, but one bomber broke through the screen to hit the light carrier *Princeton* with a 550-lb. bomb. The blazing hangar deck began exploding torpedoes chain-fashion. For hours the crew fought to save the ship, but the conflagration was uncontrollable and she had to be sunk.

With the sighting of Kurita's ships in the Sibuyan Sea, Admiral Halsey characteristically took personal charge of the battle. At 8:37 he by-passed Mitscher and ordered three of his task group commanders direct by TBS (Talk Between Ships): "Strike! Re-

peat: Strike! Good luck!" Within two hours the van of this attack
—twelve fighters and the same number of dive bombers and torpedo bombers from *Intrepid* and *Cabot*—found Kurita.

On *Musashi*, Petty Officer Second Class Shiro Hosoya was
precariously perched in an open signal booth attached to the second bridge, about halfway up its huge island structure. He was
supervisor of signalmen but during action had little to do but observe. With a mixed feeling of anxiety and awe he watched the
Americans break through the tremendous wall of antiaircraft fire
thrown up by every ship in the formation—each battleship had at
least one hundred and twenty 25-mm. guns and the cruisers carried ninety. It was like watching a show—until the enemy planes
began heading straight for him and for *Yamato*. Just ahead and to
the left, half a dozen huge geysers erupted around *Yamato*. The
great battleship was obscured and a report was relayed that she
was sinking. Hosoya refused to believe it; like *Musashi,* she was
unsinkable. He peered apprehensively through the descending
waters until he made her out again, steaming along as if on
maneuvers.

Suddenly a fountain more than two hundred feet high rose directly in front of Hosoya and drenched the men on deck below.
His booth swayed sickeningly as *Musashi* shuddered twice—once
from a bomb hit, once from a torpedo. But like her sister, she
sailed on serenely as if nothing had happened, evidence that she
truly was indestructible. Basically the same as *Yamato, Musashi*
was better constructed, had superior quarters and was worthy of
her nickname, "The Palace." She had been Yamamoto's flagship,
then Koga's, and the crew wondered a bit resentfully why Kurita
had not chosen to come aboard her for the last battle of the Japanese Navy.

At noon a second attack—twenty-four torpedo planes—swept
in toward the two superbattleships. *Musashi* took three more torpedoes but continued on course, all damage under control.

On *Yamato,* which had not yet been hit, Kurita sent another
plea for air support, at 1:15 P.M., this to his superior, Admiral
Ozawa, as well as to Manila:

WE ARE BEING SUBJECTED TO REPEATED ENEMY CARRIER-
BASED AIR ATTACKS. ADVISE IMMEDIATELY OF CONTACTS AND
ATTACKS MADE BY YOU ON THE ENEMY.

Fifteen minutes later, twenty-nine planes loomed on the horizon (they were from *Lexington* and *Essex*). To Kurita, the enemy aircraft converging on *Musashi* looked as if they were twice that number.

On *Musashi's* second bridge Chief Gunnery Officer Koshino was pleading over the voice tube with the captain, Rear Admiral Toshihira Inoguchi, to let him fire the main 18.1-inch guns, the biggest in the world, with a special spray shell called *sanshiki-dan.* "Permission denied," said Inoguchi. A dozen rounds of *sanshiki-dan* could damage a gun's bore; he wanted to save the big guns for the surface battle in Leyte Gulf.

The attackers turned out to be more aggressive than their predecessors. Dive bombers plunged down, accompanied by fighters strafing the decks. The ship became enveloped by water thrown up by near bomb-misses. Then in rapid succession four bombs crashed into *Musashi.* Fragments "like steel popcorn" ricocheted off the bridges. The air was acrid with gunpowder fumes. Another torpedo ripped into the hull.

At last *Musashi* was hurt, and perceptibly. She fell several miles behind *Yamato,* but the executive officer, Captain Kenkichi Kato, who was responsible for damage control, still remained so confident that he didn't think it necessary to report personally to the skipper. The limping ship was, however, affecting the progress of the First Striking Force. Kurita ordered fleet speed reduced to 22 knots so that *Musashi* could keep up, then sent out another request for help.

FIRST STRIKING FORCE IS ENGAGED IN SEVERE FIGHT IN SIBUYAN SEA. ENEMY AIR ATTACKS ARE EXPECTED TO IN- CREASE. REQUEST LAND-BASED AIR FORCE AND MOBILE FORCE TO MAKE PROMPT ATTACKS ON ENEMY CARRIER FORCE ES- TIMATED TO BE AT LAMON BAY.

Musashi's increased vulnerability gave Chief Gunner Officer Koshino a chance to renew his pleas to use *sanshiki-dan* in the main guns. Admiral Inoguchi argued that the ship was listing, which made it unsafe to fire the guns, but when the executive offi- cer supported Koshino, Inoguchi yielded.

Excitement spread through the ship as the huge guns—the very reason for *Musashi's* existence—were slowly trained toward the east. Sixty-five planes from *Enterprise* and *Franklin* appeared in the distance. The nine guns roared, the first time they had ever been fired at an enemy. The noise was deafening topside, and belowdecks the ship heaved as if a spread of torpedoes had smashed into her simultaneously. Koshino peered expectantly at the approaching planes but not one was falling into the sea; the formation simply spread out and kept coming.

Only six guns were firing now. The forward turret was silent. One of its guns was jammed with a projectile and the other two could not be elevated higher than 45 degrees. Bombers and torpedo planes swarmed over *Musashi*. From his signal booth Hosoya watched in horror as a line of three torpedoes plowed into the ship's port side, then a bomb exploded into the pagoda structure. Hosoya was knocked to his knees, but almost all those just above him on the command bridge were killed (by chance Inoguchi was at the top of the mast in the observation booth). Seven more torpedoes, bounding like porpoises in the choppy water, smashed one by one into the badly damaged port side.

No one seemed to be in charge of the ship until an order finally came over the voice tube: "First bridge, all killed. Captain will take command from the second bridge." It was Inoguchi, still in the observation tower, and unharmed. There were five more quick explosions, one overhead. The voice from the observation tower was weak: "Captain is wounded. Executive Officer, take command."

Musashi was listing noticeably to port, and on the second bridge Executive Officer Kato ordered the ship leveled by water ballast. Then he leaned out to the signal booth and handed Hosoya a message to transmit to *Yamato,* which was pulling away rapidly.

Electric power was out and Hosoya had to use flags; "*Musashi* capable of cruising at 15 knots. Listing to port about 15 degrees. One bomb hit first bridge, all members killed. Five direct bomb hits and twelve torpedo hits. Captain is alive."

But *Musashi*'s ordeal was not yet over. At 3:20 P.M. the attack was renewed as planes from *Intrepid, Cabot* and *Essex* joined with those still remaining from *Franklin* and *Enterprise.* Kurita's ships continued to throw up a screen of antiaircraft fire but nothing could stop the Americans boring in on *Musashi* for the kill. When they were through, she was left almost helpless, decks awash. The eerie quiet after battle was broken by a shout of *"Banzai!"* from the deck.

"What was that *banzai* for?" Kato yelled down from the second bridge.

"The enemy fleet is destroyed!" a sailor shouted back.

"Who told you that?"

"Chief Gunnery Officer Koshino."

Kato turned back to the bridge. It was just like Koshino to try to keep up the men's morale. The story spread throughout the ship and the crew's fighting spirit remained high despite the seventeen bomb and nineteen torpedo hit. But Kato himself was disconsolate. He informed Inoguchi, who had come down from the observation tower, his left arm in a sling, that the ship was "in no condition to withstand another attack." Hosoya flagged another message to the disappearing Kurita: "Speed six knots, capable of operation. Damage great. What shall we do?"

Musashi was ordered to quit the battle area with a two-destroyer escort. Since leaving Borneo, the First Striking Force had been deprived of the services of a battleship, four heavy cruisers (*Myoko* had just turned back with two damaged shafts) and two destroyers. But the rest of Kurita's fleet continued edging toward the narrows that led to San Bernardino Strait. Just before 4 P.M., however, Kurita had second thoughts. It was still light enough for several more air attacks and it would be impossible to evade them in the channel ahead. They would be trapped. Kurita reversed course and sent a lengthy explanation to Combined Fleet:

. . . WERE WE TO HAVE FORCED OUR WAY THROUGH AS SCHEDULED UNDER THESE CIRCUMSTANCES, WE WOULD MERELY MAKE OF OURSELVES MEAT FOR THE ENEMY, WITH VERY LITTLE CHANCE OF SUCCESS TO US. IT WAS THEREFORE CONCLUDED THAT OUR BEST COURSE WAS TO RETIRE TEMPORARILY BEYOND RANGE OF HOSTILE PLANES UNTIL FRIENDLY [land-based] PLANES COULD STRIKE A DECISIVE BLOW AGAINST THE ENEMY FORCE.

For an hour Kurita steamed west, but no American planes appeared. Encouraged, he decided to chance the run to San Bernardino Strait, even though there had been no reply to his request for assistance from land-based planes. At 5:15 the First Striking Force reversed course again and again cautiously filing in column between the islands of Masbate and Burias.

On *Musashi,* attempts to level the ship by emergency pumping had failed. Her bow was submerged and she crept along at a few knots. The crew transferred everything movable to the starboard aft section, but the port list grew worse. With the emergency battery-powered signal lamp, Hosoya informed Kurita that *Musashi* was taking on excess water. The answer was:

MUSASHI GO FORWARD OR BACKWARD AT TOP SPEED AND GROUND ON NEAREST ISLAND AND BECOME A LAND BATTERY.

Inoguchi tried to comply, but the listing, sinking ship could only move in circles. He told Hosoya to signal the two escorting destroyers to remove the wounded, but neither acknowledged the message.

"Why don't they come?" Executive Officer Kato fretted and irritably slapped Hosoya on the top of the head. "Try again."

Hosoya repeated the message again and again but there was no reaction. The ship was listing beyond 20 degrees, and as the skies darkened, Inoguchi ordered all men on deck. Ensign Fukujiro Shimoyama, in charge of radio operators, emerged from below with his thirty men, all in spanking clean uniforms. They were appalled at the carnage. Bodies, blasted and mutilated, covered the deck. Shimoyama's men poured gasoline on several hundred thick code books and set them afire. But they burned too slowly; finally Shimoyama had the charred books stowed in canvas bags, weighted with machine guns and tossed overboard.

In the fading light Inoguchi set down his will in a small notebook. It had been a mistake on his part, he wrote, to believe so staunchly in big ships and big guns, and he asked the Emperor and the nation to forgive his errors. He assembled his senior officers and a few petty officers on the second bridge and handed the notebook to Kato. "Give it to the commander of Combined Fleet," he said.

Kato requested permission to go down with the ship. "Damn fool!" Inoguchi muttered. "My responsibility is so great it can't even be compensated by death and I must share the ship's fate, but the executive officer is responsible for taking the crew to safety and getting them aboard a second and third *Musashi* to avenge today's battle." He extended his sword to a youthful ensign. "Thank you for your service. Signal!" Hosoya stepped forward expecting another message but the captain handed him a briefcase containing some money and seven pieces of Toraya sweet bean paste. "Thank you for your service. Do your best to the end."

His last orders to Kato were to save the Emperor's picture, lower the flag and gather all men in the stern for roll call. At about 7:15 P.M. Hosoya supervised the lowering of the flag from the mast as a sailor played the national anthem on a trumpet. The huge flag—an orange sun with sixteen white, sixteen red rays—was reverently tied around the waist of a volunteer, a strong swimmer.

By the time Hosoya and his detail had joined the others in the stern, *Musashi* listed so acutely that ammunition cases and empty shells were clattering down the deck.

"All crew abandon ship," Kato shouted. "You're on your own!"

On the high starboard side Ensign Shimoyama clutched at a rope rail as he pushed the last bag of code books into the sea. The ship took an abrupt lurch to port and the man next to him embraced him, then another hung on to the second man, and another and another, until there was a human chain of ten. Under all this weight the rope snapped and they all tumbled against a hatchway. A second chain of men tobogganed into them, and Shimoyama, dazed, gave up trying to save himself. *"Tenno Heika banzai!"* he shouted and left the rest to Fate. The next thing he knew he was in the water with no life belt.

Assistant Paymaster Kiyoshi Takahashi, a youthful ensign, held on to the rail with one hand, still clutching shoes and leggings with the other. He could see some men in the water but hesitated to join them. The ship began rolling on her side. He heard a rumble and saw an avalanche of lumber headed his way. He placed shoes and leggings neatly on the deck, as if he were to return for them later, then vaulted over the rail and scrambled over the ship's exposed bottom toward the keel. As *Musashi* continued to roll he sprinted to keep in place, as if on a treadmill. At last he reached the keel and peered down the other side. It was a long drop to the sea but he was a good swimmer. He leaped, bounced off the hull and was unconscious by the time he tumbled into the water.

Hosoya was also running shoeless over razor-sharp barnacles along the bottom of the ship, trying to keep up with her roll. His bare feet were bleeding but he felt no pain. He encountered a gaping black hole. Foaming water rushed in, sucking swimmers back into the bowels of the ship. "Torpedo hole! Follow me!" he shouted and clambered down the steep decline toward the bow. He slipped onto the barnacles, but unaware of the lacerations on his arms and legs, he worked his way to the end of the bow, which was awash. He simply continued on into the water.

Shimoyama, who had been flung safely overboard, after giving up hope, struggled to keep his head above water. A poor swimmer under ideal conditions, he panicked when he heard a monstrous sucking noise. He flailed around and saw the ship falling toward him. He was pulled into the undertow, and moments later, catapulted to the surface. Half choked, he spat out water but swallowed a mouthful of oil. He was in the middle of a huge slick. He clutched desperately at a piece of lumber and retched.

The good swimmer, Assistant Paymaster Takahashi, who had bounced off the hull, regained consciousness deep under water. Above him glowed a hole of light—too far to be reached. Suddenly a boiling vortex heaved him up. He gasped for air and swam frantically from the undertow. At a distance he turned. *Musashi* was on end, stern in air. In a daze he thought, The ship is standing straight up! He felt the concussion of an underwater explosion. The battleship slid out of sight. All at once there was nothing, not a soul in the strangely calm waters. *I am the only survivor.* He struggled through the viscous oil, collecting bits of flotsam. Then, as if in a dream, he heard distant singing and swam eagerly toward the voices.

Hosoya had also seen *Musashi* sticking up, a black silhouette against the last rays of the sinking sun. Four or five men were clustered at the end of the elevated stern. They seemed to hang on tighter as the great ship plunged. He felt himself being sucked back. There was a gigantic rumble and he flew high in the air. Life seemed to stop as he looked down—almost as if it were happening to someone else—into a great hole in the water far below. He had been gulped and spewed out. Instinctively he rolled into a ball just before splashing back into the sea. Again he was pulled under, into turbulent waters. Still in a fetal-like position, he tumbled around almost unconcerned, with no thought of breathing. Almost too late he realized what was happening and desperately clawed up. At the surface he drew in wonderful air.

The moon lit up the dark sea. There were no voices. He too imagined he was the sole survivor. Someone grabbed him from behind. Hosoya couldn't swim well and purposely sank. The grasping hand let go and when Hosoya surfaced, he was again alone. Then heads began to show up on all sides. He joined a group of men—one was Executive Officer Kato—and they started a search for anything that would float. Hot oil almost a foot deep engulfed them, blackening their faces except for white, swollen mouths and shiny eyes. For an hour Hosoya and Kato clung to the same box. The executive officer began to drowse and Hosoya punched him awake. Someone joked about hitting a superior officer. They sang the national anthem, naval marches and finally popular songs like "Shanghai Gal." After almost four hours, searchlights swept the area and the escort destroyers began picking up survivors. One, however, refused to be rescued. Chief Gunnery Officer Koshino swam away into the darkness.

3.

More than three hundred miles to the north, off Luzon in the Philippine Sea, Ozawa's Mobile Fleet was steaming south. The admiral was to have joined Kurita and Nishimura in the combined attack on Leyte Gulf, but on his way to the battle he had thought of a more effective way to use his four carriers and two semicarriers. He doubted that he could inflict serious damage with only 116 planes. The Mobile Fleet made an impressive appearance, however, and perhaps he could utilize it to draw Halsey's powerful carrier force away from the Leyte area and give Kurita a chance to slip safely through San Bernardino Strait. Ozawa radioed Combined Fleet of his intentions.

The problem had been to make his presence known to Halsey without arousing his suspicions. He did it by launching a strike at *Essex, Lexington* and *Princeton* with seventy-six planes just as

Kurita was entering the Sibuyan Sea, moments before the first attack on *Musashi*. It was a hodgepodge collection of almost thirty types of aircraft, but as they took off, the Z flag was raised as it had been twice before in the war—at Pearl Harbor and Midway. The attackers reported hitting two carriers and overflew to Luzon. They had done no damage at all, and moreover, failed in their primary mission. Halsey assumed they were part of the land-based attack on *Princeton* and didn't take the bait. Ozawa, therefore, was forced to send his two semicarriers, *Ise* and *Hyuga*, along with five other ships, farther south as a decoy.

At last American search planes sighted this force, and as Ozawa wanted, this led to the "discovery" at 4:30 P.M. of his main force. He radioed Kurita that the enemy carrier force would probably be drawn north to engage him, thus leaving San Bernardino Strait unguarded. For some reason, the message was never received.

As Ozawa had predicted, this time Halsey fell for the ruse. He knew that the Kurita fleet was steaming toward the gateway to the Philippine Sea, but thought it had been so badly mauled that it "could merely hit and run." Anyway, Admiral Kinkaid's Seventh Fleet, clustered around Leyte Gulf, had more than enough power to destroy Kurita. So why just lie off San Bernardino Strait like a cat at a mousehole and wait for the enemy to strike the first blow? The primary target was Ozawa's carriers. If he destroyed them his future operations "need fear no threat from the sea." Besides, he had no intention of letting Japan's last carrier force escape free, as Spruance had in the Philippine Sea battle; *he* would not be accused of being unaggressive.*

Just before 8 P.M. Halsey pointed on a map at Ozawa's position three hundred miles away and told his chief of staff, Robert Carney, "Here's where we're going. Mick, start them north." All that day Halsey had acted as commander of Task Force 38 as well as commander of the entire Third Fleet. In fact, he was leaving Marc Mitscher little to do.

Rear Admiral Carney wrote dispatches ordering all three of Mitscher's available carrier groups to the north. (There was a fourth, recalled from a resupply trip to Ulithi, but it was still hun-

---

* Halsey later told the author Theodore Taylor, "I wish that Spruance had been with Mitscher at Leyte Gulf and I had been with Mitscher in the Battle of the Philippine Sea."

dreds of miles to the east.) Two of these commanders were troubled by the abrupt order. Rear Admiral G. F. Bogan—alarmed by a report that the long-darkened Japanese navigation lights in San Bernardino Strait were lit—personally relayed this disquieting intelligence to one of Halsey's staff officers, who impatiently replied, "Yes, yes, we have that information." Rebuffed, Bogan decided not to recommend that he and Vice Admiral W. A. Lee stay behind with their groups to guard the strait.

"Ching" Lee himself was suspicious of Ozawa and cautioned Halsey that the Japanese carrier force might be a decoy to lure them north. The reply was a curt "Roger." A little later Bogan, too, warned Third Fleet that he was sure Kurita was coming through the strait and got the same answer.

On *Lexington,* Marc Mitscher took Halsey's latest orders to his three task groups to mean that he had been relieved, in effect, as commander of Task Force 38. "Admiral Halsey is in command now," he told his chief of staff, Arleigh Burke, and started for bed.

Commodore Burke was not willing to let it go at this. "We'd better see where that fleet is," he said, and soon word came back that Kurita was "still very much afloat and still moving toward San Bernardino." It was important enough to awaken Mitscher with the suggestion that he urge Halsey to leave two task groups behind to stop Kurita. "Does Admiral Halsey have that report?" Mitscher asked, and when the answer was affirmative, said, "If he wants my advice, he'll ask for it." He rolled over and went back to sleep.

Halsey had not altogether ignored the warnings that Kurita was probably coming through San Bernardino Strait that night. He had already sent out a message that four battleships and a score of cruisers and destroyers "will be formed as Task Force 34" under Admiral Lee to engage Kurita if he appeared. Halsey intended this "merely as a warning," but it was interpreted as an order by Admiral Kinkaid—on his flagship *Wasatch* in Leyte Gulf—who by chance intercepted the message. Assured that Halsey had "set up a plan to guard San Bernardino," Kinkaid no longer worried about Kurita. His concern lay in a different direction. A smaller Japanese surface force—it was Nishimura—was coming up toward him from the south and would probably try to slip through Surigao Strait under cover of darkness and go after the ships massed in Leyte Gulf.

Despite the fact that Kurita had been discovered prematurely and already suffered grievous losses, the plan to disrupt Mac-Arthur's invasion at Leyte Gulf was proceeding better than Combined Fleet had any right to expect. Ozawa had successfully lured Halsey to the north, leaving the strait unguarded and the American commander of shipping in Leyte Gulf complacent. Kurita could still bring more surface fire power than any other fleet in existence, and in the south Nishimura with his seven ships was approaching Surigao Strait on schedule and intact.

Kurita, however, would not be able to keep the rendezvous; the air attacks had delayed him half a day. He radioed Nishimura —on his flagship, *Yamashiro*—to proceed as planned but that he himself would not get to Leyte Gulf until 11 A.M. Nishimura took the news stoically. Like Kurita he was close-mouthed, a seagoing admiral who had never served in the ministry. He was determined to break through Surigao Strait at any cost and die a useful death. (His only son, Teiji, who had graduated at the top of his class at Etajima, had fallen in the Philippines.)

In the van, reconnoitering, was the heavy cruiser *Mogami,* along with three destroyers; they were followed by two old battleships, *Fuso* and *Yamashiro,* and the remaining destroyer, *Shigure.* Just before 11 P.M. *Shigure* sighted three PT boats. On order from Nishimura she turned into them and hit two of the boats. Nishimura radioed Kurita: ADVANCING AS SCHEDULED WHILE DESTROYING ENEMY TORPEDO BOATS.

Nishimura's was not the only Japanese fleet bound for Surigao Strait and the Decisive Battle. Thirty miles behind him came the Second Striking Force, commanded by Vice Admiral Kiyohide Shima. It was an orphan force, despite its impressive appellation, comprising two heavy cruisers, a light cruiser and four destroyers. Originally trained to be the advance guard for Ozawa, it had arbitrarily been placed under Southwest Area Force, headquartered in Manila, and assigned to escort duty. Shima had resisted the order—it would be ignominious to be left out of the coming battle —and his protest to Combined Fleet got him back into action; this time he was to join Kurita in the assault on Leyte Gulf. As he approached the Philippines from the north through the South China Sea, he still did not know exactly what role he would play. Off Lingayen Gulf he got a terse order from the commander of Southwest Area Force to "charge into Leyte Gulf," but again there were no details. A little later, however, a message from Kurita arrived, briefly outlining the joint-attack plan. On his own, Shima decided to follow Nishimura into Surigao Strait; together their two limited forces would be more effective.

Nishimura was informed of Shima's decision but knew nothing more. The two admirals were going into battle, and were from different commands, yet had never communicated with each other. And Nishimura was on radio silence. Acting independently, they would need luck to be able to join forces. As Nishimura neared the strait, PT boats struck again but all their torpedoes missed. The admiral finally radioed that he would go through the narrows between the little island of Panaon and Mindanao—the southern entry to Surigao Strait—at 1:30 A.M.

> SEVERAL TORPEDO BOATS SIGHTED BUT EN-
> EMY SITUATION OTHERWISE UNKNOWN.

Still intact, Nishimura steamed through the ten-mile portal on schedule and turned into Surigao Strait itself. Only fifty miles north lay his target—the massed enemy transports.

In the lead were two destroyers, and one mile behind came the flagship, *Yamashiro*, flanked by *Shigure* and another destroyer. Bringing up the rear, six hundred yards apart, were *Fuso* and *Mogami*. Three more PT boats darted out through darkness to launch torpedoes at the destroyers, but Nishimura's luck held. All missed and this time one boat was destroyed.

The moon had set and no wind stirred; the strait was "as calm as a graveyard." It was pleasantly warm on deck, if hot below. Magellan had sailed through these same treacherous waters, now deceptively smooth as glass, from the other direction on March 16, 1521. As if in ominous warning, there were occasional flashes of lightning.

Just ahead, Kinkaid's powerful Seventh Fleet, veiled by darkness, was waiting with apprehension mingled with expectation; no one knew for certain how big the converging Japanese forces were. Aboard the cruiser *Nashville,* General MacArthur refused the captain's request that he disembark. "I have never been able to witness a naval engagement and this is the opportunity of a lifetime. Proceed to the battle area when you wish." Kinkaid invited the general to come aboard his flagship, a transport, but the reply was final: "Transfer from a combatant ship to a noncombatant ship? Never!" The admiral was forced to keep *Nashville* out of the fight.

Tactical command of the action was under Rear Admiral Jesse Oldendorf, and to stop Nishimura and Shima's modest aggregation he had six battleships, four heavy cruisers, four light cruisers and twenty-eight destroyers. Oldendorf was a cheerful man, and reports that his PT boats had scored no hits did not ruffle him. Their main function had been to observe. Soon the Japanese would face destroyers, and then the guns of the cruisers and battleships. At 2:40 A.M. on October 25 a picket destroyer radioed: SKUNK 184 DEGREES, EIGHTEEN MILES.

Nishimura was advancing single file in battle formation. First came the four destroyers, then the two battleships, *Yamashiro* and *Fuso,* and the heavy cruiser *Mogami.* Fifteen minutes later a lookout on the destroyer *Shigure* sighted three ships four miles ahead. The flagship shot up flares, illuminating seven enemy destroyers. They closed fast, and just after 3 A.M. fired twenty-seven torpedoes. One hit *Fuso* and she sheered out to starboard. Five-inch shells were dropping all around the American destroyers, but joined by a second squadron, they came in for another attack.

At 3:20 Shigeru Nishino, captain of *Shigure,* saw phosphorescent wakes "as bright as day" directly ahead. *Shigure* and the other three destroyers heeled over violently, but their attempted evasion came too late. Nishino heard a series of quick explosions. The destroyer just ahead sank with a loud sizzling sound, like a "huge red-hot iron plunged into water"; another was left helplessly adrift and the third limped off.

One of the torpedoes struck a more important target, *Yamashiro.* Nishino heard a calm voice from the flagship say in the clear, "Our ship hit by torpedo. All ships attack!" From what Nishino could see, *Yamashiro,* about a mile and a half away, seemed undamaged. He pulled back to join other ships in a formation attack but could find nothing. What had happened to everyone?

Admiral Nishimura, unaware of the extent of the damage to his fleet, radioed Kurita and Shima from his flagship:

URGENT BATTLE REPORT NUMBER 2. ENEMY TORPEDO BOATS AND DESTROYERS PRESENT ON BOTH SIDES OF NORTHERN ENTRANCE TO SURIGAO STRAIT. TWO OF OUR DESTROYERS TORPEDOED AND DRIFTING. YAMASHIRO SUSTAINED ONE TORPEDO HIT BUT NO IMPEDIMENT TO BATTLE CRUISING.

Eight minutes later, at 3:38 A.M., there was a flash of light to the rear, followed by an awesome rumble. The damaged *Fuso,* nine miles away, had been blown in half. Both ends remained afloat, burning furiously. Twenty minutes later, with a rumble, *Michishio,* the drifting destroyer, also disintegrated.

But Nishimura would not give up. With his remaining three ships, *Yamashiro, Mogami* and *Shigure,* he continued north toward Leyte Gulf—and into the leveled guns of the Seventh Fleet. Oldendorf had caught his foe coming bow-on. He had crossed the T, as Nelson had done at Trafalgar and Togo at Tsushima, where more equal forces were involved. At 3:51 the cruisers opened fire followed by the six battleships—all but one had been hit or sunk at Pearl Harbor. This barrage was "the most beautiful sight" the commander of the American destroyer screen had ever witnessed. The blinding streams of tracers arching above his head resembled "a continued stream of lighted railroad cars going over a hill."

Both *Mogami* and *Yamashiro* returned fire even as they recoiled from hit after hit. The heavy cruiser loosed torpedoes at 4:01 A.M. and was soon deluged by shells from destroyers which had closed in. Burning and crippled, she turned back south. *Yamashiro* was also ablaze from stem to stern. At 4:09 the heavy shelling inexplicably stopped. (Oldendorf had got word that he was hitting his own destroyers.) In the hiatus *Yamashiro* too reversed course and started south after *Mogami,* but the flagship was undone. Within ten minutes she capsized and sank, taking with her Nishimura and almost the entire crew.

Thin-skinned *Shigure* was still alive. One shell had ripped through her stern but hundreds of others had missed, sending up an almost constant wall of water on either side. Nishino, benumbed by the deafening roar of battle and the jarring concussions of near misses that had knocked out every precision instrument, saw a large ship in flames to his left. It looked like a huge hunk of red-hot iron; it must be *Fuso*. He ordered right rudder, but there was no response. He brought the destroyer to a stop for repairs.

To the south, just as the first torpedoes were being launched at Nishimura, Shima's Second Striking Force had entered Surigao Strait at 28 knots. Almost immediately Shima's column was set upon by PT boats, which damaged the light cruiser *Abukuma* so severely she had to be left behind. The remaining six ships continued north. They were engulfed in a sudden squall but blindly continued to thread their way through the narrows at the same speed. At 3:25 A.M. the squall ended and Shima, who had not received Nishimura's "Urgent Battle Report Number 2" that his flagship and two destroyers had been torpedoed, ordered the Second Striking Force to go into battle formation with the flagship *Nachi* in the lead, followed by the other heavy cruiser, *Ashigara*, and the four destroyers. Rain spit spasmodically and visibility was poor, but Shima called for more speed. Everyone on *Nachi's* bridge strained to see ahead. Suddenly there came a blinding blossom of light that seemed to fill the entire strait. Some capital ship had blown up; Shima hoped it was American.

It was *Fuso*.

To encourage Nishimura, Shima said by radiotelephone, "We have arrived at battle site." His column was still bearing down at almost top speed. Ahead, two ships (they were the two sections of *Fuso*) were blazing intensely like "steel-mill flames," and Shima deduced that Nishimura's fleet had been smashed. The Second Striking Force passed to the left of the burning sections, hugging the coast to keep out of the glow.

Through the stationary telescope Shima watched destroyers dart in and out of a smoke screen. His own ships closed on another destroyer to starboard, dead in the water—a Japanese flag on its mast. It flashed out a blue signal: "I am destroyer *Shigure*. Rudder is damaged and under repair."

Nachi plunged into the smoke. In the distance came the deep, slow crump of big guns; the remnants of Nishimura must be ahead and still fighting. The column emerged through the smoke screen, only to face another. To the right was a large ship in flames, but Shima couldn't tell if it was American or Japanese. It was *Mogami.* Shima's radar detected an enemy fleet due north almost six miles. "All ships attack!" he ordered by radiotelephone.

The torpedo officer, Commander Kokichi Mori, suggested that the two heavy cruisers also launch torpedoes from the port. Shima approved, and *Nachi,* followed by *Ashigara,* turned sharply to starboard as the destroyers, which could only fire upon sighting the enemy, spurted straight ahead. Just to the left was *Mogami,* and she appeared to be dead in the water. *Nachi* launched her eight torpedoes, and moved up to hide behind the glare of *Mogami.* But as he approached, Shima saw to his surprise that *Mogami*'s prow had a wake. She was bearing down at almost 8 knots on a collision course. "Hard starboard!" he shouted, but the blazing *Mogami* moved straight at *Nachi* and there was a jarring crunch.

"This is *Mogami!*" someone called from the bridge through a megaphone. "Captain and executive officer killed. Gunnery officer in charge. Steering destroyed. Steering by engine. Sorry."

The two ships drifted slowly as if locked together, then *Nachi* cautiously turned left and the two ships parted, *Mogami* continuing south. The port side of *Nachi*'s prow was gone and engineers reported top speed would be reduced to 20 knots. Shima still wanted to follow his destroyers and attack. "Up ahead the enemy must be waiting for us with open arms," Mori objected. "Nishimura's force is almost totally destroyed. It is obvious that the Second Striking Force will fall into a trap. We may die any time." Besides, they didn't even know what Kurita was doing. "In any case, it's foolish to go ahead now."

There were still two hours left of darkness to hide their withdrawal. Shima's immediate task was to collect the remnants of Nishimura's force as well as his own. The fleeing ships were again harassed by PT boats near the south entrance of the strait. The persistent little craft were fought off, but to the rear a pursuing force of two light cruisers and three destroyers picked off the crippled destroyer *Asagumo.* This ended the surface pursuit, but Shima was not yet out of range of American aircraft. A wave of

Avengers found the straggling *Mogami,* and a bomb in the engine
room forced her abandonment. (Now only *Shigure* remained of
Nishimura's fleet.) Within an hour Shima saw a second wave of
Avengers on the horizon. In the radio room Lieutenant (j.g.)
Kameda, born in Honolulu, adjusted to the enemy cycle and
began broadcasting in English: "Hello, Charley One, hello Charley
One. Jap carrier planes attacking us. Abandon your present mis-
sion and return to base immediately."

On the bridge Shima watched as the oncoming planes abruptly
wheeled and headed back north.*

4.

At almost the same moment that Nishimura prepared to make
his foray into Surigao Strait, Kurita edged into San Bernardino
Strait two hundred miles to the north. The passage, narrower than
Surigao Strait, was difficult for a single ship to navigate even in
the daytime because of a stiff 8-knot current. Kurita had to bring
a ten-mile column of twenty-two ships through in pitch-dark; all
the navigation lights had been turned off.

As Kurita debouched into the Philippine Sea, he expected to
encounter attacks from submarines and a sizable surface force.
There was not a ship in sight. Expecting discovery momentarily,
he placed his ships in night-scouting formation as they skirted the
east coast of Samar and headed south for Leyte Gulf.

At 6:27 A.M. the sun rose in a dreary sky, and the order went
out to re-form in a circle around *Yamato.* Clouds hung low, occasional gusts of rain swept the ships, and the water was choppy.
High in the observation tower of the cruiser *Kumano,* Lieutenant
(s.g.) Shigeo Hirayama was dozing at his battle station. Like everyone else in the First Striking Force, he had had almost no sleep in
seventy-two hours. He rubbed his eyes hard and searched the
horizon. An enemy plane was approaching from the east. It looked
like a carrier-based torpedo plane. What was it doing coming
straight on?

Its pilot, an ensign named Jensen, on antisubmarine patrol, was

* There is no confirmation of this incident from American sources. It was
related by Admiral Shima.

as surprised as Hirayama. He started down toward the cruiser in a glide-bomb approach.

Simultaneously observers on *Yamato* sighted four "masts" on the horizon twenty miles to the southeast. They were soon identified as the island structures of carriers. God has come to our assistance! thought Koyanagi. This was a target worthy of their big guns. The younger officers cheered, their cheeks glistening with tears.

It had to be one of Mitscher's four powerful carrier groups. There was no alternative but to attack and Kurita wanted none. His one hope was that this task group was isolated. He closed in, altering his course slightly to 110 degrees, and radioed Combined Fleet:

BY HEAVEN-SENT OPPORTUNITY, WE ARE DASHING TO ATTACK ENEMY CARRIERS. OUR FIRST OBJECTIVE IS TO DESTROY THE FLIGHT DECKS, THEN THE TASK FORCE.

Mitscher's big carriers were far to the north—at Halsey's command—chasing the decoy, Ozawa, and what the Japanese saw was one of the Seventh Fleet's subsidiary forces, Taffy 3, whose function was to provide air cover for the amphibious shipping at Leyte. Commanded by Rear Admiral Clifton A. F. Sprague, it comprised three destroyers and four destroyer escorts, as well as six escort carriers (nicknamed "baby flattops" or "jeeps") holding no more than twenty-eight planes each and with a top speed of 19 knots. Sprague had been caught by surprise; his radar had just detected the enemy.

At 6:58 A.M. the main batteries of *Yamato* bellowed. For the first time the monstrous 3,220-lb. shells were hurled at an enemy surface target from the 70-foot-long barrels. Other ships joined in, as enthusiastic crews, on attack at last, worked their guns in a thundering chorus. Enemy destroyers tried to screen the carriers with smoke, but tiny planes could still be seen taking off from their flight decks "like bees." Kurita ordered General Attack. Breaking formation, all ships closed at optimum speed, and the chase became an unorganized scramble.

Sprague's carriers moved away sluggishly to the east, hastily launching fighters and Avengers armed with bombs. Salvos from

The BATTLE of LEYTE GULF

APPROACH OF
THE FOUR JAPANESE FORCES
23–24 OCTOBER 1944

N

SHIMA 2ND STRIKING FORCE

OZAWA FORCE

Aparri

LUZON

LINGAYEN
GULF

PHILIPPINE SEA

SOUTH
CHINA
SEA

Clark Field

Manila

Nichols Field

MINDORO

KURITA 1ST STRIKING FORCE

Musashi
sunk

SAN
BERNARDINO
STRAIT

SAMAR

MASBATE

Tacloban

PANAY

Ormoc

HOMONHON I.

Maya
sunk

CEBU

LEYTE

LEYTE GULF

Atago
sunk

Cebu
City

DINAGAT

PALAWAN

NEGROS

BOHOL

THE
DANGEROUS
GROUND

SULU

SURIGAO
STRAIT

NISHIMURA

SEA

MINDANAO

BALABAC STRAIT

Davao

BORNEO

0   Miles   200

palacios

the oncoming enemy ships fell closer and closer, sending up pink, green, red, yellow and purple geysers—the projectiles had been loaded with various dyes for identification. Their explosions had "a kind of horrid beauty" for Sprague. At 7:01 A.M. he radioed an appeal in the clear for help. To the south were two similar forces of baby flattops, Taffy 1 and Taffy 2. "Don't be alarmed," shouted the commander of Taffy 2, only thirty miles away. "Remember we're back of you. Don't get excited! Don't do anything rash!"

But these reassurances were meaningless. Sprague knew his ships could not "survive another five minutes of the heavy-caliber fire being received." Just then Taffy 3 was swallowed by a rain squall. It was a brief respite but it gave Sprague time enough to make a hard decision: he would not scatter his force but "pull the enemy out where somebody else could smack him." He turned to the south toward Taffy 2 and its planes; then, at 7:16 A.M., he ordered his three destroyers—*Hoel, Heermann* and *Johnston*—to counterattack. Possibly their sacrifice could buy time. *Johnston* (her captain was a Cherokee, Ernest E. Evans) closed to within 10,000 yards of *Kumano* and launched ten torpedoes. One hit the heavy cruiser, slowing her to 20 knots and putting her out of the battle. But *Johnston* paid for her daring as a trio each of 14- and 6-inch shells tore into her. It was, her senior surviving officer recalled, "like a puppy being smacked by a truck." She somehow remained afloat, her decks and bridge covered with dead.

Hoel was within range of two enemy columns, battleships on the left, cruisers on the right. Her captain, Commander Leon S. Kintberger, started for the big ones. Columns of green-dyed water showered *Hoel*. A shell smashed into the bridge. But the destroyer kept moving in and at 9,000 yards loosed a spread of torpedoes at the leading battleship. Kintberger swung his ship toward the cruisers, but shells knocked out the main engine and jammed the rudder hard right. He could still maneuver the ship by one engine and worked his way broadside of the cruiser column. At 7:35 A.M. his remaining five torpedoes began churning toward *Haguro,* the foremost cruiser.

In the dense smoke *Heermann,* the third destroyer, almost rammed a friendly destroyer escort and barely missed swiping *Hoel.* *Heermann* turned north, and while firing seven torpedoes at *Haguro,* sighted a battleship on the left. It was *Kongo,* which began to concentrate fire on *Heermann.* So did *Haguro* as soon as she had evaded the torpedoes. Two more Japanese battleships bore down on the destroyer, but *Heermann,* outdoing David, pressed the attack on still another adversary, the battleship *Haruna,* which was little more than two miles away. She peppered *Haruna* with 5-inch shells, and after launching her last three torpedoes, scampered away at 8:03 A.M.—miraculously still not hit by anything except shell fragments.

But the damaged *Hoel* was hemmed in by *Kongo* and several heavy cruisers. Hit at least forty times, *Hoel* continued to throw some five hundred shells at the enemy before her remaining engine was knocked out. At 8:30 A.M. she came to a stop, listing to port with one magazine on fire. Only then did Kintberger give the word to abandon ship.

Sprague's six jeep carriers had emerged from the squall in circular formation. Ten miles to the north lay the Japanese battleships, and a little closer to the northeast were four enemy cruisers. These blanketed *Gambier Bay* and *Kalinin Bay* with heavy fire, but the clumsy little carriers managed to evade every salvo. *Kalinin Bay,* however, could not escape the battleships' barrage and was hit fifteen times. Still, damage-control teams working waist-deep in oil and water kept her in formation.

Fighting back with her single 5-inch gun, *Gambier Bay* weaved around, managing to escape any damage for almost half an hour, but at last a shell struck the flight deck. Then a salvo plummeted into the water just off the carrier's port. One shell hit below the water line, flooding the forward engine room. *Gambier Bay* slowed to 11 knots, dropping out of formation.

At 8:30 A.M. Commander Evans, the Cherokee skipper of the already battered destroyer *Johnston,* saw the heavy cruiser *Chikuma* move in for the kill. "Commence firing on the cruiser, Hagen," he told his gunnery officer. "Draw her fire away from *Gambier Bay.*"

Johnston limped at 17 knots to within 6,000 yards of *Chikuma* and pumped five shells into her, but she ignored the destroyer. *Heermann,* still sound, joined the attack and forced *Chikuma* to turn some of her guns away from *Gambier Bay.* But it was too late. The carrier began to sink at 8:45 A.M.

Now Evans turned *Johnston* to face the light cruiser *Yahagi* and four destroyers which were converging on the remaining carriers. Evans closed in on *Yahagi,* which was moving into position to torpedo one of the carriers, and discharged such harassing fire with *Johnston*'s 5-inch guns—she made a dozen hits—that the light cruiser was forced to launch her torpedoes prematurely. *Yahagi*'s accompanying destroyers followed suit. Not a carrier was hit, but the Japanese jubilantly reported that "three enemy carriers and one cruiser were enveloped in black smoke and observed to sink, one after another."

Evans, who had pressured the enemy into launching their attack too soon, strutted across the bridge exclaiming, "Now I've seen everything!" But the Japanese had their measure of revenge. Cruisers and destroyers hemmed in *Johnston.* Her crew fought back until the ship was dead in the water and Evans reluctantly had to give the order to abandon her. Of the complement of 327, only 141 were picked up alive. The Cherokee skipper was not among them.

While Sprague's destroyers, aided by the four equally aggressive destroyer escorts, were blunting Kurita's surface attack, carrier planes from Taffy 2 and 3 hit the First Striking Force time and again. Three heavy cruisers—*Suzuya, Chikuma* and *Chokai*—sustained such damage that they were forced to retire.

Kurita was unaware that his advance force had been so frustrated; *Yamato*'s last two scout planes had been knocked down and her radiotelephone was out of order. Moreover, it looked from a distance through the smoke as if the advance guard had lost sight of the enemy. "Let's discontinue this chase," Koyanagi advised. "There's still Leyte Gulf to attack." Kurita concurred, and at 9:11 A.M. a message was radioed: RENDEZVOUS, MY COURSE NORTH, SPEED 20.

On the bridge of *Fanshaw Bay,* Sprague heard a signalman yell at 9:25 A.M., "Goddamit, boys, they're getting away!" The surface battle—the last of World War II—was over. Taffy 3 had not only withstood attack from the greatest array of guns afloat as well as a massive torpedo assault but inflicted serious damage on a superior force. For over an hour all was quiet. Then, at 10:50, General Quarters was again sounded on the five surviving jeep carriers. Nine enemy planes were approaching at mast level, so low that radar had failed to pick them up. They climbed to several thousand feet as American fighters tried to intercept them. Five Zero fighters with bombs lashed to their wings emerged from the milling mass and slanted down toward the jeeps. They were led by a recently married lieutenant commander, Yukio Seki. One Zero headed for the bridge of *Kitkun Bay,* its machine guns winking. Onlookers expected it to pull up; instead it drove into the port catwalk, exploded and tumbled on into the sea. Two others roared straight at *Fanshaw Bay,* also with obvious intent to crash into her, only to disintegrate at the last moment. The final two veered off from the heavy fire thrown up by *White Plains.* One, trailing smoke, banked toward *St. Lo* in a right turn as if intending to land, but the pilot pushed the little plane over, slamming it into the flight deck. Fires spread throughout the hangar deck, setting off a chain of violent internal explosions. After having survived the running battle unscathed, *St. Lo* sank.

Her survivors nicknamed the Japanese pilot "devil diver." He was a *kamikaze.* The idea for suicide attacks had recently risen spontaneously among groups of Army and Navy fliers, and several isolated efforts had been made before that day.* But it was not until Vice Admiral Takijiro Onishi arrived in Luzon—just before the American landing at Leyte—to take command of Fifth Base Air Force and learned he had fewer than a hundred operable planes that the *Kamikaze* Special Attack Corps was officially organized.

* In 1570 a Mongol emperor set sail for Japan with an invasion fleet. It looked as if Japan would easily be conquered, but a typhoon dispersed the Mongol ships. Convinced that the typhoon had been called up by the gods, the Japanese named it *kamikaze,* "divine wind."

The first Navy *kamikaze* was Rear Admiral Masafumi Arima. He took off from Clark Field on October 15, during the Formosa battle, intent on crashing his bomber into a carrier, but was shot down before he reached any American ship. The first *kamikaze* attack, however, had come a month earlier. On the evening of September 12 a group of Army pilots of the 31st Fighter Squadron located on Negros Island decided on their own to launch a suicide attack the following morning. Two were selected—First Lieutenant Takeshi Kosai and a sergeant. Captain Tatsumaru Sugiyama, one of the fifty aviation experts who had plotted to assassinate Tojo, was in charge of maintenance. He rigged 100-kilogram bombs on two fighter planes, and an hour before dawn the two pilots took off, determined to crash into carriers. They never returned. Apparently they, like Arima, were shot down before reaching a target, since there is no record on September 13 of an enemy plane ramming into an American ship.

"In my opinion," he told his commanders, "there is only one way of channeling our meager strength into maximum efficiency, and that is to organize suicide attack units composed of Zero fighters equipped with 250-kilogram bombs, with each plane to crash-dive into an enemy carrier."

Onishi's proposal was explained to the pilots. "Their eyes shone feverishly in the dimly lit room," reported one commander named Tamai. "Each must have been thinking of this as a chance to avenge comrades who had fallen recently in the fierce Marianas fighting, and at Palau and Yap. Theirs was an enthusiasm that flames naturally in the hearts of youthful men."

Onishi's *kamikaze* group was created specifically to support Kurita's raid on Leyte Gulf, and the first attack had come earlier that morning. Six suicide planes and four escorts took off from Mindanao at 6:30 A.M. and went north. While Taffy 3 was fighting off Kurita, the Special Attack planes came upon Taffy 1. One Zero crashed into *Santee* and another into *Suwannee,* but both of these jeep carriers were soon back in action. Nevertheless, all those who had seen the Japanese boring in with such fatalism were still shaken by the experience. It was a preview of things to come.

5.

It took Kurita almost two hours to collect his scattered forces —reduced from thirty-two ships to fifteen within three days—and again head south in ring formation for Leyte Gulf. The admiral and most of his staff hadn't slept since leaving Brunei and stayed alert by sheer will power. Koyanagi had difficulty moving around the bridge even with the help of a cane; he had been hit in the thigh by shrapnel the day before.

Kurita was more certain than ever that he had just encountered one of Halsey's carrier groups (Ozawa's message that he had lured Halsey north never reached First Striking Force). In addition, a report was intercepted—probably from a land-based plane—that a fleet of enemy carriers lay 113 miles north of the mouth of Leyte Gulf. Could these be Halsey's remaining task groups? In any case, Kurita would get no help from Nishimura's detached fleet that was supposed to invade Leyte Gulf from the south; Nishino, on the destroyer *Shigure,* had radioed that his was the only ship left afloat.

About 11:40 A.M. a lookout reported sighting an enemy battleship and several destroyers on the horizon. Kurita gave chase but could find nothing; perhaps the lookout had suffered from a delusion. Then a radio message to the effect that part of Kinkaid's force was making a sortie from Leyte Gulf was intercepted. It appeared likely that most of the transports had escaped. Even those which remained would have had five days to unload.

If Kurita charged into the narrow confines of the gulf to sink these transports, his own ships would be at the mercy of enemy land- and carrier-based planes. The First Striking Force might be wiped out—and for what? A few practically empty transports. This, Kurita reasoned, would be absurd. He decided instead—and he was seconded by Koyanagi and the rest of the staff—to turn north, and with the help of Japanese land-based planes, attack the enemy task force which was located less than a hundred miles away.*

The entire bridge was electrified by the decision. Forgotten was the ordeal of the past few days, which had left them bone-tired

---

* "The destruction of enemy carriers was a kind of obsession with me, and I fell victim to it." Kurita told author Masanori Ito in a unique interview after the war. "As I consider it now, my judgment does not seem to have been sound. Then the decision seemed right, but my mind was extremely fatigued. It should probably be called 'a judgment of exhaustion.' I did not feel tired at the time, but having been under great strain and without sleep for three days and nights, I was drained both physically and mentally."

The admiral refused to be interviewed for this book but consented to let Admiral Koyanagi speak for him. "I think now we should have gone into Leyte Gulf," he said. "So does Admiral Kurita. Then we thought we were doing the best thing but now, with a cool head, I realize we were obsessed by enemy task forces. Just because we got the report—and it turned out to be false—that there was a fleet of enemy carriers nearby, we shouldn't have set out after them."

If Kurita had continued on to Leyte Gulf, he would first have encountered Kinkaid's Seventh Fleet and then undergone a series of air attacks in confined waters. There was considerable shipping in the gulf—including twenty-three LST's and twenty-eight Liberty ships—but what if all these had been sunk? Most of the supplies had been landed, as Kurita had guessed, and there was on shore enough for a month's military operations. MacArthur claimed that loss of these ships would have "placed in jeopardy" the entire invasion. Still aboard were most of the steel landing mats for the airstrips, and without these he could have lost local air superiority temporarily. Also, a naval bombardment on American troops might have wreaked momentary havoc. Nevertheless, it is doubtful that MacArthur's advance would have been delayed more than a week or so.

and depressed; it was as if they were going into battle for the first
time.

At 12:35 P.M. Kurita sent out a fleet order to reverse course
and "engage in decisive battle with the enemy task force which is
in position bearing 5 degrees, distant 113 miles from Suluan lighthouse."

The news was greeted on every ship with shouts of *"Banzai!"*
The First Striking Force headed north to wage its final battle.

6.

His prey—Task Force 38—was in reality far out of range to the
north in its pursuit of Ozawa. Early that morning three American
scout planes had discovered the Mobile Force, and by 8 A.M. 180
dive bombers, fighters and torpedo planes had closed in on *Chitose*
and *Zuiho.* Only a handful of Japanese fighters came up to intercept. The rest of Ozawa's planes had been sent to the Philippines
to save them. Both light carriers were hit by bombs and *Chitose*
began to sink. Then a bomb exploded in the forward engine room
of the destroyer *Akizuki,* and a torpedo drove into the flagship,
Zuikaku.

There were no fighters to oppose the second wave. Through
heavy flak the thirty-six planes converged on the fourth carrier,
Chiyoda. Bombs exploded along her deck and, aflame, she assumed a sharp list. Ozawa's flagship could still navigate at 20
knots, but her rudder was damaged and communications were out.
Ozawa, who had had to be dragged off the stricken *Taiho* at the
Battle of the Philippine Sea, abandoned *Zuikaku* without protest.
There was no honor involved. He had accomplished his purpose
and given Kurita his chance to destroy the amphibious shipping
in Leyte Gulf.

Halsey's arbitrary actions the day before had left a worried
Admiral Kinkaid in the gulf. He tried to confirm his impression
that an emergency battle line—the newly created Task Force 34
under Admiral Lee—had been formed in front of San Bernardino
Strait, but received no reply for more than two and a half hours.

And when Halsey's answer finally arrived it jarred him—Task Force 34 was with the carriers engaging Ozawa!

By this time Kurita's fleet had hit Taffy 3, and Kinkaid replied with a plea for help: URGENTLY NEED BBS [battleships] LEYTE GULF AT ONCE.

Halsey's reaction was one of annoyance. It wasn't his job to protect the Seventh Fleet; he was carrying out a more important mission, attacking the main carrier force of the enemy. The best he could do was order Mitscher's fourth task group, which was still hundreds of miles to the east, to head for Leyte.

In the meantime Kinkaid ("I've had to fight my temper all my life") had sent Halsey another message with details of the powerful force that seemed certain to crush Taffy 3: . . . REQUEST LEE COVER LEYTE AT TOP SPEED X REQUEST FAST CARRIERS MAKE IMMEDIATE STRIKE.

This double request irritated Halsey. He had already done as much as he could and was in the middle of his own battle. Twenty-two minutes later Halsey received still another radio from Kinkaid:

. . . REQUEST IMMEDIATE AIR STRIKE X ALSO REQUEST SUP-PORT BY HEAVY SHIPS X MY OBBS [the old battleships which had bombarded Nishimura] LOW IN AMMUNITION.

This was "a new factor, so astonishing" that Halsey found it hard to accept. Why hadn't Kinkaid informed him of this earlier? Halsey replied that he was "still engaging enemy carriers" and had already sent the fourth task group of five carriers and four heavy cruisers to Kinkaid's assistance.

Little more than half an hour later yet another desperate message came from Kinkaid, this one not even in code:

WHERE IS LEE X SEND LEE

In Pearl Harbor, Nimitz was following the trials of Taffy 3, and like Kinkaid, he assumed that Task Force 34 had been detached to guard San Bernardino Strait the previous night. Now he, too, asked Halsey where that phantom task force was. A communications ensign added padding to confuse enemy decoders at the beginning and end of the message:

TURKEY TROTS TO WATER GG FROM CINCPAC . . . X WHERE IS RPT [repeat] WHERE IS TASK FORCE THIRTY-FOUR RR THE WORLD WONDERS

This dispatch reached Halsey's flagship, *New Jersey,* a moment after Kinkaid's message in the clear. The typist, Burton Goldstein, realized that TURKEY TROTS TO WATER was padding and omitted it, but THE WORLD WONDERS, despite the RR which set it off, sounded so plausible that he figured it might be a part of the text itself. So did his superior, a lieutenant, and the message was relayed to the bridge.

Infuriated by the words THE WORLD WONDERS ("as if I had been struck in the face"), Halsey slammed his cap to the deck. Carney grabbed him by the arm and said, "Stop it! What the hell's the matter with you? Pull yourself together!"

Fuming, Halsey showed him the dispatch. How could Chester Nimitz have sent "such an insult"? He ordered one of Mitscher's carrier groups to head south while the other two continued the attacks on Ozawa.

A third strike of more than two hundred planes at 1:10 P.M. set both *Zuikaku* and *Zuiho* afire. The latter steamed off at full speed, but *Zuikaku* gradually heeled over until the flight deck was awash. At 2:07 the big ship, which had survived so many battles, slid under. Mitscher's fourth wave, small like the second, concentrated on *Ise* and *Zuiho*. The rugged converted battleship managed to escape, but *Zuiho,* mortally wounded, was sent under.

It was the end of Ozawa's carriers. Three were at the bottom and the fourth, *Chiyoda,* was dead in the water. Ozawa had decoyed Halsey to the north but the shipping in Leyte Gulf remained intact. His sacrifice had been in vain.

Ten minutes after Kurita made his decision to turn away from Leyte Gulf, he was attacked by seventy fighters and Avengers from Taffy 3. *Tone* and *Nagato* were each hit by bombs but the fleet continued to search for the enemy carriers. Two more air attacks (147 sorties in all from Mitscher's still-distant fourth task group) did no damage, but Kurita was more certain than ever that his target was close by. All afternoon he pressed the search but found nothing; neither did he hear from Ozawa. By 6 P.M. he had steamed all the way back to San Bernardino Strait. There he patrolled with instructions from Combined Fleet to engage in a night battle if possible.

But the First Striking Force was low on fuel, and since no reports of enemy carriers had come in, Kurita reluctantly ordered a retirement. At 9:25 P.M. the remnants of the once mighty fleet found its way through the dark, dangerous waters of San Bernardino Strait.

The desperate plan to devastate shipping in Leyte Gulf had resulted in catastrophic losses: four carriers, three battleships, six heavy cruisers, three light cruisers and ten destroyers. About 300,000 tons of combat shipping had been sunk, more than a quarter of all Japanese losses since Pearl Harbor. Never again would the Imperial Navy play more than a minor role in the defense of the homeland.

23

The Battle of Breakneck Ridge

1.

Admiral Kurita's defeat on October 25 meant the virtual isolation of the Philippines but General Sosaku Suzuki, who was in charge of the defense of the central islands, had never been more confident. No American had flown over his headquarters island, Cebu, that day—confirmation that enemy air power had been crushed over Formosa. About noon optimistic reports of Kurita's battle off Samar began coming in: a number of American carriers had been sunk; *Yamato* and other battleships were raiding Leyte Gulf.

"General Tomochika," he told his chief of staff, "we are about to step on the center of the stage. There is no greater honor or privilege. We don't even need all the reinforcements they are sending us." Two units were coming from Luzon: the 1st Division would land at Ormoc, on Leyte's west coast, while the 26th Division landed at the port of Carigara, in the north. The two forces would merge and retake Tacloban in ten days.

Of this Suzuki had no doubt; his concern was that MacArthur

might try to surrender only his local forces, as Wainwright had done after the fall of Corregidor. "We must demand the capitulation of MacArthur's entire forces, those in New Guinea and other places as well as the troops on Leyte."

Suzuki's "air superiority" would not last long. That night, steel matting for the strips on Leyte was off-loaded but the laying on the following day was hampered by air raids and heavy rains. By nightfall every field was a quagmire. The engineers worked doggedly through the night of the twenty-seventh, and put down the last section on the Tacloban strip soon after dawn in time to welcome P-38's of the Fifth Air Force. One cracked up, but the other thirty-three landed safely.

Under persistent attacks by the U.S. 7th Division, the Japanese had retreated across the coastal plain all the way to Dagami. General Makino ordered the rear guard of his 16th Division to hold the town while the main body fell back to the foothills of the mountain range running down the island.

To the north the U.S. 24th Division was also driving west steadily. Their goal was Jaro, like Dagami at the foothills of the mountains. Held up by stiffening resistance and a river, the first GI's finally broke into the town on October 29 and turned up Highway 2—a twelve-foot-wide road with a crushed-rock and gravel surface—toward Carigara.

Poor communications continued to plague Suzuki. There were only fragmentary reports that the Americans were pushing north. He was, moreover, still ignorant of the debacle at sea. That afternoon Major Shigeharu Asaeda, General Yamashita's operations officer, flew into Cebu from Manila with more good news: the 1st Division would land at Ormoc a few days ahead of schedule, along with a battalion of the 26th Division.

Asaeda did not enlighten Suzuki about the situation confronting him. Suzuki was an able man but too honest and naïve; if he thought he was going to win he would fight much better. Asaeda, therefore, promised Suzuki continued reinforcements that he knew would never be sent, or if sent, could never arrive intact because of America's overwhelming air superiority. Suzuki had no chance to win, but why burden him with the truth? There was a saying: "The blind man fears no snake."

On the morning of November 1, eleven thousand men of the 1st Division left Manila in a driving rainstorm in four large transports escorted by six destroyers and four coastal defense ships. The 1st, also known as Gem Division, was an elite unit established in 1874 which had seen duty in the Sino-Japanese and Russo-Japanese wars. That summer it had been detached from the Kwantung Army and alerted for duty against the Americans. It had gone from northern Manchuria by rail to Shanghai, where it was trained as an emergency force.

En route to Leyte, company commanders explained to their men what lay ahead. On *Takatsu-maru* Lieutenant Minetoshi Yahiro told his platoon leaders that Americans had landed in force on Leyte and one division was heading for Carigara. Gem Division was to stop it. "We have long been preparing for this day. The hour has come when we must use all our training and skills."

Soon after sunset the throbbing noise of the engines stopped and the troops, jammed snugly in tiers of bunks, heard the clatter of chains as anchors plunged down. They had arrived at Ormoc, on Leyte. Orders were shouted; the men, their filthy uniforms crawling with lice, disentangled themselves and started up steep iron ladders to the upper decks out of stifling holds, foul with the stench of bodies.

Corporal Kiyoshi Kamiko, one of Yahiro's squad leaders, gulped in the fresh tropical air. Overhead, stars were bright pinpoints; the sea was calm. He had been a primary-school teacher before being conscripted just after Pearl Harbor. Determined and idealistic, he had enjoyed the years of training in Manchuria, accepting most of the brutalities of noncoms as necessary conditioning. He liked the comradeship of the Army, the feeling that each man depended on the next. Like the other men of Gem Division he was eager to prove himself in battle and do his duty for Japan and the Emperor.

The frightening but exhilarating rumble of distant guns came over the water. To remember the moment, Kamiko looked at his watch in the starlight. It was seven-thirty. Rope ladders tumbled over the sides of the transports, and the men, each weighed down with ninety pounds of equipment, swung awkwardly over the rail. At a flashlight signal from below, Kamiko leaped clumsily into a gently pitching boat. He landed on his back and finally realized why they had been instructed to remove their heavy ammunition belts.

On shore General Tomochika was anxiously observing the landing. He had preceded Suzuki to Leyte, to be greeted by the dismaying report that Makino's entire 16th Division was close to collapse. He stepped forward to meet Lieutenant General Tadasu Kataoka, commander of Gem Division, and his staff. "The First Division," he told them, "will proceed with the greatest possible speed along the Ormoc–Limon–Carigara road [Highway 2] and assemble to the area southeast of Carigara and prepare to attack."

Being a cavalry officer, Kataoka looked for the unexpected. What if they were attacked *before* they reached Carigara in the mountains near Limon?

"Proceed to Carigara," Tomochika answered. The possibility was ridiculous. "There's nothing to worry about."

"Is that so?" Kataoka remarked, but without sarcasm. He asked no more questions.

Yahiro Company settled down in a coconut grove, waiting for the rest of their regiment, the 57th, to come ashore. They began digging *takotsubo* (octopus traps), four and a half feet deep. The dugouts had a lateral scoop at the bottom where a man could huddle during a bombardment. In cross section a *takotsubo* looked like a Christmas stocking.

Sweat stung their eyes, and their shirts were plastered to their backs, but the warm air was preferable to the harsh winds of Manchuria. To the east the sky bloomed a pinkish glow with the unreal dawn of an exotic travel poster. The war seemed far away. Then came a distant buzzing. Someone shouted "Take shelter!" and the men leaped into their holes. The buzzing became a roar. Bombers approached in relentless formation, seeming invincible even when engulfed in black balls of ack-ack explosions.

Bombs from the planes—they were B-24's from Morotai—began to tumble toward the transports, which were still disgorging men and matériel. Zero fighters were suddenly all over the bombers, which continued sedately on course. Three Zeros burst into flames simultaneously, arching toward the ground like comets. A second wave of bombers followed shortly, their silver wings glinting in the sun.

A string of bombs fell in a great parabola toward the transport *Noto-maru*. One bomb disappeared in the smokestack. There was a dull detonation, followed by a chain of muffled blasts. The ship's whistle began to blow mournfully and without stopping. Helpless, Colonel Yoshio Miyauchi, commander of the 57th Regiment, watched the ship he and his troops had just left. He knelt on the beach and prayed, then wandered aimlessly toward the pier. His trucks, horses and most of his ammunition were on the burning ship. General Tomochika told the dazed colonel to get his men on the road to Carigara as soon as possible. He was to follow a small advance group which had left hours earlier. The division commander, General Kataoka, had already started up Highway 2 with two platoons, and Miyauchi, accompanied by an aide, now set out north on foot to regain his composure.

His regiment didn't start moving out of Ormoc until after midnight. They marched through the night strung out for miles along the narrow highway—unlike their commander, eager for battle. They were unaware of the significance of the sinking of *Noto-maru*.

In the dim light of early dawn—it was November 3—the advance group, under Major Yoshio Imada, was approaching Carigara. It unexpectedly encountered GI's of the 24th Division coming the other way. There was a brief fire fight and Imada retreated into the hills south of Highway 2.

General Kataoka learned about the skirmish just as he and his two platoons reached the heights north of Limon, a village of several score nipa huts where Highway 2 made a precipitous climb over rugged hills, then circled a commanding ridge to the right before descending again to the coast and Carigara. Kataoka ordered Major Imada to attack the advancing Americans; Imada could expect reinforcements, an antitank battalion. Then the general sent back word for Colonel Miyauchi to bring up a small field piece on the double.

This order made no sense to Miyauchi, but he loaded the gun into a truck and climbed aboard to direct operations. As the truck rumbled over the bumpy dirt road, he wondered what good one small piece of artillery would do. At Limon he listened politely to Kataoka explain how he was going to stem the enemy advance down near Carigara. The small gun was positioned to command the road where it made the sharpest turn around the ridge.

All day Miyauchi's 57th Regiment straggled north along the narrow road toward Limon, harassed by American bombing and strafing attacks. More than two hundred men were killed and scores of others were overcome by the intense heat. Darkness when it came offered little relief. Around nine o'clock the men fell out exhausted along the sides of the highway. They were attacked by mosquitoes; those who had not covered their faces before they fell asleep awoke with eyes almost swollen shut, but their eagerness was undiminished as they resumed their march, this time under dark, lowering clouds. Kamiko's battalion was the first to reach Limon, and its commander, Captain Sato, was ordered by Miyauchi to take positions north of the village near the emplaced gun.

On the other side of the mountain range Lieutenant General Walter Krueger, commander of Sixth Army, thought his advance division, the 24th, faced encirclement and annihilation. He knew from aerial observation that a large force of Japanese was marching toward Limon; and he feared the enemy might also land a large amphibious force behind the 24th Division at Carigara. Krueger reacted cautiously. Rather than push forward and take the strategic ridge, breaking through the mountain barrier which as yet was lightly defended, he ordered the 24th Division to halt and prepare to fend off a possible sea invasion in co-operation with the 1st Cavalry Division, which was on its heels.

At dusk Miyauchi's regiment started up the winding road toward the crest of the ridge. An eerie white figure approached. It was a survivor of the 16th Division, swathed in bandages, driven back all the way from Leyte Gulf. He passed silently by. He was followed by more walking wounded, helping one another or hobbling on sticks. Word spread down the ranks that General Makino's division had been annihilated.

Just ahead lay the highest point of Highway 2, where the road bent sharply to the east. The jagged hill mass on the right was covered with shoulder-high cogon grass. It was a natural fortress. Numerous spurs branched off it toward the sea to the northeast and toward the Leyte River Valley to the southwest. In between the steep rises were dense woods.

Here the march stopped. Whispered instructions were passed along to jettison all unnecessary items. The men stuffed their small battle haversacks with hardtack and five grenades each and piled their back packs near the road. Kamiko's company was ordered to take the lead, and his squad led the company—that, he thought proudly, made him the spearhead of Gem Division.

The sky lightened with dramatic suddenness. With the sun came intolerable heat. The air was acrid with powder smoke. The battlefield must be near but the ridge was silent. A rifle cracked. It was quiet again and then Kamiko heard the chirping of birds. The former schoolteacher's heart beat faster. His chest constricted. He turned to his companions. Their eyes were glittering. They had been preparing to fight for three years and were as expectant as he was. An order came up to turn off the road and climb the ridge.

On the other side, GI's were also nearing the top of the ridge. Krueger had ordered the 24th Division to reconnoiter it; the general attack south was to begin in two days.

Kamiko pushed through brush and began the ascent toward the crest. Behind, someone shouted, "Squad Leader Kamiko! Wrong direction!" It was the platoon sergeant. A grenade exploded. The sergeant stumbled, clutching his thigh. Kamiko was showered with debris. A soldier grunted, "I'm hit!" Blinded, Kamiko tripped over him. He forced himself to be calm; gradually he recovered his vision. Geysers of earth erupted on all sides. Grenades lobbed over the crest by the GI's were bounding down the slope like apples spilled from a barrel. Kamiko squirmed toward the sergeant and touched him. He felt warm, sticky blood.

While he was wondering what to do, he heard the hollow thump of mortars, then the deep cough of a machine gun. Bullets whipped through the brush, thumping into bodies and bringing cries of surprise and pain. The first squad was being wiped out without a fight! He fought a paralyzing panic and finally forced himself to shout "Fire!" Rifles crackled. Kamiko looked at his watch. It was exactly ten o'clock on November 5 in the nineteenth year of Showa. It might be his last moment as a human being.

Kamiko fired blindly round after round. He stopped to reload and peered above the brush. There was a thunderous shock, a blinding flash, and darkness. Earth and sand showered him, but he was unhurt. According to the manual, shells from the same gun never landed in the same spot, so he sprang into the newly made crater.

He was immediately joined by two comrades, a light-machine-gun team. They set up their weapon and were about to open fire when mortar rounds began bursting so close that the operator, Ogura, shouted, "It's dangerous here, Squad Leader!" and scrambled out of the hole with his gun.

The entire squad moved laterally, and frantically dug *takotsubo* among the roots of rotting palm trees. The mortar barrage ceased. Kamiko held up his helmet on a bayonet, and a hail of bullets battered the helmet "like a wind-bell." He crouched down again but the firing from the top of the ridge had stopped. He wondered why the GI's, after pinning them down, had fallen back.

Kamiko told his men to eat while they had the chance. They had hardtack but no water. He ordered a man with a slight leg injury to report the situation to the company commander, Lieutenant Yahiro, then crept along the slope to make a personal reconnaissance. The other two squads had been trapped by the mortars and machine guns and only three men in all were alive. If it hadn't been for Ogura, his squad too would have been wiped out.

At dusk he gathered his remaining five men and told them they alone held the hill. He ordered them to collect ammunition, arms and supplies from dead comrades. By midnight they were prepared for the attack that was certain to come at dawn, but their thirst had become unbearable. Kamiko remembered seeing coconut trees somewhere near the crest. He removed all clothing except for his loincloth, tied a washcloth around his head and stealthily crawled up the hill. In the moonlight he found a coconut tree and started shinnying up it.

"Squad Leader!" The whispered voice startled him and he almost lost his grasp. "Get down fast or you'll be shot!" It was Ogura, who had followed him. But Kamiko continued until he reached a cluster of coconuts. He yanked one free, dropped it with a heavy thud. He expected a burst of fire but none came. He dropped ten more before rejoining Ogura. Together they carted the coconuts back to the squad. Kamiko chopped off the tops and distributed the milk. It reminded him of a soft drink.

During the night they were joined by the 4th Squad, headed by the platoon leader himself, Warrant Officer Hakoda. A year younger than Kamiko, he looked like a schoolboy. He apologized for arriving so late. Kamiko roused his own squad before dawn. He was surprised to find that despite the heavy losses, he anticipated battle as eagerly as he had the day before. He surveyed the area. A hundred feet below was winding Highway 2. Above them loomed the crest of the ridge and he guessed one could see Carigara Bay from there. There were now nineteen men on the strategic hummock, the southeastern spur of the range.

At about nine o'clock he heard distant commands in English. Bullets pounded into the earth along the *takotsubo* line. Ogura, eyes "as big as saucers," began firing his machine gun as if possessed. The fire let up briefly and Kamiko called out the names of his men: "Aoki! Shimizu! Otsuka! Ishii!" Each shouted *"Hai!"* (Yes!) from his own hole. "If they get close enough, throw grenades," Kamiko instructed them.

Enemy fire resumed, augmented this time by the sound of heavy machine guns. "Squad Leader!" It was Aoki in the next hole. "The brush is burning!" Smoke swirled across the slope and the crackle of burning cogon grass rose above the din. "Squad Leader!" Aoki again. "The enemy is coming!"

Partially hidden by smoke, the Americans (I Company, 3rd Battalion, 21st Infantry Regiment, 24th Division) had charged over the ridge and were closing in. "Third Squad," Kamiko shouted, "fix bayonets and prepare grenades!" He heard the click of bayonets as he fastened his own and armed his grenades.

"Charge!" screamed the baby-faced Hakoda.

Kamiko was about to relay the order to his own squad, but it didn't make sense. A charge should always be preceded by some kind of covering barrage. Impulsively he yelled, "Third Squad, hold!" The enemy was still screened by the flaming brush. "Target, right oblique!" Kamiko shouted. "Fire!"

Ogura turned his machine gun to the right.

"Totsugeki!" It was Hakoda again, urging the 4th Squad to charge into the murderous fire. Hakoda fell and his new sergeant was hit. "Take command," he called out to Kamiko. The Ameri-

cans were almost upon them. It was all over. Kamiko shouted desperately, "Fire everything you have!"

Suddenly the sky overhead was split with a long screech which was cut off abruptly by an explosion on the slope ahead. Stunned, the infantrymen on both sides stopped shooting. Another big shell landed in front of Kamiko in the midst of advancing Americans. A third shell whined over, plummeting into the enemy's heavy-machine-gun positions. The three rounds had come from a single big Japanese gun just hauled into position.

Kamiko jumped to his feet and shouted, "It's ours!"

Several American machine guns resumed their chattering. A fourth shell exploded. There was silence ahead. This time the enemy machine guns remained silent.

There was no rifle fire from the *takotsubo* on the left and Kamiko crawled over to investigate. Ishii was bent over, head down. "What's the matter?" asked Kamiko and took off Ishii's helmet. His eyes were open but there was a hole the size of a bean in the middle of his forehead. The back of his head was like a burst pomegranate.

Kamiko ground his teeth in anger. Ishii was his best friend—a university man, full of spirit and compassion. He felt heat on his back and whirled around. The wind was driving the grass fire down the slope. Where was the wounded Hakoda? Kamiko began searching to save him from the flames but all he could find was an officer's leather belt, saber and pistol. Had the Americans taken Hakoda prisoner? Machine guns sent him tumbling back to his hole, clutching the platoon leader's possessions.

Aoki called out to him, "Enemy approaching!" Aoki was about to toss a grenade but Kamiko stopped him; the enemy was too far away. Kamiko crawled forward with his own grenades, followed by Ogura. He crouched, ready to stand up and throw—and die. Again a shell—this from a recently positioned four-gun battery —whistled overhead, exploded up the slope.

"Hit! Direct hit!" someone shouted excitedly. "Five or six were blown up!"

Then he heard another voice—that of the company commander, Lieutenant Yahiro! The main force of the company had arrived. Kamiko leaped to his feet. Wiping tears away with the back of one hand, he activated a grenade by slamming it on his helmet and heaved it as far up the hill as he could. His men joined him. There were five quick explosions.

"Charge!" Kamiko shouted. He felt as though nothing could stop him as he hurtled up the charred, smoldering field toward the heavy-machine-gun position with fixed bayonet. Behind pounded his squad. Dead Americans were everywhere, their bodies scorched and swollen; one seemed to be overflowing with yellow grease. Kamiko, followed by eight men, swarmed into the machine-gun emplacement. Gunners had been blown apart; cartridges on their belts were detonating like firecrackers. Every so often one of these explosions set off a grenade. Kamiko was rooted, erect. Amid all this carnage he found himself alive. It was as if he were coming out of a dream. Reality swept over him again; he crouched and once more plunged up toward the crest of the ridge. As he burst over the top he saw spread before him the breath-taking panorama of Carigara Bay. The Americans were scrambling down their side of the ridge; here and there a fleeing figure tumbled haplessly from the fusillade which followed them from the crest.

A single platoon, with the help of a dozen artillery shells, had blunted a determined enemy attack and given the strung-out regiment time to reach the front and turn the ridge into a fortress of *takotsubo,* trenches and gun emplacements.

Kamiko remembered how the samurai of the civil-war era took the head of an enemy, and reached for an American officer's helmet. The liner was wet with blood and he hesitated—was it proper for a modern man to take booty? But he still had helmet in hand when he reported to his company commander. Lieutenant Yahiro's face was black with dust and gunpowder, his arm in a sling. He grinned boyishly. "Thank you very much for enduring such hardships," he told Kamiko.

Their battalion commander, Captain Sato, called for the merits list and wrote on the first page. It was an unimaginable honor for an infantryman, the "dream flower." Usually only fliers and sailors were officially commended. Sato was curious about the American helmet. Kamiko apologized for the blood but the battalion commander put it on, waggling his head several times. "This is light and feels good." Was there one without a bullet hole?

"I'm sure I can find one," Kamiko volunteered.

"If you do, I'll use it."

Yahiro grinned as he hefted an American carbine. "This is light too. I may use it from now on."

That night Kamiko was appointed platoon leader in place of Hakoda. He couldn't sleep; the corpses of comrades lying out front unattended haunted him. From the darkness he heard someone say, "Why do American soldiers die on their backs?" Another voice answered, "The Japanese are well-mannered; even after they've died they hide their private parts." Both laughed.

Just before dawn Kamiko and the two other platoon leaders were ordered to report to the company commander's dugout. Yahiro told them that the rest of their battalion had been ambushed on the way up front and practically wiped out. So their own hummock (it had been renamed Yahiro Hill by Sato in honor of the company) had become the spearhead again—and was isolated. "Reinforcements are sure to come. When the main force of the division arrives, it will be easy to wipe out the enemy. Until then we must defend this position to the end. I hope that each platoon leader will do his best, with resolution, despite the condition of the men."

The Americans who had been forced back resumed their assault on the escarpment—it was nicknamed Breakneck Ridge—with the help of men from the 1st Cavalry Division. This time they attacked on a broader front but still concentrated on the hill where the eighty men of Kamiko's company were waiting, with orders to hold fire. When the GI's were seventy-five yards away, Lieutenant Yahiro shouted "Fire!"

The fusillade of rifle and machine-gun bullets toppled over the enemy "like bowling pins." But the onslaught was stemmed only momentarily. Kamiko grudgingly admired the Americans' ability to advance over the bodies of their comrades, throwing grenades like baseballs. The carnage along the defense line was far worse than the day before, and Kamiko doubted that Yahiro Hill could be held against such determination and firepower. He was impatient with his own single-action Model 38 rifle; it was accurate, but after every shot the five-bullet clip had to be pushed down. He shouted to Ogura to concentrate his machine-gun fire to the right where the American advance was slowing. Perhaps they could be panicked. Grenades, tossed by comrades behind him, flew overhead and bounced toward the enemy. The Americans wavered. One or two turned back and the rest followed pell-mell down the hill.

Yahiro Company had held again, but only twenty-five were alive. The survivors were sent back in relays down to a stream on the other side of Highway 2. They washed their faces in the cool water, filled canteens and ate hardtack. This, Kamiko thought, is the pleasure of nothingness.

The American failure to seize Breakneck Ridge had immediate repercussions. Major General Franklin C. Sibert, commander of X Corps, which included the 24th Infantry and 1st Cavalry divisions, came up front at noon, and without waiting to go through channels, summarily relieved a regimental commander and replaced him with his own intelligence officer, Colonel William J. Verbeck.

Verbeck quickly proved he was one staff officer who was more aggressive than the average line officer. No sooner had he taken command than he sent a company to flank the ridge. It too was pushed back. Undeterred, Verbeck ordered the 2nd Battalion, with Company L attached, to attack the ridge in force the next morning.

November 8 dawned gray. Then the skies darkened dramatically, and rain, whipped by typhoon winds, swept the ridge. Palms bent like bows, and some snapped, others were uprooted. The cogon grass lashed like a turbulent sea. Even so, Verbeck's attack began on schedule. It opened with a heavy-artillery barrage, the boom of cannons competing with the thunder and screaming wind. Infantry moved out through the beating rain, floundering on the muddy slopes. Their maps were inaccurate and it took hours for some units to get into position.

Mortar shells, however, had zeroed in on the crest of the ridge. The effect was so devastating that Yahiro ordered the company to fall back to their original *takotsubo* near the highway, and there make the final stand. The men skidded and bumped their way down to holes, which were already deep with water but nevertheless offered refuge from the mortar rounds that flew overhead.

Fog engulfed the slope; nothing could be seen beyond ten yards. As he waited, soaked and miserable, Kamiko re-evaluated the enemy. First, he was no coward; second, he could throw grenades twice as far as the Japanese; third, and most important, he always seemed to be rested. Kamiko's squad was perpetually exhausted; perhaps it was the constant battle without relief, perhaps the lack of food.

There were no mortars to lob shells over the ridge at the approaching Americans, so Yahiro ordered his men to direct steady fire on the crest line of the shrouded ridge. The strategy worked; the display of fire power discouraged the enemy from coming over the top. The defenders regained confidence, but their sense of security was short-lived. To the rear they heard an eerie grinding, thumping noise. An American tank had come around the bend of Highway 2, churning through the morass of mud, its gun spitting out shells. They were surrounded!

Two men scrambled down the hill toward the road, carrying a heavy satchel charge. The men in the *takotsubo* turned and watched the little drama as from an amphitheater until they heard shouts in English near the top of the ridge. "Use grenades!" cried Kamiko and started up the hill followed by his depleted platoon. They tossed grenades over the crest and ran back for more. Three times they scrambled up the slope. With the enemy out of sight, they returned to their holes.

But the Americans returned, as they always did. Kamiko heard something hissing at the rim of his *takotsubo*. An enemy grenade had rolled down the hill and was caught in a tent stake. He looked at Ogura and both shrugged. It was the end. But the grenade fizzled out. Others bounded over the dugouts but exploded after they were past.

On the crest above, a GI leveled his rifle at Kamiko. He crouched in his *takotsubo,* then popped up and fired. The GI fell to the ground, but in his excitement Kamiko pumped three more shells into him. A rifle barrel rose and disappeared like a periscope. It belonged to another GI who was trying to rescue his fallen comrade. Kamiko ran up to the crest and shot him, too; then sprinted back to his hole.

Pfc. Saiji Saito in the next hole leaped forward, following Kamiko's example. At the crest he, too, fired. But instead of retreating, he disappeared on the other side. Why had Saito sacrificed himself so needlessly? Kamiko wondered. Then Saito reappeared like a jack-in-the-box. He swore breathlessly as he leaped into

Kamiko's hole, "I hated him so much I had to kick his head off!"
Had Saito—a mild youngster who didn't smoke or drink—gone
mad? Was this the frenzy of the battlefield Kamiko had read about?
And yet, hadn't he himself come close to doing the same thing?

To the rear the American tank—a medium—still moved freely
on the road, raking the *takotsubo* from behind with its machine
gun and cannon. The two men with the satchel charge sprang out
of the ditch and flung the explosive under the tank's tracks. As
they leaped back to safety, there was a dull detonation and the
tank shuddered. It turned laboriously, however, and retreated
around the bend.

Without the tank the American attack faltered and once more
the GI's gave up Yahiro Hill. Without hesitation the Japanese
clambered up the muddy slope to reoccupy their positions along
the crest. This time Kamiko felt no sense of victory. The enemy,
who made retreat a tactic, would come back again and again.
What did the remnants of Yahiro Company have left to stop them?

Several hundred yards to Kamiko's right on the next hill in the
ridge, Sergeant Yoshio Noguchi's platoon had been hurt as badly
as Kamiko's by the deadly mortar barrage along the crest. He had
two 7.7-mm. machine guns left—his and the one in the next *takotsubo*—but only a few rounds of ammunition.

Crouched in the numbing water up to his waist, Noguchi heard
a cry of anguish and the operator of the second gun crawled feebly
toward him. Noguchi pulled him in. His right thigh was like "a
beehive" gushing blood. His face was pale, drained. The crawling
man had attracted steady enemy machine-gun fire. The cogon grass
all around Noguchi's *takotsubo* was mowed flat. He cautiously
checked on both sides. There was no activity. Apparently he was
the last one of his platoon. He was a hardy, experienced soldier,
a farm boy who had volunteered for service in 1938. Surrender
was out of the question. He put the barrel of his pistol to his temple.
He pulled the trigger, but the mechanism was jammed from the
mud.

Not twenty-five yards away, Americans in greenish uniforms
were coming down his line of *takotsubo*. At each hole they paused
with rifles at the ready while two of their number machine-gunned
the dead or wounded occupants. The firing grew closer and Noguchi again put pistol to head. Jammed. There was a stuttering rat-

tle of fire a few yards away and Noguchi knew he was next. A branch of palm leaves had been blown by a mortar round to the edge of his hole. With a stick he deftly pulled the palm over the mouth of the *takotsubo*. He pressed flat against the back of his dugout, water up to chin, legs outspread, then pulled the body of the lifeless machine-gun operator in front of him.

The voices were directly overhead. A shiny barrel poked between the leaves. He thought, How well they take care of their weapons. As he plugged his ears with his middle fingers he prayed the bullets would somehow miss him. He felt the concussion from a deafening series of explosions, and scores of bullets churned the water between his legs. The opposite side of the hole collapsed. Noguchi closed his eyes as mud began covering him up to the neck. The palm branch, cut in two, dropped on his head.

The voices moved away and there was a burst of fire in the next hole. Stunned almost beyond thinking, Noguchi felt no pain. Carefully he scraped the mud from his face and opened his eyes. The water in the hole was tinged red. But it was the blood of his human shield.

At last the firing stopped. What were the Americans doing now? With infinite caution he pushed his dead comrade aside and looked out, expecting to see them digging foxholes. They were building something he had never seen before—shallow, rectangular rock forts with canvas roofs.

Noguchi huddled for hours in the bloody water, afraid to make another move until well after dark. At last he painfully got to his feet. All around him were the strange squat shelters; each glowed from a dim light within. He could hear the Americans joking and eating. Cigarette smoke curled invitingly out of the cozy little structures. What kind of soldiers would have lights in the middle of a battlefield?

The lights began going out one by one, and near midnight it started to rain again. Noguchi hoisted himself out of his hole and started crawling away from the one GI he could see was on guard. He came to a wire which seemed to surround the encampment. Some kind of warning device? He crawled under without touching it, and down a steep incline. His legs were so weak and uncoordinated he had to hold on to vines to keep from falling. At the bottom he found a small stream. He drank on all fours, like a dog. Except for rain, it was the first water he had tasted in days. In the gloom he barely made out scores of bodies—comrades, canteen in hand, had met their death looking for water. In the darkness and rain he could not determine where he was. The battalion command post should be two hundred yards away, but he crawled up and down the draws for more than a mile without finding it. Exhausted, he curled up behind a bush and fell asleep.

He was wakened by voices. Through the brush he saw Americans eating breakfast. In the night he had circled around and around the knob only to climb back up to his starting place. Two GI's headed directly for him. He ducked his head, hoping they wouldn't notice him in the underbrush. Then he felt a stream of fluid splashing against his helmet. One of the Americans was urinating on him. When he looked up, the GI was adjusting his trousers as he ran after his comrades who were already marching off.

Most of Breakneck Ridge, however, still remained in Japanese hands. That morning, after heavy artillery preparation, two soaked battalions of the 24th Division resumed the attack in the driving rain. They advanced but were thrown back by a fresh Japanese battalion. Rain had become as much of a problem to the Americans as the enemy. Their supply route, Highway 2, was a swamp, and engineers were carting up loads of heavy gravel to try to make it passable. Already the GI's were suffering from "immersion foot," similar to the trench foot of Europe: the skin peeled away, leaving raw sores.

The Japanese, too, were afflicted by the endless rain. Using trenching spades, they tried in vain to bail out their *takotsubo*. Kamiko remembered that American knapsacks were waterproof and decided to use one as a bucket. He crawled over to the enemy side of the ridge, found a dead GI—as usual lying face up, mouth open—and took his knapsack. He and Ogura scooped out the water in their hole and passed the knapsack to the next *takotsubo*. Drenched to the skin and cold, they cut off the rubber tubes of gas masks and set them on fire. The smell was nauseating but there was some heat.

Kamiko awoke to another dark dawn—it was November 10. It

was nonsense to try to determine one's own deathday, yet he kept doing it. Still he had no fear at all. *"Mei ţa tzu!"* he exclaimed—a popular Chinese expression meaning "It is Fate" (similar to *"Que será será"*). There was nothing to do now except enjoy life to its last moment.

The rain increased as American shells plowed into the crest line above them. Under the constant trembling of the earth, the sides of the *takotsubo* began to crumble. It reminded Kamiko of the terrifying earthquake in 1923, which he had never been able to forget. The barrage lifted.

"First platoon, take positions on the ridge line!" Kamiko shouted and charged up the hill, an unrecognizable mass of shell holes. At the top he saw swarms of enemy soldiers halfway up the other side. They seemed numberless (they were two full battalions of the 1st Cavalry Division) and there were only a handful left in Yahiro Company to stop them. He frantically gestured to his men to return to the relative safety of their *takotsubo* down below. He called out a warning as he sped by Yahiro's dugout. He leaped into his hole a moment before bullets swept down the slope. Grenades followed, skipping down into their positions. To the right there was shouting in English. Had the 2nd Platoon been overrun?

Saito yelled, "Out of ammunition!" "Me, too!" another man called. Someone tossed them a few clips in an attempt to divide the remaining ammunition, but it was useless. Driven by anger and frustration, Kamiko plunged out of his *takotsubo,* and followed by three men, churned almost to the top of the hill before lobbing a grenade at the crest. Impulsively—perhaps to frighten the enemy—he shouted in English, "Charge, charge!"

The result was startling. An American rushed over the crest with fixed bayonet and found himself facing Kamiko. The two stared open-mouthed at each other. Neither fired. Then the GI, realizing the order had come from the wrong side, dived back over the crest.

"Company, *tenshin!*" It was the voice of Yahiro's assistant. The word meant literally "turn around and advance" and was a euphemism for "retreat." Yahiro himself repeated the word, then shouted as if in apology, "We will advance later!"

The men of the platoon next to Kamiko's, the 2nd, had never

heard the expression before—it had been created recently to cope realistically with the changing tide of war—but the urgency of the command forced them out of their holes, ready to launch the last attack.

"Tenshin! Tenshin!" Yahiro, American carbine in hand, ran out of his *takotsubo* to turn them around.

Kamiko knew the word but had never expected to hear it in battle. Paralyzed, he watched the Americans concentrate their fire on the exposed 2nd Platoon. Yahiro was firing his carbine from the hip. One GI fell. Yahiro picked off another, then was sent spinning to the ground himself. Kamiko helped drag him to a shell hole. Blood spurted from his throat. "Company Commander!" Kamiko pleaded. They held a canteen to Yahiro's mouth. He gulped once, then his head fell lifeless to the side.

Now the fate of the few men left in Yahiro Company was in Kamiko's hands. Retreat was disgraceful; in all their years of training it had been forbidden. They were going to die anyway and should take as many enemy with them as possible. "Throw all the grenades you have left!" he shouted and started up toward the crest, with five men right on his heels. Their unexpected attack caught the Americans momentarily off-guard. They fell back under the rain of grenades. We could win with one machine gun! thought Kamiko. The absurdity of that hope jerked him back to reality. He was leading his men to a meaningless death. "Follow me!" he cried and dodged back down the hill toward Highway 2 with the few survivors of the 2nd Platoon and his own men. He jumped into the ditch by the road, then looked back. Helmeted heads were poking up all along the crest.

There were eleven in the ditch and Kamiko began to lead them down the highway toward Ormoc—along the same stretch of road he had so recently led the entire Gem Division—but the shame of retreat still gnawed at his conscience. Yahiro had ordered them to fall back, yet this withdrawal was his own responsibility—and he had abandoned the body of his commander. He had valued his own life above honor, and the thought tormented him with every step he took to the rear. Then he began to feel defiant; Why die needlessly? It wouldn't help the nation.

He began to feel almost "light of heart." But his euphoria was shattered by the blast of a grenade. It had come from the west, or valley, side of Highway 2. No one was hurt and they broke into a run. How had the enemy outflanked them so fast in such rough terrain? Perhaps it might not even be possible to rejoin the main force.

A few hundred yards down the road they came to a culvert; a stream was running underneath. *Mei fa tzu!* Kamiko reminded himself. The only thing was to do one's best and not worry about the future. They were still alive. They stripped off their foul uniforms. With leggings removed, their bare legs were sickly white, like bean curd. As they scrubbed their clothes in the stream they began teasing and pushing one another as if they were back in Manchuria; then, clad only in loincloths, lay down unconcerned and before long were asleep.

They were awakened by an ominous staccato. Kamiko jumped up. Above them on the crest of the ridge he could see GI's manning a machine gun. He grabbed his rifle, and while the others snatched up what clothes they could on the run, he emptied his last clips before following them. They were chased by a few mortar rounds which detonated on contact with foliage overhead. Deep within the woods they paused to put on the clothing they had managed to salvage, and circled back to the road.

At a regimental supply depot, Kamiko checked in and the young officer in charge congratulated them for the "great victory" of their battalion. Kamiko stared at him. On the ridge they had been waiting day after day for substantial reinforcements while the 3rd Battalion was being annihilated. Didn't anyone back here at Regiment know what was going on up front?

2.

In Manila, General Yamashita knew at least that Suzuki's troops had encountered stiff opposition at the ridge. He ordered the main thrust diverted from Carigara; instead, Suzuki should turn east off Highway 2 below Limon and strike overland directly across the island to Tacloban. It was a perfunctory order. General Yamashita still questioned the advisability of waging the Decisive Battle on Leyte. It was foolhardy to drain off men and supplies that would be needed so desperately in the battle for Luzon. More-

over, he had reason to believe things were not going too well for
Suzuki at Leyte. And had American air and naval power *really*
been crippled at Formosa and Leyte?

Field Marshal Terauchi, however, remained unimpressed by these
arguments. "We have heard the opinions of Fourteenth Area
Army," he said, "but the Leyte operation will continue."

"I fully understand your intention," Yamashita replied. "I will
carry it out to a successful end."

Terauchi's confidence came in part from the relative ease with
which he had just landed 13,000 men (12,000 of them from the
26th Division) at Ormoc. Moreover, another convoy, carrying
10,000 troops, was approaching Leyte escorted by four destroyers,
a minesweeper and a submarine chaser, and screened by three
other destroyers.

Early the next morning, November 11, the convoy turned
into Ormoc Bay. But at this point Yamashita's suspicion that
American air and naval power had not been destroyed was dramatically borne out. Almost two hundred carrier planes from Task
Force 38 caught the creeping convoy before it reached the harbor.
This first wave concentrated on the six transports, which were hit
again and again. The second wave went after the destroyers, and
the third swept in, bombing the burning hulks and strafing the
men struggling in the water. The slaughter was frightful. At the
cost of nine American planes, every transport and four of the destroyers were sunk. Only a few of the 10,000 troops aboard—almost an entire division—managed to swim ashore through the
crimson sea.

The catastrophe left Terauchi unchanged, at least outwardly,
but it strengthened Yamashita's conviction that Leyte was a lost
cause. At the same time he was under orders from Terauchi to
continue the operation with vigor. His reservations were reflected
in a radio message he sent Suzuki on November 15, which came
close to predicting the abandonment of Leyte:

THE THIRTY-FIFTH ARMY WILL ENDEAVOR TO ACCOMPLISH
THE DESTRUCTION OF THE ENEMY ON LEYTE, SETTING AS ITS
MINIMUM OBJECTIVE THE DISRUPTION OF THE ENEMY'S USE
OF AIR BASES . . .

IN THE EVENT THAT FURTHER TROOP SHIPMENTS CANNOT BE

SENT, LUZON WILL BECOME THE MAIN THEATER OF FUTURE
OPERATIONS IN THE PHILIPPINES.

Suzuki, understandably, was confused. Did it mean that the
order to launch the main attack across the mountains toward
Tacloban was rescinded? He knew the ridge had to be held or the
Americans would pour down Highway 2 toward Ormoc. He therefore ordered Kataoka to counterattack. This would hold the ridge
line, and moreover, distract American attention from his own
drive over the mountains.

U. S. tanks roamed the corkscrew road almost at will. Infantry
closed in from three sides, and after bitter hand-to-hand fighting,
overran the ridge except for a few spurs at the southeastern end
still held by the rearguard of the 57th Regiment of Gem Division.
The rest of the regiment withdrew south at night, the weary men
keeping together by following the glow of phosphorescent insects
rubbed on the back of the man ahead. These men were turned
around, and at Suzuki's order, marched back to retake ground
they had just abandoned.

Kamiko found himself back on the ridge—this time at the southern end. He and Aoki had been sent as replacements to Yasuda
Company, which was dug in near the top of a rise about the size
of Yahiro Hill. Lieutenant Tatsuhide Yasuda was a mild man.
"I'm glad you arrived up here safely," he said through tight lips.
"The company has been reduced to less than one fourth, so getting
you two makes us feel we've got a million on our side." Kamiko
was given the 3rd Squad. "We've just dug in and they haven't
attacked us yet. But they will come soon. We are glad you are going to die with us."

The chattering of birds wakened Kamiko before dawn. For a
moment he thought he was back in the mountains of Chiba.
Through the dense foliage he saw something red. Was it some
gaudy tropic blossom? No, it was a huge plumed bird that belonged
in a zoo. But it was also food. He crawled to his commander's
dugout and whispered that he wanted to shoot the bird for food.
Lieutenant Yasuda shook his head; one shot would reveal their
position. They might as well have fired. The bird, flapping its great
ungainly wings, rose noisily like a loaded transport plane and instantly attracted mortar shells that continued spasmodically.

All day Yasuda Company huddled silently in their holes; their food ration was one rice ball for eight men. After dark Yasuda and his three squad leaders crept up to the ridge line. Halfway down the other side a group of Americans was eating out in the open as if it were a picnic grounds. The lieutenant suggested sending down two men to scavenge. Hunger gnawed at them more than fear, and the three squad leaders nodded approval.

Two privates were sent on the suicide mission and all night the company waited anxiously. Once they heard the crump of grenades and the rattle of machine-gun fire; they were certain their comrades had been killed. But at daybreak the two men returned, leaping into Yasuda's dugout with a poncho full of booty, as excited as schoolboys. They had ambushed an American machine-gun position in the dark and scooped up everything they could find. Their plunder turned out to be a few tins of cigarettes and boxes of ammunition that didn't fit their own weapons.

Aoki lit one of the American cigarettes. "Ah, I've forgotten the taste of tobacco," he said after a deep drag. "It makes me dizzy."

That day while enlarging his *takotsubo,* Kamiko caught a lizard. Skinned, it was light pink and reminded him of *megochi,* a fish he used to catch in the sea near his home. Aoki chopped it up with his dagger, boiled the parts in his *hango* until they were white. Kamiko found its taste a cross between fish and chicken. He finished full of vigor, almost as if he had been injected with adrenalin.

At noon Yasuda ordered Kamiko's squad to ascend a strategic knob a hundred yards to the right and relieve the squad holding it. The knob dominated the area and was constantly under fire. Its capture would compromise the regimental position. All through the afternoon the 3rd Squad kept the enemy at a distance, but the next morning the Americans pressed in close enough to lob grenades. At the height of the attack, the grenade barrage inexplicably stopped.

It was so quiet that Kamiko could hear birds singing—then a strange noise like a blow torch. A cloud of thick black smoke boiled up in front of him. "Flamethrower!" he shouted. He began heaving grenades as far and as fast as possible. At last the flame extinguished. He flopped back exhausted, puzzled about the American withdrawal. A shell landed yards ahead but did not detonate; it buried itself deep into the ground. Kamiko thought it was a dud until the earth erupted in front of him like a volcano. It was the most terrifying thing he had ever experienced; it shattered him as had the earthquake of 1923. He turned to Aoki, his face pale. "They're using some new weapon." (It was actually a delayed fuse.) The earth rumbled time and again, throwing up tons of dirt. To the left, where two men had been hiding in their *takotsubo,* there was now only level ground with three legs protruding. Kamiko felt a hot sting on his arm, then on the foot. They were minor wounds, the only wounds he had suffered in seven full days of suicidal combat. Under protest he was sent to the rear.

His regiment, reduced to less than four hundred men, had disintegrated against relentless American pressure. On November 23, GI's of the 128th Infantry Regiment of the 32nd Division broke through the mountain barrier and into Limon. The Battle of Breakneck Ridge was over. Little remained but pockets of resistance. Two days later General Kataoka ordered the remnants of Gem Division to regroup below Limon near Highway 2.

Kamiko and Aoki hobbled south along the highway. They came to a ravine that stank of death. Thousands of swollen, decomposed bodies were scattered all over the road and in both ditches. At first glance the bodies looked as if they were being attacked by snakes—they were tubes from gas masks. This was "Death Valley." Here, with deadly accuracy, American artillery had caught Japanese troops moving up to the front.

They struck off into the jungle east of the highway. At every stream they found clusters of wounded men lying like corpses, their will to live gone. Kamiko and Aoki pushed on but were obsessed by thoughts of suicide. They met seven other stragglers, led by a Sergeant Hirano, and learned that the Americans had driven a wedge below Breakneck Ridge almost to Highway 2. They would have to fight through the enemy line to rejoin their division. Hunger drove them to raid the first American position they came upon. They fled, arms loaded with GI rations, chased by a volley of rifle fire. What a difference a little food makes! Kamiko thought as he finished a piece of chocolate. They could tolerate their wounds but the lack of food had sapped their morale. If we could eat as much as the Americans, we'd still be up on the ridge fighting, he mused. Victory in battle was simply a case of supply. How could Japan win against such a rich and powerful foe?

They found an American supply parachute and were themselves almost discovered by a column of Negro soldiers carrying boxes. As Kamiko raised his rifle, he was checked by Hirano, who jerked his head. Another column was coming.

"How black they are!" Kamiko whispered; he had never before seen a Negro.

"We're all human beings, but I wonder why they're so different."

"I wonder if they think like Americans?"

"They're Americans too," said Hirano.

They worked their way over a mountain, force-marched all night through a chilling rain; by morning they approached Highway 2, directly behind the enemy front. Kamiko halted the little group. He assured them they would break through; they had food and the Japanese soldier could not be beaten at hand-to-hand combat. "If you have the bad luck to get shot, commit suicide like a man."

They started down toward the highway.

24

Debacle

1.

Organized resistance on Leyte was at the point of collapse but Yamashita in Manila directed General Sosaku Suzuki to concentrate his remaining striking power into a desperation attack (Operation WA) on American airfields. These nearly established bases were a threat to the entire Philippines as well as the supply route between the homeland and the south—Java, Malaya, Sumatra and Borneo.

There were three major forces on the island. Gem Division had lost more than three quarters of its effectives and at best could only delay the American advance down Highway 2. Makino's 16th Division, after being pushed across the coastal plain, was splintered. Some units were holding ground in the mountains west of Dagami, but the rest were scattered deep inland with the search of food their main occupation; they had been subsisting on raw insects, snails, frogs, lizards, centipedes, roots, grass—and their own sweaty belts.

The third force, the 26th Division, would have to provide the main thrust of Operation WA. Already the division, except for a battalion detached to protect Ormoc, was moving across the mountain range below Limon in a general attack toward Leyte Gulf. Suzuki ordered them to keep moving southeast, and together with the remnants of the 16th and paratroopers flown in from Luzon, attack three airfields near Burauen, a strategic village ten miles west of Dulag, at dawn on December 6.

The hastily conceived plan was compromised from the beginning. First the men of the 26th Division found it difficult to maintain the time schedule set up by Manila; Suzuki asked for a delay of two days, which was denied. Then the operation itself was vitiated by a breakdown in communications.

On December 3 meteorologists predicted an inclement weather front and Suzuki was ordered to postpone the attack for one day. But the message never reached the survivors of the 16th Division, who descended on the airstrip a mile above Burauen as scheduled, just after dawn on December 6. There were now only three hundred of them, their meager force having been further reduced by desertions. They came upon a group of sleeping American engineers bivouacked in the open, and began bayoneting them. The engineers, most of whom had never fired at an enemy, fled except for one of their cooks who killed five Japanese trying to steal food from his kitchen. The raiders held part of the field for several hours, but with no support they were driven back to the woods in the north where they dug in, cursing the paratroopers who had failed to appear.

These seven hundred 'troopers—they came from the 3rd Parachute Regiment commanded by Lieutenant Colonel Tsunehiro Shirai—were still on Luzon, preparing to board two-engine transports. The first wave of twenty-six transports, with 365 paratroopers aboard, began taking off in midafternoon. They grouped and headed south, escorted by fighters. They continued west of Leyte to avoid detection, before circling south of the island and starting up toward Leyte Gulf. The sun was setting as they turned sharply west just below Dulag and followed the Marabang River inland toward Burauen.

They ran into heavy flak, and four planes were destroyed. The others lowered to 750 feet. At six-forty the 'troopers jumped. They were supposed to concentrate at the north field, but because of darkness only Colonel Shirai and sixty others landed at the objective. The main body came down on San Pablo, the strip a mile and a half east of Burauen. They charged, shouting demoniacally in English, "Hello, where are your machine guns?" and "Surrender! Everything is resistless!" Stupefied, Americans watched as the Japanese burned parked planes and ignited gasoline and ammunition dumps.

At the north field, Shirai's force was too small to be effective. It joined the 16th Division infantrymen still hiding in the woods and waited for the second wave of paratroopers. But there would be no second wave; bad weather closed in Leyte again. Nor would there be any help from the 26th Division. A single battalion was within striking range of Burauen, and these exhausted men were intercepted and repulsed by a battalion of the U. S. 11th Airborne Division.

The paratroopers at San Pablo had discovered their mistake, however, and after ravaging that field, struck northwest to join up with Shirai at dawn. Now that he had a respectable force, almost five hundred men, Shirai regrouped. By midmorning he had seized the entire airstrip, and for three days his tenacious men held out against four American battalions. Finally overwhelmed by sheer numbers, the handful of survivors fled into the hills.

While Shirai was mounting his dawn assault on the airstrip at Burauen, an armada of destroyer-transports loaded with an entire American division, the 77th, unexpectedly appeared in Ormoc Bay. The gamble of WA had not only failed but had diverted Suzuki's best troops, the 26th Division, away from the area which was now the target for MacArthur's next strike.

Around six-forty a dozen U. S. destroyers began bombarding the beaches four miles below Ormoc. Landing craft pushed off from the destroyer-transports, and shortly after seven o'clock the first wave of men from "New York's Own" landed unopposed. It was a day of 7's—to the south the 7th Division had already crossed the waist of the island over a supposedly impassable mountain road and was coming up the coast toward Ormoc. The infantrymen were opposed only by the single battalion detached from the 26th Division to protect the city.

Suzuki had erected no obstacles on the beaches—he felt the west coast was protected by the Japanese naval base in Cebu across the narrow Camotes Sea—and was now surrounded. There was little the Japanese could do to cope with the situation. Suzuki instructed the 26th Division, and what was left of the 16th, to about-face and join him at Ormoc. Yamashita expedited the convoys already scheduled for Leyte and in addition ordered five hundred paratroopers of the 4th Parachute Regiment sent to an airfield eight miles above Ormoc near Highway 2. But they didn't arrive until dawn of December 8 and were dropped in the jungle almost five miles north of the target.

Corporal Kiyoshi Kamiko, whose group had just fought its way through the American lines to reach Highway 2, encountered half a dozen of these paratroopers, young, well equipped and eager for battle. Kamiko warned them that they would be outnumbered 10 to 1, but one youngster exclaimed, "My goal is to kill ten before I die!" and then blushed.

His naïveté appalled Kamiko. What right had Imperial Headquarters to send such children out on suicide missions? All the frustrations and doubts of the past few weeks crystallized into a decision that would have seemed treasonable on Yahiro Hill: he would escape to another island. Why die uselessly? He allowed himself to think of Japan, of its beautiful hills and rivers. He would work his way to the west coast with a few trusted companions and steal a native boat. Perhaps they could escape to Borneo. A deep roll of thunder came from the direction of Ormoc. It sounded like enemy artillery. How had the Americans got down there so fast?

Major General Andrew D. Bruce's 77th Division was driving steadily up the west coast toward Ormoc against a congeries of assorted, poorly armed service units commanded by a transportation officer, Colonel Mitsui. His force was dug in on the high ground a few miles below the city and he hoped he could hold out until the 26th Division returned. Other reinforcements were on the way by sea, and on December 9 a battalion of the 30th Division landed at Palompon, a port on the west side of the little peninsula forming Ormoc Bay. It was only fifteen air miles to Ormoc, but thirty-five miles by a winding mountain road, and Bruce's men were already on the outskirts of the city.

The following morning GI's broke through Colonel Mitsui's lines into Ormoc, a mass of choking rubble and blazing buildings. A pall of dark smoke hooded the area. That afternoon General

Bruce reported his victory to Corps Commander John R. Hodge, reminding him of a promise made by the commander of the Fifth Air Force:

. . . WHERE IS THE CASE OF SCOTCH THAT WAS PROMISED BY GENERAL WHITEHEAD FOR THE CAPTURE OF ORMOC. I DON'T DRINK BUT I HAVE AN ASSISTANT DIVISION COMMANDER AND REGIMENTAL COMMANDERS WHO DO . . .

A few hours later Bruce sent another message, referring to the 7th Division which was coming up the west coast road.

HAVE ROLLED TWO SEVENS IN ORMOC. COME SEVEN COME ELEVEN.

There were still two Japanese convoys en route to Ormoc Bay. One carried 3,000 men of the 8th Division and 900 tons of ammunition and supplies. As the five transports, three destroyers and two submarine chasers, escorted by about thirty fighters, approached the west coast of Leyte the next morning, they were attacked by Marine Corsairs which sank three transports. The remaining ships tried to pick up survivors as they turned in toward Palompon, but 700 men were drowned. Before the fleeing vessels made port, another transport was sunk by Marine and Army planes.

The final convoy—two destroyers and two transports—carried a 400-man naval detachment under Lieutenant Commander Ito, as well as nine amphibious tanks and twenty mortars. It had escaped detection and was still intact as it approached Ormoc several hours after midnight. At this point it was sighted by the destroyer *Coghlan,* which opened fire and sank a destroyer. The transports continued; one anchored near the occupied city and attempted to disembark its troops. The first barge was almost swamped by shells from the shore. "Don't shoot!" the Japanese yelled, unaware that the city was in enemy hands.

The other transport luckily made for the opposite side of the bay, where it unloaded the last reinforcements and supplies that Suzuki would get. Considering that nearly 80 percent of all the vessels dispatched to Leyte had been sunk, it was remarkable that

a total of 45,000 troops had made it safely ashore. But their effectiveness was sharply reduced by the fact that little more than 10,-
000 tons of supplies in all were salvaged.

2.

Although Leyte was not yet lost and Luzon was being fortified
for its conclusive battle, Imperial Headquarters ordered preparations expedited for the evacuation of Allied prisoners of war in
the Philippines to the homeland. There they could be used as laborers and, possibly, hostages.

Publicly the Japanese had long decried Allied treatment of prisoners while praising their own. Only a few weeks after three of
Doolittle's fliers (Lieutenants Dean Hallmark and William Farrow
and Sergeant Harold Spatz) were executed—they had been tortured
and then given a peremptory trial—the *Nippon Times* condemned
the British for the inhuman treatment they were meting out to German prisoners of war.

. . . Needless to say, the Japanese Government, actuated by consider-
ations of humanity, have, up to the present, respected the principles
contained in the International Law governing the conduct of war and
have done everything in their power with regard to the treatment
accorded to the numerous British prisoners of war in their hands.

Americans were depicted as "enjoying life at the various prisoner
camps."

On Luzon, at Cabanatuan, several survivors of the Bataan
Death March kept secret notebooks whose disclosure would probably have meant summary execution. Colonel James Gillespie, a
medical officer, described a new contingent of men marching into
the camp:

. . . Inching their way along the road came a ragged formation of
dirty, unkempt, unshaven, ragged, half naked forms, pale, bloated, lifeless. They staggered and stumbled, some plodded, others uncertain of
their balance and strength lay down only to be urged to continue by
the attendants who in many instances were only slightly more able
than those they were assisting. Limbs grotesquely swollen to double

their size. Faces devoid of expression—form or life. Aged incredibly
beyond their years. Bare feet on the stony road. Remnants of ragged
gunny sacks as loin cloths. Some stark naked. Bloodshot eyes and
cracked lips. Smeared with excreta from their bowels. Thus they came
. . . to the "end of the road," the strong, young, and alert Americans
of the 31st Infantry—the Air Corps and the A.A. The saddest sight
indeed it was and may I never see it again.

These prisoners had been forced to eat cats, dogs, baby rats
and garbage to remain alive; by now, they had lost an average of
fifty-five pounds. In the first year at Cabanatuan, 2,644 of the
complement of about 6,500 had died from malaria, dysentery,
diphtheria and other diseases. Their deaths, according to Dr.
Samuel M. Bloom, a captain, were "directly attributed to the neglect of the Japanese, the result of a deliberate policy of starvation
and the withholding of medical supplies."

Another diarist, Major Roy L. Bodine, a dentist and a veteran
of Bataan, began keeping his clandestine record the day before
MacArthur landed on Leyte. It was a day he would never forget;
his group was transferred to Manila by truck to Bilibid Prison,
where they learned they were simply being staged for shipment to
Japan. They dreaded the treatment they might receive in the
enemy homeland, but their spirits were lifted by the bombing of
the Manila area and the long-awaited news that MacArthur had
landed.* On October 28 Dr. Bodine wrote:

That added to the bombing makes us hope that the Nips won't be
able to get us out of here.
Every day they have rumors of us leaving in 2 or 3 days, but keep
putting it off. We hope and pray constantly that they can't. Really
"Sweating it Out."

Bodine's hopes were never realized. On December 12, all patients were given a cursory examination. The food improved, and
soap and toilet paper were issued—sure signs they were about to
leave. "If MacArthur gets this close and then lets us go, will really
be mad," wrote Bodine.

* At the prison camp in nearby Santo Tomás University this information
came in an underground news bulletin with the words: "Better Leyte than
never."

The next morning he and 1,618 other prisoners filed down
Quezon Avenue and past the walled city. Filipinos lined the sidewalks to watch the sad procession; many surreptitiously gave the
V sign. Luneta Park was crammed with hastily erected barracks
but the Gran Luna section, where Bodine had lived as a boy (his
father had been an Army dentist), was unchanged. As they approached the dock area he saw the effects of the recent American
bombing, and out in the bay were at least forty hulks.

At Pier 7 the prisoners began filing aboard a 15,000-ton luxury
liner built just before the war for the tourist trade, *Oryoku-maru*.*
With grim amusement Major Adrianus J. van Oosten, who
had survived a dozen jungle battles on Bataan, watched Mac-
Arthur's shiny Packard, hoisted in a cargo net, careen against the
side of a hold, smashing its fenders. Lieutenant Colonel Curtis
Beecher, a Marine, who recalled coming alongside the same pier
back in 1929 on his return from duty in China, was herded along
with seven hundred other prisoners into the dungeonlike forward
hold; its previous occupants had been horses. In a few minutes the
air was dead and hot and their uniforms became soaked with
perspiration.

The Bodine group—three hundred Army and Navy medics and
civilians—was packed amidships, three decks down. Eight buckets
of rice and pans of fish were lowered after dark. The liner began
to move. It steamed around Bataan into Subic Bay and continued
on a northern course. Suddenly, alerted to some danger ahead, it
turned back and anchored in the protective waters below Olongapo. The prisoners sat hunched in the dark, their minds churn-

---

* Seven weeks earlier a 5,000-ton freighter loaded with 1,805 prisoners
from the Philippines had been torpedoed in the South China Sea (probably
by the U. S. submarine *Shark II*). Five Americans survived, including Sergeant Calvin Graef and Corporal Donald Meyer, and they only by a remarkable series of coincidences: after hanging on to wreckage all night, they
found a lifeboat containing a keg of fresh water; while fixing the rudder, they
discovered a small compartment containing a sealed tin of hardtack; a box
floated alongside which just happened to hold pulleys and rigging that
exactly fitted their boat; finally, a pole someone had retrieved hours earlier
turned out to be their mast. Just as they were about to raise the sail a Japanese destroyer approached to within a hundred yards but for some reason
passed by without firing her machine guns. Even so, they probably would
not have made it safely to China if fortune had not continued to favor them.
After two days of sailing they were picked up by Chinese fishermen in a junk
who landed them on the only area along the coast held by Chiang Kai-shek.

ing. A couple of years more in Japan, Bodine thought, or a watery grave from subs and planes.

The condition of the seven hundred men massed in the forehold was already intolerable. The only ventilation came through a small hatch. A few pails had been tossed down to them for human waste. These were quickly filled and the hold reeked from urine and feces scattered on the deck. From the darkness came a shriek, "Oh, my God!" A man urinated into his canteen and drank the liquid. Colonel Beecher thought of the Black Hole of Calcutta; reading about it had made little impression but now he knew how horrible it must have been. An inhuman noise rose over the sighs and moans, which sounded to Major van Oosten like the gobbling of turkeys. Suddenly the sound was repeated quite close-by; the man next to him began to babble. In the shaft of starlight from the hatch, Van Oosten could see that his neighbor was losing consciousness. His puffed whitish tongue wagged between drooping lips. His eyes were glazed, unseeing. He slumped over. He was dead.

In the afterhold the other six hundred men were experiencing the same hell. They had been given a skimpy meal of rice and fish but no water. Most of them had unthinkingly emptied their canteens during the hot march through the streets. They began fanning the air in unison with mess kits but it made no difference. The men stripped in the ovenlike heat. In the darkness they shouted for water. But the guards ignored them; their own comrades had come to the Philippines in the same holds, if not as crowded. The prisoners' exertions slowly exhausted the oxygen from the air. One man, suffocating, toppled over silently with incredible restraint, but others, gasping for breath, thrashed about wildly before collapsing. A dozen, crazed by thirst, went berserk; they slashed at the throats and wrists of companions to suck blood. The panic turned the hold into bedlam. To Major Virgil Mc-Collum, another veteran of Bataan, it was "the most horrible experience imaginable and probably unprecedented in the annals of civilization." As the dim light of dawn filtered through the hatch, several score bodies lay lifeless—suffocated or murdered.

From topside the men heard excited shouting. There was the bark of antiaircraft guns, and shards of glass showered through the hatches. Bombs pummeled the ship and machine-gun bullets clattered noisily along the decks above. In the afterhold, prisoners clawed up the ladders, terrified lest they be trapped below, but were driven back by guards firing down into their midst. The bombers returned at half-hour intervals.

Amidships, Major Bodine and two friends, Captain John Hudgins and Major Bob Nelson, pushed into a little storeroom to escape stray bullets which were ricocheting through the hatch above. It was stifling but a refuge—that is, unless a bomb or torpedo made a direct hit. Bodine was a Catholic, and with death so close he prayed continuously. He said the rosary and repeated all the prayers he knew, and above the deafening clamor of shrapnel and bullets against iron, he heard Hudgins saying over and over, "Jesus save us." Packed in the little room they found it impossible to stay awake during the lull between attacks. They jerked from sleep whenever a new raid started and began drowsily mumbling another prayer.

Those in the forward hold faced another night of horror. There were shouts of "Quiet!" and "At ease!" but as the temperature reached 110 degrees, riot again erupted. It was the "worst and most brutal period" of Colonel Beecher's life. All around him men were going mad. They collided with one another in the dark, slipping and falling in the feces; the sick were trampled; wild, deadly fights erupted. Men dropped to their knees like animals to lap up sewage running in open drains.

In the rear, Major McCollum forced his way to the hull and licked the steel plates where a little moisture had condensed. The pandemonium was even worse than the first night. "Many men lost their minds," a colonel later wrote in his official report, "and crawled about in the absolute darkness armed with knives, attempting to kill people in order to drink their blood or armed with canteens filled with urine and swinging them in the dark. The hold was so crowded and everyone so interlocked with one another that the only movement possible was over the heads and bodies of others."

At about four o'clock in the morning an interpreter announced to the prisoners amidships that they were going ashore at dawn and could take along pants, shirt, canteen and mess kit—if they wanted shoes they'd have to carry them. The men crammed as much as possible in their pockets, and in the dark pawed through

musette bags for their most valuable possessions. Bodine put
his wife's rosary around his neck on top of his own, and slung his
shoes over his shoulders. At the last moment he remembered his
notebook and shoved it inside his shirt. What he most regretted
leaving behind was his dental instruments. He had carried them
all through the battles on Bataan, on the Death March and into
several camps.

Shortly after dawn the first twenty-five men, including five
wounded, started up the ladder. The interpreter was back in a few
minutes calling for another group of twenty-five. As they started
up the ladder the interpreter frenziedly waved them back: "Many
planes! Many planes!"

A bomb crashed into the rear of *Oryoku-maru*. The blast
hurled shrapnel through the afthold. Superstructure tumbled down
the hatchway, pinning screaming men. Flames swept through the
wreckage. More than a hundred of the trapped prisoners were
dead; 150 were dying.

In the forehold, the strongest scaled the forty-foot ladder and
opened the hatch covers. Nearby they discovered sacks of raw
sugar and dropped several to those below. Van Oosten wolfed
down a handful of sugar. Miraculously he seemed to feel a charge
of energy and mounted the ladder, something he was certain he
could not have done a moment before. On deck, Japanese killed
by the strafing and bombing were shrouded in straw rice sacks
and piled in a long row five bodies high. Van Oosten leaped over
the side. The cool water was invigorating and he swam toward
shore. The exercise, after two cramped days, abruptly loosed his
bowels.

A guard shouted down to the Bodine group, "All go home,
speedo!" Topside Bodine saw a beach a quarter of a mile away—
Olongapo. Hundreds of men, Japanese and Americans, were already in the water, struggling to reach land. There were shouts to
those standing indecisively at the rails that the ship was going
down. Bodine tossed a piece of four-by-four overboard and
jumped after it. Halfway, he looked back. The luxury liner looked
like a scrap heap. Four American planes came in low. One peeled
off as if to strafe, but the men in the water waved frantically and
with a waggle of the wings it zoomed off. Bodine decided to swim
back to help the others. He noticed a dangling rope ladder and

impulsively started to climb up to get the clothes he had discarded on deck. He didn't realize how weak he was until he began pulling himself up. On deck he made a bundle of his shirt, an old Filipino hat and a pair of shoes. He tied it to a 3-inch-shell crate, which he threw over the side, and jumped again.

The 1,300 surviving prisoners were shepherded to a fenced-in tennis court, where they huddled on the concrete in the sun.

3.

That morning, December 15, MacArthur took a long stride toward Luzon. At seven-thirty two of his regimental combat teams landed without opposition on Mindoro, a few miles below Luzon, and by late afternoon had pushed seven miles inland.

General Yamashita had no intention of wasting troops on the defense of Mindoro—the garrison numbered only a thousand—nor did he intend to dispatch any more reinforcements to Leyte. On December 22 he radioed his decision to Suzuki's headquarters at Cebu City:

REDEPLOY YOUR TROOPS TO FIGHT EXTENDED HOLDING ACTION
IN AREAS OF YOUR CHOICE. SELECT AREAS SUCH AS BACA-
LOD ON NEGROS WHICH ARE HIGHLY SUITABLE FOR SELF-
SUSTAINING ACTION. THIS MESSAGE RELIEVES YOU OF YOUR
ASSIGNED MISSION.

The message would not reach Suzuki himself until three days later, but he had already ordered the remnants of the 35th Army to assemble near Palompon.

Besides Suzuki, the individual most distraught by the abandonment of Leyte was perhaps Prime Minister Kuniaki Koiso. On November 8 he had publicly committed his government to victory on Leyte. In a radio broadcast to the nation he compared Leyte with the Battle of Tennozan in 1582, which had decided the issue of who was to rule Japan. Koiso had in effect guaranteed that if Japan won on Leyte, she would win the war. He learned of the decision to abandon Leyte at a particularly awkward moment—when he was on his way to an audience with the Emperor. His

Majesty asked immediately how the Prime Minister was going to explain the loss of Leyte to the people after equating it with the Battle of Tennozan. Unstrung, Koiso mumbled that he would make the best of the situation, but he knew that only some miracle could save his cabinet.

Suzuki's order to congregate in the Palompon area was thwarted by a surprise move by General Bruce's force on Christmas morning, which forced Suzuki and his staff to flee up the west coast of Leyte toward the mountains near San Isidro. They evacuated Palompon just before a reinforced battalion of the U. S. 77th Division approached the port itself from the sea in amphtracs and LCM's (landing craft, mechanized). The area was bombarded by 155-mm. guns located a dozen miles inland, and a barrage by mortar boats preceded the landing itself. At seven-twenty the first wave reached shore without opposition and had seized the town by noon. General Bruce radioed his corps commander:

THE 77TH INFANTRY DIVISION'S CHRISTMAS CONTRIBUTION TO THE LEYTE CAMPAIGN IS THE CAPTURE OF PALOMPON, THE LAST MAIN PORT OF THE ENEMY. WE ARE ALL GRATEFUL TO THE ALMIGHTY ON THIS BIRTHDAY OF THE SON AND THE SEASON OF THE FEAST OF LIGHTS.

In the afternoon MacArthur announced that the Leyte campaign was over "except for minor mopping-up operations." He turned over this last phase to Eighth Army so that Krueger's Sixth Army could prepare for the invasion of Luzon.

On Christmas night Kiyoshi Kamiko and three companions reached a beach a few miles from Suzuki's temporary headquarters. As the sounds of battle in Palompon subsided, they heard incongruous paeans of "Peace on earth, good will to men." GI's were playing Christmas carols in the hills above.

Kamiko and his comrades had fought their way to the coast through marauding bands of guerrillas and over almost impassable terrain, ranging from quicksand and swamps to precipitous ravines. (Aoki and Sergeant Hirano had become separated from the group, which at times comprised as many as fifty.) More than once their resolve to escape the island had wavered. Only hours earlier, conscience-stricken at the thought of desertion, they had left one of their party who was wounded and started down the beach toward Palompon to help defend the city. They were intercepted by a retreating Japanese officer who turned them around and ordered them to follow his unit. As they neared the coconut grove where their wounded comrade, Tokoro, lay hidden, Kamiko and his group fell behind, determined once more to escape.

In the dark they found a *banca* and rigged it with a sail they made from a tent. They loaded the little outrigger with rifles, canteens and coconuts, and clambered in.

"What about Tokoro?" someone asked under his breath.

Nakamura, a fisherman on whom they depended for navigation, warned that five would be too many, but Kamiko was against abandoning the wounded man. A voice interrupted their whispered argument: "Group Leader, I'm staying here." Tokoro was sitting on the beach a few yards away. "It's best for me."

"Group Leader, I'm staying too." Nakamura jumped out of the boat. Another man followed.

Kamiko wearily beached the stern of the *banca* and joined the others who were sitting silently with Tokoro. Finally Tokoro said he was sorry for all the trouble he had caused and hobbled off.

"The boat is too small even for the four of us," Nakamura muttered. "We can't reach another island in this thing."

"You knew that from the beginning!" Kamiko shouted. "You say you want to die on land and you *don't* want to die at sea! It doesn't matter where you die. The question is which choice offers the best chance of survival."

The others remained hunched in a tight circle on the sand, staring at the slender *banca,* which was tossing in the waves.

There was a shot. It was Tokoro. "What a pity," someone said, and another, "It's better he did that than drown."

This pushed Kamiko over the edge. He grabbed a grenade from his knapsack. "Let's follow Tokoro!" he cried. "We can't live until tomorrow. So, as you say, let's die on land. We've lived together, let's all die together! Everybody bring heads close!" He activated the grenade. In four seconds it would explode.

Nakamura lurched back. "I'll go!" he shouted.

Kamiko tossed the grenade back over his shoulder just before it detonated. He leaped to his feet. "Well, let's go!"

The *banca* sailed slowly out of the inlet in the moonlight. Nakamura, so reluctant on shore, was a new man as he deftly guided the boat toward Cebu. Abruptly the moonlight was cut off and something cold slapped his cheek. Rain. Dark clouds swirled ominously. Nakamura looked up, then said, "Let's return."

"We're at sea, Nakamura, and determined to die," said Kamiko. "So keep going."

The fragile outrigger tossed erratically. Nakamura clung stony-faced to the tiller as the others bailed with their canteens. A dark shape materialized in front of them with a roar—it must be a speed-boat transporting 35th Army headquarters to Cebu. They shouted and waved but the craft droned past. It was an American PT boat.

Just before dawn the rain stopped and the sun rose on a calmed sea. All around them were small, bare rock islets. To the south, out of the morning light, emerged the vague outline of a large island. It had to be Cebu, their first goal. Nakamura changed course, and with the wind behind it, the little *banca* cut through the water as fast as a bicycle at top speed.

Kamiko began to sing his favorite song, one he had taught his pupils:

> *"From a far-off island whose name I don't know*
> *A coconut comes floating.*
> *How many months have you been tossing on the waves*
> *Far from the shores of your native island?*
>
> *I think about tides far away*
> *And wonder when I will return to my native land."*

4.

General Suzuki had chosen to concentrate the remnants of his forces, more than ten thousand troops, on a rugged, heavily forested 1,200-foot mountain on the west coast between Palompon and San Isidro called Canguipot. Its eastern and western slopes were rocky, making it a natural fortress. Every day stragglers from the 1st Division and 68th Brigade arrived exhausted at Mount Canguipot, but those left of the 16th and 26th divisions were pinned down near Highway 2.

Many of these men had no intention of trying to reach Suzuki's position even if they could disengage themselves. Like Kamiko, they could not avoid the logic that it was senseless to die on Leyte in such circumstances. In the mountains north of Ormoc between Highway 2 and the west coast Lieutenant General Shimpei Fukue, on his own, was planning to escape from the island with his depleted 102nd Division, which had played an insignificant role in the fighting. Already fifty of his men had left by boat.

On the night of December 29, Suzuki received the first message from Fukue in more than a week: the 102nd Division was marching to the coast, where it would set sail in small boats for Cebu. The action was unprecedented in Suzuki's experience and only with difficulty was he dissuaded from court-martialing Fukue summarily. Instead he ordered the 102nd Division to remain in place; Fukue himself was to report at once to Army headquarters with his chief of staff.

But even this direct order was ignored. Fukue's answer—composed by his chief of staff, a colonel named Wada—was as infuriating as the original decision to desert: "We appreciate the efforts of Army but at the present time we are very occupied preparing for evacuation. The division commander and chief of staff are consequently unable to report to Army headquarters."

On New Year's Eve, Fukue had the effrontery to ask Suzuki to facilitate his insubordination: "All boats that were prepared for the retreat were destroyed by American planes on the night of the 30th, thus delaying our departure. Would it be possible for you to send an armored craft to aid the departure of the division commander?" Fukue and his staff, like Kamiko, managed to get across the Camotes Sea by *banca*. In Cebu City the general was relieved of his command by order of Suzuki. He accepted Suzuki's instruction to remain on the island of Cebu; there was nowhere else to go.

On Leyte, Mount Canguipot was being prepared for a long siege. Large quantities of provisions were purchased from local farmers and augmented by fern, grass and wild spinach. Salt was separated from sea water. Suzuki's plan as far as Leyte was concerned was to tie up as many enemy troops as possible, but he too was coming to doubt the usefulness of such a sacrifice. Realistically, how long could he expect Mount Canguipot to hold out? One determined assault would overrun it. Almost a hundred men were dying of starvation every day. How was that helping the empire? Moreover, Yamashita had long since given him permission to evacuate.

It was a wrenching decision for a samurai; only a week before, he would never have imagined he'd make it. Gem Division would be the first to leave. On the night of January 12, 1945, General Kataoka and his headquarters set off in three launches, safely reaching Cebu soon after dawn. In the next week 743 men—all that remained of the elite Gem Division—reached Cebu with four heavy machine guns, eleven light ones and five grenade launchers. But as Lieutenant General Robert Eichelberger's Eighth Army closed in on Suzuki, continued evacuation became almost impossible.

Except for sixteen weeks of tedious mopping up, the fighting was over. The 70,000 Japanese who came to defend Leyte against 250,000 well-armed Americans had fought as well as could be expected. They wounded 12,000 GI's and killed 3,500, but only about 5,000—one in thirteen—would live to see Japan. It was a decisive battle—for the Americans. They had destroyed an entire army and permanently crippled Japan's remaining air force and fleet. The homeland itself now lay exposed, except for two island fortresses—Iwo Jima and Okinawa.

PART SEVEN

Beyond the Bitter End

25

"Our Golden Opportunity"

1.

A relatively unpublicized war was going on in China and Burma that was frustrating and miserable for all sides—there were more than two—as well as the hundreds of millions of civilians trapped in the turmoil. Fought over a tremendous area, it was an ideological and geographical nightmare.

The British had been humiliatingly expelled from Burma in early 1942, and their attempts to return had met with limited success; forays by the Americans and Chinese into the Japanese-occupied territory had been equally inconclusive. But by the end of 1944 insatiable ambition had brought the Japanese to the point of disaster in Burma. Their dream was to topple India, that insecure pedestal of British imperialism, with the help of Chandra Bose's Indian National Army. The initial stepping stone was Imphal, a strategic city fifty miles west of the Burmese border. Not only was it the gateway to India but its occupation would be of inestimable propaganda value and an inspiration to all anti-imperialists.

For many months the Japanese military leadership in Burma, champing under orders to remain on the defensive, had been requesting an invasion of India. These appeals, and those of Chandra Bose, were heeded at last: early in 1944 Imperial Headquarters ordered the 15th Army to invest "the vital areas of northeastern India in the vicinity of Imphal." Its commander, Lieutenant General Renya Mutaguchi, regarded the capture of Imphal as the first in a series of deep thrusts into India. He had been brought to this view by an enemy, Brigadier Orde Charles Wingate, a messianic figure whose Chindits* had been harassing the Japanese commanders of Burma in a number of unorthodox stabs far behind the lines. Although opposed to earlier plans to invade India, Mutaguchi had been impressed by Wingate's raids. If an Englishman could bring troops through dense jungle and over mountains, so could he, and in far greater force. But leading a group of specially trained guerrillas over such terrain was one thing; leading an entire army was another.

Colonel Tadashi Katakura, Mutaguchi's operations officer, appreciated the obstacles: there were formidable rivers and rugged mountains to traverse; moreover, 15th Army was not logistically prepared to carry out such a long, arduous campaign with its present shortage of food, ammunition and medical supplies. Katakura forcefully pressed his misgivings—he had lost none of his bluntness since being shot in the neck during the 2/26 Incident for opposing the rebels—but Mutaguchi could not be persuaded to change the plans.

On March 8, 1944, three reinforced Japanese divisions and a division of Bose's I.N.A.—155,000 troops in all—crossed the Chindwin River and struck out across the mountains separating the two countries. On Indian soil Bose's men fell to their knees to kiss their native earth. Shouting *"Jai Hind! Jai Hind!,"* they pushed ahead toward Kohima, a city eighty miles north of Imphal, astride the British supply route. There they would turn south and march to Imphal, followed by the 31st Division after it had subdued Kohima. The other two Japanese divisions headed straight for Imphal.

The most proficient ground commander in the Far East, Lieutenant General William J. Slim of the British-Indian Fourteenth

---

* A mispronunciation of *chinthe,* Burmese for "lion."

Army, had surmised that Mutaguchi would strike at Imphal—with perhaps a single brigade diverted to Kohima—and awaited the battle in a "rather complacent mood." His plan was to let the Japanese advance to the edge of the Imphal Plain, and when they were "committed in assaults on our prepared positions," to counterattack in full force and destroy them.

"My heart sank," he later wrote, when he learned that the enemy —two divisions strong—was attacking Kohima. This not only placed an important garrison city in jeopardy but threatened his army's sole supply base and railhead at Dimapur, which lay about thirty miles to the northwest. He ordered immediate reinforcements. "As I struggled hard to redress my errors and to speed by rail and air these reinforcements I knew that all depended on the steadfastness of the troops already meeting the first impetus of attack. If they could hold until help arrived, all would be well; if not we were near disaster." What Slim feared above all was that the Japanese would by-pass Kohima and move on the railroad. An emergency line was set up on Kohima Ridge to block the road to Dimapur. Men were "scraped up" from the local administrative forces; five hundred convalescents were armed and put in the line.

But the commander of the 31st Division, Lieutenant General Kotoku Sato, directed all his forces at Kohima, where the defenders resisted so stubbornly—they were driven onto a single hill —that the Indian National Army troops alone turned south toward Imphal. On the steep hillsides south and west of that city, the other two Japanese divisions were already erecting a formidable system of earth-and-log bunkers, preparatory to launching their combined attack.

On April 18 the commander of the Indian force reported the unbelievable news that the road down to Imphal was lightly defended; his advance units were "only a stone's throw away" from the city itself. Victory was imminent; Bose had bales of new currency ready for circulation. But his dream was shattered when Sato, who had found more than he had bargained for at Kohima, refused to follow to Imphal. Instead he arbitrarily ordered his men to prepare to return to Burma; he had verbal permission (it was not meant to be taken literally) to withdraw if he weren't resupplied with food and ammunition by mid-April.

Bose was furious—without Sato backing their spearhead, the

I.N.A. troops could never break through to Imphal. He was sure it was a plot of 15th Army and accused the Japanese of purposely depriving Indians of winning the first significant victory in their own country. Mutaguchi was equally furious with Sato (and relieved him of his command), but no explanation satisfied Bose.

The Japanese at Imphal were ready to attack, and asked Bose to deliver a radio broadcast on the Emperor's birthday, offering him Imphal as a present. Bose was insulted. Perversely he now opposed any invasion of India that was not led by the I.N.A. He argued that the appearance of Indian troops would spark revolts throughout the nation, whereas Japanese invaders would only bring thousands of Indians to the side of the British.

The altercation gave General Slim a double advantage: it divided the enemy and provided time for substantial reinforcements to reach the Imphal area by rail and air. The Japanese were converging on the city from six roads, but the defenders, with strong air support, held at every point. The debilitating battle continued inconclusively week after week. Both Japanese divisional commanders became convinced it would be impossible to storm Imphal, and one even began withdrawing troops without orders.

Vice Chief of the Army General Staff Hikosaburo Hata—accompanied by Colonel Sugita and other staff officers—arrived at the front to investigate; they returned to Tokyo with disheartening conclusions for Tojo: "There is little probability that the Imphal operation will succeed."

Tojo turned on Hata, accusing him of defeatism. The Prime Minister had counted on the success of Operation U to divert the public's attention from the startling loss of the Marshalls in the Pacific. He was so beside himself with frustration that his sarcasm also seemed to include Prince Mikasa, the Emperor's brother, who sat directly in front of Hata, and a chill came over the room. Hata remained silent. "If I'd been Hata," Colonel Tanemura wrote in his Diary, "I'd have ripped off my staff insignia and fought him."

On June 5 Mutaguchi met with his superior, General Masakazu Kawabe, Burma Area Army commander. Mutaguchi had already been obliged to dismiss all three of his division commanders—something unheard of in the history of the Japanese Army (one for incompetence, one for illness, and the third for refusing to obey orders) and it was on the tip of his tongue to declare that the time had come to suspend Operation U. But he could not speak. "I was hoping," Mutaguchi later recalled, "that General Kawabe would perceive in silence what was in my heart."

Kawabe was not that perceptive. "The destiny of Subhas Chandra Bose was mine as well as his," he wrote in his memoirs. "Therefore I had to assist Mutaguchi by all means in my power. I kept telling myself so."

The day following this meeting the British won back Kohima, after sixty-four days of some of the most bitter fighting of the war. A force of Japanese and Indians still held the road to Imphal, but within two weeks the British had smashed through and started to aid their harassed comrades in Imphal.

Mutaguchi's problems were aggravated by the arrival of the monsoon. Ceaseless rains poured down, washing out the jungle trails back to Burma. Only one of his three divisions had brought adequate food supplies; the others had to subsist on grass, potatoes, snails, lizards, snakes—anything they could get their hands on, including monkeys.

Mutaguchi still could not bring himself to ask Kawabe for permission to withdraw but came close to it by inference. "If operations are to be suspended and the army is to go over to the defensive," he wrote, "it is advisable that the army be withdrawn to the line running from the high ground on the right bank of the Chindwin River through the high ground to the northwest of Mawlaik to the Tiddim area."

Kawabe's reply appeared uncompromising: he expected the 15th Army to do its duty "zealously" and fight harder. But his senior staff officer was already en route to Manila with a request for Field Marshal Terauchi to suspend the operation. Terauchi approved but word did not reach Mutaguchi until July 9. Four days later the troops began retreating toward the Chindwin River. On the long trek back over the mountains in the pounding rain, men fought one another for food. Thousands of sick and wounded fell out of the march and killed themselves with grenades. The paths were seas of mud and when a man stumbled he became half buried in slime; shoes were stolen from those struggling feebly to extricate themselves. Light machine guns, rifles, helmets, gas masks—anything useless—littered the trails. Only the will to live propelled the survivors; the men hobbled along with improvised

canes, and those who lasted out a day's march huddled together
for sleep that rarely came because of the constant downpour. Many
drowned, too feeble to raise their heads above the rising water,
and the Chindwin River itself, their goal, claimed the lives of hundreds more in its swollen waters.

In all, 65,000 men died—more than two and a half times the
number lost on Guadalcanal, and about as many as fell on Leyte.
Mutaguchi, his chief of staff and senior staff officers were relieved
of their posts, as were Kawabe and his chief of staff. The command
shake-up and the destruction of the 15th Army infected every
other unit in Burma, and by the end of the year Japanese rule was
at the point of collapse.

2.

In China, that tangled, multi-sided war continued to be a source
of frustration to everyone concerned except the Communists. The
Japanese had conquered a vast area in eastern China but were no
nearer to a final solution in their agonizingly long war in that enig-
matic country. Though they occupied one important city after another, it was like tunneling in the sand; the Nanking puppet
government of Wang Ching-wei was unable to consolidate the
victories after the Japanese troops moved on. The Japanese dominated the coast, rivers, railroads and highways, but in the expanses
between, another struggle was going on among the Chinese themselves. Chiang Kai-shek was fighting Mao Tse-tung's armies for
control while the war lords sided with whatever group was winning.

China bred dissension. Lieutenant General Joseph W. ("Vinegar Joe") Stilwell, commander of all American forces in China,
remained at incessant odds with "Old Leatherface" Chennault,
commander of 14th Air Force, an outgrowth of the American Volunteer Group, the Flying Tigers. Their argument most often
focused on the policies of the man Stilwell derisively called "Peanut"—Chiang. In a series of vituperative messages to Washington,
Stilwell charged that the aid sent to China was being criminally
wasted by the Kuomintang; moreover, its armies were expending
as little matériel as possible against the Japanese, since "Peanut"

was bent on saving men and supplies for the postwar confrontation with Mao.

This, in large part, was true. Since the second Cairo Conference, when Chiang felt his vital interests were betrayed by Roosevelt under the influence of Churchill, the Nationalist troops had been waging passive warfare against Japan. In some sectors there had been virtual truce between the Kuomintang and the Japanese for over two years. A Chinese officer at an air base in Hupeh, for example, defended his refusal to shoot at passing Japanese aircraft with the excuse that if his men did so, "the Japs would be angry and would take revenge and return and bomb the city and do a lot of damage." Another of Chiang's officers argued that it was unnecessary for the Chinese "to take up an offensive against the Japs because soon the United States will surround Japan and then the Japs will have to retreat without fighting, and so it is better to leave them alone, and get along as best we can as we are."

Although Stilwell's indignation was justified, he failed to appreciate the fact that the Kuomintang forces were more than paying for Lend-Lease assistance by tying up almost a million Japanese troops who might otherwise be used against MacArthur and Nimitz. Accordingly, Chiang not only resented Stilwell's attitude but felt he had been taken in by American Communist propaganda, which labeled the Generalissimo a fascist and pictured Mao as an agrarian reformer, not a genuine Communist. "In the mistaken belief that the Chinese Communist forces, if placed under his [Stilwell's] command, would obey his orders and wholeheartedly fight the Japanese," Chiang wrote, "he assured me that the Government could safely re-equip them on the same basis as the Government forces and set them free from combat against the Japanese from where they were being held down by the Government's blockade. Moreover, the Government, he pointed out, could thus also release its forces immobilized on blockade duty for redeployment against the common enemy. . . . Stilwell's subsequent disagreement with me was entirely brought about by the machinations of the Communists and their fellow-travelers. It almost caused the disruption of Sino-American military co-operation in the China-Burma Theater of War."

Chennault subscribed to this assessment as well as the allegation that Stilwell was spending too much time playing soldier in Burma, where he would disappear in the jungle for weeks, rifle in hand. By now the two American commanders were barely on speaking terms. A staunch advocate of ground warfare, "Vinegar Joe" thought Chennault's idea of fighting the war in China's skies was ridiculous. Wars were won on the ground. For months the two had been battling over supplies to 14th U. S. Air Force. In frustration, Chennault wrote personal letters to Roosevelt complaining he had not been given the tools promised him; nevertheless, his B-24's and fighters had provided the only bright spot in China with their effective raids on Japanese shipping and lines of communications.

Like Stilwell, though to a lesser degree, Roosevelt was becoming impatient with the Nationalists, and like Stilwell, he was primarily concerned with Burma. In early 1944 he urged Chiang and Stilwell to launch a major offensive across the Salween River into Burma. Chiang questioned the priority of such a campaign; he was far more worried about the Japanese in China. His reluctance drew stronger demands for action from Roosevelt—but still without result. The sudden thrust by Mutaguchi across the Indian border toward Imphal ended the debate as far as Roosevelt was concerned. On April 3 he radioed Chiang an implied threat to cut off Lend-Lease aid unless a Kuomintang army attacked down the Burma Road in the near future:

. . . TO ME THE TIME IS RIPE FOR ELEMENTS OF YOUR SEVENTY-FIRST ARMY GROUP TO ADVANCE WITHOUT FURTHER DELAY AND SEIZE THE TENGCHUNG-LUNGLING AREAS. A SHELL OF A DIVISION OPPOSES YOU ON THE SALWEEN. YOUR ADVANCE TO THE WEST CANNOT HELP BUT SUCCEED.
TO TAKE ADVANTAGE OF JUST SUCH AN OPPORTUNITY, WE HAVE, DURING THE PAST YEAR, BEEN EQUIPPING AND TRAINING YOUR YOKE FORCE [the Yunnan divisions]. IF THEY ARE NOT TO BE USED IN THE COMMON CAUSE OUR MOST STRENUOUS AND EXTENSIVE EFFORTS TO FLY IN EQUIPMENT AND TO FURNISH INSTRUCTUAL PERSONNEL HAVE NOT BEEN JUSTIFIED . . .

Chiang Kai-shek did not formally reply to this message but within two weeks War Minister and Chief of Staff, General Ho

Ying-chin, approved an assault across the Salween. Chennault, who also served as Chief of Staff of the Chinese Air Force, saw a far greater threat in China itself. He warned Chiang that the Japanese were about to launch an offensive on American air bases lying southeast of the Nationalist capital, Chungking. "Under the circumstances, therefore," he wrote, "it is necessary to inform your Excellency that the combined air forces in China, excluding the VLR [B-29] project, may not be able to withstand the expected Japanese air offensive and will certainly be unable to afford air support to the Chinese ground forces over the areas and on the scale desired. In order to put the air forces on a footing to accomplish these missions, drastic measures to provide them with adequate supplies and adequate strength must be taken. As the Japanese threat appears to be immediate, such measures should be taken without further delay."

He sent a similar warning to Stilwell, who replied that the threat to Imphal took precedence in the China-Burma-India theater and, therefore, Chennault's 14th Air Force must accept reductions in supplies; it would "simply have to cut" its operation. Chennault was infuriated. A week earlier he had written Stilwell that he was convinced the security of China as a base for future military operations against Japan was at stake:

. . . Since the Japanese no longer have the men and material to spare for rice raids or training exercises, it seems to me that they must now mean business. The whole logic of their situation points to this conclusion. They must make ready for eventual abandonment of their more extended commitments in order to try to hold on an interior line. To do this they must somehow neutralize the Allied China base on their flank and protect Formosa, the key to their inner defenses. The urgency of doing this has been immeasurably increased by the prospect of B-29 operations against Formosa and the Japanese Islands, which alone would be sufficient to provoke a violent reaction. . . .

At the same time he made another personal appeal to Roosevelt; an attack in eastern China was imminent and he doubted it could be withstood.

I wish I could tell you that I have no fear of the outcome. I expect the Chinese forces to make the strongest resistance they can. We shall do our best to give them, by means of airpower, a margin over the Japanese. But owing to the concentration of our resources on fighting in Burma little has been done to strengthen the Chinese armies and for the same reason the 14th Air Force is still operating on a shoe string. If we were even a little stronger I should not be worried. Since men, equipment and supplies are still very short I can say to you that we will fight very hard.

I am the more concerned since the shrewdest Chinese leaders I have consulted are convinced that any Japanese success within China will touch off violent new price rises and probably cause political unrest with inevitable effects on the energy of the Chinese resistance. I note a mood of discouragement among the more influential Chinese.

Chennault's assessment of Japanese intentions were accurate. Tokyo had already ordered the commander of the China Expeditionary Army to occupy the eastern China airfields and the three important railroads in the area. The operation, named ICHI-GO, was divided into two phases. The first would disperse the Chinese forces, "particularly the Nationalists," between the Yellow River and the Yangtze, and secure the rail lines from Peking to Hankow. After that, eleven divisions with several others in reserve would cross the Yangtze and continue southwest, seizing first Changsha, and Hengyang in Hunan Province, then Kweilin, Liuchow and Nanning in Kwangsi Province. Capture of this last city would neutralize two important 14th Air Force fields.

ICHI-GO was preceded by an intensive propaganda campaign aimed at alienating China from her Western allies and lowering the morale of the Kuomintang troops. Bales of pamphlets proclaimed that Japan's enemy was the American-British force, not Chiang's army, and her objective was the establishment of a new China. If the Chinese offered no resistance they would be treated as friends. Japanese troops, moreover, were given strict orders to cease burning, looting and raping; they were to "treat the local inhabitants with kindness and respect." The men were taught a new marching song:

> Taking loving care of trees and grass,
> The Japanese troops march through Hunan Province.
> How kind their hearts are!
> Behold, the clouds there and rivers here

Appear just as they are in our homeland.
These sights impress our soldiers' manly breasts.
With worn shoes they plod onward,
Blood streams onto the soil;
Let us defend this forest and that mountain with our blood.
Our enemies are Anglo-Americans, the white-faced demons.

ICHI-GO began on the night of April 17. The 37th Division crossed the Yellow River as Mutaguchi's men were investing Kohima. Yet, curiously, there was no co-ordination or co-operation between the two operations. That same day Stilwell told Chennault that his primary mission was the defense of the B-29 fields at Chengtu, "even at the expense of shipping strikes and support of the Chinese ground forces." Chennault wanted to throw all his planes against the oncoming Japanese. Defending Chengtu, he radioed Stilwell, presented no immediate problem, since it lay west of Chungking. Confronted with the imminent collapse of eastern China, Stilwell gave Chennault permission to use the P-47's assigned to the defense of Chengtu, and ordered B-24's of the 380th Bombardment Group to deliver fuel to the 14th Air Force.

But the additional air support hardly slowed the Japanese advance. The Chinese armies in the area had deteriorated after almost four years of inactivity. Chennault saw his failure as a predictable result of Stilwell's policies, and reported to him that he had been handicapped by "lack of tonnage for aviation supplies and a general disbelief in Japanese offensive plans."

Suspecting that Chennault was preparing a case against him, Stilwell penned a long, bitter analysis of their old antagonism:*

Chennault has assured the Generalissimo that air power is the answer. He has told him that if the 14th AF is supported, he can effectively prevent a Jap invasion. Now he realizes it can't be done, and he is trying to prepare an out for himself by claiming that with a *little more*, which we won't give him, he can still do it. He tries to duck the consequences of having sold the wrong bill of goods, and put the blame on those who pointed out the danger long ago and tried to apply the remedy.

He has failed to damage the Jap supply line. He has not caused

* It was found in Stilwell's file clipped to a radio message dated May 14, 1944.

any Jap withdrawals. On the contrary, our preparations have done exactly what I prophesied, i.e., drawn a Jap reaction, which he now acknowledges the ground forces can't handle, even with the total air support he asked for and got.

Unimpressed by the attack of 72,000 Nationalist troops into Burma in mid-May, Stilwell officially continued his complaints against Chiang. He finally forced the issue in a radio to Marshall:

CKS WILL SQUEEZE OUT OF US EVERYTHING HE CAN GET TO MAKE US PAY FOR THE PRIVILEGE OF GETTING AT JAPAN THROUGH CHINA. HE WILL DO NOTHING TO HELP UNLESS FORCED INTO IT. NO MATTER HOW MUCH WE MAY BLAME ANY OF THE CHINESE GOVERNMENT AGENCIES FOR OBSTRUCTION, THE ULTIMATE RESPONSIBILITY RESTS SQUARELY ON THE SHOULDERS OF THE G-MO. IF HE IS WHAT HE CLAIMS TO BE, HE MUST ACCEPT THE RESPONSIBILITY. . . .

SO WITH THE CHINESE THE CHOICE SEEMS TO BE TO GET REAL-ISTIC AND INSIST ON A QUID PRO QUO, OR ELSE RESTRICT OUR EFFORT IN CHINA TO MAINTAINING WHAT AMERICAN AVIATION WE CAN. THE LATTER COURSE ALLOWS CKS TO WELSH ON HIS AGREEMENTS. IT ALSO LAYS THE ULTIMATE BURDEN OF FIGHT-ING THE JAP ARMY ON THE U.S.A. I CONTEND THAT ULTI-MATELY THE JAP ARMY MUST BE FOUGHT ON THE MAINLAND OF ASIA. IF YOU DO NOT BELIEVE THIS, AND THINK THAT JAPAN CAN BE DEFEATED BY OTHER MEANS, THEN THE PROPER COURSE MAY WELL BE TO CUT OUR EFFORT HERE TO THE A.T.C. AND THE MAINTENANCE OF WHATEVER AIR FORCE YOU CON-SIDER SUITABLE IN CHINA. . . .

I REQUEST YOUR DECISION. IS MY MISSION CHANGED, OR SHALL I GO AHEAD AS BEFORE?

Washington's answer jolted Stilwell, and made official a policy which had been brewing for some time. It had been decided, Marshall replied, that operations in China and Southeast Asia would be determined by the contribution they made to campaigns in the central and southwest Pacific.

. . . JAPAN SHOULD BE DEFEATED WITHOUT UNDERTAKING A MAJOR CAMPAIGN AGAINST HER ON THE MAINLAND ON ASIA IF

HER DEFEAT CAN BE ACCOMPLISHED IN THIS MANNER. SUBSE-
QUENT OPERATIONS AGAINST THE JAPANESE GROUND ARMY IN
ASIA SHOULD THEN BE IN THE NATURE OF A MOPPING-UP OP-
ERATION. . . .

Henceforth China would be, primarily, an air base from which to bomb the Japanese mainland with B-29's. The idea for the Superfortress had been inspired by fears in 1939 that England would be overwhelmed, and there would be no air bases in Europe to attack Germany. It was a monstrous plane, dwarfing the B-17. It was 99 feet long and almost 28 feet high, with a wingspan of more than 141 feet. But it was sleek, its skin flush-riveted, and could cruise at more than 350 miles an hour at an altitude of 38,000 feet and carry four tons of bombs for 3,500 miles. From the beginning its builders had been plagued by engine trouble. An experimental model caught fire in the air, crashed and killed the entire crew. It wasn't until the summer of 1943 that the first production model took to the air—and this one, in fact, was full of "bugs."

The Marianas had been selected as the eventual base for mounting B-29 raids on Japan, but as long as these islands were in Japanese hands, Air Force planners decided to launch the first raids from China in spite of the formidable logistics problem. All fuel and supplies had to be hauled by air from India over the Hump— the Himalayas—to the four airfields in Chengtu which were still under construction. Moreover, the 4,000-mile round trip from Chengtu to Tokyo reduced the bomb-load capacity.

The B-29's were given their first test in combat before leaving India. It was a relatively short mission, but it dramatized the operational difficulties which beset the new bomber. On June 5, 1944, ninety-eight Superfortresses took off to bomb Bangkok. One crashed immediately, fourteen aborted and several others never reached the target. The remainder approached Bangkok in ragged formation. Two planes crashed on the way home, two ditched into the Bay of Bengal and forty-two landed at the wrong bases. But the mission was deemed an "operational success"; the B-29's were ready for Japan.

On June 15, ninety-two Superfortresses left for Chengtu, where they would refuel before the final long leg to Japan. Seventy-nine of the planes reached the staging area, but only sixty-eight got back into the air that afternoon. Of those, one crashed on takeoff and four others turned back because of mechanical failure. The first B-29 reached the target—the Imperial Iron and Steel Works at Yawata on the island of Kyushu—just before midnight, Chinese time. Flak was heavy and several fighters came up to intercept, but of the bombers that made it to Yawata, only six were lightly damaged. The bombing itself was a failure—a single missile hit the Imperial works—but the effect on the Japanese was indelible. The war had at last reached the homeland.

In eastern China, Japanese troops were at the gates of Changsha. The fall of this great city three days later created panic in Chungking; the War Ministry ordered the execution of several field commanders. Two Japanese divisions, the 116th and 68th, were already driving down toward Hengyang, a hundred miles farther south. They seized an adjoining airfield on June 26, and two days later assailed the walled city itself. Surrender was expected momentarily, when Major General Fong Hsien-chueh, commander of the Chinese 10th Army, confounded the Japanese and surprised the Americans by making a determined stand. His troops—supported by Chennault's fighters and bombers, which made hazardous night attacks on enemy supply convoys—flung back the Japanese day after day.

Low on food and ammunition, the invaders withdrew within a fortnight. At Kweilin, which would have been the city next in the path of the Japanese drive, victory celebrations lasted for a week, its streets acrid from the interminable explosions of firecrackers. Merchants inundated American airmen at the Kweilin base with ivory, jade, silk and lacquerware.

The Japanese were soon back in force, however, with forty thousand fresh troops. General Fong resumed his dogged defense of Hengyang, but Chiang Kai-shek no longer supported him; for some reason he distrusted Fong's superior, Marshal Hseuh Yo. The Generalissimo ordered suspension of all Chinese and American supplies to the besieged city.

Chennault turned to an old antagonist for help. He radioed Stilwell a request for permission to fly guns and ammunition to Fong. Stilwell's headquarters replied noncommittally that the proposition was being given "best treatment in this shop," but took no action.

Chennault sent another request, for 500 tons. This time the answer was definite:

IN VIEW LOCATION HSEUH YO'S FORCES, HIS MISSION, RAPIDLY
CHANGING SITUATION, CHINESE MISUSE OF EQUIPMENT THEY
HAVE AND IMPROPER EMPLOYMENT OF THEIR FORCES, YOUR
PROPOSAL TO FLY 500 TONS OF SMALL ARMS AND AMMUNI-
TION WOULD BE WASTE OF EFFORT. ENTIRE AMERICAN EFFORT
SHOULD BE CONTINUED FROM THE AIR.

Several weeks later Hengyang fell. But Chennault's 14th Air Force continued attacking the Japanese supply lines and forced the enemy to postpone their assault on Kweilin for a month.

If China—whose role in the war had been diminished—collapsed, it would release 820,000 Japanese troops. Consequently, Roosevelt dispatched a personal representative to Chungking with orders to keep China in the war by unifying all Chinese military forces, including those of the Communists, against Japan. He selected a civilian, elevated to the rank of major general, Patrick J. Hurley, a successful corporation lawyer who had been Secretary of War under President Herbert Hoover. He was hearty and affable, and had won Roosevelt's confidence by the way he had carried out wartime diplomatic missions to Russia and the Middle East.

Hurley was en route to China, via Moscow, when V. M. Molotov, Commissar of Foreign Affairs, told him that Russia wanted to be friends with Nationalist China. Hadn't he, Molotov, personally brought about the release of Chiang after the Young Marshal kidnapped him in 1936? How could China blame Russia for her own internal dissension? The Soviet Union had no interest in the Chinese Communists—they were Communists in name only. America should try to help the Chinese people improve their economy, and to unify Mao's and Chiang's armies.

Hurley, who saw life in simplistic terms, took almost everything Molotov said at face value. In Chungking he told the Generalissimo that he needn't worry about the Chinese Communists' being controlled from Russia—wasn't it obvious that they weren't really Communists at all?

Chiang was unconvinced; he had read Mao's articles and speeches. Nor could Hurley persuade Chiang to place Stilwell in command of all Chinese armed forces, as Marshall had so long been demanding. On September 25 the Generalissimo sent Hurley an *aide-mémoire* stating that his recent experiences had clearly shown him that General Stilwell was "unfitted for the vast, complex and delicate duties which the new command will entail. Almost from the moment of his arrival in China, he showed his disregard for that mutual confidence and respect which are essential to the successful collaboration of allied forces . . . Last October, I intended to ask for his recall, but when General Stilwell solemnly promised that in the future he would unreservedly obey my orders and would give me no further cause for disappointment, I withdrew my request. Unhappily, General Stilwell's solemn promise has never been implemented. . . ." Chiang promised to support any qualified replacement.

Stilwell radioed Marshall that the *aide-mémoire* was a tissue of false statements and that Chiang had "no intention of instituting any real democratic reforms or of forming a united front with the Communists."

Marshall forwarded this rejoinder to Roosevelt, whose disenchantment with the Generalissimo was evident in the reply he sent Chungking on October 5:

. . . THE GROUND SITUATION IN CHINA HAS SO DETERIORATED SINCE MY ORIGINAL PROPOSAL THAT I NOW AM INCLINED TO FEEL THAT THE UNITED STATES GOVERNMENT SHOULD NOT ASSUME THE RESPONSIBILITY INVOLVED IN PLACING AN AMERICAN OFFICER IN COMMAND OF YOUR GROUND FORCES THROUGHOUT CHINA. . . .

Chiang, in turn, tried to blame Stilwell—and Roosevelt indirectly —for the collapse in eastern China. In another *aide-mémoire* to Hurley, he charged that the disaster had been occasioned by Stilwell's insistence on an offensive in northern Burma.

. . . As I had feared, the Japanese took advantage of the opportunity thus offered to launch an offensive within China attacking first in Honan and then in Hunan. Owing to the Burma campaign, no adequately trained and equipped reinforcements were available for these war areas . . . The forces brought to bear by the Japanese in their offensive in east China were six times as great as those confronting General Stilwell in north Burma, and the consequences of defeat were certain to outweigh in China all results of victory in the north Burma campaign. Yet General Stilwell exhibited complete indifference to the outcome in east China; so much so that in the critical days of the east China operations, he consistently refused to release Lend Lease munitions already available in Yunnan for use in the East China fighting. . . .

In short, we have taken Myitkyina [Burma] but we have lost almost all east China, and in this General Stilwell cannot be absolved of grave responsibility. . . .

He took issue with the President's derogatory refusal to appoint an American commander of Chinese forces.

I am wholly confident that if the President replaces General Stilwell with a qualified American officer, we can work together to reverse the present trend and achieve a vital contribution to the final victory.

Hurley had hoped he would conciliate Stilwell and Chiang, but now he was certain that this was impossible and that Stilwell must leave China. He radioed Roosevelt:

. . . MY OPINION IS THAT IF YOU SUSTAIN STILWELL IN THIS CONTROVERSY, YOU WILL LOSE CHIANG KAI-SHEK AND POSSIBLY YOU WILL LOSE CHINA WITH HIM.

For a week the fate of the China-Burma-India theater hung in the balance as both Stilwell and Hurley bombarded Washington with conflicting advice. Finally, on October 18 (two days before MacArthur landed at Leyte), Roosevelt radioed Chiang that he was recalling Stilwell but would not appoint an American to command the Chinese forces. He did promise to send Major General Albert C. Wedemeyer, to be the Generalissimo's new Chief of Staff and to command all U. S. forces in China.

With Stilwell gone, the affable Hurley could devote his full attention to the unique problem of uniting Mao and Chiang. On November 7, against the advice of Chiang, whom he called "Mr. Shek," he flew to the Communist capital of Yenan, where his idea was already being promoted; every American official and visiting journalist had been assured by Communist spokesmen that what China needed was a coalition government based on democratic principles. The mustachioed Hurley arrived, chest loaded with medals, impressing the onlookers with his flowing mane of white hair and ramrod carriage. In a booming voice he lectured Mao Tse-tung (he pronounced it "moose dung"), Chou En-lai and their aides on five points of possible accord with the Kuomintang. The Communists were startled by his manner, but responded with nods and smiles. That evening at an elaborate banquet he astounded his sedate hosts. After toasts to Stalin, Roosevelt and Churchill, he stood up and let loose a wild Indian war whoop. John K. Emmerson and other Foreign Service experts tried to explain that it was just a quaint old American custom signifying good wishes to all.

Whatever the Communists thought, they accepted Hurley's statement with minor revisions. The five points called for unification of all military forces in China "for the immediate defeat of Japan and the reconstruction of China." The Chungking government was "to be reorganized into a coalition National Government embracing representatives of all anti-Japanese parties and non-partisan political bodies. A new democratic policy providing for reform in military, political, economic and cultural affairs shall be promulgated and made effective." The coalition regime would support the principles of Sun Yat-sen and set up a "government of the people, for the people and by the people," which would "establish justice, freedom of conscience, freedom of press, freedom of speech, freedom of assembly and association, the right to petition the government for the redress of grievances, the right of writ of habeas corpus and the right of residence." There was nothing in the document that any admirer of the Declaration of Independence would not have approved, including two additional phrases, borrowed from President Roosevelt—freedom from fear and freedom from want.

Hurley—now known as "Little Whiskers" to the Communists—flew back to Chungking with Chou En-lai, imagining that his mission was accomplished. How could anybody possibly object to such "innocuous" and noble sentiments? Molotov was right. The Chinese Reds were ersatz Communists; the Russians would never have reconciled such liberal policies with their own authoritarian practices.

Chungking greeted the document with derision, and its sponsor with a new nickname, "The Second Big Wind." "The Communists have sold you a bill of goods," T. V. Soong said to Hurley. "Never will the National Government grant the Communist request." Soong knew his brother-in-law; Chiang told Hurley that the agreement would lead to Communist domination of the coalition government. Nor could he accept Hurley's assurance that America would guarantee his position as President and Generalissimo. The coalition would be regarded by the Chinese as total defeat for the Kuomintang.

Hurley persisted in his belief that the most divergent views could be brought together by good will and persuaded the Chungking leaders to draw up a counterproposal. This stipulated that Communist forces be accepted into the Nationalist Army and that the Communist party be legalized; Mao, however, was to turn over control of his troops to the National Military Council. It subscribed to Sun Yat-sen's principles and guaranteed the various freedoms and civil liberties, "subject only to the specific needs of security in the effective prosecution of the war against Japan."

Hurley passed along this proposal to Yenan, hoping it might be acceptable. It was not. Chou En-lai felt betrayed and replied that the Communists could find no common basis in Chiang's proposition; the Yenan government would have to be accepted as an equal in a genuine coalition government.

On October 31 General Wedemeyer arrived to replace the controversial Stilwell. The strategic situation in the Pacific had altered with the crushing American naval victories off Leyte, and with the possibility that Stalin would send sixty divisions against Japan three months after Germany was defeated. But it was still important to keep Chiang's armies in the field so they could continue to tie up masses of Japanese troops. Wedemeyer radioed Marshall that the military situation was worsening; Kweilin and its airfield would soon be lost, and Kunming, the capital of Yunnan Province, would undoubtedly be the next target.

There had been some changes in the Japanese command as well. In September, General Yasuji Okamura took over the China Expeditionary Army, and although his command was vast, he took personal charge of the 6th Area Army, which was in the midst of Operation Ichi. Its aim, however, was by no means as ambitious

as Wedemeyer feared; Tokyo had no intention of driving as far
west as Chungking. The acquisition of more Chinese territory held
no attraction; the eastern China air bases did. Their seizure would
prevent long-range bombing raids on the last outposts in the Pacific
and the homeland.

Kweilin and Liuchow fell. Almost alone Chennault put up effective resistance with his B-25's and fighters. To do so, he did
not hesitate to use any means to divert supplies from the B-29
project, which he derided as the last chance of the "bomber radicals" to prove the Douhet theory of unescorted, high-altitude bombing. The results of the B-29 raids seemed to bear out Chennault's
belief that it was "a grandiose and foolish concept." After the
first disappointing attack on Japan, the big bombers hit Kyushu
four more times, as well as Manchuria and Palembang on Sumatra.
Each raid was as ineffective as the first.

Replacement of the commander of the China B-29's by Major
General Curtis LeMay—an aggressive, resourceful leader whose
Third Bombardment Division had performed brilliantly against
Germany—made little difference. He found he had inherited an
"utterly impossible situation" in China as well as "the buggiest
damn airplane that ever came down the pike." He set up a new
maintenance system, tried to teach the crews to bomb in formation,
as the B-17's had done in Europe. Despite his vigorous efforts,
a series of raids on Manchuria, Formosa, Rangoon, Singapore and
Kyushu accomplished so little that he himself was forced to admit
that his Superfortresses had not yet "made much of a splash in
the war."*

3.

In the Marianas the B-29 program was also experiencing difficulties. Beset by tropical downpours that made Saipan roads impassable, engineers had not yet completed the first 8,500-foot strip

---

* The U. S. Strategic Bombing Survey later concluded that attacks
launched by the B-29's based in China "did not warrant diversion of the effort entailed and that the aviation gas and supplies used by B-29's might have
been more profitably allocated to expansion of tactical and shipping operations of the 14th Air Force." The 800 tons of bombs they dropped were of
"insufficient weight and accuracy to produce significant results."

at Isley (formerly Aslito) Field when the first B-29, *Joltin' Josie the Pacific Pioneer,* piloted by Brigadier General Heywood ("Possum") Hansell, touched down on October 12, 1944.

"The thrill that went through all was almost electric in effect" as the great plane rolled to a halt, one witness reported. According to *Brief,* the magazine for AAF personnel in the Pacific: "The war just about stopped dead in its tracks the day *Joltin' Josie* arrived . . . The first of the B-29's had been inspected by every big gear and ogled from afar by every small fry for 5,000 miles. She was a sensation."

A few days later Brigadier General Emmett ("Rosie") O'Donnell—a B-17 veteran of the first frustrating days of war in the Philippines—arrived to open the 73rd Bombardment Wing headquarters and set up intensive unit training. After half a dozen missions over Truk and Iwo Jima, the tiny volcanic island almost halfway to Tokyo, O'Donnell's fliers were ready to strike at the Japanese capital.

The plan was an open secret, and on the morning of November 17 hundreds of vehicles converged on Isley Field. Twenty-four war correspondents and an array of still photographers and newsreel cameramen were on hand. As "Rosie" O'Donnell climbed into his B-29, dozens of flash bulbs exploded. But rain that persisted for days forced postponements until the morning of November 24.

At six-fifteen the first plane, *Dauntless Dotty,* with O'Donnell at the controls, rumbled and roared down the long runway. The wheels of the silver plane hugged the black top to its end—and onto the short coral extension. At the last moment *Dauntless Dotty* heaved up, just skimming the sea, and made a slow turn toward Tokyo. There were 110 B-29's behind her. En route, seventeen were forced back. An undercast almost obscured the target—the Nakajima airplane-engine plant at Musashino ten miles northwest of the Imperial Palace—and as the unescorted planes, swept by a 120-knot tailwind, roared over at about 445 miles an hour, they unloaded their bombs at altitudes of from 27,000 to 32,000 feet. Only forty-eight bombs, including three duds, hit the plant complex, causing slight damage; the rest blasted dock and crowded urban areas. More than a hundred assorted fighters came up to intercept the Superfortresses; one bomber was knocked down, and that by a damaged Zero whose pilot deliberately rammed into its tail.

Three days later the 73rd Wing returned. This time the engine plant was completely hidden by clouds, and the sixty-two B-29's had to go after secondary targets. Unsuccessful as these first two strikes were, they chilled Imperial Headquarters as well as the public. Important factories would not always be protected by a cloud cover, and there seemed to be no effective defense against the B-29. Already the foundations of Japan's basic industry had been undermined by persistent American submarine and air attacks on shipping. There was little crude oil for the refineries; no coke or ore for the steel mills; and the munitions plants were short of steel and aluminum. The economy could not endure continued B-29 attacks. They would somehow have to be contained.

Until such time, emergency measures would have to be taken to protect a ship which had become a source of pride and a symbol of hope to the entire nation. Combined Fleet ordered *Shinano,* sister ship of the super-battleships *Yamato* and *Musashi,* to flee Tokyo Bay for the relative safety of the Inland Sea. She had been converted into the world's largest carrier, and many navy-yard workmen were still aboard the recently launched 68,000-ton ship. Driven by 200,000-h.p. turbines, she hurriedly got underway in the late afternoon on November 28, and steamed south with her untrained crew, escorted by three destroyers.

An armored flight deck, an island, and hangar and storage spaces had been grafted onto the basic structure. *Shinano* was a seagoing armadillo, encircled at the water line by an eight-inch main belt of armor; great armored bulges below the water line reduced the effectiveness of any torpedo hit. Deadly fumes could not be drawn through the ventilating system, as they had on *Taiho.* Fire hazard had been further reduced by the elimination of wooden structures, the use of a special fire-resistant paint and the installation of a revolutionary foam extinguisher system. To fend off air attacks there were sixteen 5-inch high-angle guns, as well as one hundred and forty 24-mm. antiaircraft machine guns and a dozen multiple-rocket launchers.

Theoretically, *Shinano* was the most impregnable carrier ever launched, but there were naval engineers who privately regarded her as an ill-conceived and too hastily constructed monstrosity which was neither battleship nor carrier.

A hundred miles south of Tokyo the American submarine *Archerfish* was looking for a target. Her primary mission was to rescue crews of B-29's forced to ditch in the area, but the day's air strike had been scrubbed and *Archerfish* was free to leave her assigned station. The most likely hunting ground, decided Skipper Joseph F. Enright, was off Tokyo Bay. At 8:48 P.M., radar detected a target to the north. Through binoculars Enright made out in the moonlight a long, low shape nine miles away. It looked like a tanker. *Archerfish* headed toward the target to make a surface attack from the starboard beam. As they drew closer, Enright identified it as a carrier with three escorts. He decided to try to get ahead of the flattop, submerge and attack. He ordered course reversed and maximum speed from the four big 16-cylinder engines.

Shinano was making 18 knots, the same as *Archerfish*, but zigzagging reduced her speed enough for the stalker to move up slowly. At midnight, however, *Shinano* picked up speed and the submarine gradually fell behind. Three hours later the carrier abruptly swung around directly toward *Archerfish*. Enright waited for a few minutes to make sure it was in fact a base-course change. He ordered the bridge cleared and the diving alarm sounded. *Archerfish* slipped beneath the waves.

"Up periscope," Enright ordered. He grasped the handles and stared ahead. "I see him," he finally said. He asked the distance to the track.

"Five-five-oh yards" was the almost instantaneous answer from the executive, "Bobo" Bobczynski.

"Left full rudder. Left to course zero-nine-zero." Enright asked Plot how much time.

"He'll be here in two minutes."

Enright spun the periscope to scan the area. "Down 'scope!" he called. "Escort passing overhead!" The periscope lowered just in time to avoid a destroyer churning above them. Enright raised the periscope again on the bearing generated by the fire-control computer. It was perfect—right on the mark. At 3:17 A.M. Enright said "Fire!" The range was 1,400 yards, just forward of the carrier's beam. At eight-second intervals six torpedoes headed toward the target, running "hot, straight, and normal."

Enright watched the first two "fish" hit, then swung the periscope around to check destroyers. They were converging on *Archerfish*. "Take her down," he said.

Lookouts on *Shinano* stared helplessly as these two torpedoes, and two more, ripped into the big carrier. Captain Toshio Abe was not alarmed. Four hits were nothing; *Musashi*, basically of the same design, had taken nineteen torpedoes and many bombs before going down. He ordered the ship continued on course at 18 knots.

Musashi had indeed taken far more damage, but her veteran crew was responsible for her extended survival. Abe's inexperienced damage-control teams, hampered by the rough seas, could not stop the flow of water. Some of the compartments, moreover, lacked watertight doors. Abe could have grounded the ship or made it into port, but he held course and speed throughout the night. By dawn it was apparent even to those with blind faith in *Shinano* that she was mortally wounded. Abe reduced speed but it was too late. At 10:18 A.M., November 29, with the huge carrier listing sharply, Abe gave the order to abandon ship. Half an hour later, without having fired a gun or launched a plane, *Shinano* sank with a deafening rumble, taking with her Abe and five hundred shipmates.

The following week Japan's constant natural nemesis, the earthquake, struck the Nagoya area on Honshu Island. Its massive tremors left a long section of the rail bed in ruin, crippled a number of munitions plants and obliterated a factory in Toyohashi producing precision instruments. At the same time destruction from the air increased in effectiveness. In December, B-29's from Saipan bombed the Mitsubishi Aircraft Engine Works at Nagoya three times with such accuracy that the Japanese were forced to start moving equipment to underground sites.

4.

On January 9, 1945—the same day Superfortresses returned to Tokyo for the sixth time, and for the sixth time were ineffectual —General Krueger's Sixth Army invaded Luzon. They landed at Lingayen Gulf on the same beaches that Homma had stormed little more than three years earlier. They were expected, but there was almost no opposition and it was obvious by nightfall that General Yamashita had no intention of seriously contesting the landing. There was some concern on the part of American intelligence and operations officers that they were being drawn into a trap, but January 10 also proved to be an easy day and by dusk advance units had pushed eight miles inland. Within a week XIV Corps on the right had advanced thirty miles, losing thirty men. On the left, I Corps was making almost as good progress at the cost of 220 American casualties.

That night Yamashita finally launched a counterattack, a one-division operation designed to give him time to withdraw supplies and men to the north. He would give up the entire Central Plains —Manila Bay area and make his stand in the rugged mountains of North Luzon, where the terrain would give the defenders the advantage. It would be a battle of attrition, far from the Decisive Battle proclaimed so often.

The Japanese people, however, were told that the enemy had been lured into just such a battle on Luzon. But the reality of the situation was impossible to ignore completely, and on January 21 Prime Minister Koiso was obliged to make a rare admission to the Diet. He acknowledged that "the military developments in the Pacific theater are in a state which does not necessarily admit of optimism. However, the greatly extended supply lines of the enemy on all fronts are exposed to our attacks and in this fact, I believe, is to be found our golden opportunity to grasp victory.

"Now indeed is the time for us, the one hundred million, to give vent to our flaming ardor, and following in the footsteps of the valiant men of the Special Attack Corps, demonstrate even more spirit of sure victory in the field of production."

Imperial Headquarters was still intent on transporting prisoners of war from the Philippines to the homeland despite the sinking of two prison ships. Dr. Bodine, Major Virgil McCollum and the other survivors of *Oryoku-maru* were at sea again en route to Japan. They had left Lingayen Gulf just after Christmas in two groups—a thousand on a large freighter, *Enoura-maru,* and 236, including Bodine, on a smaller ship, *Brazil-maru.*

Major McCollum was aboard the bigger ship; sixteen prisoners died in the crowded holds on the way to Takao, Formosa—the first leg of the trip to Japan. For days the two ships remained in the harbor. It was getting cold. The threadbare parts of summer uniforms worn during the swim from the sinking *Oryoku-maru,* or thin cotton shirts and trousers issued to many who had reached shore naked, gave little protection. After a week of seemingly endless misery the men from the smaller ship were loaded onto *Enoura-maru.*

McCollum and Bodine were in the afthold with more than seven hundred others. It was seventy feet wide, ninety feet long. Halfway up one side of the vast chamber stretched a balcony. Here the Americans segregated their sick. Urine and feces dripped down from the balcony onto those below. There was little food and almost no water. The death rate rose to over ten a day.

On January 9—as General Krueger's troops came ashore at Lingayen Gulf—the prisoners heard the roar of American bombers sweeping in low. A deafening explosion rocked the ship. Bodine saw sparks fly as fragments burst through the hold. His left arm burned and he knew he was hit. He hunkered down as low as he could. At least fifteen were killed by the blast, and scores wounded.

In the forward hold, Marine Colonel Beecher was putting a spoon of rice to his mouth when slugs of metal whistled past him, burying themselves into a nearby stanchion. Heavy wooden hatch covers and steel beams cascaded onto the prisoners. Holes miraculously appeared in the side of the ship—"it was like a sieve." Dazed, Beecher shook himself. He felt nothing, then remembered from World War I that one felt no pain at the moment of being wounded. But how could he not be hit? The dead were everywhere. One corner was piled with bodies, mangled and bloody.

The carnage was indescribable. More than half of the five hundred men in the hold were killed outright. For the wounded, shrieking in pain, there was no medicine, no dressings. Nor was there any answer from topside to pleas for help. In the darkness, panic and hysteria gripped the survivors. Three of the eight field officers were dead, crushed by a single beam. "Van, you and me were not worth living," one officer remarked to Major van Oosten, "but Bob Roberts got killed. He had so much to live for and so much to do."

For two days, with little water or food, and no medical assistance, the survivors existed in a hell none would ever forget. It was like a scene from Dante's Inferno as wraithlike figures wandered dazed in the dark, stinking hull among the piles of corpses. It was not uncommon to find a man sitting on a body as he ate his pitiful meal. Finally a small Japanese medical party descended into the holds. They treated the minor cases but ignored the seriously wounded, who were "dying like flies." The dead were removed —some five hundred of them—and barged ashore for cremation.

On the afternoon of January 13 the prisoners were transferred to *Brazil-maru.* It sailed at dawn, and the next two weeks seemed to McCollum "an eternity of horror." The once-a-day ration barely kept the prisoners alive; if they were lucky, four men got a level mess kit of rice, and six men shared a canteen cup of water. The winter cold, as they proceeded north, added to their misery. They tried to keep warm by lying down spoon fashion under straw mats, "hugging each other for BTUs to keep alive." When the position became too painful a man would yell "Shift!" and the group rolled simultaneously to the other hip. Sometimes a neighbor would not turn—he was dead.

Snow fell through the open hatches, and scores of men who had survived wounds, dysentery and starvation froze to death. Sometimes life could be bought from the guards—a West Point class ring would bring an empty rice sack as a blanket—but death was becoming commonplace. When the shout "Roll out your dead!" went up in the morning, often thirty or more bodies were collected. The victims all looked alike: macabre mannikins with teeth exposed in a snarl between drawn lips, ribs almost bursting, sunken eyes, pipestem legs and arms.

In a primal urge to survive, men would jerk mats off those too weak or sick to cling to them; they fought one another like dogs over scraps of food. The prisoners were saved from chaos by the example set by a handful of officers and the three chaplains—a Lutheran, another Protestant named Nagle, and a Catholic, Father Cummings. In the end these three, worn by their exhaustive efforts, sacrificed their lives for the others.

Hardest to endure was the increasing scarcity of water, sometimes a spoonful or so a day, sometimes none. On January 24 Bodine described in his diary how he and several others stole out of the hold at night to get water condensed in the cylinders of the ship's deck engines.

. . . Finally got a half canteen and drank a cupful but got beaten with gun butt three times. Black as spades and little can be seen. Guard huddles in a little shack. If I'd been alone I'd been OK but others kept drawing his attention to me. It's a good way to get shot but worth it. Later in AM got kicked around trying to get Irons some snow from dirty deck . . . Not so many deaths last night. My bowels loosened up and had first movement since Friday. We have lost so much fat that sphincter has nothing to work on and even with formed stools can't control movements. Amount of filth in and out of clothes indescribable. Snowing rather hard this AM and temperature close to freezing. Keep praying it's our last day. We do need warmth, water, food and cleanliness. . . .

Three days later he wrote:

. . . Coldest night we've had. No chow now or no water in AM but chow small amount in PM. Suffered agony all night. Soiled pants moderately 2 times. No control due to lost fat. Father Cummings died. Kowalski gone; I am the only one left from my foot locker group. About 40 men died last night not buried. Hope ends soon. . . .

Bodine kept dreaming of waterfalls, springs and lemonade, and wakened by the bitter cold, made plans to live on a houseboat or in a house trailer or bungalow and keep a few turkeys and ducks.

On the night of January 29 the ship docked at Moji, on Kyushu Island in Japan, and the prisoners were given a physical test—the insertion of a rectal thermometer in the anus. At dawn they were lined up topside in the freezing wind and sleet to receive new clothing—shoes, wool trousers, padded jackets, socks and long cotton underwear. Those near the head of the line got the complete issue, but they had to pay a price. They were compelled to strip in the numbing cold, and with icy water from the decks running over their bare feet, they clumsily tried to dress. Guards beat them with sticks to hurry them up.

Bodine, near the end of the line, got nothing—and his shoes had just been confiscated. As he started off the ship supporting a weak comrade, both were sprayed with Lysol. They were marched through driving wet snow to an empty, unheated warehouse near the pier, where Bodine traded his broken mess-kit knife for an old pair of shoes, and was able to fill his canteen with ice-cold water from a barrel outside a window. He was issued his first square meal in more than two and a half years: a cup of steamed rice, several spoonfuls of salted fish, a large crawfish, a few slices of salted radishes, a piece of something that was peppery, and fruit that tasted like pineapple.

Six more prisoners died in the cold warehouse. Of the 1,619 who had left Manila on *Oryoku-maru,* 450 were left, and at least a hundred of these would soon die. The survivors had got water and one good meal but there was still an overriding question: What next?

5.

The same question, but in a larger sense, was about to be asked at Yalta, a seaside resort in the Crimea, where the Big Three would determine the future face not only of Europe but of the Far East as well. On January 23, just before Roosevelt left Washington, the Joint Chiefs of Staff formally advised him that Russia's entry into the war against Japan was vital to the interests of the United States. It was Marshall's opinion, as well as MacArthur's, that conquest of the 700,000-man elite Kwantung Army in Manchuria without Soviet help would cost the lives of hundreds of thousands of Americans.* A few U. S. naval intelligence experts

---

* On March 23, 1955, MacArthur charged that his views had not been sought at the Yalta Conference, and that if they had he "would most emphatically have recommended against bringing the Soviet into the Pacific war at that late date." In February 1945 he gave three listeners the opposite impression. After his conversation with MacArthur, Brigadier General George Lincoln reported: "Concerning over-all plan, General MacArthur considers it essential that maximum number of Jap divisions be engaged and pinned down on Asiatic mainland before United States forces strike Japan proper." Colonel Paul L. Freeman, Jr., recorded: "He emphatically stated that we must not invade Japan proper unless the Russian Army is previously committed to action in Manchuria." And the new Secretary of the Navy, James V. Forrestal, wrote in his diary: "He said he felt that our strength should be reserved for use in the Japanese mainland, on the plain of Tokyo, and that this could not be done without the assurance that the Japanese would be heavily engaged by the Russians in Manchuria."

—Captain Ellis Zacharias and his staff—shrewdly guessed that this Kwantung Army existed primarily on paper, since the cream of the troops had already been transferred to Leyte and other threatened sectors. But they were not heeded.

Three days later Foreign Secretary Anthony Eden sent Churchill a note from Moscow warning him to beware of the political demands which the Russians would probably make as their price for attacking Manchuria.

. . . There may perhaps be little argument about a Russian claim to recover possession of South Sakhalin which was ceded to Japan by the Treaty of Portsmouth in 1905. The Americans may look more closely at any claim to take the Kuriles. But a most difficult issue is likely to arise over Manchuria and Korea. We do not yet know what Russia's requirements are likely to be, but their conformity with the Cairo Declaration, for which we ourselves share responsibility, will be closely scrutinized by the Chinese, the Americans and others; and it is possible that these requirements can only be satisfied at the expense of incessant friction with the Chinese who may receive American support and expect ours also.

At all events there is here a potential cauldron of international dispute. It seems advisable therefore, at this stage, to go warily and to avoid anything like commitments or encouragement to Russia.

The conference opened on February 4, and its first concern was postwar Europe. The plenary meetings were lively, often heated, with Roosevelt again playing the mediator between Churchill and Stalin. The British somewhat resented Roosevelt's self-appointed role as umpire, and a few were outspoken about what they considered his appalling ignorance of the history of eastern Europe. Eden felt that Roosevelt's wish "to make it plain to Stalin that the United States was not 'ganging up' with Britain against Russia" was leading to "some confusion in Anglo-American relations which profited the Russians." Roosevelt admittedly was a consummate politician who could clearly see an immediate objective, but "his long-range vision was not quite sure." A. H. Birse, Churchill's interpreter, thought Roosevelt looked worn out. "The former self-confidence and firmness of tone, so evident at Teheran, seemed to have gone. His voice was that of a man weary in spirit . . . The good-humoured, benevolent uncle had become a shadow of his former self."

The relationship between the President and Churchill remained close, intimate as between two brothers and with the mixed feelings of brothers. Roosevelt had risked his political future to send Lend-Lease aid to Churchill in 1940 when Britain was in mortal peril—but continued to lecture his senior on the immorality of colonialism. "I believe you are trying to do away with the British Empire," Churchill once told him in private. Of this there was no doubt. "The colonial system means war," Roosevelt had confided to his son Elliott. "Exploit the resources of an India, a Burma, a Java; take all the wealth out of those countries, but never put anything back into them, things like education, decent standard of living, minimum health requirements—all you're doing is negating the value of a kind of organizational structure for peace before it begins."

On February 8 the American Chiefs of Staff were at last to take up their main concern—the war in the Pacific. They met with the Soviet Chiefs of Staff at Prince Yusupov's palace, where Rasputin was assassinated, to settle military problems in the Far East and in particular to determine what steps Russia should take once war with Japan was declared.

Six miles away at Livadia Palace, Roosevelt's headquarters, the President was cautiously approaching the same question with Stalin in the presence of Foreign Commissar Molotov, Averell Harriman and two interpreters. Livadia, built in Italian Renaissance style during Czar Nicholas' reign, was an imposing structure of honey-colored plaster trimmed with white marble. It stood more than 150 feet above the Black Sea, looking out on both water and precipitous mountains.

Roosevelt remarked that he favored intensive bombing of Japan by B-29's, thus obviating actual invasion of the homeland. Stalin interrupted him. "I'd like to discuss," he said without preamble, "the political conditions under which the U.S.S.R. would enter the war against Japan."

Roosevelt had a ready answer. There would be no difficulty, he said, regarding Russia's getting the southern half of Sakhalin Island and the Kurile Islands as a quid pro quo. As for giving the Soviets a warm-water port in the Far East, what about leasing

Dairen from the Chinese or making it a free port? Stalin was noncommittal. Instead he asked for something more—use of the Manchurian railways. Roosevelt could see no harm in that, and suggested that they be leased under Russian operation or under a joint Russian-Chinese commission.

This satisfied Stalin but he said a bit threateningly, "If these conditions are not met, it would be difficult for me and Molotov to explain to the Soviet people why Russia was entering a war against Japan, a country with which they had no great trouble."

"I haven't had an opportunity to talk to Marshal Chiang Kai-shek," said Roosevelt. "One of the difficulties in speaking with the Chinese is that anything said to them is broadcast to the world in twenty-four hours."

Stalin agreed that it wasn't yet necessary to speak to the Chinese. "Regarding the question of a warm-water port, we won't be difficult; I won't object to an internationalized free port."

They began a candid discussion of China's internal problems. America, said Roosevelt, had been attempting to keep China alive. "China will remain alive," Stalin remarked with a little smile, but he thought it strange that the Kuomintang and Communists could not maintain a united front against the Japanese.

Roosevelt replied that Wedemeyer and Hurley were making better progress than their predecessors in uniting Chungking and Yenan. The blame for the breach lay more with the Kuomintang and Chungking than with the so-called Communists.

The talk switched to Korea, and Roosevelt confidentially remarked that although he personally felt it wasn't necessary to invite the British to take part in the trusteeship of that country, they might resent not being asked.

"They most certainly would be offended," said Stalin with his feral grin. "In fact, the Prime Minister might kill us." Then to everyone's surprise he said agreeably, "I think the British should be invited."

The next morning at eleven o'clock the Combined Chiefs discussed their final military report, agreeing that for planning purposes the earliest date to expect the defeat of Germany was July 1, 1945, and the latest, December 31, 1945. The fall of Japan was set at eighteen months after the collapse of Germany.

That afternoon Roosevelt, Stalin, Churchill and their principal advisers assembled in the courtyard of Livadia Palace to be photographed. As soon as they returned to the ballroom—the site of all the plenary meetings—the new Secretary of State, Edward Stettinius, Jr., began reading the plan the three foreign ministers had drawn up that morning for dealing with territorial trusteeships in the United Nations. Before he could finish, Churchill testily cried out that he hadn't agreed to a single word of the report. "I have not been consulted nor heard the subject until now!" He was so agitated that his horn-rimmed glasses slipped to the end of his nose. "Under no circumstances will I ever consent to the fumbling fingers of forty or fifty nations prying into the life's existence of the British Empire! As long as I am Prime Minister I shall never yield a scrap of Britain's heritage!"

The following afternoon, February 10, Ambassador Harriman met Molotov at Yusupov Palace. The American ambassador was handed an English translation of the U.S.S.R.'s political conditions for going to war with Japan: the status quo was to be preserved in Outer Mongolia, and territory seized by Japan after the war in 1904–5—principally the southern part of Sakhalin Island, Port Arthur and Dairen—must be returned. Stalin also demanded control of the Manchurian railways and the Kurile Islands. In return Russia, besides declaring war on Japan, would conclude a pact of friendship and alliance with Chiang.

Harriman thought there were three amendments the President "would wish to make before accepting." Dairen and Port Arthur would have to be free ports, and the Manchurian railways operated by a joint Sino-Soviet commission. "In addition, I feel sure that the President wouldn't wish to dispose of these two matters in which China is interested, without concurrence of Generalissimo Chiang Kai-shek."

At Livadia, Harriman showed Roosevelt the draft of Stalin's proposal together with the amendments he himself had brought up. Assured he was acting in the best interests of America, the President approved the amendments, and asked the ambassador to resubmit them to Molotov.

The warm relationship between Stalin and Roosevelt, begun at Teheran, continued at Yalta until that afternoon when Churchill announced he had been "practically instructed" by his government not to mention figures in the matter of reparations, and Roosevelt said he too was afraid the mention of a specific amount (Stalin had brought up the figure of $20,000,000,000, with half going to Russia) would make many Americans think of reparations solely in terms of dollars and cents.

It seemed to Stalin that Roosevelt was ganging up with Churchill against him, and he became visibly angry. Though the matter was hastily smoothed over, Stalin was apparently so concerned by his own flare of hostility that he took Harriman aside as soon as they recessed for tea to tell him that he was prepared to meet the President halfway on the agreement to join the war against Japan. "I'm entirely willing to have Dairen a free port under international control," he said. "But Port Arthur is different. It's to be a Russian naval base and therefore Russia requires a lease."

"Why don't you discuss this matter at once with the President?" Harriman suggested, and before long Stalin and Roosevelt were huddled together conferring in hushed voices, their brief rift healed. They reached complete agreement. The only question now was how and when to tell Chiang of the accord. The President wondered if Stalin wished to take up these matters with T. V. Soong in Moscow or if he would rather that he, Roosevelt, take them up directly with the Generalissimo.

I am an interested party, said Stalin. It would be better if the President did it. When should the subject be discussed with the Generalissimo? asked Roosevelt, sensitive to the problem of secrecy. I'll let you know when I'm prepared to have this done, said Stalin, who wanted to have twenty-five more divisions in the Far East before informing Chiang Kai-shek. At that point Churchill joined them and they did not continue the discussion.

The Prime Minister did not learn of the agreement until the next morning. He was about to sign it when Eden, who was appalled by what he had just read, stopped him. In the presence of Stalin and Roosevelt the Foreign Secretary branded the agreement "a discreditable byproduct of the conference." Churchill rebuffed him; British prestige in the Orient would suffer if he followed Eden's advice. He defiantly added his signature to the accord.

A few hours later the Yalta Conference ended. At the final luncheon there was a general feeling of relief that everything had gone so well. Roosevelt was in high spirits. His cherished Declaration on Liberated Europe, the promise of self-determination for these nations, was accepted, and Stalin had agreed in writing to enter the war against Japan two or three months after the fall of Germany.*

There was an aura of quiet satisfaction among the Americans. To Ambassador Harriman it was a solid diplomatic success. Stalin had agreed to support Chiang Kai-shek and recognize the sovereignty of the Chinese Nationalist government over Manchuria. Harry Hopkins was sure that this was the dawn of a new day for everyone. The first victory of the peace had been won with the Russians proving they could be reasonable and far-seeing.

Some of the British, however, had serious reservations, particularly about the fate of Poland; Roosevelt's health had been an adverse factor of the meetings and had led him into serious errors. But it was he alone who had promoted—in the face of a reluctant Stalin and a dubious Churchill—the most lasting achievement of the conference, formation of the United Nations Organization.

The conditions of Stalin's agreement to fight Japan were known only to a few. If they had been circulated there would undoubtedly have been objections over Roosevelt and Churchill's promise that the Soviet claims for territory in the Far East "shall be unquestionably fulfilled after Japan has been defeated." Russia had, in effect, been bribed to do something she wanted very much to do. She would run no risk at all and suffer little cost in blood and matériel in attacking a beleaguered Japan once Germany was crushed. Moreover, the spoils of war—in particular the occupation of Manchuria—were a far greater inducement to join the assault than the secret pledges won from the West.

---

* Several weeks after the conference, Roosevelt summoned the American journalist and author Edgar Snow to the White House. "I got along absolutely splendidly with Stalin this time," said the President. "I feel I finally got to know the man and like him." He waved aside Snow's reservations "with airy optimism," while admitting that the Russians obviously were "going to do things in their own way in areas they occupy." Roosevelt seemed confident that future problems could be settled by mutual compromise. "I got the impression," he said, "that the Russians are now fully satisfied and that we can work out everything together. I am convinced we are going to get along."

26

"Like Hell
with the Fire Out"

1.

Several weeks before the landings at Leyte, the Joint Chiefs of Staff were persuaded—at the urgent request of Raymond Spruance and three Army generals—to proceed to Japan by way of Iwo Jima rather than Formosa. The immediate beneficiary was the Air Force. Iwo Jima was 625 miles north of Saipan and 660 miles south of Tokyo: a perfect halfway house for the VLR (Very Long Range) bombing project. Crippled Superfortresses could use it in emergencies, and from there the shorter-range P-51 Mustangs could escort the B-29's all the way to Japan.

Japanese resistance on Leyte forced a postponement of the Iwo Jima invasion, first to February 3 and then to February 19. The soft-spoken Spruance, veteran of Midway and the Marianas, was named overall commander, while Richmond Kelly Turner, who had learned so much at Guadalcanal, was made Joint Expeditionary Force commander. It was to be an all-Marine operation with "Howlin' Mad" Smith as commander of Expeditionary Troops. He in turn selected Major General Harry Schmidt to command the Landing Force, three divisions. The two assigned to hit the beaches on D-Day, the 4th and 5th, began arduous amphibious exercises in Hawaii, while the 3rd, the reserve, trained on Guam.

From the sea Iwo Jima (Sulphur Island) resembled a half-submerged whale but from the air it looked like a fat porkchop. Its most distinctive feature was an extinct volcano at the narrow (southern) end. Only 556 feet in height, it seemed more imposing, jutting as it did straight up from the sea. This was Mount Suribachi, Japanese for "cone-shaped bowl."

The island was nearly five miles long and two and a half miles wide—a third the area of Manhattan. Though its volcano was in-active, the entire island seemed to be alive with jets of steam and boiling sulphur pits. The combination of coastal cliffs and rugged Suribachi gave the appearance of another Rock of Gibraltar. Yet habitants had the queasy feeling that the island might disappear any minute into the ocean.

The fat northern part of the triangular island was a plateau some 350 feet high with inaccessible rocky shores, but at the narrow end toward Suribachi there were wide stretches suitable for amphibious landings. The beach to the east was the one selected for the Marines to assault, but what looked like black sand was volcanic ash and cinders, so light that a heavy man could sink to his knees. While the sterile soil provided little natural cover on the windswept beaches and plateau, the little hills and valleys surrounding the tableland were dense with jungle growth.

Iwo was one in a chain of islands hanging like a loose necklace from the entrance of Tokyo Bay to within three hundred miles of the Marianas: first the Izu Islands, then the Bonins, and finally the Volcanoes—three islets in a north–south line, with Iwo in the center.

The Bonins were first settled in 1830 when two New Englanders, a Genoese and twenty-five Hawaiians landed at Chichi Jima, not quite two hundred miles north of Iwo. Twenty-three years later Commodore Perry visited Chichi and took possession of it for the United States, with intent to make it a provisioning station for American naval ships and mail steamers. But President Franklin Pierce repudiated his action, and in 1861 Japan, claiming that the Prince of Ogasawara had discovered the Bonins in 1593, annexed them all.

An Englishman, Gore by name, came upon the Volcanoes in 1673 and gave Sulphur Island its name. Next a Russian explorer arrived, in 1805, but neither of these men thought the Volcanoes were worth colonizing, and it wasn't until eight decades later that the first settlers—they were Japanese—landed on Iwo. Like all the other islands in the chain it was placed under the jurisdiction of the Tokyo Prefectural Government to be administered as a part of the homeland.

By the middle of the 1930's there were almost eleven hundred colonists, living in flimsy, one-storied Japanese-style homes. The main village, Motoyama, was located a little north of the exact center of the island near the sulphur pits. Vegetables, bananas, pineapples, papayas, sugar cane and grain were grown for local consumption but the economy was based on a sugar mill and a sulphur refinery. The sugar mill did so badly that it was converted into processing medical herbs. There were two schools run by seven teachers, the Taihei-ken inn, and a bar serviced by three girls. Six times a year ships brought supplies, visitors, and news from Japan.

Of the entire chain, Iwo alone was suitable for airfields, but for years the Imperial Navy paid little attention to it except for installing radio and weather stations. In 1940 the Mabuchi Construction Company began an airfield with two strips almost a mile long near the foot of Mount Suribachi. The following spring a Navy lieutenant arrived with ninety-three men to start erecting gun positions. Two thousand civilian laborers poured onto the island.

It was not until early 1944 when the Marshalls were invaded that the island, along with Formosa, received the full attention of Imperial Headquarters. First Commander Tsunezo Wachi, the former assistant naval attaché (and secret agent) in Mexico, landed with a garrison of more than five thousand sailors. Then work commenced on a second airfield on the central plateau, and by the end of May the Army had a garrison of 5,170, thirteen artillery pieces and more than two hundred machine guns; the Navy had fourteen coast defense guns, a dozen heavy pieces and one hundred and fifty 25-mm. machine guns for antiaircraft defense. But there was a feeling of resentment between the services, and when Lieutenant General Tadamichi Kuribayashi arrived in June to set up headquarters for the 109th Division and assume overall command, he found a divided community.

The Japanese had divined American intentions long before they were conceived. "The entire Army and the nation will depend on you for the defense of that key island," Tojo had told the fifty-three-year-old Kuribayashi. Japanese estimates of American aims seemed to be confirmed a fortnight after Kuribayashi's arrival. Fifty-one carrier planes—intent only on neutralizing the island's air power—knocked down sixty-six interceptors and then bombed Iwo almost at will.

The raid was sobering to Kuribayashi. Nevertheless, he put on a show of confidence to his subordinates. "When the enemy comes here, we can contain him," he told a newly arrived major, Yoshi-taka Horie, over whiskey, "and then our Combined Fleet will come to slap his face. That is to say, our role here is a massive containing action."

Horie knew more about the Navy than most Navy men; he had worked for a year to try to improve the convoy system. "General," he said, "there is no longer any Combined Fleet. Some scattered naval forces remain, but they have no striking power. Haven't you been informed of the results of A-Go?" He described the devastating defeat off the Marianas ten days earlier.

The general accused him of being intoxicated. "This island is under the jurisdiction of the city of Tokyo!"

"When I saw this island from the air today," Horie replied, "I thought the best thing to do would be to sink it to the bottom of the sea." It could be done with enough explosives.

"You're drunk," Kuribayashi reiterated, but with less conviction. In the morning he took Horie to the beach at the foot of Suribachi. He threw himself on the black sand as if he had just stormed ashore. "This beach is wide," he said and pointed to the adjoining airstrip. "Yes, the enemy must land here. They have no alternative." For the next two hours Kuribayashi compelled Horie, who had been wounded in China, to fling himself down all over the airfield, a target while the general "shot" him time and again with a walking stick. Horie thought he had the mind of a squad leader; it was easy to believe the derogatory stories of the general's obsession with details.

But Kuribayashi must have been impressed with Horie—or at

least with the information he seemed to possess. He insisted that the major come to dinner again. They resumed their drinking, and all of a sudden Horie found himself talking about the disaster at Midway, and the pitiful state of convoy escort operations. Kuribayashi, his mind in a turmoil, tried to disparage what Horie said, and called him "a walking encyclopedia." But this resistance made Horie more persuasive. The general's face grew pale as the major disclosed the Combined Fleet's retreat from Truk to Palau, and then to the Philippines.

"The nineteenth of June [the Marianas Turkey Shoot] marked the death of Combined Fleet and Japan," said the major, his eyes glistening with tears. He tried to clear his throat. "If we could each kill ten enemies before dying, the world would realize it was really we who won the war!"

"Ah," sighed Kuribayashi, "I didn't know any of this."

"Personally I am reconciled to dying." Horie drew out a packet of potassium cyanide. Sobered, the two men sat in silence.

Kuribayashi ordered the evacuation of civilians and accelerated the program to build underground defenses in the porous volcanic rocks. He had decided to defend the island in depth rather than concentrate his efforts on annihilating the enemy on the beaches, and by midsummer Iwo was undermined with tunnels and caves. Reinforcements swelled the Army complement to 7,350 men. The Navy grew to 2,300 and received a new commander, Rear Admiral Toshinosuke Ichimaru, an experienced pilot who still limped from the crash of an experimental plane in 1926. His new combat command had inspired him to poetry:

. . .

> *Let me fall like a flower petal.*
> *May enemy bombs be directed at me, and enemy shells*
> *Mark me as their target.*
>
> *I go, never to return.*
> *Turning my head, I see the majestic mountain* [*Fuji*-san].
> *May His Majesty live as long.*

On August 10 Major Horie, who was now stationed on Chichi Jima, returned to Iwo to establish an emergency supply transportation system. He brought with him as gifts for 109th Division headquarters two bottles of water—there wasn't a spring on the island —and some vegetables. Kuribayashi was sitting on his porch in a relaxed mood, even though twenty-eight tanks had recently been sunk in transit. Most of the 145th Infantry Regiment had arrived safely, and he was pleased to find them well trained. But at dinner, after several tumblers of whiskey, he complained that he couldn't depend on his staff. There had been a growing resistance to his radical tactical plan of defense. "They react slowly to everything, and I can't restrain my impatience." What was the situation on Chichi Jima?

There were many overage officers there. One lieutenant colonel, past sixty, had asked Horie, "Why dig so many caves? We're all going to die, anyway."

"Japan has reached the end of the road," Kuribayashi reflected and poured the major another glass of whiskey.

The general's irritation with his staff embarrassed Horie the next day at the traditional morning ceremony in front of Division headquarters. After everyone had turned toward the Imperial Palace and bowed, the adjutant began reading communiqués. Kuribayashi interrupted the recital to criticize his chief of staff, Colonel Shizuichi Hori, for his bristling mustache. Later that morning Major Horie visited the headquarters of the largest unit in the 109th Division, the five-thousand-man 2nd Mixed Brigade, and was buttonholed by its commander, Major General Kotau Osuga, and the colonel with the offending mustache. For twenty minutes the two complained of Kuribayashi's arbitrary insistence on leaving the beaches undefended. That meant giving up Airfield No. 1, the only airstrip long enough for bombers.

Major Horie realized that he was largely to blame for the difference of opinion. Ignorant of the great naval defeat on June 19, these officers were still confident that the Combined Fleet would steam to their aid once the battle was joined. But he said nothing. It was not safe to tell everyone the truth.

Admiral Ichimaru was equally opposed to Kuribayashi's plan, and that afternoon he and three other naval officers confronted the general in Horie's presence. Commander Hijiri Urabe of the Third Air Fleet made it clear that he was conveying the opinions of the Navy General Staff, not his own. "The Navy wants to build pillboxes around Chidori [Airfield No. 1] and is ready to send about three hundred twenty-five-millimeter machine guns as well as the necessary building materials. The enemy can land only near Chidori. Therefore, if we defend it with pillboxes in depth, Iwo Jima will be impregnable."

It was the visitor from Chichi Jima who responded, not Kuribayashi. "How long did our guns last along the beaches at Saipan and Guam? Will you please show me just how effective the beach pillboxes at Tarawa were? Frontal defense against hundreds of naval guns and aircraft is futile. The lessons we learned at Saipan, Guam and Tinian have taught us beyond any doubt that the best defense is to snipe at the enemy from caves. We must realize we can't defend a beach." Besides, Major Horie added, the enemy's big naval guns could blow up any pillbox. "Under the circumstances, how long could we hold out on Iwo Jima?" He suggested that Navy guns and materials be utilized to strengthen the defenses of Mount Suribachi and the Motoyama area.

"I agree with Major Horie," said Kuribayashi curtly.

Urabe asked the general to reconsider, then turned to Horie with a forced smile. "I'm particularly surprised that Major Horie, who has always been considered friendly to the Navy, opposes me."

"If I hadn't read the battle reports from Guadalcanal, Saipan and Guam, I might have agreed with the Navy without hesitation. Now my conscience doesn't permit me to do so."

Kuribayashi remained opposed to strong defense of the beaches, but he needed the Navy's co-operation as well as their supplies and weapons, particularly dynamite, cement and machine guns. The next morning he suggested a compromise: the Navy could use half of the material for beach pillboxes if the remainder went to the Army. Commander Urabe more than welcomed the suggestion. "Yesterday I promised to send you enough building material for three hundred pillboxes," he said. "As soon as I return to Japan I will make every effort to get enough for three hundred and fifty."

Kuribayashi summoned all his commanders and formally announced his battle plan: they were neither to fire at landing craft nor to oppose the landing on the beaches without orders. Once the enemy pushed inland five hundred yards, automatic weapons near the airfield as well as artillery on Suribachi and the Motoyama plateau area would open up. General Osuga and Colonel Hori still contravened Kuribayashi but he overrode them. "Once the enemy invades the island," Kuribayashi said, "every man will resist until the end, making his position his tomb. Every man will do his best to kill ten enemy soldiers."

The garrison of 21,000 troops—14,000 Army, 7,000 Navy— was distributed into five sectors with 1,860 men assigned to Mount Suribachi, where they would fight independently, delaying the enemy as long as possible. Numerous caves had been dug into the slopes facing the beaches, their entrances angled as protection against blasts and flamethrowers. Inside the mountain, work was almost completed on a vast storied gallery—complete with steam, water, electricity and plastered walls.

The rest of the island was studded with thick-walled pillboxes. Many had additional protection: fifty-foot piles of sand. Big Navy coast guns were sited to enfilade the beaches, and antiaircraft guns were emplaced so that it would take a direct hit to destroy them.

The northern part of the island was a rabbit warren of natural and man-made caves; they were labyrinths of chambers and connecting tunnels, vented at the top for steam and sulphur fumes to escape. One, Brigade headquarters, located near Motoyama, could hold 2,000 troops; it was seventy-five feet deep and had a dozen entrances.

The first main line of defense—a network of dug-in positions for artillery, light machine guns and even buried tanks—ran along the southern edge of the plateau between the two airfields. A second line ran just beyond the second airfield through Motoyama.

Kuribayashi wrote home regularly. He chided his wife for visiting so much, and his eldest daughter, Yoko, for poor spelling and penmanship. When Mrs. Kuribayashi complained that life in Tokyo was getting unbearable, he pointed out that Iwo Jima was much worse.

. . . Our sole source of supply is rain water. I have a cup of water to wash my face—actually, my eyes only, then Lieutenant Fujita [his aide] uses the water. After he is through with it, I keep it for toilet purposes. The soldiers, in general, don't even have that much. Every day, after I've inspected defense positions, I dream in vain of drinking

a cup of cool water. There are a lot of flies. Also many cockroaches
crawl all over us. They are very dirty. Fortunately, there are no snakes
or poisonous reptiles.

On September 12 he started preparing her for what he knew
was coming.

. . . The enemy may land on this island soon. Once they do, we must
follow the fate of those on Attu and Saipan.

Our officers and men know about "Death" very well. I am sorry to
end my life here, fighting the United States of America but I want to
defend this island as long as possible and to delay the enemy air raids
on Tokyo.

Ah! You have worked well for a long time as my wife and the
mother of my three children. Your life will become harder and more
precarious. Watch out for your health and live long. The future of our
children will not be easy either. Please take care of them after my
death.

He also warned Yoko and his only son, Taro, that they both
faced a dismal future.

. . . The enemy landing on my island is merely a question of time.
If the defense of this island fails, then Tokyo will be raided day and
night. It is beyond words to describe the chaos, terror, heavy damage
and confusion of an air raid. Those who live idly in Tokyo can't even
imagine what it's like. Therefore, in case of a raid, the most important
thing is to keep the family together. Anyone cut off from the family
can die on the roadside. This actually happened in the great Kanto
earthquake of 1923. You must work for your family with your mother
as the central figure.

Regardless of school regulations, you must protect your home first.
You don't have to obey the regulations scrupulously because the situation will be too serious to worry about the safety of a schoolhouse.
Suppose you tried to go to your school to save it and your own home
was destroyed and your mother killed? What would you do then? You
must share the fate of your mother.

To begin with, once Tokyo is raided it means that Iwo Jima has
been taken by the enemy. It means your father is dead. In other words
you—fatherless brother and sister—must depend on your mother. It's
pitiful enough to be fatherless children but what happens if you lose

your mother? And from now on you must reconcile yourselves to living without a father.

A little later he wrote Taro a separate letter underlining his duties as the only son.

. . . The life of your father is like a flicker of flame in the wind. It is apparent your father will have the same fate as the commanders of Saipan, Tinian and Guam. There is no possibility of my survival. Therefore, you must be the central figure of our family and help Mother. Until now you have been a boy brought up in a hothouse. When I was in Tokyo I tried to give you a kind of Spartan training but perhaps you didn't realize it was done with a father's real love. In the future, you may understand.

He advised Taro to read, study, quit smoking, avoid drinking, joke at home to keep everyone in good spirits, and use both sides of a page without indentations or spaces when writing future letters.

By the end of November the underground fortifications and batteries—some eight hundred guns in all—were ready for battle. Airfield No. 2 was operational and construction was initiated on a third strip, another mile to the north. Kuribayashi had also rid himself of dissent within his own staff. He relieved his outspoken chief of staff, the mustachioed Colonel Hori, and the commander of the 2nd Mixed Brigade, General Osuga, and sent them both to an underground hospital on the island "to regain their health."

On January 21, 1945, Kuribayashi told his wife to stop praying for his return. He was destined to die on Iwo:

. . . I don't care where my grave is located. My ashes will not be returned home and my soul will remain with you and the children. Live as long as possible and please take care of the children.

He also admonished his brother to protect him from publicity.

. . . Please put a stone on my grave with these simple words: "Tomb of Lieutenant General Tadamichi Kuribayashi." Don't let any news-

papermen or magazine writers play me up in their stories. . . . I
would like my name kept clean even after my death.

2.

For six weeks Iwo Jima had been bombed daily by B-24's from
the Marianas with occasional help from Superfortresses. But the
most intensive attacks came from the sea, and by February 15,
warships had bombarded the little island with 21,926 shells. Re-
markably, there were relatively few casualties; the defenders had
moved underground. The following dawn six battleships, four
heavy cruisers and a light cruiser arrived off Mount Suribachi.
Destroyers and destroyer escorts darted in front of them, and a
dozen jeep carriers ("baby flattops"), fifty miles south of the island, sent out combat air and antisubmarine patrols.

The correspondent and author John P. Marquand (who had not
only won a Pulitzer prize for *The Late George Apley* but created
a famous Oriental detective, Mr. Moto) wrote that it would have
been hard to mistake Iwo "for anything but a Japanese island, for
it had the faint delicate colors of a painting on a scroll of silk."

The battleships and cruisers began the initial bombardment.
The shelling "turned out to be a slow, careful probing for almost
invisible targets, with long dull intervals between the firing." It
reminded Marquand of "the weaving and feinting of a fighter
watching for an opening early in the first round. To put it another
way, our task force was like a group of big-game hunters surrounding a slightly wounded but dangerous animal. They were
approaching him slowly and respectfully, endeavoring to gauge
his strength and at the same time to tempt him into action."

Except for a few unauthorized rounds, the Japanese held their
fire. Then an overcast settled over the island like a protective
cloak, and though the bombardment continued spasmodically until
late afternoon, the damage was negligible.

To the north, the homeland itself was under attack from the
sea. Planes from Mitscher's Task Force 58, which had boldly
closed to within sixty miles of the mainland, were striking at plants
near Tokyo producing aircraft frames and engines. The next morn-

ing, February 17, his bombers went after the Musashino plants, already the target of B-29's. Just before noon, however, the weather closed in, and Mitscher headed back toward Iwo Jima to back up the landing forces, cheered by the results of his foray, particularly the showing against the Japanese air defense: 341 enemy planes had reportedly been shot down and 190 destroyed on the ground, at the cost of only 49 aircraft.

At Iwo Jima the weather had improved and visibility was good. Minesweepers 750 yards from shore drew scattered fire from the island, and the heavy cruiser *Pensacola* moved in to help. This target proved too tempting for one battery commander. His guns hit the cruiser six times before she retired with 17 dead and 120 wounded. Destroyers closed in to cover gunboats armed with rockets which were a thousand yards offshore. Speedboats loaded with frogmen passed through this line.

The Japanese were shaken, as much by the enemy's nonchalance as by his display of power. Popular music floated across the water, as if from a group of people on an excursion, and they could see American sailors with towels around their necks gawking at the island like tourists. Kuribayashi had no longer any doubt that this was the landing. At 10:35 A.M. he ordered several batteries to open up on the gunboats, which retaliated with their rockets. This, in turn, brought on a barrage from big guns hidden at the foot of Mount Suribachi and at the northern end of Iwo. Several gunboats were hit, and planes laid a smoke screen while destroyers fired white phosphorus shells. The speedboats, which had continued undeterred toward the island, arced sharply near the shore line, and about a hundred frogmen flopped into the surf. They found no underwater or beach obstacles and a single mine, which was detonated.

At Airfield No. 2 there were two operable Zero fighters, armed with 60-kilogram bombs, concealed in a concrete revetment. Their pilots had been ordered to ram the largest ship they could reach, but one of them balked. "You're going to die, anyway," said a friend. The pilot insisted that his head hurt. His commander turned to a group of pilots and asked for a volunteer. One hoisted himself into the plane. The camouflage was whipped off, and the two Zeros taxied smartly from the revetment onto the strip. They managed to get into the air, but as they skimmed over Suribachi both were caught in the artillery fire and tumbled into the sea.

The second day of bombardment ended, and Kuribayashi, thinking he had repulsed a landing, radioed of his success to Tokyo. Admiral Toyoda of Combined Fleet sent his congratulations to Admiral Ichimaru:

DESPITE VERY POWERFUL ENEMY BOMBINGS AND SHELLINGS, YOUR UNIT AT IWO COOLLY JUDGED THE ENEMY INTENTIONS AND FOILED THE FIRST LANDING ATTEMPT AND SERENELY AWAITS THE NEXT ONE, DETERMINED TO HOLD IWO AT ANY COST. I AM GREATLY ELATED TO KNOW THAT, AND I WISH YOU TO CONTINUE TO MAINTAIN HIGH MORALE AND REPULSE THE ENEMY, NO MATTER HOW INTENSE HIS ATTACKS, AND SAFEGUARD THE OUTER DEFENSES OF OUR HOMELAND.

The two-day shelling caused few casualties but had uncovered Kuribayashi's hidden batteries and the extent of his defenses, enabling the Americans to revise effectively their bombardment pattern for the final day. Fire would be concentrated on the area around the southeast beach, the one the Marines would storm.

The morning sky was cloudy with bursts of rain. "Close beach and get going," ordered the commander of the Gunfire and Covering Force at 7:45 A.M. For the first time the shelling was devastating; photos indicated that half the pillboxes and most of the blockhouses on the beach had been torn from their foundations.

That evening the Marines of the 4th and 5th divisions, who had left Saipan on LST's and transports on February 15 and 16, filed their way through the chow lines, checked their gear, packs and weapons. There was no apparent tension or edginess. Everyone looked the same as the day before.

In his cabin on the command ship, *Eldorado,* "Howlin' Mad" Smith was reading the Bible. His men would suffer severe casualties when they hit the beach in a few hours. He was a Methodist but he wore a St. Christopher's medal blessed by the Pope. Several weeks earlier he had written to Lieutenant General Alexander Vandegrift, who was now Commandant of the Marine Corps, that he felt taking a fortress like Iwo Jima wasn't worth the heavy casualties his men would suffer.

. . . On two separate occasions I protested that naval gunfire is insufficient, with the result that it has been increased to some extent, but not enough, in my opinion, to suffice. I can only go so far.

We have done all we could to get ready . . . and I believe it will be successful, but the thought of the probable casualties causes me extreme unhappiness . . . would to God that something might happen to cancel the operation altogether.

At 3:30 A.M. on D-Day—February 19—the Marines had steak for breakfast. By the time they moved out on deck to the debarkation nets it was light, and through the mist they saw, looking lonely and abandoned, the island of Iwo. Mount Suribachi disappeared ominously into a low cloud.

John Marquand was atop the air lookout station on his ship. Iwo Jima had "never looked more aesthetically ugly . . . or more completely Japanese. Its silhouette was like a sea monster with the little dead volcano for the head, and the beach area for the neck, and all the rest of it with its scrubby, brown cliffs for the body. It also had the minute, fussy compactness of those miniature Japanese gardens. Its stones and rocks were like those contorted, wind-scoured, water-worn boulders which the Japanese love to collect as landscape decorations."

The transports and landing craft jockeyed over the calm waters toward their disembarkment positions. At 6:40 A.M. seven battleships, four heavy and four light cruisers began the heaviest pre-H-hour naval bombardment of the war. Five minutes later nine gunboats—LCI(R)'s—showered the Motoyama plateau with rockets while other gunboats—LCI(M)'s—pumped mortar rounds into the slopes of Suribachi. At 8:03 the bombardment let up to allow 120 carrier planes to blanket the southeast beach, Suribachi and Airfield No. 1 with rockets, napalm and explosive bombs. They climbed away as abruptly as they had appeared and the shelling resumed. This time ten destroyers joined in. The island seemed to shimmer through the burgeoning pall of dust and smoke. More planes swooped down, hosing the black sands with streams of bullets. It was the most "terrifying" bombardment the correspondent Robert Sherrod had ever witnessed. "Though I've seen this many times," he recorded in his notebook, "I can't help thinking, 'Nobody can live through this.' But I know better."

Huddled in their pillboxes, blockhouses and caves, the Japanese endured the concussions, fingers jammed into their ears. Their final instructions from Kuribayashi had been explicit:

Above all else, we shall dedicate ourselves and our entire strength to the defense of this island.
We shall grasp grenades, charge enemy tanks and destroy them.
We shall infiltrate into the midst of the enemy and annihilate them.
With every salvo we will, without fail, kill the enemy.
Each man will make it his duty to kill ten of the enemy before dying.
Until we are destroyed to the last man, we shall harass the enemy by guerrilla tactics.

From the mouth of his cave on Suribachi, Pfc. Kiyomi Hirakawa—a former government official—watched entranced as the vast flotilla of enemy ships waddled into place. How systematic and beautiful! he thought. It was the massed equipment that awed him, not the enemy himself. He knew all about the American fighting man from propaganda lectures and pamphlets. "They call themselves brave soldiers," read one such pamphlet entitled *The Psychology of the Individual American,* "yet they have no desire for the glory of their ancestors or posterity, nor for the glory of the family name. They as individuals want to be known as brave and to be given publicity. They are people who love adventure and danger. There are accounts of Americans who tried to go over Niagara Falls in a barrel. . . . They fear death, but being individualists, they do not think much about what will happen hereafter. Rather, when doing something adventurous, they are not afraid to die. They are expert liars. They are taken in by flattery and propaganda. Their desires are very materialistic. They go into battle with no spiritual incentive, and rely on material superiority."

The LST's, loaded with the first five assault waves, moved into final position 5,500 yards offshore. Slogans like *"Too Late to Worry"* were scrawled on the ramps. These lowered ponderously, and amphtracs began popping out into the sea ("It's like all the cats in the world having kittens," Marquand observed to a petty officer) and skittering toward Iwo. The first wave of sixty-nine amphtracs, each carrying some twenty men, climbed onto the beach at 9:02 A.M., two hours after H-hour, and began to crawl forward.

Twenty yards inland they encountered a steep terrace fifteen feet high in places. The amphtracs churned vigorously through the black volcanic ash, which was as loose as sugar, but only a few breasted the terrace. The others disgorged their occupants at its base, where the heavily laden men sank over their ankles in the black sand. They struggled forward through sporadic rifle fire and desultory rounds of mortar. Perhaps enemy strength had been exaggerated or the massive bombardment had driven the Japanese underground.

But once the Marines heaved themselves up the collapsing terrace, they were met by machine-gun and rifle fire from concealed pillboxes, blockhouses and caves. Mortar shells flew over their heads, crashing around amphtracs heading toward shore. Marines blown into the sea tried to swim to the beach but their heavy packs pulled them below the surface.

The 5th Division, going into action for the first time, was spewing onto the beaches on the left. One regimental combat team, the 28th, moved doggedly toward Mount Suribachi. Its job was to cut across the 700-yard-wide neck of sand to the other side of the island, isolate the volcano and storm up it while another team, the 27th, attacked the southern end of Airfield No. 1.

On the right flank two regiments of the 4th Division were to help seize the airfield and then the ridge guarding the Motoyama plateau. It was the first battle for Private Allen R. Matthews, a combat correspondent, and on the amphtrac he felt immortal, indestructible. He could picture himself grieving over the death of a friend—never a friend grieving over him. But as he scrambled onto the beach, mechanically chewing gum, his mind in a turmoil, he told himself, Run run run, get off the beach, don't hole up on the beach unless it's absolutely necessary because they're sighting on the beach and they'll get you sure as hell . . . get off the beach and run. But he couldn't. He staggered under the weight of equipment and sank into the sand. He heard nothing of the thunder of battle, but something compelled him to look to the rear. The sand spouted like a geyser of black water. His mouth was so dry that his chewing gum stuck to his teeth and tongue. He lurched forward trying to spit it out but bits clung to his lip and chin. It was nothing like the attacks he had read about. All around, men were running and stumbling in a nightmare silence. They seemed to

have no weapons, no uniforms, no faces. Suddenly he heard a noise.
"Co-o—orpsman!" wailed a voice in pain and terror. "Oh, co-o-
orpsman!" Marines weren't supposed to cry out like that. It came
from a man sitting in a shallow depression in the terrace; he was
inert, like a statue. On the left, three men were heaped oddly. They
had to be dead.

Frenzied, Matthews pumped his legs into the soft ash of the
sheer terrace, awkwardly holding his rifle aloft to keep sand out
of the breech. At last he was on top. He started for a shell crater
but wallowed helplessly in the sand. What a fine target I am! he
thought. He fell again, and rolled weakly into the hole. He swallowed for saliva but his swollen tongue scraped dryly against his
palate. He retched and at last saliva flowed. He surveyed the
scene. Now he was a veteran; he knew he too might be killed.

The first walking wounded were reporting to regimental aid
stations. One, his jaw hanging by threads of flesh, suffered himself to be bandaged but refused to be evacuated. He tried to talk,
then knelt and wrote something in the volcanic ash. The words
filled in immediately. He scuffed the sand disgustedly and allowed
himself to be led away.

The first tanks lumbered ashore at 9:30 A.M. They floundered
in the soft ash. Some managed to climb over the terrace, but more
were trapped and knocked out systematically by antitank guns.
The 4th Division in particular had been counting on their support,
and its drive toward the airfield was painfully slow. Caught in
murderous cross fire from innumerable pillboxes and blockhouses,
its troops had to subdue each one with demolitions and flamethrowers.

Second Lieutenant Benjamin Roselle, Jr., didn't land until 1
P.M. with his naval gunfire liaison team. Burdened with radio
gear, they struggled up the terrace at the extreme right end of the
battle line. Roselle's left foot was almost blown off by a mortar
round. His men put a tourniquet on his leg while he cracked jokes.
Another mortar shell landed on them, killing two of his men and
peppering Roselle's good leg with shrapnel. He was left with one
man, and the two of them hugged the ground until a third round
detonated just above them. Roselle was hit again, this time in the
shoulder. The enlisted man's right leg was blown off, and he
silently crawled down the terrace, the stump dragging behind him.

All by himself now, Roselle could think of nothing but his mother and father in Royal Oak, Michigan. A mortar barrage started walking up from the shoreline toward the terrace. Roselle felt himself lifted—and dropped. He didn't care. He glanced at his watch just as shrapnel ripped through his wrist. The watch was gone; in its place was a gaping red hole. This is what it feels like to be crucified, he thought.

To the Americans on the beach the fire seemed intense, but Kuribayashi's gunners were still firing with restraint, and many batteries up the island were not firing at all. Ammunition was husbanded; every round had to count. In his first radio report to Tokyo the general cited the commander of a platoon of antitank guns for knocking out more than twenty enemy tanks before succumbing, and requested that he be promoted posthumously to captain. He praised two other antitank commanders, an infantry officer and the entire 145th Infantry Regiment. He also reported that company funds totaling 120,000 yen were "hereby donated to the National Treasury"—the money had been burned.

By dusk thirty thousand Marines were ashore. Five hundred and sixty-six had been killed or were dying of wounds. The rest were crowded into a small beachhead, 4,400 yards long and 1,100 yards at its deepest point. They had failed to reach the first day's objectives and were digging in for the expected counterattack. But Kuribayashi was as careful of his men as he was of his ammunition. Unlike the commander at Saipan, he was not going to waste troops in futile night charges. He did something far more effective: ordered harassing mortar and artillery fire.

Throughout the night Marine ammunition dumps were detonated one by one with mystifying accuracy, as if there had been an observer within American lines. Finally a Marine heard a low clicking sound coming from the hulk of a beached Japanese transport. With a few comrades, the Marine crept up to the derelict. He made out a ghostly figure inside—a Japanese with a radio transmitter strapped on his back. Although his death brought a sharp decrease in Japanese artillery accuracy, the beach area was so crowded that casualties continued to be severe. Neither could anything stop the havoc wrought by rockets screaming out of the dark night. They were not conventional missiles. Japanese naval aviation ordnance men had somehow found a way to convert 60-

and 250-kilogram bombs into rockets, launching them electrically
along slanted wooden ramps. The "rocket" flew up the 45-degree
incline, arched some 2,000 yards in the general direction of enemy
positions and exploded on contact.

"The first night on Iwo Jima can only be described as a nightmare in hell," wrote Sherrod. By dawn dead littered the black sand.
Nowhere in the Pacific had he seen such badly mangled bodies;
legs and arms lay fifty feet from torsos. A light rain was falling.
It was cold. The naval bombardment started at 7:40 A.M., an hour
later than on D-Day. After fifty minutes the Marines attacked. On
the left, at the base of Suribachi, the going was arduous; the 28th
had made little more than two hundred yards by dark even with the
help of artillery, half-tracks, and supplementary shelling by destroyers which approached within 250 yards of land.

On the right the 4th Division broke through to Airfield No. 1,
then pivoted north and encountered Kuribayashi's first major defense line. Throughout the long day of combat, dogs brought
ashore by their Marine masters roamed the beach. One named
George was already a veteran of two previous landings. Another,
a feisty fox terrier, contemptuous of the nerve-shattering explosions on all sides, romped with a live grenade, rolling it around,
flinging it in the air. He carried it to a foxhole, scattering its occupants. He trotted after them, refusing orders to drop it. Finally he
obeyed, but as soon as a Marine reached for the grenade he would
playfully snatch it up again. They tempted him with food but he
wanted to play. The men threw sticks to distract him; he wouldn't
abandon his new toy. Finally someone thought of ignoring him.
After a few minutes the fox terrier abandoned the grenade; it was
retrieved and the battle against the Japanese resumed.

After dark the bomb-rockets again hurled into the closely packed
Marines. During a lull the men crouching in Sherrod's shell hole
felt the earth jar under them, followed by a weird noise like "someone banging on the radiator in the apartment below." It was probably a mild tremor, but no one jeered when a sergeant said, "Oh,
my God, the Japs are digging underneath us now."

3.

On the third day, February 21, the naval bombardment once more commenced at 7:40 A.M., and again the Marines launched attacks fifty minutes later with close support from carrier planes. By early afternoon the 28th Marines had blasted through formidable stone and concrete defenses, almost to the base of Suribachi. The general attack to the north also started well, particularly on the extreme left, where tanks could maneuver. Here the 5th Division pushed ahead 1,000 yards. On the right, the 4th Division encountered rugged terrain and heavier fire, and made half that distance.

At dusk the Japanese struck from the air for the first time. Five *kamikaze* based near Tokyo broke through the fighter screen around *Saratoga,* which lay thirty-five miles off Iwo Jima. The first two suicide planes were set afire but kept boring in. They skipped off the water and into the carrier. The remaining three smashed directly into *Saratoga* and exploded. Before the blazes were brought under control, five more planes appeared. Four were shot down, but the fifth dropped a bomb that tore a 25-foot hole in the flight deck. The badly damaged *Saratoga* was compelled to start directly back to America for extensive repairs. A few miles away a single *kamikaze* started fires on the jeep carrier *Bismarck Sea* which could not be contained. Blazing from stem to stern, she plunged to the bottom a few minutes after midnight.

That evening's "Home and Empire" broadcast in Tokyo mentioned the landings of enemy soldiers on Iwo Jima, and spoke of their leaders with uncharacteristic admiration:

"This man Turner is called and known as the 'Alligator' in the American Navy.* He is associated with this name because his work is very similar to that of an alligator, which lives both on land and in the water. Also, the true nature of an alligator is that once he bites into something he will not let go. Turner's nature is also like this.

"Spruance, with a powerful offensive spirit, and Turner, with ex-

* Admiral Turner was never nicknamed "Alligator." The Japanese apparently got the name from the V Amphibious Corps shoulder patch.

cellent determinative power, have led their men to a point where they are indeed close to the mainland, but they find themselves in a dilemma, as they are unable to either advance or retreat.

"This man Turner, who has been responsible for the death of so many of our precious men, shall not return home alive—he must not, and will not. This is one of the many things we can do to put to rest the many souls of those who have paid the supreme sacrifice."

The steady, cold rain continued throughout February 22 as the Marines tightened their hold on "Hotrocks," code name for Suribachi, completely surrounding the volcano except for a 400-yard stretch on the west coast. The Japanese commander, Colonel Kanehiko Atsuji, informed Kuribayashi by radio that his casualties were heavy:

NOW ENEMY IS BURNING US WITH FLAMETHROWERS. IF WE REMAIN IN OUR POSITIONS WE SHALL BE EXTERMINATED. WE WOULD LIKE TO GO OUT FOR THE FINAL ATTACK.

Suicidal attacks had dominated Japanese military philosophy since Guadalcanal, to the enemy's advantage. Kuribayashi curtly replied:

I HAD ASSUMED CHIDORI [Airfield No. 1] WOULD BE OVERRUN QUICKLY BY THE ENEMY BUT WHAT HAS HAPPENED TO MAKE MOUNT SURIBACHI FALL WITHIN THREE DAYS?

The next morning the Marines resumed the assault on the battered volcano, edging up its sheer sides in the face of concentrated fire. Where the defenders ran short of ammunition, they rolled rocks down the steep inclines. Pillboxes and underground galleries were seized. Marines bellied into smaller caves, knives in teeth, to eliminate the enemy in close combat. First Lieutenant Harold Schrier and forty men neared the summit. He had an American flag and instructions from Lieutenant Colonel Chandler Johnson, his battalion commander, to place it "on top of the hill." At about 10:15 A.M. they reached the rim of the crater, which was blanketed with dead Japanese. At the lip they were momentarily pinned down by a burst of fire from a small group on the other side. During this skirmish, somebody found a long piece of pipe. The flag—it was 54 by 28 inches—was secured to one end, and at 10:20 Lieutenant Schrier and five men, including an Indian, Louis Charlo, raised the Stars and Stripes. A photographer from *Leatherneck* magazine began taking pictures, but a sixteen-year-old, Pfc. James Robeson, disparaged his entreaty to pose: "Hollywood Marines!" Two Japanese charged from a cave, one with a grenade, the other with drawn sword. Robeson shot the latter. The other lobbed his grenade at the photographer, who leaped into the crater and tumbled down fifty feet with his camera. It was smashed but the pictures were intact.

From the beach area below, the small flag was barely visible. Men in foxholes cheered and punched one another. There were tears. Ship's whistles and horns screeched. Fortuitously James Forrestal, who had become Secretary of the Navy after the death of Frank Knox, was coming ashore with "Howlin' Mad" Smith. "Holland," Forrestal said gravely, "the raising of that flag on Suribachi means a Marine Corps for the next five hundred years."

Colonel Johnson, who had sent up the flag, turned to his adjutant: "Some son of a bitch is going to want that flag but he's not going to get it." He ordered the original brought down, and another put in its place. A much larger flag from an LST was attached to the pipe at noon. Joe Rosenthal, who had photographed the landings at Pelelieu and Guam for The Associated Press, had arrived too late for the initial flag raising. He almost missed the second in his frantic efforts to pile up stones so he could get a better vantage point. As the chubby photographer balanced himself atop his rock heap, six men started to swing up the flagpole. Rosenthal barely had time to get the shot; other photographers began suggesting different poses. One Marine stood under the waving flag, then three. Finally twenty were persuaded to yell and brandish their rifles. This was the only picture Rosenthal thought might rate a wirephoto; he sent off his film packs to Guam for routine processing.

The Marines attacking north heard the news from the beachmaster. "Mount Suribachi is ours!" he announced over the loudspeaker used to direct the unloading operations. "The American flag has been raised over it by the Fifth Marine Division. Fine work, men." The exhausted fighters took time out to turn toward the flag fluttering on top of the volcano. The loudspeaker continued, "We have only 2,630 yards to go to secure the island."

"Only," someone grunted, "only . . ."

That afternoon General Harry Schmidt came ashore, ready to direct the Landing Force, the largest body of Marines to fight under a single command, three full divisions. He met with the commanders of the 4th and 5th divisions; it was agreed that the reserve division, the 3rd, which had come ashore, would drive directly up the middle toward Airfield No. 2, with the 4th on the right and the 5th on the left. Sherrod asked General Schmidt how long the campaign would last. "Five more days after today," Schmidt replied. "I said last week it would take ten days and I haven't changed my mind."

The first line of Japanese defenses was giving way, but more than twenty-five infiltration teams charged suicidally into the Marine positions, against Kuribayashi's orders, and were wiped out to the man. Just to the rear, however, in the center of Iwo, Airfield No. 2 was heavily fortified with hundreds of pillboxes and concealed batteries. For two days it withstood almost constant pounding by ships, planes, artillery and tanks. Now it was up to the infantry of the reserve division—two battalions of the 21st Regiment. "We have got to get that field today," the commander of the 3rd Battalion told his men on Saturday, February 24. At 9:30 A.M., behind a rolling artillery barrage, the two battalions launched themselves at the seemingly impregnable positions. It was one of the most resolute charges since Pickett's at Gettysburg. The Marines flung themselves at pillboxes with grenades and bayonets. When weapons became clogged by volcanic ash, they closed the enemy with rifle butts, picks—even entrenching tools.

The Japanese—the remnants of the 145th Regiment—would not retreat, and the carnage on both sides was awesome. In minutes a Marine company lost four of its officers, but the two battalions swept onto the airfield. Beyond, the terrain changed from volcanic dunes to "a wild, barren stretch of rocky ridges, cut into crags, chasms, and gulleys." It reminded Sergeant Alvin Josephy, a combat correspondent, of "the Bad Lands of the American West—or, as someone said, like hell with the fire out." From one of the ridges a frenzied horde of Japanese poured out, flinging back the Marines, who re-formed and charged at the ridge again. For an hour and a half the two opponents battled savagely with bayonets and grenades. When it was all over, one third of the island was American.

By nightfall on Sunday the Marines had wrested most of the airfield from the Japanese and pressed on yard by yard toward Motoyama village. Kuribayashi radioed Tokyo that after one week of combat, front-line troops had averaged 50 percent losses, and most of the machine guns and 60 percent of the big guns had been destroyed.

The first picture Rosenthal had taken—the one snapped quickly as the large flag was being hoisted on Suribachi—would become the most famous picture of the war. It reached the United States in time to make the Sunday papers, where it was featured on the front page, including that of the *New York Times*. Its dramatic composition was unforgettable, symbolizing simultaneously heroism, suffering and accomplishment.*

On Monday, the Marines went into battle under clear skies for the first time since the landing. But by noon the inevitable rain resumed, and the three-division attack slowly pushed forward until advance units of the 4th Division reached a formidable rise, Hill 382, to the right of Motoyama, where they were driven off by rockets and mortar rounds. The 4th pressed on the following morning, five battalions abreast. The vicious hand-to-hand fighting continued, bringing the division's daily casualties up to 792.

All along the line Marines suffered heavily, but morale re-

---

* Three of the six Marines in the picture were to die on Iwo Jima. The others were brought back to America to help spur the Seventh War Loan Drive. One, an Indian named Ira Hayes, could not cope with the publicity. "He was a helluva good fighting man, but he wasn't the kind of guy you send on a bond tour," wrote Technical Sergeant Keyes Beech, who accompanied the three men on the tour. "He was terribly, terribly shy and ill at ease. As a defense against his own insecurity, he drank like a fish whenever he could sneak away. Maybe Hayes would have been a lush without the bond tour— but the bond tour helped. If we ever get into another war I'm going to campaign against bond tours. . . . What we used to ask ourselves, in the few minutes of privacy we had on tour, was why the hell it was necessary for us to go around on a vaudeville act to persuade a bunch of fat cats who had grown rich in the war to invest in a sure thing. . . ." During the tour Hayes made one speech from the heart. This was to the National Congress of American Indians. With tears in his eyes he told them that good things were coming out of the war and that "white men are gonna understand Indians better, and it's gonna be a better world." He died an alcoholic in 1955.

mained high. Humorous signs proliferated in caves and were
posted beside foxholes:

SURIBACHI HEIGHTS REALTY COMPANY
OCEAN VIEW
COOL BREEZES
FREE FIREWORKS NIGHTLY!

COOK WANTED

ICHIMOTO'S INN
UNDER NEW MANAGEMENT
SOON AVAILABLE TO PERSONNEL
OF THE U. S. ARMY (WE HOPE)

NOTICE: THIS FOXHOLE IS PRIVATELY OWNED
AND WAS NOT CONSTRUCTED WITH THE
HELP OF THE FEDERAL HOUSING ADMIN-
ISTRATION. NOT BUILT FOR COMFORT
BUT FOR SPEED.

The mounting casualties also revived the altercation between
the Army and the Marine Corps which had first surfaced in the
press during the battle for Saipan. The San Francisco *Examiner,*
a Hearst paper, declared in a front-page editorial on February 27
that there was "awesome evidence in the situation that the attacking
American forces are paying heavily for the island, perhaps too
heavily," and that they were "in danger of being worn out before
they ever reach the really critical Japanese areas." The editorial
went on to praise MacArthur as America's best and most successful strategist:

He wins all his objectives.
He outwits and outmaneuvers and outguesses and outthinks the Japanese.
HE SAVES THE LIVES OF HIS OWN MEN, not only for the
future and vital operations that must be fought before Japan is defeated,
but for their own safe return to their families and loved ones in the
American homeland after the peace is won.

It is our good fortune to have such a strategist as General Mac-Arthur in the Pacific War.

Why do we not USE him more, and indeed, why do we not give him supreme command in the Pacific war, and utilize to the utmost his rare military genius of winning important battles without the excessive loss of precious American lives?

Marine policy was defended the following day by another San Francisco paper, the *Chronicle:*

The recapture of the Philippines remains competent, energetic, and immensely heartening to the American people. We are proud of that job.

To slur the United States Marines in one type of operation, however, to draw odious comparisons between theirs and the type of operations conducted by General MacArthur is to raise a sinister fantasy. To hint that the Marines die fast and move slowly on Iwo Jima because Marine and Naval leadership in that assault is incompetent is an attempt at a damnable swindle of the American people.

The *Chronicle* does not propose to engage in controversy over the relative merits of our fighting forces in the various theaters of war. But neither does the *Chronicle* propose to remain mute when the United States Marines, or any force on the world battle line, is butchered at home to make a Roman holiday.

The War Department itself was searching for ways to reduce casualties on all fronts. The most controversial had already been suggested to Admiral Nimitz by General Marshall's office, which had previously made similar recommendations for the European theater of operations: the use of poison gas. There were large quantities on hand. Nimitz pondered its employment on Iwo Jima but concluded that "the United States should not be the first to violate the Geneva Convention."*

* Stanley P. Lovell of the Office of Strategic Services was sent to Pearl Harbor in late June 1944 to discuss the matter with Admiral Nimitz. When Lovell returned to Washington he learned that the proposal had been disapproved by the White House: "All prior endorsements denied—Franklin D. Roosevelt, Commander-in-Chief." Unexpected opposition had also come from London. The British, who had at first recommended the utilization of gas against certain objectives, now resolutely disfavored its use against Germany; they feared Hitler would retaliate against England. The quote from Admiral Nimitz came in an interview shortly before his death. It concluded with a rueful, "It lost many fine Marines."

General Schmidt's prediction that the battle would be over in ten days was clearly overoptimistic. The Japanese still held more than half of the island. By early afternoon of the tenth day, however, the 3rd Division broke through the second Kuribayashi line, flooding into the rubble that once was the village of Motoyama. On the right the men of the 4th Division had nearly surrounded Hill 382, but it took them two more days to secure it.

That morning—it was Saturday, March 3—the first plane set down on Airfield No. 1's dirt strip, which Seabees had repaired and lengthened to 3,000 feet during the fighting. It was a Navy C-47 hospital plane from the Marianas with medical supplies and mail. A woman, Barbara Finch of Reuters, stepped out amid exploding shells. "How the hell did you get here?" a Marine shouted, and she was pushed in a tent, then under a jeep. She was hustled back aboard the plane, which lumbered down the runway on its return to Saipan. The second plane to arrive was a Curtiss R5C carrying 2½ tons of mortar ammunition.

While the battle still raged, one of its primary aims was fulfilled. On Sunday a B-29 in distress heaved in sight; it was *Dinah Might,* which had dropped its payload on Tokyo. She was almost out of gas and the fuel selector valve would not switch to the auxiliary tanks. First Lieutenant Fred Malo dragged the field twice, then brought in the huge craft. She careened down the runway in a huge cloud of dust, sheering off a telephone pole with one wing and slamming to a stop just before she ran out of space. Faulty valve fixed, *Dinah Might* lifted off for Saipan, her eleven-man crew evangelists for the Marine Corps. (Six weeks later Malo and all but one of the crew would die—some over Kawasaki, Japan, and some on a takeoff crash at Tinian.) Admiral Spruance was watching with satisfaction from his quarter-deck on *Indianapolis;* it justified his urgent request to occupy the island.

That morning Kuribayashi relayed a rambling report to the Army Vice Chief of Staff through the radio station at Chichi Jima. Its length was mute testimony to his fear that it might be his last message.

. . . OUR FORCES ARE MAKING EVERY EFFORT TO ANNIHILATE
THE ENEMY. BUT WE HAVE ALREADY LOST MOST GUNS AND

TANKS AND TWO-THIRDS OF OFFICERS. WE MAY HAVE SOME
DIFFICULTIES IN FUTURE ENGAGEMENTS. SINCE OUR HEAD-
QUARTERS AND COMMUNICATION CENTER ARE NOW EXPOSED
TO THE ENEMY'S FRONT LINE, WE FEAR WE MAY BE CUT OFF
FROM TOKYO. OF COURSE, SOME STRONGPOINTS MAY BE ABLE
TO FIGHT DELAYING BATTLES FOR SEVERAL MORE DAYS. EVEN
IF THE STRONGPOINTS FALL, WE HOPE THE SURVIVORS WILL
CONTINUE TO FIGHT TO THE END . . . WE ARE SORRY INDEED
WE COULD NOT HAVE DEFENDED THE ISLAND SUCCESSFULLY.
NOW I, KURIBAYASHI, BELIEVE THAT THE ENEMY WILL INVADE
JAPAN PROPER FROM THIS ISLAND . . . I AM VERY SORRY BE-
CAUSE I CAN IMAGINE THE SCENES OF DISASTER IN OUR EM-
PIRE. HOWEVER, I COMFORT MYSELF A LITTLE, SEEING MY
OFFICERS AND MEN DIE WITHOUT REGRET AFTER STRUGGLING
IN THIS INCH-BY-INCH BATTLE AGAINST AN OVERWHELMING
ENEMY WITH MANY TANKS AND BEING EXPOSED TO INDE-
SCRIBABLE BOMBARDMENTS.
ALTHOUGH MY OWN DEATH APPROACHES, I CALMLY PRAY TO
GOD FOR A GOOD FUTURE FOR MY MOTHERLAND. SINCE THERE
MAY BE A GREAT CHANGE IN THE BATTLE SITUATION AND TELE-
GRAPHIC COMMUNICATIONS MAY BE CUT, I WOULD LIKE NOW
TO APOLOGIZE TO MY SENIOR AND FELLOW OFFICERS FOR
NOT BEING STRONG ENOUGH TO STOP THE ENEMY INVASION.

He recalled the glory of ancient days; how the Mongols who took
Eki and Tsushima islands were repelled on the shores of Kyushu.

. . . BELIEVING THAT MY MOTHERLAND WILL NEVER GO DOWN
IN RUIN, MY SOUL WILL ALWAYS ASSAULT THE DASTARDLY
ENEMY AND DEFEND THE LANDS OF THE EMPIRE FOREVER.
PLEASE NOTE OUR BATTLE REPORTS AND REMARKS SENT BY
TELEGRAPH. IF THEY HELP MODIFY FUTURE MILITARY TAC-
TICS AND TRAINING PLANS I SHALL BE VERY PLEASED. . . .
FINALLY I HEREBY THANK MY SENIOR AND FELLOW OFFICERS
AGAIN FOR THEIR KIND HELP DURING MY LIFE.
I WOULD LIKE TO ADD THAT WE CO-OPERATED WELL WITH
OUR NAVY UNTIL THE LAST MOMENT.

GOOD-BYE, T. KURIBAYASHI

Japanese resistance continued stronger than the Americans had expected, though there was little co-ordination among Kuribayashi's units. Desperate measures were taken to stop American flame-throwing tanks: volunteers strapped explosives on their backs and became living booby traps as they lay concealed in the path of the advancing vehicles. Their situation seemed so hopeless to Major General Sadasue Senda, who had replaced the troublesome Osuga as commander of the 2nd Mixed Brigade, that he signaled Kuribayashi for permission to launch a final general attack. Kuribayashi angrily ordered him to hold his positions; leaving the caves would merely hasten the collapse of Iwo. But Senda, who had fought against the Russians in Manchuria, proved to be even more mutinous than Osuga. On the evening of March 8 he summoned his officers to his sweltering command cave, a deep labyrinth which reeked of sulphur. There, in the 120-degree heat, he read out instructions for a general attack: a barrage of howitzers, rockets and mortars at six o'clock the next evening would precede a mass assault south toward Mount Suribachi; the Navy would support the attack on both flanks. "I will always be at the head of the troops," Senda declared. They passed around a single cup of water, to seal the order with a toast. Senda thanked them. "Let us all meet again at Yasukuni Shrine in Tokyo."

The transmittal of his order to Navy headquarters, a mile away, was by word of mouth, which led to a misinterpretation: that the attack would take place that night—since Pearl Harbor, the eighth of every month had a special significance. In the darkness almost fifteen hundred Navy men from various units started stealthily toward the line of departure armed with bamboo spears, rifles, grenades and a few light machine guns.

Lieutenant (s.g.) Satoru Omagari—in charge of the former "jet propulsion" rocket unit that had raised such havoc in the first days of fighting—led his 140 men out of their 75-foot-deep cave. He had orders to bring them to the Navy Cemetery, between airfields No. 2 and No. 3, where they would consolidate with other units. Harassed by sporadic mortar and artillery fire, and often lost in the unfamiliar terrain, Omagari arrived with fifteen men. In the sandy little valley there was chaos; more than a thousand men, hopelessly disorganized, milled around in the dark. At midnight the mob was started south toward the front-line positions of the

4th Division. They were to work cautiously through the cratered area, but undisciplined cries of *"Banzai!"* alerted the enemy. An almost instantaneous display of star-shell flares exposed the attackers. Mortar rounds threw up geysers of earth and ash. At least eight hundred men died.

The troops in Omagari's area were pinned down by machine guns. For an hour they crouched in shell holes or behind rocks awaiting the opportunity to steal back into their caves. But Omagari was not ready to give up. With several hundred men he began searching for an Army officer to lead them. He found the cave headquarters of an Army unit, the 26th Tank Regiment, but no one seemed to know anything about a general attack. The hot-blooded Omagari accused them of shirking, and almost came to blows with a captain. The argument brought out the commander's adjutant, a major. He said there would be no attack. Kuribayashi had countermanded Senda's order.

The commander himself, Lieutenant Colonel Takeichi Nishi, joined them. He was a baron from a distinguished family, and Japan's best-known horseman. In the 1932 Olympics in Los Angeles he and his horse, Uranus, had won first prize in the individual jumping event. He invited Omagari and his men to stay on as replacements, but Omagari still refused to believe the attack was canceled. He visualized his Navy comrades retaking Suribachi without him. The battle-weary Nishi was tolerant. "If one wants to die," he said, "he can do it any time. It is only fifty meters to the American positions."

Omagari impetuously left the cave, but by the time he had marshaled his men he realized it was too late to join the general attack. Downcast, he returned and offered his men to Nishi. But Omagari rejected cave warfare for himself. He volunteered to make himself a human bomb and throw himself under the treads of an enemy tank. He was promised his turn would come in a few days.

The following afternoon a patrol from the 3rd Marine Division reached the northeastern end of the island. The men washed their faces in the sea and cavorted barefoot in the surf. They brought back a canteen of salt water, and as proof that the Japanese forces had been split in two, it was sent to General Schmidt with the inscription "For inspection, not consumption." As far as Schmidt was concerned the battle was over, and he informed the Navy that he no longer needed carrier planes for close support. Admiral Turner was already on his way back to Guam.

General Kuribayashi had prevented the launching of a full-fledged general attack, but Senda, who had initiated the idea, could not be restrained. Gathering all the forces in his immediate area that night, and with a grenade in each hand, he led the charge. Around his forehead was a white band emblazoned with the Rising Sun. The attack was as futile as Kuribayashi had predicted. Almost every man died, including Senda.

By March 11 the Japanese were backed into small areas, one on the northeastern end of the island and the other on the northwest coast, where Kuribayashi and Admiral Ichimaru still held out in their deep caves while the remnants of their commands continued a suicidal defense. In the tankers' cave, not far away, Omagari waited for darkness before setting out on his final mission. After midnight he left the cave with a box of dynamite on his back. He found five bodies near a gully—a logical route of advance for American tanks—and worked his way into the stinking pile, smearing his uniform and face with blood, and draping himself with entrails. Who will be using my guts tomorrow? he wondered.

All through the day he waited, perspiring in the sun, for the clank of an enemy tank. The smell was nauseating. Huge bluebottle flies hovered overhead like buzzards. Why couldn't the end come at once and cleanly? Scenes from his childhood and treacherous thoughts interrupted his wish for death. Was this what he had been educated and trained for? He and his generation had been reared only for war to believe it was beautiful and glorious to die for the Emperor. Was lying among the dead covered with stinking guts beautiful? He had revered the forty-seven *ronin,* under the impression that they exemplified the inherent characteristics of the Japanese. If so, why had he and his comrades been bombarded with propaganda designed to make them seek death in battle?

With darkness he crept back to his cave. He tried to clean himself, but the stench of death clung tenaciously. He was irresistibly drawn back to the battlefield, where he spent another day among the corpses, agonizing over the meaning of life as a Japanese. Again no tanks appeared, and by nightfall he returned to the cave robbed of most of his illusions. He was sure of but one thing: never again would he venture out as a human bomb.

Across the island in the other pocket, Navy Lieutenant Toshihiko Ohno and his men had been driven from place to place by the advancing Americans. Ohno had commanded an antiaircraft battery of fifty-four men, but now only five were left. In some ways Ohno, who was six feet tall and slender, was more like a young American officer fresh from OCS than a typical Japanese officer. A recent college graduate, sensitive and gentle of manner, he seemed unsuited to command men, but under fire he had matured. He and his men were huddled in a pillbox about eleven feet square. The entrance was blocked and they had crawled through the gunport. They were sprawled on the concrete floor, sleeping off a feast; they had found two cases of hardtack and candy, three large bags of sugar, and a ten-gallon can half filled with water.

A noise awakened Ohno. Through the porthole he saw a Marine helmet. As he drew his pistol, the helmet disappeared. There was a hissing noise, and a grenade bounded off the floor. Someone leaped in front of Ohno and tossed a blanket over the grenade just before it detonated. It exploded upward and no one was hit. Dazed, Ohno did not at first comprehend that a bundle of dynamite sticks had just been shoved into the porthole. He snatched the smoldering blanket and used it to force the dynamite to the rear of the porthole. He leaped back, hugged the wall and shouted a warning. Everyone stuck thumbs in ears, middle fingers on noses and last two fingers over mouths. *"Tenno Heika banzai!"* he said to himself and visualized his wife and mother. "I'm ready . . ." The pillbox seemed to rise three feet in the air. It was as if his body were being pressed together by some unearthly force. He heard himself cry out, "Ahhh!"

The pillbox swirled with smoke. "Are you all right?" he asked his men. All but an enlisted man named Kitagata replied. Through a hole where the ventilator had blown out, a shaft of light illuminated Kitagata. His head was bleeding and sand peppered his skin. He moaned. A shadow interposed the foggy shaft of light; a Marine was peering down. Ohno clamped a hand over Kitagata's mouth. The shadow withdrew and someone outside shouted, "Let's go!" They were safe for the moment.

4.

On March 14 a small group of Marine officers and men stood at attention around an incinerated Japanese bunker. A colonel representing Admiral Nimitz read a proclamation:

". . . United States forces under my command have occupied this and other of the Volcano Islands. All powers of government of the Japanese Empire in these islands so occupied are hereby suspended. All powers of government are vested in me as military governor and will be exercised by subordinate commanders under my direction. . . ."

Three privates atop the bunker attached the flag to an eighty-foot pole, and as a bugler sounded Colors, raised it. There was little conversation after the ceremony. "Howlin' Mad" Smith, his eyes glistening, turned to his aide: "This was the toughest yet." In the past twenty-four days, seven Marines had won the Medal of Honor by throwing themselves on grenades to save their comrades. "Among the Americans who served on Iwo Island," Nimitz later wrote, "uncommon valor was a common virtue."

Deep underground, not far away, there was another flag ceremony. General Kuribayashi ordered the banner of the 145th Regiment burned to prevent it from falling into enemy hands. Two days later the regiment no longer existed, neither did the 2nd Mixed Brigade. At 5:35 P.M. Kuribayashi radioed Tokyo what he once more thought would be his farewell message:

THE BATTLE IS APPROACHING ITS END.
SINCE THE ENEMY'S LANDING, EVEN THE GODS WOULD WEEP AT THE BRAVERY OF THE OFFICERS AND MEN UNDER MY COMMAND.
IN PARTICULAR, I AM PLEASED THAT OUR TROOPS WITH EMPTY HANDS CARRIED OUT A SERIES OF DESPERATE FIGHTS AGAINST AN ENEMY POSSESSING OVERWHELMING MATERIAL SUPERIORITY ON LAND, SEA AND AIR.
HOWEVER, MY MEN DIED ONE BY ONE AND I REGRET VERY

MUCH THAT I HAVE ALLOWED THE ENEMY TO OCCUPY A
PIECE OF JAPANESE TERRITORY.
NOW THERE IS NO MORE AMMUNITION, NO MORE WATER. ALL
THE SURVIVORS WILL ENGAGE IN A GENERAL ATTACK.
AS I THINK OF MY DEBT OF GRATITUDE TO MY COUNTRY,
I HAVE NO REGRETS.
UNLESS THIS ISLAND IS RETAKEN, I BELIEVE JAPAN CAN NEVER
BE SAFE. I SINCERELY HOPE MY SOUL WILL SPEARHEAD A FU-
TURE ATTACK.
PRAYING TO GOD FOR THE FINAL VICTORY AND SAFETY OF OUR
MOTHERLAND, LET ME SAY "SAYONARA" EVERLASTINGLY. . . .

He ended with three of his poems:

WITHOUT AMMUNITION
IT IS SAD FOR ME TO LEAVE THIS WORLD,
HAVING FAILED TO ACHIEVE MY IMPORTANT MISSION
FOR THE MOTHERLAND.

I COULD NEVER ROT IN THE FIELDS
UNLESS MY SOUL TOOK VENGEANCE
MAY I TAKE UP ARMS, EVEN UNTO THE SEVENTH LIFE.

I WORRY OVER WHAT JAPAN'S FUTURE WILL BE
WHEN WEEDS COVER THIS ISLAND.

It seemed that Kuribayashi was ready, at last, for the general
attack. His final order was simple:

1. The battle is approaching its ultimate phase.
2. Our garrison will make a general attack against the enemy
   tonight. Starting time will be 0001 hours, 18 March, 1945.
3. . . . Everyone will fight to the death. No man will be concerned about his life.
4. I will always be at the head of our troops.

During the day code books and other secret documents were
burned in the Navy headquarters cave. Just before dusk Admiral Ichimaru summoned his able-bodied men, about sixty at
the most, to a large chamber sixty-five yards beneath the surface.

"To date," he said, "you have overcome any and all difficulties, obeyed my orders and fought gallantly against an enemy with overwhelming supplies. The loss of this island means that Yankee military boots will soon tread on our motherland. However, you are warriors of Japan. Don't be too anxious to die. Live in high spirits, kill as many enemies as possible and fight for your seventh life. Thank you."

His senior staff officer, Commander Takeji Mase, stepped forward and in a loud voice read a letter from the admiral to President Roosevelt. It charged Roosevelt with vilifying Japan by calling her "a yellow peril, a bloodthirsty nation, and a protoplasm of the military clique." America was responsible for starting the war, not Japan. "Judging from your actions, the white races—especially you Anglo-Saxons—are monopolizing the fruits of the world at the expense of the colored races. . . . Why is it that you, an already flourishing nation, nip in the bud the movement for freedom of the suppressed nations of the East? All we want is for you to return to the East that which belongs to the East." Nor could the admiral comprehend how Roosevelt dared criticize Hitler's program while co-operating with the Soviet Union, whose principal aim was the socialization of the world. "If only brute force decides who rules the world, war will go on endlessly and there will never be universal peace or happiness. When you achieve your barbaric world monopoly, remember the failure of your predecessor, President Wilson, at the height of his power."

The letter was placed in the stomach band of the communications officer, and an English version* was entrusted to Lieutenant Commander Kunio Akada.

Half an hour before midnight Admiral Ichimaru, leaving almost a hundred wounded behind, went out of the cave with his sixty men. They were immediately overwhelmed by a maelstrom of American artillery, mortar and machine-gun fire.

Kuribayashi left his cave about the same time with almost five hundred troops. But most of them had no weapons and he had no intention of leading a final charge. He merely moved a short distance to the north to a safer cave. They were joined just before

---

* It was found by the Americans and is now in the museum of the U. S. Naval Academy at Annapolis. The complete text is reproduced in the Notes.

dawn by a dozen survivors of the futile Navy assault. Among them was Admiral Ichimaru.

Colonel Nishi had never received the general-attack order, nor did he know the assault had never amounted to anything. As far as he was concerned the battle was not over, and the following night he started north to attack Marines positioned near a large rock overlooking the beach. He carried a whip, the one he had used in the Olympics, and in his breast pocket was a lock of Uranus' mane. At the foot of the rock Nishi and two hundred men, including Omagari, were pinned down by heavy fire. Dawn exposed them to a devastating rain of grenades. In the uproar Omagari heard Nishi call "Assemble!" and crept toward his position with forty others. Nishi said they were in a "hornet's nest," and they would have to find refuge in the caves along the beach.

On Chichi Jima, Major Horie had been unable to make radio contact with Iwo since the night of Kuribayashi's transfer to the new cave. On the morning of March 23, after five days, the silence was broken by a flood of messages. The operator on Iwo Jima was inexplicably on the air again with a backlog of terminal reports which came through without pause. Horie read them choked with emotion. Kuribayashi described the fighting; enemy invitations to surrender (by loudspeaker) were greeted with derision; they continued the assault despite the fact that they had been out of food and water for five days.

. . . BUT OUR FIGHTING SPIRIT STILL RUNS HIGH.
WE ARE GOING TO FIGHT RESOLUTELY TO THE END.

There was silence. It was Kuribayashi's last dispatch, but just before dusk, after almost twenty minutes' silence, the radio crackled again with the operator's final message. This time it was in the clear.

ALL OFFICERS AND MEN OF CHICHI JIMA, FAREWELL.

It was all over except for a final *banzai* charge three days later by a group of approximately 350 Army and Navy men, including 40 *battotai* (a group carrying swords). Out of the rocky gorges on the northwestern tip of the island they crawled half naked, like cavemen, to sweep down in a frenzy over anything in their path. Their wild assault surprised an Air Force and Seabee encampment. A Marine pioneer battalion, hastily summoned, drove into the melee, but it took an entire day of fierce hand-to-hand fighting before two-thirds were slaughtered and the rest dispersed.

Early the next morning, March 27, General Kuribayashi, who had been wounded while moving to another refuge, came to the mouth of his cave with a staff officer, Colonel Kaneji Nakane. Kuribayashi faced north toward the Imperial Palace, knelt and solemnly bowed three times. He stabbed himself in the abdomen and bowed his head. Nakane raised his sword and brought it down on the general's neck. He buried the body with the help of a sergeant and crawled back into the cave to inform Colonel Tadashi Takaishi, Kuribayashi's chief of staff, and Admiral Ichimaru what had happened; then he returned with Takaishi to the scene of Kuribayashi's death. The two men shot themselves.

That evening just before eleven o'clock Ichimaru, followed by ten men, also emerged into the open. A volley of machine-gun fire cut down the admiral and two officers behind him.

The Battle of Iwo Jima had cost the lives of 4,554 Marines and 363 Navy men, the greatest American toll in World War II, considering the length of the battle and the number of men involved. Of the 21,000 defenders, little more than 3,000 were alive. Of these, 216 had become prisoners of war. The others remained huddled in their sweltering, sulphuric caves like hunted animals —hungry, thirsty, desperate and bewildered. For all but a few, the only prospect ahead was death.

27

The Flowers of Edo

1.

About a year before Pearl Harbor the Japanese government had ordered the civilian population to form groups of "neighborhood societies" for the purpose of controlling the rationing and air-defense programs. Each unit comprised about a dozen families, and by now the system had wrought a drastic change in the traditional Japanese family structure. Hardship had forced families to depend more on neighbors than on close relatives, who might live miles away. Everyone, whether high born or low, took part in community air-raid drills, relaying water pails and carrying stretchers, lumber and sand. Democracy extended to food and other rationed necessities, such as clothing: women wore *mompei* (loose baggy slacks), and all men the drab khaki "national uniform." Children had taken naturally to the idea of sharing everything alike, and grownups were learning that only through co-operation could they survive.

There was a slogan, "We are all equals," which took on a new significance late in 1944 when the bombing intensified. Night raids, usually aimed at residential sections, invoked more fear than the daytime attacks. On a food-buying trip in the country, Mrs. Sumie

Seo Mishima could even stop and admire the spectacle of the approaching Bees—the popular name for Superfortresses: "In the eastern sky loomed a flight, another flight and yet another of B-29's . . . Trailing white streamers of exhaust gas, they sailed in perfect formation through the blue-gold sky . . . like shawls of pearly fish riding through the seas of the universe." This esthetic meditation was quickly shattered when the graceful-looking fish dropped their eggs. "The process of splashing the earth with showers of incendiary bullets in rhythmic rumbles of ocean breakers, and hurling heavy bombs, each pounding with a fatal thud into the depths of the globe, was repeated by each flight of planes. On almost every raid, it seemed to us, the American planes brought over new kinds of bombs and shells, which behaved differently in sound effects from those used the last time. The unaccustomed noises intensified the terrors and thrills of each new invasion."

It was an unusually cold winter and some homes had to suffer broken water pipes for months before they were repaired. The novelist Jun Takami noted in his diary that in some homes "where the upstairs toilet pipes had burst and the water poured downstairs, the people had to use umbrellas in the house, and when the water froze on the floor they were able to ice-skate on it."

Fear gave birth to new superstitions: if you ate rice balls with scallions inside, and cooked with red beans, you would never be hit by a bomb. Better yet, if you ate only scallions for breakfast you were sure not to be hit, but after a while there was an added fillip: you had to let someone else know about this trick—along the lines of the chain-letter principle—otherwise it wouldn't work. Another superstition originated when a couple who miraculously survived a close bomb hit found two dead goldfish nearby. They thought the goldfish had died for them, so they put the fish in their family Buddhist shrine and worshiped them. When word of what had happened spread and people found it difficult to obtain live goldfish, porcelain goldfish were manufactured in quantity and sold at exorbitant prices.

Although the bombing raids had wrought drastic changes in the lives of the people in the Japanese homeland, their primary purpose—to obliterate all production facilities—had not been

achieved. "This outfit has been getting a lot of publicity without having really accomplished a hell of a lot in bombing results," Curtis LeMay complained to Lieutenant Colonel St. Clair Mc-Kelway, his public relations officer, on March 6. LeMay had taken over B-29 operations in the Marianas six weeks earlier. He was glad to be out of China, with its insuperable problem of supply, but continued to be plagued by operational failures and mediocre results. The strategic bombing program, principally utilizing high explosives, which had devastated Germany with its concentrated industrial complexes, had done little to slow production in Japan, where two thirds of the industry was dispersed in homes and small factories manned by thirty workers or less.

LeMay hit upon a radical scheme for his planes: to go in low at night, stripped of most armament to increase the payload, and scatter incendiary bombs onto the tinderbox targets over a wide area. Two days later, without consulting Washington, he had field orders cut for a strike of B-29's. At briefing the following morning, March 9, the crews were informed they would attack Tokyo that night at low altitudes—from 5,000 to 8,000 feet. Their reaction of protest was audible. All guns except tail cannons would be removed; the announcement shocked the men to silence. It was suicide.

At 5:36 P.M. the first B-29 rolled down the runway of North Field on Guam and thundered into the sultry air. Fifty seconds later another was airborne, and another and another. One plane couldn't get up enough speed; its brakes were frozen and couldn't be released. Friction turned the landing gear white-hot and the brake fluid burst into flame. When the wheels melted, the gear collapsed. In a shower of sparks the huge craft slithered on its belly, careened off the runway and smashed into the coral beyond with a fearsome explosion.

At 6:15 P.M., B-29's from Tinian and Saipan began joining the elephantine procession in the air. The 333 bombers droned northward. Up ahead against the dark horizon an eruption of explosions appeared—Iwo Jima, where General Senda was about to lead the remnants of the 2nd Mixed Brigade and assorted naval units in his futile general attack. The big planes bounced in the low-level turbulence, but as they neared Tokyo the weather improved. The men, like knights getting into armor, pulled on bulky flak suits and heavy steel helmets, then peered ahead for the glow of fires to be set momentarily by the pathfinders.

Back on Guam, General LeMay paced the floor. If the raid worked the way he hoped, the war could be shortened. He would immediately inaugurate a series of similar raids all over Japan. The slaughter of civilians would be unprecedented, but Japan's industry had to be destroyed. If not, it would take an invasion to end the conflict and that might cost the lives of half a million Americans, perhaps a million.

A new moon cast a dim light but stars shone brightly over Tokyo. At midnight the pathfinders located their aiming points and prepared to mark out the heart of Tokyo with napalm-filled M47 bombs. This three-by-four-mile downtown section was once the gayest, liveliest area in the Orient, but now there was little traffic and most of the shops and theaters were boarded up. Nevertheless, 750,000 low-income workers existed in this congested city-within-a-city that was never asleep. Thousands of home factories were in constant operation.

With its profusion of wooden buildings Tokyo had continually been victim of massive fires from the time it was called Edo. These conflagrations became such an integral part of city life that they were given the poetic name "Flowers of Edo." Despite eventual modernization of the fire-fighting system, there was no guard against disaster by fire. In 1923, following the great earthquake, fire razed most of the city. Two years later Tokyo was devastated again, as it was a third time in 1932.

There were now 8,100 trained firemen and 1,117 pieces of equipment scattered throughout the city, with static water tanks for emergency use. Still, this army of firefighters was not adequate to cover the 213 square miles of the metropolitan area, particularly in time of war. The downtown section remained the most vulnerable. Few fire lanes had been cut through its crowded buildings; they would be ready in a year or two, city officials had promised.

The siren howling around midnight on March 9 sounded just the same as dozens of other alerts. Since previous raids on the city had done little damage, there didn't seem to be any cause for alarm; Radio Tokyo reported that enemy bombers were circling above the seaport of Choshi, fifty miles northeast of the capital, and that there was no immediate danger.

The pathfinders had not yet been discovered in their low sweep toward the unwary city at better than 300 miles an hour. The first two planes, crossing paths over the target, released their strings of bombs in perfect unison at 12:15 A.M. One hundred feet above the ground the M47 missiles split apart, scattering two-foot-long napalm sticks which burst into flame on impact, spreading jellied fire. In minutes a blazing X was etched in downtown Tokyo. Ten more pathfinders roared in to drop their napalm on the X. Then came the main force, three wings, in orderly but random formation, at altitudes varying from 4,900 to 9,200 feet. Searchlights poked frantically at the raiders, and puffs of antiaircraft fire detonated without effect. There was no fighter opposition.

Whipped by a stiffening wind, the fires spread rapidly as succeeding bombers fanned out toward the residential areas to unload their thousands of sticks of napalm. Flame fed upon flame, creating a sweeping conflagration. Huge balls of fire leaped from building to building with hurricane force, creating an incandescent tidal wave exceeding 1,800 degrees Fahrenheit.

Those on the ground were momentarily paralyzed by the awesome sight of the planes blanketing them like huge dragons—greenish from searchlight beams, crimson from the glare below. From the Bunkyo-ku residential district overlooking the center of the blaze, seventeen-year-old Susumu Takahashi watched clusters of bombs—they would soon be nicknamed Molotov Breadbaskets—flower over Tokyo Imperial University. He was a student at Showa Medical College, and after the air-raid alarm he had remained in the house to study for exams while the rest of the family went into the shelter. From the dull-red sky, pieces of flaming debris floated down all around Takahashi. A blaze erupted on the roof of the house and he started slapping at it with a "fire swatter"—strips of rags attached to the end of a long pole. The next house exploded into flames like a gas-filled oven. He ran to his room to pick up three books—he was still going to take the exam the next day—then looked for the family memorial tablets at their private Buddhist shrine. They were gone; his mother must have taken them earlier. He grabbed a silver-and-gold Buddha and carefully selected the best antiques—ivory figures. Out of habit, he pulled the door shut, buried the antiques in the family shelter (it was empty, the others had fled) and started up the street. To the right everything was ablaze. He ran to a main road on the left where a fire engine stood helpless, its hoses slack, surrounded by flaming buildings. There was no water.

The only way to safety was a bridge across the Kanda River but it lay beyond a wall of fire. A group of people huddled in the street, staring at the flames as if hypnotized. Charred trees and telephone poles were scattered across the road like matchsticks. The firemen shouted to make for the bridge—or die. Young Takahashi led the way, leaping over tree trunks that burned like logs in a mammoth fireplace. The others followed in single file. He was blinded by the intense light and gasped for breath. He stumbled, at the end of his endurance. Then through the roiling smoke he made out the concrete bridge, crowded with squatting people. He was safe.

Takahashi had struggled through the fringe of the conflagration. The Sekimuras lived less than two miles from the center of the fiery X. When they first saw flames near the Tokyo Station, they bundled up their four children in quilted hooded fire capes and joined a stream of people heading for one of the branches of the Sumida River. Walking through crisply burned debris that was beginning to fall like black snow reminded Mrs. Sekimura of the fires after the great earthquake of 1923, when she was twelve. The sight of bombs bursting open overhead "like bunches of bananas" entranced rather than terrified her.

They pushed their way across the bridge to escape the roaring blaze that was pursuing them "like a wild animal." A strong wind sucked into the flames swept a stinging storm of pebbles into their faces. They turned, backs to the gale, and plodded slowly away from the conflagration, fascinated at the sight of oil drums rocketing through the roof of a cable factory near the river and exploding into balls of fire a hundred feet in the air.

The center of Tokyo was as incandescent as the sun. Billowing clouds of smoke surged up, illuminated below by orange flames. Thousands crouched terrified in their wooden shelters, where they would be roasted alive, but most of those in the doomed area tried to flee—to the great Buddhist temple in Asakusa, which became their tomb, or, like the Sekimuras, toward the eleven steel bridges spanning the winding Sumida River. For a while these were escape routes, but the flames, too, crossed the river and then there was no escape for those lagging behind.

"The red glow that spread over the southeastern horizon quickly bulged up and filled the entire sky," Mrs. Sumie Mishima observed, "so that even where we were, on the opposite edge of the city, an eerie pink light settled on the earth and clearly lit up the deep-lined faces of the awestruck people. The burning seemed to go on all the night."

The tremendous thermals of heat buffeted the B-29's overhead, tossing some of them several thousand feet upward in the air. Far above, the plane carrying LeMay's chief of staff, Brigadier General Thomas Powers, cruised back and forth. He photographed the conflagration, and reported to LeMay that Tokyo was an inferno. The crews in the last waves could smell the stench of burned flesh; some men vomited. Bombing in Europe had seemed antiseptic from the air; here it was a nauseating reality.

At dawn young Takahashi looked down on the smoldering city from his vantage point in Tokyo Medical-Dental College. The center of the capital was flat wasteland except for stone statues, concrete pillars and walls, steel frames, and a scattering of telephone poles, their ends smoking like tapers. It's gone, he thought.

Mrs. Sekimura, baby on her back, set out to try to recover the belongings she had buried in the ground. The bridge was clogged with the bodies of those who had been trapped. The river itself, almost evaporated, was choked with swollen corpses and household possessions. On the other side, heat still radiating from the ground made the brisk March day feel like early summer. The places she had known most of her life had vanished. All she could recognize was the cable factory; it was twisted and deformed like melted candy. There were bodies everywhere. Some were naked, black; a few were oddly upright, crouched as if trying to run; some were clasping hands in prayer; others seated as if in contemplation. One man's head had shrunk to the size of a grapefruit. Dead covered with straw were piled high in schoolyards. The stink of death permeated the air.

At last she found the ashes of her home but the ground was too hot to dig. She looked around carefully, since it was almost impossible to buy even a piece of paper or a pair of chopsticks; if the loss of a teapot was tragic, the loss of one's possessions meant a reversal to animal life. All she could save was a *kama* for cooking rice; she picked it up with a stick so it wouldn't scorch her hands. Curiously, the sight of so much death left her untouched. She walked mechanically by the corpses of neighbors, unable to shed a tear. There were the mother and daughter who lived across the street. They were completely black except for white rings around the eyes; and they had always been so neat. Dazed, she passed the hospital and its emergency pool of water. It was filled with layer upon layer of sprawling bodies. A man stopped her and remarked that he had been in that human heap. "Everyone else is dead," he said in a toneless voice. "Miraculously I didn't even get hurt."

People poked at the layers of bodies with long sticks in search of relatives. Money spilled out of an old woman's *obi* and stuck to her wet body. Nobody reached for it. Through the gutted wall of a geisha house spilled hundreds of colorful silk kimonos. Mrs. Sekimura lifted the filmy garments tenderly in her hands; they were so expensive. What a shame such material was ruined. Not far away legs protruded awkwardly from the rubble.

Everywhere she encountered corpses in agonized positions— mothers trying to shield charred babies; husbands and wives welded together by the heat in a final embrace. Other survivors had returned and in charcoal were scrawling public messages to their loved ones on walls and sidewalks.

Sixteen square miles of Tokyo had been burned to the ground and city officials later estimated that there were 130,000 dead, almost the same carnage as at Dresden.*

The next night LeMay sent 313 bombers with napalm to Nagoya, the empire's third largest city. Massive incendiary raids on Osaka and Kobe followed in rapid succession. Within a week, forty-five square miles of crucial industrial areas had been incinerated. There could be no doubt that LeMay's new tactics would soon crush Japan's capacity to wage effective warfare. But more was being destroyed than Japanese military power. In the process a multitude of defenseless civilians had already been killed.

Americans' attitude toward bombing had undergone a complete

* The Japan War History office calculated that 72,489 died.

reversal since their sincere revulsion against the indiscriminate murder of civilians in Spanish cities and in China. At the outbreak of war in Europe, Roosevelt, reflecting the humanitarian ethics of his countrymen, dispatched messages to all belligerents urging them to refrain from the "inhuman barbarism" of bombing civilians. Even after Pearl Harbor, leaders of American air power emphasized daylight precision bombing, aimed at the destruction of selected military targets. But gradually the efficacy of this program was not borne out, and areas of bombing were enlarged to include the destruction of anything that sustained the enemy's war effort, including, if necessary, the populace itself. It was a policy which went largely unspoken and unrecorded but it seemed clear that the entire enemy population, at home as well as at the front, would have to be brutalized before it could be forced to surrender.

Public opinion accepted this metamorphosis with only an occasional outburst of moral concern. By 1945 almost every American agreed that Japan and Germany deserved every bomb that fell on their countries. *Time* magazine, for example, described LeMay's fire bombings of Tokyo as "a dream come true" which proved that "properly kindled, Japanese cities will burn like autumn leaves."

Americans in particular had little sympathy for an enemy which had attacked Pearl Harbor without warning and perpetrated such atrocities as the Bataan Death March. It was, consequently, the rare voice which spoke out in the name of humanity for the hundreds of thousands of mutilated and cremated civilians. *America,* the Jesuit weekly, doubted that mass raids squared "either with God's law or the nobility of our cause." An English pamphlet entitled *Massacre by Death* was distributed in the United States with a special introduction endorsed by twenty-eight prominent American educators and clergymen such as Harry Emerson Fosdick and Oswald Garrison Villard; it urged the readers to "examine their hearts" regarding their participation in the "carnival of death." America, including most of its clergy, rejected such exhortations. "God has given us the weapons," retorted one clergyman in the letter section of the *New York Times;* "let us use them." What was criminal in Coventry, Rotterdam, Warsaw and London had become heroic in Hamburg, Dresden, Osaka and Tokyo.

2.

Japan's last important outposts of resistance in the Philippines and Burma were in jeopardy. On Luzon, MacArthur's men had retaken Bataan and Corregidor. Nothing better illustrated the difference between the two foes than their defenses of the tiny, tadpole-shaped island. The Americans had resisted for twelve hours before Wainwright felt that further fighting was meaningless. Three years later the 5,000 Japanese defenders fought for eleven days against an aggressive, overwhelming parachute and amphibious assault. All except 20 died. Strategically it made little difference whether they had fought for eleven days or eleven hours.

MacArthur was in a sentimental mood when he journeyed to The Rock by PT boat. "Gentlemen," he said, "it has been a long way back." On the shattered remnants of the outpost he gave the order to raise the American flag. "Hoist the colors and let no enemy ever haul them down." After the ceremony he inspected the ruins. "This is atonement," he said.

Unlike Corregidor, Manila was not to have been defended at all. Yamashita moved all except security troops out of the city, but no sooner had they left than Rear Admiral Sanji Iwabuchi reoccupied Manila with 16,000 sailors. Iwabuchi had orders from his superior, Vice Admiral Denshichi Okochi, to destroy all port facilities and naval storehouses. Once there, Iwabuchi commandeered the 3,750 Army security troops, and against Yamashita's specific order, turned the city into a battlefield. By the time the Americans secured it on March 4, the capital was rubble and thousands of civilians had died, many as the result of atrocities committed by the Japanese.*

* Like General Homma, Yamashita was tried, convicted and executed on MacArthur's orders. The atrocities committed in Manila weighed heavily against him despite the fact that he had ordered the city evacuated by all troops. The trial was conducted as hastily as Homma's. MacArthur radioed from Tokyo that he doubted the need of the defense "for more time" and "urged" that the tribunal be concluded with dispatch. There was no question but that the verdict would be guilty, nor could MacArthur find any "mitigating circumstances" in his review of the case. "The proceedings were guided by that rationale of all judicial purpose—to ascertain the full truth unshackled by any artificialities of narrow method or technical arbitrariness. The results are above challenge."

But two Associate Justices of the Supreme Court condemned the findings.

But the Philippines were far from cleared. Yamashita had 170,000 well-fed, well-armed troops. Most of them defended the northern redoubt under his direct command, but there were large groups holding out in the mountains east and northeast of Manila and in the Zambales Mountains near Clark Field. Theirs was not to be the long-sought Decisive Battle but rather one of attrition. Yamashita's role was to delay MacArthur, and in the process, kill as many Americans as possible.

The GI's, incited by the deplorable state of American civilian and military prisoners at the Santo Tomás prison, set out to annihilate Yamashita's men with renewed vehemence. Posters urged them to have no mercy on the "yellow bastards." Even without such incitement, the attitude of many American soldiers toward the Japanese led to excesses. In his *Wartime Diaries,* Charles Lindbergh, who toured the Pacific, wrote: "Our men think nothing of shooting a Japanese prisoner or a soldier attempting to surrender. They treat the Jap with less respect than they would give an animal, and these acts are condoned by almost everyone. We claim to be fighting for civilization, but the more I see of this war in the Pacific the less right I think we have to claim to be civilized. In fact, I am not sure that our record in this respect stands so much higher than the Japs'."

The racial implications extended even to the victims of the Japanese—the Filipino civilians—who were disparagingly referred to as "flips" or "gooks."

There would be no battle of attrition in Burma. The British had followed the Japanese survivors of Imphal across the mountains into Burma and across the Chindwin River. On the day MacArthur's troops landed at Lingayen Gulf, January 9, they launched

---

Frank Murphy declared that the "spirit of revenge and retribution, masked in formal legal procedure for purposes of dealing with a fallen enemy commander, can do more lasting harm than all of the atrocities giving rise to that spirit." Wiley Rutledge said it "was no trial in the tradition of the common law and the Constitution," and quoted Thomas Paine: "He that would make his own liberty secure must guard even his enemy from oppression; for if he violates this duty he establishes a precedent that will reach himself."

President Truman refused to commute the sentence to life imprisonment and Yamashita was hanged on February 23, 1946, in Los Baños, a town thirty-five miles south of Manila. He was "calm and stoical." His last words were: "I will pray for the Emperor's long life and his prosperity forever!"

"We have been unjust, hypocritical, and vindictive," said Yamashita's chief counsel, Captain Adolf Reel, Jr. "We have defeated our enemies on the battlefield, but we have let their spirit triumph in our hearts."

an offensive toward Mandalay and the heart of Burma. Still drained by the Imphal disaster, the Japanese could do little to impede the British sweep south.

Ba Maw knew the war was lost and he began preparing for the postwar armed struggle to evict the British from his country. He would have to find ways to keep alive the spirit of freedom among the Burmese, coupled with a continuing hatred for the British raj. He set up a Supreme Defence Council to mobilize war activities among his people. "This is the final battle in our long struggle with British imperialism," he told them. "We have fought it three times before and lost, and so became a subject race for generations. We must now fight and win this fourth and final round with the help of Japan, for if we lose again we shall be slaves for a very long time more."

Ba Maw was successful in implanting a lasting antagonism toward the British but could not slow their drive. On March 9 they entered Mandalay, capturing the Obo railway station and Mandalay Hill, then continued south toward the capital, Rangoon.

Important as the Philippines and Burma once seemed to the Japanese military leaders, they could not escape the inevitable logic that the empire's last hope lay in the successful defense of a relatively small island just 350 miles south of the homeland—Okinawa. Admiral Tomioka, for example, believed the enemy could be beaten there with an all-out effort, and this victory would give Japan six months to negotiate a peace which would guarantee the continuing rule of the Emperor.

The fall of Leyte and Iwo Jima had left General Koiso's Cabinet at the point of collapse. Koiso had purposely been installed as interim premier, and from his first day in office his course had been uncertain. With all the prestige of his position but without genuine support from any faction, Koiso exerted almost no influence on the prosecution of the war and none at all on the subterranean efforts for peace. Unlike Tojo, he did not represent the militarists, many of whom regarded him with suspicion. Nor was he privy to the continuous and complex maneuvers of the peace groups.

Concern over the future of the nation under such leadership was so acute that the Emperor summoned Marquis Kido and suggested that it might be necessary for him to consult the former prime ministers concerning the deteriorating war situation. Only once before, on the eve of the war itself, had the Emperor convened the *jushin* to discuss anything except the selection of a new premier.

Kido had the *jushin* brought to the Emperor's office one at a time, lest the military become suspicious if they appeared as a group. It would also make it easier for each man to speak freely. But except for Konoye's, their advice was vague and poorly thought through, or simply an emotional appeal to continue the fight with determination. Konoye's appraisal was a closely reasoned, if misguided, examination of the political and military abyss into which Japan would fall unless peace were concluded shortly. His opinions were expressed in an eight-page *Memorial to the Throne,* written in his own hand with Japanese brush and read aloud to the Emperor. It is doubtful that any subject other than Konoye would have dared present such a frank evaluation directly to His Majesty. Like almost everything else concerning Konoye it was an anomaly—objective and subjective, practical and impractical. Starting with a courageous pronouncement ("Regrettable though it is, I believe that Japan has already lost the war"), he made a charge based solely on his own growing paranoia toward Communism ("The greatest danger to maintenance of Japan's imperial system comes not from defeat itself but from the threat of a Communist revolution"). Then, in an attempt to prove that Japan was about to be seized by native Reds, he accurately foresaw the course of Marxism in eastern Europe and Korea. His next historical assessment, however, was again faulted by his fixed idea: the Manchurian Incident, the China Incident and the Greater East Asian War, too, had been "a scheme consciously plotted" by Army radicals, themselves puppets of right-wing civilian extremists who were "simply Communists clothed in national essence, secretly intending to bring about a Communist revolution."

Like so many intellectuals who lean far left in their youth and grow conservative with age, Konoye saw the Red menace everywhere. He charged that those who were sponsoring the slogan "One Hundred Million Die Together" had done so at the instigation of "Communists who are trying to throw the country into confusion and bring about a revolution." Moreover, some Army leaders were so infused with pro-Soviet sentiment that they were "urging an alliance with Russia at any cost while others were calling for co-operation with Mao."

Yet the conclusion that he drew from these fanciful accusations was inescapable logic: peace could only be negotiated if the militarists ("Although they know they cannot win the war, I believe they will fight to the death in order to save face") were circumvented. "Thus if the tree is severed at the roots, its leaves and branches will wither and die." His recommendation for dealing with the die-hard militarists, however, was unrealistic, though desirable: eliminate them by a coup d'état, and then negotiate directly with America and Britain.

All its inconsistencies notwithstanding, the rambling *Memorial* stimulated both the Emperor and his chief adviser. Unlike his fellow *jushin,* Konoye had uncovered the core of the problem, and while his solution was impractical, it would eventually be transformed into an efficacious plan for peace by the pragmatic Kido.

Prime Minister Koiso's personal desire to end the war favorably was not curbed by the lack of confidence shown in him by the pacifists and militarists. Perversely, he saw peace with Chiang Kai-shek as the key to honorable negotiations with America and Britain. Moreover, his choice for go-between was a man known throughout the Far East as an intriguer, Miao Pin. An official of the Nanking puppet regime, he claimed to be in secret radio communication with the Chungking government. Koiso's own foreign minister and his most knowledgeable adviser on China, Mamoru Shigemitsu, warned that the notorious Miao was merely trying to promote his own ambitions. "To believe in his mediatory role," Shigemitsu later wrote, "was childish naïveté and betrayal of ignorance of Chinese politics."

Koiso would not listen and persuaded his war minister, Field Marshal Sugiyama, to bring Miao to Japan on a military plane. At the airport near Tokyo, Miao ignored the Prime Minister, who had invited him, and insisted on being driven directly to a meeting with a member of the royal family, Prince Higashikuni, where he tried to ingratiate himself with the Emperor. But His Majesty found such intrigue as distasteful as had Koiso's Cabinet. Miao returned ignominiously to China—subsequently to be executed by Chiang—and with him disappeared Koiso's last hope of remaining in power.

28

The Last Sortie

1.

Extending south from Japan and curving toward Formosa for 790 miles like a long tail was a chain of some 140 islands, the Ryukyus. In the middle of this archipelago lay the last important bastion guarding the homeland, Okinawa. An elongated island about sixty miles from north to south, and only two miles wide near the middle, it was an ideal staging area for invasion of Japan with its flat waist for airfields and two deep-water bays suitable for naval bases. Its climate was subtropical, moderated by the Kuroshio (the Gulf Stream of the Pacific) and the Ogasawara Current. Humidity was high all year round; rainfall was heavy and erratic with a single day's downpour occasionally equaling a month's average. From May to November two typhoons a month swept over the island.

Okinawa was a crossroads of the Orient, lying almost equidistant from Japan, China and Formosa, and had been influenced by all three as well as by the islands of the South Pacific. In 1372 it was taken over as a tributary by the founder of the Ming Dynasty. Two centuries later Japanese from Kyushu ravaged the island but allowed its inhabitants to continue sending tribute to China. This unique dual subservience existed until 1875, when

Hirohito's grandfather dispatched an invasion force which took complete control of the Ryukyus. Four years later Emperor Meiji formally annexed the archipelago, made Japanese the official language and replaced Okinawa's king with a governor. As a colony the 450,000 people of Okinawa—the majority crammed into the southern, more habitable section of the island—continued to live as they had for centuries, scratching out a meager living predominantly as farmers.

This neglect notwithstanding, Okinawa had by the outbreak of war with the West become an integral part of the empire, and was represented in the Diet as one of Japan's forty-seven prefectures. Technically its inhabitants were first-class citizens, but most mainlanders did not consider them their social equals. The Okinawans, with their mixed heritage, regarded themselves as Japanese and were as loyal to the Emperor as any Tokyo resident, though most of them still practiced Chinese ancestor worship, and their *chichi* (protective household gods in the form of fantastic lions) were as much Chinese as Japanese. Only in Okinawa did colorful porcelain *chichi,* in myriad poses and sizes, cling to the tile roofs, ready to strike down any unfriendly intruder.

For the first three years of the Pacific war, fewer than 600 troops were stationed in the Ryukyus, and it wasn't until April 1, 1944, that the 32nd Army, three full divisions and a brigade, was activated on Okinawa. At the end of the year it was significantly weakened by the transfer of the elite 9th Division to Formosa, but the Army commander—Lieutenant General Mitsuru Ushijima, a quiet and competent officer who had recently been commandant of the Military Academy—still had a sizable force: the 24th Division from Manchuria comprised 14,000 men, including several thousand Okinawan conscripts; the 62nd Division, 12,000 troops, mainly infantrymen, who had fought in China; and the 5,000 men of the 44th Independent Mixed Brigade. There was also a single tank regiment of fourteen medium and thirteen light tanks, and various artillery units with a respectable number of 22-mm. machine cannon, 75-mm. guns, 150-mm. howitzers and 81-mm. mortars, as well as twenty-four huge 320-mm. spigot mortars which belched out 675-lb. shells.

In addition, Ushijima could count on two shipping-engineer regiments, a variety of service units and 20,000 members of the

Boeitai, a home guard unit of Okinawans burning with ardor to serve their Emperor.

The withdrawal of the 9th Division forced Ushijima to formulate a new defense plan that would utilize his remaining men to the best advantage. He was almost certain that the enemy would land on the west coast just below the waist of the island along the spacious Hagushi beaches, so he concentrated his men in the south. He also began converting as many naval and service troops into front-line soldiers as possible. From sea-raiding battalions, formed to man suicide boats, he extracted 5,500 foot soldiers, and though they were poorly trained and equipped, they were eager to fight on land. Another 10,000 naval personnel were organized into a force commanded by an admiral. To free more military personnel for combat, 3,900 Okinawans were temporarily assigned to the 32nd Army as labor troops; 600 students became messengers, orderlies and communication assistants at the various headquarters. One group of enthusiastic high school students was trained to fight; 750 of them were formed into special Blood and Iron for the Emperor duty units and trained to infiltrate enemy lines and carry on guerrilla warfare.

Just above Okinawa's two largest cities, Naha and Shuri, the terrain was ideal for defense, and it was here that Ushijima erected a defense line in depth, a series of concentric fortresses, facing north and extending across the island. Numerous caves, blockhouses, and gun emplacements were carved into the ridges and hills connected by a complex system of tunnels. Even the Chinese lyre-shaped tombs which dotted the countryside were transformed into pillboxes, over the objections of the older Okinawans. As at Iwo Jima, Ushijima would let the enemy land and engage him only from prepared positions. By March more than 100,000 defenders, including the *Boeitai,* were in place. The two most experienced divisions manned the main defense line, while the third division and the 44th Independent Mixed Brigade were positioned at the southern end of Okinawa as insurance against any landing in that area. The northern half of the island was given mere token defense —two battalions.

Ushijima had correctly foreseen American plans. They would come ashore at the Hagushi beaches, although there would be a decoy landing in the south. "Iceberg" was to be a joint Army-

Navy operation under the overall command of Admiral Spruance, who had opposed the invasion of Formosa. An Army general, Simon Bolivar Buckner, Jr.—another opponent of Formosa— would lead all the ground troops. His father, one of the Confederacy's first generals, had escaped from a Union prison. The son was a Spartan and went to extreme limits to prove it. During the Aleutian campaign he had slept on a thin mattress with a sheet for cover; he trained himself to read without glasses by squinting his eyes. His Tenth Army was made up of six combat-experienced divisions, half Army, half Marine. The Army trained and rehearsed on Espíritu Santo and Leyte, while the Marines used Guadalcanal. The task of transporting the assault force of 183,000 troops and 747,000 measurement tons of cargo to the battlefield was formidable. Four hundred and thirty assault transports would have to be loaded at eleven different ports, ranging from Seattle to Leyte.

The first step, on March 24, was the capture of the Keramas, a group of small mountainous islands fifteen miles west of Naha. There were but 750 defenders to contend with, and they scattered for the hills and caves. It was obvious before dusk that the islands would soon provide a seaplane base and a fleet anchorage.

That same day a systematic naval bombardment of Okinawa began. A week later frogmen worked openly along the Hagushi beaches, clearing debris and detonating mines, while Japanese onshore watched in admiration mixed with frustration, holding fire as instructed. The climax of the bombardment came on March 31. When it ceased Rear Admiral W. H. P. Blandy, in charge of all preliminary operations, announced that the preparation was "sufficient for a successful landing." At this point, 27,226 rounds of 5-inch or larger-caliber shells had carpeted Okinawa. The effect appeared devastating but the main line of defense was still almost intact. Just before dawn on April 1, Easter Sunday, the crash of naval gunfire again wakened Ushijima's men. Those along the west coast peered out of their shelters at an awesome sight: 1,300 ships massed offshore.

It was L-(for Love) day. At eight o'clock landing craft packed with helmeted assault troops started for the beaches; LST's disgorged their armored amphibians and amphibian tractors also loaded with men and equipment. There was almost no opposition as two Army and two Marine divisions poured ashore during the morning. "This is hard to believe," wrote Robert Sherrod. "I've already lived longer than I thought I would," remarked one infantryman of the 7th Division as he reached the top of a hill. He spoke for everyone. By night more than 60,000 Americans were ashore in a beachhead not quite three miles long and a mile in depth. Except for the uncontested Guadalcanal landing, it was the least costly of any major invasion—twenty-eight dead, twenty-seven missing. "We were on Okinawa an hour and a half after H-hour, without being shot at, and hadn't even gotten our feet wet," reported the GI's favorite correspondent, Ernie Pyle. Okinawa was a piece of cake.

Tenth Army moved swiftly on all fronts, meeting some resistance around the airfields from a *Boeitai* unit, and before the end of the second day the Kadena strip was not only cleared but repaired for emergency landings. On the third day the Marines, who had swung north, spanned the narrow waist of the island. Okinawa was cut in two. The Army divisions going south continued to meet desultory resistance. At the commanding village of Shimabuku they were confronted by a pair of Japanese—trembling old men who bowed repeatedly. One was the headman, the other was Councilman Shosei Kima, a teacher. Kima had persuaded the 1,300 villagers to remain in their homes rather than flee into the countryside and risk starvation.

"You American gentleman!" Kima called out. "Me Okinawan Christian!"

The Americans warily covered the two Okinawans with their weapons. There was a tense wait of several minutes until a Nisei interpreter, Thomas Higa, arrived. *"Sensei* [Teacher]!," he shouted, seizing Kima's hand. "Kima-*sensei*, don't you remember me? My name is Taro Higa. I was one of your pupils in elementary school."

All that day the Americans pushed deeper into the island to the north and south. Where was the enemy? Lieutenant Colonel James Brown of the 12th Marine Regiment, sent a note to the divisional supply officer: "Colonel, please send us a dead Jap. A lot of my men have never seen one. We'll bury him for you."

2.

Without support from any quarter, Prime Minister Koiso's regime was doomed. Nevertheless, he continued to make frantic if futile attempts to save his cabinet. He confused the Emperor by first suggesting a drastic reorganization of it and a moment later offering to resign; he took the same proposal of reorganization to Kido, who reacted coolly; downcast, he returned to His Majesty, who, embarrassed by Koiso's flounderings, said, "Study the matter carefully."

It was a polite suggestion to step down but Koiso continued to insinuate himself. He told Prince Higashikuni he could "properly carry on the war" if he were reinstated on the active list; then he could be appointed war minister. He complained that the Army had repeatedly turned down his request to replace War Minister Sugiyama, and he was going to take the matter direct to the Emperor. Again His Majesty was noncommittal.

Koiso had exhausted every means left to save his government. Piqued, he told Kido on the afternoon of April 4 that he was going to resign the following day. The most important function of the Privy Seal was to select a new premier. By tradition Kido would first have convened the *jushin* and asked for their opinions before advising the Emperor. This time, however, a preliminary investigation had to be made at once, to ensure the selection of a man who would work for peace, yet be acceptable to the Army.

It was an exceptional step but one that had the full approval of His Majesty. On April 5, as Koiso was presenting his formal resignation to the Emperor, Marquis Kido sounded out each of the four military leaders separately. He suggested that it was perhaps time to form "an Imperial Headquarters or Conduct of War cabinet," in which the prime minister, necessarily a military man, would control not only the affairs of state but the Supreme Command. Both Army Chief of Staff Umezu and War Minister Sugiyama were cool to such a cabinet. Umezu acknowledged that the battle on Okinawa was going badly but that Japan "must be prepared to fight to the end." Sugiyama was just as pessimistic, yet held out the hope that once Russia defeated Germany she might advise her allies to make peace with Japan. Navy Chief of Staff Koshiro Oikawa was uncertain about the outcome of the war—he doubted that even a victory on Okinawa would end it; the enemy would simply attack again.

The testimony of these three indicated to Kido that the high command had privately come to realize that the war could not be won. As for the fourth man, Navy Minister Yonai's secret advocacy of peace was, of course, well known to the marquis. Besides, the minister had found a suitable candidate for the premiership: Admiral Kantaro Suzuki. The suggestion seemed ideal to Kido. The former Grand Chamberlain was a "large-scale" man, whom His Majesty affectionately called *oyaji* (old man).

Later that afternoon, at five o'clock, the *jushin*—except Baron Wakatsuki, whose train was late—assembled in the Imperial Chamber to select a premier. They were joined by Kido and the new head of the Privy Council,* who was fortuitously the Privy Seal's choice for prime minister—Admiral Suzuki. In Tojo's first session as a *jushin,* he was alert and aggressive, making it obvious from the first that he would reject any peace candidate. His fellow *jushin* all opposed him but not overtly. For fear of alerting the militarists, they could not risk an open clash.

"Koiso's resignation states that the affairs of the state as well as the Supreme Command need revision," Tojo began. "What does this mean?" It was as much a challenge as a question.

"Prime Minister Koiso doesn't give any special explanations," Kido replied.

"It is not desirable to have many changes of government during the war," Tojo said belligerently. "The next cabinet must be the last one! Now, there are two schools of thought in this nation: one that we should fight till the end to secure the future of the country; the other to bring peace speedily even at the expense of unconditional surrender. I believe we must first settle this point."

"The next cabinet must consider a wide variety of subjects," said Admiral Keisuke Okada, who like Suzuki (his private choice for prime minister) had had such a narrow escape during the 2/26 Incident. "This is the cabinet on whose shoulders will rest the destiny of our nation until the end, and which will marshal

* Yoshimichi Hara had died in 1944.

the entire strength of the nation. Questions such as peace and war cannot be determined here."

There was an uneasy pause and two of the civilians—Hiranuma and Hirota—attempted to placate Tojo. Both asserted, tongue in cheek, that the war must be fought to the end. The *jushin* began debating the requisites of the future prime minister but without naming any one person. At last, after an hour, it was President of the Privy Council Suzuki who suggested that one of the *jushin* themselves accept the post. "Since the physical strain is so great, I should like to ask Prince Konoye, the youngest in the group, to come forward."

Konoye declined; he was too compromised by the mistakes and commitments of his three past governments. Hiranuma agreed that Konoye was unacceptable on these grounds, reiterated (for Tojo's benefit) that the war must be prosecuted vigorously, and then proposed the favorite candidate of Kido and Okada—Admiral Suzuki. The response was enthusiastic.

"I agree," said Konoye.

"Very good idea," said Wakatsuki, who had arrived out of breath and apologetic. "We couldn't make a better choice."

Suzuki himself objected; he had promised his family he would not accept the post. "I think I told Admiral Okada once that if a military man goes into politics, he would only lead the nation to defeat. This is proved by the fall of Rome, the eclipse of the Kaiser and the fate of the Romanovs. Because of this principle, I cannot accept the honor. Besides, I am hard of hearing."

Hiranuma begged him to reconsider. "The public trusts your honest and loyal character."

It was difficult even for Tojo to disapprove of Suzuki—he was a devout Taoist, free of ambition; he came from a solid military background; his brother was a respected general—but he lacked one vital qualification. Tojo began by praising the admiral but challenged his tenet that the military should avoid politics. "The enemy is getting impatient. He will try a bold strategy; he is likely to attempt landing somewhere on Japan proper. Home defense will then become a vital matter. The government and the high command must be fused into one. Therefore the premier must be a soldier on the active list." He proposed Field Marshal Shun-roku Hata.

Kido restrained himself. "What is your opinion, Mr. Hirota?"

"We must have someone from the Army or Navy who can control and lead them."

"Your opinion, please, Admiral Okada?"

Okada refused to endorse anyone except Suzuki, who had been summarily rejected by Tojo. "I know of no one," he said, "so I can say nothing."

Kido acknowledged that the homeland would soon be a battlefield and the new cabinet would need the full confidence of the nation. But there he parted company with Tojo. "Personally," he said, "I hope that His Excellency Suzuki will rise to the occasion." He turned directly to Tojo. "We must look at the situation in a wider perspective than yours."

Tojo glared at Kido. Until now he had curbed his bitterness toward the Privy Seal, whom he blamed for his own downfall. "Be very careful, otherwise I'm afraid the Army will *soppo o muku* [turn its head away]! If it does, the new cabinet will fall."

The phrase infuriated rather than intimidated Kido. "It is very serious to have the Army turn its head away from us," he said. "Do you yourself feel that way?"

"I can't say that I don't."

Kido stood his ground. "The atmosphere at this meeting is really quite antimilitaristic. Perhaps the people will turn their heads away from the Army!"

Tojo's threatening posture also provoked Okada to action. "At a time as critical as this," he exclaimed indignantly, "how dare a man who once accepted the imperial command to be premier say that the Army might turn its head away!"

Tojo realized he had gone too far. "I'm sorry," he said. "I take back what I just said. I meant to say that the Army will find such a choice disagreeable."

Tojo was isolated. The whole trend of the meeting had turned against him.

"Keeping all this in mind," Kido summed up, "I will present my views to the Emperor and ask for his decision." A few minutes later, at eight o'clock, the meeting was adjourned, and the members filed to a nearby room for dinner. Before they were through, Kido asked Suzuki to return with him to the conference room. "If you form a government," Kido told him, "we would have to ask you to carry out extremely important tasks." Once more Suzuki demurred; he didn't think he was fit for the job and he lacked confidence.

Kido persisted. The times were too perilous to decline on the grounds that a military man should not become involved in politics. "It is beyond that, Admiral. We must recommend someone to the Emperor whom he trusts implicitly."

Suzuki capitulated. "If the Emperor orders me to form a new cabinet, I will do it," he said. There was no emotion, not a trace of reluctance in his voice. At ten o'clock the seventy-eight-year-old admiral, his back bowed with age, entered the Emperor's study. His Majesty, who was alone except for Grand Chamberlain Hisanori Fujita, said simply, "I order you to form a cabinet." He omitted the traditional admonitions and conditions.

"I am very pleased to be so honored by His Majesty's offer but I beg to decline as I did at the *jushin* meeting held late this afternoon." Within an hour he had changed his mind twice. "I am merely His Majesty's humble naval officer and have had no experience in political affairs. Further, I have no political opinions. My motto has been to abide by the adage of Emperor Meiji to the effect that military men should never interfere in politics. Therefore, begging His Majesty's pardon, I must refrain from accepting His Majesty's offer."

The Emperor smiled understandingly. "I know, Suzuki, what you're trying to say and appreciate your position, but at this critical moment there is no one but you for this task. That is why I have asked you."

As he slowly backed away, Suzuki said, "With His Majesty's permission, I wish to think it over fully," but the Emperor's sincerity had already decided him to once more change his mind. As a result of more than seven years' service as Grand Chamberlain, he had also interpreted correctly the unspoken words of His Majesty: to end the conflict as soon as possible.*

* The Emperor was equally sensitive to Suzuki's aims. After the war he told Kido's chief secretary, Marquis Yasumasa Matsudaira, "I was aware of Suzuki's sentiments from the very beginning of his appointment as premier, and likewise I was convinced that Suzuki understood my sentiments. Consequently I was in no hurry at the time to express to him my desires for peace."

3.

That evening on the Inland Sea, farewell parties enlivened the superbattleship *Yamato* and nine other ships of the Second Fleet. Its commander, Vice Admiral Seiichi Ito, had been ordered by Admiral Soemu Toyoda, commander of Combined Fleet, to lead these remnants against enemy vessels anchored off Okinawa. Toyoda informed all commanders in Combined Fleet of the suicide sortie:

THE FATE OF OUR EMPIRE TRULY RESTS UPON THIS ONE AC-
TION. I HAVE CALLED FOR THE ORGANIZATION OF A SURFACE
SPECIAL ATTACK UNIT FOR A BREAKTHROUGH OPERATION OF
UNRIVALED BRAVERY SO THAT THE POWER OF THE IMPERIAL
NAVY MAY BE FELT IN THIS ONE ACTION IN ORDER THAT THE
BRILLIANT TRADITION OF THE IMPERIAL NAVY'S SURFACE
FORCES MAY BE EXALTED AND OUR GLORY HANDED DOWN TO
POSTERITY. EACH UNIT, REGARDLESS OF WHETHER OR NOT IT
IS A SPECIAL ATTACK UNIT, WILL HARDEN ITS RESOLVE TO
FIGHT GLORIOUSLY TO THE DEATH TO COMPLETELY DESTROY
THE ENEMY FLEET, THEREBY ESTABLISHING FIRMLY AN ETER-
NAL FOUNDATION FOR THE EMPIRE.*

The party Rear Admiral Keizo Komura gave for commanding officers of his Second Destroyer Squadron aboard his flagship, the light cruiser *Yahagi,* was boisterous. Each ship had taken on just enough fuel for a one-way trip, but knowledge of this and the certainty of their death seemed to free the officers from care. Komura and Captain Tameichi Hara, skipper of *Yahagi,* left their comrades singing the fraternal "Doki no Sakura" and went on an impromptu tour of the ship. In the sailors' quarters they found men sleeping peacefully in their hammocks. In an engine room a machinist's mate sweating diligently over a generator told Hara,

* After the war Admiral Toyoda said, "I knew very well what the fate would be of warships without air cover, and that the probability of success was very slight. Nevertheless, we had to do everything to help our troops at Okinawa."

"I changed watches with my buddy who likes to drink." He wanted to be absolutely sure there would be no power failure at Okinawa.

Hara clambered topside, overwhelmed with emotion and alcohol. He felt tremendously happy as he clung to a post for support. *"Nippon banzai!"* he yelled, tears streaming down his cheeks. *"Yahagi banzai! Nippon banzai!"*

Vice Admiral Ryunosuke Kusaka, Toyoda's chief of staff, veteran of Pearl Harbor, Midway and the carrier battles off Guadalcanal, had vehemently opposed the suicide sortie of the Second Fleet; *Yamato* could be used to better advantage in the battle for the mainland. But he was the one selected to fly to the Inland Sea on the morning of April 6 (the fleet would depart that evening for its rendezvous with destiny) to explain personally the significance of the mission. Ito understood; he wanted advice on one matter. "What should I do if we are so badly damaged on the way that we can't proceed?"

Kusaka could not help him. "You'll have to decide that for yourself." They drank a last cup of *sake*.

"I see," said Ito. "Please do not be uneasy about me. My mind is calm. I have no regrets and am leaving willingly." He asked Kusaka to address his senior officers. Kusaka told them it was Combined Fleet's last chance as well as the nation's. They must break through the American naval force off Okinawa and ground their ships on the island. *Yamato*'s big guns—their range was 25 miles—could devastate the enemy positions.

There were private doubts but no one voiced them. The captain of *Yamato,* however—Rear Admiral Kosaku Ariga—was eager. With a perpetual grin, he slapped his stomach every time Kusaka made a point. Captain Hara wrote his family that he was going on a surface attack mission:

. . . It is a great responsibility as well as a great honor to be skipper of a ship in this sortie to Okinawa. Know that I am happy and proud of this opportunity. Be proud of me. Farewell.

Extra supplies were off-loaded from the ships. The sick as well as the midshipmen were compelled to disembark against their will. The sun shone through the mist as the fleet weighed anchor at 3 P.M. Hara's cruiser, *Yahagi,* got under way first, followed by four destroyers, and finally *Yamato* with four more destroyers.

As the ten-ship column slowly proceeded south through the Inland Sea, the first of ten mass air raids was launched against ships clustered off Okinawa. For almost four hours, 341 bombers dropped their explosives in conventional style while 355 *kamikaze* plummeted down on the Americans. By dark three destroyers, an LST and two ammunition ships had been sunk, and ten other ships heavily damaged.

On *Yamato,* Admiral Ito was elated by reports that thirty enemy ships had been seen going down, while another twenty were afire. Overhead Kusaka followed the column in a floatplane as far as his fuel would allow, then waved an arm in farewell as the little plane banked away. That evening *Yahagi*'s thousand-man crew assembled on her deck to hear Captain Hara read a final message from Admiral Toyoda exhorting them to fight to the end—the fate of the nation rested "on this operation." As the shouts of *"Banzai!"* subsided, Hara added practical strictures of his own, which scandalized most of the crew: "Our mission appears suicidal, and it is. But I wish to emphasize that suicide is not the objective. The objective is victory. You are not sheep whipped to a sacrificial altar. . . . Once this ship is crippled or sunk, do not hesitate to save yourselves for the next fight. There will be other battles. You are not to commit suicide. You are to beat the enemy!"

This time there were no *banzai.* A perturbed lieutenant broke the silence: he had been taught at the Academy to die with his ship. Hara understood his concern. "In feudal times," he said, "lives were wasted cheaply, but we are in the twentieth century. The code of *bushido* says that a warrior lives in such a way that he is always prepared to die." But this didn't mean that their lives should be forfeited meaninglessly. "We are to win this war and not think of dying." He called on them to turn the tide of battle. There was a spontaneous cheer for the Emperor and *Yahagi.*

At 8 P.M. the Second Fleet cautiously picked its way through the mines of Bungo Strait and sortied into the Pacific. Ito ordered a course at 20 knots down the coast of Kyushu. (His column had already been sighted by two American submarines.) At dawn the ten ships entered the open sea below the island. They shifted into a ring formation with *Yamato* in the center, and began zigzagging south toward Okinawa at 24 knots. The last escort planes turned back, and as the coast of Kyushu dropped out of sight, the fleet was alone.

Rain from low leaden clouds swept the Japanese ships at 8 A.M. An hour later one of the destroyers, *Asashimo*, dropped out of the ring, signaling that she was having engine trouble but would try to make repairs. Before long she too was out of sight. Slowly the overcast broke and at 11:30 a seaplane appeared about ten miles to the east. It was American. Then came a warning from an island lookout station ahead that 250 enemy planes were winging south.

Admiral Spruance, still in command of Fifth Fleet, had told Marc Mitscher, Task Force 58, to let the enemy ships continue south, leaving them to the guns of surface units, but Mitscher wanted this opportunity to demonstrate once and for all that his airmen could sink the most formidable ship afloat; naval airmen claimed that they had sunk *Musashi* in the Philippines, but submarines could possibly have done it. The unexpected appearance of *Yamato,* her sister ship, "provided a clean-cut chance to prove, if proof was needed, aircraft superiority."

Mitscher sent off planes from Task Groups 58.1 and 58.2, then turned to his chief of staff. "Inform Admiral Spruance that I propose to attack the *Yamato* sortie group at 1200 unless otherwise directed." The message to Spruance read: "Will you take them or shall I?" Spruance scribbled on his message blank: "You take them."

On *Yahagi*'s bridge, shortly after noon, Admiral Komura saw the approaching planes first. "Here they come!" he exclaimed to Captain Hara. Rapidly the ships opened formation as crews scrambled to battle stations. The fleet was abruptly blanketed by a rain squall, but only for ten minutes. A lookout on *Yahagi* called out, "Planes on port bow!"

Hara turned. Planes, more than forty of them, were diving out of a low thick cloud. *Yamato*'s 150 antiaircraft and machine guns hesitated momentarily, then the sky erupted with black puffs, crisscrossed by tracers. But the Americans burst through this wall of flak. Two bombs crashed near *Yamato*'s mainmast. A torpedo ripped into the battleship's port side.

The 8,500-ton *Yahagi* heeled sharply in the rain to avoid the resolute assault, but at 12:45 P.M. she staggered from a bomb. Almost immediately a momentous shudder ran through the ship; a torpedo had plunged into her port side just below the waterline. The cruiser coasted to a stop, helpless and dead in the water, as a second group of attackers dropped out of the clouds. A bomb detonated on the forecastle, another in the stern; a torpedo rammed into the starboard bow. *Yahagi* vibrated violently, as if, thought Hara, she were made of paper.

The planes climbing away through patches of clear sky seemed almost cocky, and in the abrupt, unearthly quiet, Hara surveyed his wrecked cruiser in dismay. Admiral Komura wanted to transfer to one of the destroyers and continue on to Okinawa. The destroyer *Isokaze* was signaled to come alongside to take on survivors, but as she slowly closed, the hapless destroyer was caught by a second wave of planes bursting through a cloud. *Yahagi*, too, was raked by machine-gun bullets. Komura refused to escape in a cutter. He would die on *Yahagi* rather than on some nameless little boat.

A few miles away the twisted decks of *Yamato* were jammed with butchered bodies, a tangle of intestines, limbs, torsos. Blood coursed down the scuppers. The sides of the battleship had buckled and she had slowed to 18 knots. But Admiral Ariga kept her on course to Okinawa. At 1:35 P.M. a third wave—it looked like 150 planes—swept in, concentrating on the damaged port side. *Yamato* heeled and swerved, but two more torpedoes—the fifth and sixth—drove into the left side while seven or more bombs exploded on the center deck. Machine-gun bullets swept the ship "like rain," annihilating half of the antiaircraft gun crews. Steering was damaged and the list increased to 15 degrees.

At 1:50 the officer supervising water control phoned the bridge: "We have reached maximum water level. To prevent further listing we must flood the starboard engine rooms." This meant cutting speed to 9 knots, but the commander of air defense had been pleading for half an hour to correct the listing so he could fire his guns. The executive officer, Captain Jiro Nomura, hesitated but a moment. "Flood the engine rooms," he said.

Slowly the battleship began to level. Then another torpedo hit the port and the listing resumed. At 2 P.M. *Yamato* took her eighth torpedo, this one on the starboard side. An urgent call came from the emergency steering room: "Too much water here. We can no longer steer—" The steering commander's voice was cut off.

"Bring the ship north!" Admiral Ariga shouted. Traditionally a dead man was faced north; Ariga wanted to do the same for the dying *Yamato*. But the men in the emergency steering room had drowned at their posts, and the ship began circling slowly to port, out of control, just as the fourth wave appeared. The temporary hospital on the bow was obliterated. Three more torpedoes knifed into the hulk. Listing increased to 18 degrees; speed slowed to 7 knots.

The cruiser *Yahagi* was rapidly settling, her decks already awash. She had absorbed thirteen bombs and seven torpedoes. Everywhere he looked Captain Hara saw destroyers either sinking or in flames. Two seemed unharmed and they were darting protectively around *Yamato*. Admiral Komura felt water creeping up his legs. He glanced at his watch—it was 2:05. Just then he was sucked under. He knew it was the end of his life but he remained conscious, engulfed in swirling water, for what seemed an eternity before he shot to the surface. As he paddled through the oily water he saw a black-faced man. It was Hara. At the crest of a wave Hara got a glimpse of *Yamato* six-odd miles away. Planes swarmed around her like gnats. But she was moving, a beautiful sight!

On *Yamato*'s bridge Executive Officer Nomura noticed red lights flash on the warning board. He approached to see where the danger was. Half a dozen lights glowed—gun turret No. 1 and at least five ammunition storerooms. Were they going to have a chain explosion? Of the 1,170 rounds for the big guns, 3 had been fired. If the remaining shells detonated, the "unsinkable" *Yamato* would burst at the seams. A backup warning device began its ominous buzzing, then another, and another and another. He heard Ariga shout at him, "Can't we pump water into the ammunition rooms?" and his voice seemed to be "tearing his throat." It was impossible. The water control command post was destroyed. Nomura waited for the explosion that would obliterate them all.

He thought with a measure of satisfaction, Well, that's all right. It will be a samurai's hara-kiri.

Shortly after 2:15 P.M. the twelfth torpedo struck the port side, as if, Nomura thought, "we had received the *coup de grâce.*" If the order to abandon ship wasn't given without delay, the crew would be lost. But no instructions came from Admiral Ariga. Nomura lurched up the narrow spiral staircase to the second bridge, where he could survey the ship. Normally the top deck was twenty-five feet above water level; the port side of the deck was awash. It was incongruous to see men sitting at the bow smoking and eating hardtack. Inexplicably, Nomura was annoyed at their nonchalance.

Towering water columns geysered on either side of the ship. Nomura's eyes swept the superstructure. Something was missing. The flag! He took another look; the mast itself was gone. Were the pictures of the Emperor and Empress safe? During a battle they were kept in the main gun command post, the most armored place aboard ship. Nomura phoned the gun commander and learned he had locked himself in his cabin with the pictures lest they float away when the ship sank.

With *Yamato* listing more than 30 degrees, Nomura phoned Ariga. "The end is near," he said. It was time for the entire crew to come topside. Ariga, in turn, informed Admiral Ito over the voice tube that there was no longer any prospect of correcting the list.

"Fleet Commander, your person is valuable. Please leave the ship with the crew. I alone will remain." Ariga gave orders to assemble on the upper deck, then phoned Nomura, who was still on the second bridge. "Executive Officer," he said hoarsely, "leave the ship immediately and report the details of the action to Combined Fleet." Nomura's protest was curtly ignored by Ariga. "I'm remaining with the ship. Be sure to get home alive."

"Captain," Nomura insisted, "I'm staying with you."

"Executive Officer, that is an order." He hung up and told a crewman to lash him to the compass post. Sailors started tying each other to the bridge binnacle. "What are you doing?" Ariga shouted angrily. "You young men jump in and swim for it!"

Ito refused to leave the ship too. He shook hands with Chief of Staff Morishita, and while his staff looked on "with ten thousand feelings," the admiral balanced his way along the listing deck, opened the door of a spiral staircase and disappeared. His aide made a move to follow but Morishita shouted, *"Baka!* Young men should live to serve the Emperor!"

At 2:25 P.M. the listing increased rapidly until the great ship was rolling on her beam ends. Cries of *"Banzai!"* were drowned out by the rush of water. *Yamato* was on one side, like a foundered whale. Lights blacked out as gun wreckage, ammunition, pieces of bodies slid inexorably into the sea. Men struggled up the almost vertical deck, slipping on their comrades' blood. At the top they clambered over the starboard rail, where they clustered on the side of the ship.

Executive Officer Nomura felt himself being pulled under water by a titanic force. In the clear sea he saw other men "dancing about" in the whirlpool. Below was a bottomless dark blue. The light above diminished. Close to death, he felt his sense of awareness becoming unexpectedly clear. He tumbled deeper and deeper in agony. Bright red flashes shot through the water. A series of concussions slammed him like battering rams. It was as if "heaven and earth were blowing up." The ammunition was exploding under water. Nomura was propelled to the surface. Balls of fire arched across the waves. He rolled over on his back and floated. The end of *Yamato,* he thought; the end of the Imperial Navy.

Aboard the destroyer *Yukikaze* its captain, Commander Tochigi Terauchi, watched in despair as *Yamato*—it stood for "Japan"—rolled over and disappeared. He signaled Captain Masayoshi Yoshida, the new senior officer of the fleet, who was aboard the destroyer *Fuyutsuki:* "Recommend we proceed with mission."

"Pick up survivors and then we will decide course of action" was the answer.

Yukikaze's torpedo officer wanted to lower a cutter for survivors but Terauchi stopped him. "This is no ordinary mission," he shouted. "This is a suicide attack. Even with *Yamato* gone we should continue." He signaled Yoshida again, requesting reconsideration, then ordered his men to pick up survivors but only those who could be used in the attack. "Ignore the wounded!"*

Those in the water faced a double hazard—abandonment and

---

* *Yamato* had a crew of 3,332, of whom 269 survived.

bullets from strafing American planes which systematically stitched a pattern of death across the battle area. Hara watched in wonder as a flying boat skimmed the surface and settled to taxi speed nearby. It churned toward a patch of water dyed green. An American pilot scrambled out of a life raft into the plane, and as it heaved out of the sea like an aged goose, Hara felt envious.

It was hours later, near dusk, when Hara himself, along with Admiral Komura and other survivors of *Yahagi,* was finally picked up by the destroyer *Hatsushimo.* Komura took time to clean his oily face and put on a borrowed uniform before he wrote out a message for Combined Fleet: "We are now heading for Okinawa." His entire fleet consisted of two sound destroyers; two other destroyers had survived and both of them were limping back to Japan. But before Komura's message could be transmitted, Combined Fleet canceled the entire Okinawa mission. *Hatsushimo* reversed course for home. It was Komura who had sent the first planes over Pearl Harbor—the search planes from *Chikuma*—and he had survived the last sortie of the Japanese Navy. He had seen the beginning and the end. "I've had enough," he muttered.

4.

In Tokyo that night Hajime Suzuki, the only son of the next prime minister, could not sleep. His father, who had miraculously survived the 2/26 Incident (the bullet that had pierced his heart was still lodged in his back), undoubtedly faced danger from radical young officers again. But Hajime was no longer a child and felt he should become his father's shield. Early the next morning Hajime told Suzuki that he would quit his job at the Agriculture Ministry and become his personal secretary. "Don't accompany me to death," said the admiral. "I have come a long way but you still have far to go." Hajime could not be dissuaded—personal aspirations would be meaningless in a defeated Japan.

Suzuki summoned Admiral Keisuke Okada to his house and asked him to serve as munitions minister in the new cabinet. Okada was as appalled by the suggestion (he had been retired from the Navy for seven years and remained anathema to the radical officers) as he was by the confusion in the Suzuki household. The admiral was surrounded by well-meaning amateurs who could hardly use a telephone properly, let alone help him select a cabinet. Okada phoned his son-in-law, Hisatsune Sakomizu, who had spirited him out of the Prime Minister's (Okada's) official residence in 1936. "I am now at Admiral Suzuki's, helping him form a cabinet," he began. Sakomizu, with his shrewd grasp of both politics and the military, was "the only one" who could prevent Suzuki from making disastrous mistakes. Within the hour Sakomizu left his post at the Finance Ministry to become cabinet secretary.

Suzuki's greatest strength was a conviction that he was best qualified to end the war, but he had not yet made up his mind how to go about it. If he announced such a "defeatist" policy, even to his cabinet, he would be forced out of office or assassinated. For a while he would have to play *haragei* (the "stomach game"), that is, to dissemble, to support the war while seeking peace. As a result, Konoye refused a cabinet post when Suzuki would not give any assurance that he would "work for peace." On the other hand, he was quick to promise Marshal Sugiyama that he would carry on the war to its ultimate end, and moreover, told reporters, "Now is the time for every one of the hundred million people to cast away what holds them down and to become the glorious shields for the defense of the national structure. I, of course, will deal with the national administration and am prepared to fall as the spearhead of you, the people. I ask you, the people, to manifest a new fighting power with the courageous and furious will to drive ahead over my body, and thus to put the Imperial Mind at ease."

At the time, Suzuki did not reveal his stratagem to anyone, but his son, Hajime, intuitively understood his father and informed close friends, in a written announcement, of his true intentions.

The Cabinet was invested on April 7, though the most significant position, that of foreign minister, had not been filled. The other selections had been based on advice by fellow *jushin* and Sakomizu, but after considerable thought Suzuki's preference for the man who would have to engineer peace negotiations was Shigenori Togo. Investigation indicated that Togo, who had held the post at the time of Pearl Harbor, had opposed going to war and later resigned in opposition to Tojo's "dictatorial and high-handed policies."

Togo was rusticating in Karuizawa, the favorite resort town of diplomats near the Japanese Alps, when he got a phone call from a go-between—the governor of Nagano Prefecture—transmitting Suzuki's offer. Togo's reply was blunt: Not until he had discussed the matter with the new Prime Minister and "reached an agreement of views." He would not return to public life unless he had a free hand. In Tokyo, however, he found Suzuki unwilling to abandon *haragei,* even in a confidential conversation with someone who shared his own views. "I assume you took office with some definite things in mind," Togo told him in his heavy Kyushu accent, "since it will be anything but easy to manage the affairs of state now, with the war effort in its last throes."

Suzuki's answer could not have alienated Togo more: "I think that we can still carry on the war for another two or three years."

Togo declined the post. "Even if I felt able to accept the grave responsibility of our diplomacy, the Prime Minister and I would be unable to co-operate effectively so long as we held divergent views on the prospects for the war."

But the matter did not end there. Too many others saw Togo as an advocate for peace and each in turn brought pressure upon him. Within twenty-four hours he was importuned by half a dozen leaders, including two *jushin* and the Emperor's chief adviser. Admiral Okada, for instance, argued that Suzuki's policy was not "necessarily rigid" and Togo could "help mold it," and Okada's son-in-law, Sakomizu, excused Suzuki: it would have been too hazardous for him to speak of an early peace at their initial meeting. "Such language, coming from one in the Prime Minister's position and in those circumstances, might have had undesirable repercussions."

Togo could not understand such circuity. If Suzuki had agreed with him about peace, why couldn't he have let him know in their private conversation? If Suzuki did not even trust the man he wanted as foreign minister, how could they possibly co-operate in the critical days ahead?

The next appeal came from the office of the Privy Seal. Matsudaira, Kido's chief secretary, revealed that the Emperor himself was hoping the war would end. This concerted effort brought Togo a second time to Suzuki, who now realized he must be more candid. "So far as the outcome of the war is concerned," he told

Togo, "your views are quite satisfactory to me. And as to diplomacy, you shall have a free hand."

Togo remained reluctant. He demanded assurance that the Cabinet would support peace negotiations if a study showed that the war could not be continued for three more years at least. Suzuki dropped all pretense. Without qualification he accepted Togo's condition. To the rest of the world, however, the admiral continued *haragei,* pretending to be as dedicated to a fight to the bitter end as a Tojo.

5.

After a week on Okinawa, the two American Army divisions pressing south had still encountered nothing but enemy outposts and were far ahead of schedule.

Admiral Turner was so confident that he radioed Nimitz at noon on April 8:

> I MAY BE CRAZY BUT IT LOOKS LIKE THE JAPS HAVE
> QUIT THE WAR, AT LEAST IN THIS SECTION.

DELETE ALL AFTER "CRAZY" was Nimitz' sardonic reply.

The Army troops were about to encounter the formidable defense system above Shuri. Here the island was four miles wide, a series of rolling limestone hills pocked with natural caves, dotted with burial tombs and broken by terraces, escarpments and ravines. Since the hills ran generally from east to west, the Americans faced successive natural lines of defense.

That afternoon, persistent enemy fire brought Buckner's east flank to a complete halt while his west flank was delayed by a hill mass extending east for a thousand yards from the coast to Highway 5, a road running through the middle of the defense system all the way down to Shuri. This land elevation was Kakazu Ridge, two hills connected by a saddle. It didn't look like much of an obstacle, for it was neither high nor jagged, merely a squat hump covered with grass, brush and small trees.

But this chunky, ugly hill was one of the keys of the Shuri defense, and when the Americans stormed up to its crest on the morning of April 9 they were met by a spirited defense. By late afternoon, out of ammunition and their ranks decimated, they fell back. The next two days were a bloody stalemate as the Americans on both flanks repeatedly attacked and were thrown back.

It was the battle Ushijima wanted, but being on the defense rankled his impatient subordinates; they had persuaded him, against his better judgment, to approve a six-battalion assault the following night, April 12, in conjunction with another mass *kamikaze* raid. The 22nd Regiment (of the 62nd Division) would attack on the left, and on the evening of the eleventh its commander, Lieutenant Colonel Masaru Yoshida, who had been in Okinawa less than a month, assembled his officers to outline the mission. "You will be traveling in darkness over bad roads and under heavy shelling; the secrecy of our plans must be maintained to the last. March in a sinuous 'eel line.' Although you are going to an unfamiliar place, do not make any noise when you arrive, but dig *takotsubo* in hard ground and camouflage them skillfully by dawn tomorrow."

It was raining heavily as the men, toting 110-lb. packs, started toward the front on the muddy roads.

Early the following morning 185 *kamikaze,* accompanied by 150 fighters and 45 torpedo planes, began assaulting the ships around Okinawa. Then came 8 two-engine bombers; underneath them hung a new weapon, the *oka* (cherry blossom) bomb. Powered by three booster rockets, this one-way glider looked like a torpedo with small wings, and the pilot could dive its ton of tri-nitro-anisol explosives at more than 500 knots.* The new suicide weapon was

* There were other suicidal measures, but all were relatively unsuccessful. Miniature submarines, which received so much publicity, were involved in six verified raids: Pearl Harbor; Sydney Harbor, May 31, 1942; the Guadalcanal area, November 23 and December 7, 1942; off Madagascar, May 31, 1942; and west of the Mindanao Sea, January 5, 1945. Twenty-eight submariners died and insignificant damage was inflicted. A new two-man submarine, *Kairyu* (Sea Dragon), with a range of 250 miles and a payload of two aviation-type torpedoes, was in production. By the end of the war there were 230, but not one was used.

Another notable failure was the *kaiten* (turn toward Heaven), a human torpedo which was brought close to the target on the deck of a conventional submarine. An early model penetrated the Ulithi lagoon and sank the oiler *Mississinewa* carrying 400,000 gallons of aviation gas. This success spurred improvements, and the final *kaiten* model was fifty-four feet long and carried a warhead of 3,000 pounds of high explosives. Such a charge, the inventors

nicknamed *baka* ("stupid") bomb by the Americans, but it didn't
lessen the terror it spread instantly throughout the fleet. At about
2:45 P.M. one dropped from the belly of its mother ship and ar-
rowed into the destroyer *Mannert L. Abele,* which had just been
staggered by a *kamikaze* hit. The ship jackknifed in two and
sank almost instantly. Another *oka* exploded on the destroyer
Stanly. In the meantime, *kamikaze* and conventional planes sank
LCS(L)-33 and damaged a battleship, three destroyers and eight
other ships.

The assault on the ground was less successful. It opened with a
concentrated artillery and mortar barrage, which lifted at midnight.
Japanese infantrymen began infiltrating into the American positions, but the glare of NGF star shells caught them in the open and
within an hour the counterattack faltered. For the first time Warrant Officer Kaname Imai of the 22nd Regiment, the son of a
Shinto priest, heard the word "retreat" from his battalion commander. He repeated it, but his men stood uncomprehending.
"After me!" called Imai and started trotting forward as if on the
attack. His men followed and so did several other platoons, as he
swung back to the rear.

---

claimed, could sink any warship afloat, and a submarine carrying four *kaiten*
on its back could approach a U. S. anchorage and sink four large ships in a
single attack. That was the prophecy and hope. Hundreds of *kaiten* were
launched against Allied vessels but they sent only one more to the bottom,
the merchant vessel *Canada Victory.* The destroyer escort, *Underhill,* was
hit by a *kaiten,* then sunk accidentally by friendly forces. Almost nine hundred Japanese died in the *kaiten* program.

Equally futile was Operation Flying Elephant, an ambitious program to
launch thousands of large hydrogen balloons, equipped with incendiary
bombs, against the heavily wooded northwest section of the United States.
Over Japan the balloons would be caught up in the jet stream at 33,000 feet
and travel eastward at 120 miles an hour, reaching Washington, Oregon or
Montana in approximately forty-eight hours. The balloons, which had a lifting power of 300 kilograms at sea level, were manufactured in a number of
Tokyo movie theaters and a *sumo* stadium by a work force of paperhangers,
schoolgirls and women from the *iromachi* (red-light districts). The balloons
were fashioned out of rice paper strengthened with *konnyaku* (devil's-tongue
root, an important ingredient in sukiyaki); the entire *konnyaku* crop was
requisitioned. Each balloon required 600 strips of paper, pasted together to
form a sphere. Several million workers were involved in the production of
10,000 balloons. On November 1, 1944, the commanders of the launching
sites in Chiba, Ibaraki and Fukushima prefectures were ordered to "initiate
the attacks on North America!" A staff officer was dispatched to the Ise
Shrine to pray for success. In the next six months 9,300 balloons were released into the jet stream. The results were disappointing: a few minor forest
fires were started in the Pacific Northwest.

In Warm Springs, Georgia, it was still April 12. After lunch President Roosevelt sat for a water-color portrait at the clapboard cottage called the Little White House, two miles from the Warm Springs Foundation. At 1:15 P.M. he closed his eyes and said quietly, "I have a terrific headache." He slumped over unconscious.

Dr. James Paullin, former president of the American Medical Association, arrived, after a two-hour race over back roads, to find the President "in a cold sweat, ashy gray and breathing with difficulty." His pulse was barely perceptible and four minutes later his heart sounds disappeared completely. Dr. Paullin gave him an intracardiac dose of adrenalin. The President's heart beat a few times, then stopped forever. It was 3:55 P.M.

The Nazis looked upon his death as a last-minute reprieve from defeat. "Fate has laid low your greatest enemy. God has not abandoned us," Goebbels feverishly told Hitler over the phone. "Twice he has saved you from savage assassins. Death, which the enemy aimed at you in 1939 and 1944, has now struck down our most dangerous enemy. It is a miracle!"

Japan's new leader, on the other hand, did not rejoice. Prime Minister Suzuki broadcast his condolences to the American people, expressing his "profound sympathy" over the loss of a man who was responsible for the "Americans' advantageous position today."* Japanese propagandists did take advantage of the situation, however, to promote a story that Roosevelt had died in anguish—and altered his last words from "I have a terrific headache" to "I have made a terrific mistake."

Otherwise little attention was devoted to Roosevelt's death except on editorial pages. "It is Heaven's punishment," said the *Mainichi*. "As the incarnation of American imperialism, he has had a cursed influence on the whole of mankind." The *Asahi Shimbun* quoted Admiral Nomura, who had worked so hard for peace in Washington, as saying, "This may be a foolish thing, but I had a dream four or five days ago. I was at the White House and when I went into Roosevelt's room there was a coffin there. The adjutant pointed to the coffin and told me Roosevelt was in there. This dream has come true. But no matter who dies, the American

* Suzuki's broadcast was not reported in the Japanese press, and even his son knew nothing of it until after the war.

war drive will undergo no change and we must be determined to fight it out to the finish."

The news reached Okinawa at dawn on the thirteenth. "Attention! Attention! All hands!" loudspeakers blasted on American ships. "President Roosevelt is dead. Repeat, our Supreme Commander, President Roosevelt, is dead." There was shock amounting to disbelief, and Admiral Turner was compelled to issue official confirmation. Beyond the grief loomed new concerns. Would his death affect the conduct of the war? Would his successor, Harry Truman, also demand unconditional surrender?

Japanese Army propagandists on Okinawa, taking a cue from the homeland, printed leaflets which linked the President's demise with the fate of the Americans on the island.

We must express our deep regret over the death of President Roosevelt. The "American Tragedy" is now raised here at Okinawa with his death. You must have seen 70% of your CVs [aircraft carriers] and 73% of your Bs [battleships] sink or be damaged causing 150,000 casualties. Not only the late President but anyone else would die in the excess of worry to hear such an annihilative damage. The dreadful loss that led your late leader to death will make you orphans of this island. The Japanese special attack corps will sink your vessels to the last destroyer. You will witness it realized in the near future.

One GI looked up from the leaflet as blasts of gunfire from American ships reverberated from Nakagusuku Bay and exclaimed, "Where the hell do they think that stuff's coming from?"

Few Japanese shared Goebbels' illusion that Roosevelt's death presaged a turn in the tide of war. Territories they had conquered in the first months of the conflict had been retaken or were falling. Nowhere was this more evident than in the Philippines. Yamashita still held his northern redoubt, but MacArthur was firmly entrenched on western Mindanao and was preparing a full-scale sweep across the island.

General Sosaku Suzuki had been forced to abandon Leyte to join the 743 men who had already been evacuated to Cebu. Almost all of the 12,000 or so left behind, including General Makino of the 16th Division, were fated to die—by starvation, suicide or at the hands of the enemy. Americans had already landed on Cebu by the time Suzuki reached the capital, and he decided to chance the perilous trip to Mindanao, where there were almost two full divisions of able-bodied troops as well as 12,000 Japanese civilians. Why not gather all these people in the mountains northwest of Davao? There they would be able to fight off the enemy indefinitely, and moreover, establish a self-sufficient society, intermarrying with the natives. It would be a paradise with absolutely no discrimination. His enthusiasm was shared by General Tomochika, his chief of staff. Between them they drew up a constitution and picked a temporary name for the "dream nation"—the Suzuki Kingdom.

"In case I die en route," Suzuki told Tomochika just before they embarked in five *bancas* on April 10, "you must take my place as Thirty-fifth Army commander and carry on our project." He memorialized the ordeal they faced with a poem:

> *Do not starve to death,*
> *Go into the fields;*
> *Even though we die bravely,*
> *It will not stop the forward advance,*
> *For I am the commander,*
> *And fortunately I am still able to serve;*
> *Give me many glories.*

It took six days for the little flotilla, often beset by storms, to reach southern Negros. With dark they set out on the last long lap, across the open water to Mindanao. There was no wind and the tide ran against them, but resolute paddling brought them to the main current. All but Suzuki's boat were swept into the Mindanao Sea, and by ten o'clock they were far ahead out of sight. Exhausted, Suzuki and his companions could no longer best the current, and their *banca* drifted back toward Negros. In the morning an American plane discovered them near a lighthouse.

"Jump!" cried the general's aide, First Lieutenant Tokujo Watano, and leaped over the side. But Suzuki remained in the *banca*. As bullets ripped up the water toward the dugout, Watano saw his general, sword in hand, lean over as if committing harakiri. It was the end of Suzuki and of his dream kingdom.*

* Only Tomochika's boat reached Mindanao, and shortly the island was dominated by MacArthur. "What started as a dream," Tomochika later remarked, "ended in a nightmare."

29

The Iron Typhoon

1.

On the day of Roosevelt's death Kantaro Suzuki's Cabinet authorized the organization of a Volunteer Army of men from fifteen to fifty-five and women from seventeen to forty-five for the mainland battle. Newspapers continued to write confidently of Okinawa, whose fall would necessitate the use of the volunteers. "The enemy did the very thing we expected when we were working out the details of our plans for dealing with him," said a retired admiral named Endo. "The strategy under which we have allowed the enemy to invade the Okinawan islands has much in common with the strategy of fighting with our backs to the wall. We could not resort to this strategy unless we were fully conscious of our power to thrust at the enemy's vitals while letting him thrust at our less vital parts."

But General Ushijima's 32nd Army had already been dealt a more grievous wound. In two weeks of fighting, almost seven thousand of its best troops had fallen, and although the Shuri line was holding, Marines had overrun the northern half of the island—which was defended by two battalions—except for Motobu Peninsula. On April 16 they seized Yae-take, a rugged 1,200-foot peak

which dominated the peninsula, after an arduous three-day struggle, virtually ending the campaign in northern Okinawa.

A few miles west of the peninsula lay Ie Shima, an oval-shaped
island five miles long, flat except for an extinct volcano which rose
dramatically 600 feet near the center where the last Japanese
troops in the area were garrisoned. Occupation of the island was
assigned to the Army, and at eight o'clock that same morning, after
a naval bombardment, GI's clambered over the high dunes toward
the airfield, the main objective of the invasion. On their approach
to the volcano they encountered a maze of tunnels, bunkers, caves
and spider holes. From these positions the outnumbered garrison,
buttressed by hundreds of civilian volunteers, gave the 77th Division the toughest opposition yet.

Ernie Pyle temporarily left the Marines on Okinawa to be with
the GI's, for whom he had a special affinity. On April 18 he was
on his way up front in a jeep with a regimental commander when
the road was swept by machine-gun bullets. Pyle, a frail little man,
leaped into a ditch. As he raised his head to get a look, he was hit
in the temple. He died instantly and was buried nearby.*

Back on Okinawa the Marines sat around that evening reciting
favorite passages from his columns. "It seems a shame such a big
guy had to get it on such a lousy little island," said a corporal.
They checked his bedroll, which he had left behind. It contained a
single personal item—a chain of colored sea shells. They wrapped
it and forwarded it to Pyle's widow, "That Girl."

North of the Shuri line the Army had been readying a general
attack on its defense system. "It is going to be really tough," predicted Major General John Hodge, commander of XXIV Corps.
"There are sixty-five to seventy thousand fighting Japs holed up in
the south end of the island, and I see no way to get them out except blast them out yard by yard."

The Navy was brought in to help. At five-forty the next morning
six battleships, six cruisers and eight destroyers began bombarding
the five-mile defense complex extending across the island. Twenty

* Today a monument marks the place. It reads: "At this spot the 77th
Infantry Division lost a buddy, Ernie Pyle, 18 April 1945." "More than any
other man," President Truman eulogized, "he became the spokesman of the
ordinary American in arms doing so many extraordinary things."

minutes later, twenty-seven battalions of artillery—324 pieces in all—sounded off, digging up front-line positions before lifting 500 yards to the rear. At six-thirty the artillery lowered, splattering the front lines for another ten minutes. It was the greatest single concentration of artillery in Pacific warfare—19,000 shells.

The artillery elevated once more while assault platoons of two divisions, the 7th in the east and the 96th in the center, rushed forward. Fifty minutes later another division, the 27th, assaulted Kakazu Ridge on the west end of the line.

Incredibly, the unprecedented bombardment left the Japanese relatively intact, and though all three units attacked aggressively, all three were thrown back. Casualties were high, particularly in the 27th Division sector, where twenty-two tanks were destroyed in futile charges against formidable Kakazu Ridge. By late afternoon XXIV Corps had lost 720 dead, wounded and missing. During the next four days the two divisions on the flanks made negligible gains in slow, grinding advances, but the GI's of the 96th did manage to drive forward more than 1,000 yards—only to face the heart of the Shuri defenses, a rugged little escarpment that stuck up like a segment of the Great Wall of China. This was Maeda Ridge, which, with its forbidding sheer cliffs, proved to be a fortress in fact as well as in appearance. The GI's were promptly repelled. General Buckner, the Tenth Army commander, rejected a proposal to make an amphibious landing behind the Japanese lines: the reefs in the south were too dangerous, the beaches inadequate for supplies, and any beachhead could be contained by the multitude of Japanese in the area.

Buckner's reasoning was logical—but incorrect. Much as Ushijima feared such a maneuver ("It would bring a prompt end to the fighting"), he was compelled to transfer his rear-guard division north to beef up the Shuri line. These replacements began marching up front at night, and by the evening of April 25 most of them were in position to relieve the casualty-ridden defenders. They arrived in time to face the brunt of a renewed American attack on Maeda. It too failed. One company of the 96th Division scaled up to the top at a prohibitive cost of eighteen casualties in minutes. Another company formed a human chain to breast the ridge, but the three key men at the top were cut down by machine-gun bullets.

To their left, at the eastern terminus of Maeda, GI's gained the tops of two rolling hills and caught more than five hundred Japanese out in the open at the very moment when American tanks and armored flamethrowers rolled up Highway 5, which curved around the end of the ridge. The cross fire annihilated the Japanese.

Fearing that the enemy might break through in force and come up behind the escarpment, Ushijima sent a curt directive to 62nd Division: "The enemy with troops following tanks has been advancing into the southern and eastern sectors of Maeda since about 1300. The 62nd Division will dispatch local units . . . attack the enemy advancing in the Maeda sector with a view to repulsing him decisively." Ushijima also ordered the 24th Division to help its neighbors seal up this hole regardless of the division boundary and to "put its main strength northeast of Shuri this evening." Maeda had to be held at all costs.

On the morning of April 27 American infantry, tanks and flamethrowers, working in close co-operation, again assaulted the remaining Japanese positions at the eastern end of Maeda, and before dusk held the two rolling hills. With the entire eastern segment of the escarpment in enemy hands, Ushijima ordered a regiment of the 24th Division to clear the entire ridge at once. The task of seizing the center portion was given to a battalion commanded by one of the youngest captains in the Imperial Army, Tsuneo Shimura. Most of his six hundred men had never before seen battle. For example, a few weeks earlier nineteen-year-old Shuzen Hokama was still going to the Normal School in Shuri, but like so many patriotic Okinawans he volunteered for front-line duty.

As the battalion slowly wound through the ancient capital that evening, the men had to pick their way around a hundred bodies tossed "like rag dolls" in the street opposite a large Christian church—a naval shell had hit a wagonful of ammunition. Hokama saw pieces of flesh sticking to a stone wall, and blood was splattered over the cobblestones. Leaving the town, the men continued north in two files along a muddy road until shells scattered them into the fields. During a rest each soldier was given a slice of canned pineapple—"a final good taste" before death.

They failed to reach the line of departure until well after mid-

night, and it was almost three o'clock in the morning by the time
Captain Shimura launched a two-company attack. Almost immediately mortar rounds lobbed over the ridge into the ranks. Shimura
ordered the men to proceed cautiously through the mortar screen.
As soon as they started up the steep incline in the first pasty light
of day, tanks appeared to the right on Highway 5 like questing
tigers. All their guns opened fire simultaneously, and more than a
hundred men were killed in the first moments. The survivors took
cover in Chinese tombs and rude air shelters, or behind rocks.
Shimura and seven others found safety in a tomb, where they hid
for the rest of the day.

The tanks finally departed with the last rays of sunlight. Shimura
emerged to find one third of his men dead, but Regiment still insisted that he take the cliffs that night. He marked his back with
white strips and led his men forward along a dry streambed. Halfway up the incline he stumbled across a camouflaged opening.
Crouched inside the cave were fifty men—the remnants of the Kaya
Detachment. Armed only with a few rifles, they had been driven
off the escarpment. Shimura's entrance was greeted with excla-
mations and tears. Colonel Kaya embraced Shimura with relief.
"From now on I'm leaving everything up to you," he said. He
wouldn't discuss the battle or what he knew of the enemy's positions; instead he proffered a cup of *sake,* which the captain refused.

Shimura left the cave in disgust and brought his men to the lip
of the crest. They remained hidden until dawn, when they suddenly launched grenades, and under cover of fire from light machine guns burst over the edge, screeching and brandishing their
glistening bayonets. Their momentum carried them to the summit
of the ridge, a jutting piece of limestone that resembled a castle
turret—it had already been nicknamed "Needle Rock" by the GI's.
Here they overran the handful of Americans at the center of the
escarpment, and then spread out along a front of two hundred
yards, positioning themselves behind rocks or in small caves. Their
quick success was due as much to their élan as to the debilitating
struggle that had seesawed along the ridge for four days. The
American units facing them had been reduced to about 40 percent
combat efficiency, and some platoons were down to half a dozen
men.

The fighting near the west coast was not as fierce as that on the escarpment but had been almost as costly to both sides. The next day, April 30, the 1st Marine Division began relieving the 27th Infantry Division, which had suffered 2,661 casualties in less than two weeks. Down the line of Marines slouching ahead the word was passed: "Doggies coming back." The Marines straightened up and smartly raised weapons to their shoulders. But the GI's (to one Marine they looked "dirty and dispirited, turned into zombies") ignored their parading replacements. A passing Marine made a sarcastic remark but was silenced by his comrades; perhaps they would come out the same way—those who survived.

Fresh Army troops were also moved up to Maeda Ridge. Time and again GI's, carrying satchel charges, scaled the heights with ropes and grapnels but were repeatedly driven back by the Japanese, who emerged from an intricate network of caves. Shimura held his positions near Needle Rock against a dozen resolute assaults, and his defense was so impressive that Regiment ordered him to go on the attack himself. That night he was to retake the first rolling hummock to his right, called Satan Hill by the Japanese. He sent the 5th Company. The men reached the hill soon after midnight and sent up flares to signal that they had taken the objective. But since they could not dig *takotsubo* in the rocky soil, they were caught unprotected at first light and were annihilated to the last man.

The enemy soldiers had been on the island for a month and their number had grown to 170,000. Okinawa had been transformed into a Little America. Roads had been widened and improved—to accommodate the tens of thousands of vehicles that swarmed ashore—supply dumps set up, antiaircraft guns emplaced, and phone service established linking all Army and Navy installations.

The Japanese, who had been taught to despise the Americans, were impressed by their rational way of fighting. They were dressed sensibly, had endless quantities of ammunition and food, and seemed to turn war into an adventure. Even the enemy's tattoos intrigued the Japanese.

In a cave a hundred feet beneath the ancient Shuri Castle, where Commodore Perry had been received in state by the King of Okinawa almost a century before, Ushijima's chief of staff, Lieutenant

General Isamu Cho, vociferously demanded another all-out counterattack. He was a hearty man who smoked and drank to excess. His Army career—like that of Tsuji—had been studded with acts of *gekokujo*. He had participated in the abortive Brocade Flag Revolution of 1931. Afterward he was transferred to Manchuria, where his penchant for intrigue prolonged the border fighting with Russia at Changkufeng in 1938. His temper was short, and it was not unusual for him to slap his orderly, his aide or a junior officer in a line unit. Now arguing with Ushijima, he brandished his long cigarette holder as if it were a weapon.

Ushijima listened politely. He often exhibited such deference that it made those around him uneasy—with the exception of Cho, whose present belligerence had been aggravated by the *sake* they had all consumed in the past hour. Ushijima's reservations were supported only by his operations officer, who alone debated Cho's repeated demands for a decisive strike. Colonel Hiromichi Yahara —a grim-faced man with the nickname "Sobersides"—refused to be intimidated. "To take the offensive with inferior forces against overwhelmingly superior enemy forces is reckless and will lead to early defeat." Moreover, he went on, they would have to attack an enemy which held commanding ground. The sensible course was to continue current operations. He thought annihilation was inevitable, but invaluable time could be won for Imperial Headquarters by a strategic holding action. A counterattack would at best inflict light casualties on the enemy, and thousands of His Majesty's troops would be sacrificed in vain. But the Japanese instinct to attack when cornered was irrepressible. The commander of the 62nd Division sprang to his feet and aggressively backed Cho, as did the other division and brigade commanders who had been frustrated by the defensive tactics forced upon them. With misgivings, Ushijima ordered the offensive to begin in two days.

It was a complicated and ambitious plan—co-ordinated with another massive *kamikaze* attack on shipping and supported by tactical bombers—to drive a wedge five miles north into the American lines. Two regiments, their way cleared by a heavy artillery barrage, would start the assault east of Highway 5 while a third stormed down from Maeda Ridge, and with considerable tank support press on along the highway to the heights beyond. The 44th Independent Mixed Brigade would follow for half a mile before turning left toward the west coast. To mislead the enemy there would also be two amphibious landings behind the American lines, one on the west coast and the other on the east coast.

At dusk on May 3, artillery began to pound enemy front-line positions, and *kamikaze* planes struck at U. S. shipping, sinking the destroyer *Little* and *LSM-195,* and damaging four other ships. Just after midnight an attack by sixty conventional bombers on Tenth Army's rear areas coincided with the two amphibious forces' advance up the coasts in barges. The western unit mistakenly landed near a Marine company. Alerted by shouts of *"Banzai!"* the Marines turned on the surprised Japanese a murderous mortar barrage and concentrated machine-gun and rifle fire. The few who escaped were hunted down and killed. The sole captive was a carrier pigeon. It was released carrying a typical Marine taunt: "We are returning your pigeon. Sorry we cannot return your demolition engineers." The amphibious force plowing up the east coast was sighted by a naval patrol which illuminated the area with star shells. Most of the barges were destroyed, and the score of men who made it to shore were eliminated.

An hour before dawn the Japanese artillery barrage reached a deafening climax which continued for half an hour. Then two red flares shot up: the signal to attack. Japanese infantrymen surged forward pell-mell. On the right, two thousand were soon caught in the open terrain by American artillery. Those who survived tried to forge ahead but were systematically picked off on the exposed flatland.

The successful outcome of the assault in the center was dependent on armored support. But since accurate enemy artillery fire had immobilized all the medium tanks, no more than nine light ones managed to pull behind the spearhead, Captain Koichi Ito's 600-man battalion. Ito's troops pierced the American lines in the predawn gloom but were pinned down by automatic-weapons fire. The nine tanks tried to close up but artillery found their range one by one. Ito decided to go on without tank support and led his scattered battalion toward the first objective, a hill mass one mile northeast of Maeda near the town of Tanabaru.

Fragmentary reports reaching 32nd Army headquarters later in the morning claimed impressive victories and touched off celebrations in the cave under the wreckage of Shuri Castle. However, no one but Ito had made a substantial breakthrough, and he was ordered to assault the hill above Tanabaru that night. With his men he pushed ahead along either side of Highway 5 until they were blocked by enemy shells. Since Ito now had armored support —the tanks had come up under cover of darkness—he was able to continue. Six tanks were destroyed during the fierce fire fights that followed, but Ito and his men covered the long, arduous mile through the American lines to Tanabaru. He mined the road running through town and by dawn had set up a perimeter defense on the slope of the hill. Then he radioed in the clear—his code men were dead—that he and almost 450 of his troops had reached the objective. He was ordered to stay in place.

By noon of May 5 it was obvious even to the blustery Cho that the counterattack, which he had fathered, had failed. Now he saw no hope at all for Okinawa; defeat was certain.

Ito was still lodged above Tanabaru but he was under constant pressure from all sides. During the day a hundred more of his detachment had been killed by flamethrowers, mortars and grenades. The next morning the American assaults continued and were repulsed by sacrificial measures. There were now fewer than 150 of the 600 men who had started the offensive, and Ito was preparing himself for death when a message wrapped around a rock hurtled into his *takotsubo*. It was from his radioman: an order had just been received to fall back. On taking leave of the wounded, he distributed grenades among them before he assembled his able-bodied men at the foot of the hill. At midnight they moved south in the darkness but the one mile of enemy territory took its toll. Only Ito and a dozen others broke through.

The Japanese had struck with every resource they could muster but were easily crushed by Hodge's XXIV Corps. The success coincided with a much more significant achievement. At high noon on May 8 every American artillery piece and naval gun fired three volleys—Germany had surrendered.

Defeating the Japanese in an open, wasteful charge was one thing, but dislodging them from dug-in defenses was devastating. Maeda Ridge had turned into a bloody version of "King of the Hill," with first one side holding the crest and then the other. One GI battalion, the 1st of the 307th Infantry Regiment, lost more

than half its men in eight days, including eight company commanders in a thirty-six-hour period.

The Japanese losses were far more grievous. Young Captain
Shimura, for example, had once had 600 men on the ridge line;
now there were fewer than 150 left and most of them were severely
wounded. Still he refused to withdraw on order; he wanted to die
where most of his men had been killed. Regiment insisted that he
was to fall back, and a staff officer of the 24th Division sent a personal message in code with the argument that he would "find other
suitable battlefields to die on." Shimura told his men of the order
but he was going to remain as a guerrilla. "Those who wish to stay
with me, can. We'll stick it out here on this ridge until we die."
Some of the men went underground and the rest withdrew, leaving
Maeda Ridge to the Americans.

With the fall of Maeda, the American offensive slowly ground
forward all across the island. Two full Marine divisions (III Amphibious Corps) now held the western flank: after an arduous battle the 6th had seized Sugar Loaf Hill, the western anchor of the
entire defense line, less than a mile from Shuri, and the 1st Division, which had been in battle since Guadalcanal, advanced
through Wana Draw, a narrow, rocky passage leading to the center of the former capital. Farther east, all the way to the coast, the
three divisions of XXIV Corps, advancing slowly, captured Chocolate Drop, Flattop and other hills just east of Shuri. By dusk on
May 21 the city itself was invested from three sides but as darkness
overtook the fighting, so did torrential rains. Wana Draw became
a swamp. Tanks and amphibian tractors churned helplessly in
mud. All along the front, foxholes carved out of the clay slopes
began to disintegrate, and those on lower ground had to be bailed
constantly like leaky boats. For almost a full week the downpour
continued. Little food could be brought up front; sleep in the constant deluge was impossible; the dead could not be buried and
were left to decompose.

The respite granted him by the rain notwithstanding, General
Ushijima decided to abandon Shuri. More than sixty thousand of
his troops had been killed in the bloody defense of the city. The
62nd and 24th divisions and the 44th Independent Mixed Brigade
—the heart of his army—had been shattered by relentless enemy

naval gunfire, artillery fire and bombings, as well as infantry and tank assaults. He overrode protests against any retreat, however localized, on the grounds that an attempt to make a stand at Shuri would accelerate the fall of Okinawa.

2.

In the May issue of the commercial magazine *Jitsugyo-no-Nippon,* Rear Admiral Etsuzo Kurihara wrote:

Some people favor the method of letting the enemy cut our skin while we cut the enemy's body, and of letting him cut our body while we cut his bone. I am opposed to such a calculating strategy. Rather, I am in favor of letting the enemy cut our bone while we cut the enemy's bone. Each Japanese can do this. This method will give rise to a great tenacity among our people. This is the tactics of our Special Attack Corps.

Kamikaze tactics had been tried against the Americans since the battle for Leyte Gulf, but at Okinawa they became an integral part of the defense. Since the Easter landing six massive *kamikaze* attacks, involving more than fifteen hundred planes, had been loosed at the hundreds of American vessels concentrated around the island. Several hundred of these planes had careened through dense flak and exploded on their targets, sending to the bottom almost a score of American ships and seriously damaging some twenty-five others. Grim as the figures were, they did not tell the true story of death, terror and heroism on either side. It was blood-curdling to watch a plane aim relentlessly at your ship, its pilot resolved to blast you and himself to hell.

The seventh *kamikaze* raid, on May 25, co-ordinated with Ushijima's withdrawal from Shuri and was preceded by a suicide unit of saboteurs which was brought by five bombers to Yontan Airfield in central Okinawa. Four of the two-engine planes were shot down, but the fifth made a belly-landing on the field. Americans watched incredulous as its occupants disgorged and scattered to the flight line lobbing grenades and incendiaries into parked planes. Seven aircraft were destroyed, twenty-six others damaged, and two fuel dumps containing 70,000 gallons of gasoline set ablaze before the raiders were killed.

Offshore, *kamikaze* were already sweeping in toward the transport area, and in the next twelve hours 176 Special Attack planes bored in on their targets. They sank *LSM-135* and the destroyer escort *Bates*. Four other ships had to be scuttled, scrapped or decommissioned as a result of damage.

The fanaticism of these fliers was frightening to Americans in its finality, yet "there was a hypnotic fascination to a sight so alien to our Western philosophy," Vice Admiral C. R. Brown observed. "We watched each plunging *kamikaze* with the detached horror of one witnessing a terrible spectacle rather than as the intended victim. We forgot self for the moment as we groped hopelessly for the thought of that other man up there." Out of this almost morbid fascination came a welter of theories and rumors: *kamikaze* fliers went into battle like priests in hooded robes; they were drugged; they had to be chained to their cockpits; they were an elite group trained from youth for suicide. They were, in fact, average young Japanese who were volunteers. Their goal was to die a meaningful death and they were convinced that the Special Attack system was the best possible way to overcome Japan's inferior productivity vis-à-vis America. One man could damage or sink a carrier or battleship and take a thousand enemies with him.

Ensign Yasunori Aoki, born in Tokyo twenty-two years earlier, believed in their slogan: "One plane, one warship." His love of nature had led him to Agricultural and Forestry College on Formosa. Faced with conscription, he joined the Imperial Navy "for its glamor," learned to fly, and by early 1945 was an instructor at Kochi on the island of Shikoku. There, volunteers were sought for the Special Attack Corps. Each flier, instructor as well as student, was told to write his name on a piece of paper. Those who wished to volunteer would place a circle above their name; those who declined, a triangle. There was no coercion and several unhesitatingly drew triangles, but Aoki felt it would be cowardly. Besides, since no one would survive the war, he preferred to die as a flier; he might even sink a ship.

The volunteers were trained to skim the water at 30 feet, then climb and fire at a control tower. They flew the *Shiragiku* (White Chrysanthemum), a slow, bulky, two-seat trainer. Aoki, as commander of his plane, became its navigator, although, in his opinion, one was not needed; but without a superior in the second seat, perhaps the pilot would be tempted to turn back.

The weeks went by quickly. The training was absorbing and the mission itself was so far in the future that it seemed unreal. But once the training ended, Aoki began to realize that he was under sentence of death; the sense of doom grew as the planes were remodeled for the mission. An extra fuel tank was lashed inside the cabin, and a 250-kilogram bomb fixed to either wing. As he surveyed his own aircraft Aoki could not help thinking, This is the plane that is going to take me on a one-way trip.

On May 25 his group was transferred to Kanoya on Kyushu, a staging area for the last flight to Okinawa. The finality of his fate overwhelmed him. His comrades' appearance of serenity gave him a feeling of inferiority. At dusk Aoki watched a flight of *kamikaze* leave for Okinawa—his own group was next. He returned disconsolate to the barracks, an elementary school, where he found to his amazement half a dozen men who he thought had just taken off. Their refusal to go assuaged his own burden of shame; he could never be *that* cowardly.

The following noon he was lying in the grass watching the planes of his group being wheeled out and prepared for the mission. Suddenly the ground around him erupted; the Americans were bombing the base. Aoki didn't move. It made no difference if he was killed, he told himself; he hoped he would live in a more peaceful time in his reincarnation. But as he sauntered back to the barracks, life, which had seemed too cheap moments before, became more precious than ever. An extra day of living would be priceless; even an extra hour, a minute, a second. He stopped to watch the antics of a fly. "How lucky you are to be alive," he said aloud. After supper the group gathered for a briefing on next day's mission. Each crew was to pick its own altitude and course. The majority chose to take an indirect course to the east or west. Aoki suggested going to Okinawa direct. His pilot, a seventeen-year-old named Yokoyama, was agreeable.

They went to bed early and Aoki awoke, composed, just before dawn. I'm all right! he thought. May 27, his last day on earth, was brilliant and clear, and he felt extraordinarily refreshed and keen. He had already put aside fingernail clippings and a lock of hair for his family. Now he wrote postcards to each of his parents, his four younger sisters and his younger brother. "Our divine country will not be destroyed," he told them, and then prayed that Japan would survive total defeat.

Late that afternoon his group was given a ceremonial supper. An administrative officer proposed a toast. Aoki downed his *sake* in one gulp before noticing that his drinking friends sipped theirs. A newsreel cameraman asked the young men to pose. They donned leather helmets decorated with the emblem of the Rising Sun; a few banded their helmets with *hachimaki*. Linking arms, they sang lustily "Doki no Sakura" ("Class of Cherry Blossoms").

At final inspection a captain stopped in front of Aoki and wondered why his face was crimson. "Don't you feel well?" It was merely the *sake*, explained Aoki. "If you don't feel well," said the captain solicitously, "you can stay behind and join a later group."

"I'm all right, sir."

The fifteen crews piled into a truck and were followed by well-wishers. At the field they incongruously slipped into life jackets emblazoned with large Rising Suns. Aoki's pockets were empty except for a picture of his family and two small wooden *omamori*, Buddhist good luck charms, which he hoped would help him achieve his mission.

Just before dusk there was a farewell ceremony conducted by a rear admiral. During his speech Aoki heard a group of staff officers at the side chatting and laughing. He bitterly resented their treating such an occasion so casually. Their chief instructor solemnly wished them success. "There is an observation post on Okinawa that will confirm the results of your mission," he said. "Tonight there is a full moon. It will be watching you, so you won't be alone. I will join you later; please wait for me." The thirty men shed tears unashamedly. They knew he wished he were going with them, and were grateful that a fellow airman had prevented their last moments on earth from being commonplace.

As the fifteen planes taxied into position, there was a flutter of handkerchiefs, caps and flags from the little crowd along the runway. Over the roar of the engines Aoki heard someone shouting, "Aoki! Aoki!" He turned in his seat. There behind the plane, chasing after him, gesticulating and weeping, was one of the pilots who had refused to take off on the previous flight. Aoki felt embarrassed and resentful; it was like being pursued by a woman. But he smiled and called out, "Follow us!" as the old trainer gathered speed and lifted off the field. Its climb prolonged the fading sunset. How beautiful! Aoki thought.

At 3,000 feet the young pilot took a course almost directly south for Tori Shima (Bird Island), which lay sixty miles west of Okinawa. Here they would turn left straight for the transport area. Ahead a single plane was veering off on its indirect course. Below was a green light marking Sada Point. This was the last light in the homeland and Aoki watched it intently until it vanished. He peered down at a small island. Streaks of white smoke curled up. Some housewife was cooking dinner for her family. He couldn't help thinking, You're living and I am going to die.

A layer of clouds forced Yokoyama to descend to 2,200 feet, but the air was so turbulent underneath that he lowered to 1,000 feet. They droned on monotonously hour after hour. The estimated time of arrival at Bird Island passed. Aoki motioned Yokoyama to continue and rechecked his watch. It was eleven-thirty. The attack was scheduled to start at midnight; they would never make it on time. After five minutes he ordered Yokoyama to turn east and start his descent. Aoki scattered tinfoil to jam enemy radar, then pulled a toggle which set the propellers on the two bombs spinning. The bombs were now armed and would explode on contact. The cloud cover above had become scattered and Aoki saw the reflection of the moon in the water. There was a flash of lightning. Another. No, some enemy ship was shooting at them. Yokoyama pulled the trainer up to 300 feet; Aoki strained to see the ship but was blinded by the angry flash of antiaircraft fire perhaps no more than a mile away. It would take a minute to reach the ship, and the ack-ack fire was becoming more accurate.

"Break right!" he ordered.

Bright streaks of fire stitched toward them. Tracers! There was a roar, and what looked like a Grumman flashed by. *Shimatta,* he thought—damn it! There was not so much as a pistol to fight it off, and if Yokoyama tried to turn away he would present an easier target. Aoki pulled open his canopy, raised himself and looked around. The Grumman was gone. He told the pilot to head back toward Okinawa. Almost immediately they came upon a destroyer cruising unconcerned in front of them in a southerly direction. "Dive!" Aoki shouted. Yokoyama had been trained to dive counterclockwise to avoid crashing into any friendly plane but now he would have to go in clockwise, something he had never done before.

Not a shot came up from the destroyer as they approached from the stern. Aoki was still out of his seat, arms crossed on the canopy, chin on arms, staring fixedly at the destroyer. He was serene as he waited for the explosion of oblivion. They were now so close that even if the American fired it would be too late. He was content; his death would be meaningful.

Neither he nor Yokoyama said a word as the lumbering old trainer roared toward the destroyer. There was a crash as they hit the water. Aoki found himself still in the plane—by a double coincidence still alive. Since Yokoyama had never before stalked a moving target, it had managed to pull out from under him. But why hadn't the bombs exploded on contact?

"*Buntaicho* [Commander], come over here!" Yokoyama was standing on top of the settling plane. Aoki heaved himself out of the cockpit just before the aircraft plunged nose first beneath the waves, and inflated the life jacket that had seemed so pointless. They were alone in the darkness—no ships, no planes.

"What shall we do?" asked Yokoyama.

Having already forsaken life, Aoki found it difficult to answer. He felt no joy whatsoever at being alive. At dawn they could distinguish a strip of land in the distance. It must be Okinawa. Aoki suggested that they swim for it, but they were cut off by an enemy destroyer. They lay motionless in the water as if dead, their arms locked together. As the destroyer pulled alongside they closed their eyes and opened their mouths. A grappling hook caught Yokoyama's trouser leg. "Kick it off!" Aoki shouted but the pilot couldn't shake loose and was hauled in like a fish, with Aoki still clutching his arm. Aoki started up the rope dangling over the side of the ship; he was caught now but would escape or commit suicide later.

"You're climbing up!" Yokoyama exclaimed, incredulous.

On deck they refused cigarettes and bread. Yokoyama glared at Aoki with resentment. They were transferred to a larger ship, and once it became obvious that escape was impossible, Aoki demonstrated to his pilot how to commit suicide by biting the tongue and choking on the blood. With tongue extended, Aoki punched his chin again and again. For all the pain, there was very little blood. Then he tried to strangle himself with a thick strand of twisted string. A guard rushed in as he was blacking out. He concluded that it was his fate to live and became a model prisoner.*

3.

On the eve of Aoki's suicidal mission, General Ushijima began withdrawing his headquarters from Shuri, along with what was left of the 62nd Division and the 27th Tank Regiment, leaving a defense shell out front. The heavy rain covered the retreat but made it a trial, particularly for the walking wounded. They had had no medicine and almost no food or water since evacuation from the front. In small groups those who could stand moved off into the drenching rain, shepherded by young Okinawan nurses who had recently attended the Normal School, and hanging onto ropes for guidance in the darkness.

The movement in the enemy rear area was not discovered by the Americans for another twenty-four hours. Then artillery and naval support ships began interdicting roads and junctions. The following day, May 27, General Buckner dispatched new instructions to III and XXIV Corps:

Indications point to possible enemy retirement to new defensive positions with possible counteroffensive against our forces threatening his flank. Initiate without delay strong and unrelenting pressure to ascertain probable intentions and keep him off balance. Enemy must not repeat not be permitted to establish himself securely on new position with only nominal interference.

Aggressive combat patrols probed along the entire Shuri front, but the shell protecting the retreat held and patrols reported there was no indication of Japanese withdrawal. Tenth Army intelli-

---

* When Aoki returned to Japan in late 1946, he was greeted by his uncle, a lieutenant general, with joy and understanding—and for the first time Aoki was glad to be alive. "I've had two lives," he later said. "Now every moment is precious."

gence concurred: "It now looks as though the Japanese thinks holding the line around north of Shuri is his best bet. . . . It is probable that we will gradually surround the Shuri position."

The Army predicted a siege, but the Marines would not wait. The 1st Division stormed Shuri Ridge on May 29 and found it lightly defended. They swept on to the ruins of the castle. Here the defense stiffened, but that evening the Tenth Army intelligence officer re-evaluated the situation: he was now certain that the "enemy was holding the Shuri lines with a shell, and that the bulk of the troops were elsewhere."

Behind a curtain of almost constant rain, Ushijima had escaped with most of his forces and had established new headquarters nine miles due south of Shuri Castle in a cliffside cave overlooking the rugged coast of the island. But the withdrawal had been costly to the Okinawans. In panic, hordes of civilians had fled south behind the troops and had been slaughtered by shells and bombs. Thousands were left dead along the quagmire roads.

On the last day of May, Marines and GI's cautiously entered the former capital from two sides. Shuri lay in ruins, ravaged by mortars, 1,000-lb. bombs and almost two hundred rounds of artillery and naval gunfire. Only two structures—the concrete Normal School and the Methodist church—remained. Buried in the smoldering rubble were hundreds of civilians and their scattered possessions. The stench of rotting flesh penetrated the sharp odor of smoke.

Shuri Castle itself, which it had taken ten thousand laborers eight years to construct, was almost completely demolished by naval shells. Its massive ramparts were toppled like a child's play blocks. Two large bronze bells, battered by shell fire, were at least recognizable. On them was inscribed:

. . . Behold! What is a bell? A bell is that which sounds far, wide and high. It is a precious Buddhist instrument, bringing order to the daily routine of the monk. . . .

It will always toll on time, to herald the approaching darkness or the hour of dawn. It will startle the indolent into activity that will restore honor to his name. And how will the bell sound? It will echo far and wide like a peal of thunder, but with utmost purity. And sinful men, hearing the bell, will be saved.

General Buckner was jubilant that the enemy had abandoned the formidable defense system. "Ushijima missed the boat on his withdrawal from the Shuri line," he told his staff that evening. "It's all over now but cleaning up pockets of resistance. This doesn't mean there won't be stiff fighting but the Japanese won't be able to organize another line."

However, Ushijima had found another natural barrier six miles below Shuri. It was a coral escarpment—dominated by two adjoining hills, Yuzadake and Yaeju-dake—which transversed most of the southern tip of Okinawa like a huge wall. It was loftier and more rugged than Maeda Ridge. Here, backs to the sea, the Japanese would make their last stand.

On June 1 the Americans began to close in. Progress was slow as they slogged forward through ankle-deep mud. Thick cloud formations blanketed the lowlands stretching below the formidable barrier as the flanks fanned out to seize the peninsula on either side. The one to the east, Chinen, was lightly defended, but Oroku Peninsula, which jutted out just below Naha, was held by two thousand Navy troops. Under orders from Ushijima, they had abandoned their installations on the peninsula, after destroying most of their equipment and heavy weapons, and moved south; but there, below the new natural defense line, they found civilians occupying most of the caves they were supposed to fortify. Rather than force out the Okinawans, as the Army was doing, they returned to the peninsula, where, with small arms, they held off aggressive Marine amphibious and land attacks.

At long last, on June 5, the rain ended but it had left its mark. The approaches to the Yuza-Yaeju wall were a morass of soft clay through which American tanks could not negotiate. It was not until June 10 that the 96th Division launched an assault on Yaeju, renamed "the Big Apple" by the GI's. It took two days of concentrated artillery fire and intense close combat for one regiment to establish firm positions on the northern slope of the Big Apple.

Ushijima had almost no artillery to keep the foe at bay; nor did his infantry reinforcements, slowed by poor communications, arrive in time. The Americans consolidated each gain before the Japanese could counterattack effectively, and by midnight on June 13 the entire eastern half of the ridge line had begun to collapse.

The stubborn sailors on Oroku Peninsula had also succumbed

at last to Marines of the 6th Division, but the savage struggle had cost the Americans 1,608 casualties. On June 15 the bodies of Rear Admiral Minoru Ota, the Japanese commander, and five of his staff were found in his subterranean headquarters. They were sprawled, throats cut, on an elevated platform covered with blood-soaked mattresses.

Almost a thousand Japanese were being killed every day as the battle fragmented into a series of fierce contests for caves. That same evening Colonel Hitoshi Kanayama, commander of the 27th Regiment of the 7th Division, gathered his officers and noncoms in his command cave. From a small dais he announced that Division was to launch a general attack at dawn. But he could not obey the order. There were fewer than a hundred men left in his regiment and he imagined other units were just as depleted. It was impossible to carry on organized warfare any longer.

Kanayama poured gasoline on the regimental flag and touched a match to it. As the standard flared up, he said, "During the past three months you men have gone through unspeakable hardships. I thank you all for having fought so well. I am now dissolving the regiment. You will act on your own. Those who wish to return to the homeland are free to make the attempt. I am going to die here, but you are not to share my responsibility."

These words left his subordinates bewildered; they resented being left on their own. Drawing a dagger, Kanayama gazed at his men and again admonished them not to "follow" him. Purposefully and without sound he slashed his abdomen in the ritual pattern. As the blood pumped out, his head fell forward. His adjutant, Captain Sato, brought his raised sword down sharply, severing Kanayama's head. Then Sato shot himself. Another officer, a first lieutenant named Adachi, drew his pistol. *"Tenno Heika banzai!"* he cried out before he pulled the trigger.

4.

The fighting had degenerated into a cruel hunt as the Americans went after their entombed prey with grenades, satchel charges and flamethrowers. By June 17, Ushijima's 32nd Army was dazed and shattered. Discipline had evaporated. Survivors committed acts that would have been unthinkable a few days before: they challenged their officers; fought like savages in their caves for food and water; murdered and raped civilians.

In Headquarters cave, deep within a craggy, precipitous cliff near the tip of the island, General Ushijima stoically waited for the end. It was a long cave, near the top of the cliff, with one end facing the sea more than two hundred feet below, and the other overlooking the village of Mabuni—and the approaching enemy. Ushijima had just finished reading a surrender appeal from Buckner which had been dropped behind the lines:

The forces under your command have fought bravely and well, and your infantry tactics have merited the respect of your opponents. . . . Like myself, you are an infantry general long schooled and practiced in infantry warfare. . . . I believe, therefore, that you understand as clearly as I, that the destruction of all Japanese resistance on the island is merely a matter of days. . . .

While this bid for surrender brought a faint smile to Ushijima's face, Cho broke into derisive, almost uncontrollable laughter— how could a samurai even consider such a proposal? The rapidly deteriorating situation had wrought a disturbing transformation in Cho. Ushijima would lie thoughtfully on his cot, reading or writing poetry, but Cho paced the cave like a caged animal, often grabbing his sword as if he had just seen an enemy.

Ushijima remained himself. He was particularly considerate to the young Okinawan students who served as his personal aides; he patted them paternally on the head and questioned them about their families. His sense of humor was sharpened by adversity. Once when Cho strode up to the end of the cave facing Mabuni and urinated into the wind, Ushijima said with a laugh, "You'd better hurry. Your thing is too big a target for the enemy."

At noon on June 18 his opponent, Simon Bolivar Buckner, roamed far forward to observe a fresh unit of Marines moving into battle. He watched for an hour; then as he started down from his observation post, a Japanese shell exploded directly overhead. A fragment shattered a mound of coral, and freakishly, one jagged piece of coral flew up and embedded itself in the general's chest. Ten minutes later he died.

Ushijima's last order written from the cave urged his men "to fight to the last and die for the eternal cause of loyalty to the Emperor," but not in a suicide charge. He instructed survivors of the 32nd Army to filter through enemy lines in civilian clothes and join the small band of guerrillas in the north of the island. With darkness the first groups tried to get through but were detected. The area was illuminated by flares and star shells, and those who weren't killed immediately were forced to go to ground again.

At noon the following day an explosion rocked the north entrance of Ushijima's cave. American tanks had approached Mabuni and were firing directly on cave openings in the hill rising below the village. Jinsai Higa, an Okinawan who had served in New Guinea before illness forced him to return to Naha, was giving Ushijima a haircut. Cho approached the general as the barber was putting away his utensils, and said, "Thank you very much." What for? asked Ushijima. "You took my advice when I didn't think you would. You let me have my way on the counterattack."

"I thought it would be easier that way," Ushijima replied. "It was always my policy to leave decisions up to my subordinates."

"At one time I thought of committing hara-kiri if you didn't approve of my plan," Cho said gruffly. "But you let me do it—and with a smile. You made it so easy for me and I want to thank you before we part in this world."

Civilians and soldiers alike faced extermination in the hundreds of caves that honeycombed the southern tip of the island. Two miles west of Ushijima's headquarters a group of Okinawan student nurses—turned out of their hospital when it was disbanded —had found refuge with scores of civilians in an underground cave. Nobuko Yamashiro was only seventeen. She was trying desperately to save her dying sister, Yoshiko, also a nurse. But there was no food or water in the cave and she was afraid to venture outside. The nurses had been driven from cave to cave, and on the evening of the eighteenth were ordered by soldiers to move once again—to find "a safer refuge" farther south.

Resentful and weary, the nurses started up the ladder leading to the cave opening. A shout of "Enemy attack!" was cut off by the rattle of firing. Blue sparks showered those on the ladder. Gas! Acrid smoke billowed into the cave. Choking and blinded, the occupants groped toward the ladder. Nobuko gagged as if something clutched her throat. She cried out painfully for her sister. Hell must be like this, she thought. Grenades exploded thunderously. Then there was silence.

"Now we are all going to die," said a calm masculine voice. "Let us sing 'Umi Yukaba.'" As they tried to sing their favorite patriotic song Nobuko fainted. She came to with a strange sense of euphoria; never before had she wakened with such a wonderful feeling of well-being. She struggled to get up from the floor, but her body weighed too much. Why? People were moaning all around her; she must be wounded too. Her left thigh and neck began to throb, and she discovered that she had been hit by shrapnel.

She tried again and again to rise. Where was her sister? Fighting an overpowering desire to sleep, she commanded herself to stay awake; she knew she would die if she succumbed. She pulled up her legs, and in a fetal position rolled over on her knees. Crawling among the bodies sprawled on the cave floor, she began examining them carefully one by one. At the foot of the ladder she looked up. An American soldier stood silhouetted against a startlingly blue sky. She stifled a cough and crept back into the blackness to continue the agonizing search. When she found her sister at the rear of the cave she was dead.

Amplified pleas to surrender from tanks and from boats cruising offshore were far more effective than they had been at Saipan and Iwo Jima. Masses of civilians and a substantial number of soldiers abandoned their subterranean hiding places. Before nightfall more than four thousand Okinawans and eight hundred military had surrendered. The soldiers came out, as they had been instructed, stripped to their loincloths. One marched up to the lines of the 7th Infantry Division, saber in hand. He stood stiffly at attention, saluted and handed over his weapon to Sergeant Alvin Hannah. Another carried two small dictionaries—one English–Japanese, the other Japanese–English. After a bit of sampling he exclaimed cheerfully, "Me vanquished, miserable, dishonorable, depraved."

As Ushijima radioed his farewell message to Imperial Headquarters on the evening of June 21, Cho was composing one of his own which he hoped could be delivered by hand. "Our strategy, tactics and methods were all utilized to the utmost and we fought valiantly, but they had little effect against the superior material strength of the enemy," he wrote, adding that he was departing this life "without regret, fear, shame or obligations."

Their last duties completed, the two generals now readied themselves for death. A grim-faced Colonel Yahara asked Ushijima for permission to commit suicide. The general gently but firmly refused the request. "If you die there will be no one left who knows the truth about the battle of Okinawa. Bear the temporary shame but endure it. This is an order of your Army commander."

Soon after sunrise on June 22 Ushijima asked Higa to give him the final ritual haircut. His sense of humor had not deserted him. As the barber revolved him from side to side, Ushijima joked, "I'm a human rotary machine." By noon the Americans had occupied the upper part of the cave. After a few hours the general opened a can of pineapple—the last food in the cave—and shared it with anyone, soldier or civilian, who happened to pass by.

Late in the afternoon Ushijima and Cho kneeled ceremoniously side by side. Cho deliberately lowered his head so as to expose his neck. Captain Sakaguchi, a fifth-grade *kendo* expert, brought down his sword, but his injured right hand wavered and the blade did not go deeply enough. Sergeant Kyushu Fujita seized the sword and severed the spinal column.

"The Okinawans must resent me," Ushijima said regretfully as he bared his abdomen and stoically cut himself. His spinal cord was severed and seven of his staff, using pistols, committed mass suicide.

The same day at Tenth Army headquarters near the Kadena airfield, representatives of Tenth Army, the two corps and the divisions stood at attention as the band played "The Star-Spangled Banner." The color guard raised the Stars and Stripes, denoting that the island of Okinawa was secure.

But for thousands of Japanese soldiers and civilians, still hiding from the Americans, the ordeal was far from over. Thirteen-year-old Shigeru Kinjo crept out of the cave where his family had found shelter and got his first close glimpse of the enemy. They were naked from the waist up, hairy like animals. It is the end, thought Shigeru. He discredited the enemy leaflets claiming that no prisoners would be killed; they would have their noses and ears cut off. Back in the cave he rejoined the family, which sat huddled in a close circle. Someone activated a grenade against a rock and threw it in their midst. Shigeru thought the world had exploded. He heard his sister mutter something, then her death rattle.

"I'm not dead," said a voice and then, pleadingly, "Explode another!"

A second detonation rocked the little cave. Pieces of flesh struck Shigeru. Still a few survived but no one suggested a third grenade. Someone did propose that they cut their arteries and bleed to death, but no one acted. They remained apathetically in the cave all night. In the morning a voice shouted in English, "Come out!" Almost immediately a can tumbled into the cave spewing white smoke. Two more tear gas canisters exploded. Suffocating, Shigeru crawled out into the open, both legs bleeding profusely. He felt himself being lifted onto a soldier's back. At the village of Makabe the enemy soldier (a Marine) lowered Shigeru and opened a can of clams. It had a Japanese label but the boy was certain the clams were poisoned and refused to eat them. The soldier said something, then cut Shigeru two bamboo canes, and as the youngster hobbled toward a collecting station he wondered, When will the murdering begin?

A mile to the northwest the Americans had been trying to clear a multilevel labyrinthian cave with smoke bombs for more than a week. At least three hundred soldiers and eight hundred civilians were bottled inside. Petty Officer Shikichi Miyagi had escaped from Oroku Peninsula after Admiral Ota's death to find his wife Betty, a Hawaiian, and had succeeded. Now the smoke became so suffocating that Miyagi—one of the most celebrated karate experts in Okinawa, the home of karate—toted his unconscious wife piggyback deep into the cave through hip-high mud.

The mud became a stream and soon water was up to Miyagi's shoulders. The water revived Betty, and when Miyagi could no longer touch bottom he gave her the glowing candle that was guiding them and swam through the water with the collar of her dress in his teeth. Every few yards he lowered his feet to rest but they sank into gummy mud and he flailed frantically to keep head above water. The nightmare seemed endless—he had no idea how long—until his feet touched solid ground and he could relieve his tortured muscles. Together the Miyagis pulled themselves onto a bank. Then they noticed a cold breeze—there had to be an entrance nearby—and saw a light ahead. It was a candle in the center of half a dozen civilians.

The ordeal left them with one conviction: they would rather die on the surface in the sunlight than smother in the dark. At the entrance they heard American voices. Betty shouted "Hello!" and said that she was from Hawaii and that her older brother was with her.

"We've come to save you," someone shouted back. "Come out!"

They emerged from the cave and found themselves in a cul-de-sac, twenty feet deep. Above them a circle of rifles rimmed its lips. Ropes tumbled down, followed by a dozen Marines hand over hand. Instead of being killed the Miyagis were hauled swiftly to the top. They could scarcely believe what was happening. Americans, smiling broadly, pressed K rations, water and cigarettes on them. A lieutenant pumped Miyagi's hand. Marines embraced them, rubbed cheeks with them, and then began bringing cans of gasoline to the cave mouth. Miyagi tried to stop them. Gesturing excitedly, he explained that the burning gasoline would kill not only the Japanese soldiers in the higher lateral but the civilians in the lower level as well. He volunteered to go back into the cave and bring out the civilians. Clad in brand-new Marine fatigues, he fought his way into the cave past armed Japanese guards, and persuaded all eight hundred civilians to surrender.

Farther south, at the very end of the island in thorny brush near the shoreline, thirteen Okinawan student nurses led by Seizen Nakasone, an instructor at the Normal School, were preparing for suicide that night—thousands of civilians had already killed themselves with grenades, motivated in equal proportion by a desire to die as true Japanese and by fear of the enemy. The girls sat in a circle singing "Sayonara," a haunting song composed by their young music teacher. In a turmoil Nakasone went off by himself to sort out his thoughts. How futile to die with nobody knowing anything about it! The dew on the trees shone in the moonlight, beautiful and mysterious.

At dawn he noticed Americans in green fatigues stealthily approaching. These were the Anglo-Saxon devils, yet he no longer feared them. Why should he and the girls kill themselves? He hastened to his students and found them huddling in a tight circle.

"Nakasone-sensei, is it all right to die now?" asked one who held a grenade. From the first she had urged suicide.

Nakasone asked them to wait—he was hoping to stall them until the Americans arrived. Two of the youngest girls whimpered for their mothers and were allowed to leave the circle. Again the girl with the grenade asked if the time had come. Again Nakasone said to wait. He started toward the beach to intercept the enemy. One GI wrote "Food—Water" on a piece of paper. Nakasone, followed by the GI's, returned to the girls and tried to convince them that the Americans, who began to close in, wouldn't harm them in any way. But they remained terrified of the "foreign devils" until they noticed one soldier cradling a rifle in one arm and a baby in the other and crooning repeatedly, "Don't cry, baby." One by one the girls left the circle—all except the resolute girl with the grenade. Nakasone wrenched it from her hand. She raced to the beach and flung herself into the water. Soldiers dragged her out, bleeding from coral cuts and still struggling. Nakasone, imagining he was the only Okinawan man who had surrendered, stifled his sense of shame. At least he had saved his students.

But Nakasone was far from alone. In the next week at least 3,000 soldiers and labor troops heeded the pleas of Petty Officer Miyagi and other Japanese volunteers like him who time and again went deep into the earth to save their comrades. Those who refused were trapped in their caves by flamethrowers and demolitions, and during the same period, 9,000 military were exterminated.

On July 2 the Okinawan campaign was officially declared ended. In almost exactly three months Americans had lost 12,520 GI's, Marines and sailors, dead or missing. It was their greatest toll in the Pacific.

The Japanese lost 110,000 troops. In addition, civilian casualties reached unprecedented proportions. Caught between two armies, approximately 75,000 innocent men, women and children died. And their sacrifice was in vain. Japan had lost the last major battle she could fight outside the homeland itself.

30

The Stragglers

1.

Even with the mainland threatened, millions of troops continued to occupy large segments of the crumbling Japanese Empire. The bastion at Rabaul, long by-passed, still stood, and the horde of soldiers in China controlled most of that country. But the men in Burma, the Philippines and the leapfrogged islands of the Pacific were lost to Japan. Few would ever return to the homeland. Those who did not commit hara-kiri or die in a last suicidal charge were abandoned, sick and starving, living from day to day, driven by the will to survive.

Corporal Kiyoshi Kamiko, the former schoolteacher, was one of these. Since sailing away from Leyte in a *banca,* he had escaped capture and death a dozen times. By April he had reached Negros, the large island west of Cebu, but before he could resume his voyage to freedom, he was conscripted by an Army unit and forced to help man a defense against the Americans who had recently landed. Kamiko, however, had not given up his dream of a new life on Borneo and persuaded six others to desert and come with him. He promoted himself to sergeant, and on the morning of April 30 led the way into the dense jungle toward the southwest coast.

But each rugged mountain was succeeded by another, and for a month they had no food other than snails and crabs. There was little relief from poisonous insects except urine applied to the swollen areas, and when they were asleep, leeches crept into their eyeballs and began sucking blood. They stuck painfully until, big as marbles and black with blood, they fell off. The men ate them; nothing went to waste in the jungle.

Food became an obsession, and they remembered a story about a cook serving his unit soup made from an executed Filipino. "The thought of eating human flesh is disgusting," someone remarked. "But I understand it tastes very good as long as you don't know it."

"When a man is really starving," said a recruit named Yabuki, "he'll eat anything." Had Yabuki ever eaten human flesh? "No, I haven't, but I worked in a crematorium on Hokkaido and there a man soon lost the feeling that he was handling human flesh. If you're squeamish you can't be a cremator. One day an ordinary fellow came to me secretly and asked for burned brains." What for? "I understand they're very beneficial if you're sick."

The conversation repelled Kamiko and he feared Yabuki might get the idea of eating Mayama, a tubercular recruit who was so thin that his puttees kept slipping down his legs. One night Kamiko overheard Yabuki whisper, "Anyway, he'll soon die," and on wakening discovered that both Yabuki's and Mayama's beds of leaves were empty. Kamiko found them at a stream. Mayama was drying his skeleton frame after a bath while Yabuki, crouched behind a rock with drawn sword, watched him like a hunter would his prey. Kamiko shouted a warning and the commotion brought the others. Yabuki, his eyes gleaming strangely, dropped his sword and exclaimed, "Forgive me!" Kamiko beat him savagely until his hands were raw. Yabuki submitted docilely, finally toppling back, his face covered with blood.

On their continued march Yabuki tried to rationalize what he had done. Mayama, he argued, was dying from tuberculosis but could not kill himself. "It would not be murder if I killed him. I would only be helping him to die sooner." Then he added, "What nonsense just to let his body rot! It would please the spirit of Mayama that his body was used to save his hungry comrades."

That night Kamiko dreamed he was attending a funeral on a

warm spring day with larks flying in the sky. "Do you want to bury him or cremate him?" asked a young man wearing *montsuki,* a ceremonial garment. It was Usui, a pale, poetic recruit.

"Please let me do it if you are going to cremate him," said a man in work clothes—Yabuki.

"The enemy will discover us by the fire," warned the head of the village—another member of the group, Nakao. A middle-aged woman, attended by girls, said, "Let us now prepare the meal." They made a soup that tasted like *satsuma-jiru* (a soy bean soup with pork and vegetables). "Very good," said the woman.

"Yes, of course," said one of the girls, "the meat is Mayama."

"So? This is Mayama?" asked another girl and laughed merrily. "How nice."

It was all so pleasant and natural that in the morning Kamiko felt happier than he had since landing on Negros. He wondered why, until he vaguely remembered having had a delightful dream. Even after he realized that he had dreamed of eating Mayama, the sense of well-being continued. He felt no distaste, not the slightest sense of guilt, and in the days to follow he found himself muttering as he marched, "I want to eat Mayama. I want to eat Mayama."

They crossed another mountain. At the foot they forded a swollen river. The feeble Mayama was swept away, but clung to a rock with his last strength and was saved by the others. They encountered an insane Japanese soldier lurking near ten dead comrades. Beyond were empty U. S. foxholes filled with abandoned equipment. They put on American uniforms and shoes, and retrieved a box of K rations, "a gift of the gods." They also found four kinds of cigarettes—Camel, Lucky Strike, Chesterfield and Philip Morris —proof, thought Kamiko, that they had "rejoined the human race."

Within a mile they came to a village where they were ambushed by guerrillas—fourteen thousand Filipinos under Lieutenant Colonel Salvador Abcede had controlled two thirds of the island since the beginning of the year. The Japanese were backed up against a river. Cornered, they leaped into the rushing water. Mayama struggled weakly in the current until his head finally disappeared. Downstream Kamiko and the others emerged on the opposite bank and scrambled up a steep hill. Behind them almost three hundred guerrillas fanned out in pursuit. But at the top of the hill the Japanese were trapped again. Filipinos astride buffaloes closed in on them from another rise, shooting and shouting. There was a burst of machine-pistol fire. Three men fell and two of them begged Kamiko—who had the only rifle—to kill them. They didn't want to die at the hands of the enemy.

"I'll avenge you and then die with you!" Kamiko crouched behind a fallen tree. He had three grenades. He would toss two and save the last for himself. One of the wounded men, Nakajima, again pleaded with Kamiko to shoot him. He called out that he wanted to help him, but since Nakajima lay hidden in the tall grass, Kamiko couldn't see where he was without exposing himself. Nakajima managed to raise himself in a sitting position, and Kamiko saw him point to his forehead with one finger. Kamiko took aim, closed his eyes and fired.

The buffaloes thundered toward the crest. In one moment I will be dead, thought Kamiko. Twenty-four years old . . . never had a woman . . . Kiyoshi Kamiko will have disappeared . . . Mother, forgive me.

"You missed!" Kamiko could hardly believe his ears; it was Nakajima's voice. "Shoot me again!" But before Kamiko could pull the trigger, dismounted guerrillas swarmed over Nakajima.

Guerrillas were lurching behind a bush above Kamiko. They shouted to their comrades below that they had discovered another one. The leader of the main group—a big man wearing a panama hat—rushed forward, a rifle with fixed bayonet in his left hand.

Kamiko saw his mother's face. He suddenly got up and aimed at the big man who was lunging at him. Startled, the Filipino tried to shift his gun to his right hand. Kamiko hesitated—the man was so close and suddenly so helpless—then fired. A bright red blotch instantly stained the guerrilla's shirt. He staggered and collapsed.

All at once there was silence. Kamiko looked around him. There wasn't a Filipino in sight. (According to Nakao, who watched hidden in the grass, the three men directly behind the big Filipino were simultaneously bowled over, apparently all felled by Kamiko's single bullet. The other guerrillas panicked "at the fantastic sight" and disappeared.) Kamiko, who never dreamt he would survive the skirmish, hastily collected the three grenades and the bullets he had placed on the grass and leaped over the bush. There was a crackle of gunfire as bullets whizzed by like angry bees. But he scrambled safely up the hill, rifle cradled in arms. At the top there was a ravine. Without hesitation he leaped into space. He bounced like a ball but still clung to the rifle. Stunned, he hid behind fallen trees just as curious faces poked over the edge of the ravine. One Filipino started down on a thick vine but gave up halfway.

Utterly exhausted, Kamiko fell asleep. He woke with a bright full moon shining down on him. He climbed up the ravine. The hillside was empty. He found a field of onions and ate a dozen before he dozed off again.

Crazed by fatigue and attacks of malaria, he followed a highway that seemed to lead to the coast until he dropped from exhaustion. He was wakened by the deafening roar of trucks—U. S. vehicles going in the opposite direction. Now he knew he was heading for the coast and Borneo, but he lost track of the days. He was so weak he could hardly put one foot in front of the other. He made hazy plans to ambush an American truck for K rations with his last grenade, and rehearsed killing himself with his rifle by pushing the trigger with his toe. But no truck passed and he fell asleep.

He heard a voice saying as from a great distance, "It's a Japanese soldier. He's dead." He wanted his rifle but couldn't move. His head throbbed and he was getting fainter. He knew he was dying. "Mother, *sayonara*," he mumbled. A moment later (in fact, it was days) he saw stars shining and heard the buzz of conversation. Someone—a man in uniform—was speaking Japanese but Kamiko couldn't make out the words because of the clamor of locusts. Gradually he realized that the sound of locusts was in his own head and that the stars were rays of sunlight coming through holes in a tent. The tent was American and so was the soldier. Kamiko knew he was captured, and that his dream of Borneo was also an illusion.*

* Kamiko and Nakao survived. So, incredibly, did Mayama. Soon after publication of his book, *I Did Not Die on Leyte*, in 1965, Kamiko encountered Mayama on a street in Tokyo. When Kamiko revealed that another of their group had survived, Mayama recoiled in fright. He said, however, that he had never been afraid of being eaten by Kamiko. "Because," he explained, "you were a teacher."

2.

There were more stragglers concentrated per square mile on Iwo Jima than on any other island in the Pacific. When Iwo Jima was officially declared secure in mid-March, Marines estimated there were not more than three hundred Japanese left alive in the caves; there were close to three thousand. Those who finally emerged after dark to prowl for provisions and safer caves found an unrecognizable landscape. Seven thousand Seabees had laid down twenty miles of roads, erected extensive housing, built breakwaters and piers, and levelled the central plateau near Motoyama to make a 10,000-foot runway, the longest in the Pacific. Scavengers often crossed paths at night without exchanging a word, but when the new moon shone (a time of sentiment to the Japanese) they would reminisce furtively about home, family and food—and finally wonder how they would die: hara-kiri or a suicide attack.

Escape from Iwo Jima was virtually impossible but there were those with the audacity to try. Ohno, the young Navy lieutenant who had escaped apparent death by dynamite in a pillbox, was one of these; he still had visions of becoming a trader or diplomat. By April 2 he had improvised a compass by magnetizing a wax needle with the magnet in a telephone receiver, and with four others collected enough material for a raft—eighteen-foot planks, empty water drums, one half of an American pup tent for a sail and the other half torn in strips, for rope—and laboriously buried it in the sand so it could hastily be assembled on the first moonless night. Hopefully they would sail north at six knots and in twelve hours catch the *Kuroshio,* which swept up past Japan.

On the first completely overcast night they hastened to the beach with their supply of food and water, and began building the raft. They estimated it would take two hours, but by the time they had erected the mast and attached the shelter half it was midnight. Too late, said Kitagata, formerly a fisherman from Hokkaido, who would navigate. Moreover, the waves were running high. He held back until Ohno drew his sword and threatened to kill him.

Kicking energetically, the five men managed to propel the bulky craft through six-foot-high breakers, coming in at long regular intervals. Thirty yards offshore a towering breaker smashed into the raft. Ohno found himself alone and thrashed desperately. Another breaker crashed down; he was torn away and knocked out. He came to on the beach. Kitagata was staring down at him almost accusingly. One of the men was sprawled in the wreckage of the raft; his skull was split open. The survivors buried him in the sand and returned disconsolately to their cave, all hope of escape gone.

In a cave at the base of Mount Suribachi, the last twenty-two survivors of that battle had withstood everything. Neither flamethrowers nor burning gasoline had been able to dislodge them, but when sea water came gushing at them from hoses, they were forced to surface. Private Kiyomi Hirakawa was next to the last in line and the exit caved in before he was half out. He flailed for his life through the sand but was held back by the last man clutching his legs. Hirakawa was wrenched to safety by those already out, and as he vainly burrowed for the man below, they disappeared up the beach. Hirakawa patiently waited until dawn, but only five of his comrades returned. They had been ambushed by the enemy. Four of them went underground again but the fifth man and Hirakawa decided to stay in the fresh air and terminate their nightmare existence with a grenade.

The sunrise was beautiful, the ocean a deep green, the grass glistening with dew. They found a cigarette butt dropped by some GI—the Army had just taken over from the Marines. They lit it with a book of U. S. matches and hunkered down behind a rock sharing puffs. Not twenty yards away GI's began issuing from tents to wash and brush their teeth, and noticed the smoke curling from behind the rock. The two Japanese were signaled to come out. They didn't move; they wanted at least one American to draw closer so they could all die with the single grenade.

Several GI's approached cautiously and flipped two lighted cigarettes near the rock. Hirakawa retrieved his—the first whole cigarette he had seen in more than a month. Two packs landed at their feet. Certain they would die at any moment, the two strag-

glers frantically smoked one after another. Two apples bounced
to the base of the rock. Hirakawa, already dizzy from the cigarettes, devoured his but couldn't taste it.

An American started to move slowly toward them with a couple
of beer bottles. This is the last treat before death, thought Hirakawa, and reached for his grenade. The GI stopped fifteen feet
away. He put down the bottles and tipped his hand to pantomime
drinking. He was too far away to be killed by the grenade. The
two Japanese moved forward but the GI stepped back. Hirakawa
put the bottle to his mouth. It was water! Ambrosia after the sul-
phurous drippings they had subsisted on in the cave.

While the two stood indecisively savoring the water, a Japanese cadet in American uniform arrived breathless. He told them
that the entire garrison on Iwo Jima had been listed as dead in
Japan. "Why should we die twice?" the youngster reasoned. "It
doesn't make sense."

Life had suddenly become possible for Hirakawa. I'm "dead"
already, he rationalized, and now have the chance for a second
existence, almost like reincarnation.

The two men surrendered. They were given a shower and clean
fatigues, and they watched incredulous as an American doctor
tenderly dressed a Japanese enlisted man's leg, allowing blood
and pus to stain his own uniform. No Japanese doctor would
ever do that, thought Hirakawa. How could he fear Americans
after that? What a waste, those terrible months in the cave, he
thought. Why did so many of us die so needlessly?

Misfortune still plagued Lieutenant Ohno. Two of his men—
Yamakage and Matsudo—had left one evening for food and ammunition but never returned, and he was alone with Kitagata.
For endless hours they endured a solitary confinement in their
cave, punctuated occasionally by jarring explosions of grenades
tossed at random by patrolling GI's. The two fugitives were so
close to Seabee work parties that they could hear jazz music piped
over a loudspeaker, and once it seemed they would surely be discovered by Americans gossiping overhead when Kitagata farted.

One unrealistic hope sustained them: there would be a major
Japanese counterattack from the sea on May 27, Navy Day. That
morning they celebrated with the last of their stolen food—a can

of ham and eggs and fruit punch—and confidently waited hour after hour for the arrival of the Combined Fleet. As the sky darkened, so did their spirits. They brooded for two days and then impulsively left their cave armed with three grenades apiece and a determination to make their own deaths as costly as possible. The darkened island seemed deserted until they intercepted two wandering GI's, who fled before Ohno could activate the first grenade —the two "GI's" were his own men, Yamakage and Matsudo.

They returned discouraged to their cave and slept. Ohno was alerted by a hissing. Grenade! He seized a blanket and was only half covered before it exploded. At first he thought he was unharmed, then he saw that his clothes were smoldering. A phosphorus grenade had showered him with burning red specks. He brushed at them frantically; bits stuck under his fingernails. In agony he dug his inflamed fingers into the ground. A package of dynamite tumbled through the cave entrance. The two men were thrown to the dirt by the thumping concussion. Through the clearing smoke they saw the entrance blasted wide open. Ohno, sword in one hand and grenade in the other, started forward. Kitagata seized him. "Useless," he whispered.

The throaty rumble of a motor and clanging gears preceded an avalanche of earth. Then everything was dark. They had been sealed in by a bulldozer. They crept back to an emergency exit and at dusk once more came to the surface with their six grenades. A complex of tents had magically mushroomed nearby and Kitagata thought grenades were not sufficient for a "proper" assault. He wanted to search for land mines buried during the battle. After five hours they were still empty-handed. Now Kitagata refused to attack altogether, but Ohno remained resolved to end it all that night. "You need only one grenade to kill yourself," he said. "Give me the other two."

Kitagata refused even that. Cowering in the predawn fog, Ohno smeared himself with stolen toothpaste and Lux soap so he would smell like an American. As he hung a necklace of three grenades around his neck he said, "We'll meet at Yasukuni Shrine." He began crawling toward the barbed-wire fence enclosing the tents. Near the gate he reached for his sword but it had slipped out of its scabbard; he cursed himself for not carrying it in his teeth like a movie commando.

In the dim light he was confident he could deceive the sentry with his "Yankee odor." But there was no guard to fool. He picked up a stone to activate the grenades and made for the largest tent, one enclosed by screen. He peered inside—a mess hall. Creeping to the next tent, he cautiously rolled up a canvas side. A man, bare to the waist, was lying on a cot a few feet away sleepily scratching his hairy chest. Ohno struck the grenade and waited for the hiss. The fuse apparently had deteriorated after several months in damp caves. He tried a second. This one hissed briefly but fizzled out.

He tied the two duds to the third grenade and tried to activate it. Again nothing happened. Tears of vexation came to his eyes. There were no weapons in the tent, not even a trenching tool. What kind of soldiers were these? It was growing lighter now and he slipped into another tent. Two of the four field cots were occupied—but no guns. Someone approached, whistling a tune. Ohno ducked behind an empty cot just before the whistler, a tall, heavyset man, stalked into the tent. He went directly to Ohno's cot and started making it. Certain he had been discovered, Ohno sprang to his feet—a scraggy apparition with Medusa hair. The big American plunged out of the tent with a shrill scream. The two men on the cots leaped at Ohno and clung to him until the whistler returned with half a dozen armed men. At bay, waiting to be shot, Ohno asked the whistler in stumbling English for his name—it would be an interesting tale to tell in Heaven. The big man, his face still drained, reluctantly mumbled "Bill." The other GI's burst into laughter. One of them said, "Please," and casually motioned Ohno to follow. Inexplicably Ohno felt as if he had found new friends. He turned to Bill and said, "How is Gary Cooper?"*

Not far from where Ohno was enjoying hot cakes and coffee, Lieutenant Satoru Omagari, who had spent two full days trying to blow himself up along with an American tank, again failed to kill himself—this time he thrust a pistol into his mouth and pulled

---

* On November 30, 1946, ashes marked with Ohno's name were delivered to his father. That same day, Ohno himself arrived home after almost a year and a half of imprisonment in Hawaii. "What a remarkable day!" exclaimed the father as they bowed. "Suddenly I have two sons."

the trigger. There was an empty click. He had long since given his troops permission to surrender, but few had done so. It would have meant eternal disgrace to a man's family, and he himself would become a *musekimono* (an outcast), one whose name was erased from the census register of his town or village. Legally he ceased to exist and the only way to get employment would be to move away and assume a false name.

Even Omagari allowed himself to contemplate surrender, but as an officer he knew that such an act could be punishable by death after the war. Driven from hiding place to hiding place by the Americans, he decided to return with his men to the Navy Aviation cave, whose occupants guarded its entrances against Japanese as well as Americans: their *hikocho* (squadron leader), a lieutenant, and his staff refused to share the spacious cave and its plentiful supply of food and water with anyone.

Now at night Omagari and his men nevertheless surprised the guards at one entrance and broke in. There were at least 150 sailors in the rambling cave and they pressed around the interlopers, curious about what was going on above—few of them had seen daylight in the past two months. They were being terrorized by the *hikocho*'s regime; enlisted men were sent out systematically on assault missions and not allowed to return lest they "draw enemy attention to the cave." They wanted Omagari to help rid them of their commander. Perhaps he would encourage the lieutenant to steal an American plane for escape from the island—a plan the *hikocho* was tentatively considering.

He talked eagerly of his plan to the newcomers, and Omagari's encouragement sounded so genuine that the lieutenant and four of his followers left the cave to find a plane. Their departure was celebrated with song, *sake* and whiskey, but the revelry was interrupted by a commotion near the rear entrance. The *hikocho*'s party was clamoring to get back in—they had quickly discovered that it was impossible to approach the flight line. They were blocked by an irate group of enlisted men. "You yourself made the rule that once a man left, he couldn't return," one of them shouted.

As their new senior officer, Omagari told the sailors, as he had previously told his own men, that they were on their own. Life in the cave became relaxed with the evaporation of military dis-

cipline. In the intense heat the men reverted to nakedness, but
the officers did retain a measure of dignity by wearing their
loincloths.

Within days the cave was discovered by the Americans. Grenades and smoke bombs drove the occupants into its deepest
recesses. As the attacks intensified, a large group decided to flee
the island by raft. Everyone was captured almost immediately,
and several were released so they could return to the cave to persuade their comrades to surrender. Their appeals failed and the
assaults continued. Omagari was singled out by loudspeaker: "I
want to talk with you. Will you come out?" It was a fellow officer,
but Omagari ignored him. An American took the microphone
and announced that the cave would be flooded the next day.

The sailors refused to believe that there was enough water on
the island for such an operation. "Let them pour it in," someone
boasted. "We'll drink it!" As sea water was pumped into the cave
the men scrambled to lateral tunnels which were slightly higher.
Then with a crump, fire raced across the torrent; gasoline had
been poured on top of the water and ignited. Only those who
had retreated to the highest lateral survived.

The following day a yellowish beam probed the smoke-filled
cavern. Omagari fumbled for a light machine gun, then saw it
was one of his own petty officers with a flashlight. He was wearing
an American uniform. Two more Japanese, also in GI fatigues,
came forward. They had cigarettes. They had been treated well
by the enemy and said there were many Japanese prisoners, including a major. Then they left to allow their countrymen to make
their own decision. No one spoke until a sailor said, "I think I'll
leave, too."

"If you want to live," said Omagari, "surrender." One by one
the men excused themselves with formal bows and filed out of
the cave. Finally Omagari was left with an old friend, Ensign
Kakuta, who was severely wounded.

"What shall we do?" Omagari asked him.

Kakuta was delirious and raved like a madman until Omagari
suggested that they die at once together. "I don't want to die,"
Kakuta replied in a flash of sanity.

Neither did Omagari. But he couldn't turn himself over naked
to the enemy. He found a bolt of cotton loincloth material, and

taking leave of Kakuta, crept out of the cave, pistol in hand. Half a dozen Americans, grinning broadly, came toward him. A baby-faced first lieutenant stretched out his hand.

"Wait," Omagari said in Japanese. "I am an officer and must be clothed before I greet you." He modestly turned his back, ripped off six feet of material and adroitly fashioned himself a loincloth. Then he too extended a hand.

He remained composed until after he had showered, then he broke down. It was the first time he had ever wept. He refused to talk and had no appetite. After supper the other prisoners riotously celebrated their resurrection with bawdy songs. He decried their behavior, and his depression increased to the point where he no longer wanted to live. He vowed that when he returned to the cave in the morning to bring out Kakuta, he would kill himself.

He made the mistake of confiding his plan to a fellow officer, who informed the Americans. Omagari was put under restraint. Like Yasunori Aoki, the *kamikaze* flier, he bit his tongue to choke on his own blood. He too failed. Then he tried to strangle himself with his bare hands, but each attempt became feebler. It was weeks before he finally accepted the degradation of surrender.

But hundreds of other stragglers on Iwo Jima could not yet bring themselves to consider surrender. Nor could they bring themselves to commit hara-kiri. They continued to hide beneath the crust of the little island, like dead souls on a distant planet. Among them were Ohno's two men—Yamakage and Matsudo. Six years later they were the last of the Iwo Jima garrison to surrender.*

---

* They held out until 1951. Yamakage returned to Iwo Jima with Stuart Griffin, a historian at Tachikawa Air Base and later columnist for the *Mainichi*. They had come to find the diary Yamakage insisted he had kept for five years. The two men methodically searched Yamakage's last cave, and finding nothing, Griffin expressed doubt that there had ever been a diary. That evening Yamakage disappeared to continue the quest for the notebook. In the morning he returned dejected, with torn hands.

Just before their plane was to leave, Griffin and Yamakage were driven to the summit of Mount Suribachi to take pictures. At the crest Yamakage started trotting with eyes on the ground. He paused, turned and slowly walked back. Then he again loped toward the edge of the cliff overlooking the sea. He picked up speed, threw both arms in the air, shouted something and jumped. Griffin ran to the edge of the cliff. There was a drop of twenty yards to a rocky ledge covered with sand, and he saw an indentation as if something had hit it. Out of sight, a hundred yards below on another ledge, lay the body of Yamakage.

He and Matsudo were by no means the last stragglers in the Pacific to surrender. In the next six years men were found all the way from Saipan to Mindoro. Two soldiers on Guam surrendered almost sixteen years after the liberation of that island. Perhaps there are more to come; they have been reported in the Philippines, New Guinea and Guadalcanal.

PART EIGHT

"One Hundred Million Die Together"

31

In Quest of Peace

1.

The American landing on Okinawa coincided with the final convulsions of the Third Reich. While Count Folke Bernadotte risked his life on trips to and from Germany to arrange peace in Europe through Gestapo chief Heinrich Himmler, other Swedes were endeavoring to bring an end to the war in the Pacific through various channels, some of them spurious.

Widar Bagge, the Swedish minister to Japan, was approached by Mamoru Shigemitsu, foreign minister in the Koiso Cabinet, with a suggestion that Sweden intercede on Japan's behalf with the United States. It came to nothing because of opposition from Shigemitsu's successor, Shigenori Togo, who was convinced that a much more influential go-between than Sweden could be found.

A private effort was introduced by another Bernadotte, Prince Carl, grandnephew of the King of Sweden, and Eric Erickson, a shipbroker who had business ties with Japan. The two urged Major General Makoto Onodera, the Japanese military attaché in Stockholm, to seek peace through Sweden. On his part Prince Carl would request the King to send "a confidential, friendly letter to the Emperor of Japan suggesting peace be negotiated as soon as possible."

Prince Carl also informed the Swedish Foreign Minister, Christian Günther, of the plan. Günther was not at all pleased, since it by-passed the regular channel, Bagge, and he protested to the Japanese minister in Stockholm. Presently General Onodera received a peremptory cable from Tokyo:

JAPAN'S POLICY IS TO FIGHT TO THE END, BUT WE HAVE INFORMATION THAT SOMEONE IS CONDUCTING A PEACE MOVE IN NORTHERN EUROPE. YOU ARE TO INVESTIGATE THE MATTER AND REPORT YOUR FINDINGS.

There were also two peace efforts of a more substantial nature being mounted in Switzerland. Both involved Allen W. Dulles, OSS representative for the area of Germany, southeastern Europe and parts of France and Italy with headquarters in Berne. The first was initiated by a German, Dr. Fritz Hack, a man of mystery who could have come out of a spy novel. He was a friend of Japan who felt it had been "stupid" for Japan to start the war. He enlisted the aid of Commander Yoshiro Fujimura, the naval attaché in Berne, who had come to realize that Japan had no chance of victory and felt that it was his duty to help bring peace no matter what the personal risk. They were joined by two other Japanese —Shigeyoshi Tsuyama, the European representative of the Osaka Shipping Line, and Shintaro Ryu, the European correspondent of the *Asahi Shimbun.*

The four conspirators held a series of clandestine meetings with representatives of Dulles and convinced them of their own political reliability. Moreover, they had access to a Navy Type 94 code machine with which they could communicate directly with Navy Headquarters in Japan without having to go through diplomatic channels. On May 3 Dr. Hack was informed by the Dulles office that the U. S. State Department authorized the commencement of direct peace negotiations with the Fujimura group.

The self-appointed peacemakers painstakingly composed a message addressed to Navy Minister Yonai and the new Chief of Staff, Admiral Soemu Toyoda, informing them that Dulles had offered to act as mediator and described him as "a leading political figure of America who has long associated with Lippmann and Stettinius, and especially enjoys the confidence of President

Roosevelt and is directly connected with the President." They had confused Dulles with his brother, John Foster, but did accurately state that Dulles had been "guiding the American political warfare for nearly all of Europe with Switzerland as his base, and particularly noteworthy is the fact that it was largely through his efforts that separate peace was effected with North Italy in early May." Instructions were "requested immediately."

Near midnight on May 8, the day of Germany's surrender, Fujimura and Tsuyama cautiously entered the darkened legation building, and with the aid of a flashlight, climbed up to the code room on the third floor. First Tsuyama set the machine for the proper date and hour, then he began typing the message in romanized Japanese. The machine automatically transmitted this in code.

In the next eight days, six more telegrams were secretly dispatched reporting Germany's surrender and the plans to move American and British units from Europe to the Far East, along with the admonition to seek peace before it was too late. After thirteen days of silence from Navy Headquarters, the conspirators sent another telegram to Yonai and Toyoda urgently requesting an early reply to the first message, since the United States was "pressing" them for an answer. It came two days later and was signed by the Naval Affairs Bureau chief:

. . . THE PRINCIPAL POINT OF YOUR NEGOTIATION WITH MR. DULLES FULLY UNDERSTOOD, BUT THERE ARE CERTAIN POINTS WHICH INDICATE AN ENEMY PLOT, THEREFORE WE ADVISE YOU TO BE VERY CAUTIOUS.

Incredulous, the Fujimura group saw the answer as a subterfuge. They in turn requested concrete evidence of "enemy machinations" and insisted that the Dulles agency was a reliable political organ directly connected with the President.

MR. DULLES AND ALL OTHERS ARE EXPECTING A SINCERE REPLY FROM JAPAN. EVEN IF WE CONCEDE A GREAT DEAL AND ADMIT IT TO BE AN ENEMY PLOT, WOULD IT NOT BE MORE ADVANTAGEOUS TO AVOID THE SAD PLIGHT OF GERMANY WHICH LOST EVERYTHING? ARE THERE ANY MEANS WHICH

PROVIDE BETTER CONDITIONS THAN THIS FOR JAPAN AT
PRESENT?

Navy Headquarters did not reply. Nor did they so much as
acknowledge continued requests for action. They had not ignored
the flood of messages from Switzerland. In fact, these had created
violent disagreement among the naval leaders. Three men were
strongly in favor of accepting the Dulles proposal—the Chief of
Operations, the head of the Naval Affairs Bureau, and Admiral
Sokichi Takagi (erstwhile plotter to kill Tojo), who offered to
fly to Switzerland to open negotiations. But Chief of Staff Toyoda,
as well as the rest of his staff, was strongly opposed. The Dulles
proposal was either a "trial balloon to sound out Japan's fighting
spirit or a plot to lower morale."

The lack of response from Tokyo drove Fujimura to extremes.
He volunteered to fly to Japan to explain in person the importance of Dulles' position in establishing a reliable high-level contact between the two belligerents. Dulles, however, feared that
such a journey would compromise the negotiations and suggested
that the Japanese send a fully authorized representative to Switzerland. America would guarantee safe air transportation. Fujimura
transmitted this promising offer directly to Yonai in words so
strong that they verged on the insulting.

Yonai was at last spurred to action. He took the proposal to
the Foreign Minister. With some trepidation—Togo too knew little
about Dulles—he asked Yonai to explore the proposal more thor-
oughly, and the admiral dispatched a message to Berne that
seemed to give approval:

YOUR POINT IS FULLY UNDERSTOOD. THE PAPERS RELATING
TO THE AFFAIR HAVE BEEN REFERRED TO THE FOREIGN MIN-
ISTER AND YOU ARE REQUESTED TO TAKE PROPER MEASURES
IN CLOSE CO-OPERATION WITH THE MINISTER AND OTHER PER-
SONS CONCERNED AT YOUR PLACE.

Despite the vague phraseology, this was the first encouragement
the conspirators had received from Tokyo, although it meant that
negotiations were now in the hands of the Foreign Ministry. But
their enthusiasm began to dim as days passed without receipt of

specific instructions from either Togo or Yonai on how to proceed. This procrastination had a similar effect on the Americans. It seemed increasingly apparent either that the men they were dealing with in Switzerland had little influence or that Tokyo had no interest in pursuing negotiations through Dulles. Togo's silence, however, was due to another cause. The Navy's reservations had become too strong; Admiral Toyoda had grown more convinced than ever that Fujimura ("only a commander in the Navy," at that) was the victim of American duplicity. Moreover, the Japanese leaders were already considering opening a channel to negotiations in a completely different direction.

While Japan searched hesitatingly for peace, her cities were being reduced to ashes. LeMay's campaign to destroy the homeland's industrial centers had reached a cataclysmic climax. Nagoya was a ruined city, and 34.2 square miles of Tokyo had been incinerated in four devastating raids, after which the usual greeting between friends was simply, "Not burned out yet?"—nothing else seemed to matter. On May 23, in the afternoon, 562 B-29's headed back to lay waste the area along the west side of Tokyo harbor that included residential as well as industrial communities. Pilots had been instructed to avoid the Palace, "since the Emperor of Japan is not at present a liability and may later become an asset." Another five square miles were destroyed that night. Thirty-six hours later 502 Superfortresses returned to hit the heart of Tokyo with 3,262 tons of incendiaries.

Once again a fire storm seared the capital, and by dawn 16.8 square miles of the financial, commercial and government district lay in ruins, including the detention house of Tokyo Army Prison. Among the tens of thousands of incinerated victims were sixty-two imprisoned Allied airmen. The uncontrollable flames reached the Imperial Palace. Flying debris leaped the moat, setting brushwood fires which spread to several buildings, including the Palace itself. Twenty-eight members of the staff died, but the Emperor and Empress were safe in their underground shelter. Because of the bombings, they now resided in the *obunko* (the imperial library), a long one-story building fronted by a row of imposing pillars half a mile from the Palace in the imperial garden. It was connected by a long tunnel to the *obunko* annex, an underground complex. Outside the Palace walls, the pavilions of the Dowager Empress, the Crown Prince and other royal personages were completely destroyed, as were the Foreign Ministry, the Prime Minister's official residence, and the Navy Department and Greater East Asia Department buildings.

More than half of the sprawling city was gutted, a wasteland, like Nagoya. Radio Tokyo had often broadcast an overoptimistic ditty, which now seemed more irrelevant than ever:

> *Why should we be afraid of air raids?*
> *The big sky is protected with iron defenses.*
> *For young and old it is time to stand up;*
> *We are loaded with the honor of defending the homeland.*
> *Come on, enemy planes! Come on many times!*

During the attack the Bees had buzzed the skyline of Tokyo with impunity, since the antiaircraft guns had long since ceased to operate, and deafened the ears of the people with their "thundering boom." This time the incendiaries, descending in "hissing and rattling bundles," set fire to the Mishimas' house. It burned slowly because it was filled with books. Poking in the embers, Mrs. Sumie Mishima found "layers upon layers of ashes of different colors. The Chinese books of the Sung and the Ming dynasty, with their softly creamed paper and beautiful woodprinted scripts, had turned into glistening snow-white powder of the finest quality imaginable. . . . The modern books produced coarse ashes in various shades of dingy gray." Mrs. Mishima put the white ashes in a broken jar, and her family found them "the cleanest possible toothpowder."

Four nights later LeMay turned to nearby Yokohama, the nation's fifth largest city; after the 517 raiders left, 85 percent of the metropolitan area was in flames. With the Tokyo–Yokohama area in ruins, the B-29's concentrated on Osaka and Kobe, and within two weeks both cities had been eliminated as targets. More than a hundred square miles of the principal cities were obliterated; Phase I of LeMay's Urban Area Program was accomplished. Two million buildings—almost one third of all construction—were razed, and at least thirteen million people left homeless.

2.

Even before Tokyo's second catastrophic fire storm, Prime Minister Suzuki had instructed Cabinet Secretary Sakomizu to make a confidential study of Japan's resources to see whether the nation could possibly continue the war. A special investigatory bureau was set up which included military and civilian experts from the Cabinet Planning Board, the Foreign, Finance and Munitions ministries, and the Army and Navy.

Their findings revealed that the situation was more critical than anyone had realized. Every aspect of Japanese life, civilian as well as military, was affected by the lack of basic raw materials. Steel production was less than 100,000 tons per month, two thirds below the official estimate. Similarly, aircraft production had dropped to a third of its quota because of shortages in aluminum and bauxite, and lack of coal had curtailed munitions production by 50 percent. Shipping was down to 1,000,000 tons, and the entire transportation system was crippled by fuel shortages and lack of manpower to handle cargo. The Sakomizu report predicted that in weeks there would be no rail transportation between cities, construction of steel ships would end and the chemical industry would collapse.

In a desperate attempt to replenish diminishing oil reserves, ersatz aviation fuel was being made from pine trees,* and since the population was faced with the specter of starvation—the rice harvest was the smallest since 1905—the government devised a plan to convert acorns into food. "The entire people will be called upon to give their aid. Schoolchildren and evacuees in particular will be enjoined to collect the maximum goal of five million *koku* [5.2 bushels] of acorns." The official daily food ration—when it could be obtained—had fallen below 1,500 calories, two thirds of the minimum Japanese standard. Those in the cities suffered most,

* The pine root oil project required a work force of millions to grub out the pine roots, as well as more than 37,000 small distillation units, each capable of producing 3 to 4 gallons of crude oil per day. Production eventually reached 70,000 barrels a month, but the process of refining was so difficult that little more than 3,000 barrels of aviation gasoline were produced by the end of the war.

and millions went into the country each Sunday to barter kimonos, jewelry, furniture, anything of value, for sweet potatoes, vegetables and fruit.

The Sakomizu report was released to a newly inaugurated "inner cabinet" officially titled the Supreme Council for the Conduct of the War but commonly called the Big Six, since it was comprised of the Prime Minister, the Foreign Minister and the four military chiefs. The implications of the report were unassailable, and on May 12, at a meeting of the Big Six, Admiral Yonai made a suggestion that could have caused his expulsion a week earlier. He proposed that they ask Russia to mediate a settlement of the war. Togo, who was as anxious to negotiate a peace as anyone else in the room, snapped that Yonai didn't know much about Russia if he imagined she would really help Japan. Suzuki, however, could see no reason why they shouldn't at least sound out the Soviets.

The forbidden subject of peace was at last out in the open, but one of the military men apprehensively suggested that they keep their discussions within the confines of the room—lest the morale of the armed forces be "seriously shaken." In this conspiratorial atmosphere they candidly discussed possible mediation by Switzerland, Sweden, China or the Vatican and concluded that these channels would undoubtedly end in the Allies' demand for unconditional surrender. General Yoshijiro Umezu, the Army Chief of Staff, saw the Soviet Union with its power and prestige as the best possible go-between for Japan. General Korechika Anami, the War Minister, concurred: the Soviets would prefer a strong Japan to emerge from the war as a buffer between their Asian possessions and the United States.

The undiplomatic Togo accused them of being unrealistic. "The matter of Japan must have been discussed at the Yalta Conference," he said, "so it is probably hopeless to try and get the Soviets on our side now. Judging from past Russian actions [recently he had told Sakomizu, "The Soviet Union is not to be trusted"], I think it's even going to be difficult to keep her from joining the war. It would be better, in my opinion, to negotiate directly with the United States for a cease-fire."

But Suzuki, who was still playing *haragei,* backed the generals.

"Stalin seems to be like Saigo,* and I believe he will make every effort on our behalf if we ask him." Togo, who was from Kyushu, saw no similarity but when it became evident that the Army was willing to negotiate through Russia alone, he agreed to write up a draft memorandum to that effect. He presented it to the Big Six on May 14:

It should be clearly made known to Russia that she owes her victory over Germany to Japan, since we remained neutral, and that it would be to the advantage of the Soviets to help Japan maintain her international position, since they may have the United States as an enemy in the future.

The memorandum warned that Russia, having achieved her victory over Germany, might demand a price "much beyond our imagination," and Japan should be prepared to give up Port Arthur, Dairen, the railways in South Manchuria and the northern portions of the Kuriles.

Togo expected opposition from the military at the prospect of giving up so much territory, but the Big Six approved the draft unanimously and instructed him to initiate negotiations. Togo reckoned that the straightest line to Moscow would go through a former premier and foreign minister, Koki Hirota, who had many ties with diplomats of the Soviet Union. Togo asked him to sound out the Soviet ambassador, Yakov Malik, who was staying at Gohra, a resort town in the Hakone area, a two-hour drive from Tokyo.

Hirota was to try to convince Malik to reverse the recent Soviet decision not to extend their Neutrality Pact,* and ask for help in ending the war. The devastating May 25 fire bombing of Tokyo

---

* The samurai hero from Kyushu who arranged with rebel troops a peaceable transfer of the city of Edo in 1867.

* On April 5, 1945, the Soviet government had announced that it could not renew its pact with Japan because the situation had "basically altered" since it was signed. *A Short History of the U.S.S.R.* states that the pact "ran out on April 5, 1945." It did not terminate until April 13, 1946, and according to its terms, a full year's notice had to be given if either party did not wish to renew it. Unaware of the secret provisions in the Yalta agreement, the Japanese felt assured of a twelve-month period of grace, during which time they might get the Russians to sign a new pact. Perhaps the Soviet historians made a mistake; perhaps they were attempting to obscure the fact that when Russia declared war on Japan on August 8, 1945, she was violating a treaty.

delayed Hirota's departure, and it was not until June 3 that he finally reached Gohra. That evening he strolled around the mountain village like any other vacationer and stopped, as if by chance, at the Gohra Hotel, a comfortable European-type establishment, to chat with Malik.

"It is very fortunate that Japan and the Soviet Union have not exchanged blows in this war," Hirota said affably, and congratulated Malik on his country's victory over Hitler. He assured Malik that the Japanese people earnestly desired friendly relations with both the Soviet Union and China. Malik was guarded—he implied that there were those in Japan who showed considerable antagonism to the Soviet Union—but he did invite Hirota to dinner at the hotel the next evening.

Over the table Hirota concentrated on Japan's desire to resuscitate the Neutrality Pact. "Japan wishes to promote friendly relations with the Soviet Union even before it terminates. That's why we are currently trying to figure out how to go about it."

Malik replied that Russia had consistently maintained a peaceful policy but that her distrust of Japan was based on the many belligerent acts of the past and the anti-Soviet feeling in Japan.

Hirota pointed out that there was "an increasing number of people who are beginning to understand the attitude of the U.S.S.R. . . . Japan wishes to find means to maintain peace with the Soviet Union for a long time to come." When Malik wondered if this was simply Hirota's personal opinion, the answer was: "I want you to know that what I just told you reflects the attitude of the Imperial Government as well as the people."

Malik pondered this for a moment, then said he wanted a few days to think the matter over before giving an answer. Hirota was encouraged; he had dealt with the Russians before and knew they were inherently cautious. He reported to Togo that "the atmosphere of the talks was friendly, that the Russian side responded satisfactorily and the conversations looked hopeful."

But hopes for a negotiated peace were dashed the following morning—it was June 6—at another Big Six meeting when Togo was handed a document composed by the Supreme Command entitled *The Fundamental Policy to be Followed Henceforth in the Conduct of the War*. It demanded an official reaffirmation of carrying the war to its ultimate conclusion:

With a faith born of eternal loyalty as our inspiration, we shall—thanks to the advantages of our terrain and the unity of our nation—prosecute the war to the bitter end in order to uphold our *kokutai* [national essence], protect the imperial land and achieve our goals of conquest.

There followed a list of steps that would have to be taken, including all-out preparations for defense of the mainland and organization of a national volunteer army. Togo read on in consternation. No one had consulted him about this. If accepted, it ensured Japan's destruction. Ironically, Sakomizu's devastating report was attached, and items from it had been quoted out of context with the ostensible purpose of giving weight to the Supreme Command's position.

Togo stood up painfully—he had been suffering from pernicious anemia for five years. "Going through these items," he said, waving the Sakomizu report, "I can find no reason for continuing the war. As far as I can see, there is no relation between your draft proposal and the detailed items submitted." He ridiculed all the Supreme Command's theories, including the one that the nearer the battlefield came to Japan, the more advantageous it would be. And what about the strained will of the hard-pressed people?

At this Admiral Toyoda lost his composure. "Even if the Japanese people are weary of the war, we must fight to the last man!"

General Anami was furious. "If we cannot fulfill our responsibility as advisers to the Throne," he exclaimed, "we should offer our sincere apologies by committing hara-kiri!"

Another hour passed. Without any support Togo could no longer delay the decision, and the resolution to fight to the end was passed. On his way out, Tog confronted Admiral Yonai. "I expected support from you today," he complained, "but I got none."

Two days later, on June 8, an imperial conference was convened to present the Supreme Council's resolution to the Emperor for his approval. It was held in the Imperial Household Ministry because of fire damage to the Palace. In attendance, besides the Emperor, were the Big Six, President of the Privy Council Hiranuma, the Munitions Minister, the Agriculture and Forestry Minister, and four secretaries including Sakomizu.

Unprepared for what he was hearing, the Emperor sat silent on his dais "with a grave look on his face." Togo alone expressed reservations but they were muted, apparently out of consideration for His Majesty, and at the conclusion of the stilted discussion, even he did not respond to Suzuki's request for summary opinions on the new policy. "Well, then," said the Prime Minister, "I conclude that no one has any particular objection to the plan."

The thirteen members rose, bowed to the Emperor and backed out of the room. As the Emperor emerged from the meeting Marquis Kido was puzzled by the concern on his face and wondered why. "They have made this decision," His Majesty replied and showed the Privy Seal a copy of the new policy. It was as great a surprise to Kido as it had been to Togo, and it undermined his faith in Suzuki. Now it was apparent that he could no longer depend on the aging Prime Minister, even with the support of Togo, to take the initiative for peace. As confidential adviser to the Throne, tradition required Kido to remain above politics. In the past he had circumvented this restriction indirectly, but now somehow he had to take positive action.

The problem seemed insoluble. All that afternoon and into the night he searched for a solution. Ideally the initiative should come from the Army, whose power could thwart other peace movements. The solution was inescapable: there was one source no one could oppose—the Throne. Kido decided to confront the Emperor with candor. He felt that in the crisis, such an unprecedented approach was necessary to persuade His Majesty to end the war by personal intervention. At last the Privy Seal dropped off to sleep.

In the morning he marshaled his arguments in a paper entitled *Tentative Plan to Cope with the Situation.* At 1:30 P.M. he presented himself to the Emperor. "Under the circumstances," he said, "I consider any peace move almost impossible, but I will, with His Majesty's gracious permission, try to address myself to the problem. These are my ideas."

The Emperor studied the document. The first four paragraphs summed up the situation: reports on production indicated that it was unlikely war could be waged by the end of the year; further, the devastation wrought by the bombings, aggravated by the growing food shortage, would create serious unrest throughout the nation.

5. Based on the above, I believe Japan must resolutely move toward a resumption of peace by terminating hostilities. How shall this objective be attained? That is the question which calls for cautious study.

6. It is almost certain, in the light of various announcements, speeches and articles made public by the enemy in their peace offensive, that the enemy's main object is to overthrow the so-called *gumbatsu*, that is, military clique.

7. Although it is customary to start negotiations with a proposal of peace from the military, followed by negotiations on the part of the government, this would be almost impossible at the present stage in Japan's current condition. Moreover, if we wait for a more favorable opportunity, it may be too late. Then Japan would share Germany's fate and her minimum demands—the security of royal family and retention of our national essence—might not even be met.

8. Exceptional and unprecedented measures have to be taken—and we do so with awe and trepidation—but I believe the only possible course is to ask His Majesty to intervene for the sake of the people and initiate termination of hostilities in the following manner:

9. Start negotiations with an intermediary power with His Majesty's personal message. . . .

10. The message should cite the Imperial Rescript on the Declaration of War [December 8, 1941] and emphasize His Majesty's constant desire for peace and his decision to end the war—bearing the unbearable in view of the heavy damages we have sustained in the war—on reasonable terms. The minimum peace terms are:

Honorable peace (this may, inevitably, be the minimum term)

If guarantee is obtained that the Pacific be truly pacific . . . Japan will renounce her right of occupation and claim of leadership for all occupied areas, provided that the nations and peoples therein attain their independence. The Japanese armed forces in these occupied areas will be withdrawn by Japan on her own accord. . . .

11. As for armament limitation, Japan must be prepared to meet demands for a pretty heavy reduction. We must be contented with minimum armament for national defense.

This is my personal opinion, candidly expressed. It contains only the essential points.

The Emperor appeared to be "greatly satisfied" by what he read, and Kido asked permission to discuss the proposal with the Prime Minister and other leaders; he would need the support of key men in the Cabinet before the Emperor could be openly involved. His Majesty approved: "Do it at once."

Kido, however, felt it was wiser to wait for a few days. The Diet was in session and the entire Cabinet was too involved in politics. On the morning of June 13, the final day of the proceedings, Kido intercepted Suzuki on his way to the Diet Building. He briefly outlined his peace plan and got a promise from Suzuki to return as soon as the Diet was adjourned.

In the meantime Kido talked to Admiral Yonai. He was the only one of the four military chiefs the Privy Seal was sure would not betray the peace plan. He asked the admiral to read the proposal. Yonai reacted with his usual caution. "Of course, very good idea," he said with restrained enthusiasm, "but I wonder how the Prime Minister really feels about the war?"

So did Kido.

The object of their conjecture was just rising from his seat to address the House of Peers and House of Representatives. Suzuki was far more committed to peace than he had indicated to Kido, and was about to prove it in public. He began by referring to a speech he had made in San Francisco twenty-seven years before when he commanded the training fleet. His listeners, who were prepared to indulge the reminiscences of an old man, were shocked by the point he was making.

"The gist of my speech was: 'Japan is not warlike. She is the most peace-loving nation in the world. There is no reason why she and the United States should come to war, but if they do, the conflict will be a long one and end disastrously. The Pacific Ocean,

as the name suggests, should be the Sea of Peace with no troop transports permitted on its surface. However, if such an unhappy event should come to pass, both sides will be meted out punishment by the gods.' "*

A wave of indignation swept the vast hall. The word "peace" and the desirability to achieve it had been publicly proclaimed by the head of the government, and the effect was not mitigated by Suzuki's concluding exhortation that the nation must fight to the end and that unconditional surrender would mean the ruin of the Japanese race. As he turned from the podium the hostility erupted into boos, threatening gestures, and cries of "Down with the Suzuki Cabinet!" One Diet member, however, elbowed his way to Cabinet Secretary Sakomizu. "Now I understand what the Prime Minister means in his heart," he said tearfully. "Please continue!"

If Suzuki heard the jeers, he ignored them as he absently waved at the audience. Forcing his way through the pressing crowd, he started for the Imperial Household Ministry to make the traditional report to the Emperor. Then he proceeded down the corridor to Kido's office, where he read the Privy Seal's unique plan in its entirety. Suzuki promised to do everything he could to further its aims, but like Yonai, he seemed to have some reservations: "I wonder what Admiral Yonai thinks about all this?"

"Yonai said the same thing about you," Kido told him. This struck Suzuki as comical, but Kido was perturbed. How was it that at such a critical point in the war neither the Prime Minister nor his Navy Minister knew what the other "had in his stomach"?

Suzuki's pledge to help Kido did not alter his public stance. At a press conference the following morning he spoke like a militarist. "If our hundred million people fight with the resolve to sacrifice their lives, I believe it is not at all impossible to attain the great goal of preserving the essence of Japan. . . . None of our fighting men can understand how it is that Germany, with such a large army left, was not able to hold out until the end. In quan-

---

* Suzuki had submitted the speech to his cabinet two days earlier and was urged to eliminate the phrase "Sea of Peace," and the reference to retribution; the Americans alone should be punished by the gods. But Suzuki ignored both suggestions. He told his son just before the Diet session that there would be no point in making a speech with such deletions; he hoped that the United States would take his words as a subtle peace feeler.

tities of arms and supplies, we may not compare favorably with the enemy, but our determination as we stand on the firing line is peculiar to us alone. With this formidable strength we must fight to the end, the entire population uniting as one body."

Kido now summoned the third member of the Cabinet whose support was vital, Foreign Minister Togo. The Privy Seal did not show him the written proposal but confided to him that the Emperor was deeply disturbed by the decision presented to him at the latest imperial conference. Togo pointed out that he had opposed the suicidal Army plan at the Big Six meeting.

"I know," said Kido. "I have some ideas of my own about peace and I need your help." He indicated that the Emperor might possibly make a public statement calling for peace.

Togo was ready to do anything he could, and said he would be extremely gratified "if the Emperor were to say now that we should work to end the war without delay, for there could be no greater aid to the attainment of my purpose than such words from the Throne."

It was not Kido's intention to involve the other three military chiefs, but on impulse one day he found himself telling War Minister Anami about his proposal. It happened as a result of Anami's casual remark as he left the Privy Seal's office: "I hear you're resigning. Is it true?"

Perhaps the fact that they had once been very intimate—Anami was military aide to the Emperor when Kido was chief secretary to the Privy Seal—led Kido to say, "I'm not resigning, but if I tell you what's on my mind you may ask me to resign."

"What is it?" Anami wanted to know.

Kido revealed the entire peace plan and the part the Throne would play in it. His instinct was sound. Anami was not antagonistic; in fact, he "agreed in principle" with the Privy Seal's line of action. He had considerable reservations, however, about its timing. It would be more advantageous, he pointed out, for Japan to sue for peace "after the United States has sustained heavy losses in the Mainland Beach Operation."

Then Kido belittled the fact that thousands of planes had been collected to be thrown against the invaders. "When they are gone, what will you do?" Since Japan did not have more strength than to destroy one third of the American landing force, it would be better to come to terms before the invasion. Anami recognized the authority of Kido's tactical conclusions—his own secret files* —and although he would not support the Kido plan, he promised not to oppose it "too vigorously" before the Big Six.

The unexpected opportunity to sound out Anami had been "assistance from Heaven." Now Kido felt he had the backing he needed to confront the Supreme Council. On June 22 the Emperor, at the instigation of his Privy Seal, abruptly summoned the Big Six to the *obunko* annex. He signified the unique informality of the occasion by speaking first. "This is not an imperial command," he said simply, "but merely a discussion. At the last meeting of the Supreme Council it was decided to adopt a new policy and prepare the homeland for defense. But now I have deemed it necessary to consider a move toward peace, an unprecedented one, and I ask you to take steps at once to realize my wish." General Umezu and Admiral Toyoda, the two men Kido had not consulted, were staggered.

The Emperor asked if they had considered initiating negotiations. He already knew the answer—Togo had privately kept him informed. Suzuki struggled to his feet and allowed as how the government had given thought to negotiations. Togo gave a full account of Hirota's conversations with Malik.

"When will an envoy be sent to the Soviet Union?" the Emperor asked. "Is there any chance of success?"

Togo estimated that envoys would probably arrive in Moscow before mid-July. He warned, however, that Japan would no doubt be forced to make numerous concessions to Stalin.

The Emperor turned to the two Army representatives, who had remained silent. Anami kept his word to Kido: he did not object to any attempt "to save the situation," but expressed his fear that it would be construed as a sign of weakness if Japan appeared too anxious to end the war. Army Chief of Staff Umezu,

* Top-secret information was often channeled to Kido and other proponents of peace by a special group of influential aides who were endeavoring to reform the Big Six into a peace body. The group was composed of Colonel Sei Matsutani, Suzuki's first secretary; Toshikazu Kase, Togo's secretary; Marquis Yasumasa Matsudaira, Kido's aide and secretary; and the redoubtable Admiral Takagi, who represented Yonai. These four conferred frequently, occasionally changing the meeting place to prevent being tracked down by the *kempeitai*. Their favorite rendezvous was a secluded room in the Diet Building.

on the other hand, was openly distressed: any proposal of peace would have incalculable impact at home and abroad and should be "treated with the utmost caution."

"Does treating the proposal 'with the utmost caution' imply acting only after having struck another blow at the enemy?" the Emperor asked. Umezu said no. "It is all very well to be cautious, but if we are too cautious we will miss our opportunity."

"Well, the sooner the better, then," Umezu conceded.

It was the first palpable step toward peace.

On June 24 Hirota, at Togo's bidding, once more visited Malik. This time Hirota abandoned the language of diplomacy and made a direct request to have the moribund Neutrality Pact superseded. Malik remained evasive however; there was no need for another pact, he said, since the previous one was still in effect.

In desperation, Hirota offered rubber, tin, lead and tungsten in exchange for oil. "If the Soviet Army and the Japanese Navy were to join forces," he said, "Japan and the Soviet Union together would become the strongest force in the world!"

Understandably, Malik was not impressed; the bulk of the Imperial Navy was resting on the bottom of the sea. He replied that Russia didn't have enough oil for her own needs. Brusquely he questioned the necessity for further meetings unless Japan came up with some "concrete plan."

In less than a week Hirota returned with one in writing: in return for a new nonaggression treaty and oil, Japan promised to give Manchuria her independence and relinquish her fishing concessions in Soviet waters. Malik remained noncommittal; he would get back to Hirota when he got an answer from Moscow. Then he asked if it was true that Japan and America were conducting peace negotiations in Sweden.

"Of course not," Hirota exclaimed. Japan would surely consult the Soviet Union before engaging in any negotiations at all.

Hirota's ingenuous answer was close to the truth: Japan had turned down two offers to negotiate in Sweden, and the Fujimura channel in Berne had been abandoned as well. But a new, more prestigious peace venture was getting under way in Switzerland. It was inspired by a remark made by Lieutenant General Seigo Okamoto, the military attaché, to two Japanese bankers—Kojiro

Kitamura and Kan Yoshimura, officials of the Bank for International Settlements in Basel. "Japan intends to fight to the end," he had told them. "However, she can't fight an extended war, and if there is any peace move on the part of the Americans, I would like to negotiate with them."

Such words from a general in such a sensitive position had an electrifying effect on the two civilians. Perhaps it was possible, after all, to save Japan from total ruin? But how could the militarists back home be persuaded to countenance these negotiations?

"Chief of Staff Umezu and I are very close friends," Okamoto said confidently. "In the Nomonhan Incident [on the Manchurian border in 1938] he was my Army commander. So he will listen to what I say."

The bankers agreed to "sound out" the Americans. But who was there with sufficient prestige to act as go-between? They settled on Per Jacobsson, a director of their bank and known for his proficiency as a negotiator in international disputes. Like so many Swedes before him, Jacobsson was responsive. He was well thought of by the Americans, and easily made direct contact with a Dulles operative.

Jacobsson told the two bankers that the Americans fully appreciated the respect in which the royal family was held by the Japanese; that was why they had sedulously avoided bombing the Imperial Palace. The conditions for any peace talks would, of course, have to be unconditional surrender. Yoshimura objected to the term even in a purely military sense. It was better than continuing a hopeless war, argued Jacobsson. The Kaiser's surrender in 1918 had prevented Germany from being totally occupied, as it was now, and had, furthermore, led to the retention of the German government. It was likely that both the Constitution and the Throne could be saved even after unconditional surrender.

On July 10 Jacobsson was back talking to the Americans, this time to Gero von S. Gaevernitz, Dulles' German-born second-in-command who had masterminded the surrender of all German forces in Italy. Gaevernitz re-emphasized the necessity for unconditional surrender but also held out hope that the Japanese might be able to retain their Emperor. No, the latter item could not be put in writing. The only ones who could do that were President Truman and Churchill. It would take weeks.

"Could not Allen Dulles tell what his [own] impression is?" asked Jacobsson.

"He would not be authorized to do so."

"Have you never done or said anything without authorization?"

Gaevernitz conceded the possibility. "But suppose Allen Dulles made such a statement and suppose a leakage occurred in Tokyo. The result might be that Dulles could no longer be used by the State Department." Instead Gaevernitz proposed that Jacobsson exaggerate a bit and tell the Japanese that he was "in direct contact with the Americans responsible for these surrender negotiations." He added that in his opinion "these talks ought not to be carried on with anybody else than those present. No other Americans. If the Japanese approached the U. S. Military Attaché that would only muddle matters. He might not want to go on with the talks. And no Swiss."

Now the next step was up to the Japanese. But General Okamoto, whose words had instigated the conspiracy, refused to involve Tokyo until he was assured of the fate of the royal family and the Constitution. These restrictions did not discourage Jacobsson. He had just received word from the Americans that in a few days he was to meet Dulles himself in Germany, and confident of his own powers of persuasion, he felt he might persuade Dulles to allay Okamoto's fears.

While these scattered efforts went on, the Japanese militarists completed their final plans for suicidal defense of the homeland —Operation Decision (KETSU-Go). More than ten thousand planes—most of them hastily converted trainers—had been collected. Two thirds of these would be thrown into the battle for Kyushu; the rest would be reserved to repel any landing near Tokyo. In the face of the bloody lessons of Tarawa and Saipan, the plan was to crush the Americans on the beaches with fifty-three infantry divisions and twenty-five brigades—a total of 2,350,-000 troops. These would be backed by almost 4,000,000 Army and Navy civilian employees, a special garrison force of 250,000, and a 28,000,000 civilian militia. This last mammoth force would evolve from the national volunteer military service law for men from fifteen to sixty and women from seventeen to forty-five which had been unanimously passed at the final Diet session. The military spokesmen, whose impressive testimony had ensured passage of the bill, later showed Suzuki and his cabinet a display of the weapons that would be used by the volunteers: muzzle-loading rifles and bamboo sticks cut into spears stacked beside bows and arrows from feudal times.

3.

The negotiations initiated by the Japanese government itself were being ignored. A week had gone by and Moscow had not replied to Hirota's overtures. It was the Emperor who lost his patience, and he sent for Prime Minister Suzuki on July 7. "It will not do to miss the opportunity of exploring the Soviet Union's real intentions," he said. Couldn't Russia be asked directly to mediate? Why not dispatch the special envoy with a personal message from the Throne?

Konoye was the Emperor's obvious choice for such a mission. He was summoned to Tokyo on July 12 from his summer home in Karuizawa. Dressed as a commoner in simple khakis—the national civilian uniform—he waited with mixed emotions in the *obunko* for the Emperor to ascend from his underground office. His Majesty's appearance was unsettling—he looked pale, exhausted and ill-groomed. Contrary to court protocol, the two were alone. Kido's hope that this would encourage frankness was borne out by Konoye's reply to the question: What did the former prime minister think should be done about the war? "The people are tired of war," Konoye replied candidly. "They all wish His Majesty would condescend to act in their behalf and do something to relieve their plight. There are even those who say His Majesty is to blame. It is necessary to end the war as soon as possible."

The Emperor told him to make preparations to leave for Moscow. Though Konoye was privately opposed to relying on Russia as a go-between, he was willing to take any step to rectify his past mistakes. He brought up the occasion of the signing of the Tripartite Pact, when the Emperor had warned him that it would eventually lead to war with Britain and America. "At that time,"

Konoye went on, "His Majesty graciously told me I would have to share the consequences with him, the good things as well as the bad. Now if it is the imperial command"—he was choked with emotion—"I am prepared to risk my life for His Majesty's sake."

As soon as Konoye left, the Emperor was rejoined by Kido. He turned to the Privy Seal and said with satisfaction, "This time he appears to be resolute."

Even as the Emperor was sounding out Konoye, Ambassador Naotake Sato in Moscow was advised of the prince's imminent arrival:

HIS MAJESTY IS EXTREMELY ANXIOUS TO TERMINATE THE WAR AS SOON AS POSSIBLE, BEING DEEPLY CONCERNED THAT ANY FURTHER CONTINUATION OF HOSTILITIES WILL ONLY AGGRAVATE THE UNTOLD MISERIES OF THE MILLIONS UPON MILLIONS OF INNOCENT MEN AND WOMEN IN THE COUNTRIES AT WAR. SHOULD, HOWEVER, THE UNITED STATES AND GREAT BRITAIN INSIST ON UNCONDITIONAL SURRENDER, JAPAN WOULD BE FORCED TO FIGHT TO THE BITTER END WITH ALL HER MIGHT IN ORDER TO VINDICATE HER HONOR AND SAFEGUARD HER NATIONAL EXISTENCE, WHICH, TO OUR INTENSE REGRET, WOULD ENTAIL FURTHER BLOODSHED. OUR GOVERNMENT THEREFORE DESIRES TO NEGOTIATE FOR A SPEEDY RESTORATION OF PEACE, PROMPTED AS WE SINCERELY ARE BY SOLICITUDE FOR THE WELFARE OF MANKIND. FOR THIS PURPOSE PRINCE KONOYE WILL PROCEED TO MOSCOW WITH A PERSONAL MESSAGE FROM THE EMPEROR AND IT IS REQUESTED THAT THE SOVIET GOVERNMENT KINDLY PROVIDE HIM WITH TRAVEL FACILITIES.

Sato knew the Russians well enough to doubt that anything good would come of this maneuver; at one time he had spent almost nine years in St. Petersburg and had been ambassador in Moscow since early 1942. In what way, he reasoned, would the Soviets profit from a speedy end to the war in the Pacific? Molotov had shown no interest in the Hirota-Malik conversations. Why would he be interested now? His assessment was confirmed as soon as he phoned the Kremlin and requested an appointment with the Foreign Commissar. Molotov was about to leave for an Allied conference in Germany and was too busy. Would Deputy Commissar Alexander Lozovsky do?

Lozovsky (his real name was A. S. Dridso) was as uncooperative as Malik had been with Hirota. He politely side-stepped every attempt Sato made to get prompt approval for Konoye's visit. The most Lozovsky would say was that a reply would take at least several days.

Sato cabled a report to Togo, with the caustic observation that if Konoye was merely coming to enunciate "previous abstractions, lacking in concreteness," he had better stay home, and the following day added some unpalatable advice:

. . . A PEACE TREATY BY NEGOTIATION IS SOMETHING WHICH CANNOT WIN THE SUPPORT OF THE SOVIET UNION. IN THE FINAL ANALYSIS, IF OUR COUNTRY TRULY DESIRES TO TERMINATE THE WAR, WE HAVE NO ALTERNATIVE BUT TO ACCEPT UNCONDITIONAL SURRENDER OR SOMETHING VERY CLOSE TO IT.

The question of Japan's surrender was also being pursued by Per Jacobsson and Allen Dulles in Germany. The OSS now had headquarters at Wiesbaden in a champagne factory that once supplied wine to Himmler. The stench was so penetrating, however, that Jacobsson's meeting with Dulles and Gaevernitz took place in their billets, a snug two-story stucco house.

Dulles' primary concern was whether the Japanese negotiators were sincere. Jacobsson was certain that they were and that the peace party in Japan was doing its best, but Dulles remained suspicious. "Isn't this perhaps a trick of the war party to strengthen morale? To try to show how unreasonable the Americans are?"

Jacobsson resented the implication that he was an accessory to a deception. He curtly conceded that he did not have Dulles' experience in negotiating but that he had a reputation for being trustworthy. "I even persuaded De Valera to negotiate with the British in 1935–37."

They argued for hours in stifling heat and retired with nothing resolved. At breakfast Jacobsson renewed his appeal to maintain the Throne—the crux, he felt, of the negotiations. The position of the Emperor should depend solely on how he conducted himself. He could disassociate himself from the military, and if he then came out with a peace move, something could be worked out. This way the American public would be able to distinguish between the royal family and the war clique.

Dulles could not, even by inference, commit his government to such a policy. If, however, the Emperor took the lead in effectuating a surrender and removed Japanese troops from foreign soil, Americans would be more prone to let him continue to reign. It was merely an opinion but one from a man of position, and Dulles' parting words emphasized his sincerity. "We very much appreciate that you have come here," he told Jacobsson. "Don't think we do not." Then he made a phone call to Potsdam, a city just west of Berlin, where President Truman and his advisers had just arrived to meet with Churchill and Stalin in the final conference of the war.

32

"That Was Not Any Decision That You Had to Worry About"

1.

On the morning of July 15, *Augusta,* the cruiser that had brought Roosevelt to his historic meeting with Churchill off Newfoundland to promulgate the Atlantic Charter, docked at Antwerp with Harry S. Truman. A little after noon he was aboard the presidential plane, *The Sacred Cow,* bound for Potsdam and the meeting code-named "Terminal."

War had forced an uneasy alliance between capitalism and Communism, and the advent of peace exposed the underlying antagonisms between East and West. The union forged at Yalta was already disintegrating. Stalin had broken his promise to honor the Declaration of Liberated Europe by attempting to communize all territory liberated by the Red Army in eastern Europe. He himself suspected the West of plotting behind his back: witness the "anti-Soviet" negotiations recently concluded by the Dulles group in North Italy.

There was no doubt how the new President intended to handle the Russians. Molotov had already found his frankness disconcerting. "The United States is prepared to carry out loyally all the agreements reached at Yalta and only asks that the Soviet government do the same," he had told the Foreign Commissar at their first meeting in Washington. "But I want it clearly understood that this can be only on a basis of the mutual observation of agreements and not on the basis of a one-way street."

"I have never been talked to like that in my life!" Molotov exclaimed angrily.

"Carry out your agreements, and you won't get talked to like that," said Truman.

Truman's goals for "Terminal" were clear. He wanted to establish just political and economic principles for the occupation of Germany, enforce the Declaration on Liberated Europe (particularly in reference to Poland) and solve the reparations problem. All of these would be on the agenda of the plenary sessions. But termination of the war in Asia would require equal though unofficial attention. To Truman, this "most urgent" problem at Potsdam could not be settled around the formal conference table but required a private encounter with Stalin. At the behest of Marshall and MacArthur he was to insinuate the Soviets into the war against Japan as soon as possible. He was to do this even with the secret knowledge that an atomic bomb would soon be tested in New Mexico.

He had brought with him a draft declaration calling on the Japanese to surrender. It had been instigated by a diplomat who had strived to prevent the war, Joseph Grew. Appalled by reports of the fire bombings in Tokyo, he had called on Truman on May 29 (he was Acting Secretary of State while Stettinius attended the United Nations conference in San Francisco) with the plea that the President issue a proclamation informing the Japanese that unconditional surrender did not mean the end of the imperial system. Without such assurance, he said, it was doubtful that the Japanese would ever surrender. He was supported by Far Eastern experts in the State Department, such as Eugene Dooman, Joseph Ballantine and Professor George Blakeslee.

"I've already given thought to the matter," Truman replied, "and it seems to me a sound idea." He wanted Ambassador Grew to consult the Joint Chiefs and the Secretaries of War and Navy before a final decision was made.

Stimson and Forrestal "liked the idea," and so did Marshall, but the Chief of Staff feared that a public proclamation "at this time would be premature." Stimson thought the wording would depend on the successful testing of the atom bomb. The Secretary of War had become increasingly preoccupied over the use of the bomb. He headed a group of prominent civilians known as the Interim Committee which included three noted scientists and which had been set up to advise the President on the political, military and scientific questions that the unleashing of atomic energy would raise. He put his conclusions to the committee, which met two days later with General Marshall and a four-man advisory Scientific Panel. "Gentlemen," he said, "it is our responsibility to recommend action that may turn the course of civilization. In our hands we expect soon to have a weapon of wholly unprecedented destructive power. Today's prime fact is war. Our great task is to bring this war to a prompt and successful conclusion. We may assume that our new weapon puts in our hands overwhelming power. It is our obligation to use this power with the best wisdom we can command. To us now the matter of first importance is how our use of this new weapon will appear in the long view of history."

One of the Scientific Panel members, Dr. J. Robert Oppenheimer, the physicist responsible for the design and testing of the bomb, estimated that a single atomic explosion would probably kill twenty thousand people. The mention of this figure appalled Stimson. The objective, he interjected, should be military destruction, not the lives of civilians. For example, Kyoto, one of the cities on a list of targets, should not be bombed; it was a cultural center and its shrines were revered. His knowledge of the ancient city was fortuitous; recently the son of a friend, a student of the Orient, had told him at length of the charms of Kyoto.

There was no question in General Marshall's mind that the bomb should be used to end the war quickly and save American lives, but he did not want to use the prestige of his office to influence the committee. He said that he hoped the bomb would not have to be dropped; it would prematurely reveal to the Soviets the new power America possessed and diminish its deterrent effect in the postwar world.

When they adjourned for lunch Dr. Arthur Holly Compton, another of the consulting scientists, turned to Stimson on his left and asked if some nonmilitary demonstration couldn't be arranged to impress the Japanese. The possibility was debated at the table. If an isolated place in Japan were announced in advance, the plane carrying the bomb might be shot down. Moreover, what if the demonstration bomb didn't work? Innumerable things could go wrong. And if a test were made on neutral ground, the Japanese leaders might think it was faked. The conclusion was that the bomb should be used as soon as possible "against such a target as to make clear its devastating strength"—without warning.

The three scientists on the Interim Committee—Vannevar Bush, James B. Conant and Karl Compton—concurred but a number of other scientists working on the bomb were dismayed at their recommendation. They were led by Dr. James Franck, a refugee from Germany and a Nobel-prize physicist. He and seven other well-known scientists submitted a report to the committee:

. . . If the United States were to be the first to release this new means of indiscriminate destruction upon mankind, she would sacrifice public support throughout the world, precipitate the race for armaments, and prejudice the possibility of reaching an international agreement on the future control of such weapons.

Much more favorable conditions for the eventual achievement of such an agreement could be created if nuclear bombs were first revealed to the world by demonstration in an appropriately selected uninhabited area. . . .

After a long, searching weekend at the Los Alamos Scientific Laboratory in New Mexico, Arthur Compton, Oppenheimer and the other two members of the Scientific Panel—Ernest Lawrence and Enrico Fermi—drew up their answer to the Franck Report. "Our hearts were heavy," Compton recalled, "as on June 16 we turned in this report to the Interim Committee."

. . . Those who advocate a purely technical demonstration would wish to outlaw the use of atomic weapons and have feared that if we use the weapons now our future negotiations will be prejudiced. Others emphasize the opportunity of saving American lives by immediate military use and believe that such use will improve the international prospects, in that they are more concerned with the prevention of war than with the elimination of this special weapon.

We find ourselves closer to these latter views: we can see no acceptable alternative to direct military use.*

In Washington, Stimson and the Assistant Secretary of War, John J. McCloy, were preparing for a crucial meeting with the Joint Chiefs of Staff and the President to determine whether to blockade and bomb Japan into submission or whether to land on the main islands. McCloy opposed both plans. For weeks he and Grew had privately discussed the future of Japan and had come to the same conclusion: that she should be offered an honorable surrender. McCloy had promised to use his influence on Stimson and now said, "We should have our heads examined if we don't consider a political solution." America had command of the sea and air and, in addition, possessed the atomic bomb. Japan should be allowed to keep the Emperor on a constitutional basis and also have access to but not control over vital raw materials.

The President, McCloy went on, should send the Emperor, or the Suzuki government, a personal message outlining this offer, with the threat that if it was not accepted the United States would have no alternative but to employ a new weapon, the atomic bomb, on Japan. Such a procedure would probably bring about the end of the war without further casualties, and if not, America would be in a better moral position if she had to use the bomb. As McCloy spelled out the form and substance of the proposal, Stimson was in apparent agreement saying he thought it a statesmanlike way to proceed and would advocate it at the meeting. On Sunday evening, however, he phoned McCloy. "Jack," he said, "I'm not up to going to that meeting tomorrow." He was plagued with one of his migraine headaches. "I'll arrange with the White House to have you take my place."

Just before three-thirty on Monday, June 18, McCloy arrived at the conference room in the White House. The President's chief of staff, Admiral Leahy, was there, along with two of the Joint

---

* In an address at Notre Dame University on February 6, 1967, Dr. Edward Teller voiced regret over this decision: "We could have exploded the bomb over Tokyo at a safe altitude and done nothing more than shake the windows. We could have demonstrated in a wonderful way that man's technical ingenuity can stop a most horrible war."

Chiefs—King and Marshall—but Arnold was represented by Lieutenant General Ira C. Eaker. Then Stimson, looking worn and in pain, entered. He had dragged himself out of bed.

Truman called for opinions from each, beginning with Marshall. The Army Chief of Staff insisted that there was no choice but to invade the main islands. The initial landing, on the island of Kyushu on November 1, would involve 766,700 troops. Losses would be heavy, but air power alone, he said, was simply not enough to conquer Japan. Speaking for the Air Force, Eaker confirmed this judgment; the air arm had not been able to subdue the Germans. Admiral King also supported Marshall.

To McCloy's chagrin, Stimson nodded assent. However, he also suggested that some alternatives should be explored. "I do think that there is a large submerged class in Japan who do not favor the present war and whose full opinion and influence have not yet been felt . . . I feel something should be done to arouse them and to develop any possible influence they might have before it becomes necessary to come to grips with them." But he said nothing about the message to the Emperor which he had indicated to McCloy he would propose.

Truman turned to Leahy. The admiral, blunt as always, denounced Roosevelt's Casablanca formula. "I do not agree with those who say that unless we obtain the unconditional surrender of the Japanese that we will have lost the war. I fear no menace from Japan in the foreseeable future, even if we are unsuccessful in forcing unconditional surrender. What I do fear is that our insistence on unconditional surrender will only result in making the Japanese more desperate and thereby increase our casualty lists. I don't think this is at all necessary."

Truman didn't believe the public was ready to accept relaxation of the demand for unconditional surrender. As for the Kyushu operation—and here McCloy thought he sounded somewhat reluctant—he said that he was "quite sure that the Joint Chiefs should proceed." But they were not to invade the main island of Honshu without consulting him. Nor did he want matters to have progressed to such an extent that he "would have no alternative" but to approve such an invasion.

With that, the meeting was apparently over and the conferees, in a resigned mood, started to get to their feet. The President stopped them. "No one is leaving this meeting without committing himself. McCloy, you haven't said anything. What is your view?"

McCloy looked at Stimson questioningly. Stimson nodded. Mc-Cloy repeated what he had told the Secretary of War, including the sentence "We should have our heads examined if we don't consider a political solution." Admiral King glared at him, but Truman was impressed. "Well, this is just what I wanted considered," he said. "Spell out the message you think we should send."

Verbally McCloy composed a message to the Emperor promising continuation of the imperial regime and ending with a threat to use the atomic bomb. The last two words had an electrifying effect. McCloy "sensed the chills that ran up and down the spines" of his listeners. Everyone in the room knew about the bomb, but it was such a secret that except in private conversations, it was rarely mentioned.

Truman said that the use of the atomic bomb was a "good possibility," as if the subject had never before been brought up at a formal meeting he had attended. He asked everyone to remain in the room; it was time the matter was placed on the table. The talk concentrated on the feasibility of the bomb itself and on the question of whether the Japanese should be warned before it was used. Although there was considerable discussion about the unpredictability of the bomb—"How do we know it will go off?" . . . "It would be a great fiasco if it did not work" . . . "What would happen if we gave the warning and it would not work?"—everyone seemed to take for granted that it would be dropped if necessary. Without any formal statement, the decision to use the bomb had, in essence, just been confirmed. Truman told McCloy to "give further thought to this message but don't mention the bomb at this stage."

Sobered by the finality of the moment, Stimson left the meeting more resolved than ever to see that Japan was given a realistic chance to surrender. With the help of Grew and Forrestal he began marshaling all arguments in favor of warning Japan before the bomb was used. Concurrently McCloy, Dooman and Ballantine set to work on the text of a declaration to the Japanese outlining surrender terms, to be issued jointly by America, Britain and China. Paragraph 12 contained the sole exception to unconditional surrender and the one most vital to the Japanese—the possibility of retention of the Emperor:

The occupying forces of the Allies shall be withdrawn from Japan as soon as these objectives have been accomplished and there has been established in accordance with the freely expressed will of the Japanese people a peacefully inclined and responsible government. This may include a constitutional monarchy under the present dynasty if the peace-loving nations can be convinced of the genuine determination of such a government to follow policies of peace which will render impossible the future development of aggressive militarism in Japan.

On Monday morning, July 2, Truman gave general approval to the declaration, but James F. Byrnes, the new Secretary of State, questioned the last sentence of Paragraph 12. So did Cordell Hull. It sounded "too much like appeasement," he advised Byrnes. "The Emperor and the ruling classes must be stripped of all extraordinary privileges and placed on a level before the law of everybody else." Public opinion coincided with this view. In a recent Gallup poll one third had favored executing Hirohito, and 37 percent wanted him put on trial, imprisoned for life or executed. Only 7 percent believed he should be left alone or used as a puppet.

On the way to Potsdam aboard *Augusta,* the President and Byrnes made the final decision to eliminate the controversial sentence. At the same time Truman privately re-examined the decision to use the bomb. There had been no doubt among the leaders of the Allies, including Churchill, that the bomb should be dropped once it was ready. In a sense Truman's decision was inevitable. "As far as I was concerned," General Leslie Groves, overseer of the Manhattan Project, later wrote, "his decision was one of non-interference—basically, a decision not to upset the existing plans." Nevertheless, one man would have to push the button and that was the President, and Truman now accepted the responsibility with confidence. After all, it was purely a military weapon, he reasoned, and it had to be used.*

* To a question posed in an interview by the author in 1958 that the decision must have come only after considerable soul-searching, President Truman replied, "Hell, no, I made it like"—he snapped his fingers—"that!"

A year later, on April 28, 1959, he told a seminar at Columbia University,

2.

The actual site of the conference was a pleasant town surrounded by woods on the outskirts of Potsdam. Almost totally untouched by the war, Babelsberg had been a summer resort and the playground of Germany's movie colony. It reminded Major General John Deane, head of the U. S. Military Mission in Moscow, of a ghost city. On Sunday, July 15, Truman was installed in a three-story stucco house, once the home of a movie producer now in a Russian labor battalion. Located on Griebnitz Lake, "the Little White House," as it was nicknamed, was surrounded by groves of trees and an elegant garden which, like the house, showed signs of neglect. Churchill was billeted nearby in similar seedy splendor; Stalin was a mile away.

The conference, scheduled to open on Monday, July 16, was postponed until the next day because Stalin had suffered a slight heart attack. The one question about the bomb that remained—would it work?—was answered Monday evening at seven-thirty by a cable from Washington addressed to Stimson:

OPERATED ON THIS MORNING, DIAGNOSIS NOT YET COMPLETE BUT RESULTS SEEM SATISFACTORY AND ALREADY EXCEED EXPECTATIONS. LOCAL PRESS RELEASE NECESSARY AS INTEREST EXTENDS GREAT DISTANCE. DR. GROVES PLEASED. HE RETURNS [to Washington] TOMORROW. I WILL KEEP YOU POSTED.

The atomic bomb had been successfully exploded in Alamogordo, New Mexico. Groves and his deputy, Brigadier General

---

"The atom bomb was no 'great decision.' It was used in the war, and for your information, there were more people killed by fire bombs in Tokyo than dropping of the atom bombs accounted for. It was merely another powerful weapon in the arsenal of righteousness. The dropping of the two bombs stopped the war, saved millions of lives. It is just the same as artillery on our side. Napoleon said that victory is always on the side of the artillery. It was a purely military decision to end the war."

At the end of the seminar, a student again pressed him. "That was not any decision that you had to worry about," the President retorted. "It was just the same as getting a bigger gun than the other fellow had to win the war and that's what it was used for. Nothing else but an artillery weapon."

Thomas Farrell, had watched the explosion from a distance of ten thousand yards. Awed by the stupendous blast Farrell exclaimed, "The war is over!" "Yes, it is over," said Groves, "as soon as we drop one or two on Japan!"

Stimson cabled back: I SEND MY WARMEST CONGRATULATIONS TO THE DOCTOR AND HIS CONSULTANT. The timing could not have been better as far as the President was concerned. The following noon Generalissimo Stalin (he had just been given the new title) arrived at the Little White House with Molotov and his interpreter, Pavlov.

Stalin chatted amiably for a few moments with Truman and Byrnes, then brought up the subject that was foremost in the President's mind: the war in the Pacific. He confided that the Japanese had requested him to mediate a peace but he had made no definite reply, since they were not ready to accept unconditional surrender. Both Truman and Byrnes knew every detail of the Japanese overture—the messages flying between Togo and Sato had been intercepted and decoded—but they pretended they were hearing it for the first time. Unprompted, Stalin announced that the Red Army would be prepared to attack early in August. The only obstacle was settlement of minor matters with Chiang Kai-shek, such as disposition of Dairen.

Dairen should be maintained as an open port, said Truman. If we get control of it, Stalin replied reassuringly, it will be. At lunch Stalin was expansive. He praised the wine. It was a propitious observation: when the Filipino waiter whipped the towel from the bottle, a California label came into view.

The first plenary session opened at ten past five in Cecilienhof Palace, one-time residence of Crown Prince Wilhelm and recently used as an army hospital. Beautifully furnished, the spacious two-story brownstone building on the lake reminded General Deane of an estate in Newport or Grosse Pointe.

The conferees settled around an imposing oaken table in the palace reception room which was decorated with the flags of the three nations. At Stalin's suggestion Truman (Churchill's interpreter thought he looked like a "polite but determined Chairman of a Board Meeting") took the chair. The initial discussions focused on Europe's postwar problems. Afterward at his quarters Churchill confided to Lord Moran, "Stalin is very amiable but he is opening his mouth very wide." He noted that the Generalissimo had switched to cigars, perhaps after the heart attack. "He says he prefers them to cigarettes. If he is photographed smoking a cigar with me everybody will say it is my influence. I said so to him." Moran asked the Prime Minister if he thought Truman had real ability. "I should think he has. At any rate, he is a man of immense determination. He takes no notice of delicate ground, he just plants his foot firmly on it." In illustration he stamped both bare feet solidly on the floor.

A few hours later Stimson received another report from the Interim Committee:

DOCTOR HAS JUST RETURNED MOST ENTHUSIASTIC AND CONFIDENT THAT THE LITTLE BOY IS AS HUSKY AS HIS BIG BROTHER. THE LIGHT IN HIS EYES DISCERNIBLE FROM HERE TO HIGHHOLD [Stimson's home on Long Island] AND I COULD HAVE HEARD HIS SCREAMS FROM HERE TO MY FARM.

The officers decoding this coy subterfuge figured the seventy-seven-year-old Stimson had become a father and wondered if the conference would adjourn for a day to celebrate. "The little boy" was, of course, the plutonium bomb just exploded in New Mexico and "his big brother" the untested uranium gun-type bomb that would be dropped on Japan.

Success at Alamogordo had aggravated the distress of scores of scientists who had made it possible. Dr. Leo Szilard (like Dr. Franck, a refugee from the Nazis) submitted a petition to the Interim Committee drawn up by himself and signed by fifty-seven Chicago scientists. It urged that the Japanese be given suitable warning and the opportunity to surrender.*

* Szilard had gone much further in an early draft of this petition, calling for an outright ban on the use of atomic bombs: "Once they were introduced as an instrument of war it would be difficult to resist the temptation of putting them to such use. . . . Thus a nation which sets the precedent of using these newly liberated forces of nature for purposes of destruction may have to bear the responsibility of opening the door to an era of devastation on an unimaginable scale."
Few of his colleagues would endorse this draft on the grounds that if the bomb was not used they would be guilty of allowing the war to drag on and the slaughter to continue. Others completely disagreed with Szilard and countered with their own petitions. One such concluded: "In short, are we to go on shedding American blood when we have available a means to speedy victory? No! If we can save even a handful of American lives, then let us use this weapon—now!"

At lunch on Wednesday, Truman sounded out Churchill on the question of apprising the Russians about the bomb. Churchill suggested that if Truman was "resolved to tell," he should explain that he had been waiting for the successful test. Then he would have an answer to the question, Why did you not tell us this before? Churchill also offered other advice. The phrase "unconditional surrender" bothered him; it could lead to tremendous loss of American lives. Couldn't it be expressed in another way so that the Allies got "all the essentials for future peace and security, and yet left the Japanese some show of saving their military honour and some assurance of their national existence, after they had complied with all safeguards necessary for the conqueror."

"I don't think the Japanese have any honor after Pearl Harbor," Truman retorted. "At any rate they have something for which they are ready to face certain death in very large numbers, and this may not be so important to us as to them."

That afternoon Truman met with Stalin. The President made no mention of the bomb, but Stalin had a secret to confide that was already known to Truman. The Generalissimo showed him the Emperor's confidential message requesting that Prince Konoye be received as an emissary of peace. Stalin wondered if he shouldn't ignore it; the U.S.S.R. would "eventually" declare war on Japan.

Innocently Truman told him to do what he thought best. Stalin suggested he "lull" the Japanese to sleep: what if he told the Japanese government that the message was so vague about Konoye's visit that he couldn't give a concrete reply?

So it was that Molotov's deputy in Moscow, Alexander Lozovsky, after keeping Ambassador Sato waiting for five days, at last sent him a confidential letter: the Emperor's proposal was so vague and Prince Konoye's mission so unclear that his government did not feel it could reply definitely to either question. Sato followed up his report to Tokyo with a plea to accept peace on any terms as long as the Emperor remained on the throne:

I REALIZE THAT IT IS A GREAT CRIME TO DARE TO MAKE SUCH STATEMENTS, KNOWING THEY ARE CONTRARY TO THE VIEWS OF THE GOVERNMENT. THE REASON FOR DOING SO, HOWEVER, IS THAT I BELIEVE THAT THE ONLY POLICY FOR OUR NATION'S SALVATION MUST COINCIDE WITH THESE IDEAS.

But his superiors back home were not yet ready to go that far, and if they had, the Americans would have given no formal assurance regarding the Emperor.

In Switzerland, however, Per Jacobsson was more determined than ever to open a channel for negotiations. He had finally succeeded in overcoming General Okamoto's reluctance to trust any American promises not in writing—by sophistry: the Americans had broken their written promises after World War I; now they were refusing to put promises in writing because they intended to keep their word. It appealed to Oriental logic and General Okamoto agreed to cable Tokyo a "strong recommendation" to end the war.

As a result of Okamoto's positive action Allen Dulles flew to Potsdam to give Stimson a firsthand report of the Japanese overtures. Dulles did not expect an immediate response, nor did he get it. He was satisfied, nevertheless, that the very real possibility of negotiations through Okamoto had been pointed out to "authoritative American quarters in a timely and, I believe, effective method." But the American leaders, now in possession of the ultimate weapon, were already determined to accept nothing short of unconditional surrender, and were no longer capable of considering negotiations even as the most peace-minded Japanese saw them.*

On July 21 Stimson read aloud to Truman and Byrnes a detailed report from eyewitnesses describing the awesome spectacle

---

* This hardened position was belied on July 18 in a startling letter to the editor which appeared in the Washington *Post* signed "An Observer." The writer proclaimed that American military law, based upon historical precedents, clearly specified that conquest or occupation did not affect the sovereignty of a defeated nation. Its suggestion that the United States was open to negotiations through regular diplomatic channels created a minor furor in the capital. Knowledgeable reporters interpreted it as an official trial balloon. They had been privately informed, indeed, that it was the work of Ellis Zacharias, a maverick Navy captain and head of Op-16-W, a secret naval operational intelligence agency concerned mainly with psychological warfare. As an "official spokesman," Zacharias had for some time been assuring the Japanese by radio that unconditional surrender was largely a military term and did not mean the end of Japan's way of life. But the writer of the letter was actually one of his assistants, Ladislas Farago, who had spontaneously, on his own, decided to mitigate the unconditional surrender formula. Zacharias, when he learned of his subordinate's enterprise, approved of it and, moreover, repeated the advice to the Japanese in a subsequent broadcast.

at Alamogordo. Both were "immensely pleased" and Truman was "tremendously pepped up." The following morning Stimson brought the report to Churchill, who was exhilarated. The Prime Minister leaned forward. "Stimson, what was gunpowder?" he asked rhetorically, brandishing his cigar. "Trivial. What was electricity? Meaningless. This atomic bomb is the Second Coming in wrath." Suddenly he remembered something amusing. "Now I know what happened to Truman yesterday. I couldn't understand it. When he got to the meeting after having this report he was a changed man. He told the Russians just where they got on and off and generally bossed the whole meeting." His excitement went beyond the scientific triumph. It would no longer be necessary to invade Japan. "Now all this nightmare picture had vanished," he later wrote. "In its place was the vision—fair and bright indeed it seemed—of the end of the whole war in one or two violent shocks. . . . Moreover, we should not need the Russians."

As far as Churchill and Truman were concerned, the decision to drop the bomb had been made. But three American military men continued to debate the issue. Beyond his moral reservations, Admiral Leahy suspected that the scientists and others in the program wanted to use the bomb "because of the vast sums that had been spent on the project." General "Hap" Arnold claimed that conventional bombing alone could end the war, even in the face of Marshall's insistence that it was either the bomb or a costly invasion. General Dwight Eisenhower also took vehement issue with Marshall's conclusion. He told Stimson privately that Japan was already defeated. Dropping the bomb was "completely unnecessary." Moreover, America should avoid rousing world condemnation by using a weapon which, in his opinion, "was no longer mandatory as a measure to save American lives."

On the evening of July 23, Churchill was host at a banquet. Many of the innumerable toasts and speeches were drowned out by the Royal Air Force Band. Mischievous, Churchill whispered to Leahy that it was his retaliation for being "bored to tears" by classical music at the Truman and Stalin banquets.

The President said he hoped he had been fair at the conference and would endeavor to be so in the future. Stalin immediately got to his feet. "Honesty adorns the man," he said and spoke at length in praise of Truman. King leaned over to Moran and whispered, "Watch the President. This is all new to him, but he can take it. He is a more typical American than Roosevelt, and he will do a good job, not only for the United States but for the whole world."

The toasts became more effusive. Churchill addressed the Soviet leader as Stalin the Great, and he in turn startled his listeners with "Here's to our next meeting in Tokyo!" After dessert Stalin began moving methodically around the big table collecting autographs on his menu.

Socially the banquet was an unqualified success, but the morning after revived doubts about the continuing unity of the Big Three. Field-Marshal Brooke, now Lord Alanbrooke, glumly noted in his diary: "One fact that stands out more clearly than any other is that nothing is ever settled!" The Big Three were no longer drawn together by the bonds of a common cause.

Truman's morning began with the news that the bomb should be ready by August 4–5, almost certainly no later than August 10. Before lunch he reviewed the final report of the Combined Chiefs, who recommended that Russia be brought into the war as soon as possible in order to eventuate the earliest possible surrender of Japan. This conclusion was a reflection of their conservative attitude toward an untried weapon. Secretary of State Byrnes, however, had no misgivings. Like Churchill, he saw the bomb as a means to end the war. It made Russia's entry, which would surely complicate the postwar settlements in Asia, unnecessary. At lunch he was so persuasive that Truman agreed that while Stalin had to be informed of the bomb, he should be told in a casual way. Otherwise the Generalissimo might realize its full import and move into Manchuria against the Japanese before the date he had promised —"early in August."*

After adjournment of the plenary that afternoon, Truman singled out Stalin and offhandedly mentioned, without using the words "nuclear" or "atomic," that America had "a new weapon of unusual destructive force." Just as casually Stalin replied that he

* Within two hours the Combined Chiefs of Staff would hear General Alexei E. Antonov, Chief of Staff of the Red Army, announce that "Soviet troops were now being concentrated in the Far East and would be ready to commence operations against Japan in the last half of August. The actual date, however, would depend upon the result of conferences with Chinese representatives which had not yet been completed."

was glad to hear it and hoped the Americans would make "good use of it against the Japanese."*

Churchill, who shared Byrnes's desire to keep Russia out of Asia, sidled up to Truman. "How did it go?" he asked conspiratorially.

"He never asked a question."

Within twenty-four hours the operational order to drop the first atomic bomb was on its way to General Carl A. ("Tooey") Spaatz, the new commander of the Strategic Air Forces:

The 509 Composite Group, 20th Air Force will deliver its first special bomb as soon as weather will permit visual bombing after about 3 August 1945 on one of the targets: Hiroshima, Kokura, Niigata and Nagasaki. To carry military and civilian scientific personnel from the War Department to observe and record the effects of the explosion of the bomb, additional aircraft will accompany the airplane carrying the bomb. The observing planes will stay several miles distant from the point of impact of the bomb. . . .

A day later the heavy cruiser *Indianapolis* dropped anchor a thousand yards off Tinian Island in the Marianas. Numerous small craft swarmed around the warship, and high-ranking officers of all services climbed aboard to watch the unloading of its top-secret cargo, a metal cylinder about eighteen inches in diameter and two feet high—the heart of the first practical atomic bomb. It weighed several hundred pounds and contained U-235, a derivation of uranium metal, shielded by lead. The momentous occasion was marred by a slight miscalculation. The wire on the winch lowering the cylinder to an LCT was six feet short and the onlookers —GI's and brass alike—jeered the sailors. But at last the ticklish job was over and the U-235 was safely ashore. *Indianapolis'* grave responsibility was over.**

* In 1946 Alexander Werth, war correspondent in the Soviet Union for the Sunday *Times* of London, asked Molotov if the Soviets had been told about the bomb at Potsdam. Molotov looked startled, thought for a moment and then said: "It's a tricky subject, and the real answer to your question is both Yes and No. We were told of a 'super-bomb,' of a bomb 'the like of which had never been seen'; but the word *atom* was not used.'"

** Less than four days later *Indianapolis* was hit by three torpedoes from the submarine *I-58*, skippered by Lieutenant Commander Mochitsura Hashimoto. She sank in twelve minutes. There were no lifeboats and few life rafts. Incredibly, *Indianapolis* was not missed for almost four days and, conse-

On July 25 the opposition Labour party challenged Churchill's leadership at the polls for the first time since the war began. Churchill flew home, and though still confident his Conservative party would get a substantial majority in the election, he carried with him a feeling of foreboding. "I dreamed that life was over," he told Moran. "I sat—it was very vivid—my dead body under a white sheet on a table in an empty room. I recognized my bare feet projecting from under the sheet. It was very life-like." Then he added, "Perhaps this is the end." He went to bed still confident of victory but was wakened "with a sharp stab of almost physical pain." He was suddenly convinced he was beaten and thought: "The power to shape the future would be denied me. The knowledge and experience I had gathered, the authority and goodwill I had gained in so many countries, would vanish."

By noon on the twenty-sixth it was obvious that the Labour party would win; Clement Attlee would be the new Prime Minister and return to Potsdam in his stead. "It may be a blessing in disguise," said Mrs. Churchill at luncheon.

"At the moment it seems quite effectively disguised."

The bomb was on Tinian, the orders for its use were cut. Now all that remained was to dispatch the final warning to Japan, the Potsdam Proclamation.* On the day of Churchill's defeat, President Truman ordered the Office of War Information in Washington to beam the message in the open to Japan. It threatened "the utter devastation of the Japanese homeland" unless Japan surrendered unconditionally, but made no mention of the atomic bomb; nor did it contain the controversial paragraph about retaining the Emperor. It limited Japanese sovereignty to the four main islands, but did promise that the Japanese would not be "enslaved as a race or destroyed as a nation" and would be allowed "to maintain such industries as will sustain her economy" and permitted access to raw materials. Moreover, the occupying forces

---

quently, only 316 of her crew of 1,196 were rescued. It was the most controversial sea disaster in American naval history.

* The State Department makes a distinction between the Potsdam Proclamation (the July 26 document demanding that Japan surrender unconditionally) and the Potsdam Declaration (the Allied policy statement concerning Europe), although both are usually referred to as "the declaration."

would be withdrawn as soon as a new order was established and there was convincing proof that Japan's war-making capabilities were destroyed.

China and Britain had approved the proclamation, but not until that night was it shown to the Russians, who were understandably surprised and annoyed. Molotov immediately got on the phone with a request that the release of the declaration be postponed for a few days. Too late, Byrnes replied apologetically, it has already been issued. He hurriedly added, "I deemed it inappropriate to consult the Soviet Union about the document when your government was not at war with Japan."

Japanese monitors picked up the broadcast of the proclamation on the morning of July 27, Tokyo time. Togo's first reaction was that "it was evidently not a dictate of unconditional surrender." Perhaps the Emperor's personal desire for peace had become known to the Allies and moderated their attitude. There were, of course, some ambiguities but it was clearly desirable to enter into negotiations with the Allies for clarification and "revision—even if it should be slight—of disadvantageous points in the declaration." He reported at once to the Emperor urging that the ultimatum be "treated with the utmost circumspection, both domestically and internationally." He worried particularly about what might happen if Japan let it be known that she intended to reject it. In subsequent reports to the Big Six and then to the entire Cabinet, Togo recommended the same course as he had outlined to the Emperor. Admiral Toyoda countered that they should issue a statement at once proclaiming that "the government regarded the declaration as absurd and would not consider it."

Prime Minister Suzuki supported Togo, but everyone agreed that the proclamation had to be announced in the newspapers. The military wanted an official rejection to accompany the press release, but Suzuki suggested that they ignore the ultimatum. A compromise was reached: they would allow the papers to publish an expurgated version, without comment or criticism.

In the morning, however, several newspapers disregarded instructions and did editorialize, much to the discomfort of the Foreign Ministry. The *Mainichi* headlined the story LAUGHABLE MATTER and the *Asahi Shimbun* declared: "Since the joint declaration of American, Britain and Chungking is a thing of no great moment, it will merely serve to re-enhance the government's resolve to carry the war forward unfalteringly to a successful conclusion!"

Togo thought the military were responsible—the editors would never have had the courage to defy the government on their own —and they countered his accusation with renewed insistence that the declaration be refuted in definite terms. Once more a compromise was reached: the Prime Minister would read a statement belittling the Allied terms without rejecting them. At four o'clock Suzuki told reporters, "The Potsdam Proclamation, in my opinion, is just a rehash of the Cairo Declaration, and the government therefore does not consider it of great importance. We must *mokusatsu* it." The word means literally "kill with silence" but as Suzuki later told his son, he intended it to stand for the English phrase "No comment," for which there is no Japanese equivalent. Americans, however, understandably applied the dictionary meanings: "ignore" and "treat with silent contempt." On July 30 the *New York Times* headline read: JAPAN OFFICIALLY TURNS DOWN ALLIED SURRENDER ULTIMATUM.

The use of the atom bomb was inevitable, but for the Americans a question still remained: Would the Russians declare war *before* the bomb brought about a quick Japanese surrender? Only days before, General Antonov had postponed Soviet entry until "the last half of August." Now, after issue of the proclamation, Molotov pressed for a letter formally inviting Russian participation in the war. Truman stalled for forty-eight hours but finally, on the last day of July, sent Stalin the draft of an ambiguous invitation stating that "it would be proper for the Soviet Union to indicate its willingness to consult and cooperate with other great powers now at war with Japan with a view to joint action on behalf of the community of nations to maintain peace and security."

In a covering note, which attempted to shift the onus of the initiative on the Russians, Truman said he would send them a formal, signed copy after Stalin had reached an agreement with Chiang Kai-shek. "If you decide to use it, it will be all right. However, if you decide to issue a statement basing your action on other ground or for any other reason prefer not to use this letter, it will be satisfactory to me. I leave it to your good judgment."

"Terminal" was over. Truman, Attlee and Stalin publicly expressed their gratification, but there was an underlying atmosphere of weariness and disappointment. Truman, suspicious of Russian motives, privately resolved not to allow them "any part in the control of Japan" or to reveal anything about the bomb until there was some agreement on control and inspection. "You never saw such pig-headed people as are the Russians," he wrote his mother. "I hope I never have to hold another conference with them—but, of course, I will."

Leahy was proud of the way Truman had stood up to Stalin, particularly in refusing to be "bulldozed into any reparations agreement that would repeat the history of World War I," but continued Soviet objections to proposals important to the future peace of Europe had left the admiral with "serious doubts that any peace treaties acceptable to our government could be negotiated." Byrnes too was dissatisfied. The concessions won from Stalin depended on the Russians' carrying out their part of the bargain, and by this time Byrnes had "little confidence in their pledges."

"Terminal" had offered a unique opportunity to the victors of the war to further order and justice in a world torn by conflict for a decade. Instead, however, it created new conflicts for the post-war world.

3.

In Moscow, Ambassador Sato once more tried to convince Tokyo that the U.S.S.R. had no intention of intervening on Japan's behalf:

. . . I BELIEVE THAT STALIN FEELS THAT THERE IS ABSO-LUTELY NO NECESSITY FOR MAKING A VOLUNTARY AGREE-MENT WITH JAPAN. ON THIS POINT I SEE A SERIOUS DIS-CREPANCY BETWEEN YOUR VIEW AND THE ACTUAL STATE OF AFFAIRS.

But the Japanese leaders could not face the truth. They seemed immobilized by a common wishful conviction that the Soviet Union would come to the assistance of Japan. Even the pragmatic

Kido expected a favorable reply once Molotov and Stalin returned to Moscow. Togo continued to press Sato:

> . . . IT IS REQUESTED THAT FURTHER EFFORTS BE EXERTED TO SOMEHOW MAKE THE SOVIET UNION ENTHUSIASTIC OVER THE SPECIAL ENVOY. . . . SINCE THE LOSS OF ONE DAY RELATIVE TO THIS PRESENT MATTER MAY RESULT IN A THOUSAND YEARS OF REGRET, IT IS REQUESTED THAT YOU IMMEDIATELY HAVE A TALK WITH MOLOTOV. . . .

While the Japanese waited hopefully for Russia to solve their problems, the first atomic bomb was ready for delivery, waiting only for good weather, and others were en route. Rather than explore peace with a Japan that desperately sought it, American leaders were resolved to bring a summary end to the war—and avenge the humiliation of Pearl Harbor as well as the countless atrocities committed throughout the Pacific—with a weapon already weighted with controversy.

The bomb was assembled in an air-conditioned bomb hut on Tinian on the first day of August. It was ten feet long and twenty-eight inches in diameter, and except for its size, resembled an ordinary bomb.

The men who would drop it, the 509th Group, had been training under such secrecy that only their commander, Colonel Paul W. Tibbets, Jr., knew what their mission was to be. Their area was surrounded by barbed-wire fences and protected by machine guns. A general needed a pass to enter.

For all the stringent security measures, the 509th seemed to be doing very little. Ocasionally they flew off in threes to dump a single bomb on enemy territory. They were derided by the other outfits on the island. One anonymous satirist wrote:

> *Into the air the secret rose,*
> *Where they're going, nobody knows.*
> *Tomorrow they'll return again,*
> *But we'll never know where they've been.*
> *Don't ask us about results or such,*
> *Unless you want to get in Dutch.*
> *But take it from one who is sure of the score,*
> *The 509th is winning the war.*

On the morning of August 5, the weather was forecast as favorable for takeoff after midnight. The previous night Captain William Parsons, a Navy ordnance expert who was responsible for arming the bomb, had witnessed four B-29's crash in succession on takeoff. He told General Thomas Farrell, in command of the secret project, that if the plane carrying the bomb failed to get into the air safely, an atomic explosion might be set off that would ravage the entire island.

"We will just have to pray that it doesn't happen."

"Well, if I made the final assembly of that bomb after we left the island, that couldn't happen." Farrell asked if he had ever before assembled a bomb under these conditions. "No, but I've got all day to try it."

"Go ahead and try it."

Late in the afternoon the bomb, scrawled with rude crayoned messages for the Emperor, was rolled out of its air-conditioned building into the glaring sunlight and transferred to the bomb bay of a B-29 named *Enola Gay* after Colonel Tibbets' mother. At dusk Parsons climbed into the stifling fuselage. Squatting beside the bomb, he practiced the final assembly hour after hour.

"For God's sake, man," said Farrell when he saw Parsons' bleeding hands, "let me loan you a pair of pigskin gloves. They're thin ones."

"I wouldn't dare. I've got to feel the touch."

At 7:17 P.M. Farrell radioed Groves: JUDGE [Parsons] TO LOAD BOMB AFTER TAKEOFF. . . . Shortly after 10 P.M. six crews were summoned to a Quonset assembly hut for briefing. Soberly they watched Tibbets stride up to a platform. "Tonight is the night we have all been waiting for," he said. "Our long months of training are to be put to the test. We will soon know if we have been successful or failed. Upon our efforts tonight it is possible that history will be made." They were to drop a bomb containing a destructive force equivalent to 20,000 tons of TNT. (The crew of *Enola Gay* had been told three days earlier what they would carry.) "Because this bomb is so powerful, we must use different tactics from those we have employed when using ordinary bombs." He explained that three weather planes would take off first and cover the three selected cities so the target could be changed at the last minute. An hour later *Enola Gay,* followed by two escort planes with scientific and photographic equipment, would leave. All three would rendezvous over Iwo Jima a few minutes after dawn.

At a final midnight briefing each man was issued a pair of adjustable arc welder's goggles to protect his eyes from the intense flash of the explosion. The crews bowed their heads in awed silence absorbing the words of Chaplain William Downey, a husky twenty-seven-year-old Lutheran: ". . . We pray Thee that the end of the war may come soon, and that once more we may know peace on earth. May the men who fly this night be kept safe in Thy care, and may they be returned safely to us. . . ."

The men solemnly filed into the mess hall for preflight supper, and were handed menus embellished with GI humor:

> Look! Real eggs ("How da ya want them?")
> Rolled oats ("Why?")
> Milk ("No fishing")
> Sausage ("We think it's pork")
> Apple butter ("Looks like axle grease")
> Butter ("Yep, it's out of again")
> Coffee ("Saniflush")
> Bread ("Someone get a toaster")

After the three weather planes lifted off into the night at 1:37 A.M., a crowd of well-wishers and photographers gathered around *Enola Gay,* and scores of flashbulbs popped, causing some apprehension that Japanese guerrillas in the hills might radio Tokyo that something extraordinary was taking place.

Enola Gay and her two escorts taxied to their runways. From the North Field control tower William Laurence, science editor of the *New York Times* and the sole newspaperman covering the story, watched intently, at General Farrell's side, as *Enola Gay* slowly rumbled down the runway. She accelerated to 180 miles an hour, but burdened by her extra weight, seemed earthbound. The onlookers, remembering the four Superfortresses that had crashed the night before, strained to help lift the plane into the air.

Tibbets was holding the nose down to build up speed but his co-pilot, Captain Robert A. Lewis, thought it was "gobbling a little too much runway," and began to put back pressure on the wheel.

At last, with only a few yards of the oiled coral left, the huge aircraft soared up into the darkness.

In the tower, General Farrell turned to a Navy officer. "I never saw a plane use that much runway," he said. "I thought Tibbets was never going to pull it off."

It was exactly 2:45 A.M., August 6. It would be a day to remember.

33

Hiroshima

1.

Once *Enola Gay* had climbed to 4,000 feet, Captain Parsons lowered himself into the bomb bay and while his assistant, First Lieutenant Morris Jeppson, a Mormon, illuminated the bomb with a flashlight, he cautiously inserted the explosive detonating charge through the bomb's tail. It was almost half an hour before Parsons said, "Okay, that'll do it."

Jeppson removed a green plug from the bomb, replacing it with a red one. The electrical circuit was completed; the bomb was ready to be dropped. In the rear compartment Tibbets tried to sleep—he had been awake for twenty-four hours—but it was impossible, and after fifteen minutes he started to crawl back through the narrow thirty-foot tube that led to the front compartment. The tail gunner, Staff Sergeant George R. Caron, in a Brooklyn Dodgers baseball cap, held him back. "Say, Colonel," he asked, "are we splitting atoms today?"

"You're pretty close, Bob."

Tibbets relieved his co-pilot. Lewis left the cockpit for a snack and noticed little green lights on a black box. He asked Parsons "what the hell" they meant. They indicated that the bomb was okay; red lights meant trouble.

Tibbets watched Mount Suribachi, scarred from battle, slowly rise out of the sea in the dawn light. He moved the throttles forward and *Enola Gay* began to climb. It was 4:52 A.M. In minutes the plane had reached 9,000 feet, where she was joined by her two escorts. Below on Iwo Jima—the emergency stand-by base— awaited Tibbets' security chief, Major William Uanna. Tibbets called him by voice radio: "Bud, we are proceeding to target."

Tibbets picked up the intercom and told everyone to remain at his station until the bombing was over. Once Japan was sighted, he said, their conversation would be recorded. "This is for history, so watch your language. We're carrying the first atomic bomb."

Most of the crew had never heard the word "atomic" before. Its very sound was chilling.

Their primary target was Hiroshima on the southeast coast of Honshu, Japan's principal island. From this, the empire's eighth largest city, 120,000 civilians had been evacuated to the countryside, but 245,000 still remained. The city was almost unscarred by the war. Like the people of Dresden before them, the citizens of Hiroshima felt that their city was to be spared, though it was headquarters of 2nd General Army and was an important military port of embarkation. Their reasons for hope of immunity ranged from the naïve to the preposterous: they were exempt because they had numerous relatives in the United States; their city, like Kyoto, was so beautiful that the Americans wanted it as a residential area after the war; President Truman's mother lived nearby. They had taken little notice of 720,000 leaflets fluttering from the sky two days before, warning them that their city among others would be obliterated unless Japan surrendered at once. At 7:09 A.M. (an hour earlier than Tinian time), sirens blasted for a long minute. It was the third air-raid warning since midnight and few took to the shelters. The latest alert had been set off by *Straight Flush,* a weather plane bearing a cartoon of a Japanese soldier being flushed down a toilet. It was on the same course that Tibbets would take if the weather conditions at Hiroshima were favorable enough. If not, Tibbets would be sent to Kokura or Nagasaki.

From the distance Hiroshima appeared to be blanketed by an undercast, but by the time *Straight Flush* reached the bombing point the observer-bombardier, First Lieutenant Kenneth Wey, could see Hiroshima clearly through his bombsight. It was flat and consisted of six long slender islands lying in the delta of the Ota River. From 32,000 feet the city resembled the fingers of a deformed hand. On the southern tips docks jutted into the beautiful Inland Sea. The delta itself was rimmed by small mountains.

At 7:25 *Straight Flush* turned back toward its base, Tinian, harassed by scattered flak that burst far short of the target. The pilot, Major Claude Eatherly,* ordered the radio operator to send out the following message: "Low clouds, 1 to 3/10ths. Middle cloud amount, 1 to 3/10ths. Advice: Bomb primary."

Enola Gay had just reached its bombing height of almost 32,000 feet, and Co-pilot Lewis noted in the log he was writing at the request of *New York Times* correspondent William Laurence: "Well, folks, it won't be long."

Tibbets was informed of Eatherly's message and turned to his navigator, Captain Theodore ("Dutch") Van Kirk: "It's Hiroshima." At 7:50 (their watches read 8:50) the big aircraft reached Shikoku Island. Just beyond was Honshu—and Hiroshima. The crew hurriedly strapped on their flak suits. The radar and IFF (Identification, Friend or Foe) were switched off. The ship remained on autopilot. Parsons sent word up front that the lights were still green, then crawled forward to the cockpit where he looked over Tibbets' shoulder through a large opening in the clouds. A sprawling city lay below. "Do you agree that's the target?" Tibbets asked.

"Yes," said Parsons with a nod.

It was 8:09 A.M. "We are about to start the bomb run," Tibbets announced over the intercom. "Put on your goggles and place them up on your forehead. When the countdown starts, pull the goggles over your eyes and leave them there until after the flash."

Lewis added another line to his log, the only in-flight record

* After the war Major Eatherly was exploited by a number of "Ban the Bomb" groups which claimed he was a martyr, an "American Dreyfus," jailed and hounded because of expressed guilt for his part in the Hiroshima bombing. A rash of books and articles made numerous false claims (at least one of which originated with Eatherly himself): that he personally selected Hiroshima as a target; that he was given the D.F.C.; that he flew through the bomb cloud at Hiroshima; that he commanded the bombing of Hiroshima; that he participated in the bombing of Nagasaki.

of the mission: "There will be a short intermission while we bomb our target."

The instrument plane, *The Great Artiste,* dropped back 1,000 yards. The other escort, *Number 91,* began circling to mark time and position itself for photographs.

Enola Gay's bombardier, Major Thomas Ferebee, was leaning forward, left eye pressed to the Norden bombsight, his mustache flaring to either side. At 8:13 plus thirty seconds Tibbets said, "It's yours." Ferebee's bombsight required flight corrections in autopilot as the Superfortress headed west 31,600 feet over Hiroshima at a ground speed of approximately 285 miles an hour. The clouds had scattered and Ferebee could clearly distinguish what was already so familiar from target photographs—the seven tributaries of the Ota River which formed the six islands. The aiming point, the center of Aioi Bridge, crept to the cross hairs of the bombsight.

"I've got it," he said. In forty-five seconds he sent the bombing radio-tone signal through the intercom. The crew pulled down their dark glasses—all except the two pilots and Ferebee, who could not have seen through the bombsight with them.

At 8:15 plus seventeen seconds the plane's bomb-bay doors automatically swung open. The release of the bomb was timed electrically through the bombsight according to the information Ferebee fed into it. His finger was at a toggle button ready to push if the bomb failed to release. The radio tone stopped abruptly and he watched the elongated missile drop bottom first, flip over and hurtle nose down on Hiroshima. Nine thousand pounds lighter, the plane lunged upward. Tibbets banked violently to the right until he had come around more than 150 degrees, then nosed down to pick up speed.

The bomb-bay doors of *The Great Artiste* gaped open and three packs tumbled out. Almost immediately each one flowered into a parachute; dangling below was a cylinder resembling a fire extinguisher—it was a transmitter sending back data.

Tibbets ordered everyone to "make sure those goggles are on." The bomb was set to detonate in forty-three seconds, and at thirty-five he slipped on his own glasses.

Hiroshima was serene and so was the sky above it as the people continued on their daily routine. Those who noticed the three parachutes imagined that the plane had been hit and that the crew was bailing out or that more propaganda leaflets had been jettisoned. One man, remembering how the last leaflets had shimmered down in the sun, thought, The Americans have brought us some more beautiful things.

Several hundred yards north of Aioi Bridge (Ferebee's target), Private Shigeru Shimoyama, a recent draftee, looked up and idly peered through his thick glasses at one of the drifting chutes. He was standing outside his barracks, a huge wooden structure once a warehouse. He had been in Hiroshima four days and was already "bored to death." He wished he were back in Tokyo making school notebooks. All at once a pinkish light burst in the sky like a cosmic flash bulb.

Clocks all over Hiroshima were fixed forever at 8:15.

The bomb exploded 660 yards from the ground into a fireball almost 110 yards in diameter. Those directly below heard nothing, nor could they later agree what color the *pika* (lightning) flash was—blue, pink, reddish, dark-brown, yellow or purple.

The heat emanating from the fireball lasted a fraction of a second but was so intense (almost 300,000 degrees Centigrade) that it melted the surface of granite within a thousand yards of the hypocenter, or ground zero—directly under the burst. Roof tiles softened and changed in color from black to olive or brown. All over the center of the city numerous silhouettes were imprinted on walls. On Yorozuyo Bridge ten people left permanent outlines of themselves on the railing and the tar-paved surface.

Moments later came an unearthly concussion that obliterated all but a few solid, earthquake-proof buildings within two miles. Ferebee had been almost on target, little more than 300 yards off the intended drop point.

Private Shimoyama was 550 yards north of ground zero. He was not directly exposed to the *pika* flash or his life would have been puffed out, but the blast hurled him into the vast barnlike warehouse, driving him into the collapsing roof beam where five long nails in his back held him suspended several feet off the ground. His glasses were still intact.

Five hundred yards farther north Captain Hideo Sematoo, a company commander, had just cantered up to his office and was removing his riding boots. The building fell on top of him and ignited. He thought of the seven years he had fought in Manchuria, China, Singapore, Malaya and New Guinea. How miserable to be burned to death rather than die in battle! *"Tenno Heika banzai!"* he shouted. As the flames reached for him, the wreckage above him was pulled away and he wrenched himself free. Nauseated, he looked at an eerie yellow sky. The ground was flat as far as he could see. Everything was gone—towering Hiroshima Castle and 2nd General Army headquarters. Instinctively he stumbled and crawled toward the main branch of the Ota River. There, crowded along the banks, were hundreds of dazed patients and nurses from the Army Hospital. Their hair was burned off, their skin charred a dark brown. He felt chilly.

A thousand yards on the other side of the hypocenter, Mrs. Yasuko Nukushina was trapped in the ruins of the family *sake* store. Her first thought was of her four-year-old daughter, Ikuko, who was playing outside somewhere. Unaccountably, she heard Ikuko's voice beside her: "I'm afraid, Mama." She told the child they were buried and would die there. Her own words made her claw desperately at the wreckage. She was a slight woman, four feet six inches tall, but in her frenzy she broke free into the yard. All around was devastation. She somehow felt responsible; "her" bomb had also destroyed the neighborhood. People drifted by expressionless and silent like sleepwalkers in tattered, smoldering clothing. It was a parade of wraiths, an evocation of a Buddhist hell. She watched mesmerized until someone touched her. Grasping Ikuko's hand, she joined the procession. In her confusion she had the illusion that vast numbers of planes were roaring over the city, dropping bomb after bomb without cessation.

Fourteen hundred yards east of ground zero at the presbytery of the only Catholic church in the city, Father Superior Hugo Lassalle, a German, had heard a plane overhead. He went to the window. The empty sky glared yellow—and the ceiling dropped. Cut and bleeding, Father Lassalle found his way to the street. It was dark. The entire city was covered by a blanket of dust. With another German priest he began searching through the rubble for residents of the mission.

Half a dozen blocks south, fifteen-year-old Michiko Yamaoka had just left home for work at the telephone office. She remembered "a magnesium flash," then a faraway voice calling "Michiko!"

Her mother. "I'm here," she answered but didn't know where that was. She couldn't see—she must be blind! She heard her mother shout, "My daughter is buried under there!" Another voice, a man's, advised the mother to escape the flames sweeping down the street. Michiko begged her mother to save herself and heard running steps diminish to silence. She was going to die. Then came a shaft of light as concrete blocks were pushed aside by soldiers. Her mother was bleeding profusely, one arm skewered by a piece of wood. She ordered Michiko to escape. She herself was staying to rescue two relatives under the ruins of their house.

Michiko moved through a nightmare world—past charred bodies —a crying baby sealed behind the twisted iron bars of a collapsed reinforced-concrete building. She saw someone she knew and called out.

"Who are you?" the other girl asked.

"Michiko."

The friend stared at her. "Your nose and eyebrows are gone!"

Michiko felt her face. It was so swollen that her nose seemed to have disappeared.

In the same area, 350 young girls from the Girls Commercial School had been working in an empty lot, clearing an evacuated area. They wore blue *mompei* and jackets but no hats or fire hoods, and those who turned, curious, toward the *pika*—almost 300 of them—were instantly doomed. Twelve-year-old Miyoko Matsubara's instinct was to bury her face in her arms. She regained consciousness in unimaginable desolation—no people, no buildings— only limitless rubble. Where were her *mompei*? All she had around her waist was a white cloth belt and it was on fire. (Everyone wearing dark clothing who was exposed to the *pika* suffered primary thermal burns but the cruel flash reflected harmlessly off white material.) She started to beat out the flames with her right hand but to her horror she saw strips of skin, her skin, dangling from it.

Mrs. Tomita had given birth to a baby girl that morning. Together with her husband, Torao, she was admiring their newborn daughter, Hiroko, when an intense light filled the window. Mrs. Tomita remembered a whooshing noise before losing consciousness. She came to on the floor. Her husband was gone. The baby in her little red dress was lying on top of the sewing machine— alive but unnaturally silent. Mrs. Tomita wrapped diapers tightly around her distended stomach—the midwife had told her to move as little as possible—and walked out into the street with the baby. Torao was hysterically digging in the ruins for their other two children. He found the elder daughter still alive, but her brother was hopelessly buried somewhere under the mass. There was a shout that more planes were on the way and the family sought shelter in a ditch trickling with foul water.

Less than a mile south of ground zero the main building of Hiroshima University stood intact amid the devastation. The hands of its huge clock, which faced the campus, had stopped at 8:15. But the bomb, which had stilled so many other clocks and watches at that time, had nothing to do with it; several days previously it had stopped prophetically at that catastrophic moment.

Two student nurses, who were ill in bed at a wooden dormitory of the Red Cross Hospital across the street, neither saw nor heard the bomb. Their first sensation was that their lungs were collapsing. Kyoko Sato crawled out of the caved-in building into a maelstrom of dust. A muffled call, "Sato-*san!*" led her to her friend, whom she pried loose from the debris. Together they tried to cross the highway to report to the hospital but couldn't penetrate the solid stream of silent humanity moving away from the city, half naked and bleeding but without hysteria, not even tears. The unreality of it was terrifying.

Dr. Fumio Shigeto, head of internal medicine at the hospital, never reached his office that morning. On his way to work, he was waiting for a trolley at the end of a long line which bent around the corner of the Hiroshima railway station, 2,000 yards east of the hypocenter. The flash seemed to turn a group of girls ahead of him white, almost invisible. An incendiary bomb! As he dropped to the sidewalk, covering eyes and ears, a heavy slate slammed into his back. Whirls of smoke blotted out the sun. In the darkness he groped blindly to reach shelter before the next wave of attackers came on. Fearing poison gas, he covered his mouth with a handkerchief.

A breeze from the east gradually cleared the area as though it were dawn, revealing an incredible scene: the buildings in front of the station were collapsed, flattened; half-naked and smoldering bodies covered the ground. Of the people at the trolley stop he alone, the last one in line, was unhurt, protected by the corner of the station building. Dr. Shigeto started for the hospital but was stopped by an impenetrable wall of advancing flames. He turned and ran for open space—toward an Army drill ground behind the station. He saw scores of survivors milling around, crying hysterically, and to ease the pain of their burns they extended their arms from which dangled long curls of skin.

A nurse approached him; he must be a doctor because he carried a black bag and had a trim little mustache. She begged him to help another doctor and his wife lying on the ground. His first thought was: What if this mob of desperate people discovers I am a physician? He couldn't help them all. "Please treat my wife first," said the injured doctor, who was bleeding profusely. Shigeto gave the woman a camphor shot for shock, followed by another injection to stop the bleeding. He rearranged the bandages the nurse had applied and then turned to the other wounded, treating them until he ran out of medicine and supplies. There was nothing else he could do. He fled toward the hills.

2.

Enola Gay's crew members saw a pinpoint of purplish red light miles below them instantly expand into a ball of purple fire. This exploded into a chaotic mass of flames and clouds emanating smoke rings of fog. A white column of smoke emerged from the purple clouds, rising rapidly to 10,000 feet, where it bloomed into an immense mushroom which seethed turbulently as it continued climbing to almost 50,000 feet.

A shock wave rocked *Enola Gay*. Tibbets thought it was anti-aircraft fire and shouted "Flak!" Parsons yelled that it was shock and added, "We're in the clear now." Co-pilot Lewis cast a backward glance at the flash, even though he had removed his dark glasses seconds before the explosion to look at the instrument panel. Ferebee had become so fascinated by the long trajectory of the bomb that he forgot to pull down his goggles. It was as if a photographer's flash bulb had gone off in his face. Tibbets swept off his goggles, scanned the panel and banked the ship back toward Hiroshima to observe the results.

"Holy Moses, what a mess!" Sergeant Caron, the tail gunner, exclaimed over the intercom.

"My God," said Lewis, "what have we done?" He jotted the words "My God!" in his log. It looked as if Hiroshima had been "torn apart," and made him feel as if they were "Buck Rogers twenty-fifth-century warriors."

The navigator, "Dutch" Van Kirk, was stunned at first, next filled with pride and finally relieved that it was all over. There were cheers over the intercom; it meant the end of the war. Then the crew began to think of the people on the ground.

Tibbets ordered the radio operator to send a message in the clear that the primary target had been bombed visually with good results. Parsons sent another, this one in code:

RESULTS CLEAR CUT, SUCCESSFUL IN ALL RESPECTS. VISIBLE EFFECTS GREATER THAN TRINITY [the test at Alamogordo]. CONDITIONS NORMAL IN AIRPLANE FOLLOWING DELIVERY, PROCEEDING TO PAPACY [Tinian]. . . .

A few miles away the scientists in *The Great Artiste* were glued to their blast-recording gear. In the photo plane Dr. Bernard Waldman, a physicist from Notre Dame, was in the bombardier's seat, operating a special high-speed movie camera he had brought from America. There hadn't been time to test it in the air. He had counted to forty after the bomb dropped and turned on the camera. As the plane banked away First Lieutenant Russell Gackenbach, the navigator, also snapped a series of pictures with his pocket camera.

On the ground, two and a half miles south of the hypocenter, former news photographer Gonichi Kimura was working outside a stable for the Army when he saw a strong flash to his left and simultaneously felt a searing blast of heat. At first he thought the Hiroshima Gas Company's tank had exploded, but since he soon discovered that it was still standing, he felt intuitively that some special bomb must have been dropped and decided to take pictures as soon as he could get to his camera, which was stored in the warehouse nearby. By the time he had crawled through the wreckage of the stable, the narrow white column of smoke from the bomb had changed to pink and the top started to swell, making it look like a mushroom, and it kept growing massively.

At the warehouse Kimura found all the windows shattered from the blast, and there was so much broken glass on the floor where his camera was kept that he could not even step inside, but he managed to stretch in and pull the drawer open. The trees outside the warehouse were in the way, so he returned to the stable to take his first pictures of the atomic cloud—"indeed, a gruesome sight"—which was now covering most of the sky. Fires which had broken out in the western part of the city were spreading rapidly, and he finished his roll of film from the roof of a factory.* Kimura escaped the bomb without injury, but he never saw his wife again —he had left her at home after breakfast that morning.

Those near the hypocenter never heard the explosion of the bomb. With distance, the noise grew perceptible, then shattering. From three miles it sounded like the rumbling of unworldly thunder; at four miles it was a distant moan which grew into a jarring boom. Near the port of Kure, twelve miles to the southeast, Tadahiko Kitayama thought a nearby ammunition dump had detonated, and several miles offshore, salvagers attempting to raise the four-man submarine *Koryu,* which was stuck in the bottom mud, heard a deafening "thunderbolt" clap. Moments later they noticed a B-29 coming from the direction of Hiroshima.

For a quarter of an hour the atmosphere above Hiroshima was churned by cosmic forces. Then huge drops of rain began to plummet down. The rising cloud column had carried moisture sufficiently high for water vapor to condense, and stained by radioactive dust, fall in large drops. The "black rain," weird and almost supernatural, horrified the survivors. Was it some kind of poisonous oil that would stick to the skin and slowly kill them? It pelted down on the half-naked people, leaving gray streaks on their bodies, releasing in many of them a sense of awareness of the unimaginable disaster that had been visited on Hiroshima. Mrs. Tomita tried to

* Kimura developed the films himself at home. They were overexposed but usable, and one is reprinted in the picture section of this book. Waldman's film was ruined when it was processed in the well-equipped photo laboratory at Tinian. The equipment had to be kept at 70 degrees but the refrigeration unit malfunctioned, subjecting the film to excessive heat stripping the emulsion. The pictures in Lieutenant Gackenbach's little camera were excellent.

protect her two-hour-old baby, but little Hiroko was soaked by the fallout. She still had not uttered a sound since the blast.*

The deadly rain, which had changed into a foggy, yellowish drizzle, spread to the northwest. Almost none fell on the area to the east where the fires were more intense, and Dr. Yoshimasa Matsuzaka, a skin specialist and head of the city's civil defense, was trying to bring some order out of chaos. Ignoring his own wounds, he put on his civil defense uniform which his wife had rescued from the wreckage of his office, and leaning on his son, marched toward the East District police station holding high a Rising Sun flag on a long stick. The sight of the determined little procession extending first-aid treatment—Mrs. Matsuzaka and three nurses brought up the rear—calmed the people. The group set up a first-aid station in front of the police headquarters—it was 1,200 yards from the hypocenter—and long lines of injured and burned began to form outside the shell of the station house.

From his destroyed home less than half a mile away the police chief, Shiroku Tanabe, was desperately trying to get to the station. But he was impeded by thousands of refugees (they looked "as if they had crawled out of a pool of blood") streaming away from ground zero. By the time Tanabe reached the station house, it had caught fire. He took command and organized a bucket brigade to a nearby "fire pool." Though half the building was ablaze, Dr. Matsuzaka and his indomitable first-aid team continued to treat the injured and to urge them to seek refuge outside the city.

All over town, charcoal braziers full of hot coals (housewives had been preparing breakfast) ignited the tinderbox rubble. These thousands of small fires were whipped into fury by a cyclonic wind that was sucked in toward the hypocenter with such force that large trees were uprooted. Blasts of flame—they could have come from monster blowtorches—erratically ripped off corrugated roofs as if they were cardboard, blasted houses apart and twisted metal bridges. Telephone poles ignited explosively.

Near the site of Hiroshima Castle four men staggered through the burning streets with a massive portrait of the Emperor; they

---

* Miraculously the entire family, except for the boy who was never found, survived with few ill effects. Hiroko was nicknamed "Pikako" (little *pika*), and grew to be an attractive, healthy young woman—a local tennis champion. The Tomitas rebuilt on the ruins of their former home.

had rescued it from the inferno of the 2nd General Army communications center and were trying to get it safely out of the city. At the sight of the picture, lines of apathetic refugees broke into cries of "The Emperor's portrait!" The burned and bleeding saluted or bowed low. Those unable to get to their feet clasped hands in prayer. As the picture was trundled through Asano Sentei Park to a waiting boat moored on the river, towering pine trees flamed into torches. Wounded soldiers on the banks, waiting to be rescued, struggled to attention and saluted as the boat headed upstream for safety through a shower of flaming debris.

Their commander, General Fujii, was incinerated in the first minutes at his quarters near the castle but Private Shigeru Shimoyama, who was closer to ground zero, was still alive even after being impaled on the spikes of a roof beam. He painfully pulled himself free from the spikes, and using his head as a battering ram, relentlessly slammed at the roof, blinded by streams of blood, until he broke through. Thick stifling clouds of dust swirled about him, but he could tell that some irresistible force had swept across the city like the hand of a vengeful giant. At the river he watched scores of wounded making the long frantic leap from its banks. What did they think they were doing? The surface of the water was covered with carmine scum. From blood? Shimoyama kept telling himself to remain calm. He was no stranger to disaster; he had almost been killed in the earthquake of '23, the Doolittle raid and the Tokyo fire bombing of April 13. He started up the river against the wind; it would help keep the fires behind him.

Directly in his path was a cavalry horse standing alone. It was pink; the blast had seared off its skin. It looked at him pleadingly and followed with a few faltering steps. The pitiful sight fascinated Shimoyama, and he had to force himself to press on (he would dream about the pink horse for years afterward). Half a dozen other soldiers were also purposefully following the bank north, but it was as if each man was solitary, preoccupied with his own survival. Civilians, some almost naked, tried to keep up with them, but as the dull rumble of flames behind grew louder, the soldiers quickened their pace, leaving the others far behind.

Several miles upstream Shimoyama forded the river where the water only came up to his neck. As he proceeded into the suburbs where the havoc of the bomb had not reached, he was obsessed by one thought—that it was an atomic bomb. He must get home and see his daughter before he died of the effects. In 1943 a brother-in-law of his had informed him that the Japanese were working on one and for the past few days, oddly, there had been so much talk in his barracks about such a bomb that if a man lost his temper someone would say, "He's like an atomic bomb." He passed scores of high school girls, horribly burned, sprawling on either side of the road. Long strips of skin hung in ribbons from their faces, arms and legs. They reached out in supplication for water. But what could he do? Farther up the road, villagers were laying sliced cucumbers on the burns of other survivors and carrying those most seriously hurt to first-aid stations in vegetable carts.

The first fragmentary reports that came into Tokyo indicated simply that Hiroshima had suffered an unprecedented disaster. Imperial Headquarters could not raise the 2nd General Army communications center for fuller details.

Marquis Kido immediately informed the Emperor that Hiroshima had been laid waste by some secret weapons. "Under these circumstances we must bow to the inevitable," said His Majesty. He could not hide his anguish. "No matter what happens to me, we must put an end to this war as soon as possible. This tragedy must not be repeated." But both agreed that the psychological moment had not yet come for the Emperor to take personal action.

In the dying light of dusk the fires began to subside and from a distance Hiroshima looked peaceful, like the gigantic encampment of a quiescent army on the plain. And high overhead, stars appeared startlingly bright against the darkening sky. The flow out of the city had been reversed as the first trickle of help entered from the outside.

Dr. Shigeto of the Red Cross Hospital, who had fled the holocaust, was back. Going from one first-aid station to another, he was told that water was harmful for those suffering burns. On the contrary, he announced, it flushed the poison from burns out of the system. He had signs put up: YOU MAY GIVE WATER. DR. SHIGETO, VICE DIRECTOR, RED CROSS HOSPITAL.

As he penetrated deeper into the ravaged city, he found his way blocked by smoldering rubble. Although there seemed to be no passable road, he saw to his astonishment a large charcoal-burning truck come rumbling, out of the smoke, its cab crowded with men. He recognized the driver, a *sake* manufacturer from his suburb. He had braved the inferno to carry emergency food and *sake* to his customers, but found their stores burned down. Shigeto started past the truck. "There's not a living soul in there!" the driver called out. "Not an animal. What use is a doctor?" Shigeto was forcibly lifted into the truck.

The doctor had to borrow a bicycle to cover the last mile home. He came unexpectedly upon a woman, a baby on her back, wandering on the dark road. When she saw him she began to weep hysterically. It was his wife, and in his memory, she had already placed a burning candle on the family Buddhist shrine.

Outside the city, first-aid stations were powerless to help the hundreds dying every hour. Seven-year-old Shizuko Iura was close to death but no one had heard her cry or complain. She continually asked for water, which her mother gave her against the advice of attendants. Why not ease her dying? "Father [he was a sailor on some Pacific island] is far away from home in a dangerous place," Shizuko said as if she saw him in a vision. "Please stay alive, Mother. If both of us die, he will be very lonely." She mentioned the names of all her friends and relatives. When she came to her grandparents she added, "They were good to me." She cried "Papa, Papa!" and died.

That day perhaps 100,000 human beings perished in Hiroshima, and an equal number were dying from burns, injuries and a disease of the atomic age, radiation poisoning.*

* Professor Shogo Nagaoka, the first curator of the Peace Memorial in Hiroshima, concluded that at least 200,000 died as a result of the bomb. This figure was corroborated by Drs. Naomi Shohno and K. Sakuma after an extensive study.

Twenty-two of the victims were American prisoners of war, and included several women. This was revealed to a Japanese newspaper in July 1970 by Hiroshi Yanagida, a *kempei* warrant officer, who had guarded the Americans. There were twenty-three prisoners in all. The twenty-third, a young soldier, was pulled out of the rubble alive, but he was killed by an angry mob of Japanese survivors.

3.

At 2:58 P.M., local time, *Enola Gay* touched down on Tinian's North Field. Several hundred officers and men rushed to surround the aircraft as the crew emerged. General "Tooey" Spaatz strode up and pinned a D.S.C. on Tibbets, who embarrassedly poked his pipe up a coverall sleeve as he stood at attention. The crew was interrogated in the officers club, a Quonset hut, over lemonade laced with bourbon. An intelligence officer asked Navigator Van Kirk for the exact drop time. He replied, "At 091517K"—seventeen seconds past schedule.

"Why were you late?"

Everyone laughed. General Farrell left the interrogation to send his first full report (an earlier bulletin had been transmitted based on the initial reports radioed from *Enola Gay*) to General Groves:

. . . FLASH NOT SO BLINDING AS TRINITY BECAUSE OF BRIGHT SUNLIGHT. FIRST THERE WAS A BALL OF FIRE CHANGING IN A FEW SECONDS TO PURPLE CLOUDS AND FLAMES BOILING AND SWIRLING UPWARD. FLASH OBSERVED JUST AFTER AIRPLANE ROLLED OUT OF TURN. ALL AGREED LIGHT WAS INTENSELY BRIGHT. . . .

ENTIRE CITY EXCEPT OUTERMOST ENDS OF DOCK AREAS WAS COVERED WITH A DARK GRAY DUST LAYER WHICH JOINED THE CLOUD COLUMN. IT WAS EXTREMELY TURBULENT WITH FLASHES OF FIRE VISIBLE IN THE DUST. ESTIMATED DIAMETER OF THIS DUST LAYER IS AT LEAST THREE MILES. ONE OBSERVER STATED IT LOOKED AS THOUGH WHOLE TOWN WAS BEING TORN APART WITH COLUMNS OF DUST RISING OUT OF VALLEYS APPROACHING THE TOWN. DUE TO DUST VISUAL OBSERVATIONS OF STRUCTURAL DAMAGE COULD NOT BE MADE.

JUDGE [Parsons] AND OTHER OBSERVERS FELT THIS STRIKE WAS TREMENDOUS AND AWESOME EVEN IN COMPARISON WITH TR [Trinity]. ITS EFFECTS MAY BE ATTRIBUTED BY THE JAPANESE TO A HUGE METEOR.

In Washington, Groves had received the preliminary message just before midnight, August 5. Because of the hour he did not awaken General Marshall; he went to sleep in his office to be on hand when the more detailed report came in. It arrived at 4:15 A.M., and three and a half hours later Chief of Staff Marshall transmitted the information by scrambler telephone to Stimson at his home on Long Island. The Secretary of War agreed that Truman's prepared statement concerning the bomb should be released to the press that morning.

It announced that a revolutionary bomb had been dropped on Hiroshima, which was described as an important Army base. "It is an atomic bomb. It is a harnessing of the basic power of the universe. The force from which the sun draws its power has been loosed against those who brought war to the Far East." America was prepared to obliterate all Japanese factories, docks, communications. "It was to spare the Japanese people from utter destruction that the ultimatum of July 26 was issued at Potsdam. Their leaders promptly rejected that ultimatum. If they do not now accept our terms, they may expect a rain of ruin from the air, the like of which has never been seen on this earth."

Truman was aboard *Augusta* on his way home from Potsdam. Army Captain Franklin Graham interrupted the President at lunch in the after mess hall to hand him a short dispatch from Stimson saying that the "big bomb" had been dropped on Hiroshima, apparently with success. Truman looked up. "Captain Graham," he remarked, "this is the greatest thing in history," and lapsed into silence. Within minutes another message arrived. It quoted the report from Parsons that the results had been "clear cut, successful in all respects."

Truman had kept the first dispatch to himself. Now he brusquely shoved his chair back and strode over to Byrnes at a nearby table. "It's time to get on home!" he said cryptically. He picked up a fork and rapped it sharply against a glass. The room went silent and he told the sailors about the new weapon. The President left for the officers wardroom, the cheers of the enlisted men following him down the companionway. "Keep your seats, gentlemen," he told the startled officers. "We have just dropped a bomb on Japan which has more power than twenty thousand tons of TNT. It was an overwhelming success. We won the gamble!"

At his home in Tokyo, Cabinet Secretary Sakomizu was in bed half asleep when the Domei News Agency phoned about the Truman announcement. The words "atomic bomb" brought him wide awake. He was shocked, but realized at the same time that this was the "golden opportunity" to end the war. No nation could defend itself against atomic bombs. It wouldn't be necessary to blame the military or the munitions makers for losing the war. He picked up the phone to call the Prime Minister.

... and Nagasaki

1.

In Hiroshima the mysterious effects of radiation were making themselves known at dawn on August 7. Shogo Nagaoka, formerly a geologist at the university, was trying to get through the rubble to the campus. A recent draftee, he had deserted his Army unit out of concern for the fate of the university and had been traveling for hours. He could hardly fathom the endless devastation. At the Gokoku Shrine near the hypocenter he slumped exhausted at the foot of a stone lantern. He felt a stinging sensation —it was radiation—and sprang to his feet. Then he noticed a strange silhouette on the lantern and that some of its surface was melted. An awful and sudden realization came to him: an atomic bomb! Japan had to surrender at once.

At scores of aid stations doctors were mystified. Their patients' symptoms were so bizarre that it was suspected an acrid poison gas had been used to spread bacillary dysentery. Some victims were scorched on just one side of the face; oddly, some had the shadow of a nose or ear stenciled on their cheek. Like Nagaoka, Dr. Shigeto of the Red Cross Hospital had heard of atomic energy and guessed that the victims were suffering from primary radiation. He checked the walls of the hospital with a simple X-ray indicator. The count was so low, however, that he concluded it was safe to remain.

The aftereffects were unpredictable. Private Shimoyama, one of those closest to ground zero, had been near-sighted before the *pika*. Now as he peered through his glasses everything seemed slightly blurred to him. Was he going blind? When he finally removed his glasses he discovered that he had regained perfect vision. But his hair was falling out and he was suffering from the same sickness that had struck thousands of others. First they felt nauseated and vomited; diarrhea and fever followed. Other reactions were erratic. Some victims were covered with brilliant spots—red, green-yellow, black and purple—and lived; others whose bodies had no apparent marks died abruptly. One man escaped with a slightly burned hand and ignored it until he began vomiting blood. He put his injured hand in water for relief and "something strange and bluish came out of it, like smoke."

Terror of the unknown, intensified by vague feelings of guilt and shame, swept over the survivors: they were alive because they had ignored pleas of relatives and neighbors for help and left them trapped in burning wreckage. The anguished voices of those who had died kept haunting them. Parents who had lost children blamed themselves, and children who had lost parents felt this was punishment for some wrongdoing. The tragedy had cruelly shattered the intricate and intimate structure of Japanese family life.

In Tokyo the Army's fanatic reluctance to accept the responsibility of surrender led them to question the significance of the complete destruction of a major city. They saw no merit in Foreign Minister Togo's suggestion that Japan accept the Potsdam Proclamation even when he pointed out with logic that the bomb "drastically alters the whole military situation and offers the military ample grounds for ending the war."

"Such a move is uncalled for," War Minister Anami countered. "Furthermore, we do not yet know if the bomb was atomic." They only had Truman's word for it. It might be a trick. Dr. Yoshio Nishina, the nation's leading nuclear scientist, should be sent at once to investigate Hiroshima.

As Dr. Nishina and Lieutenant General Seizo Arisue, chief of

Intelligence, were about to board a plane at Tachikawa Air Base, an air-raid siren began its banshee howl. Arisue ordered Dr. Nishina to wait until the All Clear sounded, but he and several subordinates took off immediately. Their plane arrived over Hiroshima just before dusk. The general had seen many cities laid waste by fire bombings—usually there was smoldering debris, smoke from emergency kitchens and some signs of human activity —but below him stretched a lifeless desert. No smoke, no fires, nothing. There wasn't a street in sight.

The pilot turned and shouted, "Sir, this is supposed to be Hiroshima. What should we do?"

"Land!"

The plane touched down on a sod strip near the harbor. As Arisue descended he noticed that the grass, a strange clay color, was leaning toward the Inland Sea; it looked as if it had been pressed by some giant hot iron. The party was met by a lieutenant colonel who saluted smartly. The left half of his face was severely burned, the right half untouched. Arisue was taken by motorboat to Army Maritime Transport Command. At the dock he was greeted by Lieutenant General Hideo Baba, a friend since the Military Academy, who reported that there was no water or electricity in Hiroshima. The two generals sat in the open at a long wooden table lit by candles. Baba had difficulty controlling his voice. He described how his daughter had perished on her way to high school. "Not my daughter alone, but thousands of other innocent children were massacred. This new bomb is satanic, too atrocious and horrible to use." He covered his face with his hands.

Arisue put his arm around his friend. "Please remember that we are military men," he finally said. Baba apologized for breaking down. He told Arisue that there was "a persistent rumor" that the Americans were going to drop another of the new bombs on Tokyo.*

* The fear that Tokyo was to be the next atomic target was "confirmed" the following night by a captured American fighter pilot downed near Osaka. Lieutenant Marcus McDilda didn't have the slightest idea what atomic energy was until an interrogator, a general, jabbed the tip of a sword into the American's lip and threatened to cut off his head. McDilda obliged. In his Florida drawl he described how atoms were split into pluses and minuses, which were then separated by a lead shield encased in a box thirty-six feet long and twenty-four feet wide. When the box was dropped from a plane,

People were returning to the city in ever-increasing numbers. Work groups began collecting bodies and incinerating them with whatever wood they could find. The stench was nauseating, somewhat like broiled sardines, but some of the workers had developed a perverse craving for the smell; it actually stimulated their appetites.

Dr. Nishina's plane arrived over Hiroshima the following afternoon. He surveyed the city and instantly concluded that an atomic bomb alone could have wreaked such havoc. He informed General Arisue that it had been an uranium-type bomb similar to the one he was trying to develop. Should he continue work on his bomb?

Arisue didn't answer.

The destruction of Hiroshima made Japan's unrealistic hope for a negotiated peace through the good offices of the Soviet Union more urgent than ever. Togo cabled Ambassador Sato in Moscow:

THE SITUATION IS BECOMING SO ACUTE THAT WE MUST HAVE CLARIFICATION OF THE SOVIET ATTITUDE AS SOON AS POSSIBLE. PLEASE MAKE FURTHER EFFORTS TO OBTAIN A REPLY IMMEDIATELY.

In the afternoon on August 8 the ambassador requested an immediate audience with Molotov, who had been avoiding him for several weeks. He was granted an appointment at eight that evening but moments later he was inexplicably asked to move up the meeting to five o'clock. Sato forced himself to remain calm as he entered the rambling Kremlin complex a few minutes before five. He was ushered into Molotov's study, but before he could greet the Foreign Commissar in Russian as was his custom, Molotov cut him off with a wave of the hand. "I have here, in the name of the Soviet Union, a notification to the Japanese government which I wish to communicate to you."

Sato's instinct told him this was a declaration of war. Although

---

the lead shield melted and the pluses and minuses reunited with a monstrous explosion that could lay waste to an entire city. Awed, his inquisitors wanted to know the next target. McDilda thought quickly. "I believe Kyoto and Tokyo. Tokyo is supposed to be bombed in the next few days."

he'd been expecting it, the reality of it was a blow. Molotov left his desk and sat down at the head of a long table. Sato was directed to a chair at the other end. With set expression Molotov began to read a document:

"After the defeat and capitulation of Hitlerite Germany, Japan remained the only great power which still stands for the continuation of the war.

"The demand of the three powers, the United States, Great Britain and China, of July 26 for the unconditional surrender of the Japanese armed forces was rejected by Japan. Thus the proposal made by the Japanese Government to the Soviet Union for mediation in the Far East has lost all foundation.

"Taking into account the refusal of Japan to capitulate, the Allies approached the Soviet Government with a proposal to join the war against Japanese aggression and thus shorten the duration of the war, reduce the number of casualties and contribute toward the most speedy restoration of peace.

"True to its obligation as an Ally, the Soviet Government has accepted the proposal of the Allies and has joined in the declaration of the Allied powers of July 26.

"The Soviet Government considers that this policy is the only means able to bring peace nearer, to free the people from further sacrifice and suffering and to give the Japanese people the opportunity of avoiding the danger of destruction suffered by Germany after her refusal to accept unconditional surrender.

"In view of the above, the Soviet Government declares that from tomorrow, that is from August 9, the Soviet Union will consider herself in a state of war against Japan."

Controlling his agitation, Ambassador Sato politely expressed regret that the Soviet Union was breaking a nonaggression pact almost a year before it expired. Now, as a favor, could he cable the information to his government? Molotov emerged from behind the impersonal façade: Sato could send any cables he wished, and in code. He said he personally regretted what had happened. "I have been quite satisfied with your actions as Japanese ambassador the past few years and am pleased that we two could maintain good relations between our governments until today in spite of the difficulties facing us."

"I am grateful for the good will and hospitality of your government," Sato replied in halting Russian, "which has enabled me to stay in Moscow during this difficult time. It is indeed a sad thing that we shall have to part as enemies. But this cannot be helped. At any rate, let us part with a handshake. It may be the last one."

They shook hands, but almost immediately the telephones at the Japanese embassy were disconnected and all radio equipment confiscated. Sato wrote out a message in plain Japanese text and sent it to the cable office.

2.

The bombing of Hiroshima had undoubtedly inspired the Russians to advance their timetable to enter the war, but for months 1,600,000 troops under the command of Marshal A. M. Vasilievsky had been assembling along the Manchurian border. They faced a Kwantung Army, half their size, which had been stripped of all armor and antitank guns, and whose average efficiency was not quite 30 percent of a prewar front-line unit.

Two hours after Molotov read the declaration of war to Sato, two Soviet armies crossed into Manchuria from the west. At the same time another army, based in Vladivostok, invaded from the east. Roads were muddy and streams overflowed their banks from a day-long downpour, but the three great Russian columns converged inexorably on Tsitsihar, Taonan and the cosmopolitan city of Harbin.

Shortly after his meeting with Sato, Molotov informed Ambassador Averell Harriman that war with Japan would start at midnight. The Soviet Union had decided to honor its pledge to the day to enter the Pacific war three months after the defeat of Germany.

Later in the evening Harriman and George Kennan found Stalin in a talkative mood. He announced that the first Soviet units had already advanced ten or twelve kilometers into Manchuria. "Who would have thought that things would have progressed so far by this time!" he exulted.

Harriman asked him what effect the atomic bomb would have on the Japanese. Stalin was confident that the enemy was looking for any pretext to form a new government that could arrange a surrender. Harriman's reminder of how fortunate the Soviets were to be on the side that had developed the bomb set Stalin off on an affable discussion of atomic energy. He seemed undisturbed that the allies had scored a scientific triumph. There was no hint that the previous day he had summoned five of Russia's foremost nuclear scientists to the Kremlin and ordered them to develop their own bomb as soon as possible regardless of the cost; he had put Lavrenti P. Beria, General Commissar of State Security and the most feared man in the Soviet Union, in overall charge of the project.

It was understandable that Americans as a whole regarded the atomic bomb primarily as a deliverance from four costly years of war. A few, however, saw beyond the common exultance. Admiral Leahy thought it was an inhuman weapon to use on a people that was already defeated and ready to surrender, and that Americans "had adopted an ethical standard common to the barbarians of the Dark Ages."*

Stimson also remained gravely concerned. That afternoon he had showed the President a photo which graphically illustrated the "total destruction" of Hiroshima. He said they must make every effort to persuade Japan to surrender as quickly as possible, and success depended largely on the manner in which the Japanese were approached. "When you punish your dog," he said, "you don't keep souring on him all day after the punishment is over; if you want to keep his affection, punishment takes care of itself. In the same way with Japan. They naturally are a smiling people and we have to get on those terms with them. . . ."

But Truman was not prepared to go beyond the Potsdam Proclamation. He was not unmoved by the photo of Hiroshima, and recognized "the terrible responsibility such destruction placed

---

* In his dissenting, and largely ignored, opinion at the Tokyo Tribunal, Justice Radhabinad Pal of India declared that "if any indiscriminate destruction of civilian life and property is still illegitimate in warfare, then, in the Pacific war, the decision to use the atom bomb is the only near approach to the directives of the German Emperor during the first World War and of the Nazi leaders during the second World War. Nothing like this could be traced to the credit of the present accused."

upon us here and himself." At the same time, a second atomic bomb would have to be used presently. No top-level meeting had been convened to discuss the necessity of a second bomb, no attempt made to determine if the first bomb or Russian entry into the conflict had quickened Japan's intent to surrender. If there were any moral compunctions felt by anyone of influence, except Stimson, they were not expressed to the President; and he felt none. He was ready to drop two bombs, three—and more, if it meant saving American lives.

On Guam, thirty-two copies of orders for the second raid were mimeographed. The decision on how and when to use subsequent bombs was now in the hands of the Joint Chiefs of Staff. Takeoff time would be early the next morning, August 9. There were two possible targets, both on the island of Kyushu: the primary was "Kokura Arsenal and City," and the secondary, "Nagasaki Urban Area."

On nearby Saipan, sixteen million leaflets designed to persuade the Japanese to surrender were being turned out by the Office of War Information printing plant. The very first propaganda had been ineffective. Obsolete, archaic phrases were used; drawings showed Japanese men wearing kimono left side over right like women, and pictured chopsticks placed one on each side of a plate like a knife and fork; the Japanese characters were often ludicrously inept: "freedom of speech" became "freedom of words," and "freedom of want"—"freedom from desire." But these mistakes had been rectified, and since the beginning of the year American leaflets had made an impact on the population. The present one, in particular, would have an indelible effect on public morale:

TO THE JAPANESE PEOPLE

America asks that you take immediate heed of what we say on this leaflet.

We are in possession of the most destructive explosive ever devised by man. A single one of our newly developed atomic bombs is actually the equivalent in explosive power to what 2,000 of our giant B-29s can carry on a single mission. This awful fact is one for you to ponder and we solemnly assure you that it is grimly accurate.

We have just begun to use this weapon against your homeland. If you still have any doubt, make inquiry as to what happened to Hiroshima when just one atomic bomb fell on that city.

Before using this bomb to destroy every resource of the military by which they are prolonging this useless war, we ask that you now petition the Emperor to end the war. Our President has outlined for you the thirteen consequences of an honorable surrender. We urge that you accept these consequences and begin work of building a new, better and peace-loving Japan.

You should take steps now to cease military resistance. Otherwise, we shall resolutely employ this bomb and all our other superior weapons to promptly and forcefully end the war.

Evacuate your cities now!

Even before the pamphlets were delivered, newspapers in Japan were warning that "new-type" bombs had been used at Hiroshima which "should not be made light of." The enemy, said the *Nippon Times,* now appeared to be "intent on killing and wounding as many innocent people as possible due to his urgent desire to end the war speedily." An editorial titled "A Moral Outrage Against Humanity" revealed that the new bomb possessed "unprecedented power. Not only was the greater part of the city wiped out, but an extraordinary proportion of the inhabitants have been either killed or wounded."

On the afternoon of August 8 Major Charles ("Chuck") Sweeney, who had piloted the instrument plane *Great Artiste* over Hiroshima, was informed that he was to drop the second bomb, using another aircraft. Unlike the bomb used at Hiroshima, this was a spherical plutonium missile, ten feet eight inches long and five feet in diameter, called "Fat Man" after Churchill. Colonel Tibbets told Sweeney and his crew that "Fat Man" would make the first bomb obsolete. He wished them luck.

For their mission Sweeney and his crew would use *Bock's Car,* while her regular pilot, Captain Frederick Bock, Jr., would fly the instrument plane.* *The Great Artiste* was unofficially being pre-

---

* This last-minute switch of planes was to confuse historians. By mistake the official communiqué announced that *The Great Artiste* had dropped the bomb and this was incorporated in most accounts, including several written by eyewitnesses. The error was discovered in 1946 when plans were made to retire *The Great Artiste,* because of her historical role, and it was learned that the serial number of the plane carrying the bomb was different.

pared for an unscheduled double role: three young scientists—
Luis Alvarez, Philip Morrison and Robert Serber—were attaching
a personal appeal, signed by them, to the canisters which would
be parachuted over the target to gather data. Each envelope was
addressed to Professor Ryokichi Sagane, a Japanese nuclear scientist whom all of them had known and worked with in the thirties
at the University of California Radiation Laboratory.

To: Prof. R. Sagane.
From: Three of your former scientific colleagues during your stay
in the United States.

We are sending this as a personal message to urge that you use your
influence as a reputable nuclear physicist, to convince the Japanese
General Staff of the terrible consequences which will be suffered by
your people if you continue in this war.

You have known for several years that an atomic bomb could be
built if a nation were willing to pay the enormous cost of preparing
the necessary material. Now that you have seen that we have constructed the production plants, there can be no doubt in your mind,
that all the output of these factories, working 24 hours a day, will be
exploded on your homeland.

Within the space of three weeks, we have proof-fired one bomb in
the American desert, exploded one in Hiroshima, and fired the third
this morning.

We implore you to confirm these facts to your leaders, and to do
your utmost to stop the destruction and waste of life which can only
result in the total annihilation of all your cities if continued. As
scientists, we deplore the use to which a beautiful discovery has been
put, but we can assure you that unless Japan surrenders at once, this
rain of atomic bombs will increase manyfold in fury.*

At 3:49 A.M. *Bock's Car* rumbled down the long runway. Unlike the first bomb, "Fat Man" could not be assembled in flight
and was fully armed at takeoff. The B-29's ground run seemed

---

* Professor Sagane did not read the letter until after the war. Had he
received it immediately he would have tried to persuade a group of influential
scientists to join him in a protest, but the letter was deliberately kept from
him. The day after the bombing one of his former students, a naval officer,
informed him with visible agitation that a letter from several Americans,
addressed to the professor, had just been turned over to the Navy. However,
an Army officer instructed Professor Sagane to discount any rumor he might
hear that the Navy had found a letter "about the atom bomb" because there
was no such letter.

interminable but its nose finally lifted, and lumbering off to the north in the darkness, it was closely followed by *The Great Artiste* and the photograph plane.

The mission seemed jinxed from the start. Sweeney discovered that the fuel selector to the 600 gallons of gas in his bomb-bay tank was inoperative. With that reserve unavailable, *Bock's Car*'s range was dangerously restricted, but Sweeney decided to keep going. At 8:09 A.M. Tokyo time, one minute ahead of schedule, a small island appeared ahead through a break in the clouds. It was Yakushima, off the south coast of Kyushu, where *Bock's Car* was to rendezvous with her escorts.

Three minutes later another B-29 loomed out of the clouds. It was *The Great Artiste*. The two planes circled for forty-five minutes but the photograph plane did not appear. "The hell with it," Sweeney told his co-pilot. "We can't wait any longer." He waggled his wings and headed for the primary target. Kokura, a port on the northeast coast of Kyushu, was reported clearly visible. But the city turned out to be partially obscured by smoke and haze, and Bombardier Kermit Beahan, who had been ordered to make a visual drop, could not find the aiming point. He called back to Sweeney, "We'll have to make another run."

"Pilot to crew," Sweeney announced. "No drop. Repeat. No drop." He banked sharply and they came in for a second attempt. Captain Beahan squinted into the rubber eyepiece of the Norden MK 15 bombsight. All he could see was dense smoke. "I can't pick up the aiming point," he said.

"No drop," Sweeney told him. "Repeat. No drop."

They came in from the east. Here, too, Kokura was hidden. The flight engineer reported that fuel was "getting critical," with just about enough to get them back to Iwo Jima. "Roger," Sweeney acknowledged, but turned to the weaponeer—the officer in charge of "Fat Man," Commander Frederick Ashworth—and said, "We'll go on to secondary target, if you agree." The Navy man nodded. "Proceeding to Nagasaki," Sweeney told the crew and turned southwest. The Nagasaki weather plane had reported only two-tenths cloud cover over the city.

Nagasaki, a city of 200,000, spread over precipitous hills, like San Francisco. Its bay faced the East China Sea. It was a fabled port of spectacular beauty, particularly now, for a touch of autumn had come early and many of the trees were brilliant with reddish browns and yellows. The center of town fronted the bay which was formed by the Urakami River flowing into it from the north. With the centuries, Nagasaki had expanded from this nucleus into several valleys, including the one fashioned by the river which had become an industrial complex employing 90 percent of the city's labor force.

In 1571 the Portuguese had helped build it from a fishing village into Japan's chief port for foreign trade, and introduced tobacco, firearms and Christianity. The new faith became so widespread that the government took brutal steps to repress it. All missionaries were either killed or forced to leave the country, but in the seventeenth century 37,000 of their followers rebelled against religious persecution. They rallied around a castle near Nagasaki, and with the help of guns on a few Dutch vessels, held off the armies of the central government for three months before being slaughtered almost to a man.

Their faith survived, however, and Nagasaki remained the most Europeanized, the most Christian city in Japan, a harmonious blend of the cultures of East and West with its numerous Christian churches and schools, hundreds of Western-type houses, and such tourist attractions as Glover's Mansion, the legendary home of Madame Butterfly overlooking the harbor.

Shigeyoshi Morimoto was on his way home to Nagasaki, a nervous and shaken man. Only three days before, he had miraculously escaped death in Hiroshima, where he had been working for the past months making antiaircraft kites for the Army. He had been shopping for paint brushes less than 900 yards from ground zero when the bomb exploded, and the wreckage of the flimsy store protected him from the *pika*. He had fled the city, along with three assistants, in a coal car bound for Nagasaki and safety. All night long they talked compulsively about "the bomb." Had Japan been punished by some supernatural force for attacking Pearl Harbor? By the time the freight train made its steep, dramatic descent into the Nagasaki terminal, Morimoto had an unshakable premonition that the bomb would follow him to his own home. He had to warn his wife. As he approached his shop, which was in the center of town, it was almost 11 A.M.

Misfortune continued to dog *Bock's Car.* As it neared the target it encountered deteriorating weather. The cloud cover over Nagasaki would probably be nine-tenths. Sweeney told Commander Ashworth that with the reduced fuel they couldn't make more than one pass and suggested dropping "Fat Man" by radar. Ashworth hesitated; he was supposed to jettison the bomb into the ocean if he couldn't find the target visually. What a waste that would be, he thought, and decided to disobey orders. "Go ahead and drop it by radar," he told Sweeney, "if you can't do it visually."

The drop point, chosen for maximum devastation of the city, was on high ground near Morimoto's kite shop. An explosion here should wipe out the center of town, the port area and reach up into the factories of the Urakami Valley. Nagasaki appeared on the radar scope at 11 A.M. Bombardier Beahan shouted to Sweeney, "I've got it. I see the city." So he would be able to bomb visually, after all. Through a break in the cloud cover he could see the oval rim of an outdoor stadium on the banks of the Urakami River. It was almost two miles northwest of the scheduled hypocenter but would have to do. He trained his cross hairs on the stadium, and seconds later, at 11:01 A.M., the plane lurched upward.

"Bombs away," Beahan reported over the intercom, then corrected himself, "Bomb away."

Morimoto, the kite maker, was breathlessly telling his wife that a terrible bomb had been dropped on Hiroshima and that he feared Nagasaki would be next. He began to describe the *pika:* "First there is a great blue flash—" A blinding blue flash cut off his words. He flung back a trap door in the floor and shoved his wife and infant son into their shelter. As he pulled down the heavy lid there was a terrifying tremor, like an earthquake.

If there had been no clouds overhead, the Morimoto shop, directly under the original drop point, would have been obliterated but the bomb exploded several hundred yards northeast of the stadium and the river, almost exactly between the Mitsubishi Steel and Arms Works and the Mitsubishi Torpedo Factory.

Hajime Iwanaga, who would be fourteen the next day, was bathing in the Urakami River near the torpedo factory. He saw a black object (it was an instrument canister) drop from a plane and burst into a parachute. He called out "Friendly plane!" to a comrade and exuberantly ducked his face in the water as the *pika* flashed. Seconds later he emerged into a blinding world. Something warm clung to his left shoulder. It was yellowish. Mystified, he touched it and saw skin come off. He splashed toward the bank as the sky darkened ominously, and was reaching for his clothes when two dark-green spheres, the size of baseballs, streaked at him. One struck his shirt, set it afire, and disintegrated. As he clambered up the bank he heard a comrade in the river shriek in agony, "Mother!" Huge raindrops pummeled him for a moment.

Taeko Fukabori, a year older, was helping pump water out of a large natural cave which served as a public air-raid shelter. She was hurled into the mud and remembered hearing how people had been buried alive in a bomb raid the week before at the shipyards. Terrified, she groped her way toward the exit. Outside (the cave was less than 200 yards from ground zero) she found herself right in hell. Bodies of workers at the entrance were so charred that she could not distinguish their backs from their fronts. A person without hair and blackened body—it was impossible to tell if it was man or woman—walked by, seemingly oblivious, with only a burning string around the waist.

Taeko started up the eastern slope of the valley to get home to her mother. A soldier stopped her and said that direction was impassable. She followed him across the railroad tracks to the river, unaware that the right side of her face and her right shoulder were burned. Inexplicably, she was suddenly certain that her family on the hill was safe.

Farther up the slope, adjacent to the municipal prison and less than 275 yards from the hypocenter, twelve-year-old Kazuko Tokai had crawled into the small, unfinished family shelter to rest. Two feet of dirt above it saved her from the *pika*. She felt an indescribable sensation on her body and heard a crackling noise like the sizzling of a broiling steak. She crawled outside, into darkness. Confused—she thought that it was night—and unable to feel or smell a thing, she began walking aimlessly.

As the dust cleared, Kazuko found herself at a crumbled wall— all that was left of Urakami Prison. She turned around to get back home. The house had disappeared. Kazuko freed her mother, who was buried under tiles, and together they located Mr. Tokai in the rubble. His skin came off like a glove as they pulled him out.

Near the top of the slope in a seventy-bed tuberculosis sana-
torium—1,500 yards from ground zero—Dr. Tatsuichiro Akizuki
was inserting a long needle into the side of a male patient when he
heard an eerie noise, as if a huge plane were roaring down at them.
It was going to hit the hospital! "Drop on the floor!" he yelled.
He withdrew the needle and plunged to the floor. There was a
white flash and debris rained on him. He struggled to his feet, unharmed. The air was filled with choking dust from pulverized
plaster.

He feared all the patients on the second and third floors were
dead, and he started for the staircase with one of the nurses.
Patients were coming down, frightened but only superficially
wounded. Through a window he saw yellow smoke in Urakami
Valley. The cathedral was on fire: so was the vocational high
school. The sky was red and a murky yellow. He was drawn outside to the garden. Eggplant leaves and potato plants were smoldering. It had to be similar to the bomb used at Hiroshima. The
president of Nagasaki Medical College had seen the wreckage in
that city, and just the day before, had excitedly described it at a
student–faculty meeting.

At the bottom of the valley Hachiro Kosasa had gone into the
storehouse of the torpedo factory to get some metal material when
he sensed something vaguely odd. He turned and saw the windows
aglow with colored lights—a gas tank must have exploded. He
dropped to the floor as the ceiling collapsed. Unaware of deep cuts
in his head, legs and thigh, he staggered toward the plant infir-
mary, but it was gone. In the twilight gloom people milled around
helplessly. His instinct was to escape, try to get home. Weak from
loss of blood, he tied his legging around his thigh as a tourniquet,
and driven by fear that his body might not be found by relatives
and given a proper funeral, he headed south toward the Mitsubishi
Steel and Arms Works. Soon his leg no longer supported him and
he continued the journey on hands and knees.

At the steel works, which stretched for almost a mile down to
the railroad station, sixteen-year-old Etsuko Obata had started a
new job that morning filing machine parts on the second floor. The
concussion knocked her unconscious; when she came to, she found
herself suspended in wreckage six feet above the ground floor. She
was carried to a truck bound for the University Hospital up on

the eastern slope, but fires forced the "ambulance" to detour south, toward the station. This avenue too became blocked by spreading fires, and the patients were instructed to get out and walk. Etsuko lowered herself painfully onto the highway. The sun looked big and red, burning red. She tried to crawl under the truck for shelter but couldn't. Incongruously, there was a heavy shower, the raindrops hissing into the fires and hot earth.

Overhead, the crews in the two B-29's saw "a giant ball of fire rise as though from the bowels of the earth, belching forth enormous white smoke rings." Correspondent William Laurence in *The Great Artiste* watched a fiery column shoot two miles into the sky. He began scribbling frantically as the pillar of fire became "a living thing, a new species of being, born right before incredulous eyes." A giant mushroom billowed at the top, even more alive than the towering pillar. It seethed and boiled in white fury like a thousand geysers. In seconds it broke free from the stem and a smaller mushroom took its place. It was, Laurence thought, like a decapitated monster growing a new head.

In *Bock's Car* the rear gunner shouted over the intercom to Sweeney, "Major, let's get the hell out of here!"

As Sweeney swung the plane away from the terrible sight, Copilot Albury called to the bombardier, "Well, Bea, there's a hundred thousand Japs you just killed."

Beahan didn't answer.

The men began to unbend from the tension. While removing their cumbersome flak suits they shouted congratulations to one another, and the radio operator sent Sweeney's first report back to Tinian:

BOMBED NAGASAKI 090158Z VISUALLY WITH NO FIGHTER OP-POSITION AND NO FLAK. RESULTS "TECHNICALLY SUCCESSFUL" BUT OTHER FACTORS INVOLVED MAKE CONFERENCE NECESSARY BEFORE TAKING FURTHER STEPS. VISIBLE EFFECTS ABOUT EQUAL TO HIROSHIMA. TROUBLE IN AIRPLANE FOLLOWING DE-LIVERY REQUIRES US TO PROCEED TO OKINAWA. FUEL ONLY TO GET TO OKINAWA.

The victims of Nagasaki were not all Japanese. A work party of Allied prisoners at the Steel and Arms Works was caught in the blast and a number of them died. A POW camp a mile away was badly damaged and no one would ever know how many perished. Even forty miles away at the Senryu Camp, Dr. Julien M. Goodman, a surgeon captured on Bataan, felt the concussion. There was a deep rumble, followed by a blast of air. The earth trembled. Within moments there was another tremor, and an Australian physician, Dr. John Higgin, remarked, "This must be the beginning of a great naval barrage." The shock waves and tremors continued for almost five minutes. The inexplicable phenomenon transformed the camp. The prisoners were called into the mess hall and informed that no more work details would be sent to the coal-mine shafts.

A Japanese seaplane was heading directly for Nagasaki through clouds at 10,000 feet. Ten minutes earlier a report had come in to the naval air base at Sasebo of a "great bombing" on nearby Nagasaki, and the pilot, a twenty-year-old cadet, had made an unauthorized takeoff to investigate. Cadet Nobukazu Komatsu had heard Truman's announcement about Hiroshima by short wave. Perhaps this, too, was an atomic bomb.

The plane broke out of the clouds and was confronted by a huge column of black smoke. At the top, "like the head of a monster," was a massive, swelling ball changing colors kaleidoscopically. Drawing closer, Komatsu realized that the colors were an illusion caused by the sun's rays. He started circling around the cloud; everything below was obscured. He shouted to his two companions, "Let's cut into the cloud!"

It was like an oven. Komatsu slid open the cockpit window and extended his gloved hand—it was like plunging his arm into live steam. He jerked it back, slammed the window shut, and found his glove covered with "sticky dust." One of his comrades cried out; Chief Petty Officer Umeda was vomiting. The darkness and heat intensified. The third man, Cadet Tomimura, opened his window for relief. A blast of heat swept into his face. He screamed and shut the window just before the seaplane burst into sunlight again. Their faces were covered with grayish dust.

His head throbbing, and fighting nausea, Komatsu descended in circles. Below, Nagasaki was a mass of flames and dark billowing clouds. He reduced power to go lower for pictures but the heat forced him to turn toward the bay. There he would land in the harbor and continue to explore the city on foot.*

3.

Ambassador Sato's report to Tokyo that the Soviet Union had declared war was never transmitted, Molotov's promise notwithstanding. The Russians themselves, hours later, broadcast the news. It was monitored by the radio room of the Foreign Ministry before dawn that morning, while *Bock's Car* was still hundreds of miles from Nagasaki. Smashed was Togo's last tenuous hope for negotiations through the U.S.S.R., which he had pressed so hard, despite a conviction that it was hopeless. Japan had been stabbed in the back without warning—he was as indignant as Cordell Hull had been on Pearl Harbor day. He took the information personally to Prime Minister Suzuki, berating him for his failure to call an emergency meeting of the Big Six the previous day. Togo's anger was unnecessary. This time Suzuki did not argue or play with words; his reaction was simple and straightforward. "Let us end the war," he said. But first he wanted to make certain that the Emperor would approve an immediate surrender. At the *obunko* he found His Majesty agreeable to acceptance of any terms that would lead to peace.

With this assurance Suzuki called to order an emergency meeting of the Big Six. It was 11 A.M., one minute before "Fat Man" fell on Nagasaki. "Under the present circumstances," Suzuki began, "I have concluded that our only alternative is to accept the Potsdam Proclamation and terminate the war. I would like to hear your opinions on this."

No one spoke.

"Why are you all so silent?" asked Admiral Yonai. "We won't accomplish a thing unless we speak frankly."

The other three military men resented Yonai's willingness to discuss surrender, yet the Russian invasion of Manchuria had shaken them more than the bombing of Hiroshima.**

---

* Umeda died of leukemia two years later; Tomimura also died of leukemia in 1964; Komatsu still suffers from anemia.

** After the war Admiral Toyoda said, "I believe the Russian participation

An officer entered the room with the report that a second atomic bomb had been dropped. This disquieting news, coupled with that from Manchuria, brought the pent-up resentment of Anami, Umezu and Toyoda into the open. They knew in their hearts that surrender was inevitable but adamantly refused to accept the Potsdam Proclamation even if the Emperor was allowed to reign. They insisted, in addition, that war criminals be tried by the Japanese themselves, that the Army be demobilized by Japanese officers, and that the occupation force be limited.

Togo impatiently tried to make them acknowledge the reality of the situation. With Japan so close to collapse, the Allies would undoubtedly reject such stipulations and the entire effort for peace would be endangered. Could the military offer any hope of victory? War Minister Anami could not, but he still wanted Japan to fight one more great battle—on the mainland. Could you keep the enemy from landing? Togo persisted.

"With luck we will be able to repulse the invaders before they land," Umezu answered. "At any rate, I can say with confidence that we will be able to destroy the major part of an invading force. That is, we will be able to inflict extremely heavy damage on the enemy."

Togo pressed him: What difference would that make? The enemy would simply launch a second or third assault if necessary. There was nothing to do but sue for peace with a minimum of counterdemands. After three hours the issue remained unresolved. Suzuki adjourned the meeting and reported its inconclusive results to Marquis Kido. "There is but one solution," he told the Privy Seal. "We must ask the Emperor to make the decision."

It was a bold suggestion; powerful though the Emperor was, his role did not encompass initiation of policy. But Kido also realized that only an extraordinary act of the Throne could save Japan. Without hesitation the Privy Seal explained the situation to the Emperor. His Majesty, too, saw the necessity for defying tradition.

---

in the war against Japan rather than the atom bombs did more to hasten the surrender." The official British history, *The War Against Japan,* supports this contention: " . . . for it brought home to all members of the Supreme Council the realization that the last hope of a negotiated peace had gone and there was no alternative but to accept the Allied terms sooner or later."

The Cabinet meeting that afternoon did no more to settle the issue than the Big Six had that morning. The military again lined up against the civilians—all except Yonai, who maintained that nothing could be gained by continuing the war. "Therefore we must forget about 'face' and surrender as quickly as possible, and begin to consider at once how best to preserve the country."

His words incensed his fellow officers. Anami had difficulty in containing his animosity. "That we will inflict severe losses on the enemy when he invades Japan is certain," he said, "and it is not impossible to reverse the situation and pull victory out of defeat." Furthermore, Army units in the field would not submit to demobilization. "Our men will simply refuse to lay down their arms. They know they are forbidden to surrender. There is really no alternative for us but to continue the war."

Four civilian ministers—Agriculture, Commerce, Transportation and Munitions—differed. The people were on the verge of exhaustion; the rice crop was the poorest in years; the country no longer had the strength to fight.

Anami interrupted impatiently. "Everyone understands all that, but we must fight to the end no matter how great the odds against us!"

At the mouth of the Urakami River the globular gas tanks near the railroad station lifted into the air like monstrous fireballs, crashed back to earth and shot up again. Drum cans rocketed much higher. Just to the north, survivors were dazedly working their way from ground zero. A naked man, expressionless, was carrying a boy with entrails spilling from his stomach. A cat, its hair burned kinky, was licking intestines hanging from a horse.

Midori Nishida was a messenger girl at the Steel and Arms Works whose hair had been set afire by the *pika*. She sought to escape across the Ohashi railroad bridge just above the stadium, unaware that she was heading into the center of destruction. The ties had burned out and she inched across, balancing on the twisted rails. The river below was filled with bodies. The buttocks of one woman near the bank were blown up like balloons. Nearby a black-and-white cow covered with raw spots of pink was placidly lapping water.

At one point Midori almost fell and asked for help from a girl coming the other way. It was a classmate, but Midori's scorched appearance frightened her; she burst into tears and refused to touch Midori. Resentfully Midori edged her way to the east bank. She passed a charred naked man standing like a statue with arms and legs spread apart. He was dead. Beyond she saw bales of charcoal. She was almost on them before she realized they were human beings. Their faces were huge and round as if pumped up with gas. There were no buildings, only flat, smoldering rubble. Near the hypocenter she encountered someone else from her class, a boy. He didn't recognize her until she spoke. "Are you really Nishida-*san?*" he said.

All around them, agonized voices pleaded for help. Midori felt irresistibly drawn to them and in panic fled back toward the river. With her new companion she picked her way south along the bank until they found a place shallow enough to ford. They passed a mother and daughter seated on a scorched *futon*. The girl was leaning forward, dead, her head drooping in the water. The mother stared at her blankly. Why didn't she pull her daughter out of the water? Midori wondered and continued south past the Steel and Arms Works, unaware that the soles of her sneakers were burned through.

As twilight began to obscure the visual horror of Nagasaki, thousands of survivors were unable to leave the blasted area because of wounds or inertia. Little Kazuko Tokai, whose scanty earth refuge 275 yards from ground zero had saved her from injury, was huddled with her mother and father in an empty public shelter near the ruins of their home. Just before the stars appeared, Kazuko's father died. Her mother's voice became hoarse and barely discernible. "Don't die!" Kazuko begged in the darkness. There was no answer, nor could Kazuko rouse her. She, too, was dead. The girl waited. She heard no sound from anywhere in the vast nothingness. I'm the only one left alive, she thought.*

* Americans put the death toll at 35,000; the officials of Nagasaki, at 74,800.

35

"To Bear
the Unbearable"

1.

In Tokyo that evening the Cabinet continued the fruitless debate. As spokesman for the militarists, Anami seemed as adamant as ever, but Sakomizu suspected that the War Minister was playing his own game of *haragei*. If Anami really meant what he said, all he had to do was resign and the Cabinet would be dissolved —whoever followed would have to be subservient to the militarists. Just before eleven Prime Minister Suzuki, who had scrupulously avoided getting involved in the argument, adjourned the meeting. It was clear that the Cabinet itself was unable to reach a decision. Now the last recourse was to call upon the Emperor.

Minutes later in his private office the Prime Minister instructed Sakomizu to arrange for an immediate imperial conference. First it would be necessary to obtain the *kaki ban* (handwritten seal) of the Army and Navy Chiefs of Staff. With foresight Sakomizu had already persuaded Admiral Toyoda and General Umezu to put their seals on a request for the meeting—he had told them, quite reasonably, that it might have to be called at a moment's notice.

The two officers had assumed that a conference with the Emperor would be held only if a unanimous decision was reached. Sakomizu did not ask Umezu or Toyoda for confirmation of their approval, since he knew they would not give it. Nor did he inform his chief that he had acquired the seals under provisional circumstances.

Within the hour the puzzled conferees—they had been summoned hastily without full explanation—began arriving singly at the *obunko*. They stepped out of their cars in the bright moonlight and were escorted by one of the chamberlains down a steep, mat-lined stairway to the long tunnel which led to the *obunko* annex, the imperial underground complex. Built into the side of a hill, it consisted of half a dozen rooms, the largest a conference chamber, poorly ventilated, sweltering. It was spare and gloomy with a ceiling supported by steel beams, and walls paneled in dark wood.

In addition to the Big Six—along with four secretaries, including the ubiquitous Sakomizu—the aged Baron Hiranuma, President of the Privy Council, had been summoned. In the anteroom their anger and confusion focused on Sakomizu. Toyoda, Umezu and two military secretaries pressed around him, their swords clanging ominously, and accused him of obtaining their *kaki ban* under false pretenses.

The Cabinet Secretary could not calm them even when forced to lie: "We are not going to make any decision at this conference." He escaped his accusers only when the conferees were instructed to take their seats in the conference room at two long parallel tables. At the head of the tables on a dais was a much smaller one covered with gold-lined brocade behind which was a chair and a six-panel gilt screen.

At ten minutes before midnight the Emperor entered. He appeared tired and concerned. He lowered himself heavily into the chair on the dais. The conferees bowed and sat down, avoiding looking directly at him. Several of the older men began coughing, increasing the feeling of uneasiness. At Suzuki's request, Sakomizu read the Potsdam Proclamation. The disturbing words stuck in his throat.

Suzuki briefly reviewed the recent debates in the Supreme Council and Cabinet, and then called on each member of the Big Six in turn for a statement. Despite the oppressive heat Togo was self-possessed. He quietly declared that the Potsdam Proclamation should be accepted at once so long as *kokutai,* the national essence, could be maintained. Admiral Yonai was just as contained. "I agree with Foreign Minister Togo," he said evenly.

His unequivocal concurrence enraged War Minister Anami, the next in line. "I oppose the opinions of the Foreign Minister!" he exclaimed. The Army could not agree to surrender unless the Allies allowed Japan to demobilize her own troops, try her own war criminals and limit the occupation force. "If not, we must continue fighting with courage and find life in death." His cheeks glistened with tears and his voice became strident as he pleaded for a last decisive battle in the homeland. "I am quite sure we could inflict great casualties on the enemy, and even if we fail in the attempt, our hundred million people are ready to die for honor, glorifying the deeds of the Japanese race in recorded history!"

The shaven-headed Umezu got to his feet. It would be unthinkable, he announced sternly, to surrender unconditionally after so many brave men had died for the Emperor.

Admiral Toyoda should have been the next to speak but Suzuki, seemingly confused but perhaps by design, asked Baron Hiranuma for his opinion. Anami and Umezu eyed him suspiciously—he might be well known as an ultranationalist, but like most of the *jushin,* he was probably a "Badoglio"—as he posed a series of pointed questions ending with one which called for a direct answer from the military: Could they continue the war?

Umezu assured him that further atomic attacks could be stemmed by antiaircraft measures. "We have been preserving our strength for future operations," he said, "and we expect to counterattack in time."

The legalistic Hiranuma appeared unimpressed. He agreed more or less with Togo, but he said they should negotiate with the Allies for the Army's demands. He turned to the Emperor. "In accordance with the legacy of His Imperial Forefathers, His Imperial Majesty is also responsible for preventing unrest in the nation. I should like to ask His Majesty to make his decision with this point in mind." The crusty old man sat down.

When Toyoda finally spoke he tried to re-emphasize the militarist position, but his conclusions were ambiguous: "We cannot say that final victory is a sure thing, but at the same time we do not believe that we will be completely defeated."

For more than two hours the old arguments had been repeated almost word for word. As Toyoda finished, Suzuki again got to his feet, slowly and deliberately. It appeared to Sakomizu that he was at last going to reveal the convictions he had repressed so long. What he said, however, astonished his listeners even more: "We have been discussing this matter many hours without reaching a conclusion. The situation is indeed serious, but not a moment has been spent in vain. We have no precedent—and I find it difficult to do—but with the greatest reverence I must now ask the Emperor to express his wishes."

He turned toward his ruler. He asked that the Emperor decide whether Japan should accept the Potsdam Proclamation outright or demand the conditions the Army wanted. Unaccountably, he stepped away from his chair toward His Majesty. There were gasps.

"Mr. Prime Minister!" Anami exclaimed, but Suzuki seemed not to hear him and advanced to the foot of the Emperor's small podium, his large shoulders bent with age. He stopped and bowed very low. With an understanding nod His Majesty bid Suzuki to sit down. The old man couldn't catch the words and cupped a hand to his left ear. The Emperor beckoned him to return to his place.

As soon as Suzuki was seated the Emperor himself got to his feet. His voice, usually expressionless, was noticeably strained. "I have given serious thought to the situation prevailing at home and abroad and have concluded that continuing the war means destruction for the nation and a prolongation of bloodshed and cruelty in the world." The others listened with heads bowed. "I cannot bear to see my innocent people suffer any longer. Ending the war is the only way to restore world peace and to relieve the nation from the terrible distress with which it is burdened." He paused.

Sakomizu glanced up at His Majesty, who was gazing thoughtfully at the ceiling as he wiped his glasses with a white-gloved thumb. The Cabinet Secretary felt tears flooding his eyes. The conferees were no longer sitting stiffly in their chairs but had thrown themselves forward—some arms outstretched, prostrate on the tables, sobbing unashamedly. By now the Emperor had regained his composure. He resumed speaking in a voice choked with emotion but was again forced to stop. Sakomizu wanted to cry out, "We now all understand His Majesty's wishes. Please do not condescend to say another word."

"It pains me," the Emperor was saying, "to think of those who served me so faithfully, the soldiers and sailors who have been killed or wounded in far-off battles, the families who have lost all their worldly goods—and often their lives as well—in the air raids at home. It goes without saying that it is unbearable for me to see the brave and loyal fighting men of Japan disarmed. It is equally unbearable that others who have rendered me devoted service should now be punished as instigators of the war. Nevertheless, the time has come when we must bear the unbearable. When I recall the feelings of my Imperial Grandsire, the Emperor Meiji, at the time of the Triple Intervention [by Russia, Germany and France in 1895], I swallow my own tears and give my sanction to the proposal to accept the Allied proclamation on the basis outlined by the Foreign Minister."*

He had finished. Suzuki stood up, as did the others. "I have respectfully listened to His Majesty's gracious words," he said.

The Emperor started to reply but instead nodded. Slowly, as if burdened with some intolerable weight, he left the room.

"His Majesty's decision," said Suzuki, "should now be made the unanimous decision of this conference." Of course, it had not been a decision in the Western sense, merely an expression of his wish. But to a loyal Japanese—and all eleven men in the room were that—his wish was tantamount to a command. The minutes of the meeting were recorded, and the conferees, still shaken by the Emperor's anguish, began affixing their signatures, thus approving acceptance of the Potsdam Proclamation with the proviso that the Allies recognize the lawful status of the Emperor.

All but Baron Hiranuma. As usual something bothered him;

* In his talk with Grand Chamberlain Fujita in January 1946, the Emperor pointed out the difference between the decisions to start the war and end it, and how it affected his role as emperor. "At the time of surrender, there was no prospect of agreement no matter how many discussions they [the Big Six] had. In addition to the intense bombings, we had suffered atomic bombs, and the ravages of war were suddenly accelerated. Lastly, when Suzuki asked me, at the imperial conference, which of the two views should be taken, I was given the opportunity to express my own free will for the first time without violating anybody else's authority or responsibilities. . . ."

he objected to the phrasing of the stipulation "the status of our Emperor is one ordained by God." He was adamant that the exact wording of the Constitution—"the supreme power of the Emperor" —be substituted.

Hiranuma added his signature at two-thirty. The momentous meeting was over and the military had approved what amounted to unconditional surrender. But in the absence of His Majesty, their frustration and sense of betrayal were directed at Suzuki. "You didn't keep your promise, Mr. Prime Minister!" shouted Lieutenant General Masao Yoshizumi, who had sat in as a secretary. "Are you happy now?"

Anami stepped between them.

There was one more formality—approval by the entire Cabinet. It was convened at once at Suzuki's home, where the ministers also drafted identical notes to each of the Allies accepting the Potsdam Proclamation "with the understanding that the said declaration does not compromise any demand which prejudices the prerogatives of His Majesty as a Sovereign Ruler."*

It had been a long evening. Suzuki went upstairs to bed. Sakomizu didn't leave but slumped down in an armchair and was soon asleep. The others wearily headed home through the dark, quiet streets of Tokyo. Everyone but Togo. Debilitated by pernicious anemia, he was probably the most exhausted of all. Light was just faintly coming from the east as his car stopped at the makeshift Foreign Ministry, where he wanted to record the Emperor's words which burned in his mind. He dictated them to his unofficial secretary, his son-in-law Fumihiko Togo, who, despite the family ties, remained in awe of the old man. He had rarely seen him exhibit any emotion, but as Togo recited what His Majesty had said his eyes filled with tears.

August 10 dawned hot and muggy in Tokyo. At Army Headquarters on Ichigaya Heights more than fifty officers of the War Ministry waited in an air-raid shelter for the appearance of General Anami. The emergency summons of so many important of-

---

* The wording in English was imprecise. Later Shunichi Matsumoto, Vice Minister to Togo, called it misleading. It should have read: "We accept the Potsdam Proclamation. We understand that this acceptance does not affect the position of the Imperial Household."

ficers aroused lively speculation. Was the War Minister going to announce the merger of the Army and Navy? Was it something about the atomic bomb or was he going to report on last night's imperial conference?

At nine-thirty Anami, flanked by two high-ranking officers, strode down the long tunnel from the Headquarters building and into the bunker. As he mounted a little platform, riding crop in right hand, the audience clustered about him in a semicircle. Quietly he said that last night's imperial conference had decided to accept the Potsdam Proclamation.

Incredulous, several shouted "No!" Anami held up his hands for quiet. "I do not know what excuse I can offer," he said, "but since it is the wish of His Majesty that we accept the Potsdam Proclamation there is nothing that can be done." He told them of the Army's minimum demands and regretted he had been unable to get them accepted. He promised, however, to make another attempt, and he asked for their help to keep order in the Army whatever happened. "Your individual feelings and those of the men under you must be disregarded."

A major stepped forward. "What about the duty of the military to protect the nation?"

Ordinarily a gentle man, Anami brandished his crop at the major. "If anybody disobeys Anami's order, he will have to cut Anami down!"

Lieutenant Colonel Masao Inaba of the Military Affairs Bureau approached the general with a plan to keep order in the Army. "Regardless of whether we end the war or not," he said, "we must send out instructions to keep fighting, particularly with the Soviet troops advancing in Manchuria."

"Write it out," said Anami.

It still remained for the Cabinet to decide how much the public should be told. The military was unwilling to reveal the Emperor's decision for fear it would immediately undermine Japan's will to fight and bring chaos. A compromise was reached: they would merely issue a vague statement that would help prepare the people for surrender. It was composed by Kainan Shimomura, President of the Information Board, and his staff. It boasted of victories, condemned the new bomb as ruthless and barbarous, and warned that the enemy was about to invade the homeland. The last paragraph alone gave an indication that the public was about to face an unprecedented situation:

In truth, we must recognize that we are now beset with the worst possible situation. Just as the government is exerting its utmost efforts to defend the homeland, safeguard *kokutai*, and preserve the honor of the nation, so too must the people rise to the occasion and overcome all manner of difficulties in order to protect the national essence of their empire.

On the other hand, there was no hint at all of surrender in Inaba's instructions to the officers and men of the Army, to fight the holy war to the end:

We are determined to fight resolutely, although we may have to chew grass, eat dirt and sleep in the fields. It is our belief that there is life in death. This is the spirit of the great Nanko, who wanted to be reborn seven times in order to serve the country, or the indomitable spirit of Tokimune, who refused to be swayed and pressed on vigorously with the work of crushing the Mongolian horde.

Shortly after Inaba sent the message to the War Minister for approval, two perturbed lieutenant colonels—one a press officer, the other Masahiko Takeshita, Anami's brother-in-law—burst into Inaba's office with the information that the Cabinet was about to issue a public statement hinting at surrender. Since this would create confusion among the troops, they must broadcast Inaba's exhortation at once. Inaba turned his wastebasket upside down and retrieved a crumpled sheet of paper, the original draft of his statement. Because it was in Anami's name he hesitated releasing it without the War Minister's approval. But the two colonels convinced him there was no time, and copies of the instructions were sent immediately to all local radio stations and newspapers.

The two conflicting statements, issued almost simultaneously, baffled the editors and station managers and forced Togo to take precipitous action. Anami's statement would undoubtedly lead the Allies to believe that Japan was resolved to continue hostilities. The formal notes informing the Allies of Japan's willingness to surrender were being processed through sluggish diplomatic channels, and a few hours' delay might mean a third atomic bomb. Why not send out the official note immediately as a news story? There was a good possibility some military censor, if he recognized the contents of the message, might hold it up. To circumvent this it was decided to transmit the Japanese proposal in English in Morse code. By the time the censors translated the message, it would, hopefully, be too late.

Saiji Hasegawa, foreign news editor of Domei, agreed to accept the hazardous assignment of relaying the message. He put it on the transmitters at 8 P.M. beamed first to the United States, then to Europe. He waited tensely, praying that its contents would not be monitored.

Almost at that moment the streets of Tokyo were disrupted with a rash of exploding grenades. The Army dissidents, including Colonel Inaba, hoped to create a disturbance that would necessitate the proclamation of martial law throughout the city. With Tokyo under military control, the Emperor might be influenced to change his mind and continue the war. But the city, so inured to bombings, ignored the fitful explosions.

In Nagasaki leaflets fluttered down on the razed city, tardily warning its citizens to evacuate.

2.

On the other side of the world it was still the morning of August 10. At 7:33 A.M. the Morse code message sent out by Hasegawa—providentially the Japanese Army censors hadn't bothered to check it—was picked up by American monitors. President Truman summoned Leahy, Byrnes, Stimson and Forrestal to his office and read them the message. Since it was from an unofficial source, he asked them each in turn if it could be considered as an acceptance of the Potsdam Proclamation. If so, should they let the Emperor continue to reign? For weeks a number of influential men, including Harry Hopkins, Archibald MacLeish and Dean Acheson, had been urging abolishment of the imperial system.

But three of his four advisers in the room opposed such drastic counsel. To the ailing Stimson, retention of the Emperor was a practical matter. He pointed out that the Allies would need Hirohito's help to effect the surrender of the scattered Japanese armies. "Something like this use of the Emperor must be made in order to save us from a score of bloody Iwo Jimas and Okinawas all over China and the New Netherlands." Leahy had "no feelings about little Hirohito" but supported Stimson.

Byrnes, however, was against retreating "from our demand for unconditional surrender. That demand was presented to Japan before the use of the bomb and before the Soviet Union was a belligerent. If any conditions are to be accepted, I want the United States and not Japan to state the conditions." Forrestal countered that the Japanese could be reassured "by an affirmative statement on our part in which we could see to it that the language of surrender accorded fully with our intent and view."

Japan's offer to surrender aggravated Stimson's concern over the continued loss of life. He proposed that they call a bombing halt—carrier-based planes and B-29's from the Marianas were still blasting Japanese cities; there were growing misgivings in America over the use of the atomic bomb. "We must remember," Forrestal added, "that this nation will have to bear the focus of the hatred by the Japanese."

Truman remained noncommittal. He decided to wait until the official surrender came through diplomatic channels, but he ordered Byrnes to start drafting an answer at once. The Secretary of State weighed every word, aware that he spoke for Russia, China and Great Britain as well as his own country. Shortly before noon he was informed that the Swiss embassy had just received the official Japanese offer to surrender. As soon as this message arrived he personally brought it, along with his draft to Japan, to the White House. Truman called an emergency meeting of the Cabinet and at 2 P.M. began reading Byrnes's reply. Stimson was pleased by its conciliatory tone (". . . it was a pretty wise and careful statement and stood a better chance of being accepted than a more outspoken one"). It stated that from the moment of surrender, the authority of the Emperor and the Japanese government to rule the state would be subject to the Supreme Commander of the Allied Powers and that the ultimate form of government of Japan would be established by the freely expressed will of the Japanese people. Everyone agreed that this should reassure the Japanese about the future position of their Emperor without compromising the basic principle of unconditional surrender.

First, however, the message to Tokyo had to be approved by the Allies, and copies were cabled to the U.S. ambassadors in London, Moscow and Chungking with a request that they secure quick compliance.

Admiral King sent word of the negotiations to Nimitz at Pearl Harbor, and recalling the first alert dispatched by the Navy ten days before the "day of infamy," his message began: THIS IS A PEACE WARNING. . . .

The more General Anami reviewed the events of the past thirty-six hours, the more resentful he grew toward Suzuki and Togo. As he drove to his office on the morning of August 11, after archery practice in his garden, he grumbled about the Prime Minister to his secretary, Colonel Saburo Hayashi. The appearance in his office of half a dozen disgruntled officers—including his sister's husband, Colonel Takeshita—elicited more specific complaints: the imperial conference had been so impromptu that Togo alone had been prepared to present his proposal to the Emperor; and why was Baron Hiranuma at the meeting? Anami left the impression that the conferees had been maneuvered into approving surrender.

These accusations were vaguely expressed but they encouraged the dissidents to commit another act of *gekokujo,* and a score of them gathered secretly in the War Ministry itself to plan a coup. Takeshita, as senior officer, warned them that what they were doing was punishable by death. First, he suggested, they must isolate the Emperor from those urging him to seek peace. Then they would enlist Anami to advise the Emperor to continue the war. A hard-fought Decisive Battle on the mainland could inflict such losses on the Americans that an honorable peace might be arranged. If not, they would carry on the war as guerrillas in the mountains.

The conspirators took up the plan enthusiastically. They would use the troops stationed in Tokyo to surround the Palace grounds. They would cut the lines of communication and occupy broadcasting stations, newspapers and key governmental buildings.

Then they would arrest the "Badoglios" like Suzuki, Togo and Kido.

Takeshita was confident that Anami would eventually join them and, in turn, bring Umezu. Then the two local commanders, Lieutenant General Takeshi Mori of the Konoye Division and General Shizuichi Tanaka of Eastern District Army, would have to cooperate. With the Army Chief of Staff and the War Minister supporting the coup, they would not fail—as had the small group of officers who briefly seized Tokyo in 1936. It would, in essence, be an Army operation. They would be acting lawfully under its highest commanders for the good of the nation.

This concept of legality was a perversion of the teachings of Professor Kiyoshi Hiraizumi, who had incalculable influence over the officer corps. In 1926, at the age of thirty-one, he became an assistant professor at Tokyo Imperial University. His main interest was Japanese history, his main purpose to preserve the spirit of the leaders of the Meiji period. When Communism began sweeping the campus he countered by establishing his Green-Green School.* The essence of his teaching was that each nation has its own tradition, history and morality and other nations should respect the differences. He taught that Japanese society was based on complete loyalty and obedience to parents, nation and Emperor, and Green-Green evolved into an ultranationalist school with Shinto as its bone, Confucianism as its flesh and *bushido* as its blood.

Hiraizumi was a slender, mild little man who looked what he was, a professor of history, but in his first lecture at the Military Academy he made a dramatic entrance, striding up to the platform with a sword. He put it aside and spoke softly, never using his hands or contorting his face for effect. Somehow he electrified every young officer in that audience and each succeeding audience with his burning sincerity. What they heard about the Imperial Way and their country so imbued them with the spirit of self-sacrifice to Emperor and country that his sayings were often on the lips of those going off on *kamikaze* missions.

* The name was inspired by a line from a poem written by a Chinese patriot just before his execution by Mongol raiders: "Evergreens in the snow are even greener." That is, the man under fire who remains "green" is truly pure.

High-ranking officers remained his disciples. While he was prime minister, Tojo often sought his advice and Anami still held him in the highest regard. Takeshita and others in the conspiracy had attended the Green-Green School and believed they were now acting out what Hiraizumi preached. Wouldn't unconditional surrender destroy *Yamato damashii* and *kokutai*? Consequently, it was perfectly proper to defy the Emperor's decision for peace, since it was a mistaken and ill-advised judgment. In fact, true faithfulness to the Throne made temporary disobedience to the Emperor imperative.

3.

With one exception the Allies immediately accepted Byrnes's proposed reply to Japan. The Soviet government was "skeptical" about the Japanese offer: Molotov found it neither unconditional nor concrete. Therefore, the Red Army was continuing its advance into Manchuria.

Harriman, however, pressed for a quick answer and Molotov complied—with one proviso: "The Soviet Government also considers that, in case of an affirmative reply from the Japanese Government, the Allied Powers should reach an agreement on the candidacy or candidacies for representation of the Allied High Command to which the Japanese Emperor and the Japanese Government are to be subordinated."

Harriman "took firm exception" to this stipulation; his government would never agree to it. He was not even exactly sure what it meant. Molotov explained that the High Command in the Far East should consist of two people, an American and a Russian general.

Harriman's reaction was sharp and unequivocal. The United States had carried the main burden of the Pacific war for four years and by doing so had kept Japan off Russia's back. The Soviets had been in the war two days. Therefore it was unthinkable that the Supreme Command should be anyone other than an American. Molotov answered heatedly but Harriman remained firm; he would send the suggestion to Washington but he knew that it would be unacceptable.

Harriman returned to his office still angry. He was called to the phone. It was M. Pavlov, Molotov's secretary, who said that the Foreign Commissar had checked with Stalin and that there had been a misunderstanding: "consultation" had been intended, but not necessarily "approval." Harriman again warned that the words "or candidacies" would not be acceptable in Washington. A few minutes later Pavlov called again to say that Stalin was agreeable to deletion of the offending words and would confirm it in writing.

With peace so imminent, Forrestal and Stimson once more tried to persuade President Truman to cease all air and naval action against Japan as a humane gesture. Truman would not hear of it. Pressure, he said, should be maintained so the Japanese wouldn't be encouraged to request further concessions. He did promise to suspend further atomic missions unless Tokyo's reply was unsatisfactory. Two more atomic bombs were ready on Tinian, and drops were tentatively scheduled for August 13 and 16. General Spaatz acknowledged that battered Tokyo was too poor a target for a conventional bombing, and he was still eager to drop an atomic bomb on the capital.*

While the Byrnes reply was officially being processed through Switzerland, it was also being broadcast to the Orient by short wave from San Francisco for its propaganda effect on the Japanese civilian population. The man who had clandestinely transmitted Japan's answer to the Potsdam Proclamation, Saiji Hasegawa of Domei, was informed by a monitoring station of the Allied counter-proposal just after midnight of the eleventh. He notified the Foreign Ministry and then phoned his close friend Sakomizu. The sleepy Cabinet Secretary was anxious to know what it said. "We don't have the complete text yet," Hasegawa replied, "but it doesn't look too good."

For more than two hours Sakomizu waited impatiently until the full English text was delivered to him:

With regard to the Japanese Government's message accepting the terms of the Potsdam proclamation but containing the statement,

---

* There was a persistent rumor abroad in Tokyo that the capital was going to be hit by an atom bomb on August 13.

"with the understanding that the said declaration does not comprise any demand which prejudices the prerogatives of His Majesty as a sovereign ruler," our position is as follows:

From the moment of surrender, the authority of the Emperor and the Japanese Government to rule the state shall be subject to the Supreme Commander of the Allied powers, who will take such steps as he deems proper to effectuate the surrender terms.

The Emperor will be required to authorize and ensure the signature by the Government of Japan and the Japanese Imperial General Headquarters of the surrender terms necessary to carry out the provisions of the Potsdam Declaration, and shall issue his commands to all the Japanese military, naval and air authorities and to all the forces under their control wherever located to cease active operations and to surrender their arms, and to issue such other orders as the Supreme Commander may require to give effect to the surrender terms.

Immediately upon the surrender the Japanese government shall transport prisoners of war and civilian internees to places of safety, as directed, where they can quickly be placed aboard Allied transports.

The ultimate form of the Government of Japan shall, in accordance with the Potsdam Declaration, be established by the freely expressed will of the Japanese people.

The armed forces of the Allied Powers will remain in Japan until the purposes set forth in the Potsdam Declaration are achieved.

It wasn't as negative as Hasegawa had indicated. The Allies didn't reject outright the Japanese demand to retain the Emperor, but his ultimate fate was not indicated and this *would* give the war party grounds to reject the entire proposal. Sakomizu was joined by Vice Foreign Minister Matsumoto, who had raced through the streets of Tokyo. His face fell as he read the note.

Its vagueness regarding the national essence was compounded by two typographical errors in the fifth paragraph. Byrnes had written "The ultimate form of government of Japan," but the monitor had transcribed it to read "The ultimate form of the Government of Japan." Did the capital *G* refer exclusively to civilian administration, or did it include the Emperor? And was there any particular connotation to "the"? Matsumoto took the optimistic view that "the Government" excluded His Majesty; the best thing to do was "gulp down" the note as a whole lest the militarists break it into parts that could be disputed interminably. While Matsumoto took his recommendation to Togo, Sakomizu headed for

Suzuki's home. The old Prime Minister listened to the new proposal and the reasoning, then said gravely, "In any case, we must end the war."

At the *obunko,* Kido explained the problems the note presented to the Emperor. "That's all beside the point," said His Majesty. "It would be useless if the people didn't want an emperor. I think it's perfectly all right to leave the matter up to the people." His serenity was like "a blow on the head" to Kido. What had concerned the Privy Seal so much had evaporated under the Emperor's absolute confidence in his subjects.

Sakomizu's fears about the reaction of the military were justified. The Army and Navy Chiefs of Staff saw in the Byrnes reply ample excuse to continue the war and were the first—even before Togo—to reach the Emperor with their objections.

His Majesty indicated their conclusions were premature; no formal Allied answer had yet been received. "We will be sure to study it after it arrives," he said, putting them off. "We can probably make another inquiry about those points still in doubt."

But he himself had already reached a conclusion. He advised Togo, who arrived at the *obunko* two hours later, that the Allied proposal was satisfactory and should be accepted. His reaction was as welcome to Suzuki as it had been to Togo, but eventual acceptance of Allied terms was far from assured. The phrasing regarding the Emperor disturbed conservatives like Baron Hiranuma, whose anxiety about *kokutai* brought him to Suzuki's home. First he strenuously objected to the statement that "the authority of the Emperor and the Japanese Government to rule the state shall be subject to the Supreme Commander of the Allied powers." The words "subject to" he translated as slavery. He also took exception to the paragraph declaring that the ultimate form of government be established by the people. That was unbearable. The Emperor was a deity and could not be subject to the will of the populace.

That afternoon the full Cabinet met to discuss the Byrnes reply. Togo saw no reason not to accept it. Paragraph 2 left the position of His Majesty unimpaired in principle and paragraph 5 allowed the people of Japan to select their own form of government. "It is impossible," he argued, "to conceive that the overwhelming loyal majority of our people would not wish to preserve our traditional system." Moreover, if they demanded revisions in the phraseology it was quite likely that those among the Allies antagonistic to the imperial system might demand the abolition of the imperial house.

But General Anami (moments before, he had been cornered in his own office by the young dissidents who demanded that the proposal be rejected: "If you cannot bring that about, you should commit hara-kiri!") stood firm and was supported in his resistance by Hiranuma and two other civilians under the baron's influence, the Interior and Justice ministers. There were others who sided with Togo, but Admiral Yonai alone spoke out. After more than an hour's unproductive debate Suzuki—who had remained silent, reluctant perhaps to stand against such formidable opposition—finally said, "If disarmament is forced upon us, we have no alternative but to continue the war."

The outspoken Togo, incredulous at Suzuki's vacillation, managed to control his temper. He had to find some way to postpone the decision. "Inasmuch as the official reply of the Allies has not yet arrived," he said (as the Emperor had said before him), "we had better continue our discussion after receipt of it." There was no objection. Togo followed Suzuki into his private office, berating him. What a time to bring up the question of disarmament! he shouted. "Unless we are resigned to rupture of the negotiations for peace, there is no alternative to acceptance of their reply as it stands," he said. Wasn't the Prime Minister aware that the Emperor wanted the war ended and that the question at issue involved the very existence of the imperial house? "If you persist in this attitude, I may have to report independently to the Throne!"

Togo returned to his own office more depressed than angry. He told Matsumoto that he might have to resign. The Vice Minister begged him to do nothing hastily. "Although a formal reply from the Allies is expected at any moment," he suggested, "why don't we pretend it didn't arrive until tomorrow morning.* Tonight, please go home and rest." Scarcely listening, Togo nodded

* The message from Washington, routed through Berne, arrived at the Foreign Ministry moments later, at 6:40 P.M., but the Telegraph Section chief, following Matsumoto's instructions, postdated it 7:40 A.M., August 13, and kept it in his basket.

consent and dejectedly started for his car. He had to inform Marquis Kido of Suzuki's "betrayal."

The Privy Seal phoned Suzuki's office and requested his presence. He was informed that the Prime Minister was not available but would report to the Imperial Household Ministry as soon as he was free. An hour passed, two, and Kido's anxiety grew. Finally, at 9:30 P.M., Suzuki arrived, grumbling about the "Hiranuma crowd" who were setting themselves up as guardians of *kokutai.*

"I don't intend belittling the argument of those who are anxious to jealously guard the national essence," said Kido, "but on the basis of careful study, the Foreign Minister assures us that there is nothing objectionable in the paragraph in question. . . . Should we turn down the Potsdam Proclamation at this stage and should the war be continued, a million innocent Japanese would die from bombings and starvation." Suzuki's defensive posture relaxed, and Kido continued, "If we bring about peace now, four or five of us may be assassinated but it would be worth it. Without wavering or hesitation, let us carry out the policy to accept the Potsdam Proclamation!"

"Let us do it!" Suzuki suddenly exclaimed.

In the Cabinet meeting General Anami had been unequivocally opposed to acceptance of the Allied proposal but privately he was beset by doubt. How could he go against the will of the Emperor? Like the dissidents who had accosted him that afternoon, he believed the honorable course for Japan was to continue the war, but with His Majesty's permission. Perhaps he could persuade Prince Mikasa to help change his brother's mind. With his secretary, Colonel Hayashi, he drove to the shelter that had become the prince's home after his palace was destroyed.

Anami was disconcerted by Mikasa's hostile reception. He was aware there had been an imperial family meeting that afternoon but not that Mikasa, as well as all the other princes of the blood, had pledged their support to the Emperor in his decision. Hastily Anami added that he was anxious to forestall headstrong younger officers who opposed surrender.

"Since the Manchurian Incident the Army has at times acted not quite in accordance with the imperial wish," said the prince.

"It is most improper that you should still want to continue the war when things have reached this stage." Chastened, Anami departed, leaving Mikasa wondering how such a responsible officer could ignore His Majesty's instructions. Was this feeling prevalent at Army Headquarters? Later several Army staff officers called on Prince Mikasa. One happened to be an old schoolmate, and they talked in the garden outside the shelter. When Mikasa told his friend about Anami's request, he asked why the prince didn't speak to the Emperor. His booming voice and argumentative manner gave Mikasa the impression that he was being threatened. Their raised voices alarmed the princess, who was in the shelter, and made her fear for her husband's safety.

Shaken by Mikasa's reaction, the staff officer tried to placate the prince: Anami could control the unruly officers; moreover, the Army would remain a disciplined force under the War Minister's leadership. "There is no need to be concerned about a rebellion."

Anami could not fall asleep. Long after midnight he awakened his secretary and sent him to his staunchest ally, the Army Chief of Staff, with a suggestion that General Umezu ask Field Marshal Shunroku Hata to intercede with the Emperor on behalf of the Army's senior officers. "You must forgive me," Umezu told Hayashi as he paced the floor, "but I now favor acceptance of the Potsdam Proclamation."

Even after Umezu's dramatic change of heart, Anami made yet another private attempt to sway the Emperor. Early in the morning—it was August 13—he unceremoniously interrupted the Privy Seal's breakfast, literally "bounding" into the room. Kido had never seen him so distraught. Words poured out of him. The Allied terms would destroy the soul of Japan. There should be a final Decisive Battle. "Couldn't you just once more request the Emperor to reconsider acceptance of the note?"

"I cannot do that," Kido replied. He disputed Anami's charge that leaving the choice of government up to the people would mark the end of the national essence. He went further. "Supposing the Emperor does change his mind, rescind the peace proposal of the tenth, and issue a proclamation for a final Decisive Battle?" The Allied powers would undoubtedly regard His Majesty as a fool or a lunatic. "It would be unbearable to subject him to such insults."

Anami got control of himself. "I understand how you feel," he said. "In your position, you must protect the Emperor."

"The Army is very powerful," said Kido with sympathy, "and you will have a difficult job to keep it under control."

Anami forced a smile. "You have no idea what it's like in the War Ministry." They shook hands.

At 9 A.M. the Big Six continued the debate which the Cabinet had been unable to resolve the previous day. The session was still deadlocked when a phone call from the *obunko* interrupted proceedings. The Emperor had been informed of Anami's emotional visit to Kido and now he wanted to see the two Chiefs of Staff, Umezu and Toyoda.

Negotiations were under way to end the war, the Emperor told them, and in his oblique manner implied that he wanted as little bloodshed as possible until a decision was made. He asked what air operations would be conducted during the negotiations. Umezu replied they would only fire when fired upon. The Emperor nodded approval.

The two officers bowed themselves out and returned to the Big Six conference. If the Emperor had summoned them for the dual purpose of saving lives and influencing the debate, it had no immediate effect on the deliberations of the Big Six. However, that afternoon at the Cabinet meeting the majority of members now favored acceptance of the Allied demands; moreover, the leader of the opposition, General Anami, purposefully let it be known privately, in a typically Japanese roundabout way, that he was not as adamant as he appeared.

He pushed away from the conference table and signaled Sakomizu to follow him into the next room, where he phoned the chief of the Military Affairs Bureau, the short-tempered General Masao Yoshizumi. "I'm at the Cabinet meeting," said Anami, "and every one of the ministers is being brought over to your views. So all of you people stay where you are until I get back." Sakomizu was mystified. The situation was just the opposite. Anami winked. "I am right here with the Cabinet Secretary," Anami continued, "and if you want you can speak to him directly about how things are going in the meeting." Suddenly Sakomizu understood. Anami was playing *haragei* to quiet his rebellious insubordinates at Army Headquarters.

But Anami's words, which were intended to forestall the dissidents, had the opposite effect. The Cabinet meeting was dramatically disrupted at 3:45 P.M. A messenger brought in a copy of an Army communiqué which would be released by newspapers and radio stations in fifteen minutes: "The Army, upon receipt of a newly issued imperial command, has renewed offensive action against the United States, the United Kingdom, the Soviet Union and China."

"I don't know anything about this!" Anami exclaimed. He immediately phoned Umezu, who had left earlier to return to Army Headquarters. The Chief of Staff was as outraged as Anami. An imperial command needed approval of both the War Ministry and the General Staff, and neither he nor Anami had given it. It must have been approved by his deputy and Anami's deputy despite the War Minister's specific instructions by phone to General Yoshizumi to do nothing. Umezu issued an order to quash the communiqué and it was stopped minutes before it was to be broadcast.

The meeting resumed, but Anami had momentarily lost interest in the proceedings. Even as the two civilians who also opposed immediate surrender—the Interior and Justice ministers—almost alone persisted in demands for better terms, the War Minister seemed perturbed and lost in reverie.

"Byrnes's reply," Togo insisted, "unquestionably represents the least common denominator of the terms of the several Allies, and it is imperative that we accept them as they now stand, if we are to bring about peace for the sake of the reconstruction of Japan and the welfare of the human race."

Another quibble over semantics resulted. Exasperated, Suzuki broke in. "Are the military leaders intent on upsetting our efforts to terminate the war by deliberately grumbling over Byrnes's reply? Why can't we interpret it as we see fit?" They must make a final decision. A number of ministers had refrained from expressing their opinions and now he wanted each one to speak out clearly. He pointed at the Justice Minister. He, of course, agreed with Anami and Toyoda, as did the Interior Minister. Several were reluctant to take a positive position—as Suzuki himself had been—but he questioned them testily until all but one approved surrender. Now Suzuki too had to declare himself.

"I have made up my mind," he said, "to end the war at this critical moment in compliance with the wishes of the Emperor. On examining the Allied reply, I found some points that seemed unacceptable but when I carefully perused them I discovered that the United States had no ill will toward us in laying out these conditions, and I feel they have no intention of changing the status of the Emperor. I believe I must end the war as desired by His Majesty, so I will fully report to the Throne what we have discussed here, and ask for his final decision."

There was no question what the decision would be. But Anami, whose position made him personally responsible for the outcome of the war, was torn by conflicting loyalties and unable to accept the inevitable. After the Cabinet was dismissed he followed Suzuki to his office, where a naval doctor was waiting to see the Prime Minister. "Won't you please give me two more days before calling another imperial conference?" Anami asked.

"I'm sorry," replied Suzuki. "This is our golden opportunity and we must seize it at once." After Anami left, the Prime Minister turned to the doctor. "If we delay," he said, "the Russians may occupy Hokkaido as well as Manchuria, Korea and Sakhalin Island. That would deal this country a fatal blow. We must act now while the negotiations are confined primarily to the United States."

"But General Anami might kill himself."

"I know," said Suzuki. "I am sorry."

The emerging leader of the conspirators was not Anami's brother-in-law, Colonel Takeshita, but an officer he outranked, Major Kenji Hatanaka. Hatanaka outwardly appeared to be the antithesis of a revolutionary. He was quiet, studious and modest, but his unshakable dedication to *kokutai* and his unwillingness to compromise gave him unchallenged authority. Anami's support remained the key to success, since every level of command would trust him, and that evening the conspirators had been invited to meet with him at his residence. Twice before, Hatanaka had arranged go-betweens to enlist Anami in the conspiracy. First he thought he had persuaded Takeshita to intercede with his brother-in-law, but the colonel's reluctance to use his privileged position proved too strong. Next he asked Professor Hiraizumi, whose philosophy of national honor permeated Army Headquarters, to speak to the War Minister, although Hiraizumi had written him a letter requesting that he and the other rebels "refrain from acting rashly at their own discretion" and be guided instead by Anami. Hatanaka, always an optimist, hoped that the professor would advise Anami to join the plot but, in fact Hiraizumi was going to urge him to obey the Emperor implicitly. Hatanaka personally escorted Hiraizumi to the anteroom of the War Minister, but the professor never got to see him. After a long wait he was informed that Anami was in conference at the Palace and would not be back for some time.

At 8 P.M.—the August night was still and muggy—the inner circle of conspirators crowded into Anami's modest one-story wooden house, now serving as official residence after the fire bombings. Hatanaka first wanted to alienate the general from those advocating surrender and reported the rumor that the "Badoglios" were planning to assassinate him. Anami, amused, smiled tolerantly. Nor did the plan for the coup itself seem to impress him: Kido, Suzuki, Togo and Yonai were to be imprisoned, martial law proclaimed and the Palace isolated. To accomplish all this, four generals—Anami, Umezu, Tanaka and Mori—would have to cooperate. Anami ignored the treasonous nature of the plan but faulted the staff work. For instance, how were they going to handle communications?

Takeshita persisted. "We must carry out the plan!" he exclaimed. Besides, it had to be before the imperial conference formally agreed to accept the Byrnes note. Anami's noncommittal manner left the conspirators unsure of his intentions. Colonel Okikatsu Arao was discouraged, but Takeshita would not give up.

In order not to antagonize the group, Anami promised to use his influence "first thing in the morning" with Umezu—who he knew had already resolved to support the Emperor. But the young officers wanted more immediate action. This time Anami put them off by agreeing to see one of their number, Colonel Arao, at midnight when, he implied, he might give the coup fuller consideration. As he accompanied them to the porch, he called out solicitously,

"Be careful! You may be under surveillance. You had better return in separate groups instead of all together."

Takeshita waited with his brother-in-law until the others had left. Was Anami going to join them? asked the colonel, presuming on their relationship. "One cannot reveal one's true thoughts in the presence of such a large group," answered the general. He said no more, but Takeshita departed with renewed optimism.

The Army and Navy Chiefs of Staff—Umezu and Toyoda—had not felt direct pressure from the conspirators but were unable to repress resurgent qualms about accepting unconditional surrender. They called Foreign Minister Togo from a dinner party for a private meeting in the underground conference room of the Prime Minister's official residence. But Togo remained unwilling to consider any last-minute stipulations. He repeated time and again, "Impossible!" There was a hubbub outside and Sakomizu, who had arranged the meeting, apologetically ushered in Admiral Onishi, organizer of the *kamikaze* corps. He approached Admiral Toyoda and in a choking voice confessed that he had just begged Prince Takamatsu to ask his brother to continue the war. But he had of course been no more successful than Anami had been with Prince Mikasa. Instead Takamatsu said, "You military people have already lost the Emperor's confidence!" Onishi's eyes brimmed with tears. "We must submit a plan to gain victory to His Majesty and ask him to reconsider his decision. We must throw ourselves headlong into the plan and make it come true. If we are prepared to sacrifice twenty million Japanese lives in a 'special attack' effort, victory will be ours!" His impassioned appeal brought no response and he turned, desperate, to Togo.

"If we had any realistic hope of victory no one would for a moment think of accepting the Potsdam Proclamation," said the Foreign Minister. "But winning one battle will not win the war for us."

Air-raid sirens began screeching. It was an excuse for Togo to adjourn the meeting. As he drove home through the blacked-out streets he ruminated on what Onishi had said about sacrificing twenty million lives. The final decision for peace had to be reached the next day. "We could bear anything," he later wrote, "if it promised a return; the arrows and bamboo spears of which the military men were prattling promised none."

36

The Palace Revolt

1.

As the sky east of Tokyo began to lighten on August 14 a lone B-29, high overhead, droned toward the center of the city disgorging a trail of missiles. One by one they burst, releasing clouds of fluttering pamphlets. The text had been hastily drafted in Washington by the Office of War Information, translated into Japanese characters and radiophotoed to Saipan.

TO THE JAPANESE PEOPLE

These American planes are not dropping bombs on you today. They are dropping leaflets instead because the Japanese Government has offered to surrender, and every Japanese has a right to know the terms of that offer and the reply made to it by the United States Government on behalf of itself, the British, the Chinese, and the Russians. Your government now has a chance to end the war immediately.

The Japanese conditional acceptance of the Potsdam Proclamation was quoted, as well as Byrnes's reply.

Marquis Kido took one of the pamphlets, which had landed on the Palace grounds, to the *obunko*. He told the Emperor that if

they fell into the hands of the troops who knew nothing of the negotiations, they could cause an uprising. His Majesty should con-
voke an imperial conference without delay so he could inform the
councilors of his determined desire to end the war immediately.

The Emperor glanced through the leaflet and instructed his
Privy Seal to find Suzuki at once. Fortunately the Prime Minister
was already in the anteroom. Under the circumstances, Suzuki
said, it would take too much time to obtain the seals of the two
Chiefs of Staff; instead, he would have to request the Emperor to
take the unprecedented step of mustering the imperial conference
on his own authority. Kido saw the necessity of this emergency
measure. Moreover, he decided that another unprecedented step
was called for: he would accompany Suzuki when he saw the Emperor. Never before had the Privy Seal been present at a private
audience between Prime Minister and Emperor. His Majesty not
only agreed to call the meeting at 10:30 A.M. but went much further. If there was a deadlock he would "command" the Cabinet to
accept the terms of the Byrnes note.

That morning Anami was again urged to take a stand regarding the conspiracy. At his midnight meeting with Colonel Arao he
had hedged to such a degree that his secretary, Colonel Hayashi,
who had advised him to be frank with Arao, said curtly, "From
the way you just talked I couldn't tell if you were for their plan or
not." Now, with the coup hours away, the rebels descended on
Anami at Army Headquarters with demands for his immediate
assistance. Once more Anami could not bring himself to give them
a straight no; he left them in his office with the excuse that he had
to sound out the Army Chief of Staff.

Umezu was in no such state of indecision. He told Anami that
it would be sacrilege to employ armed troops on the Palace
grounds. On the way back to his own office Anami was intercepted
by the conspirators. He could no longer avoid the issue. "After
discussing the matter with the Chief of Staff," he said, "I've decided
not to support your action." He refused to discuss it further and
summarily strode out of the building, where a car was waiting to
take him to the Prime Minister's underground conference room
for a Cabinet meeting.*

---

* During air raids and alerts, Cabinet meetings were held in a safer place,
the Telephone Operations office in the Akasaka section.

It had hardly begun before it was announced that they were to transfer en masse to the *obunko* annex for an emergency imperial conference, the first fully attended meeting with the Emperor since the historic one of December 1, 1941. They were not even given time to change into formal clothes; the Munitions Minister, for example, had to borrow a necktie from an Imperial Household staff official and have it tied by the Welfare Minister. For the second time in five days the military had been maneuvered into a confrontation they were not prepared for, and Suzuki bore the brunt of their resentment.

As they filed into the restricted underground conference room they saw that the tables had been removed and replaced by two long rows of chairs to accept their increased number. They waited uneasily in the steaming and claustrophobic chamber. At about 10:50 the Emperor, dressed in Army uniform and wearing white gloves, entered with General Hasunuma, his chief military aide-de-camp.

Suzuki apologized to the Emperor for the fact that his cabinet had not unanimously approved acceptance of the Byrnes note. He indicated the three principal dissenters—Toyoda, Umezu and Anami—and asked them to state their arguments directly to His Majesty. Umezu called for a continuance of the war. If surrender meant the end of the national essence, then the entire nation should be sacrificed in a final battle. His words were echoed by Admiral Toyoda. Anami, whose emotions constricted his voice, wanted to fight on unless the Allies definitely promised to guarantee the Emperor's safety. There was still a chance to win, and if not, at least the war could be ended on better terms.

The Emperor waited but no one else got to his feet. Finally he nodded. "If there are no more opinions," he said, "I will express mine. I want you all to agree with my conclusions. I have listened carefully to all of the arguments opposing Japan's acceptance of the Allied reply as it stands, but my own view has not changed. I have studied internal as well as international conditions and have come to the conclusion that we cannot continue the war any longer." His gloved hand brushed tears from his cheeks. The sight unnerved several of the conferees, who were unable to stifle sobs. "I have studied the Allied reply and concluded that it virtually acknowledges the position of our note sent a few days ago. I find it quite acceptable. Some seem to question the Allied motives in regard to the supreme power of the Emperor, but I agree with the Foreign Minister. I do not believe the note was written to subvert our *kokutai:* I realize full well how difficult it will be for the loyal officers and men of the Army and Navy to surrender their arms to the enemy and see their country occupied, and perhaps stand accused of being war criminals." His voice broke and he stopped momentarily. "So many died in battle and their families still suffer. . . . I think of all these with such sympathy." Again he raised glove to cheek. "All these feelings are so hard to bear, but I cannot let my subjects suffer any longer. I wish to save the people at the risk of my own life. If the war continues our entire nation will be laid waste, hundreds of thousands more will die. I cannot endure this, and the decision I must now make is like the one made by Emperor Meiji at the time of the Triple Intervention when he bore the unbearable and endured the unendurable. Now I must do it and together we must all unite to rebuild Japan into a peaceful country." He paused again. Two of the ministers had collapsed uncontrollably to the floor.

"It is my desire that all of you, my ministers of state, bow to my wishes and accept the Allied reply forthwith. The people know nothing about this situation and will be surprised to hear of my sudden decision. I am ready to do anything. If it is for the good of the people I am willing to make a broadcast. I will go anywhere to persuade the officers and men of the Army and Navy to lay down their arms. It is my desire that the Cabinet at once draw up an imperial rescript to end the war."

In their anguish and grief the conferees clung to each other. Suzuki struggled to his feet, apologized again, stepped in front of the dais and bowed. The Emperor rose and wearily headed for the door.

Just before Umezu left Army Headquarters for the meeting, two of the conspirators had burst into his office and berated him. In an attempt at conciliation he told them that he didn't "absolutely" disapprove of the coup. They started headlong down the hallway to Colonel Takeshita's office. "Umezu is going along with us!" one of them shouted. Anami had to be advised of this development at once and Takeshita drove to the Prime Minister's. He discovered to his consternation that the Cabinet meeting had been interrupted for an emergency conference with the Emperor. At the Palace grounds he was forced to wait at the Imperial Household Ministry, and then, after an interminable interval, was informed that everyone had returned to the Prime Minister's underground chambers to resume the Cabinet meeting. At the Prime Minister's he again had to wait. The Cabinet was having lunch.

When the meal was over, General Anami headed for the men's room followed by his secretary. The War Minister was unnaturally animated. "We have just received information," he exclaimed to Colonel Hayashi, "that the United States fleet is outside Tokyo Bay! What do you think about attacking them with everything we have?" Hayashi became exasperated with War Minister Anami's continued vacillation. It was as though he had not attended the imperial conference. "It won't do," he said. "In the first place it's only a rumor that the U. S. fleet is outside Tokyo Bay. Secondly, the Emperor has just demanded an end to the war."

A man of deep convictions, Anami was emotionally torn by his capacity to see the merits of the facts on all sides. He decided to return to Army Headquarters for a few minutes before the Cabinet meeting reconvened, and face the conspirators. As he passed through the anteroom he ran into his waiting brother-in-law. "General Umezu has changed his mind!" Takeshita burst out.

Anami's face brightened. "Is that so?" he said with quickened interest. Then, remembering that it was all over, he added dejectedly, "But everything has already been decided."

The colonel pleaded with him to use his influence at the Cabinet meeting, but Anami shook his head. "Then at least resign from the Cabinet," Takeshita persisted. If he did, the Suzuki government would be dissolved and could not terminate the war.

"Get me some ink," Anami said with renewed enthusiasm. "I will write my resignation." But again he changed his mind—peace was inevitable whether he left the Cabinet or not. "And if I resign," he added, "I will never again see the Emperor."

Anami found his office at Ichigaya Heights occupied by at least fifteen conspirators. There was no pretense left in the War Minister. "A council in the imperial presence has just been held," he said, "and the Emperor has finally decided to end the war."

His apology for not meeting their expectations was acknowledged by an embarrassed silence. "The entire Army must act in complete accord with this decision," he said. "Japan will face difficult times, but no matter how arduous life becomes, I ask you to do your utmost to preserve the national essence."

A lieutenant colonel, Masataka Ida, challenged him. Why had he changed his mind?

General Anami closed his eyes, remembering the harrowing experience that morning in the *obunko* annex. "I could not oppose the decision once His Majesty made it." He told them that the Emperor, with tears in his eyes, had turned to him expressly and said, "Anami, I understand it is particularly difficult for you, but you must bear it!" He gazed at the bitter faces around him but this time made no attempt to mollify them. "The decision stands and must be obeyed," he said with dignity and determination. "Those who are dissatisfied will have to cut me down first!"

Clearly, there was nothing more to be said. Major Hatanaka broke down. Tears coursed down his cheeks and he sobbed. Anami was moved, but without a word he turned and left the room. The others followed him out one by one, heads bowed.

Anami returned to a Cabinet meeting which was more subdued than any in memory. Suzuki had reprimanded his ministers for twice forcing the Emperor to make the decision for peace; it was an affront to His Majesty. There was no rebuttal to his harsh words. Bowing to the Emperor's will, each of the fifteen ministers signed the document accepting the Potsdam Proclamation unconditionally.

One crucial problem remained: How should the decision be presented to the nation? President of the Information Board Kainan Shimomura suggested that the Emperor broadcast an imperial rescript. It was distasteful, but words about capitulation would be believed only if they came from his mouth. The cabinet unanimously agreed, with one proviso: it would be presumptuous to ask His Majesty to speak directly to his subjects over the airwaves. It should be a recording.

2.

The rumor Anami had heard that an American fleet lay off Tokyo Bay swept through Army Headquarters. Enemy troops were preparing to land; paratroopers were about to drop on all important airports. Panicked officers hauled files to the courtyard and set fire to classified documents. A colonel from Okinawa, brandishing his two-handed dress sword, charged into the office which translated English-language broadcasts and newspapers. He accused the translators of promulgating defeatism. Slashing his sword at them, he shouted, "You deserve to die for misleading us!" but he was overcome with tears and left abruptly, slamming the door.

General Takeshi Mori, commander of the Konoye Division, which guarded the Palace grounds, loosed his frustrations on the chief of Intelligence. He stormed into General Seizo Arisue's office shouting, "Kill yourself! I'll commit hara-kiri after I see you dead!" Arisue reminded him it was his duty to guard the Emperor. "That is my business. I'll defend His Majesty. Then I'll kill you!" Shaken, Arisue walked over to the office of the Chief of Operations, General Shuichi Miyazaki, who also had been threatened by Mori. "He was out of his mind," said Arisue.

Discipline was disintegrating on all levels. *Kempei* noncoms assigned to the building had deserted, taking clothing and food with them; junior officers insulted their superiors; some senior officers closeted themselves behind their doors with whiskey and *sake*. Disruption had one positive effect: it unified the Army leaders. Anami, Umezu, Hata and Sugiyama all put their seals to a terse declaration which amounted to a credo: "The Army will act in accord with the imperial decision to the last." All section chiefs were instructed to report to Conference Room I, where War Minister Anami would address them.

At 3:30 P.M. Anami climbed a small platform. "The Emperor has decided to end the war," he told the standing audience. "It is, therefore, proper that we abide by the imperial wish. His Majesty is confident that the *kokutai* will be maintained and he has expressed that conviction to the field marshals. Difficulties lie ahead for all of us, but you officers must face the fact that death does not absolve you from your duty. You must stay alive, even if it means eating grass and sleeping on thorns and rocks."

Anami's speech destroyed the possibility of any coup involving high-ranking officers. Only the unshakable Major Hatanaka and several die-hard comrades remained resolved to act. Moreover, they still had a good chance of seizing the Palace grounds; two majors of General Mori's division—one was Tojo's son-in-law Hidemasa Koga—still espoused their cause. There was one new objective, however, of the highest priority. They would have to intercept the recording the Emperor was to make before it was delivered to the NHK (Japan Broadcasting Corporation) Building.

All afternoon Hatanaka had been bicycling around Tokyo in the sweltering heat, attempting to revitalize the conspiracy. His obsession led him to the sixth floor of the Dai Ichi Insurance Building, where General Shizuichi Tanaka, commander of Eastern District Army, had a suite. Unannounced, he strode into the general's private office. Tanaka ordered him to get out. The general's fury left Hatanaka speechless. He saluted smartly, whirled around and left.

His resolution had not dissipated, however, and he pedaled back to Ichigaya Heights to re-enlist those who had abandoned the conspiracy. First he went to Colonel Ida; the solution, Ida had decided, after hearing Anami's pronouncement, was for the leading officers at Army Headquarters to commit mass suicide in apology to the Emperor and the nation—but few were willing to join him.

Hatanaka asked Ida to follow him up to the roof, where they could talk freely. He had "something important" to say: he planned to occupy the Palace grounds that night. "Most of the battalion and company commanders of the Konoye Division have already agreed," he said persuasively.

"It won't work," Ida replied. "The Emperor has already made his decision. And what about the commander of the Konoye Division?"

"I'm not sure of Mori," Hatanaka conceded, "but we must bring him in somehow." Ida doubted that General Mori could be won over. "I know, but that can't stop me. The Emperor himself probably is not sure whether accepting the Potsdam Proclamation will mean maintenance of the national essence. How can we obey the Emperor's order when we're fifty percent uncertain of its outcome?" Any Japanese having such doubts, he rationalized, and not rising up in this most critical time of history, would leave a stain on national honor. "That's why I must test this by acting now. If the coup d'état fails, it will prove that the Emperor's decision was correct. If it succeeds, then it will prove that I was right. I must do something. I can't just sit and wait."

Ida could not go along with this reasoning, but he admired Hatanaka for risking his life for an ideal. "If you're serious about it, go ahead," he said. "I can't stop you."

But Hatanaka wanted more than approval. "I would appreciate your help." Ida said he would have to think it over, but he had no intention of changing his mind.

On the stairway Hatanaka encountered Colonel Masao Inaba, who had written the unauthorized exhortation to the troops to go on fighting. Inaba would not even pretend he would consider supporting the new conspiracy. "The Cabinet has already signed the surrender document," he said, "and the Emperor is going to broadcast tomorrow. It's useless. Give it up."

Exactly what the Emperor would say in this broadcast—the imperial rescript—was still being debated by the Cabinet. Anami could not tolerate the phrase "the war situation is growing more unfavorable for us every day." How could he endorse such a statement? It would brand all the communiqués from Imperial Headquarters as lies. Besides, they hadn't yet lost the war.

Yonai confronted him with the catastrophic losses of Burma and Okinawa, and another lengthy argument was averted by Sakomizu, who diplomatically suggested that they change the wording to read "the war situation has developed not necessarily to Japan's advantage."

During a recess Anami returned to his residence near the Diet Building to change into dress uniform for the ceremonious signing of the document. As he was about to leave the little house, Field Marshal Shunroku Hata and former Prime Minister Tojo appeared. It was obvious that after the surrender they would all be tried as war criminals, and Tojo wanted everyone to testify that they had fought a defensive war. Hata had a different request: he wanted to give up the rank of field marshal.

As the Cabinet worked to approve the final wording of the rescript, two officials at the Household Ministry were making copies with brush; one would be the official document, another would be used by the Emperor at the recording. His Majesty was shown the finished version and requested five minor changes. It would take several hours to make new copies, since the rescript contained about eight hundred characters.* Instead the copyists wrote the alterations on slips of paper that were pasted onto the original. Then came a phone call from the Prime Minister's—another change, the one requested by Anami. This was followed by the frustrating discovery that a clause had been omitted from one of the copies.

At last, at 8:30 P.M., the Emperor, in the presence of Prime Minister Suzuki, signed the patchwork document and affixed his seal. Still the formal surrender to the Allies could not be transmitted until the entire Cabinet had signed it. It took almost an hour and a half to collect all the signatures. At about 11 P.M. the last man, the Transportation Minister, arrived at the Prime Minister's conference room and signed. Surrender was official. A secretary phoned the Foreign Ministry and identical cables in English were sent to the Japanese legations in Switzerland and Sweden. The ministers in those countries were instructed to transmit the following message to the United States, Great Britain, the Soviet Union and China:

With reference to the Japanese Government's note of August 10 regarding their acceptance of the provisions of the Potsdam declaration and the reply of the Governments of the United States, Great Britain, the Soviet Union, and China sent by American Secretary of State Byrnes under the date of August 11, the Japanese Government have the honor to communicate to the Governments of the four powers as follows:

1. His Majesty the Emperor has issued an Imperial rescript regarding Japan's acceptance of the provisions of the Potsdam declaration.

2. His Majesty the Emperor is prepared to authorize and ensure the signature of his government and the Imperial General Headquarters of the necessary terms for carrying out the provisions of the Potsdam declaration. His Majesty is also prepared to issue his commands to all

* The final draft of the rescript had 815 characters. By coincidence it was to be broadcast on 8/15, that is, August 15.

the military, naval, and air authorities of Japan and all the forces under their control wherever located to cease active operations, to surrender arms and to issue such other orders as may be required by the Supreme Commander of the Allied Forces for the execution of the above-mentioned terms.

The Cabinet ministers sat numb around the table. There were no more decisions to make. Suzuki got up and left the room. Anami, in his full uniform, rose and approached his old antagonist, Togo. He squared his shoulders and said in a dignified tone, "I have seen the Foreign Minister's draft of the communication to the Allied powers regarding the occupation and disarmament, and I am grateful beyond description. Had I known that the matter would be dealt with in that way, I should not have felt it necessary to speak so zealously at the imperial conference."

Togo thought this was being overly polite and replied rather stiffly that he had always been sympathetic to the conditions for surrender proposed by the military.

Anami buckled on his sword, and with cap under his arm he entered Suzuki's private office. He saluted the Prime Minister. "Ever since the peace talk started, I have given you a great deal of trouble and I am here to express my regrets. What I did was only so that our *kokutai* could be maintained—that was all. I hope you understand this and I deeply apologize."

"I am fully aware of that," said Suzuki and went up to Anami, who was blinking the tears from his eyes. He grasped the general's hand. "But Anami-*san,* please rest assured that the Imperial Household will always be blessed by peace, for His Majesty always prayed for peace at the spring and autumn festivals of his imperial ancestors."

3.

In the Household Ministry a four-man crew from NHK had been waiting since midafternoon to record the Emperor's announcement of surrender. Daitaro Arakawa, the director of engineering at NHK, had set up equipment in adjoining rooms on the second floor. Only once before had His Majesty's voice been recorded; on December 2, 1928, through an acoustical freak, NHK microphones had inadvertently picked up the young Emperor's voice fifty yards away when he was reading a rescript to the Army.

At 11:30 P.M. the Emperor was escorted to the microphone, which stood in front of two gold-foiled screens. Chamberlain Yasuhide Toda, whose voice somewhat resembled the Emperor's, said a few words into the microphone so the engineers could judge how to modulate the volume for His Majesty.

"How loudly shall I speak?" the Emperor asked.

President of the Information Board Shimomura said that his ordinary voice, which was loud, would be adequate. But the Emperor unconsciously lowered his voice as he spoke the words in the unique, imperial language:

"TO OUR GOOD AND LOYAL SUBJECTS

"After pondering deeply the general trends of the world and the actual conditions obtaining in Our Empire today, We have decided to effect a settlement of the present situation by resorting to an extraordinary measure.

"We have ordered Our Government to communicate to the Governments of the United States, Great Britain, China and the Soviet Union that Our Empire accepts the provisions of their Joint Declaration.

"To strive for the common prosperity and happiness of all nations, as well as the security and well-being of Our subjects, is the solemn obligation which has been handed down by Our Imperial Ancestors, and which We lay close to heart. Indeed, We declared war on America and Britain out of Our sincere desire to ensure Japan's self-preservation and the stabilization of East Asia, it being far from Our thought either to infringe upon the sovereignty of other nations or to embark upon territorial aggrandizement. But now the war has lasted for nearly four years. Despite the best that has been done by everyone —the gallant fighting of military and naval forces, the diligence and assiduity of Our servants of the State and the devoted service of Our one hundred million people—the war situation has developed not necessarily to Japan's advantage, while the general trends of the world have all turned against her interest. Moreover, the enemy has begun to employ a new and most cruel bomb, the power of which to do damage is indeed incalculable, taking the toll of many innocent lives. Should We continue to fight, it would not only result in an ultimate collapse and obliteration of the Japanese nation, but also it would lead to the total extinction of human civilization. Such being the case, how are We to save the millions of Our subjects; or to atone Ourselves before the hallowed spirits of Our Imperial Ancestors? This is the reason why We have ordered the acceptance of the provisions of the Joint Declaration of the Powers.

"We cannot but express the deepest sense of regret to our allied nations of East Asia, who have consistently co-operated with the Empire toward the emancipation of East Asia. The thought of those officers and men as well as others who have fallen in the fields of battle, those who died at their posts of duty, or those who met with untimely death and all their bereaved families, pains Our Heart night and day. The welfare of the wounded and the war-sufferers, and of those who have lost their homes and livelihood, are the objects of Our profound solicitude. The hardships and sufferings to which Our nation is to be subjected hereafter will certainly be great. We are keenly aware of the inmost feelings of all ye, Our subjects. However, it is according to the dictate of time and fate that We have resolved to pave the way for a grand peace for all the generations to come by enduring the unendurable and suffering what is insufferable.

"Having been able to safeguard and maintain the structure of the Imperial State, We are always with ye, Our good and loyal subjects, relying upon your sincerity and integrity. Beware most strictly of any outbursts of emotion which may engender needless complications, or any fraternal contention and strife which may create confusion, lead ye astray and cause ye to lose the confidence of the world. Let the entire nation continue as one family from generation to generation, ever firm in its faith of the imperishableness of its divine land, and mindful of its heavy burden of responsibilities, and the long road before it. Unite your total strength to be devoted to the construction for the future. Cultivate the ways of rectitude; foster nobility of spirit; and work with resolution so as ye may enhance the innate glory of the Imperial State and keep pace with the progress of the world."

His Majesty turned and said, "Was it all right?" An engineer in the other room embarrassedly replied that he was sorry but a few words were not clear. The Emperor, who was showing increased interest in the proceedings, knew he had stuttered several times and said he wanted to do it again. This time his voice was pitched too high and he skipped a character. "I'm willing to make another," he said obligingly, but it was thought that this would be "too great an ordeal" for him.

It was decided that the second version would be the official one, and the first used only in an emergency. The two sets of two 10-inch disks each were carefully placed in separate cardboard containers, then put in a cotton bag that someone found in the room. Now the problem was: Where would be the safest place to keep them? The obvious place—the radio station—would be vulnerable in case there was any truth to the rumor about an uprising; the Household Ministry would be more secure. Consequently, the records were locked in a small safe on the second floor.

These precautions were well taken. The Palace grounds were about to be sealed from the outside world by rebel troops, and already a general had been assassinated. Rebuffed at Army Headquarters, Hatanaka had gone to Colonel Toyojiro Haga, commander of the Second Regiment of the Konoye Division, and by swearing that Generals Anami, Umezu, Tanaka and Mori had joined the conspiracy, won his reluctant support. Then Hatanaka bicycled back to Ichigaya Heights, where he awakened Colonel Ida—for the past week many officers had been sleeping at Army Headquarters. Again Hatanaka grossly exaggerated his backing: "The regimental commanders of Konoye Division have all agreed to come in with us! The only one left to convince is the division commander." He doubted that Mori would listen to him (the general had been one of his instructors at the War College and still regarded him as a "student"), but Ida, as a lieutenant colonel, might be heeded. Hatanaka swore that if Mori refused to join then, he would abandon his entire plan.

Ida still endorsed the purpose of the revolt, and he convinced himself that he should go along with Hatanaka. If General Mori could be persuaded to join them, he assured himself, that "would help to prove we were right." Moreover, if trouble started, Ida would be on hand to stop it.

On bicycles the two men followed the dark streets to the Konoye Division barracks, which were located just outside the Palace compound only a few hundred yards from the *obunko*. A flat tire prevented them from reaching Mori's office until 11 P.M. and the general had just left to inspect the grounds. Even when Mori returned they were kept waiting in the orderly room; the general was visiting with his brother-in-law, Lieutenant Colonel Michinori Shiraishi. Shortly after midnight Hatanaka impatiently stood up.

"Never mind about his visitor," he said. "Let's go in and see Mori." Ida followed him to the general's office. At the door Hatanaka stopped. "You go in by yourself," he said. At the same time he would try to re-enlist Colonel Takeshita's help with his brother-in-law. He left Ida so exasperated that he almost returned to Army Headquarters. But Ida knocked at the door and entered.

General Mori (a scholarly, solemn man with the appropriate nickname *Osho-san,* "head monk") had berated two generals that afternoon at Army Headquarters for their part in losing the war. He greeted Ida affably, and without asking why he had come, began a philosophic monologue on life and religion. It was half an hour before Ida could find an appropriate opening. Ordinarily, he said, a loyal Japanese obeyed any order of the Emperor, such obedience was a virtue. But today it was the duty of the loyal subject to advise His Majesty to reconsider his decision. "It is not true loyalty to the Emperor to obey him blindly." Mori listened perturbed, but with growing interest. Ida pressed him. "If you are absolutely convinced that the Allies have guaranteed to maintain the national essence, then obey the Emperor, but if you are uncertain, shouldn't you so advise His Majesty?" But it would be too late unless the recording His Majesty made was seized. He urged Mori to mobilize the Konoye Division at once.

"I'm not sure what is right," Mori said dubiously. "I would like to go to Meiji Shrine, where I can cleanse myself of all impure thoughts. Then I can tell who is correct—you or me." Colonel Kazuo Mizutani, the general's chief of staff, entered. "You came in at the right moment," said Mori and turned to Ida, who was dripping with nervous perspiration. "Ask him what he thinks."

Mizutani suggested that they talk in his office while the general changed clothes to go to the shrine. In the corridor they encountered Major Hatanaka—thanks to his persuasiveness, Colonel Takeshita had agreed to see Anami once more—and several other conspirators.

Ida said that he and General Mori were going to the Meiji Shrine, but first he had to see Colonel Mizutani for a moment.

"This is all a waste of time!" Hatanaka exclaimed irritably.

It wouldn't take long; Ida ordered Hatanaka to wait in Mori's office.

But Hatanaka was in no mood for delay. Impatience had brought him to the point of recklessness. In fact, he was ready to cut Mori down if he rejected them. He strode into Mori's office, followed by several other aggressive sympathizers. Ignoring military courtesy, Hatanaka abruptly asked—rather, insisted—that the general join them. But Mori would not be rushed; he would decide only after he had visited the shrine.

His procrastination was intolerable. Captain Shigetaro Uehara, of the Air Academy, advanced on him with drawn sword. Colonel Shiraishi lunged to shield his brother-in-law, General Mori. Uehara struck him down. Another rebel officer, a major, slashed viciously at the prone Shiraishi, almost beheading him. Uehara's impulsive attack unleashed the pent-up emotions of days of frustration. Hatanaka leveled his pistol at Mori and pulled the trigger. The general collapsed into the blood flowing from Shiraishi's body and died.

Ida and Mizutani heard the shot and a clattering of feet. They ran into the corridor. There was Hatanaka, his face drained, pistol still in hand. Instantly Ida guessed what had happened. *"Baka-yaro!"* he shouted. Why couldn't Hatanaka have waited; Mori might have joined them after he had visited the Meiji Shrine.

"I did it because there was no time left," Hatanaka muttered. "I'm sorry." He bowed his head but he had lost none of his determination. He begged Ida to make another appeal to General Tanaka. With Mori dead, the division was now under his command.

Ida had reluctantly accompanied Hatanaka to the Konoye Division to prevent violence, but now that the worst had happened he had become, in effect, an accessory to assassination, committed to a course he had resisted. With Mori's death, serious opposition to the coup within the Konoye Division was eliminated and its troops would shortly occupy the Palace grounds. Accompanied by an almost hysterical Colonel Mizutani, Ida speeded by staff car to the Dai Ichi Building, headquarters of Eastern District Army. Mizutani rushed into Tanaka's inner office while Ida, without mentioning Mori's murder, requested Tanaka's chief of staff, Major General Tatsuhiko Takashima, to cooperate with the rebels. Takashima's reaction seemed almost one of embarrassment—it was like "jumping from fire into ice water"—and Ida's too-easily-won confidence evaporated.

The phone rang. It was Major Koga, Tojo's son-in-law, reporting that the Konoye Division had just revolted and would never surrender. Eastern District Army must join them. General Takashima went into Tanaka's private office, leaving Ida with one of the staff officers with whom he continued to argue. But the staff officer maintained that there was not the slightest possibility that General Tanaka would oppose the Emperor. His certainty brought Ida back to reality. Soberly he said, "I will do my best to withdraw the troops before dawn."

An order had already been issued to regimental commanders of the Konoye Division—it bore General Mori's seal but it had been placed there by Hatanaka. The instructions, actually written by Major Koga, directed the troops to occupy the Palace grounds, thus "protecting" the Emperor and *kokutai;* one company was sent to the NHK Building to control what was broadcast. Contingents totaling more than a thousand men cordoned the Palace grounds. The majority, as in the 2/26 uprising, had no idea that they were acting as insurgents. In appearance all that seemed to be taking place was an emergency reinforcement of the permanent guard posts. Within minutes all of the great gates clanged shut and the Emperor was isolated from the outside.

Nor was anyone, no matter what his rank, allowed to leave the grounds without Hatanaka's permission. Inside the Imperial Household Ministry, the Emperor had finished his recording, and President Shimomura and the NHK crew drove away. As their cars approached the Sakashita Gate, barely a hundred yards away, soldiers with fixed bayonets halted them. One peered into the first car. He had been alerted to look for the President of the Information Board. Shimomura's secretary acknowledged who they were and the entire contingent was taken under escort to a small wooden guardhouse for interrogation. One of the group disclosed that the recording had been turned over to a chamberlain for safekeeping. A search party was sent to the Imperial Household Ministry.

On the fourth floor of the ministry Kido was routed from his cot by Chamberlain Yasuhide Toda. The Privy Seal had been kept half awake by a succession of noises—air-raid sirens, the thud of bombs in the distance,* announcement from the loudspeaker in the hall reporting damage, and most recently the crunch of marching feet on gravel.

Toda informed him that rebel soldiers were in the building looking for Kido and the recording, and that the *obunko* itself was surrounded. The Privy Seal remained calm. "I expected something like this," he said. "The Army is *shoganai yatsu* [damn foolish]." Since Kido's appearance was little known outside Palace circles, Toda suggested that he move to the court physician's night-duty quarters, where he could pose as a doctor. No sooner was Kido stretched out on the doctor's bed than he began brooding about how humiliating it would be to be killed while hiding like Kira in *The Forty-seven Ronin.* He returned to his office, where he hastily collected his most secret documents, tore them to bits and flushed them down the toilet.

He was interrupted by another plea to seek sanctuary. Chamberlain Yoshihiro Tokugawa importuned him to join the Imperial Household Minister in a storage room in the basement. The clatter of soldiers' boots echoed down the corridor and Kido allowed himself to be led down a dark staircase.

Chamberlain Toda, who thought he had left Kido safely in the physician's office, now tried to make his way on foot to the *obunko* to alert the court staff; all phone connections had been severed. He feared that the short cut to the *obunko,* a small tunnel, would be guarded, and as he started on a circuitous route, half a dozen soldiers appeared out of the darkness. Toda explained he was a chamberlain, but the commanding officer was unimpressed. Shoving a pistol in his chest, he said, "Go back; the road is blocked."

Toda returned to the ministry. At the entrance he ran into Tokugawa, and together they started back for the *obunko,* this time by way of the tunnel. As expected, there were sentries guarding the other end, but there was no officer in charge. Imperiously they announced that they were chamberlains on duty, and were allowed to pass. At the *obunko* they roused the court ladies but instructed them not to awaken the royal family. Tokugawa, a short man, tried to pull down the iron shutters over the windows, but they were so rusty that it required several husky bodyguards to

---

* During the day, 821 Superfortresses had left the Marianas to bomb the Tokyo area. General Spaatz had wanted "as big a finale as possible."

finish the job. As he and Toda started back to the Household Ministry a second lieutenant called out to halt, but they broke into a run and escaped.

The main entrance of the ministry was now guarded by a heavy-machine-gun crew and they entered separately by side doors. On the second floor Toda was apprehended by rebel soldiers with bayonets who were escorting a bound prisoner, an NHK official.

"Who are you?" one of the soldiers asked.

"I am a chamberlain," Toda replied.

The soldier turned to his prisoner. "Did you give the records to this chamberlain?"

"No, it was a much taller man with a big nose."

The man he had given them to was Tokugawa, who in fact was smaller. Shortly after re-entering the ministry, Tokugawa had been caught by the second lieutenant who had tried to stop him near the *obunko*. He ordered soldiers to take the chamberlain to the guardhouse.

But Tokugawa, whose ancestors had once ruled Japan for more than 250 years, haughtily refused to go. "If you have any business with me," he said, "I'll discuss it here." Two other rebel officers were attracted by the altercation. "Cut him down!" one of them shouted. "It won't do you any good to kill me," said Tokugawa with dignity.

"I wouldn't rust my sword on you," the second lieutenant sneered, but obviously he was impressed by Tokugawa's bearing and tried to justify the coup. It had been necessary, he said, to occupy the Palace grounds because the Emperor's advisers had misled him. "Those men are *keshikaran* [outrageous]!" Tokugawa merely stared at him. Incensed, the lieutenant yelled, "Don't you have the Japanese spirit?"

"I am a chamberlain," Tokugawa said proudly. "You are not the ones defending the country. To defend our nation, everyone has to co-operate."

A noncom slapped Tokugawa's face so hard that his glasses were knocked awry and hung on one ear. Tokugawa called to a Palace policeman (the small police force had been powerless to resist the rebels openly), "Get in touch with the aides-de-camp!" The second lieutenant seized the policeman, but Tokugawa, who acted as though he were in charge, stopped him with an indignant

"He's on duty." The policeman was released. Another rebel officer politely asked Tokugawa the way to the Privy Seal's office.

Tokugawa gave the directions but added, "I doubt that you'll find him there." Then he turned and strode away. No one tried to stop him. He went into the office of the Emperor's military aides.

"They're like madmen," warned Admiral Toshihisa Nakamura, the Emperor's naval aide. "Be careful." He wanted to know where Kido really was.

"I'm not disclosing to anyone where he is," said Tokugawa. He could not trust any senior officer who merely secluded himself in an office during such an emergency. "Rest assured he's safe."

Major Hatanaka had succeeded in isolating the Emperor, but his recording could not be found. Moreover, Colonel Ida, whom he had sent on a vital mission, was back with a disconcerting report: there would be no help from the outside. "Eastern District Army won't go along," he said. In fact, Ida himself no longer thought the coup was feasible. "Once the men of the Konoye Division discover that their commander has been killed, they'll refuse to continue. If you try to force this thing through, there will be chaos. There's no other alternative: withdraw all troops before dawn." Hatanaka tried to interrupt, but Ida held up his hand. "Face the facts; the coup has failed, but if you pull out all the troops quickly the people will never know what happened." It would all pass like "a midsummer night's dream."

Hatanaka's face sagged. "I understand," he said.

"I'm going to report what has happened to the War Minister," Ida went on. Would Hatanaka promise to withdraw the troops? Hatanaka nodded. But the effect of Ida's reasoning dissipated with his departure, and Hatanaka's spirit of revolt flared as bright as ever. He returned to the control point of the uprising, the Konoye barracks, where Colonel Haga, commander of the 2nd Regiment, was growing suspicious of Mori's prolonged absence. Hatanaka tried to parry the colonel's questions but Major Koga could no longer remain silent. He confessed to his superior that Mori was dead and urged him to take command of the division.

How did Mori die? demanded Colonel Haga. Neither Hatanaka nor Koga professed to know. Perturbed as he was, Colonel Haga would have continued his reluctant alliance with the dissidents but for a phone call that moment from Eastern District Army headquarters. Tanaka's chief of staff, General Takashima, wanted to know exactly what was going on in the Palace grounds. Haga could not give specific answers and handed the phone to Hatanaka.

"This is Major Hatanaka, Your Excellency," he said in a trembling voice. "Please understand our ardor."

It was lucky that Takashima had reached the ringleader. He remembered Hatanaka from the War College as a bright, naïve idealist, and decided "to admonish him gently and reason with him rather than order or reprimand him." He said he understood how the dissidents felt, but the Emperor had issued his order and Eastern Army* was going to obey it. "Do not use any force now that there's no prospect of success. It will only cause further needless sacrifices. . . . In Japan it is both pragmatic and highly moral to obey His Majesty's order." He paused. "Did I get through to you?"

Everything Ida had just predicted was materializing. Hatanaka's voice broke. "I understand very well, Your Excellency. I'd like to think it over. I have one more request. Please give us ten minutes to broadcast before His Majesty goes on the air." He wanted to tell the people why the young officers had revolted.

Takashima said that would be "irresolution," and as many lives as possible should be saved. "We have reached the point where the final outcome cannot be changed. Hatanaka, do you understand me?" There was no answer. Then Takashima heard a faint sobbing.

Even hearing one side of the conversation confirmed Haga's suspicions. He raged at Hatanaka and Koga for claiming support of Eastern District Army, and he too ordered them to end the rebellion at once or they would have to kill him.

As he had before when forcefully confronted, Hatanaka verbally capitulated but privately had not given up. He was all set to pursue a new tactic. He would prevent the Emperor's broadcast at the NHK Building, which was occupied by his troops, and instead make a personal plea to the nation himself.

Colonel Takeshita found War Minister Anami at his modest residence near the Diet Building. He had come as much out of

---

* General Tanaka commanded two units simultaneously, Eastern District Army and 12th Army Group. Together they were popularly known as Eastern Army.

fear that his brother-in-law might take his life as to fulfill his promise on behalf of the dissidents. Anami was sitting at a table in the living room writing his will. To one side a bed of mats was laid out. Over it hung a canopy of mosquito netting. The general hastily folded the document and said somewhat accusingly, "What do you want?"

Takeshita could see he was preparing himself for death. It was pointless to talk of the uprising, so he chatted inconsequentially with Anami for some time over *sake*. Finally the general said casually, "I'm thinking of killing myself tonight."

"It may be proper for you to commit suicide," Takeshita replied, "but it doesn't have to be tonight, does it?"

Anami seemed relieved. "I thought you would try to talk me out of it. I'm pleased you approve." He showed Takeshita the will, which was dated August 14. "The fourteenth is the anniversary of the death of my father and the twenty first is the date my son was killed in action. I debated which date I should pick, but the twenty first is too late. I could not bear to hear the Emperor's broadcast tomorrow."

They talked about personal matters until two in the morning, when a distant volley of gunfire in the direction of the Palace grounds reminded Takeshita of his promise to Hatanaka. He outlined the latest rebel plan.* But Anami was preoccupied with his own death—as far as he was concerned, the coup was a foregone failure. In another attempt to delay his brother-in-law, Takeshita questioned whether he could perform the disembowelment ritual of *seppuku* with so much *sake* in him.

"I have a fifth-degree rank in *kendo,* so I won't fail," he said confidently. "*Sake* makes you bleed more profusely. That way you are certain of dying. Should anything go wrong, I want you to as-

* Hatanaka was not the only officer who had planned an insurrection. Some forty men, led by the commander of the Yokohama Guards, drove up to Tokyo to assassinate the "Badoglios" in the government. They barricaded the Prime Minister's office just before dawn on Aguust 15. They had hoped to trap Suzuki and other ministers inside, but the Prime Minister was asleep at home. The rebels set fire to the empty building and headed for the Suzuki house. The Suzukis escaped in a car—it had to be pushed to get started—just before the rebels arrived. Again the would-be assassins became arsonists and at gunpoint prevented firemen from saving the house. Frustrated, the gang headed for Baron Hiranuma's residence, which they also set afire. The aged baron, leaving his false teeth behind, escaped through a garden gate, the only one not covered by his pursuers.

sist me." He stripped to the waist and wrapped a band of white cotton around his belly. But the preparations for the ceremony were suspended by the arrival of Colonel Ida, who had come to inform the War Minister about Hatanaka. But he said nothing, not wishing to "upset" a man about to commit suicide.

"Come in," said Anami. "I am getting ready to die." Did Ida approve?

"I think it would be *kekko* [fine]." Ida told the War Minister, and added that not only had he himself advocated mass suicide, but Anami's example would end all confusion in the Army and terminate any other plots. Ida bowed his head and held back his tears. "I will accompany you shortly," he said.

Anami reached over and slapped Ida's cheek sharply. "It's enough with me; you must not die!" he said and enfolded him in a long embrace. Both men broke down. "Don't die," said Anami in little more than a whisper. "I depend on you for the future of Japan. Do you understand?"

"Yes, sir, I understand." But Ida still intended to kill himself.

"Let's have a farewell drink," Anami suggested, suddenly cheerful. As the three men sipped *sake* they were again interrupted, this time by Colonel Hayashi, who appeared with the general's jacket draped over his arm. He said brusquely, "General, you are urgently requested at the ministry. We should leave immediately."

Annoyed, Anami turned and said, "You make too much noise. Get out!"

The three resumed their drinking. Anami showed Ida two scrolls. One was signed "War Minister Korechika Anami" and read:

> *Believing in the eternity of our Divine Land,*
> *with my death I apologize to the Emperor*
> *for the great crime.*

The other was a *waka*, a thirty-one-syllable poem:

> *Having received great favors from the Emperor,*
> *I do not have even half a word to leave*
> *in the hour of my death.*

"General, it will soon be dawn," Takeshita reminded him.

"I will go now," said Anami. "Farewell."

As soon as Colonel Ida had bowed himself out of the room, Anami once more asked Takeshita to give him the *coup de grâce* if he failed to kill himself. He placed his uniform neatly in an alcove, embraced his brother-in-law and made a final request—that the uniform be put on his body.

There was yet another interruption, around four o'clock. Lieutenant General Sanji Okido, chief of the *kempeitai*, had come to see the War Minister. Anami told Takeshita to handle the matter. He moved off the straw mat to the corridor and sat cross-legged facing the Imperial Palace. According to the etiquette of *seppuku*, if he stained the tatami with his blood it meant that he considered himself blameless. He deliberately thrust the dagger deep into his abdomen, then slashed twice—to the right and straight up. This was *kappuku*, so excruciatingly painful that few could force themselves to do it. He sat erect as the blood flowed onto the floor and soaked the two scrolls at his side. He heard someone approach, and called out loudly, "Who's that?"

It was Hayashi. Anami groaned and his secretary rushed back to the reception room to get Takeshita. "Tell my sister he's committed hara-kiri," said Takeshita. In the corridor he found the general leaning forward slightly, a dripping dagger in his right hand; with the left he was searching for the jugular vein. Suddenly he plunged the dagger into his throat. Curiously, almost no blood flowed from the wound and Takeshita said, "Can I assist you?"

"*Muyo* [No need]," Anami grunted. "Go away."

Takeshita withdrew, but the general's groans made him go back. "Are you in pain?" he asked. Anami was unconscious. Takeshita picked up the dagger and drove it all the way into the nape of his neck. He draped Anami's coat, heavy with medals, over the dying man.

4.

It was now early morning, another sultry day, August 15. Troops still occupied the Palace grounds; the original orders had not yet been rescinded.

At 6:15 Chamberlain Toda once more tried to regain entrance to the *obunko,* but this time he was unsuccessful. A young officer had orders to let no one in, whoever he was. Toda pretended he had to escort the Emperor to safety, since the air-raid alert was still on, but to no avail. He was finally allowed to pass through on orders of an older officer who reasoned that since the rebels might have to invade the *obunko* en masse to search for the recording which had still not been located, what difference would it make if a single man entered now?

Inside, Toda informed Grand Chamberlain Hisanori Fujita that the insurgents might break in at any moment and that there would probably be a hand-to-hand fight. They had to awaken the Emperor. At 6:40 he appeared in his dressing gown. The events of the previous evening distressed him. "Don't they understand my true intentions yet?" There were tears in his eyes. "Assemble all the Konoye Division officers and men and I will talk to them myself."

A mild-mannered chamberlain, Yasuya Mitsui, was selected to go through the cordon and contact the military. He had not gone fifty yards before an elderly officer stopped him with the question, "Are you a chamberlain?"

It was General Tanaka. A man of culture and a strict disciplinarian, he had gone to Oxford and had once, like Tojo, commanded the *kempeitai* in the Kwantung Army. He had come in person to restore order; he had already arrested one of the majors in the conspiracy and had commanded Colonel Haga to withdraw all his men to their original stations.

"Don't be afraid," he said to the chamberlain. He bowed and extended a large calling card; Mitsui brought out his own. The two bowed again. "I'm sorry for causing so much trouble," said the general. "Within the hour everything will be under control. Please don't worry. All the troops will be withdrawn."* The chamberlain unceremoniously sprinted back to the *obunko.*

---

* On the evening of August 24, wearing full uniform, Tanaka shot himself at his desk. Previously he had told General Takashima that the revolt had little to do with his decision to take his own life. It was primarily because he felt responsible for the burning of the Imperial Palace and the lives lost in the Tokyo fire raids. He had to apologize to the Emperor. He said that no one else in the Eastern District Army should commit suicide: "I will take the responsibility for everyone."

Major Hatanaka had been in personal control of the NHK Building for two hours. At gunpoint he had ordered Morio Tateno, who was about to broadcast the early-morning news, to give him the microphone so he could talk to the nation. Tateno invented several excuses: an imminent air raid made it impossible to transmit without permission from Eastern District Army; in addition, it would take time to inform local stations to stand by for a national hookup.

Tateno went into the control room and asked for a line to General Tanaka's office. The engineer understood the ruse. He began talking into a dead phone whose line had already been cut by the rebels. He pretended he couldn't get through. Hatanaka waited, resigned, but one of his lieutenants, irritated by the continued delay, jabbed at the engineer with his pistol and threatened to shoot if he didn't hurry. Hatanaka intervened. "I have to convey my feelings to the people," he told Tateno. It was more of a supplication than a demand. He held out a fistful of papers scrawled in pencil. Tateno read the first characters: "Our unit has been defending the Palace. . . ."

Tateno asked them to be patient. "We are doing our best to contact Eastern District Army." The charade was cut short by the ringing of another phone in the booth. The engineer listened for a moment and looked uncertainly at Tateno. It was Eastern District Army and they wanted to talk to "the officer in the studio."

Hatanaka took the phone and listened passively. He had gone back on his word to give up the revolt and now faced a direct order to desist. Still, he pleaded for the opportunity to make a final explanation to the public, but it was obvious to Tateno that the request was denied. Dejected, Hatanaka put down the receiver. It was all over.

At 7:21 A.M. Tateno made a special announcement to the nation: "At noon today the Emperor will broadcast his rescript. Let us all respectfully listen to the voice of the Emperor. Electric power will be transmitted to those areas not served during daylight hours. The public shall be given access to radio sets in all plants, railroad stations and government offices. The broadcast will be heard at noon today." The circle is complete, Tateno thought. At the same microphone on the morning of December 8, 1941 he had made the first announcement that war had begun.

The organized opposition to surrender was over, but numerous intransigent individuals and groups remained ready to give up their lives to prevent it. The Palace staff still feared that there would be another attempt to destroy the Emperor's recording. Even getting the disks from the safe on the second floor through the Household Ministry to the courtyard was risky. One set, stamped COPY, was placed in a square lacquer box bearing the imperial crest and carried ostentatiously through the dark labyrinthian corridors by a ministry official, Motohiko Kakei. The other set, stamped ORIGINAL, was put in the lunch bag of a chamberlain who slung it over his shoulder. Both messengers reached the ground floor safely. Then Kakei wrapped the lacquer box in a purple *furoshiki* and set out for the studio in a Palace limousine. The lunch bag was handed over to another official, who was driven off in a metropolitan police car. The copy was delivered without incident to the stand-by studio in the basement of the NHK Building. The ORIGINAL set was taken to the office of the chairman of NHK, where it was locked in a safe.

With the arrival of *kempeitai,* sent as a result of Hatanaka's phone conversation with Eastern District Army, all the rebels left the NHK Building without protest. Hatanaka did not return to Army Headquarters. His one thought was to prove his sincerity and bring his violent actions to a proper close. With one companion who had remained steadfast from the beginning, Lieutenant Colonel Jiro Shiizaki, he gravitated toward the spacious plaza in front of the Imperial Palace. Here, in a last futile gesture, they passed out leaflets calling on the people to prevent the surrender. At 11:20 A.M. Hatanaka drew the pistol that had killed General Mori and fired a bullet into his own forehead. Shiizaki thrust a sword into his middle, then put a pistol to his head and pulled the trigger.

In Hatanaka's pocket a poem was found:

> *I have nothing to regret*
> *now that the dark clouds have disappeared*
> *from the reign of the Emperor.*

The broadcast, even without the presence of His Majesty, was ceremonial. Studio 8 was crowded with NHK staff members as well as official witnesses from the Cabinet, the Information Board, the Household Ministry and the Army. At almost the same moment that Hatanaka killed himself, the chairman of NHK took the records marked ORIGINAL out of his safe. It was suggested that they be tested, but would it be respectful to the Emperor? The consensus was that it would be wise to rehearse to avoid any mishaps.

The Emperor's voice roused a *kempei* lieutenant who was standing outside Studio 8. Drawing his sword, he shouted, "If this is a surrender broadcast, I will kill every one of you!" He was seized by an Army lieutenant and herded off by guards.

Inside the studio Chokugen Wada, Japan's most popular announcer, sat pale and tense at a table behind a microphone, watching the second hand of a clock sweep around to join the other hand at twelve. At exactly noon he said, "This will be a broadcast of the gravest importance. Will all listeners please rise. His Majesty the Emperor will now read his imperial rescript to the people of Japan. We respectfully transmit his voice."

After the reverent strains of the national anthem, "Kimigayo," ended, there was a pause followed by the voice that few had heard: "To Our Good and Loyal Subjects: After pondering deeply the general trends of the world and the actual conditions obtaining in Our Empire today, We have decided to effect a settlement of the present situation by resorting to an extraordinary measure. . . ."

37

The Voice
of the Crane

1.

An entire nation listened attentively, awed by the high-pitched, almost unreal voice. The strange imperial language, coupled with poor reception, allowed few of His Majesty's subjects to understand exactly what he was saying. It was evident only that a surrender, or something equally catastrophic, had occurred.

"Cultivate the ways of rectitude; foster nobility of spirit; and work with resolution so as ye may enhance the innate glory of the Imperial State and keep pace with the progress of the world."

There was silence. The listeners, who had stood or kneeled quietly, faces contorted, could no longer control their emotions. Millions wept, perhaps more people simultaneously than at any other moment in the world's history. Yet underlying the humiliation and sorrow was an undeniable sense of relief. The terrible burden of years of war, death and destruction was at last over.

At the *obunko* the Emperor had intently followed his own words on a prewar RCA radio. At the Household Ministry, Kido reacted with mixed emotions, secretly triumphant that what he had been striving for so diligently was finally achieved.

In a dingy auditorium at Army Headquarters hundreds of officers, including General Umezu—resplendent in dress uniforms, complete with white gloves, decorations and swords—still stood at attention, tears coursing down their cheeks. But for some officers the war was not yet over. Not far from Tokyo at Atsugi Air Base, Navy Captain Yasuna Kozono, commander of the 302nd Air Group, climbed to a platform near the runway to address his pilots. The order to surrender, he said, meant the end of the national essence, and to obey it would be treason. Join me and destroy the enemy, he cried. Scores, inflamed by his words, shouted back, "*Banzai!*" And at Oita Air Base on northeastern Kyushu, Admiral Matome Ugaki, Yamamoto's former chief of staff and now commander of all naval *kamikaze* units, was equally resolved to die fighting. He felt responsible for Yamamoto's death—he could not forget the sight of his chief plunging to his doom—and had recently written to Captain Watanabe: "I must pay for it." The Emperor's words increased his shame. Now more than ever it was his duty to follow all those Special Attack men he had sent off to die.

The Voice of the Crane* reached troops thousands of miles from the homeland, as far away as Harbin, Manchuria. Tomomi Yamato, a staff officer, was chagrined to discover that the voice of the man who was more than mortal wavered with hesitancy. How could he have bowed so many times in the direction of the Imperial Palace? But infected by the sobs around him, he could not stifle his own. Out of habit he turned toward the imperial crest above the door of the headquarters building and made his last salute as a Japanese soldier. Then he put on civilian clothes to avoid capture by the approaching Soviets.

On Okinawa, Captain Tsuneo Shimura, the battalion commander whose troops had held Maeda Ridge so stubbornly, was still fighting as a guerrilla. He was trying to steal an American vehicle in order to break through to the north when the sky above was suddenly filled with tracers. It was beautiful, like fireworks, and he thought for a moment it was the Japanese counterattack he had dreamed of. But scouts returned with a report of an American victory celebration. They were drinking beer and shooting in the air. What new disaster had befallen Japan?

---

* The crane is the symbol for the Emperor or the Throne, in the same manner that the Crown is synonymous with the reigning monarch in England.

Words alone, even the Emperor's, could not bring an abrupt end to the emotions war had engendered for more than four years. In Fukuoka, on the island of Kyushu, some sixteen captured B-29 crewmen were trucked to a hill near a crematorium where eight of their comrades had been beheaded four days earlier. The Americans were forced to strip and then were led one by one into the woods and executed.

No reply to Japan's offer to surrender had yet been received from America, but Navy units were ordered to cease fire before midnight. The Army, however, was reluctant to proceed without a formal reply from Washington. At the last Suzuki Cabinet meeting that afternoon it was learned that it would take twelve days to notify troops isolated in New Guinea and the Philippines. The Allies had to be advised of this communication problem.

Suzuki said he was ashamed that he had "troubled His Majesty twice for his august decision." Now, however, it was necessary to form a new cabinet as soon as possible. Shortly before three o'clock Suzuki tendered the resignation of his entire cabinet to the Emperor. For the last time Kido, at the behest of the Emperor, was requested to select a new prime minister. In consultation with the *jushin* he had already decided that Prince Higashikuni was the best choice. The prince, however, had discouraged such overtures; politics had financially ruined his father. He was, moreover, a man of rare independence. When he was a second lieutenant at the War College he declined an invitation to attend a dinner given by Emperor Meiji; he quarreled with the crown prince (later Emperor Taisho); and he had to be persuaded by a field marshal to retain his membership in the royal family. A few years later he married the Emperor Meiji's daughter, Princess Toshiko, but he still aspired, above all else, to be a private and free citizen.

But today the Emperor approved of Kido's selection—as a member of the royal family, his uncle-in-law was above politics and immune to attack.

"As I told you last night," Prince Higashikuni informed Kido's emissary, "I had no intention whatever of accepting the premiership. But in these circumstances and with the situation so perilous, I believe I will think it over."

At Oita Air Base on Kyushu, Admiral Ugaki was preparing for the final *kamikaze* mission of his command. In his diary he called for vengeance:

There are many causes which have brought Japan to this situation. I must assume responsibility. However, to take a broad view, the main cause was the difference in strength between the two nations [Japan and America]. I hope that not only military men but the whole Japanese people will endure hardships, stir up the *Yamato* spirit and do their utmost to rebuild the nation so that Japan can have her revenge in the future. I, too, have made up my mind to serve our country forever with the spirit of Masashige Kusunoki.

Ugaki arrived at the airfield in a uniform stripped of all insignia, carrying a pair of binoculars and a short samurai sword given him by Yamamoto. The plan was for a three-plane strike, but eleven small bombers were on the ramp. Ugaki mounted a small platform and asked the assembled fliers if they were "all so willing to die with me?" Every hand shot up. He climbed into the cockpit behind the pilot of the leading plane. Warrant Officer Akiyoshi Endo, whom he had replaced, protested, "You've taken my seat!"

"I have relieved you," said Ugaki with the suggestion of a smile. Undeterred, Endo scrambled up and tried to wedge himself in beside the admiral. Ugaki good-naturedly moved over.

Four of the bombers had to turn back because of engine trouble but the rest continued on toward Okinawa. At 7:24 P.M. Endo radioed back an impassioned farewell message from Ugaki:

I alone am to blame for our failure to defend the homeland and destroy the arrogant enemy. The valiant efforts of all officers and men of my command during the past six months have been greatly appreciated.

I am going to make an attack at Okinawa, where my men have fallen like cherry blossoms. There I will crash into and destroy the conceited enemy in the true spirit of *bushido,* with firm conviction and faith in the eternity of Imperial Japan.

I trust that the members of all units under my command will understand my motives, will overcome all hardships of the future and will strive for the reconstruction of our great homeland, that it may survive forever.

Long live His Imperial Majesty the Emperor!

Minutes later Endo advised that the plane was diving toward a target.*

The bodies of Anami and the two rebel leaders, Hatanaka and Shiizaki, were brought to a building adjoining Army Headquarters for memorial services. Hundreds of mourners filed by to honor them, particularly Anami, who had given his life to bring order to the nation.

Early that evening Colonel Ida, Hatanaka's reluctant ally, came to pay his respects. He had written his will and said farewell to his wife. In his office next door he lay down to prepare himself spiritually for death. When all was quiet he rose and walked down the darkened corridor to Anami's office. Here, as was fitting, he would commit suicide. At the door a major named Sakai called to him.

"What are you doing here, Sakai?"

"What about you?"

"Never mind," Ida told him. "Just leave me alone."

Sakai said that he had been ordered to "keep an eye on" the colonel. "If you want to die, you'll have to kill me first."

Ida was annoyed. "Can't you understand the feelings of a samurai?" But Sakai persisted and their argument dissipated Ida's resolve. When one misses the time for hara-kiri, he thought ruefully, it is gone forever.

They returned to Ida's office, where they stretched out on adjoining cots and talked for hours. In the morning Ida was awakened by a macabre request. His wife and her father (his name was Ida and he had adopted his son-in-law) had come to claim the body. Awkwardly Ida tried to explain what had happened, but on his wife's face appeared an inquiring look as if she were asking: Why are you still alive?

In another section of Tokyo the creator of the *kamikaze* corps, Admiral Takijiro Onishi, lay mortally wounded by his own hand in his home. He sent for his associate and friend, Yoshio Kodama, whose sword he had borrowed the night before. Kodama found Onishi still conscious, though he had slit his abdomen and stabbed himself in the chest and throat. He seized Kodama's hand. "What I want to tell you is written in my will on the top of the desk.

---

* This was the last report of the seven planes. Curiously, there is no U. S. record of any *kamikaze* attack on that date.

There's also a letter to my wife; she is in the country." He smiled faintly. "I thought your sword was sharper. It didn't cut very well."

The weapon was on the floor, and Kodama picked it up. "Your Excellency," he whispered, "I will go with you."

"*Bakayaro!*" Onishi shouted in a surprisingly strong voice. "What would you gain by dying now? Instead— There is another letter on my desk. Take it to Atsugi Air Base at once and bring those headstrong men under control. That will do more good for Japan than dying here." His forehead was covered with perspiration and he gasped for words. "Many of the nationalists will rise up. Stop them!"

Kodama found the letter on the desk. In it the man who a few days before had pleaded with Admiral Toyoda and Foreign Minister Togo to sacrifice twenty million lives in a final defense of the homeland apologized for his failure to bring victory. He wanted the young people of Japan to find a moral in his death. "To be reckless is only to aid the enemy. You must abide by the spirit of the Emperor's decision with utmost perseverance. Do not forget your rightful pride in being Japanese. You are the treasure of the nation. With all the fervor of spirit of the Special Attackers, strive for the welfare of Japan and for peace throughout the world."

Beside the letter was a *haiku,* Onishi's last poem:

> *Refreshed,*
> *I feel like the clear moon*
> *after a storm.*

Kodama turned back to the admiral, who was vomiting blood, and begged Onishi to stay alive until he brought back his wife—it would take about five hours. Onishi smiled wanly. "Is there anything more stupid than a military man committing suicide and then prolonging death just to wait for his wife?" He reached for Kodama's hand. "*Sayonara.*"

2.

The knowledge that he was the Emperor's "personal choice" for prime minister made it almost impossible for Prince Higashikuni to refuse. "I can't think of my own welfare in this critical situation," he resignedly told Kido on the morning of August 16, "and if I can be of any service to the country I shall be pleased to accept the post." Before making up his mind, however, he wanted to know what the current situation was.

Kido informed him that General MacArthur required a liaison officer representing the Japanese government sent to Manila promptly. "So it is expedient to form a cabinet as soon as possible. At the present time we have no means to deal with the Americans, and the Allies might regard any delay with suspicion and make our situation even more difficult." The previous night's attempted coup made it necessary to select someone respected by the Army. "If you do not accept the post, you will cause His Majesty great anxiety."

Higashikuni pondered: it would be onerous to lead a defeated nation, but he knew he could control the riotous acts of dissident Army men through colleagues in the service—he held the rank of general—and once Japan's future was settled, he could step down. "I will humbly accept the imperial order to form a cabinet," he said.

Before noon a note accepting the Japanese surrender offer arrived from Washington and Imperial Headquarters issued orders to all Army and Navy units to cease hostilities. In addition, the Emperor instructed three members of his family to tour overseas commands and reassure the troops that he had made the decision to surrender of his own free will. Prince Tsunenori Takeda, a lieutenant colonel, would cover the forces in Korea and Manchuria; Prince Yasuhiko Asaka, a colonel, the China Expeditionary Army and the China Area Fleet; and Prince Haruhito Kanin, son of the former Army Chief of Staff, Shanghai, Canton, Saigon, Singapore, Indochina and Nanking. The three men left Haneda Airport in identical white twin-engine Mitsubishi Ki-57 Army transports.

Overt acts of rebellion still plagued the homeland itself. The pilots at Atsugi Air Base dropped thousands of leaflets on the Tokyo area accusing the *jushin* and the Suzuki government of misleading the Emperor. Their leader, Captain Kozono, remained firm even when confronted by an admiral. He charged that the Emperor must be insane to surrender; the war had to continue. But the mutiny collapsed. That night the distraught Kozono began raving about Amaterasu, the Sun Goddess, and had to be restrained. Injected with morphine, he was placed in a strait jacket and taken to a naval hospital.

The spirit of rebellion also permeated Oita Air Base, whence Admiral Ugaki had taken off on Japan's last *kamikaze* mission. Ugaki's replacement, Admiral Ryunosuke Kusaka, veteran of Pearl Harbor and Midway, summoned all senior officers; a group of younger officers crowded into the room, uninvited and belligerent. Kusaka said he knew there were some among them who, out of patriotism, thought the war should continue—but "as long as my eyes are black [i. e., as long as he lived] I will not tolerate any rash action." Those intent on revolt would first have to "cut me to pieces." He closed his eyes expecting to be killed. For what seemed an eternity there was silence. Then Kusaka heard sobbing and opened his eyes.

"Your speech has cooled our heads," one of the young officers admitted. He and several others promised to control their men. Kusaka glanced around the room. "How about you older officers? Do any of you disagree with me?" No one spoke up. "If anyone changes his mind, come and see me any time. I have no guards at night. It's very hot and I shall sleep naked [unprotected]."

That night he was awakened by a voice shouting, *"Chokan! Chokan!"* (Commander in chief!). It was a feverish commander with drawn pistol and sword. He had just "had a revelation": unless Japan waged the final battle she would have no future. "According to God, you are the only one to lead us."

Kusaka looked at him levelly. "You believe in God's prophecy but I cannot—perhaps I haven't had enough religious training. In any case, the Emperor himself ordered me to carry out these duties and I cannot trust in God, only myself." He sensed that time itself would take care of the young man's problem and suggested that he fly up to Tokyo and report this revelation to the commander of Combined Fleet, the Navy Minister and the Prime Minister.*

The new Prime Minister lay awake that night burdened by his unwanted responsibility. Prince Higashikuni recalled a long-

* The commander was received by Admirals Ozawa and Yonai. Before seeing Higashikuni, he sat down on a bench to rest and dropped off to sleep. He awakened too late for his appointment and reasoned, "It must have been God's will that I fell asleep," and that he had misinterpreted the revelation.

forgotten incident twenty-five years before in France. He had told an aged fortuneteller that he was a simple painter, but she looked up from his palm and said, "It is a lie. You will become prime minister of Japan." With a laugh he admitted that he was a prince and an officer. "In Japan, members of the royal family and Army men as a rule are not allowed to become politicians. So how can I become prime minister?"

"Japan will have a revolution or some great trouble and you will become prime minister."

At eleven o'clock the next morning, August 17, he presented his suggestions for Cabinet ministers to the Emperor. Yonai alone retained his post. Togo had declined to stay on as foreign minister and would be succeeded by his predecessor, Mamoru Shigemitsu. Prince Konoye was to be a minister without portfolio. Those and the other choices were agreeable to His Majesty.

The new government's first task was to send a mission to Manila to arrange with General MacArthur for the surrender of Japanese troops in the field. The man selected to lead it was Lieutenant General Torashiro Kawabe, Umezu's deputy. Since there was still fear that rebel pilots might intercept the delegation, elaborate precautions were taken. A little after dawn on August 19 the sixteen members arrived at Haneda Airport, where they boarded several small planes. After a few minutes over Tokyo Bay they descended for a landing at Kisarazu Air Base. Here two war-weary and bullet-punctured, cigar-shaped Mitsubishi bombers—the type known as "Bettys" to the Allies—were waiting. In accordance with instructions from MacArthur they had been painted white and marked with large green crosses.

Only after the delegates were on board did the pilots open sealed orders: their destination was Ie Shima, the tiny island where Ernie Pyle had died. Together the Bettys droned south. Over Kyushu the anxious delegates watched a formation of planes heading straight for them. But they had American markings, and the passengers relaxed as two bombers and a dozen fighters surrounded them protectively. The Japanese planes radioed the password; "Bataan," and the reassuring reply was, "We are Bataan's watchdog. Follow us." For an hour and a half the incongruous group continued over the South China Sea until Ie Shima's peak heaved in sight. The first bomber landed smoothly on the Birch airstrip, but the pilot of the second forgot to lower his landing flaps. The plane flared neatly over the runway but landed jarringly on the coral. It taxied uncertainly to its parking position. As soon as the delegates appeared, hundreds of GI's and Navy men pressed around them, snapping pictures.

The sixteen Japanese transferred to an American plane, a four-engine C-54, where they were given box lunches. Two GI's passed out cups of orange juice. Katsuo Okazaki, the ranking Foreign Ministry representative, ordered his secretary by hand signals to tip the Americans $10 apiece.

The C-54 arrived at Nichols Field shortly before dusk. General Kawabe led the group across the ramp to the nearest American, Colonel Sidney Mashbir, chief of MacArthur's staff of translators. As Mashbir saluted he saw Okazaki come toward him with extended hand—they were prewar acquaintances. Mashbir swung up his right fist with thumb up as an informal greeting; to avoid the onus of shaking hands with an enemy he had practiced this gesture twenty times in front of a mirror. The colonel then escorted the delegation to Major General Charles Willoughby, head of Mac-Arthur's Intelligence Division. Thousands of soldiers, civilians and newsmen closed in, and the clicking of cameras seemed to Okazaki "like machine guns fired at strange animals."

Willoughby shared his car with Kawabe and on the way into Manila affably asked what language he would prefer to converse in. Kawabe suggested German—coincidentally it was Willoughby's native language. Their rapport was immediate, and to Kawabe, unexpected.

Curious groups had gathered along the narrow streets leading to Dewey Boulevard. GI's hollered *"Banzai!"* good-naturedly, but the Filipinos were hostile. There were shouts of *"Baka!"* Rocks were thrown; they bounced off the cars while the Japanese pointedly looked straight ahead.

As soon as they had settled in the Rosario Apartments, a two-story building near the Manila Hotel, they were served a turkey dinner, which they remembered "with relish" years later. Afterward they were shuttled to City Hall, where they were escorted to seats at a large conference table facing their American counterparts. Kawabe sat directly opposite MacArthur's chief of staff, Sutherland, who read out General Order Number One. It enumerated the authorities to which the scattered Japanese armed forces would surrender. Those in China, Formosa and northern Indo China would capitulate to Chiang Kai-shek, while those in Manchuria, southern Sakhalin and northern Korea would surrender to the Russians. All other forces would be taken over by the British and Americans. Formal surrender would take place on an American warship in Tokyo Bay in early September. Japanese delegates were ordered to reveal the placement of all troops and ships, the location of airfields, submarine and *kaiten* bases, ammunition dumps and minefields.

The next morning the conference reconvened. Sutherland handed Kawabe a draft of the *Instrument of Surrender* to be issued by the Emperor. Kawabe dropped it on the table, then picked it up gingerly as if, an American naval officer observed, it were deadly poison. He thrust it at his aide, Second Lieutenant Sadao Otake, a graduate of New York University, where he was called Roy, and said *"Yakuse!"* (Translate!).

The first words—"I, Hirohito, Emperor of Japan"—made Otake turn pale. The Emperor never used the word *watakushi* for "I," but one that was his alone, *Chin*—the royal "We." Kawabe listened to the translation with folded arms and eyes closed tight as if in pain, and at the word *owari* (the end), he slapped the table and said *"Shimai!"* (Finished!).

Mashbir, an expert on Japan, realized how offensive the bald words written for the Emperor were to the Japanese—it was obvious that they were "dying right there in their chairs." At the Rosario, while the delegates were packing for the return to Japan, he and Willoughby tried to reassure Kawabe and Okazaki. "I am sure," Mashbir said in Japanese, "that it's not the intention of the Supreme Commander to degrade or debase your Emperor in the eyes of your people." He told them to disregard the wording of the declaration—he would take up the matter personally with General MacArthur. He advised them to draw it up themselves "in the normal form of an imperial rescript and ending in the approved and customary manner." Mashbir explained to Willoughby what he had promised the Japanese. The general couldn't understand why the Japanese were so upset.

"General Willoughby," Okazaki said in English, "it is of the utmost importance. It is impossible for me to explain to you how important it really is!"

As the delegation was leaving the Rosario, Otake introduced himself to a Nisei standing guard. The guard, in turn, said his name was Takamura. In America, Otake had married a Nisei of the same name. "Do you have a sister named Etsuyo?" he asked. The guard nodded and Otake said, "I'm her husband." They shook hands. "Look me up in Japan," Otake said to his brother-in-law as the car drove off.

General Sutherland agreed that Mashbir had acted properly in permitting the Japanese to reword the document but wanted him to explain it to MacArthur. The commander in chief put his arm around the colonel's shoulder and said, "Mashbir, you handled that exactly right. As a matter of fact, I have no desire whatever to debase him [the Emperor] in the eyes of his own people." Orderly government could best be maintained through Hirohito. He wondered if His Majesty would call on him in Tokyo. "If he does, it will be the first time that a Japanese emperor ever called on anyone, won't it?"

"Yes, sir, it will be, and I'm sure that he'll do exactly that."

At Ie Shima the delegates discovered that one of the Mitsubishis was unable to take off for Japan. Otake ridiculed the possibility of sabotage expressed by several delegates—it was the plane that had pancaked coming in. Kawabe, Okazaki and six others boarded the other bomber and settled down for the long flight home. Okazaki began dictating a memorandum to a junior official, Harumi Takeuchi (who would later become ambassador to the Philippines). But General Kawabe sat preoccupied, marveling at the respect they had been shown by the Americans. "If human beings were to sincerely exercise justice and humanity in their relations with one another," he later wrote, "the horrors of war in all likelihood could be avoided, and even if a war unfortunately broke out, the victor would not become arrogant and the suffering of the losers would be alleviated immediately. A truly great cultural nation is the first requisite."

In the darkness following sunset, cold air whistled in through bullet holes in the fuselage. The passengers began drinking whiskey to keep warm and eventually fell asleep. At about eleven they were wakened by the pilot. A fuel tank had sprung a leak and they were heading for the nearest land. If they didn't make it, the bomber would float only briefly. They were to put on life jackets.

Their overriding concern was the documents—the Americans might interpret their loss as a ruse to delay the surrender formalities. The papers were entrusted to Okazaki, an athlete who had represented Japan in the 1924 Olympics in Paris.

The engines began missing and the plane descended. Through the window Takeuchi saw the sea just below shimmering in the moonlight. He tried to tie his life jacket but his fingers were too cold. Silently everyone except Okazaki put his hands against the seat in front of him and lowered his head. Okazaki was clutching the precious papers with both hands. The bomber bounced into the sea, water spraying over the windows. It skipped like a flat stone until it hit something and stopped abruptly.

Oil cans tumbled over Takeuchi and he heard someone say, "We are all right." He felt something sticky on his face. He thought it was blood, but it was oil. The pilot unlatched a side door. Whitecaps lashed against the plane, and Takeuchi hoped he could make it out before they sank. Then he realized that, incongruously, the pilot was standing in water up to his knees.

Okazaki, dazed from a blow on his forehead, stumbled out of the aircraft on his own and waded ashore. Ahead, in the moonlight, was Mount Fuji.

3.

The United States was having more trouble with her allies than with Japan. Stalin wanted a greater share of the spoils of war. In a cable to Truman he proposed that the Japanese on the Kuriles, which had been "awarded" to the Soviets at Yalta, as well as those on the top half of Hokkaido, the northernmost home island, be surrendered to the Russian Far East commander.

. . . THIS LATTER PROPOSAL HAS A SPECIAL MEANING FOR THE RUSSIAN PUBLIC OPINION. AS IT IS KNOWN, THE JAPANESE IN 1919-1921 HELD UNDER OCCUPATION OF THEIR TROOPS

THE WHOLE SOVIET FAR EAST. THE RUSSIAN PUBLIC OPINION
WOULD BE SERIOUSLY OFFENDED IF THE RUSSIAN TROOPS
WOULD NOT HAVE AN OCCUPATION REGION IN SOME PART OF
THE JAPANESE PROPER TERRITORY.
GREATLY I WISH THAT MY MODEST SUGGESTIONS AS STATED
ABOVE WOULD NOT MEET ANY OBJECTIONS.

Rankled, Truman replied that while he could go along with
the Kurile proposal, he would like it to be understood that America wanted an air base on one of the Kurile islands. About Hokkaido, however, he was adamant; present arrangements for the
surrender of the Japanese on all four of the main islands must
stand.

Stalin, in turn, was indignant. Two days later, on August 22,
he replied that he "did not expect such an answer" regarding
Hokkaido; and nothing had been mentioned at Yalta about a
permanent American air base in the Kuriles.

. . . DEMANDS OF SUCH A NATURE ARE USUALLY LAID BEFORE
EITHER A CONQUERED STATE, OR SUCH AN ALLIED STATE
WHICH IS IN NO POSITION TO DEFEND WITH ITS OWN MEANS
CERTAIN PARTS OF ITS TERRITORY AND, IN VIEW OF THIS, EX-
PRESSES READINESS TO GRANT ITS ALLY AN APPROPRIATE
BASE. I DO NOT BELIEVE THAT THE SOVIET UNION COULD BE
INCLUDED AMONG SUCH STATES . . . AS YOUR MESSAGE DOES
NOT STATE ANY MOTIVES FOR A DEMAND TO GRANT A PERMA-
NENT BASE I HAVE TO TELL YOU FRANKLY THAT NEITHER I
NOR MY COLLEAGUES UNDERSTAND WHAT CIRCUMSTANCES
PROMPTED SUCH A DEMAND TO BE MADE OF THE SOVIET
UNION.

Truman's "first inclination was to let this message with its strong
undercurrent of antagonism go unanswered," but he reconsidered
and terminated the altercation with the explanation that the United
States merely wanted a temporary base in the Kuriles for emergency use during the occupation of Japan.

The question of China, however, was not so easily resolved.
Four days before the Japanese accepted the Potsdam Proclamation, Chu Teh, commanding general of the Communist forces,

announced falsely that Japan had surrendered unconditionally and ordered Red units to occupy whatever towns and cities they could. Chiang Kai-shek charged that this was "an abrupt and illegal action" and ordered Chu Teh to desist from independent movement against the Japanese. The Communist radio thereupon branded Chiang a fascist. "We want to announce to our three great allies, the people of China and the world that the Chungking High Command cannot represent the Chinese people and the Chinese troops which really oppose the Japanese. The Chinese people demand that anti-Japanese troops in liberated China under Commander in Chief Chu Teh have the right to send their representatives directly to participate in accepting a Japanese surrender by the Allies."

Red Chinese plans for postwar domination were hobbled by their ideological comrades in Moscow. On the day before Japan's surrender, Molotov signed accords with Nationalist China. It was an affront that would plague Soviet–Red China rapport for decades.

In the meantime Russia was intent on establishing herself on the Asian mainland in force. The Red Army had already seized much of Manchuria against almost no opposition from the weakened Kwantung Army. Each occupied city was plundered. Tons of wheat, flour, rice, kaoliang (grain sorghum) and soybeans were shipped back to the Soviet Union along with machinery, rolling stock, paper, printing machines, photographic and electric equipment. Chairs, desks, telephones, typewriters were cleared from every office. Carloads of broken furniture and countless crates of broken glass were dispatched westward as if junk itself were a treasure to the Soviets.

The Japanese prisoners of war were stripped of all valuables, including the gold fillings in their teeth. Rape, pillage and murder became commonplace, but these atrocities were not inspired by hatred or vengeance. The conquerors, like their predecessors Attila and his Huns, were enjoying the booty of war.

4.

The unreasoning spirit to resist capitulation did not die with Hatanaka and Ugaki. Late in the afternoon of August 22, ten

young men with white bands around their foreheads, calling themselves the *Sonjo Gigun* (the Righteous Group for Upholding Imperial Rule and Driving Out Foreigners), occupied Atago Hill,
within sight of the American embassy. With pistols and grenades
they threatened a cordon of police sent to disperse them. In the
pouring rain they linked arms and sang the national anthem.
Three times they shouted *"Tenno Heika banzai!"* And then there
was a multiple roar as five grenades exploded almost simultaneously. Everyone lay dead. Their leader had left a note of farewell: "The cicada rain falls in vain on defeated hills and streams."
A few days later the wives of three of the dead rebels climbed
to the top of Atago Hill and also attempted suicide. Two died.
In a wave of self-destruction, eleven transport officers belonging
to a Buddhist sect killed themselves in front of the Imperial Palace, and fourteen students committed hara-kiri at the Yoyogi
parade grounds.

Other rebels continued sporadic attacks on communication centers. The NHK station at Kawaguchi was briefly occupied by a
major and sixty-six soldiers from a communication school; some
forty civilians, including ten women, seized the broadcasting station in Matsui and then attacked the post office, a power station,
the local newspaper and the prefectural government office.

The announcement that American forces would shortly occupy
the country invoked new fears and unrest. Wild rumors made
the population panicky: the Chinese were landing at Osaka; thousands of American soldiers were already looting and raping in
Yokohama. Girls and family treasures were evacuated to the
country or the mountains. Newspapers ran columns of advice on
how to get along with the American troops. Women were told:
"Don't go out at all in the evening. Keep watches and other valuables at home. When in danger of being raped, show the most
dignified attitude. Don't yield. Cry for help." They were cautioned
to avoid "provocative acts" such as smoking or going without
socks. Some factories issued poison capsules to women workers.

Soon after dawn on August 28, forty-five C-47's approached
Mount Fuji with the American advance party, commanded by
Colonel Charles Tench, a member of MacArthur's staff. At Atsugi
Air Base the lead plane taxied to a stop and the first conqueror
ever to step on Japanese soil emerged in the person of Colonel

Tench. From the edge of the ramp a mob of shouting Japanese headed for him, and for a moment he thought he was about to be cut down by fanatics. Then he noticed a small reception party near the plane. A short officer stepped forward and announced that he was Lieutenant General Seizo Arisue.* As the two walked toward a tent in the reception area, Japanese cameramen and U. S. Signal Corps photographers recorded almost every step. In the tent Colonel Tench went pale when Arisue offered him orange punch. To show it wasn't poisoned the general drained a glass of it before Tench hesitantly took a sip.

Within forty-eight hours Atsugi was occupied in force by the 11th Airborne Division, whose four-engine transports touched down every two minutes for hours. No sooner was the air base secured than another C-54 appeared in the distance. It was *Bataan,* with General of the Army Douglas MacArthur on board. He was discussing the fate of Japan with his Military Secretary, Brigadier General Bonner Fellers, who had visited the country numerous times. "It's very simple," said MacArthur. "We'll use the instrumentality of the Japanese government to implement the occupation." Among other things, he was going to give Japanese women the right to vote.

"The Japanese men won't like it."

"I don't care. I want to discredit the military. Women don't want war."

The big transport touched down at 2:19 P.M. MacArthur, the first to leave the plane, paused at the top of the ladder and Fellers heard him mutter, "This is the payoff." He lit his corncob and descended, pipe clenched between teeth. General Robert Eichelberger, who had preceded him by a few hours, came up to him

---

* Two hours earlier, three blue American fighter planes had hurtled down at Atsugi. One dropped a large tube. Arisue stood paralyzed and watched it tumble down, fearing it had been dropped by radical Americans who wanted to continue the war. The tube landed on the grass without exploding. When it was gingerly brought to Arisue, he noticed a cap at one end. The cap was unscrewed, thus "deactivating" the missile; inside, there was a rolled cloth. It was a fifteen-foot banner:

WELCOME U. S. ARMY
U. S. Navy

A note requested the Navy's banner be attached to the side of a hangar where MacArthur's officers would see it on disembarking. Arisue, "afraid to allow anything that might cause ill feeling and trouble," ordered it hidden.

and they shook hands. "Bob," said MacArthur, grinning broadly, "from Melbourne to Tokyo is a long way, but this seems to be the end of the road."

A line of dilapidated cars was waiting to take the MacArthur group to temporary headquarters in Yokohama. At the head of the column was a red fire engine, which reminded General Courtney Whitney of the Toonerville Trolley. It lunged forward with a startling explosion, and the motorcade clanged and crawled the fifteen miles to Yokohama. The entire length of the road was lined with almost thirty thousand Japanese soldiers, who stood on guard, their backs to MacArthur.

The Americans were quartered at the New Grand Hotel, a luxury establishment erected after the earthquake of 1923. At dinner Whitney warned his chief that the steak might be poisoned, but MacArthur laughed and brushed it off with "No one can live forever." Later that evening he told his staff, which had congregated in his room, "Boys, this is the greatest adventure in military history. Here we sit in the enemy's country with only a handful of troops, looking down the throats of nineteen fully armed divisions and seventy million fanatics. One false move and the Alamo would look like a Sunday-school picnic!"

The following day Lieutenant General Jonathan W. Wainwright was flown in from a POW camp in Manchuria. When MacArthur, who was having dinner, heard that Wainwright was in the lobby, he immediately went downstairs to greet the most famous survivor of Bataan. The officer who had lost through surrender more troops than any other American commander stood haggard and aged far beyond his years. His hair was snow-white, his uniform hung loose on his skeletal frame and he supported himself with a cane. He tried to smile. MacArthur embraced him but Wainwright was unable to speak. "Well, Skinny," said MacArthur with emotion, putting his hands on the other man's shoulders.

Wainwright got out one choked word, "General." While photographers took pictures, he found his voice: he believed he was in disgrace for surrendering the Philippines.* But MacArthur reassured him; Wainwright could have anything he wanted.

---

* In his *Reminiscences,* MacArthur states that he was "shocked" to find this out, apparently forgetting the messages he sent Marshall in 1942 about Wainwright, including one which declared he believed his successor had "temporarily become unbalanced."

"General, the only thing I want now is command of a corps," Wainwright said huskily. "That is what I wanted right in the beginning."

"Why, Jim, your old corps is yours when you want it."

Only a token occupation force was sent to ravaged Tokyo. The newsmen who accompanied it wanted above all to interview Tokyo Rose. She was finally located by correspondents Harry Brundige and Clark Lee through a Japanese newsman named Yamashita who brought her to the Imperial Hotel on the morning of September 1. She wore slacks and her hair was in pigtails. With her was a solemn young Portuguese-Japanese.

"This is Iva Ikuko Toguri, your Tokyo Rose. And this is her husband, Philip d'Aquino."

"Are you really Tokyo Rose?" Brundige asked.

"The one and only," she said with a smile.

Brundige offered her $2,000 for an exclusive first-person story for *Cosmopolitan* magazine which he would ghost-write, with the proviso, however, that she stay away from all other correspondents—as well as Army Intelligence and the CIC—until the story appeared. She agreed, and Brundige tapped out seventeen pages of notes on his portable typewriter. What emerged was the ironic story of an intelligent, scholarly young woman with a degree in zoology from UCLA who had sold out the country she loved for the country she hated—for $6.60 a month—because the alternative to propaganda broadcasting was work in a munitions factory.

After graduation from UCLA, Iva had gone to Japan, under protest, to see her mother's sister who was ill—her mother was too sick to make the trip. She found she disliked almost everything about Japan, including rice and her relatives, but before she could go back home the war broke out. She supported herself as a secretary, which led to a job as typist with the Japanese Broadcasting Corporation. At the behest of an American Army captain—an ex-radio commentator who had himself been persuaded to return to his old trade, for the other side—she agreed to make fifteen-minute daily broadcasts to the Allied soldiers. In her capacity as disk jockey she met and became friends with American POW's who were broadcasting propaganda for the Japanese. (They were subsequently pardoned because they had been

forced to it under "immediate threat of death or bodily harm.")
Iva used to bring food, medicine, cigarettes—whatever she could
scrape up for the prisoners. "It was manna from heaven," she
said later, "to be among people who thought and felt as I did."

The editor of *Cosmopolitan,* however, was astounded that
Brundige had negotiated with a traitor and by return cable demanded an explanation. Disgusted, Brundige turned over his
scoop to Lee. He submitted his own version to the International
News Service, which released it at once.*

5.

At Navy Secretary Forrestal's instigation, the formal surrender
ceremonies took place on the battleship *Missouri* in Tokyo Bay
on September 2, just three days after MacArthur's arrival. Truman
was particularly pleased by the choice. *Missouri,* one of the four
largest battleships in the world, had been named after his own
state and christened by his daughter, Margaret.

On September 1 Commander Horace Bird, *Missouri*'s gunnery
officer, conducted a dress rehearsal on the ship's deck. He gathered three hundred sailors to represent the dignitaries. Everything
went smoothly until the band began the "Admiral's March," signaling Nimitz' arrival. "Nimitz" did not appear. The admiral's
stand-in, a burly chief boatswain's mate nicknamed "Two-Gut,"
was immobilized by his role. He stood transfixed, scratching his
head. "I'll be damned!" he said in an awed voice. "Me an
admiral!"

The next morning Commander Bird watched the dawn with
disappointment. It was cool and gray. At about 7:30 a destroyer
lay to, and correspondents from all over the world clambered
aboard the battleship. Each was given a position, but the intimi-

---

* Mrs. D'Aquino was arrested on a charge of treason. At the grand jury
session in September 1948 Lee and Brundige "poured it on the Army captain
who taught Rose her broadcasting business"—to them, he was guiltier than
she was—and the jury demanded an indictment for the captain as well as
Tokyo Rose. Informed that the captain was not under the jurisdiction of the
court, the jury refused to charge her. When the prosecution assured the jury
that the captain would also be brought to justice, Iva was indicted. She was
tried, convicted as a traitor, sentenced to ten years in prison and fined
$10,000. The captain was never tried; he was promoted to major.

dated Japanese alone remained in place. The Russians were particularly obstreperous, roaming around the ship "like wild men."

For the Americans the moment brought back vivid memories. Robert Trumbull of the *New York Times* would never forget the hectic morning in Pearl Harbor when he worked for a Honolulu paper, nor would Webley Edwards, in charge of the pool broadcast on *Missouri,* who had announced by radio from Honolulu on December 7, "This is the real McCoy!"

Destroyers pulled alongside *Missouri,* discharging Allied generals and admirals including Halsey, Helfrich, Turner, Percival, Stilwell, Wainwright, Spaatz, Kenney and Eichelberger. At 8:05 Nimitz was piped aboard, followed shortly by MacArthur. There was so much excitement that the arrival of the two senior American officers went generally unnoticed. Commander Bird rushed ahead of them calling out, "Gentlemen, General MacArthur and Admiral Nimitz are approaching." Bird was ignored. In desperation he shouted, "Attention, all hands!" As one the assembled admirals and generals snapped to attention. In the immediate silence, waves could be heard lapping around the water line.

Now the destroyer *Lansdowne,* named after the commander of the dirigible *Shenandoah,* appeared with the eleven Japanese delegates. There had been a controversy about who would lead the Japanese. It was intolerable to think that Prime Minister Higashikuni, a member of the royal family, should be subjected to such humiliation, and Prince Konoye, who had risked his life for two years for peace, could not bring himself to face the shame of the moment. The onerous responsibility fell on the new foreign minister, Shigemitsu, who regarded it as "a painful but profitable task," and was honored that the Emperor had entrusted him with it. Army Chief of Staff Umezu was there under duress; it had taken a personal appeal from His Majesty. Navy Chief of Staff Toyoda ordered his operations officer, Admiral Tomioka, to take his place. "You lost the war," he said, "so you go"; Tomioka acquiesced but had already made up his mind to commit hara-kiri after the ceremonies.

The Japanese delegates were not even sure of protocol once they were on board. Should they salute, bow, shake hands or smile? Their adviser, Colonel Mashbir, had told the military to salute; the civilians should merely take off their hats and bow.

"And I suggest that all of you wear a *shiran kao* [nonchalant face]."

Mashbir started up *Missouri*'s gangway at exactly 8:55, followed by a Japanese civilian in a tall silk hat, cutaway and ascot. He was laboriously pulling himself up, groaning with every step. It was Foreign Minister Shigemitsu, whose left leg had been blown off by an assassin's bomb in Shanghai years before. His new artificial limb caused him excruciating agony. Bird, watching from above, expected the grim-faced general behind the man in the silk hat to give him a hand—it was Umezu, who regarded Shigemitsu as a detestable "Badoglio" and refused to take notice of his plight. Bird himself stepped down to offer a hand. Shigemitsu shook his head but then stiffly allowed the American to assist him momentarily.

Shigemitsu's painful progress across the quarter-deck to the ladder leading to the ceremony deck made him the center of attraction. An American correspondent noted that the onlookers watched him "with savage satisfaction." Shigemitsu shook off Bird's further offer of assistance and awkwardly mounted the ladder, his face a mask.

Once the Japanese were in place, the entire company came to attention for the invocation by the ship's chaplain. They remained at attention while a record of "The Star-Spangled Banner" was played over amplifiers. In the long uneasy pause that followed, Toshikazu Kase (previously Matsuoka's and now the new Foreign Minister's secretary), discovered several miniature Rising Suns painted on a nearby bulkhead, apparently to indicate destroyed Japanese planes or submarines. As he counted them, Kase's throat constricted. Beside him Admiral Tomioka was consumed by wonder and anger—wonder that the Americans showed no sign of contempt for the Japanese and anger at the presence of the Soviet delegates; they were part Asian, yet they had ignored Japan's plea to act as peacemaker and then stabbed her in the back in Manchuria.*

* On the same day Generalissimo Stalin made an important radio broadcast to the Russian people. He said they had had a special account to settle with Japan ever since she seized southern Sakhalin and strengthened her grip on the Kuriles in 1904.

"But the defeat of the Russian troops in 1904 during the Russo-Japanese War left bitter memories with our people. It was a dark stain

General MacArthur appeared, walking briskly with Nimitz and Halsey across the deck to a table covered with documents. The British had offered one used at the Battle of Jutland, but since it was too small, Bird had substituted a battered mess table covered with a coffee-stained green felt cloth; the documents had been arranged to hide the stains. Wainwright and Percival stepped to MacArthur's side behind the table.

"We are gathered here," MacArthur said, "representatives of the major warring powers, to conclude a solemn agreement whereby peace may be restored. The issues, involving divergent ideals and ideologies, have been determined on the battlefields of the world and hence are not for our discussion or our debate. Nor is it for us here to meet, representing as we do a majority of the peoples of the earth, in a spirit of distrust, malice or hatred. But rather it is for us, both victors and vanquished, to rise to that higher dignity which alone benefits the sacred purposes we are about to serve, committing all our people unreservedly to faithful compliance with the understanding they are here formally to assume."

Tomioka was impressed by the absence of rancor or retribution in MacArthur's words. General Yatsuji Nagai, who had accompanied Matsuoka to Berlin and Moscow, couldn't take his eyes away from MacArthur. How young-looking and fit he was in contrast to Umezu! Had the psychological impact of losing the war prematurely aged the Chief of Staff? Colonel Ichiji Sugita, who had interpreted at an earlier surrender ceremony, stared fixedly at another Allied officer, General Percival. Their eyes met and held, both apparently remembering the painful scene at the Ford factory in Singapore.

"It is my earnest hope," MacArthur continued, "—indeed the hope of all mankind—that from this solemn occasion a better world shall emerge out of the blood and carnage of the past, a world founded upon faith and understanding, a world dedicated to the dignity of man and the fulfillment of his most cherished wish for freedom, tolerance and justice."

---

on our country's honor. Our people waited with confidence for the day when Japan would suffer defeat and the stain could be wiped out. We of the older generation have been waiting for this day for forty years. Now it is here. Today Japan has conceded her defeat and signed the documents of unconditional surrender. . . ."

Almost as if on cue the clouds parted, and in the distance the peak of Mount Fuji sparkled in the sun. MacArthur indicated a chair at the opposite side of the table. Shigemitsu limped forward and sat down. He fumbled uncertainly with his hat, gloves and cane, giving the impression of stalling. Halsey wanted to slap him and say, "Sign, damn you! Sign!" MacArthur, however, realized that Shigemitsu was confused, and turning to his chief of staff, said sharply, "Sutherland, show him where to sign." Shigemitsu signed. Next Umezu marched forward stiffly, and without bothering to sit down, scrawled his name. Using separate pens, MacArthur now signed as Supreme Commander of the Allied Powers. Then in turn Nimitz and the other allies signed for their respective countries: General Hsu Yung-chang for China, Admiral Sir Bruce Fraser for the United Kingdom, Lieutenant General K. Derevyanko for the Soviet Union, General Sir Thomas Blamey for Australia, Colonel L. Moore-Gosgrove for Canada, General Jacques Leclerc for France, Admiral C. E. L. Helfrich for the Netherlands and Air Vice-Marshal Sir L. M. Isitt for New Zealand.

The dignity of the occasion was marred briefly by an inebriated delegate—it was not an American—who obtrusively began making faces at the Japanese. Shigemitsu stared him down and without expression slowly and deliberately put on his top hat. The other Japanese civilians followed suit. Perhaps it was a coincidence, thought Mashbir, but it struck him as an effective example of Oriental subtlety.

The last signatures were inscribed and MacArthur again addressed the assemblage. "Let us pray," he said, "that peace now be restored to the world and that God will preserve it always. These proceedings are now closed." He walked over to Halsey and put his arm around his shoulders. Bird was close by and thought he heard MacArthur say, "Bill, where in the hell are those airplanes?" As if in answer came a rumble in the distance. Thousands of carrier planes and B-29's swept over *Missouri* in an inspiring exhibition.

MacArthur left the ceremony deck for another microphone which would broadcast his message to America. "Today the guns are silent," he said. "A great tragedy has ended. A great victory has been won. The skies no longer rain death—the seas bear only commerce—men everywhere walk upright in the sunlight. The entire world is quietly at peace. The holy mission has been completed. . . .

"A new era is upon us. Even the lesson of victory itself brings with it profound concern, both for our future security, and the survival of civilization. . . . Military alliances, balances of power, leagues of nations, all in turn failed, leaving the only path to be by way of the crucible of war. . . .

"The utter destructiveness of war now blots out this alternative. We have had our last chance. If we do not devise some greater and more equitable system, Armageddon will be at our door. . . ."

MacArthur's words were in a very real sense a pledge that the United States would treat the fallen enemy with understanding and compassion. And throughout Japan itself, the populace was beginning to recover from the anguish of an almost intolerable fate. "If we allow the pain and humility to breed within us the dark thoughts of future revenge," the *Nippon Times* advised its readers in words that were meant to be inspiring and proved to be prophetic, "our spirit will be warped and perverted into a morbidly base design. . . . But if we use this pain and this humiliation as a spur to self-reflection and reform, and if we make this self-reflection and reform the motive force for a great constructive effort, there is nothing to stop us from building, out of the ashes of our defeat, a magnificent new Japan free from the dross of the old which is now gone, a new Japan which will vindicate our pride by winning the respect of the world."

Epilogue

1.

Six days after the ceremonies on *Missouri,* MacArthur came to Tokyo. At noon, on September 8, he strode to the terrace of the U. S. embassy, where an honor guard from the 1st Cavalry Division was attaching a historic flag to the halyards of the flagpole. "General Eichelberger," he said sonorously, "have our country's flag unfurled, and in Tokyo's sun let it wave its full glory as a symbol of hope for the oppressed and as a harbinger of victory for the right." To the sound of bugles the flag, which had flown over the Capitol Building in Washington on Pearl Harbor day, climbed up the staff.

If the reality of MacArthur the Conqueror's arrival, accentuated by the American colors which waved humiliatingly within sight of the Imperial Palace, was fairly incomprehensible to the Japanese people in all its implications, the defeat was intolerable to the military, who were directly responsible for the failure to stop the enemy. Moreover, many of them expected to stand trial, and within three days MacArthur issued orders for the arrest of the first forty alleged war criminals.

There was one name on the list which was recognized by everyone—Hideki Tojo. Almost immediately Tojo's modest home in Setagaya was besieged by correspondents and photographers. They crowded before the stone walls which fronted the house. Confined in his office, Tojo sat writing at a large desk. The room was dominated by a full-length portrait of the former premier in full military regalia. On another wall hung a tiger skin sent by an admirer from Malaya.

The crowd outside continued to grow while newsmen pushed into the garden itself, and by midafternoon the crush had become so overwhelming that Tojo told his wife to get out of the house at once with their maid; the children had already been evacuated to Kyushu. Mrs. Tojo was reluctant to go. "Take care of yourself," she said, fearing he might commit suicide. "Please, take care of yourself," she repeated and bowed. His answer was a noncommittal grunt.

She left by the back door with the maid. They circled around the wall and came up the street toward the driveway. Ahead was a confused mass of cars and people. The crowd blocked any view of her home, so she entered the garden of the house across the street which was on a slight rise. It belonged to a doctor named Suzuki who had earlier marked Tojo's chest with charcoal to indicate the location of his heart. Over the wall she could see that American soldiers—they were MP's—had already surrounded her house. An officer shouted, "Tell this yellow bastard we've waited long enough. Bring him out!" Suddenly she heard a muffled shot and the soldiers began breaking into the house. Even from across the street she recognized the sound of splintering wood. It was 4:17 P.M.

Major Paul Kraus and the arresting party, followed by George Jones, a reporter for the *New York Times,* broke into the office. Tojo, his jacket off, stood wavering beside an easy chair. Blood stained his shirt. In his right hand he still held a .32-caliber Colt, which now confronted the intruders.

"Don't shoot!" Kraus called out.

Tojo gave no indication that he had heard, but the gun clattered to the floor and he collapsed into the chair. He motioned to a Japanese police guard who had followed the Americans into the office and asked for water. He emptied the glass in a few gulps and wanted more.

In the garden across the road Mrs. Tojo knelt, repeating a Buddhist prayer. She imagined his agony and tried to prepare herself for the moment the Americans would bring out his body. Instead an ambulance appeared and a Japanese doctor rushed into the house.

At 4:29 Tojo's lips moved. Two Japanese interpreters, who accompanied the press, began to record his words. "I am very sorry it is taking me so long to die," he murmured. His face was contorted in pain but those of the Americans staring down at him showed no sympathy. "The Greater East Asian war was justified and righteous," he said. "I am very sorry for the nation and all the races of the Greater Asiatic powers. I would not like to be judged before a conqueror's court. I wait for the righteous judgment of history." His voice grew stronger but his words were not always distinct. "I wished to commit suicide but sometimes that fails." His bullet had entered almost exactly where Dr. Suzuki had marked his chest, but it had just missed his heart.

As medics transferred him to a divan, Tojo whispered, "I did not shoot myself in the head, because I wanted the people to recognize my features and know I was dead." He was taken to the 48th Evacuation Hospital in Yokohama, and in the evening General Eichelberger came to his bedside. Tojo opened his eyes and tried to bow. "I am dying," he said. "I am sorry to have given General Eichelberger so much trouble."

"Do you mean tonight or for the last few years?"

"Tonight. I want General Eichelberger to have my new saber."

Tojo lived to stand trial as a major war criminal*; but the fol-

---

* Near the end of the tedious proceedings, which took place at the Army Headquarters building on Ichigaya Heights, Tojo and Yoshio Kodama watched two American planes from the exercise yard of Sugamo Prison. "Kodama," the general said, "this trial will be meaningful only if there is no more war. As you see above, they are practicing to go against the Russians. By the time the trial ends there will be uneasy relations between the Soviets and the United States. If there is another war, a war crimes trial like this is really meaningless."

On November 12, 1948, Tojo was sentenced to death. In prison he had become a changed man. Religion now dominated his life and he was nicknamed *Tera-kozo* ("the Buddhist priestling"). A few hours before his execution he told Dr. Shinsho Hanayama, a Buddhist priest and one of the prison lowing morning Marshal Sugiyama was more accurate in his aim. He shot himself in the heart at his office. When his wife learned of his death, she followed the example of the wife of General Maresuke Nogi, who had led all troops in the Russo-Japanese War and later killed himself in apology for the death of his men. She knelt before a Buddhist shrine in her room, drank a thimbleful of cyanide and fell on a small dagger.

Trial at the hands of the victors was anathema to the Japanese leaders, but it was particularly repugnant to an aristocrat like Prince Konoye with his inordinate sense of pride. He too preferred

---

chaplains, that he had much to be thankful for: his body would soon become part of the soil of Japan; his death would be not only an apology to the Japanese but a move toward peace and the rebuilding of Japan. He said it was time that he died, since he had few teeth left, his eyes were failing and his memory was poor. And it was better to die than spend the rest of his days in prison, the victim of worldly passions. Finally, it was joyful to die in the knowledge that he would be reborn in Amida's paradise. He had even developed a sense of humor. With a grin he held up a Cannon washcloth and said, "Kannon-sama [the Buddhist Goddess of Mercy] has finally appeared."

In his final testament Tojo called on the Americans not to alienate the feelings of the Japanese or infect them with Communism. Japan had been the sole bulwark in Asia against Communism, and now Manchuria was becoming a base for the communization of the continent. The Americans had also divided Korea, which he prophesied would lead to great trouble in the future.

He apologized for the atrocities committed by the Japanese military and urged the American military to show compassion and repentance toward the civilians of Japan, who had suffered so grievously from indiscriminate air attacks and the two atomic bombs. He predicted that a third world war was bound to break out because of the conflicting interests of the United States and the Soviet Union, and since the battlefields would be Japan, China and Korea, it was the responsibility of the Americans to protect a helpless Japan.

The testament closed with two poems:

> *Although I now depart,*
> *I shall return to this land,*
> *as I have yet to repay*
> *my debt to my country.*

> *It is time for farewell.*
> *I shall wait beneath the moss,*
> *until the flowers are fragrant again*
> *in the islands of Yamato* [Japan].

He walked up the thirteen steps to the gallows with dignity. Just after midnight on December 22, the trap was sprung.

death to such humiliation. Facetiously he told a friend, "I'm a lazybones and I might find life in prison easy and carefree"—for thirty years he had never even carried a wallet nor squeezed a wet washcloth when he took a bath—"but I could never stand the shame of being called a war criminal."

The night before Konoye was to leave for Sugamo Prison his younger son, Michitaka,* searched his father's bedroom for weapons or poison. Although he found nothing, he was still worried, so before going to bed, he returned to his father's room. They talked at length about the China Incident, the negotiations with America, and the heavy responsibility Konoye felt toward the Emperor and the people. Michitaka thought his father should record these personal feelings. Konoye wrote for some time with a pencil—there was no writing brush available—then handed the script to his son. "This is not worded properly," he said, "but it expresses how I feel right now."

Michitaka sensed that this might be their last moments together. "For a long time I've only given you trouble and failed to be filial to you. I apologize."

Konoye rebuffed the overture. "What does 'to be filial' mean?" he asked and turned away. They sat in silence. Finally Michitaka said, "It is quite late now. Please go to sleep." He hesitated. "You will leave tomorrow?"

Konoye did not reply, but Michitaka continued to gaze at him entreatingly. Konoye returned the look as if saying, his son thought, "Why do you still ask me such a question? I was under the impression that you understood everything." Michitaka had never before seen such a "strange, distasteful" expression on his father's face, and for the first time he perceived his intention to die.

"If you need anything during the night, please call me," Michitaka said. "I'll be in the next room."

Just before dawn Michitaka managed to fall asleep but was soon awakened by his mother's excited voice. He tried to get up but was momentarily paralyzed. He remained seated, eyes closed, body trembling. At last he rose and entered his father's bedroom.

---

* Konoye's eldest son, Fumitaka (called "Butch" at Princeton), had been captured by the Russians in Manchuria. He died in a prison camp not far from Moscow.

Konoye was stretched out, looking calm and serene, as if sleeping. There was no sign of anguish on his patrician face. He was dead. A brownish bottle, empty, lay beside his pillow.

Americans considered Japan's titular leader, the Emperor, along with Tojo, to be the one most responsible for the war. Now he was even being reviled by some of the liberated Japanese press, who branded him a lecher as well as a warmonger. There were demonstrations outside MacArthur's headquarters advocating his removal. The Supreme Commander ignored these and similar demands from the Russians and segments of the American and Australian press. To bring the Emperor to trial would provoke guerrilla warfare throughout the nation and perpetuate a military government.

MacArthur was more than determined to treat the Emperor with respect—against the advice of his own staff, who wanted him summoned peremptorily to Allied headquarters as a show of power. "To do so," the general said, "would be to outrage the feelings of the Japanese people and make a martyr of the Emperor in their eyes. No, I shall wait and in time the Emperor will voluntarily come to see me. In this case, the patience of the East rather than the haste of the West will best serve our purpose."

The soundness of MacArthur's intuition was borne out. Two weeks after Tojo's attempted suicide, the Emperor himself requested an interview. Wearing cutaway, striped trousers, button shoes and top hat, he drove up to the American embassy with Grand Chamberlain Fujita. He stepped out of his ancient limousine and was greeted by a salute from General Fellers. As Fellers' hand came down, the Emperor seized it. A young Japanese interpreter explained that His Majesty was pleased to see the general.

"I am honored to meet you," Fellers replied. "Come in and meet General MacArthur." The Emperor nervously allowed himself to be escorted into the embassy by Fellers and up the spacious staircase to MacArthur's office on the second floor.

To put His Majesty at ease MacArthur mentioned that he had been presented to his father, Emperor Taisho, after the Russo-Japanese War, then thoughtfully dismissed everyone except his interpreter. They sat down before an open fire, unaware that the general's wife and young son, Arthur, were peering out at them from behind the red curtains. The general extended an American cigarette, which His Majesty took with thanks, his hands trembling while MacArthur lit it.

Kido's last advice to the Emperor before he left for the embassy had been not to assume any responsibility for the war, but now he did just that. "I come to you, General MacArthur, to offer myself to the judgment of the powers you represent as the one to bear sole responsibility for every political and military decision made and action taken by my people in the conduct of this war."

MacArthur was moved, as he later described the scene, "to the marrow of my bones. He was an Emperor by inherent birth, but in that instant I knew I faced the First Gentleman of Japan in his own right."

2.

World War II was over, but it had left in its wake more problems than it had solved. Asia, in the throes of an extensive revolt, was discarding the shackles of Western domination. Warfare would be transformed from a global conflict into fragmented nationalist struggles of liberation.

Ironically, one of Japan's most cherished war aims was being achieved. Asia was at last freeing itself from the white man. Great Britain had already lost Burma and was being pried loose from India. In the Dutch East Indies, Achmed Sukarno and Mohammed Hatti, who had supported the Japanese during the conflict, were mounting an irresistible independence movement.

In China the war had settled the contest for supremacy between the Communists and the Western-dominated Kuomintang. With the extensive destruction of property and loss of capital, Nationalist industry was at a standstill. Prices were more than two thousand times the level of 1937; on the foreign exchange the Chinese currency had dropped more than 70 percent in value within a month of Japan's surrender. Inflation had practically wiped out China's middle class and left intellectuals disillusioned. Beset by such difficulties, the Nationalists could not answer the needs of the people, and unlike the Communists, they were not willing to divide the land. For better or for worse—and it could not be much worse for the common man—China's only hope was Mao.

Land reform was also the keystone of the new government of Indochina. During the war the Viet Minh (Independence League), led by Ho Chi Minh, a Communist, fought the French and Japanese with the sympathy and support of Great Britain and the United States, to emerge as the dominant nationalist movement in the country. Peace brought the abdication of the playboy emperor, Bao Dai, and the Viet Minh proclaimed a new nation, the Republic of Vietnam, with a Declaration of Independence borrowed from America. But the United States, which had pledged independence for Indochina during the war, had already changed her policy. On August 24, 1945, President Truman informed General de Gaulle that he favored the return of Indochina to France. In the republic's first election, in January 1946, the Viet Minh won a majority in the new assembly, but French troops in the country, with the help of reinforcements from France shipped in American transports, seized Saigon, and Bao Dai was eventually restored as ruler. Puppet monarchies were also established in Cambodia and Laos, and all these governments were recognized by the United States.

American support of French colonialism indicated that her leaders intended to follow Britain's antiquated East of Suez policy —self-determination for nations of Europe but not for Asia—convinced that Asians did not know what was best for themselves and world security. America still had not learned that she had spent her blood and treasure to help win two disparate wars: one against Fascism in Europe, and the other against Asian aspirations. And the course of world history was irrevocably determined for the next two, three, perhaps four decades.

Several months after the war an aged woodman, his face deeply creased by the years, stopped in front of the Dai Ichi Building, MacArthur's new headquarters. Strapped to his back was a towering bundle of kindling. First he bowed low to MacArthur's standard, then he turned and bowed just as low to the Imperial Palace on the other side of the plaza. American bystanders watched with perplexed amusement as if he were a living paradox

of the inscrutable Orient. But the Japanese who saw him understood. He was acknowledging without reservations the temporal
power of today's *shogun* while revering what was eternal across
the avenue.

Acknowledgments

This book could not have been written without the co-operation of hundreds of people in Asia, Europe and the United States, particularly those who permitted themselves to be interviewed. Libraries contributed immeasurably to the book: the National Archives and Records Service, Alexandria, Virginia (Wilbur Nigh and Lois Aldridge); the National Archives (John E. Taylor); the Library of Congress; the main branch of the New York Public Library; the Danbury (Connecticut) Public Library; the Diet Library in Tokyo; the Library of the U. S. Embassy Annex in Tokyo (Mrs. Yuji Yamamoto); the Houghton Library, Harvard University (Marte Shaw and W. H. Bond); the Yale University Library (Judith A. Schiff); and the Franklin D. Roosevelt Library (Elizabeth Drewry, William Stewart, Jerome Deyo, Robert Parks, Mrs. Anne Morris and Joseph Marshall).

Numerous agencies, organizations and individuals made substantial contributions to this book:

The United States: Lieutenant Colonel Gerald M. Holland, Lieutenant Commander Herbert C. Prendergast and Anna Urband of the Magazine and Book Branch, Office of the Assistant Secretary of Defense; Betty Sprigg, Audio-Visual Division, Directorate for Defense Information; Roland F. Gill, Historical Reference Section Headquarters, Marine Corps; Brigadier General Hal C. Pattison, Judge Israel Wice, Charles B. MacDonald, Charles Romanus, Detmar H. Finke and Hannah Zeidlik of the Office of the Chief of Military History, Department of the Army; the Departments of Navy and Air Force; Arthur G. Kogan, Historical Division of the Department of State; six fellow authors: Michael Erlanger, Walter Lord, Martin Blumenson, Ladislas Farago, Tom Mahoney and Tom Coffey; my two typists, Isabelle Bates and Helen Toland; my special research assistant, Dale P. Harper; Myron Land and Robert Meskill of *Look* magazine; Colonel Ray M. O'Day, *Chit & Chat;* Professor John McV. Haight, Jr., Lehigh University; James O. Wade, World Publishing Company; Japan National Tourist Organization, New York City; William Henry Chamberlin; Pearl Buck; John J. McCloy; Mark Wohlfeld; Major Robert C. Mikesh; Virgil O. McCollum; Jean Colbert, WTIC, Hartford, Connecticut; Marty Allen; Captain Joseph W. Enright; Dr. Roy L. Bodine, Jr.; and Jean Ennis, Cynthia Humber, Elizabeth Kapuster, Sono Rosenberg, Anthony Wimpfheimer, Donald Klopfer and Bennett Cerf of Random House, Inc.

Germany: The late Gero von S. Gaevernitz; and Karola Gillich, my German representative.

Guadalcanal: Brian D. Hackman, J. C. Glover and Dominic Otuana of the Geological Survey Department, British Solomon Islands.

Philippines: Aurelio Repato; C. Bohannon; J. A. Villamor; Eduardo Montilla; and Secretary of Foreign Affairs Carlos Romulo.

Okinawa: Dr. Samuel Mukaida, Samuel H. Kitamura and Joseph S. Evans, Jr., of Public Affairs Department, U. S. Civil Administration of the Ryukyu Islands; and Eikichi Yamazato.

Thailand: Sol Sanders, the *U. S. News and World Report.*

Iwo Jima: A. B. Truax, the U. S. Coast Guard; and U. S. Air Force.

Republic of China: James Wei, director of the Government Information Office.

Guam: Rear Admiral Horace V. Bird.

Hawaii: Colonel James Sunderman and Major Mart Smith, U. S. Air Force; and Captain W. J. Holmes.

Saipan: Tony Benavente; and the civilian pilot who flew me throughout the Marianas.

Tinian: Henry Fleming.

Malaya: Abdul Majid bin Ithman.

New Guinea: John Robertson.

Japan

Tokyo: Prince Takahito Mikasa; Ambassador Edwin O. Reischauer, John Emmerson and George Saito of the U. S. Embassy; Colonels Susumu Nishiura and Hiroshi Fukushige; Lieutenant Colonels Yutaka Fujita and Masao Inaba; Commander Kengo Tominaga, Kazue Ohtani, Kenji Koyama and Captain Masanori Odagiri of the Japan Self-Defense Force War History Office; Rear Admiral Sadatoshi Tomioka, Historical Research Institute; Robert Trumbull, the *New York Times;* Denroku Sakai, the *Asahi Shimbun;* Tatsuo Shibata, editor-in-chief of the *Mainichi Daily News;* Shinji Hasegawa, director of the *Japan Times;* Kyo Naruse, president of Hara Shobo; Lewis Bush and Hiroshi Niino, NHK; John Rich, NBC; Ernest Richter, managing editor, *Pacific Stars and Stripes;* Dr. Kazutaka Watanabe, New Family Center; Taro Fukuda, Japan Public Relations, Inc.; Tomohiko Ushiba, former private secretary to Prince Konoye; Mrs. Fumimaro Konoye, widow of Prince Konoye; Toshio Katsube, Tokyo Fuji Co.; Kazuaki Arichi of the Foreign Ministry; Captain Sadae Ikeda, who arranged interviews with survivors of *Musashi;* Yoshimichi Itagawa, who arranged interviews with veterans in Hokkaido; Koichi Narita, who, together with Kiyoshi Kamiko, arranged trip to Leyte; Commander Suguru Suzuki; Mrs. Junko Kawabe, widow of General Masakazu Kawabe; Mrs. Yoshii Kuribayashi, widow of General Tadamichi Kuribayashi; Mrs. Haruko Ichimaru, eldest daughter of the late Admiral Toshinosuke Ichimaru; Mrs. Yoshie Onishi, widow of Admiral Takijiro Onishi; Yoshio Kodama; Captain Atsushi Oi of the Air-Sea Technical Research Association; Mrs. Sadako Fushimi, widow of Prince Hiroyoshi Fushimi; Mrs. Toyoko Dantani, widow of Sergeant Minoru Dantani (Iwo Jima); Petty Officer Iwao Matsumoto and Sergeant Shinya Ryumae, veterans of Iwo Jima; Lieutenant Colonel Shigeharu Asaeda; Major Iwao Takahashi, son-in-law of the late General Sosaku Suzuki; Mrs. Chitose Tsuji, widow of Colonel Masanobu Tsuji; Seizo Yamanaka, Mannesmann Aktiengesellschaft liaison office in Japan; Yoichi Nagata; Den Oshima; Motoji Tokushima; Keizaburo Matsumoto; Beiji Yamamoto; Mrs. Kimiko Matsumura; Toshio Haneda; Mrs. Keiko Ohtake; and the following translators; Kanji Motai, Tsuneo Oki, Toshio Nagasaki, Kiichiro Kumano and Toshihiko Kasahara.

Oiso: Marquis Koichi Kido, who arranged interviews with a number of officials in the Imperial Household Ministry and made numerous suggestions.

Hiroshima: Shogo Nagaoka, co-ordinator and guide; Mrs. Barbara Reynolds, Hiroshima Friendship Center; Mayor Shinzo Hamai; Masao Niide, chief of the Foreign Affairs Section, City Hall; Seigo Wada, Municipal Government, who arranged a number of interviews.

Nagasaki: Shogo Nagaoka, co-ordinator and guide; Deputy Mayor Kaoru Naruse; Mayor Tsutomu Tagawa, Toshiyuki Hayama and Sunao Tanaka, who arranged a number of interviews.

Osaka: Gen Nishino, the *Mainichi.*

Kyoto: Dr. Yoichi Misaki, who arranged interviews with survivors of the 16th Division and Koichiro Hatanaka.

Matsuyama: Toyoshige Miyoshi.

Hokkaido: Daisuke Kuriga, who arranged research interviews.

Kure: Shinji Chiba, who arranged trips to Kure, Etajima, Iwakuni and Hashirajima; and Captain Arashi Kamimura, commander, Educational Troops, Maritime Defense Agency, Kure.

Etajima: Admiral Toshihiko Tmota, Superintendent of Naval Academy; and Seizo Okamura, curator of Naval Academy Gallery.

Iwakuni: Colonel Hideo Nakamura, commanding officer, Iwakuni Air Base, Japan Self-Defense Force; Lieutenant William M. Bokholt, Marine Corps Air Station; Hajime Takahashi, harbor master, Iwakuni; Mrs. Yoshiko Kugiya, proprietress of Kugiman Inn.

Hashirajima: Hisaro Fujimoto; Tsutae Fujiyama; and Isamu Horimoto.

Yokosuka: Vice Admiral Nobuo Fukuchi, commandant, Memorial Battleship *Mikasa;* Rear Admiral Frank L. Johnson, Captain Tom Dwyer and Douglas Wada, U. S. Naval Forces in Japan. Mr. Wada arranged a number of special interviews and acted as interpreter.

Finally I would like to thank six people who contributed most outstandingly to the book: my chief assistant and interpreter, my wife Toshiko; my two representatives in Japan, Tokiji Matsumura and Major Yoshitaka Horie; my copyeditor, Mrs. Barbara Willson, not only for correcting mistakes but for suggesting innumerable improvements in style and content; my agent, Paul Revere Reynolds, who gave me the idea for this project and was a constant source of encouragement throughout the five years it took to complete it; and my editor, Robert Loomis, who labored so diligently with me for more than sixteen months on the final draft that the finished manuscript could properly be called a collaboration.

Sources

A. Interviews

(Rank at time of action)

Lieutenant Heijiro Abe, Pearl Harbor and Midway (2 interviews)
Valeriano Abello, Leyte
Yasuharu Agaria, Okinawa
Dr. Tatsuichiro Akizuki, Nagasaki
Zoilo Andrade, Leyte
Ensign Yasunori Aoki, *kamikaze* flier (3 interviews)
Antonio Aquino, Bataan
Daitaro Arakawa, NHK
General Sadao Araki*
Colonel Okikatsu Arao, Palace revolt
Major Shigeharu Asaeda, Tsuji's assistant (4 interviews)
Lieutenant (j.g.) Wahei Asami, *Musashi*
Yoshinori Ataka, Hiroshima
Prime Minister Clement Attlee*
Tony Benavente, Saipan

* deceased

Admiral Thomas Binford, Battle of Java Sea
Commander Horace V. Bird, *Missouri*
Admiral C. C. Bloch, Pearl Harbor
General Clifford Bluemel, Bataan
Paul C. Blum, peace move in Switzerland
Major Roy L. Bodine, Jr., prisoner of war
C. T. R. Bohannan, Philippines
Charles Bohlen, Yalta and Potsdam (2 interviews)
Ordnanceman 3rd Class Donald Briggs, Pearl Harbor
Corporal Durward Brooks, Clark Field
Lewis Bush, British prisoner of war
Captain Richard Carmichael, Pearl Harbor
Corporal Roy Castleberry, Bataan
Chen Cheng,* Minister of War, Nationalist China
Shinji Chiba, navigation instructor
Dr. Shigeko Chihara, Okinawa
Colonel Jim Cushing,* Cebu
Hisaji Dai, Hiroshima
Hiroaki Daido, Hiroshima
Sergeant Dwayne Davis, Clark Field
Major James P. S. Devereux, Wake Island
General Akio Doi, Soviet expert (3 interviews)
Eugene Hoffman Dooman, adviser to Ambassador Grew*
Allen Dulles*
Hideo Edo, Mitsui Real Estate Co., Ltd. (2 interviews)
Private George E. Elliott, Jr., Pearl Harbor
John Kenneth Emmerson, consular staff in Yenan
Mrs. Tsuyako Eshima, Nagasaki
Ramon Esperas, Leyte
Admiral Frank Jack Fletcher
Hisaro Fujimoto, Hashirajima
Commander Yoshiro Fujimura, peace move in Switzerland (2 interviews)
Colonel Nobuo Fujisawa, aviation maintenance officer
Lieutenant Yoshimi Fujiwara, Iwo Jima
Tsutae Fujiyama, Hashirajima
Taeko Fukabori, Nagasaki (Mrs. Furukawa)
Captain Nobuo Fukuchi, Personnel Bureau, Navy Ministry

* deceased

Admiral Shigeru Fukudome
Commander Shizuo Fukui, naval construction expert
George A. Furness, IMTFE counsel
First Sergeant Noboru Furukawa, Leyte (2 interviews)
Gero von S. Gaevernitz,* peace move in Switzerland
Jesse Gaines, Pearl Harbor
Lieutenant Wilmer Earl Gallaher, Midway
Commander Minoru Genda, Pearl Harbor and Midway (2 interviews)
Stuart Griffin, Iwo Jima
J. C. Glover, Guadalcanal
Vicente Guerrero, Saipan
Brian D. Hackman, Guadalcanal
Colonel Tatsuo Haki, Bataan
Ryuji Hamai, Hiroshima
Shinzo Hamai,* mayor of Hiroshima (2 interviews)
W. Averell Harriman, U. S. ambassador to Moscow
Saiji Hasegawa, Domei
Shinichi Hasegawa, Yonosuke Matsuoka's secretary
Colonel Takushiro Hattori,* Army General Staff (3 interviews)
Toshiyuki Hayama, Nagasaki
Mrs. Matsuyo Hayashi, Hiroshima
Colonel Saburo Hayashi, Palace revolt
Tosaku Hayashiya, Tokyo fire bombing, May 25, 1945
Jinsai Higa, General Ushijima's barber
Professor Kiyoshi Hiraizumi, teacher of the Imperial Way (2 interviews)
Private Kiyomi Hirakawa, Iwo Jima
Lieutenant Colonel Takashi Hirakushi, Saipan (2 interviews)
Lieutenant (s.g.) Shigeo Hirayama, Battle of Leyte Gulf
Matao Hisatomi, correspondent on Leyte
General Ho Ying-chin, Chief of Staff, Chinese Nationalist Army
Private Shuzen Hokama, Okinawa (2 interviews)
Admiral Ernest Holtzworth, Pearl Harbor
Jiro Homma, peace move in Sweden
Major Yoshitaka Horie, Iwo Jima, etc. (4 interviews)
Naoki Hoshino, Tojo Cabinet (3 interviews)
Morisada Hosokawa, Prince Konoye's secretary and son-in-law

* deceased

Petty Officer Shiro Hosoya, *Musashi* (2 interviews)

Lieutenant Colonel Masataka Ida, Palace revolt (2 interviews)

Major Einosuke Iemura, Guadalcanal

Tsuyako Iju, Okinawa

Captain Sadae Ikeda, *Musashi* (2 interviews)

Lieutenant Haruki Iki, sinking of *Repulse*

Professor Seiji Imabori, Hiroshima

Warrant Officer Kaname Imai, Okinawa

Colonel Takeo Imai, Marco Polo Bridge incident and Bataan (2 interviews)

General Hitoshi Imamura,* Java and Guadalcanal

Major Kumao Imoto, Army General Staff and Guadalcanal (2 interviews)

Lieutenant Colonel Masao Inaba, Palace revolt (2 interviews)

Sergeant Kenichi Inagaki, Leyte (2 interviews)

Dr. Masaru Inaoka, Iwo Jima

Genji Inoue, Leyte

Sukemasa Irie, Chamberlain to the Emperor

Ryoichi Ishizaki, Leyte

Yoshimichi Itagawa, The Wounded Soldiers' Association of Japan

Captain Koichi Ito, Okinawa

Colonel Tsuneo Ito, War History Office

Pfc. Waichi Ito, Leyte (2 interviews)

Commander Haruki Itoh, Guadalcanal

Mrs. Fukiko Iura, Hiroshima

Colonel Hideo Iwakuro, peace negotiations in Washington (3 interviews)

Mrs. Chiyo Iwamiya, proprietress of Iwamiya Inn, Mitsukue, Shikoku

Hajime Iwanaga, Nagasaki

Rikuro Iwata, student factory worker

Tomoko Iwata, student factory worker

Miyoko Jahana, Okinawa (Mrs. Toguchi)

Colonel Nobuhiko Jimbo, Philippines (2 interviews)

General Albert Jones,* Bataan

Hideko Kakinohana, Okinawa (Mrs. Yoshimura)

Corporal Kiyoshi Kamiko, Leyte (3 interviews)

Lieutenant (s.g.) Arashi Kamimura, *Shimakaze*

* deceased

Shinichi Kamimura, chief, Chinese Section, Foreign Ministry, Marco Polo incident
Lieutenant Hisamichi Kano, Philippines
Osanaga Kanroji, High Priest, the Meiji Shrine
Toshikazu Kase, assistant to Matsuoka and Togo
Colonel Tadashi Katakura, 2/26 Incident, Burma, etc. (5 interviews)
Captain Kenkichi Kato, *Musashi*
Toshio Katsube, Tokyo fire bombing, March 10, 1945
Seigo Kawasaki, Okinawa (2 interviews)
Okinori Kaya, Tojo Cabinet (3 interviews)
Marquis Koichi Kido (4 interviews)
Gonichi Kimura, Hiroshima
Ikuko Kimura, employed by Shigenori Togo
Shigeru Kinjo, Okinawa
Kojiro Kitamura, peace move in Switzerland
Tadahiko Kitayama, Hiroshima, etc. (2 interviews)
Shunzo Kobayashi, Matsuoka's defense counsel at IMTFE
Yoshio Kodama, associate of Tsuji, Onishi, etc. (4 interviews)
Keizo Kohno, Burma
Yuichiro Kominami, Tokyo fire bombing, March 10, 1945
Captain Keizo Komura, Pearl Harbor to Okinawa (2 interviews)
Michitaka Konoye, younger son of Prince Konoye (2 interviews)
General Haruo Konuma, Guadalcanal (3 interviews)
Hachiro Kosasa, Nagasaki (2 interviews)
Mrs. Hachiro Kosasa, Nagasaki
Lieutenant Commander Choichi Koyama, *Hatsuyuki*
Admiral Tomiji Koyanagi, Guadalcanal, Marianas and Leyte (2 interviews)
Sachiko Kuda, Okinawa (Mrs. Omi)
Mrs. Yoshiko Kugiya, proprietress of Kugiman Inn
Lieutenant (s.g.) Kazutoshi Kuhara, Pearl Harbor, etc.
Captain Hiromu Kumano, Imphal campaign
Daisuke Kuriga, Sakhalin
Pfc. Noboru Kuriyama, Okinawa
Mrs. Saburo Kurusu
Admiral Jinichi Kusaka, commander, Southeast Area Fleet
Admiral Ryunosuke Kusaka (6 interviews)
Father Hugo Lassalle (Makibi Enomiya), Hiroshima

Yeoman C. O. Lines, Pearl Harbor
Tokuzo Makiminato, Okinawa
Toraichi Masuda, Leyte
Tsuneo Mataba, naval salvage expert
Miyoko Matsubara, Hiroshima
Shigeharu Matsumoto, managing editor of Domei
Lieutenant Hirata Matsumura, Pearl Harbor
Cadet Hisashi Matsumura, information on prisoners of war
Kenichiro Matsuoka, son of Yosuke Matsuoka
Colonel Sei Matsutani, Army General Staff
Dr. Yoshimasa Matsuzaka, Hiroshima
John J. McCloy, The Assistant Secretary of War
Yates McDaniel, Singapore
Prince Mikasa
Admiral Gunichi Mikawa, Battle of Savo Island
Dr. Yoichi Misaki, Leyte (2 interviews)
Shizuko Miura, Saipan (Mrs. Sugano)
Petty Officer Shikichi Miyagi, Okinawa (3 interviews)
Shuji Miyahara, student mobilization
Mieko Miyahira, Okinawa
Colonel Yoshio Miyauchi, Leyte
Commander Kazunari Miyo, Navy General Staff (2 interviews)
Eduardo Montilla, Leyte
Captain Joseph Moore, Clark Field
Chiematsu Mori, Shikoku
Lieutenant (j.g.) Juzo Mori, Pearl Harbor
Shigeyoshi Morimoto, Nagasaki
Mrs. Shigeyoshi Morimoto, Nagasaki
Pfc. Hiroshi Morishima, Leyte (2 interviews)
Professor Ichiro Moritaki, Hiroshima
Dr. Tadashi Moriya, Leyte
Colonel William Morse, Philippines
Baron Yonosuke (Ian) Mutsu, Domei
General Yatsuji Nagai, Matsuoka trip to Germany, and *Missouri*
    (2 interviews)
Professor Shogo Nagaoka, Hiroshima and Nagasaki (3 interviews)
Captain Ko Nagasawa,* Java Sea, Coral Sea and Midway (2 in-
    terviews)

* deceased

Lieutenant (s.g.) Masanao Naito, *Musashi*
Chomei Nakachi, Okinawa
Fumihiko Nakajima, Marianas
Pfc. Hideichi Nakamura, Leyte (2 interviews)
Yukio Nakamura, secret service agent, Marco Polo Bridge incident
Seizen Nakasone, Okinawa
General Akira Nara,* Bataan (2 interviews)
Kaoru Naruse, Nagasaki (2 interviews)
Ricardo P. Negru, Leyte
Hiroshi Niino, NHK (2 interviews)
Fleet Admiral Chester Nimitz*
Ambassador Haruhiko Nishi, Foreign Minister Togo's deputy (2
    interviews)
Midori Nishida, Nagasaki
Masao Nishikawa, Leyte
Sergeant Kunio Nishimura, Leyte (2 interviews)
Gen Nishino, Guadalcanal (5 interviews)
Commander Shigeru Nishino, Battle of Surigao Strait
Colonel Susumu Nishiura, secretary to Tojo (2 interviews)
Zenso Noborikawa, Okinawa
Yeoman Second Class Mitsuharu Noda, *Yamato* and Saipan
First Lieutenant Sajibei Noguchi, Imphal campaign
Sergeant Yoshio Noguchi, Leyte (3 interviews)
Admiral Kichisaburo Nomura,* ambassador to the United States
Admiral Naokuni Nomura, German-Japanese military co-operation
Mrs. Fumiko Nozaki, Okinawa
Shinichi Nozaki, Okinawa
Mrs. Yasuko Nukushina, Hiroshima
Etsuko Obata, Nagasaki
Admiral Sueo Obayashi, Battle of the Philippine Sea
Mikio Ogawa, Leyte
Kiwamu Ogiwara, Matsuoka's *shosei*
Captain Toshikazu Ohmae, Battle of the Philippine Sea, etc. (2
    interviews)
Ensign Toshihiko Ohno, Iwo Jima (4 interviews)
Captain Atsushi Oi, naval expert
Seizo Okamura, curator of Naval Gallery, Etajima
Pfc. Kazuyuki Okumura, Leyte

* deceased

Ryoko Okuyama, Saipan (Mrs. Miura)
Ensign Satoru Omagari, Iwo Jima (4 interviews)
Yeoman Heijiro Omi, Admiral Yamamoto's chief orderly (2 interviews)
Kunio Ono, Hiroshima
Takeshi Ono, Manchuria
General Makoto Onodera, peace move in Sweden
Yoshiko Ooganeku, Okinawa (Mrs. Kitashiro)
Colonel Adrianus van Oosten, prisoner of war
Tokuo Ootowa, Hiroshima
Chosei Osato, Okinawa
General Hiroshi Oshima, Japanese ambassador to Germany
Chief Petty Officer Mitsukuni Oshita, sinking of *Hiyo*
Sergio Osmeña, President of the Philippines
Masahide Ota, Okinawa
Lieutenant Sadao (Roy) Otake, surrender mission to Manila
Sayao Otsuka, midget-submarine training
General Eugen Ott, German ambassador to Japan
Dominic Otuana, Guadalcanal
Second Lieutenant Robert Overstreet, Pearl Harbor
Jose S. Pangelinan, Saipan
Joe Price, Leyte
Robert Price, Leyte
Vicente Quintero, Leyte (2 interviews)
Ambassador Edwin O. Reischauer
First Lieutenant John Rich, Saipan and Iwo Jima (2 interviews)
Admiral Francis Rockwell, Philippines
General Carlos Romulo, MacArthur's staff (2 interviews)
Shintaro Ryu,* peace move in Switzerland
Manuel Sablan, Saipan
Sheriff Mariano Sablan, Saipan
Mayor Vicente D. Sablan, Saipan
Dr. Ryokichi Sagane,* Nagasaki
Pfc. Koichi Saijo, Okinawa (2 interviews)
Petty Officer Haruyoshi Saima, Battle of Cape Esperance
Ensign Kazuo Sakamaki, Pearl Harbor
Joe Sakisat, Saipan

* deceased

Hisatsune Sakomizu, secretary to Prime Ministers Okada and
    Suzuki (2 interviews)
Tomie Sanada, Hiroshima (Mrs. Fujii)
General Sadamu Sanagi, Philippines
Colonel Fabian Sanchez, Cebu
Commander Naohiro Sata, Pearl Harbor
General Kenryo Sato, adviser to Tojo (7 interviews)
Kyoko Sato, Hiroshima (Mrs. Heiya Yamamoto)
Naotake Sato, Japanese ambassador to Russia (2 interviews)
General Shozaburo Sato, 2/26 Incident
Petty Officer Taro Sato, *Musashi*
Captain Manuel Segura, Cebu
Emi Sekimura, Tokyo fire bombing, March 10, 1945 (Mrs. Seo)
Mrs. Yoshie Sekimura, Tokyo fire bombing, March 10, 1945
Captain Hideo Sematoo, Hiroshima
Tatsuo Shibata, editor-in-chief, the *Mainichi Daily News*
Pfc. Toshio Shida, Okinawa
Lieutenant Yoshio Shiga, Pearl Harbor and Battle of the Santa
    Cruz Islands (3 interviews)
Dr. Fumio Shigeto, Hiroshima
Admiral Kiyohide Shima, Battle of Surigao Strait (3 interviews)
Ensign Fukujiro Shimoyama, *Musashi*
Private Shigeru Shimoyama, Hiroshima (5 interviews)
Captain Tsuneo Shimura, Okinawa (2 interviews)
Cesario Sipaco, Leyte
John H. Skeen, Jr., General Homma's defense counsel
Sturmbannführer (Major) Otto Skorzeny, Teheran
Admiral W. W. Smith, Pearl Harbor
Admiral Raymond Spruance*
Admiral Harold Stark
Kamekichi Sugimoto, Nagasaki
Major Mitsuo Suginoo, Guadalcanal
Colonel Ichiji Sugita, Singapore and *Missouri* (2 interviews)
Captain Tatsumaru Sugiyama, aviation officers' plot against Tojo,
    etc. (2 interviews)
Captain Eijiro Suzuki, Pearl Harbor (2 interviews)
Hajime Suzuki, son of Prime Minister Suzuki

* deceased

Commander Suguru Suzuki, Pearl Harbor
Pfc. Tadashi Suzuki, Guadalcanal
General Teiichi Suzuki, President of the Cabinet Planning Board
  (2 interviews)
Admiral Sokichi Takagi, Navy Ministry
Hachiro Takahashi, Burma
Lieutenant (s.g.) Katsusaku Takahashi, sinking of *Repulse*
Ensign Kiyoshi Takahashi, *Musashi*
Dr. Shingo Takahashi, Leyte
Dr. Susumu Takahashi, Tokyo fire bombing, March 10, 1945
Chiyo Takamori, Hiroshima (Mrs. Takeuchi)
General Tatsuhiko Takashima, chief of staff to General Seiichi
  Tanaka
Lieutenant Colonel Masahiko Takeshita, Palace revolt (2 inter-
  views)
Harumi Takeuchi, peace mission to Manila
Shiroku Tanabe, Hiroshima
Commander Yahachi Tanabe, Midway
Lieutenant Commander Tomonobu Tanaka, sinking of *Soryu*
Morio Tateno, NHK announcer
Nobuyuki Tateno, Japanese literature
Corporal Shinjiro Terasaki, Leyte (2 interviews)
Commander Masamichi Terauchi, *Yukikaze*
Yasuhide Toda, Chamberlain to the Emperor
Junji Togashi, *Mainichi* reporter
Fumihiko Togo, son-in-law and adopted son of Shigenori Togo
Mrs. Hideki Tojo (2 interviews)
Hitoshi Tokai, Nagasaki
Kazuko Tokai, Nagasaki (Mrs. Tanaka)
Yoshihiro Tokugawa, Chamberlain to the Emperor
Captain Sadatoshi Tomioka, Naval General Staff (5 interviews)
Admiral Toshihiko Tomita, Etajima
Mrs. Yoshiko Tomita, Hiroshima
General Yoshiharu Tomochika, Leyte (2 interviews)
Chief Petty Officer Hisao Tomokane, *Shimakaze*
Commander Shukichi Toshikawa, Battle of Java Sea
Staff Sergeant Frank Trammell,* Clark Field
Colonel Jesse Traywick, Jr., Philippines

  * deceased

President Harry S. Truman
Robert Trumbull, Pearl Harbor and *Missouri* (2 interviews)
Sadako Tsutsumimachi, Hiroshima (Mrs. Tochida)
Seiyu Uema, Okinawa
Takeshi Usami, Grand Steward of the Imperial Household
Tomohiko Ushiba, Prince Konoye's secretary (2 interviews)
General Takaji Wachi, C/S Generals Homma and Yamashita
Captain Tsunezo Wachi, Mexico and Iwo Jima
Petty Officer Tadashi Wada, *kamikaze* pilot trainee
Wang Chia-yu, Nationalist China Ministry of Information
General Wang Shu-ming, Flying Tigers
Commander Yasuji Watanabe,* on Yamamoto's staff (3 interviews)
Second Lieutenant William Welch, Pearl Harbor
Kiichiro Yamada, Leyte (2 interviews)
Sadahiro Yamada, Leyte
Taro Yamada, naval ordnance expert
Senji Yamaguchi, Nagasaki
Major Chikuro Yamamoto, Guadalcanal
Lieutenant (s.g.) Heiya Yamamoto, *Akizuki*
Mrs. Makiko Yamamoto, widow of Commander Yuji Yamamoto
Lieutenant (s.g.) Masahide Yamamoto, Guadalcanal sea battles
Michiko Yamaoka, Hiroshima
Nobuko Yamashiro, Okinawa (Mrs. Oshiro)
Eikichi Yamazato, Okinawa
Kayo Yasuo, Okinawa
Major Jesus Ybanez, Cebu
Shigeru Yoshida,* Japanese ambassador to Great Britain
Shozaburo Yoshida, Rabaul (3 interviews)
Ensign Takeo Yoshikawa, Pearl Harbor
Hajime Yukimune, Hiroshima

B. Documents, Records and Reports

Foreign Relations of the United States: Diplomatic Papers. The Far East: 1931, Vol. III; 1932, Vols. III and IV; 1933, Vol.

* deceased

III; 1934, Vol. III; 1935, Vol. III; 1936, Vol. IV; 1937, Vols. III and IV; 1938, Vols. III and IV; 1939, Vols. III and IV; 1940, Vol. IV; 1941, Vols. III and IV. Washington: Department of State, 1946–1956.

Papers Relating to the Foreign Relations of the United States: Japan, 1931–1941. 2 vols. Washington: Department of State, 1943.

Peace and War: United States Foreign Policy, 1931–1941. Washington: Department of State, 1946.

International Military Tribunal for the Far East, Dissenting Judgement (Justice Radhabinad Pal). Calcutta: Sanyal, 1953.

International Military Tribunal for the Far East. *Interrogations* (listed in Notes).

Japan Defense Agency. Archives of the War History Office. Unpublished manuscripts and records which are the source of the series of histories being written by the War History Office.

Japan International Politics Association. "Records of the Meetings of the Liaison and Imperial Conferences." Compiled by Dr. Jun Tsunoda, and others. Published in 7 vols. by Asahi Shimbun, Tokyo, in 1962–1963, under the title *The Road to the Pacific War.*

Japan Ministry of Foreign Affairs. Archives and Documents Section. "The Circumstances relating to the Termination of the War and Relative Historical Materials." Unpublished manuscript and materials. Published version: *Historical Records of the Surrender.* 2 vols. Tokyo: Shimbun Gekkan, 1952.

——. *Chronological Tables and Major Documents pertaining to Japan's Foreign Relations.* 2 volumes. Tokyo: Nihon Kokusai Rengo Kyokai, 1955.

——. Archives 1868–1945, microfilmed for the Library of Congress, 1949–1951. Compiled by Cecil H. Uyehara. Washington: Photoduplication Service, Library of Congress, 1954.

Japanese monographs and studies. U.S. Department of the Army. Office, Chief of Military History Archives (listed in Notes).

The NHK File on the Emperor's recording and the Palace revolt.

Pearl Harbor Attack. Hearings before the Joint Committee on the Investigation of the Pearl Harbor Attack, Congress of the

United States, Seventy-ninth Congress. Washington: U.S. Government Printing Office, 1946.

Takashima, Tatsuhiko. "Notes," a report by Major General Tatsuhiko Takashima. Unpublished.

U.S. Strategic Bombing Survey (USSBS). *The Effects of Strategic Bombing on Japanese Morale.* Washington: U.S. Government Printing Office, 1947.

——. *Interrogations of Japanese Officers, Navy.* Unpublished.

——. *Interrogations of Japanese Officials.* 2 vols. Washington: U.S. Government Printing Office, 1946.

——. *Japan's Struggle to End the War.* Washington: U.S. Government Printing Office, 1946.

C. Official Histories

AUSTRALIA

Wigmore, Lionel. *The Japanese Thrust.* Canberra: Australian War Memorial, 1957.

GREAT BRITAIN

History of the Second World War (United Kingdom Military Series). London, Her Majesty's Stationery Office:

Ehrman, John. *Grand Strategy,* Vol. VI. 1956.

Gwyer, John M.A., and J.R.M. Butler. *Grand Strategy,* Vol. III, Part 1, 1964.

Kirby, Woodburn S. *The War against Japan,* Vols. I and V. 1957 and 1969.

JAPAN

Defense Agency, War History Office. *Advance Operations into Malaya.* Tokyo: Asagumo Shimbun, 1966.

UNITED STATES

Department of the Air Force. *The Army Air Forces in World War II:*

Craven, W. F., and J. L. Cate, eds. Vol. IV, *The Pacific—Guadalcanal to Saipan;* Vol. V, *The Pacific—Matterhorn to Nagasaki.* University of Chicago Press, 1950 and 1953.

Department of the Army. Publications of the Office of the Chief of Military History. Washington, U.S. Government Printing Office:

Appleman, Roy E., James M. Burns, Russell A. Gugeler and John Stevens. *Okinawa: The Last Battle.* 1948.

Cannon, M. Hamlin. *Leyte: The Return to the Philippines.* 1954.

Conn, Stetson, Rose C. Engelman and Byron Fairchild. *Guarding the United States and Its Outposts.* 1964.

Crowl, Philip A. *Campaign in the Marianas.* 1960.

——, and Edmund G. Love. *Seizure of the Gilberts and Marshalls.* 1960.

Greenfield, Kent Roberts, ed. *Command Decisions.* New York: Harcourt, 1959.

Matloff, Maurice. *Strategic Planning for Coalition Warfare: 1943–1944.* 1959.

——, and Edwin M. Snell. *Strategic Planning for Coalition Warfare: 1941–1942.* 1953.

Miller, John, Jr., *Guadalcanal: The First Offensive.* 1949.

Morton, Louis. *The Fall of the Philippines.* 1953.

——, *Strategy and Command: The First Two Years.* 1962.

Romanus, Charles F., and Riley Sunderland. *Stilwell's Command Problems.* 1956.

Romanus and Sunderland. *Stilwell's Mission to China.* 1953.

——. *Time Runs Out in CBI.* 1959.

Smith, Robert Ross. *The Approach to the Philippines.* 1953.

——. *Triumph in the Philippines.* 1963.

Watson, Mark Skinner. *Chief of Staff: Prewar Plans and Preparations: 1941–1942.* 1950.

Williams, Mary H., compiler. *Chronology: 1941–1945.* 1960.

Department of the Navy

Marine Corps. Washington, U.S. Government Printing Office for Historical Branch, Marine Corps.

Bartley, Lt. Col. Whitman S. *Iwo Jima: Amphibious Epic*. 1954.
Hoffman, Major Carl W. *Saipan: The Beginning of the End*. 1950.
Hough, Lieutenant Colonel Frank O., Major Verle E. Ludwig, and Henry I. Shaw, Jr. *Pearl Harbor to Guadalcanal*. 1958.
Nichols, Major Charles S., Jr., and Henry I. Shaw, Jr. *Okinawa: Victory in the Pacific*. 1955.
Zimmerman, Major John L. *The Guadalcanal Campaign*. 1949.

Navy. Boston, Little, Brown:

Morison, Samuel Eliot. *History of the United States Naval Operations in World War II*. Vol. III, *The Rising Sun in the Pacific*, 1948; Vol. IV, *Coral Sea, Midway and Submarine Actions*, 1949; Vol. V, *Struggle for Guadalcanal*, 1949; Vol. VI, *Breaking the Bismarcks Barrier*, 1950; Vol. VII, *Aleutians, Gilberts and Marshalls*, 1951; Vol. VIII, *New Guinea and the Marianas*, 1953; Vol. XII, *Leyte*, 1958; Vol. XIII, *The Liberation of the Philippines*, 1959; Vol. XVI, *Victory in the Pacific*, 1960.

D. Newspaper and Magazine Articles (listed in Notes)

E. Biographies, Diaries, Memoirs, Studies of History

Academy of Sciences of the U.S.S.R., Institute of History. *A Short History of the U.S.S.R.*, Part II. A. Samsonov, ed. Moscow: Progress Publishers, 1965.
Adams, Henry H. *1942: The Year That Doomed the Axis*. New York: McKay, 1967.
Agawa, Hiroyuki. *Isoroku Yamamoto*. Tokyo: Shincho Sha, 1966.
Alperovitz, Gar. *Atomic Diplomacy: Hiroshima and Potsdam*. New York: Simon & Schuster, 1965.
Arnold, H. H. *Global Mission*. New York: Harper, 1949.

Attiwell, Kenneth. *Fortress*. Garden City, N.Y.: Doubleday, 1960.

Attlee, Clement R. *As It Happened*. New York: Viking, 1954.

——, and Frances Williams. *Twilight of Empire: Memoirs of Prime Minister Clement Attlee*. New York: Barnes, 1962.

Baker, Richard Terrill. *Darkness of the Sun*. New York: Abingdon-Cokesbury, 1947.

Ba Maw. *Breakthrough in Burma*. New Haven: Yale University Press, 1968.

Barbey, Daniel E. *MacArthur's Amphibious Navy*. Annapolis, Md.: U.S. Naval Institute, 1969.

Beach, Edward L. *Submarine*. New York: Holt, 1952.

Beard, Charles A. *President Roosevelt and the Coming of the War*. New Haven: Yale University Press, 1948.

Belote, James H., and William M. *Corregidor: The Saga of a Fortress*. New York: Harper, 1967.

Benedict, Ruth. *The Chrysanthemum and the Sword*. Boston: Houghton Mifflin, 1946.

Bennett, Henry Gordon. *Why Singapore Fell*. Sydney: Angus & Robertson, 1944.

Birse, A. H. *Memoirs of an Interpreter*. London: Michael Joseph, 1967.

Bisson, T. A. *Japan in China*. New York: Macmillan, 1938.

Blum, John Morton. *From the Diaries of Henry Morgenthau, Jr.*, Vol. II, *Years of Urgency, 1938–1941;* Vol. III, *Years of War, 1941–1945*. Boston: Houghton Mifflin, 1965 and 1967.

Bodine, Major Roy L., Jr. *Jap POW Diary*. Unpublished.

Bosworth, Allan R. *America's Concentration Camps*. New York: Norton, 1967.

Brooks, Lester. *Behind Japan's Surrender*. New York: McGraw-Hill, 1968.

Browne, Cecil. *From Suez to Singapore*. New York: Random House, 1942.

Bryant, Arthur. *Triumph in the West*. New York: Doubleday, 1959.

——. *The Turn of the Tide* (the diaries of Lord Alanbrooke). New York: Doubleday, 1957.

Burtness, Paul S., and Warren Ober, eds. *The Puzzle of Pearl Harbor*. Evanston, Ill.: Row, Peterson, 1962.

Busch, Noel F. *The Emperor's Sword*. New York: Funk & Wagnalls, 1969.

Bush, Lewis. *Clutch of Circumstance*. Tokyo: Okuyama, 1956.

——. *Japanalia, A Concise Cyclopedia*. Tokyo: Tokyo News Service, 1965.

Butow, Robert J. C. *Japan's Decision to Surrender*. Stanford University Press, 1954.

——. *Tojo and the Coming of the War*. Princeton University Press, 1961.

Byas, Hugh. *Government by Assassination*. New York: Harper, 1958.

Byrnes, James F. *All in One Lifetime*. New York: Harper, 1958.

——. *Speaking Frankly*. New York: Harper, 1947.

Bywater, Hector C. *The Great Pacific War*. London: Constable, 1925.

Caidin, Martin. *A Torch to the Enemy*. New York: Ballantine, 1960.

Chamberlin, William Henry. *Japan over Asia*. Garden City, N.Y.: Blue Ribbon, 1942.

Chen Cheng. *Outline of the Course of Eight Years of Resistance*. Unpublished.

Chennault, Claire Lee. *Way of a Fighter*. New York: Putnam, 1949.

Chiang Kai-shek. *Soviet Russia in China*. New York: Farrar, Straus, 1958.

Chinnock, Frank W. *Nagasaki: The Forgotten Bomb*. New York: World, 1969.

Churchill, Winston S. *The Second World War,* Vol. III, *The Grand Alliance;* Vol. IV, *The Hinge of Fate;* Vol. V, *Closing the Ring;* Vol. VI, *Triumph and Tragedy*. Boston: Houghton Mifflin, 1950, 1951 and 1953.

Ciano, Count Galeazzo. *Ciano's Diaries, 1939–1943*. Hugh Gibson, editor. Introduction by Sumner Welles. New York: Doubleday, 1946.

Clarke, Hugh, and Takeo Yamashita. *To Sydney by Stealth*. London: Horwitz, 1966.

Cohen, Jerome B. *Japan's Economy in War and Reconstruction*. University of Minnesota Press, 1949.

Compton, Arthur Holly. *Atomic Quest*. New York: Oxford University Press, 1956.

Cordero, Colonel V. N. *My Experiences during the War with Japan*. Privately printed.

Craig, William. *The Fall of Japan*. New York: Dial, 1967.

Crowley, James B. *Japan's Quest for Autonomy*. Princeton University Press, 1966.

Davis, Burke. *Get Yamamoto*. New York: Random House, 1969.

——. *Marine!* Boston: Little, Brown, 1962.

Davis, Kenneth S. *Experience of War*. Garden City, N.Y.: Doubleday, 1965.

Deakin, F. W., and G. R. Storry. *The Case of Richard Sorge*. New York: Harper, 1966.

Deane, John R. *The Strange Alliance*. New York: Viking, 1947.

Dunn, Frederick S. *Peace-Making and the Settlement with Japan*. Princeton University Press, 1963.

Dyess, William. *The Dyess Story*. New York: Putnam, 1942.

Eden, Anthony. *The Memoirs of Anthony Eden, Vol. III, The Reckoning*. Boston: Houghton Mifflin, 1965.

Edmonds, Walter D. *They Fought with What They Had*. Boston: Little, Brown, 1951.

Eichelberger, Robert L. *Our Jungle Road to Tokyo*. New York: Viking, 1950.

Falk, Stanley L. *Bataan: The March of Death*. New York: Norton, 1962.

——. *Decision at Leyte*. New York: Norton, 1966.

Farago, Ladislas. *The Broken Seal*. New York: Random House, 1967.

——. *Burn after Reading*. New York: Walker, 1961.

Feis, Herbert. *Between War and Peace*. Princeton University Press, 1960.

——. *The China Tangle*. Princeton University Press, 1953.

——. *Contest over Japan*. New York: Norton, 1968.

——. *Japan Subdued*. Princeton University Press, 1961.

——. *The Road to Pearl Harbor*. Princeton University Press, 1950.

Feldt, Eric A. *The Coast Watchers*. New York: Oxford University Press, 1946.

Fitzgerald, C. P. *The Birth of Communist China*. Baltimore, Md.: Penguin, 1964.

Forrestal, E. P. *Admiral Raymond A. Spruance, USN: A Study in Command*. Washington: U.S. Government Printing Office, 1966.

Forrestal, James. *The Forrestal Diaries*. Walter Millis, ed. New York: Viking, 1951.

Friedlander, Saul. *Prelude to Downfall: Hitler and the United States, 1939–1941*. New York: Knopf, 1967.

Fuchida, Mitsuo, and Masatake Okumiya. *Midway, The Battle That Doomed Japan*. Annapolis, Md.: U.S. Naval Institute, 1955.

Garfield, Brian W. *The Thousand-Mile War: World War II in Alaska and the Aleutians*. Garden City, N.Y.: Doubleday, 1969.

Glines, Carroll V. *Doolittle's Tokyo Raiders*. New York: Van Nostrand, 1964.

Grew, Joseph C. *The Diary of Joseph C. Grew* and *The Papers of Joseph C. Grew*. Cambridge: Houghton Library, Harvard University.

———. *Ten Years in Japan*. New York: Simon & Schuster, 1944.

———. *Turbulent Era*. 2 vols. Boston: Houghton Mifflin, 1952.

Gunnison, Arch. *So Sorry, No Peace*. New York: Viking, 1944.

Halsey, William F., and J. Bryan III. *Admiral Halsey's Story*. New York: McGraw-Hill, 1947.

Hara, Tameichi, Fred Saito and Roger Pineau. *Japanese Destroyer Captain*. New York: Ballantine, 1961.

Hashimoto, Mochitsura. *Sunk*. New York: Holt, 1954.

Hattori, Takushiro. *The Complete History of the Greater East Asia War*. Tokyo: Hara Shobo, 1966.

Hearn, Lafcadio. *Japan: An Interpretation*. New York: Grosset & Dunlap, 1904.

Heinrichs, Waldo H., Jr. *American Ambassador: Joseph C. Grew and the Development of the U.S. Diplomatic Tradition*. Boston: Little, Brown, 1966.

Hersey, John. *Hiroshima*. New York: Knopf, 1946.

Hewlett, Richard G., and Oscar E. Anderson, Jr. *The New World*. University Park, Pa.: The Pennsylvania State University Press, 1962.

Higashikuni, Prince Toshihiko. *The War Diary of a Member of the Royal Family*. Tokyo: Nihon Shuho Sha, 1957.

Holmes, W. J. *Undersea Victory*. Garden City, N.Y.: Doubleday, 1966.

Homma, Masaharu. *The Diary of Masaharu Homma.* Unpublished.

Horie, Yoshitaka. *End of the Ogasawara Army Corps.* Compiled by Major Horie for the Association of Veterans of the Ogasawara Corps. Tokyo: Hara Shobo, 1969.

———. *Fighting Spirit—Iwo Jima.* Tokyo: Kobun Sha, 1965.

Hosokawa, Morisada. *Information Never Reached the Emperor.* 2 vols. Tokyo: Dokosha Isobe Shobo, 1953.

Hsu Kai-yu. *Chou En-lai.* Garden City, N.Y.: Doubleday, 1968.

Huie, William Bradford. *The Hero of Iwo Jima.* New York: New American Library, 1962.

———. *The Hiroshima Pilot.* New York: Putnam, 1964.

Hull, Cordell. *The Memoirs of Cordell Hull.* 2 vols. New York: Macmillan, 1948.

Hunt, Frazier. *MacArthur and the War against Japan.* New York: Scribner, 1944.

Ike, Nobutaka. *Japan's Decision for War: Liaison and Imperial Conference Records, March–December, 1941.* Stanford University Press, 1967.

Ind, Allison. *Allied Intelligence Bureau.* New York: McKay, 1958.

Inoguchi, Rikihei, Tadashi Nakajima and Roger Pineau. *The Divine Wind.* Annapolis, Md.: U.S. Naval Institute, 1958.

Iriye, Akira. *Across the Pacific.* New York: Harcourt, 1967.

———. *After Imperialism.* Cambridge: Harvard University Press, 1965.

Ismay, Hastings Lionel. *The Memoirs of General Lord Ismay.* New York: Viking, 1960.

Ito, Masanori. *The End of the Imperial Japanese Navy.* New York: Norton, 1962.

Ito, Masashi. *The Emperor's Last Soldiers.* New York: Coward-McCann, 1967.

James, David H. *The Rise and Fall of the Japanese Empire.* London: Allen & Unwin, 1951.

Johnston, Stanley. *Queen of the Flat-Tops.* New York: Dutton, 1942.

Jones, E. Stanley. *A Song of Ascents.* Nashville, Tenn.: Abingdon Press, 1968.

Joya, Mock. *Things Japanese.* Tokyo: Tokyo News Service, 1958.

Jucker-Fleetwood, Erin E., ed. *The Per Jacobsson Mediations.* Basle: Basle Centre for Economic and Financial Research.

Kahn, David. *The Code-Breakers*. New York: Macmillan, 1967.

Kahn, E. J., Jr. *The Stragglers*. New York: Random House, 1962.

Kamiko, Kiyoshi. *I Didn't Die on Leyte*. Tokyo: Shuppan Kyodo Sha, 1966.

Karig, Walter, and others. *Battle Report,* Vol. I, *Pearl Harbor to Coral Sea;* Vol. IV, *The End of an Empire*. New York: Rinehart, 1944 and 1948.

Kase, Toshikazu. *Journey to the Missouri*. New Haven: Yale University Press, 1950.

Kato, Masuo. *The Lost War*. New York: Knopf, 1946.

Kennan, George F. *Memoirs, 1925–1950*. Boston: Little, Brown, 1967.

Kenney, George C. *General Kenney Reports*. New York: Duell, Sloan & Pearce, 1949.

Kido, Koichi. *Diary of Koichi Kido*. 2 vols. Tokyo: Tokyo University Press, 1966.

——. *The Relevant Documents of Koichi Kido*. Compiled by the Society for the Study of the Kido Diary. Tokyo: Tokyo University Press, 1966.

King, Ernest J., and Walter Muir Whitehill. *Fleet Admiral King*. London: Eyre & Spottiswoode, 1953.

Kiyosawa, Kiyoshi, and others. *Diaries in Darkness*. Tokyo: Shuei Sha, 1966.

Knebel, Fletcher, and Charles W. Bailey II. *No High Ground*. New York: Harper, 1960.

Kodama, Yoshio. *I Was Defeated*. Japan: Radiopress, 1959.

Kolko, Gabriel. *The Politics of War*. New York: Random House, 1968.

Konoye, Fumimaro. *The Konoye Diary*. Compiled by Kyodo Press. Tokyo: Kyodo Press, 1968.

——. *My Efforts towards Peace*. Tokyo: Nippon Dempo Tsushinsha, 1946.

Koyanagi, Tomiji. *The Kurita Fleet*. Tokyo: Ushio Shobo, 1956.

Kurzman, Dan. *Kishi and Japan*. New York: Obolensky, 1960.

Kusaka, Ryunosuke. *The Combined Fleet: Memoirs of Former Chief of Staff Kusaka*. Tokyo: Mainichi Shimbun, 1952.

Lamont, Lansing. *Day of Trinity*. New York: Atheneum, 1965.

Langer, William L., and S. Everett Gleason. *The Undeclared War*. New York: Harper, 1953.

Laurence, William L. *Dawn over Zero*. New York: Knopf, 1946.

Leahy, William D. *I Was There*. New York: Whittlesey, 1950.

Leckie, Robert. *Challenge for the Pacific*. Garden City, N.Y.: Doubleday, 1965.

LeMay, Curtis E., with MacKinlay Kantor. *Mission with LeMay: My Story*. Garden City, N.Y.: Doubleday, 1965.

Lifton, Robert Jay. *Death in Life: Survivors of Hiroshima*. New York: Random House, 1968.

Lockwood, Charles A., and Hans Christian Adamson. *Battles of the Philippine Sea*. New York: Crowell, 1967.

Lord, Walter. *Day of Infamy*. New York: Holt, 1957.

——. *Incredible Victory*. New York: Harper, 1967.

Lu, David J. *From the Marco Polo Bridge to Pearl Harbor*. Washington: Public Affairs Press, 1961.

MacArthur, Douglas. *Reminiscences*. New York: McGraw-Hill, 1964.

Mallaby, George. *From My Level*. New York: Atheneum, 1965.

Marquand, John P. *Thirty Years*. Boston: Little, Brown, 1945.

Mashbir, Sidney Forrester. *I Was an American Spy*. New York: Vantage, 1953.

Matthews, Allen R. *The Assault*. New York: Simon & Schuster, 1947.

Miller, Thomas G., Jr. *The Cactus Air Force*. New York: Harper, 1969.

Mishima, Sumie. *The Broader Way*. New York: John Day, 1953.

Moorad, George. *Lost Peace in China*. New York: Dutton, 1949.

Moore, Frederick. *With Japan's Leaders*. New York: Scribner, 1942.

Moran, Lord (Sir Charles Wilson). *Churchill: Taken from the Diaries of Lord Moran*. Boston: Houghton Mifflin, 1966.

Myers, Hugh H. *Prisoner of War, World War II*. Metropolitan Press.

Naeve, Virginia, ed. *Friends of the Hibakusha*. Denver, Colo.: Swallow, 1964.

Nakasone, Seizen. *Tragedy of Okinawa*. Tokyo: Kacho Shobo, 1951.

Neumann, William L. *America Encounters Japan: From Perry to MacArthur*. Baltimore: The Johns Hopkins Press, 1963.

Newcomb, Richard F. *Abandon Ship!* New York: Holt, 1958.

——. *Iwo Jima*. New York: Holt, 1965.

——. *Savo*. New York: Rinehart, 1961.

Nishino, Gen. *Isle of Death: Guadalcanal*. Tokyo: Masu Shobo, 1956.

Nomura, Jiro. *Sea of Lamentation*. Tokyo: Yomiuri Shimbun, 1967.

Ogata, Sadako N. *Defiance in Manchuria*. Berkeley: University of California Press, 1964.

Okumiya, Masatake, and Jiro Horikoshi, with Martin Caidin. *Zero*. New York: Dutton, 1956.

Okuyama, Ryoko. *Left Alive on Saipan, the Island of Suicide*. Tokyo: Hara Shobo, 1967.

Omura, Bunji. *The Last Genro*. Philadelphia: Lippincott, 1938.

Pacific War Research Society. *Japan's Longest Day*. Tokyo and Palo Alto, Calif.: Kodansha International, 1968.

Peffer, Nathaniel. *The Far East*. Ann Arbor: University of Michigan Press, 1958.

Pogue, Forrest C. *George C. Marshall: Ordeal and Hope*. New York: Viking, 1966.

Potter, E. B., and Chester W. Nimitz, eds. *The Great Sea War*. Englewood Cliffs, N.J.: Prentice-Hall, 1960.

Prange, Gordon. *Tora, Tora, Tora*. Tokyo: *Reader's Digest* of Japan, 1966.

Rappaport, Armin. *Henry L. Stimson and Japan, 1931–1933*. University of Chicago Press, 1963.

Reischauer, Edwin O. *Japan Past and Present*. Rev. ed. New York: Knopf, 1964.

Romulo, Carlos. *I Saw the Fall of the Philippines*. New York: Doubleday, Doran, 1943.

Roosevelt, Eleanor. *This I Remember*. New York: Harper, 1949.

Roosevelt, Elliott. *As He Saw It*. New York: Duell, Sloan & Pearce, 1946.

Roosevelt, Franklin D. *Papers*. Franklin D. Roosevelt Library, Hyde Park, N.Y.

Saito, Dr. Yoshie. *Deceived History: An Inside Account of Matsuoka and the Tripartite Pact*. Tokyo: Yomiuri Shimbun, 1955.

Sakai, Saburo, with Martin Caidin and Fred Saito. *Samurai!* New York: Dutton, 1957.

Sakomizu, Hisatsune. *The Prime Minister's Official Residence under Machine-Gun Fire*. Tokyo: Kobun Sha, 1965.

Sansom, G.B. *The Western World and Japan*. New York: Knopf, 1951.

Sato, Kenryo. *The Greater East Asia War Memoirs*. Tokyo: Tokuma Shoten, 1966.

Sato, Naotake. *My Eighty Years Reminiscences*. Tokyo: Jiji Press, 1964.

Schroeder, Paul W. *The Axis Alliance and Japanese-American Relations, 1941*. Ithaca: Cornell University Press, 1958.

Seward, Jack. *Hara-kiri*. Rutland, Vt., and Tokyo: Tuttle, 1968.

Sherman, Frederick C. *Combat Command*. New York: Dutton, 1950.

Sherrod, Robert. *Tarawa*. New York: Duell, Sloan & Pearce, 1944.

Sherwood, Robert E. *Roosevelt and Hopkins*. New York: Harper, 1948.

Shigemitsu, Mamoru. *Japan and Her Destiny*. New York: Dutton, 1958.

Shimomura, Kainan. *Notes on the Termination of the War*. Tokyo: Kamakura Bunko, 1948.

Shirer, William L. *The Rise and Fall of the Third Reich*. New York: Simon & Schuster, 1960.

Slim, William J. *Defeat into Victory*. New York: McKay, 1961.

Smith, S. E., compiler & ed. *The United States Marine Corps in World War II*. New York: Random House, 1969.

——, compiler & ed. *The United States Navy in World War II*. New York: Morrow, 1966.

Snell, John L., ed. *The Meaning of Yalta*. Baton Rouge: Louisiana State University Press, 1956.

Snow, Edgar. *Red Star over China*. New York: Random House, 1938.

Stafford, Edward P. *The Big E*. New York: Random House, 1962.

Stimson, Henry L. *The Diary of Henry L. Stimson* and *The Papers of Henry L. Stimson*. New Haven: Yale University Library.

——, and McGeorge Bundy. *On Active Service in Peace and War*. New York: Harper, 1947.

Storry, Richard. *The Double Patriots*. Boston: Houghton Mifflin, 1957.

Sugano, Shizuko. *The End at Saipan*. Tokyo: Shuppan Kyodo Sha, 1959.

Sugiyama, Gen. *Notes of Field Marshal Sugiyama*. Compiled by the Army General Staff. Tokyo: Hara Shobo, 1967.

The Biography of Kantaro Suzuki. Compilation Committee for the Biography of Kantaro Suzuki. Tokyo: Privately printed, 1960.

Suzuki, Takeshi. *Sun over the Raging Seas*. Compilation Committee of Confidential Documents concerning Prime Minister Suzuki. Tokyo: Privately printed, 1960.

Takagi, Sokichi. *History of Naval Battles in the Pacific*. Tokyo: Iwanami Shoten, 1949.

———. *Memoir of the Termination of the War*. Tokyo: Kobundo, 1948.

Takahashi, H. *A History of the Minami Organization*. Unpublished.

Takahashi, Masaye. *The 2/26 Incident*. Tokyo: Chuo Koron Sha, 1965.

Takami, Jun. *Diary of Jun Takami*. Tokyo: Keiso Shobo, 1964.

Takeshita, Masahiko. Diary of Lieutenant Colonel Masahiko Takeshita. Unpublished.

Taleja, Thaddeus. *Climax at Midway*. New York: Norton, 1960.

Tanemura, Sako. *Secret Diary of Imperial Headquarters*. Tokyo: Diamond Sha, 1952.

Tansill, Charles Callan. *Back Door to War*. Chicago: Regnery, 1952.

Tarling, Nicholas. *Southeast Asia, Past and Present*. Melbourne: Cheshire, 1966.

Taylor, Theodore. *The Magnificent Mitscher*. New York: Norton, 1960.

Terasaki, Gwen. *Bridge to the Sun*. Chapel Hill: University of North Carolina Press, 1957.

Terasaki, Ryuji. *Navy Spirit: Life of Commander Jisaburo Ozawa*. Tokyo: Tokuma Shoten, 1967.

Togo, Shigenori. *The Cause of Japan*. New York: Simon & Schuster, 1956.

Toland, John. *But Not in Shame*. New York: Random House, 1961.

———. *The Flying Tigers*. New York: Random House, 1963.

──. *The Last 100 Days*. New York: Random House, 1966.

Tolischus, Otto D. *Tokyo Record*. New York: Reynal & Hitchcock, 1943.

Tomioka, Sadatoshi. *The Outbreak and Termination of the War*. Tokyo: Mainichi Shimbun, 1968.

Trefousse, Hans Louis. *What Happened at Pearl Harbor?* New York: Twayne, 1958.

Tregaskis, Richard. *Guadalcanal Diary*. New York: Random House, 1943.

Truman, Harry S. *Memoirs*, Vol. I, *Year of Decisions*. Garden City, N.Y.: Doubleday, 1955.

Tsuji, Masanobu. *Guadalcanal*. Tamba-shi, Nara: Yotoku Sha, 1950.

──. *Singapore: The Japanese Version*. New York: St. Martin's, 1960.

Ueda, Toshio, ed. *Treatise on the Termination of the Pacific War*. Compiled by Japan Diplomatic Association. Tokyo: Tokyo University Press, 1958.

Ugaki, Matome. *Record of Sea Battles: Diary of the Late Vice Admiral Matome Ugaki*. 2 vols. Compiled by Rear Admirals Kanji Ogawa and Toshiyuki Yokoi. Tokyo: Nippon Shuppan Kyodo, 1952–1953.

Ulam, Adam B. *Expansion and Coexistence*. New York: Praeger, 1968.

United States Marine Corps Combat Correspondents. *Semper fidelis: The U.S. Marines in the Pacific, 1942–1945*. Edited and arranged by Patrick O'Sheel and Gene Cook. New York: Sloane, 1947.

Uno, Kazumaro. *Corregidor: Isle of Delusion*. Privately printed.

Vandegrift, A. A. *Once a Marine: The Memoirs of General A. A. Vandegrift*. As told to Robert A. Asprey. New York: Norton, 1964.

Van Slyke, Lyman P., ed. *The Chinese Communist Movement: A Report of the United States War Department, July 1945*. Stanford University Press, 1968.

Wainwright, Jonathan. *General Wainwright's Story*. Garden City, N.Y.: Doubleday, 1946.

Weller, George A. *Singapore Is Silent*. New York: Harcourt, 1943.

Werth, Alexander. *Russia at War, 1941–1945*. New York: Dutton, 1964.

White, Theodore H., and Annalee Jacoby. *Thunder out of China*. New York: Sloane, 1946.

White, W. L. *They Were Expendable*. Boston: Little, Brown, 1942.

Whitney, Courtney. *MacArthur: His Rendezvous with History*. New York: Knopf, 1956.

Willoughby, Charles A. *Shanghai Conspiracy*. New York: Dutton, 1952.

Wohlstetter, Roberta. *Pearl Harbor: Warning and Decision*. Stanford University Press, 1962.

Yabe, Teiji. *Fumimaro Konoye*. 2 vols. Compilation-Publication Society of the Biography of Fumimaro Konoye. Tokyo: Privately printed, 1951–1952.

Yamamoto, Kumaichi. *Memoirs of the Greater East Asia War*. Manuscripts left by the late Kumaichi Yamamoto. Japan: Privately printed, 1964.

Yamamoto, Tomomi. *Four Years in Hell*. Japan: Asian Publications, 1952.

Yanaga, Chitoshi. *Japanese People and Politics*. New York: Wiley, 1956.

Yokota, Yutaka, with Joseph D. Harrington. *The Kaiten Weapon*. New York: Ballantine, 1962.

Yoshida, Shigeru. *The Yoshida Memoirs*. Boston: Houghton Mifflin, 1962.

Young, Arthur N. *China and the Helping Hand 1937–1945*. Cambridge: Harvard University Press, 1963.

Notes

The main sources for each chapter are listed below with explanatory details. The books which proved of overall value, and which will not be referred to again, are: *Record of Sea Battles: Diary of the Late Vice Admiral Matome Ugaki,* compiled by Rear Admirals Kanji Ogawa and Toshiyuki Yokoi; *Outbreak and Termination of the War,* by Sadatoshi Tomioka; *Japan and Her Destiny,* by Mamoru Shigemitsu; *Roosevelt and Hopkins,* by Robert E. Sherwood; *A Collection of War Memoirs and Notes,* compiled by the Japanese Foreign Ministry; *The Combined Fleet: Memoirs of Former Chief of Staff Kusaka,* by Admiral Ryunosuke Kusaka; *Secret Diary of Imperial Headquarters,* by Colonel Sako Tanemura; *The Complete History of the Greater Asia War,* by Colonel Takushiro Hattori; *Greater East Asia War Memoirs,* by General Kenryo Sato; *Japanalia: A Concise Cyclopedia,* by Lewis Bush; *Things Japanese,* by Mock Joya; *The Sugiyama Notes,* compiled by the Army General Staff; and *The Diary of Koichi Kido.* The last book is the unexpurgated edition of the diary and runs from January 1, 1930, through December 15, 1945; it was published in 1966 along with *Relevant Documents of Koichi Kido.* An English translation of the diary is being prepared by

Robert J. C. Butow and will be invaluable to historians and students of the Pacific war. The version of *The Kido Diary* used at the International Military Tribunal for the Far East (hereafter referred to as IMTFE) was not only incomplete but inaccurately translated.

1 Gekokujo

The events leading up to the 2/26 Incident are based on interviews with Naoki Hoshino, Yoshio Kodama, Generals Teiichi Suzuki, Kenryo Sato, Sadao Araki and Akio Doi, and the following books: *Defiance in Manchuria,* by Sadako N. Ogata; *After Imperialism* and *Across the Pacific,* by Akira Iriye; *From the Marco Polo Bridge to Pearl Harbor,* by David J. Lu; *Japan in China,* by T. A. Bisson; *I Was Defeated,* by Yoshio Kodama; *Government by Assassination,* by Hugh Byas; *Japan over Asia,* by William Henry Chamberlin; and *The Double Patriots,* by Richard Storry.

The 2/26 Incident: interviews with Hisatsune Sakomizu, Marquis Koichi Kido, Generals Tadashi Katakura,* Sadao Araki, Kenryo Sato and Shozaburo Sato; correspondence with William Henry Chamberlin; "Witness to the 2/26 Assassination," by Y. Arima in the *Weekly Shincho* magazine; *The Prime Minister's Official Residence under Machine-Gun Fire,* by Hisatsune Sakomizu; *The Biography of Kantaro Suzuki;* BYAS; STORRY; CHAMBERLIN; *The Last Genro,* by Bunji Omura; *The 2/26 Incident,* by Masaye Takahashi; and a secret report, "An Account of Major Katakura's Accident in the 2/26 Incident," by General Tadashi Katakura.

Information on the Emperor comes from interviews with his youngest brother (Prince Mikasa); Marquis Kido; Junji Togashi; Chamberlains Sukemasa Irie, Yoshihiro Tokugawa and Yasuhide Toda; and Osanaga Kanroji, one of His Majesty's instructors and currently High Priest of the Meiji Shrine.

Material on Sorge is based on an interview with Tomohiko Ushiba; *Shanghai Conspiracy,* by Charles A. Willoughby; and *The Case of Richard Sorge,* by F. W. Deakin and G. R. Storry.

* Throughout the Notes, the highest military rank attained will be given; Major Katakura, for example, became a general. Enlisted ranks are omitted.

2 To the Marco Polo Bridge

Interviews with Arashi Kamimura, Yukio Nakamura, Generals Sadao Araki, Akio Doi, Kenryo Sato, Teiichi Suzuki, Ho Ying-chin and Takeo Imai; articles in the April 15, 1952, issue of *The Reporter* by Charles Wertenbaker and in the May 1963 issue of the *Journal of Asian Studies* by James B. Crowley; IMTFE, *Dissenting Judgement* (Justice R. A. Pal); OGATA; *Red Star over China,* by Edgar Snow; CHAMBERLIN; *Soviet Russia in China,* by Chiang Kai-shek; *The Birth of Communist China,* by C. P. Fitzgerald; *Chou En-lai,* by Hsu Kai-yu; *The Chinese Communist Movement: A Report of the U. S. War Department, July 1945,* edited by Lyman P. Van Slyke; KODAMA; *Lost Peace in China,* by George Moorad; BISSON; *Japan's Quest for Autonomy,* by James B. Crowley; and *A Short History of the U.S.S.R.,* Part II, compiled by the Academy of Sciences of the U.S.S.R., Institute of History.

Eight books were used throughout Chapters 2 to 7: *With Japan's Leaders,* by Frederick Moore; *American Ambassador,* by Waldo H. Heinrichs, Jr.; *The Road to Pearl Harbor,* by Herbert Feis; LU; *Turbulent Era* and *Ten Years in Japan,* by Joseph C. Grew; and *Tojo and the Coming of the War,* by Robert J. C. Butow, an accurate and objective study of the events leading to Pearl Harbor based primarily on Japanese sources.

Both Chinese Communist and Kuomintang sources put the date of the signing of the Communist-Kuomintang agreement at July 15, 1937, but the Central Chinese Communist Party of Inner Mongolia announced several years ago that the original document had been found in Mongolia and was dated July 5.

3 "Then the War Will Be a Desperate One"

Early relations between Japan and the United States: cited material; and *America Encounters Japan: From Perry to MacArthur,* by William L. Neumann.

Differences between East and West: unpublished articles by Dr. Kazutaka Watanabe.

Matsuoka: interviews with Kenichiro Matsuoka, Kiwamu Ogiwara, Toshikazu Kase, Shunzo Kobayashi and General Yatsuji

Nagai; *Yosuke Matsuoka,* by T. Furukaki; *Deceived History: An Inside Account of Matsuoka and the Tripartite Pact,* by Dr. Yoshie Saito.

Iwakuro mission: interviews with Major General Hideo Iwakuro; "Fight for Peace," by General Iwakuro, in the August 1966 issue of *Bungei-Shunju;* "Taking Part in the Japan–U. S. Negotiations," a pamphlet by General Iwakuro; and *The Broken Seal,* by Ladislas Farago.

Negotiations between Japan and the United States (which extend to Chapters 4, 5 and 7): interviews with Eugene Dooman; Generals Hiroshi Oshima, Kenryo Sato and Teiichi Suzuki; Michitaka Konoye; Tomohiko Ushiba; Zenjun Hirose; Colonel Susumu Nishiura; Naoki Hoshino; and Marquis Kido; "Germany and Pearl Harbor," by Hans Louis Trefousse, in the *Far Eastern Quarterly; Fumimaro Konoye,* by Teiji Yabe; the Konoye Family Book (privately printed); *My Efforts Towards Peace,* by Fumimaro Konoye; *Memoirs of the Greater East Asia War,* by Kumaichi Yamamoto; *The War Diary of a Member of the Royal Family,* by Prince Higashikuni; *The Axis Alliance and Japanese-American Relations, 1941,* by Paul W. Schroeder; *The Diary of Joseph C. Grew* and the Grew Papers (courtesy of the Houghton Library, Harvard University); *The Diary of Henry L. Stimson* and the Stimson Papers (courtesy of the Yale University Library); *Peace and War: United States Foreign Policy 1931–1941,* compiled by U. S. Department of State; *The Undeclared War,* by William L. Langer and S. Everett Gleason; *Foreign Relations of the United States* (hereafter referred to as FRUS) *1940,* Vol. IV, *The Far East;* FRUS, *1941,* Vol. IV, *The Far East;* FRUS, *Japan 1931–1941,* Vols. I and II; *The Memoirs of Cordell Hull,* Vol. II; *On Active Service in Peace and War,* by Henry L. Stimson and McGeorge Bundy; *The Cause of Japan,* by Shigenori Togo; *President Roosevelt and the Coming of War,* by Charles A. Beard; *Back Door to War,* by Charles Callan Tansill; NEUMANN; *From the Diaries of Henry Morgenthau, Jr.,* Vol. II, *Years of Urgency 1938–1941,* by John Morton Blum; *Japanese People and Politics,* by Chitoshi Yanaga; *Prelude to Downfall: Hitler and the United States 1939–1941,* by Saul Friedlander; and IMTFE . . . JUSTICE R. A. PAL.

The dialogue in the liaison and imperial conferences was re-

constructed from recollections of those attending and on detailed
official notes found in the War History Office Archives of the Japan
Defense Agency by a group of scholars headed by Dr. Jun Tsunoda
of the National Diet Library. These notes were published as a
supplementary volume to the *Asahi Shimbun*'s seven-volume work
The Road to the Pacific War. The records of sixty-two of these
conferences, held between March and December in 1941, were
translated into English by Nobutaka Ike, professor of political
science at Stanford University, and published under the title *Japan's
Decision for War*.

4 "Go Back to Blank Paper"

See Notes for Chapter 3. Material also based on interviews
with Eugene Dooman; Tomohiko Ushiba; Okinori Kaya; Ad-
miral Kichisaburo Nomura; Marquis Kido; Naoki Hoshino; Gen-
erals Hideo Iwakuro, Kenryo Sato and Teiichi Suzuki; Shigeharu
Matsumoto; Yoshio Kodama; Mrs. Hideki Tojo; and Prince
Konoye's mistress; the Papers of President Roosevelt, at the
Franklin D. Roosevelt Library, Hyde Park; "The Hull-Nomura
Conversations: A Fundamental Misconception," by Robert J. C.
Butow, in the *American Historical Review* (July 1960); KODAMA;
Kishi and Japan, by Dan Kurzman; and *Tokyo Record,* by Otto
D. Tolischus.

The cable from Ambassador Grew to Secretary of State Hull
on September 29, 1941, is a paraphrase by the State Department
of the original text.

5 The Fatal Note

See Notes for Chapter 3. There were also interviews with
Marquis Kido; Tomohiko Ushiba; Naoki Hoshino; Okinori Kaya;
Mrs. Saburo Kurusu; Admiral Kichisaburo Nomura; Generals
Kenryo Sato, Hiroshi Oshima and Teiichi Suzuki; and Ambas-
sador Haruhiko Nishi, who brought to my attention the errors made
in the American translations of Japanese diplomatic messages.
The footnote on page 180 is based on "How Stimson Meant to
'Maneuver' the Japanese," by Richard N. Current, in the *Missis-
sippi Historical Review* (June 1953).

6 Operation Z

Interviews with Admirals Ryunosuke Kusaka, Shigeru Fukudome and Sadatoshi Tomioka; Captains Naohiro Sata, Yasuji Watanabe, Tsunezo Wachi, Kazunari Miyo, Atsushi Oi and Eijiro Suzuki; Commanders Heijiro Abe, Yoshio Shiga and Suguru Suzuki; Lieutenant Juzo Mori; Ensign Takeo Yoshikawa; Mitsuharu Noda, Heijiro Omi, Yoshio Kodama, Sayao Otsuka; Mrs. Chiyo Iwamiya; Generals Kenryo Sato, Minoru Genda; and Admiral Sadamu Sanagi; Colonels Kumao Imoto and Takushiro Hattori; Lieutenant Colonel Shigeharu Asaeda; letter from Carl S. Sipple to Walter Lord (February 28, 1957); "The Combined Fleet and My Memoirs of the Navy," a magazine article by Heijiro Omi; "The Inside Story of the Pearl Harbor Plan," by Robert E. Ward, in *U. S. Naval Institute Proceedings*—hereafter referred to as USNIP (December 1951); "Combined Fleet Secret Operations Order No. 1"; *Tora, Tora, Tora,* by Gordon Prange (published in Japan in 1966); *The Great Pacific War,* by Hector C. Bywater; *Isoroku Yamamoto,* by Hiroyuki Agawa; *Get Yamamoto,* by Burke Davis; *Day of Infamy,* by Walter Lord; *The End of the Imperial Japanese Navy,* by Masanori Ito; *The Emperor's Sword,* by Noel F. Busch; FARAGO; *Singapore: The Japanese Version,* by Masanobu Tsuji; *History of United States Naval Operations in World War II,* Vol. III, *The Rising Sun in the Pacific,* by Samuel Eliot Morison; *The Fall of the Philippines,* by Louis Morton; DEAKIN & STORRY; and WILLOUGHBY.

7 "This War May Come Quicker Than Anyone Dreams"

See Notes for Chapter 3. There were also interviews with Admirals Ryunosuke Kusaka, Keizo Komura, Kazutoshi Kuhara, Sadatoshi Tomioka, Kichisaburo Nomura, Gunichi Mikawa and Harold Stark; Captains Yasuji Watanabe, Naohiro Sata and Kazunari Miyo; Commanders Yoshio Shiga, Hirata Matsumura, Saguru Suzuki, Heijiro Abe; Lieutenant Juzo Mori; Ensign Takeo Yoshikawa; Heijiro Omi, Mitsuharu Noda; Generals Minoru Genda, Kenryo Sato, Teiichi Suzuki and Hiroshi Oshima; Colonel Kumao Imoto; Lieutenant Colonel Shigeharu Asaeda; Frank

Trammell; George Elliott, Jr.; Ambassador Haruhiko Nishi; Ikuko Kimura; Fumihiko Togo; Mrs. Saburo Kurusu; the late Bernard Baruch; Mrs. Yoshiko Kugiya; Marquis Kido; Naoki Hoshino; Okinori Kaya; United States Strategic Bombing Survey (hereafter referred to as USSBS) Navy interrogation #29 (Captain M. Fuchida); "Political Survey Prior to Outbreak of War," a report by Admiral Sadatoshi Tomioka; IMTFE documents #1079 (Kazuji Kameyama) and #2597 (Tateki Shirao); an interview with Vice Admiral Frank E. Beatty in the *National Review* (December 13, 1966); *The Lost War,* by Masuo Kato; *A Song of Ascents,* by E. Stanley Jones; PRANGE; *Bridge to the Sun,* by Gwen Terasaki; FARAGO; LORD; TOLISCHUS; ITO; *The War against Japan,* Vol. I, by Major-General S. Woodburn Kirby; *Grand Strategy,* Vol. III, Part I, by J. M. A. Gwyer and J. R. M. Butler; *Chief of Staff Prewar Plans and Preparations,* by Mark S. Watson; MORTON; MORISON, *The Rising Sun; What Happened at Pearl Harbor?,* by Hans Louis Trefousse; *Pearl Harbor: Warning and Decision,* by Roberta Wohlstetter; TSUJI; *Sunk,* by Mochitsura Hashimoto; *The Puzzle of Pearl Harbor,* by Paul S. Burtness and Warren U. Ober; and *But Not in Shame,* by John Toland. The last book was also used throughout Chapters 8 to 13.

The rare conversation between Grand Chamberlain Fujita and the Emperor appears in *Sun over the Raging Seas,* the Suzuki Family Book, which was privately printed in 1969. Chamberlain Fujita revealed this information because he felt he would soon die and wanted it recorded for posterity.

8 "I Shall Never Look Back"

Interviews with Admirals Chester Nimitz, C. C. Bloch, Ernest Holtzworth, W. W. Smith, Harold Stark, Kichisaburo Nomura, Keizo Komura, Gunichi Mikawa, Ryunosuke Kusaka and Sadatoshi Tomioka; Captains Yasuji Watanabe, Eijiro Suzuki, Kazunari Miyo and Naohiro Sata; Commanders Heijiro Abe, Hirata Matsumura and Yoshio Shiga; Lieutenant Juzo Mori; Ensigns Takeo Yoshikawa and Kazuo Sakamaki; Generals Minoru Genda, Joseph H. Moore and Richard Carmichael; Colonels Susumu Nishiura, Takushiro Hattori, William Morse and William Welch; Lieutenant Colonel Shigeharu Asaeda; and Major Durward Brooks;

Lieutenant Robert Overstreet; Heijiro Omi; Mitsuharu Noda; Jesse Gaines; C. O. Lines; Donald Briggs; Dwaine Davis; Baron Ian Mutsu; Marquis Kido; Robert Trumbull; Okinori Kaya; Morio Tateno; Yates McDaniel. Also USSBS Navy interrogations #6 and #29 (Captain M. Fuchida); memorandum by Ferdinand Mayor on his conversation with Kurusu on December 7, 1941; "Records of the Meeting of the Inquiry Committee of the Privy Council, December 8, 1941"; article on Pearl Harbor by Robert Trumbull in the *New York Times Magazine* (December 4, 1966); PRANGE; LORD; KATO; TSUJI; *Way of a Fighter,* by Claire Lee Chennault; *The Flying Tigers,* by John Toland; *The Second World War,* Vol. III, *The Grand Alliance,* by Winston Churchill; MORI-SON, *The Rising Sun;* WOHLSTETTER; TREFOUSSE; *Ciano's Diaries;* MORTON; *This I Remember,* by Eleanor Roosevelt; *As He Saw It,* by Elliott Roosevelt; *They Fought with What They Had,* by Walter D. Edmonds; and BURTNESS & OBER.

9   "The Formidable Years That Lie Before Us"

Interviews with President Sergio Osmeña; Generals Hiroshi Oshima, James Devereux and Carlos Romulo; Admirals Chester Nimitz and Ryunosuke Kusaka; Captains Tsunezo Wachi and Masamichi Fujita; Commanders Katsusaku Takahashi and Choichi Koyama; Lieutenants Haruki Iki and Sadao Takai; and Carl Mydans; "Japanese Victory: The Sinking of Force Z," by David Mason, in *History of the Second World War* magazine, Vol. II, No. 13; IMTFE document #4002 (General Oshima); *The Turn of the Tide,* by Arthur Bryant; *From Suez to Singapore,* by Cecil Browne; GWYER & BUTLER; KIRBY; *Samurai,* by Saburo Sakai; *The Memoirs of Anthony Eden,* Vol. III, *The Reckoning; The Rise and Fall of the Third Reich,* by William L. Shirer; CHURCHILL; *Churchill: Taken from the Diaries of Lord Moran; Strategic Planning for Coalition Warfare: 1941–1942,* by Maurice Matloff and Edwin M. Snell; and *So Sorry, No Peace,* by Arch Gunnison.

10   "For a Wasted Hope and Sure Defeat"

Interviews with Carl Mydans; Generals Akira Nara, Takeo Imai and Ichiji Sugita; Colonels Kumao Imoto and Susumu

Nishiura; Antonio Aquino, President Sergio Osmeña; Lieutenant Colonel Shigeharu Asaeda; Admirals Sadatoshi Tomioka and T. H. Binford; Captains Ko Nagasawa and Kazunari Miyo; Commander Shukichi Toshikawa; correspondence with Admiral C. E. L. Helfrich; "Operations of Malaya Campaign, from 8th December, 1941, to 15th February, 1942," official report by Lieutenant-General A. E. Percival; "Japanese Victory: The Conquest of Malaya," by Arthur Swinson, in *History of the Second World War* magazine, Vol. VI, No. 11; "Malayan Campaign," a report by Shigeharu Asaeda; "Statement on the Malayan Campaign," by General Tomoyuki Yamashita at his trial in Manila; *Battle Report: Pearl Harbor to Coral Sea*, by Walter Karig, and others; *The Rise and Fall of the Japanese Empire*, by David H. James; *Fortress*, by Kenneth Attiwell; *Singapore Is Silent*, by George Weller; CHURCHILL, Vol. IV, *The Hinge of Fate; Why Singapore Fell*, by H. G. Bennett; TSUJI; KIRBY; *The Japanese Thrust*, by Lionel Wigmore; *George C. Marshall: Ordeal and Hope*, by Forrest C. Pogue; MORISON, *The Rising Sun;* MORTON; *Doolittle's Tokyo Raiders*, by Carroll V. Glines; and *MacArthur and the War Against Japan*, by Frazier Hunt.

Stories filed by Japanese reporters praising Colonel Takechi for his crossing of Mount Natib were approved by General Nara. He never revealed the facts—not until 1960, and then, he told me, "only because I went to Amherst and you went to Williams."

11   "To Show Them Mercy Is to Prolong the War"

Interviews with Generals Albert M. Jones, Clifford Bluemel, Takeo Imai, Akira Nara and Carlos Romulo; Colonels Susumu Nishirua, Takushiro Hattori, Kumao Imoto and Nobuhiko Jimbo; Antonio Aquino; Roy Castleberry and numerous survivors of the Bataan Death March; correspondence with Captain John Bulkeley and Mark Wohlfeld; "A Strange Order Received at the Bataan Battle Front," an unpublished article by Lieutenant General Takeo Imai; "Dawn of the Philippines," privately printed pamphlet by Nobuhiko Jimbo; "Bataan Death March," doctoral thesis of Stanley Lawrence Falk; the Homma Diary (unpublished); documents for the defense at General Homma's trial; MORTON; *I Saw the Fall of the Philippines*, by Carlos Romulo; *MacArthur: His*

Rendezvous with History, by Courtney Whitney; *They Were Expendable,* by W. L. White; *The Dyess Story,* by William Dyess; and *General Wainwright's Story,* by Jonathan M. Wainwright.

12 "But Not in Shame"

Interviews with General Takaji Wachi; Colonels Jesse T. Traywick, Jr., Nobuhiko Jimbo, Susumu Nishiura and Takushiro Hattori; Admiral Sadatoshi Tomioka; Captains Yasuji Watanabe and Kazunari Miyo; Lieutenant Hisamichi Kano; John H. Skeen, Jr.; Gen Nishino and Heijiro Omi; THE HOMMA DIARY; the Homma documents; "Corregidor—A Name, A Symbol, A Tradition," by Colonel William C. Braly, in the *Coast Artillery Journal* (July-August 1947); POGUE; *Corregidor: Isle of Delusion,* by Kazumaro Uno; *Corregidor: The Saga of a Fortress,* by James H. and William M. Belote; WAINWRIGHT; and HUNT.

In *But Not in Shame* I concluded that the atrocities committed on the Death March had not been "purposefully planned and executed." Colonel Ray O'Day, one of the survivors of the march, took issue with me after publication of the book and put me in touch with Colonel Nobuhiko Jimbo. With new information from Colonel Jimbo and Gen Nishino I approached commanders on Bataan such as General Imai and received corroboration of Colonel O'Day's charges.

13 The Tide Turns

Interviews with Admirals Ryunosuke Kusaka, Frank Jack Fletcher, Chester Nimitz, Raymond Spruance, Keizo Komura, Sadatoshi Tomioka; Captains Ko Nagasawa, Kazunari Miyo, Yasuji Watanabe; Commanders Yahachi Tanabe, Heijiro Abe and Yoshio Shiga; Lieutenant Wilmer Earl Gallaher; Ensign Kazuo Sakamaki; General Minoru Genda; Colonels Susumu Nishiura and Takushiro Hattori; Mitsuharu Noda and Heijiro Omi; USSBS Navy interrogations #39 (Captain H. Ohara), #4 (Captain Taijiro Aoki) and #1 (Captain Takahisa Amagai); "I Sank the *Yorktown* at Midway," by Yahachi Tanabe, with Joseph D. Harrington, in USNIP (May 1963); "Never a Battle Like Midway," by J. Bryan III in the *Saturday Evening Post* (March 26, 1949); "Torpedo

Squadron 8," in *Life* (August 31, 1942); *Incredible Victory,* by Walter Lord; *Admiral Raymond A. Spruance, USN: A Study in Command,* by Vice Admiral E. P. Forrestal; *Climax at Midway,* by Thaddeus Taleja; *Midway—The Battle That Doomed Japan,* by Mitsuo Fuchida and Masatake Okumiya; ITO; *Combat Command,* by Admiral Frederick C. Sherman; *Queen of the Flat-Tops,* by Stanley Johnston; MORISON, Vol. IV, *Coral Sea, Midway and Submarine Actions;* and *The Code-Breakers,* by David Kahn.

In my version of the Battle of Midway in *But Not in Shame,* Gallaher and McClusky attack *Akagi,* while Best attacks *Soryu* and Leslie goes after *Kaga.* This account was based on interviews and after-action reports, but since then Walter Lord, while researching *Incredible Victory,* became convinced that the American fliers, who had only fragmentary information about the Japanese carriers, were mistaken. Mr. Lord's conclusions, I believe, are correct. Incidentally, Mr. Lord and I interviewed several naval men in Japan simultaneously in 1966 and later exchanged notes.

14 Operation Shoestring

Interviews with Admirals Gunichi Mikawa and Sadatoshi Tomioka; Commander Haruki Itoh; General Haruo Konuma; Colonel Kumao Imoto; Haruyoshi Saima; Brian Hackman; J. C. Glover; and Gen Nishino; "A Brief History of Geological and Geophysical Investigations in the British Solomon Islands 1881–1961," a report by J. C. Glover; *Guadalcanal Diary,* by Richard Tregaskis; *The Coast Watchers,* by Eric A. Feldt; SAKAI; and POGUE.

The following books were used throughout Chapters 14 to 17: *Isle of Death: Guadalcanal,* by Gen Nishino; *The Guadalcanal Campaign,* by Major John L. Zimmerman, USMCR; *Pearl Harbor to Guadalcanal,* by Lieutenant Colonel Frank O. Hough, USMCR, Major Verle E. Ludwig, USMC, and Henry I. Shaw, Jr.; *The Great Sea War,* edited by E. B. Potter and Fleet Admiral Chester W. Nimitz; *Semper Fidelis,* by Marine Corps combat correspondents (hereafter referred to as SEMPER FIDELIS); *1942: The Year That Doomed the Axis,* by Henry H. Adams; MORISON, Vol. V, *The Struggle for Guadalcanal; Guadalcanal: The First Offensive,* by John Miller, Jr.; *Savo,* by Richard F. Newcomb;

The Big E, by Edward P. Stafford; *Once a Marine: The Memoirs
of General A. A. Vandegrift, U.S.M.C.,* as told to Robert B.
Asprey; *Challenge for the Pacific,* by Robert Leckie; *The Army
Air Forces in World War II,* Vol. IV, *The Pacific: Guadalcanal
to Saipan,* edited by Wesley F. Craven and James L. Cate; ITO;
The United States Navy in World War II and *The United States
Marine Corps in World War II,* compiled and edited by S. E. Smith.

15 Green Hell

See Notes for Chapter 14. Additional sources were interviews
with General Haruo Konuma and Gen Nishino; "Guadalcanal,"
by Koji Mori, in the *Mainichi* (August 5, 1967); *Guadalcanal,*
by Masanobu Tsuji.

According to Brian Hackman, who recently mapped Guadalcanal for the British Solomon Islands Protectorate, two rivers near
Henderson Field are spelled incorrectly by U. S. Army and Marine
historians: "Matanikau" and "Lunga" should be Mataniko and
Lungga.

The Japanese operation to retake Guadalcanal was called KA.
Some Western historians have assumed this stood for "Guadalcanal," in the mistaken belief that it was the first syllable of the
Japanese for "Guadalcanal." *Ka* is merely a letter in the Japanese
alphabet.

16 "I Deserve Ten Thousand Deaths"

See Notes for Chapter 14. Also, interviews with Gen Nishino;
Generals Haruo Konuma and Hitoshi Imamura; Admirals Keizo
Komura, Ryunosuke Kusaka, Jinichi Kusaka, Sadatoshi Tomioka
and Tomiji Koyanagi; Captains Ko Nagasawa, Toshikazu Ohmae
and Masahide Yamamoto; and Commander Yoshio Shiga; USSBS
Navy interrogation #16 (Commander Masatake Okumiya); "Ja-
pan's Losing Struggle for Guadalcanal," by Vice Admiral Raizo
Tanaka, with the assistance of Roger Pineau, in USNIP (August
1956); TSUJI, *Guadalcanal; The Cactus Air Force,* by Thomas
G. Miller, Jr.; *Admiral Halsey's Story,* by Fleet Admiral William
F. Halsey and J. Bryan III; *Marine! The Life of Lieutenant General Lewis B. (Chesty) Puller,* by Burke Davis.

17 The End

See Notes for Chapter 14. Also, interviews with Gen Nishino; Generals Kenryo Sato, Hitoshi Imamura, Chikuro Yamamoto, Haruo Konuma and Teiichi Suzuki; Colonels Kumao Imoto, Mitsuo Suginoo and Susumu Nishiura; Major Einosuke Iemura; and Captain Masahide Yamamoto; Admirals Tomiji Koyanagi and Sadatoshi Tomioka; Captain Yasuji Watanabe; Commander Haruki Itoh; and Tadashi Suzuki; USSBS Navy interrogation #33 (Lieutenant Commander Horishi Tokuno); "Miraculous Total Evacuation of Japanese Troops from Guadalcanal," unpublished article by Haruki Itoh; "The Retreat from Guadalcanal," a memorandum by Rear Admiral Tomiji Koyanagi; IMTFE documents #62081 and #55452 (Colonel Joichiro Sanada); TSUJI, *Guadalcanal; General Kenney Reports,* by George C. Kenney; and *Our Jungle Road to Tokyo,* by Robert L. Eichelberger.

To avoid standing trial as a war criminal, Colonel Tsuji went underground in Thailand, immediately after the surrender, disguised as a Buddhist priest. He made his way secretly to Japan and hid for thirty months with friends such as Yoshio Kodama. He surfaced when the tribunals ended, and in September 1952 was elected to the Diet from the first district in Ishikawa Prefecture. He was re-elected in 1956 but resigned three years later to run for the House of Councilors, to which he was elected. As he was taking his seat General Kawaguchi shouted at him, "Tsuji-*san,* you are not qualified to represent the people. Have shame!" Kawaguchi had been feuding with Tsuji ever since his emergence. "I can't bear to see a man of such complete immorality writing best sellers, riding high and becoming *nouveau riche*," he told Gen Nishino. "My patience is running out." The two antagonists finally had a face-to-face debate before a capacity audience at Town Hall in Kanazawa. Kawaguchi not only accused Tsuji of lying about the Guadalcanal campaign but charged him with atrocities against prisoners in Singapore and the Philippines. Tsuji denied the accusations but admitted he had erred in calling Kawaguchi a coward for leaving his troops on Guadalcanal; he had not known the facts when he made the charge.

In 1961 the Japanese government sent Tsuji to Southeast Asia to investigate the political and military situation. He arrived in Bangkok on April 4 and continued on to Laos where he vanished. Several months later it was reported that Tsuji had entered Red China, and in December the Japanese Red Cross requested the Red Chinese Red Cross to locate him. He never was found and his mysterious disappearance has resulted in numerous sensational rumors: he was working for the Communists; he was working against the Communists; he was in the Middle East; he was in Japan incognito. Mrs. Chitose Tsuji believes her husband is dead, but Shigeharu Asaeda—who had accompanied him on numerous postwar trips to interview Nasser, Mao, Chou En-lai, and other Asian and Middle East leaders—reports there is a slight possibility that he is in a Red Chinese prison.

18 Of Mice and Men

Interviews with Generals Hitoshi Imamura, Hideo Iwakuro and Kenryo Sato; Admirals Jinichi Kusaka and Ryunosuke Kusaka; Captains Atsushi Oi and Yasuji Watanabe; Hachiro Takahasi; Major Yoshitaka Horie; and Yoshio Kodama; "Fragments from F.D.R.," by Edgar Snow, in *Monthly Review* (March 1957); "The Social Perception of Skin Color in Japan," by Hiroshi Wagatsuma, in *Daedalus* (Spring 1967); letter from Pearl Buck to Mrs. Roosevelt, December 12, 1941 (in the Franklin D. Roosevelt Library); "The Race Barrier That Must Be Destroyed," by Pearl Buck, in the *New York Times Magazine* (May 31, 1942); Elmer Davis letter (Franklin D. Roosevelt Library); "I Shot Down Yamamoto," by Colonel Thomas Lanphier, Jr., in *Reader's Digest* (January 1967); "Why Japan's Anti-Submarine Warfare Failed," by Captain Atsushi Oi, in USNIP (June 1952); *Guarding the United States and Its Outposts,* by Stetson Conn, Rose C. Engelman and Byron Fairchild; *Strategy and Command: The First Two Years,* by Louis Morton; *Strategic Planning for Coalition Warfare: 1943–1944,* by Maurice Matloff; *America's Concentration Camps,* by Allan R. Bosworth; *A History of the Minami Organization,* by Hachiro Takahashi; *Memoirs of an Interpreter,* by A. H. Birse; *I Was There,* by Fleet Admiral William D. Leahy; KENNEY; DAVIS, *Get Yamamoto; Fleet Admiral King,* by Ernest J. King and Walter Muir Whitehill; *The Thousand-Mile War: World War II in*

Alaska and the Aleutians, by Brian W. Garfield; MORISON, Vol. VII, *Aleutians, Gilberts and Marshalls; Seizure of the Gilberts and Marshalls,* by Philip A. Crowl and Edmund G. Love; MORISON, Vol. VIII, *New Guinea and the Marianas; Global Mission,* by H. H. Arnold; HALSEY & BRYAN; KODAMA; *Southeast Asia, Past and Present,* by Nicholas Tarling; *Breakthrough in Burma,* by Ba Maw; EDEN; LORD MORAN; *The Memoirs of General Lord Ismay; Triumph in the West,* by Arthur Bryant; CHURCHILL, HINGE OF FATE, and Vol. V, *Closing the Ring.*

19 To the Marianas

Saipan: interviews with Shizuko (Miura) Sugano, Mitsuharu Noda, Mariano Sablan, Manuel Sablan, Joe Sakisat, John Rich, Vicente Guerrero, Tony Benavente, Jose Pangelinan and Colonel Takashi Hirakushi; *The End at Saipan,* by Shizuko (Miura) Sugano; *Campaign in the Marianas,* by Philip A. Crowl; SMITH, *U. S. Marine Corps;* SEMPER FIDELIS; MORISON, *New Guinea and the Marianas;* and *Saipan: The Beginning of the End,* by Major Carl W. Hoffmann, USMC.

The Koga case: interviews with Jim Cushing, Admiral Shigeru Fukudome, Colonel Fabian Sanchez, Major Jesus Ybanez, Captain Manuel Segura and Mrs. Yuji Yamamoto; "The Capture of Admiral Koga," a newspaper article by Gregorio M. Mercado; *Allied Intelligence Bureau,* by Colonel Allison Ind.

Miscellaneous: interviews with Generals Kenryo Sato and Eugen Ott; Admirals Jinichi Kusaka, Ryunosuke Kusaka and Sokichi Takagi; Major Yoshitaka Horie; Captain Tsunezo Wachi; Marquis Kido; Yoshio Kodama; and Hideo Edo; "The Failure of the Japanese Convoy Escort," by Yoshitaka Horie, in USNIP (October 1956); article by George Sansom in *International Affairs* (October 1948); MATLOFF; FORRESTAL; *Tarawa,* by Robert Sherrod; CROWL & LOVE; *History of Naval Battles in the Pacific,* by Admiral Sokichi Takagi; *Undersea Victory,* by W. J. Holmes; *Japan's Economy in War and Reconstruction,* by Jerome B. Cohen; and *The Diary of Fumimaro Konoye.* The last book is a secret diary kept by Prince Konoye from June 21, 1944, through July 24, 1944, while under surveillance by the *kempeitai.* He dictated the entries to his secretary, Fukumatsu Ueno, who kept the document (a thick university notebook) with him at all times because of its explosive contents—at the time, Prince Konoye was plotting to overthrow Tojo and end the war. While escaping from a fire bombing in Tokyo in April 1945, Ueno lost the diary and it was presumed to have burned. According to Konoye's mistress, the prince (who had once said that all diaries were useless) wept when he learned of the loss.

In October 1967 the notebook was found among the effects of a man who had just died; there was no connection between him and Ueno or Prince Konoye. The handwriting was authenticated as Ueno's, and the diary was returned to the Konoye family; it is now at the Yomei Library in Kyoto. In 1968 the diary was published in Tokyo by Kyoto Press.

As the war progressed, Tojo became increasingly convinced that the independence of the Supreme Command was contributing to Japan's military reverses. After the war he told interrogators, "I am not saying that the independence of the Supreme Command is a bad thing. There are some good points about it too; for example, being able to conduct operations without political interference. It was a good thing in 1890, when the Constitution was established for the High Command to be untrammeled, but these days, when the influence of a single action is felt around the world, a certain amount of control by the political authority is necessary. However, under the Japanese system it was impossible."

20 "Seven Lives to Repay Our Country!"

Battle of the Philippine Sea: interviews with Admirals Sueo Obayashi and Ryunosuke Kusaka; Captains Toshikazu Ohmae and Shigeo Hirayama; and Mitsukuni Oshita; USSBS Navy interrogations #9 (Vice Admiral Takeo Kurita) and #3 (Vice Admiral Jisaburo Ozawa); "The Shokakus," by Hajime Fukaya, in USNIP (June 1952); *The Magnificent Mitscher,* by Theodore Taylor; FORRESTAL; *Battles of the Philippine Sea,* by Charles A. Lockwood and Hans Christian Adamson; GARFIELD; KING & WHITEHILL; MORISON, *New Guinea and the Marianas;* and POTTER & NIMITZ.

Saipan: interviews with Shizuko (Miura) Sugano, Ryoko Okuyama, John Rich, Mitsuharu Noda and Colonel Takashi Hirakushi; "A Lone Survivor at Saipan—Isle of Death," by Ryoko Okuyama, in *Fujin Koron* (December 1966), and *Left Alive on Saipan, the Island of Suicide,* by the same author; SUGANO; CROWL; SEMPER FIDELIS; SMITH, *U. S. Marine Corps;* CRAVEN & CATE; HOFFMANN.

Miscellaneous: interview with Marquis Kido; THE KONOYE DIARY; and *Information Never Reached the Emperor,* by Morisada Hosokawa.

21 "Let No Heart Be Faint"

Leyte: interviews with President Sergio Osmeña; Generals Carlos Romulo and Yoshiharu Tomochika; Admiral Ryunosuke Kusaka; Lieutenant Colonel Shigeharu Asaeda; Eduardo Montilla, Bob Price, Joe Price, Cesario Sipaco, Valeriano Abello, Vicente Quintero, and the following members of the 16th Division: Waichi Ito, Shinjiro Terasaki, Sadahiro Yamada, Kiichiro Yamada, Kazuyuki Okumura, Hideichi Nakamura, Noboru Furukawa, Dr. Yoichi Misaki, Kunio Nishimura and Hiroshi Morishima; "The True Facts of the Leyte Operation," a monograph by Major General Yoshiharu Tomochika; "Souvenir Program on the 13th Anniversary Celebration Leyte Landing of the American Forces of Liberation," compiled by the Tacloban Lions Club; "Lovely Americans," by Robert Shaplen, in *The New Yorker* (November 28, 1944); "35th Army Operations, 1944–1945" (official report); *Command Decisions,* prepared by Office of the Chief of Military History; TAYLOR; MATLOFF; HALSEY & BRYAN; KING & WHITEHILL; *End of the Ogasawara Army Corps,* compiled by Yoshitaka Horie, and others; *The Approach to the Philippines,* by Robert Ross Smith; *Leyte: The Return to the Philippines,* by M. Hamlin Cannon; *Decision at Leyte,* by Stanley L. Falk; *Reminiscences,* by General Douglas MacArthur; and *MacArthur's Amphibious Navy,* by Daniel E. Barbey.

Miscellaneous: interviews with Prince Mikasa, Prime Minister Shigeru Yoshida, Marquis Kido, General Kenryo Sato, Admirals Naokumi Nomura and Sokichi Takagi, Colonel Sei Matsutani, Morisada Hosokawa, and Mrs. Hideki Tojo; "Strategic Aspects of the Battle off Formosa," by Vice Admiral Shigeru Fukudome, in USNIP (December 1952); IMTFE documents #58228 and #53405

(Admiral Keisuke Okada); *Memoir of the Termination of the War,* by Sokichi Takagi; *The History of the Great Rightists,* by Bokusui Arakara; HOSOKAWA; THE KONOYE DIARY; *Diaries in Darkness* (diaries of civilians), compiled by Kiyoshi Kayosawa, and others; and COHEN.

22   The Battle of Leyte Gulf

Interviews with Admirals Tomiji Koyanagi, Kiyohide Shima, Keizo Komura and Ryunosuke Kusaka; Captains Toshikazu Ohmae and Tatsumaru Sugiyama; Shigeo Hirayama, Kenkichi Kato and Sadae Ikeda; Commander Shigeru Nishino; Lieutenants Heiya Yamamoto, Wahei Asami and Masanao Naito; Ensign Fukujiro Shimoyama; Kiyoshi Takahashi, Shiro Hosoya, Taro Sato and Hisao Tomokane; "The Japs Had Us on the Ropes," by Rear Admiral C. A. F. Sprague and Lieutenant Philip H. Gustafson, in *American* magazine (April 1945); "With Kurita in the Battle for Leyte Gulf," by Rear Admiral Tomiji Koyanagi, in USNIP (February 1953); "Battle Stations Submerged," by Lieutenant Commander R. C. Benitez, *loc. cit.;* USSBS Navy interrogations #69 (Rear Admiral Chiaki Matsuda), #58 (Commander Kokichi Mori), #55 (Vice Admiral Jisaburo Ozawa), #41 (Commander Tonosuke Otani), #35 (Rear Admiral Tomiji Koyanagi) and #9 (Vice Admiral Takeo Kurita); *The Kurita Fleet,* by Tomiji Koyanagi; MORISON, Vol. XII, *Leyte;* ITO; *The Divine Wind,* by Rikihei Inoguchi, Tadashi Nakajima and Roger Pineau; FALK, *Leyte;* LOCKWOOD & ADAMSON; TAYLOR; HALSEY & BRYAN; and *Battle Report: The End of an Empire,* by Walter Karig, and others.

23   The Battle of Breakneck Ridge

Interviews with Generals Tomochika and Miyauchi; Lieutenant Colonel Shigeharu Asaeda; Kiyoshi Kamiko, Yoshio Noguchi, Noboru Furukawa and Hiroshi Morishima; "Staff Studies of the Japanese 35th Army on Leyte," by Colonel Toshii Watanabe; "Operations of the 1st Japanese Division on Leyte," a report by Colonel Junkichi Okabayashi; TOMOCHIKA, "Leyte Operation"; *I Didn't Die on Leyte,* by Kiyoshi Kamiko; FALK, *Leyte;* and CANNON.

In August 1966 I accompanied a Japanese party (fifty survivors and relatives of soldiers who had died) to Leyte. The survivors collected the remains of comrades who had fallen, and the entire party conducted a number of Shinto memorial services at the battle sites. Kamiko and Noguchi re-enacted their battle experiences on Breakneck Ridge.

24 Debacle

Leyte: interviews with Generals Yoshiharu Tomochika and Yoshio Miyauchi; Captain Arashi Kamimura; Kiyoshi Kamiko, Yoshio Noguchi, Hiroshi Morishima, Noboru Furukawa, Eduardo R. Bugho (and other members of the 4th Leyte Warfare Guerilla Brigade), Ricardo P. Negru and Zoilo Andrade; two reports: "The Relief of Lieutenant General Shimpei Fukue of His Command of the 102nd Division" and "35th Army Operations, 1944–1945."

Prisoners of war: correspondence with Calvin Graef, Donald Meyer, Colonel James O. Gillespie, Colonel Curtis Beecher; Lieutenant Colonels Virgil O. McCollum and Adrianus J. van Oosten, and Major Roy L. Bodine, Jr.; "Notebook" of Colonel James O. Gillespie; "Five Came Back," by Gene Weeks, in *Hence* (July–August–September 1946); an address, "Medical Experience in Japanese Prison Camp," delivered by Major Samuel M. Bloom at Mount Sinai Hospital, New York, on May 15, 1945; *Jap POW Diary* (unpublished), by Major R. L. Bodine, Jr.; "Hell Ships," unpublished article by A. J. van Oosten; official report by Lieutenant Colonel O. O. Wilson; *Prisoner of War, World War II,* by Hugh H. Myers; and *My Experiences during the War with Japan* (privately printed), by Colonel V. N. Cordero.

25 "Our Golden Opportunity"

Burma: interviews with Generals Hideo Iwakuro and Tadashi Katakura; and Captain Hiromu Kumano and Sajibei Noguchi; "Retreat to the Chindwin," by General Iwaichi Fujiwara, in *History of the Second World War* magazine, Vol. 5, No. 10; *Defeat into Victory,* by General William J. Slim; BA MAW.

China: interviews with John Emmerson and Vice President Chen Cheng; "Propaganda Used against China by the China Expeditionary Army during ICHI-GO [Operation Ichi]," a report by Lieutenant Colonel Tadao Inoue; CHENNAULT; The Stilwell Papers; *Thunder out of China,* by Theodore H. White and Annalee Jacoby; *Outline of the Course of Eight Years of Resistance* (unpublished), by Chen Cheng; *Stilwell's Mission to China, Stilwell's Command Problems* and *Time Runs Out in CBI,* by Charles F. Romanus and Riley Sunderland; *The China Tangle,* by Herbert Feis; *China and the Helping Hand 1937–1945,* by Arthur N. Young; FITZGERALD; VAN SLYKE; HSU KAI-YU; and CHIANG KAI-SHEK.

Prisoners of war: see Notes for Chapter 24.

Yalta: interviews with Ambassador W. Averell Harriman and Charles Bohlen; SNOW, "Fragments from F.D.R."; *The Last 100 Days,* by John Toland; FRUS, *The Conferences at Malta and Yalta 1945;* KING & WHITEHILL; EDEN; *The Meaning of Yalta,* by John N. Snell, and others; LEAHY; and BIRSE.

Miscellaneous: interviews with General Yoshiharu Tomochika, and with Shizuo Fukui; correspondence with Captain John F. Enright; "Statement on the Philippine Operations in 1944–1945," by General Tomoyuki Yamashita at his trial; *"Shinano:* The Jinx Carrier," by Lynn Lucius Moore, in USNIP (February 1953); THE KONOYE DIARY; HOSOKAWA; *Mission with LeMay,* by General Curtis E. LeMay, with MacKinlay Kantor; *Triumph in the Philippines,* by Robert Ross Smith; and *Submarine,* by Edward L. Beach.

26   "Like Hell with the Fire Out"

Interviews with Major Yoshitaka Horie, Captain Tsunezo Wachi, Dr. Masaru Inaoka, John Rich, Toshihiko Ohno, Satoru Omagari, Kiyomi Hirakawa and Yoshimi Fujiwara; a series of interviews conducted by Major Horie for this book in 1970; "Translation of Diary Found on Dead Japanese Officer on Iwo Jima" by a patrol from C Company, 147th Infantry, March 27, 1945; "A Japanese Remembers Iwo Jima," by Toshihiko Ohno, in the *New York Times Magazine* (February 14, 1965); "Iwo Jima," by Yasuo Kato in *Jiji Shimpo* (February 18, 1952); "Prisoners of War," article by Yoshitaka Horie; *Fighting Spirit— Iwo Jima* (unpublished), by Yoshitaka Horie; HORIE, *End of the Ogasawara;* SEMPER FIDELIS; *Iwo Jima: Amphibious Epic,* by

Lieutenant Colonel Whitman S. Bartley; *Iwo Jima,* by Richard F. Newcomb; *The Hero of Iwo Jima,* by William Bradford Huie; MORISON, Vol. XV, *Victory in the Pacific;* VANDEGRIFT (with ASPREY); *Thirty Years,* by John P. Marquand; and *The Assault,* by Allen R. Matthews.

The letter Rear Admiral Toshinosuke Ichimaru addressed to President Roosevelt was found by a Marine in a cave in the northern part of the island. It is now in the museum of the U. S. Naval Academy in Annapolis. It is reprinted here in full:

> Rear Admiral T. Ichimaru of the Japanese Navy sends this note to Roosevelt. I have one word to give you upon the termination of this battle.
>
> Approximately a century has elapsed since Nippon, after Commodore Perry's entry to Shimoda, became widely affiliated with the countries of the world. During this period of intercourse, Nippon has met with many national crises, as well as the undesired Sino-Japanese War, Russo-Japanese War, the World War, the Manchurian Incident, and the China Incident. Nippon is now, unfortunately, in a state of open conflict with your country. Judging Nippon from just this side of the screen, you may slander our nation as a yellow peril, or a blood-thirsty nation, or maybe a protoplasm of military clique.
>
> Though you may use the surprise attack on Pearl Harbor as your primary material for propaganda, I believe you, of all persons, know best that you left Nippon no other method in order to save herself from self-destruction.
>
> His Imperial Highness, as clearly shown in the "Rescript of the Founder of the Empire" "Yosei" (Justice), "Choki" (Sagacity) and "Sekkei" (Benevolence), contained in the above three-fold doctrine, rules in the realization of "Hakko-ichiu" (the universe under His Sacred Rule) in His Gracious mind.
>
> The realization of which means the habitation of their respective fatherlands under their own customs and traditions, thus insuring the everlasting peace of the world.
>
> Emperor Meiji's "The four seas of the world that are united in brotherhood will know no high waves nor wind" (composed during the Russo-Japanese War), won the appraisal of your uncle, Theodore Roosevelt, as you yourself know.
>
> We, the Nippon-jin, though may follow all lines of trade, it is through our each walk of life that we support the Imperial doc-

trine. We, the soldiers of the Imperial Fighting Force take up arms to further the above stated "doctrine."

Though we, at the time, are externally taken by your air raids and shelling, backed by your material superiority, spiritually we are burning with delight and enjoying the peace of mind.

This peacefulness of mind, the common universal stigma of the Nippon-jin burning with fervour in the upholding of the Imperial Doctrine may be impossible for you and Churchill to understand. I hereupon pitying your spiritual feebleness pen a word or two.

Judging from your actions, white races, especially you Anglo-Saxons at the sacrifice of the coloured races, are monopolizing the fruits of the world.

In order to attain this end, countless machinations were used to cajole the yellow races, and to finally deprive them of any strength. Nippon in retaliation to your imperialism tried to free the oriental nations from your punitive bonds, only to be faced by your dogged opposition. You now consider your once friendly Nippon a harmful existence to your luscious plan, a bunch of barbarians that must be exterminated. The completion of this Greater East Asia War will bring about the birth of the East Asia Co-Prosperity Area, this in turn will in the near future result in the everlasting peace of the world, if of course, it is not hampered upon by your unending imperialism.

Why is it that you, an already flourishing nation, nip in bud the movement for the freedom of the suppressed nations of the East. It is no other than to return to the East that which belongs to the East.

It is beyond our contemplation when we try to understand your stinted narrowness. The existence of the East Asia Co-Prosperity sphere does not in anyway encroach upon your safety as a nation; on the contrary, will act as a pillar of world peace insuring the happiness of the world. His Imperial Majesty's true aim is no other than the attainment of this everlasting peace.

Studying the condition of the never ending racial struggle resulting from mutual misunderstanding of the European countries, it is not difficult to feel the need of the everlasting universal peace.

Present Hitler's crusade of "His Fatherland" is brought about by no other than the stupidity of holding only Germany, the loser of the World War, solely responsible for the 1914–1918 calamity and the deprivation of German's re-establishment.

It is beyond my imagination of how you can slander Hitler's

program and at the same time cooperate with Stalin's "Soviet Russia" which has as its principal aim the "socialization" of the world at large.

If only the brute force decides the ruler of the world, fighting will everlastingly be repeated, and never will the world know peace nor happiness.

Upon the attainment of your barbaric world monopoly, never forget to retain in your mind the failure of your predecessor President Wilson at his heights.

27   The Flowers of Edo

Interviews with Rikuro Iwata, Emi Sekimura, Yoshie Sekimura, Tosaku Hayashiya, Yuichiro Kominami and Susumu Takahashi; USSBS Navy interrogation #28 (Major Hiroshi Toga); KIYOSAWA; *The Diary of Jun Takami; The Broader Way,* by Sumie Mishima; LeMay (with KANTOR); *A Torch to the Enemy,* by Martin Caidin; CRAVEN & CATE, Vol. V, *The Pacific: Matterhorn to Nagasaki;* SMITH, *Triumph;* PRINCE HIGASHIKUNI; HOSOKAWA; and BA MAW.

28   The Last Sortie

The last sortie: interviews with Admirals Keizo Komura and Ryunosuke Kusaka; Commander Tochigi Terauchi; and Lieutenant Akira Yunoki; "Okinawa Area Naval Operations," Japanese Monograph #83 (OCMH); USSBS Navy interrogation #32 (Commander T. Miyamoto); *Sea of Lamentation,* by Captain Jiro Nomura; FORRESTAL; ITO; and *Japanese Destroyer Captain,* by Captain Tameichi Hara.

Okinawa: interviews with Admiral Sadatoshi Tomioka; Colonels Tsuneo Ito, Tsuneo Shimura, and Koichi Ito; Warrant Officer Kaname Imai; Dr. Shigeko Chihara; Shuzen Hokama, Hisashi Matsumura, Shikichi Miyagi, Mrs. Fumiko Nozaki and Zenso Noborikawa; "Okinawa: A Key to the Western Pacific," by Hyman Kublin, in USNIP (December 1954); "Unexpected Meeting of Teacher and Pupil of Opposite Sides Saves 1,300 Villagers," in the *Okinawa Times* (June 22, 1963); *Okinawa: The Last Battle,* by Roy E. Appleman, James M. Burns, Russell A. Gugeler and John Stevens; MORISON, *Victory;* and *Okinawa: Victory in the*

Pacific, by Major Charles S. Nichols, Jr., USMC, and Henry I. Shaw, Jr.

Miscellaneous: interviews with Morisada Hosokawa, Marquis Kido, Hajime Suzuki, Hisatsune Sakomizu and General Yoshiharu Tomochika; letter from Mamoru Shigemitsu to Gordon W. Prange, February 5, 1950, concerning resignation of the Koiso Cabinet and the Miao Pin affair; IMTFE documents #55127 (Baron Kiichiro Hiranuma), #61636 (Yasumasa Matsudaira) and #55906 (Kuniaki Koiso); "Operation 'Flying Elephant,'" by Mitsutoshi Kondo in *This Is Japan* (1966 edition); *The Kaiten Weapon,* by Yutaka Yokota (with Joseph D. Harrington); HOSOKAWA; PRINCE HIGASHIKUNI; and TOGO.

29   The Iron Typhoon

Interviews with Colonels Tsuneo Shimura, Tsuneo Ito and Koichi Ito; Warrant Officer Kaname Imai; Nobuko Yamashiro, Toshio Shida, Jinsai Higa, Eikichi Yamazato, Seigo Kawasaki, Masahide Ota, Mieko Miyahira, Shikichi Miyagi, Sachiko Kuda, Hideko Yoshimura, Chosei Osato, Seizu Uema, Tokuzo Makiminato, Chomei Nabachi, Tsuyako Iju, Shinichi Nozaki, Shuzen Hokama, Miyoko Toguchi, Yoshiko Kitashiro, Noburo Kuriyama, Yasuharu Agarie, Shigeru Kinjo, Seizen Nakasone, Yasuo Kayo, Koichi Saijo and Yasunori Aoki; *The Operations of the 7th Infantry Division in Okinawa,* a unit history prepared by Historical Division, U. S. War Department Special Staff; NICHOLS & SHAW; APPLEMAN; INOGUCHI; and *Tragedy of Okinawa,* by Seizen Nakasone.

There is a question about the time of death of Generals Ushijima and Cho. The account in *Okinawa: The Last Battle,* the most authoritative book on the battle, is based on information from a prisoner who heard it from other prisoners. It claims that the suicides occurred at 4 A.M., June 22. Higa, who still lives in Okinawa, testified that he gave Ushijima a haircut four hours later. Higa learned of the suicides from Kuzono's orderly, *Jotohei* Kimura, who witnessed them. Higa returned to the command cave and saw the bodies "lying around like tuna fish." There is another story that Ushijima and Cho committed suicide on a ledge outside the cave. But the bodies were found by Americans inside the cave. See photograph in picture section.

30 The Stragglers

Interviews with Kiyoshi Kamiko, Masaru Inaoka, Toshihiko Ohno, Satoru Omagari and Stewart Griffin; KAMIKO; *The Emperor's Last Soldiers,* by Masashi Ito; and *The Stragglers,* by E. J. Kahn, Jr.

Colonel Nishi's body was never found. Some survivors believe he was wounded in a charge on Airfield No. 2, and after telling his aide to turn him toward the Imperial Palace, shot himself in the head; others claim he died on the north beach. The Baroness Nishi prefers to believe the latter; it would be insupportable to imagine his body "run over" by innumerable American bombers.

31 In Quest of Peace

Interviews with Admirals Sadatoshi Tomioka and Sokichi Takagi, Ambassador Naotake Sato, Gero von S. Gaevernitz, Allen Dulles, Paul Blum, Yoshiro Fujimura, Shintaro Ryu, General Makato Onodera, Kojiro Kitamura, Jiro Homma, Hajime Suzuki, Hisatsune Sakomizu, Marquis Kido and Prime Minister Shigeru Yoshida; "Unmaterialized Peace Movement in Sweden Now Exceedingly Regretted," unpublished article by General Makoto Onodera; "The Japanese Peace Effort in Sweden," unpublished article by General Onodera; "The Mysterious Dr. Hack," by Gero von S. Gaevernitz, in *Frankfurter Allgemeine Zeitung* (August 31, 1965); IMTFE documents #61477 (Suemasa Okamoto), #64118 (Yoshiro Fujimura), #54483 (Shigenori Togo), #61978 (Vice Admiral Zenshiro Hoshina), and #61338 (General Masao Yoshizumi); *The Per Jacobsson Mediation,* edited by Erin E. Jucker-Fleetwood; *Japanese-U.S.S.R. Diplomatic Negotiations,* compiled by Research Department, Japanese Foreign Ministry; *Journey to the Missouri,* by Toshikazu Kase; *The Yoshida Memoirs,* by Shigeru Yoshida; MORISON, *Victory;* LeMay (with KANTOR); and *Russia at War,* by Alexander Werth.

The following books were used in Chapters 31 through 36: *Japan's Decision to Surrender,* by Robert J. C. Butow; *Behind*

Japan's Surrender, by Lester Brooks; *The Fall of Japan,* by William Craig; HOSOKAWA; CRAVEN & CATE, *Matterhorn to Nagasaki;* SAKOMIZU; SUZUKI BIOGRAPHY; *Historical Records on the Surrender,* 2 vols., compiled by the Japanese Foreign Ministry; and *Notes on the Termination of the War,* by Kainan Shimomura.

According to the *History of the Great Patriotic War of the Soviet Union,* there had been peace-feelers before Hirota approached Malik. "First of all, two private persons approached the Russians on behalf of the Japanese Government—Mr. Mijakawa, the Japanese Consul General in Harbin, and Mr. Tanakamuru, a fishing magnate.

"On March 4 [1945], the same Tanakamuru called on Mr. J. Malik, the Soviet Ambassador in Tokyo, saying that neither Japan nor the United States could start speaking of peace. A 'divine outside force' was necessary to bring about a peace settlement, and the Soviet Union could play that role.

"After the formation of the Suzuki Government, these peace-feelers became even more explicit. Foreign Minister Togo asked Mr. Malik on April 20 to arrange for him a meeting with Mr. Molotov."

In 1953 Allen Dulles told Fujimura that if the Japanese had accepted the Fujimura-Dulles proposal, the "present tragedy in Korea" could have been avoided. "The history of the world," he said, "would have been different."

32 "That Was Not Any Decision That You Had to Worry About"

Interviews with President Harry S. Truman, Ambassador Charles Bohlen, Eugene Dooman, John J. McCloy, Prime Minister Clement Attlee, Allen Dulles, Ladislas Farago, Ambassador Naotake Sato, Marquis Kido, Hajime Suzuki and Saiji Hasegawa; "The Decision to Use the Atomic Bomb," by Henry L. Stimson, in *Harper's* (February 1947); correspondence with John J. McCloy, Major Robert Lewis and Colonel Thomas W. Ferebee; GREW, *Turbulent Era;* HEINRICHS; BIRSE; *The Strange Alliance,* by John R. Deane; TOLAND, *Last 100 Days; My Eighty Years Reminiscences,* by Naotake Sato; JUCKER-FLEETWOOD; *Year of Decisions,* by Harry S. Truman; *Speaking Frankly* and *All in One*

Lifetime, by James F. Byrnes; *The* [James] *Forrestal Diaries,*
edited by Walter Millis; LEAHY; OCMH, *Command Decisions: Japan
Subdued,* and *Between War and Peace,* by Herbert Feis; STIMSON
& BUNDY; THE STIMSON DIARY; *Burn after Reading,* by Ladislas
Farago; *The New World,* by Richard G. Hewlett and Oscar E.
Anderson, Jr.; *Atomic Diplomacy: Hiroshima and Potsdam,* by
Gar Alperovitz; *Day of Trinity,* by Lansing Lamont; *Atomic
Quest,* by Arthur Holly Compton; *Abandon Ship!,* by Richard F.
Newcomb; *Dawn over Zero,* by William L. Laurence; WERTH;
Experience of War, by Kenneth S. Davis; CHURCHILL, Vol. VI,
Triumph and Tragedy; LORD MORAN; *Twilight of Empire:
Memoirs of Prime Minister Clement Attlee,* as set down by Frances
Williams; *As It Happened,* by Clement R. Attlee; *Memoirs,* by
George F. Kennan; and GRAND STRATEGY, Vol. VI, by John Ehr-
man. IMTFE document #503 (Shigenori Togo) was used for
Chapters 32 to 36.

Late in July 1945 the Zacharias office in Washington proposed
a bold plan to send General Oshima, who had recently been captured in southern Germany, to Tokyo on a secret mission of peace.
The party—to be led by a hero of adventure movies, Douglas Fair-
banks, Jr.—would proceed to Japan by submarine. Forrestal and
Admiral King approved the mission but were overridden by others
close to Truman.

33 Hiroshima

Interviews with Kyoko Sato, Michiko Yamaoka, Hiroaki Daido,
Mrs. Fukiko Iura, Mayor Shinzo Hamai, Dr. Fumio Shigeto,
Sadako Tsutsumachi, Shiroku Tanabe, Tomie Fujii, Hisaji Dai,
Ryuji Hamai, Tadahiko Kitayama, Mrs. Matsuyo Hayashi, Ryo
Fukumaru, Yoshinori Ataka, Tokuo Ootowa, Chiyo Takamori,
Mrs. Yasuko Nukushina, Dr. Yoshimasa Matsuzaka, Shogo
Nagaoka, Kunio Ono, Gonichi Kimura, Captain Hideo Sematoo,
Mrs. Yoshiko Tomita, Father Hugo Lassalle (Makibi Enomiya),
Miyoko Matsubara, Shigeru Shimoyama, Tsuneo Mataba and Dr.
Bernard Waldman; correspondence with Major Robert Lewis and
Colonel Thomas W. Ferebee; "Dr. Teller Urges More A-
Explosive Use," by Roger Birdsell, in the South Bend *Tribune*
(February 7, 1967); "Story of the Atomic Bomb," unpublished

article by Dr. Ryokichi Sagane; "Delayed Effects Occurring within the First Decade after Exposure of Young Individuals to the Hiroshima Atomic Bomb" (Atomic Bomb Casualty Commission pamphlet), by Robert W. Miller, M.D.; "Determination of the Burst Point and Hypocenter of the Atomic Bomb in Hiroshima" (ABCC), by Edward T. Arakawa and Shogo Nagaoka; *Hiroshima,* by John Hersey; *Hiroshima Pilot,* by William Bradford Huie; TRUMAN; and THE STIMSON DIARY.

The following pamphlets and books were used for Chapters 33 and 34: "Residual Radiation in Hiroshima and Nagasaki" (ABCC), by Edward T. Arakawa; "Actual Facts of the A-Bomb Disaster" (ABCC), by Drs. Naomi Shohno, Yukio Fujimoto and Fukashi Nakamura; "Human Radiation Effects" (ABCC), by Drs. Kenneth G. Johnson and Antonio Cicco; "Geological Study of Damages Caused by Atomic Bombs in Hiroshima and Nagasaki" (ABCC), by T. Watanabe, S. Nagaoka, and others; *No High Ground,* by Fletcher Knebel and Charles W. Bailey II; *Friends of the Hibakusha,* edited by Virginia Naeve; LAURENCE; *Death in Life,* by Robert Jay Lifton; and FEIS, *Japan Subdued.*

34 . . . and Nagasaki

Interviews with Shogo Nagaoka, H. Yukimune, Professor Seiji Imabori, Dr. Tatsuichiro Akizuki, Etsuko Obata, Hachiro Kosasa, Dr. Ryokichi Sagane, Kaoru Naruse, Kamekichi Sugimoto, Hitoshi Tokai, Kazuko Tokai, Shigeyoshi Morimoto, Toshiyuki Hayama, Senji Yamaguchi, Hajime Iwanaga, Mayor Tsutomu Tagawa, Taeko Fukakori, Midori Nishida, Hajime Suzuki, Marquis Kido, Ambassador Naotake Sato, Hisatsune Sakomizu, Tomio Yamamoto, Saiji Hasegawa and Admiral Sadatoshi Tomioka; "Notes on the Nagasaki Atom Bomb," unpublished article by Yoshiko Araki; "Unforgettable Evacuation," unpublished article by Yoshiko Kato; "Record of Operations against Soviet Russia," Japanese Monograph #155 (OCMH); correspondence with Dr. Julien M. Goodman; and *Nagasaki, The Forgotten Bomb,* by Frank W. Chinnock, the only full-length account of the Nagasaki bombing.

Shogo Nagaoka, with nine children and little money, dedicated his life to the study of the atomic bombings. He was forced to sell most of the family possessions, including his wife's kimonos. It was he who set up the museum in Hiroshima's Park of Peace and was its first curator.

35 "To Bear the Unbearable"

Interviews with Professor Kiyoshi Hiraizumi; Prince Mikasa; Marquis Kido; Admiral Sadatoshi Tomioka; General Masahiko Takeshita; Colonels Saburo Hayashi, Masao Inaba and Okikatsu Arao; Fumihiko Togo; Hajime Suzuki; and Saiji Hasegawa; IMTFE documents #57670 (Admiral Soemu Toyoda), #60745 (Yasumasa Matsudaira), #61883 (General Yatsuji Nagai), #61636 (Yasumasa Matsudaira), #62049 ("The Unpublished Record on Termination of the War, Kept by the Japanese Navy General Staff"), #61481 (Shunichi Matsumoto), #61475 (Marquis Kido), #53437 (Admiral Zenshiro Hoshina), #59496 (Colonel Makoto Tsukamoto), #55127 (Kiichiro Hiranuma); "The Reason Why the Affair Happened," unpublished article by Colonel Masataka Ida; *The Takeshita Diary* (unpublished), by Masahiko Takeshita; KING & WHITEHILL; THE FORRESTAL DIARIES; BYRNES, *One Lifetime* and *Speaking Frankly;* TRUMAN; THE GREW DIARY; THE STIMSON DIARY; *Treatise on the Termination of the Pacific War,* compiled by the Japan Diplomatic Association; general editor, T. Ueda.

36 The Palace Revolt

Interviews with Marquis Kido; Professor Kiyoshi Hiraizumi; General Tatsuhiko Takashima; and Colonels Masahiko Takeshita, Saburo Hayashi, Masao Inaba, Okikatsu Arao and Masataka Ida; Hajime Suzuki; Morio Tateno; Daitaro Arakawa; and Chamberlains Yoshihiro Tokugawa and Yasuhide Toda; IMTFE documents #61978 (Admiral Zenshiro Hoshina), #56367 and #50025A (Masahiko Takeshita), #61338 (General Masao Yoshizumi); "Notes," a report by General Tatsuhiko Takashima; "Anami," an unpublished article by Colonel Masataka Ida; "Army Minister General Korechika Anami," a speech delivered at the Defense Training School on November 11, 1964, by General Masahiko Takeshita; *Hara-kiri,* by Jack Seward; documents from the NHK File on the Palace revolt; and KIRBY, *The War against Japan,* Vol. V.

37 The Voice of the Crane

Interviews with Generals Bonner Fellers, Yatsuji Nagai, Masahiko Takeshita and Ichiji Sugita; Admirals Horace V. Bird, Sadatoshi Tomioka and Ryunosuke Kusaka; Colonels Tsuneo Shimura and Masataka Ida; Baron Ian Mutsu; Ambassador Harumi Takeuchi; Roy Otake; Takeshi Ono; Robert Trumbull; Yoshio Kodama; Marquis Kido; IMTFE document #50025A (Masahiko Takeshita); IDA, "Anami"; "Welcome U. S. Army Signed U. S. Navy," by Hal Drake, in *Pacific Stars and Stripes;* "The End of World War II," unpublished article by Rear Admiral Horace V. Bird; an article on Tokyo Rose by Harry T. Brundige, in *American Mercury* (January 1954); "An Account of the Honorable Deaths of the Righteous Army for the Cause of Reverence for the Emperor and Expulsion of Foreigners: Twelve Patriots and Patriotesses of Atago Hill," article by Katsuichi Ohba; "Going down to Manila," article by Katsuo Okazaki; "The Emperor's Courier," unpublished article by Robert C. Mikesh; *Four Years in Hell,* by Tomomi Yamamoto; MACARTHUR; EICHELBERGER; *I Was an American Spy,* by Sidney Forrester Mashbir; WHITE & JACOBY; documents from the NHK File; PRINCE HIGASHIKUNI; INOGUCHI; TRUMAN; FEIS, *China Tangle;* VAN SLYKE; KASE; MORISON, *Victory;* and KATO.

Admiral Tomioka was so impressed by MacArthur's speech at the surrender ceremonies that his resolve to commit hara-kiri weakened. Moreover, one of his former teachers urged him to live so he could write an objective history of the war; no one else, he said, was as qualified. With the help of Admiral Yonai, Tomioka collected important documents—including the original rescripts of the Emperor—which had been ordered destroyed, and hid them. He wanted to preserve them as proof "that the millions who had died had done so for the Emperor; otherwise their souls would never be comforted." Since then he has devoted his life to the history of the Pacific war and is currently head of the Historical Research Institute in Tokyo. The Emperor's rescripts and many other high-echelon documents are still in his library.

Epilogue

Interviews with Michitaka Konoye, Marquis Kido, Mrs. Hideki Tojo and General Bonner Fellers; Tojo story by George E. Jones, in the *New York Times* (September 12, 1945); "Tragedy in Vietnam," by Frederick L. Schuman in *The Berkshire Review* (Spring 1968); BUTOW, *Tojo;* EICHELBERGER; YOUNG; *The Politics of War,* by Gabriel Kolko; and FEIS, *Contest.*

Index

About the Author

To research this book, JOHN TOLAND and his wife, who is Japanese, spent 15 months traveling through the Far East—Japan, Iwo Jima, Okinawa, Taiwan, the Philippines, Guam, Saipan, Singapore, Malaya and Thailand. Included among the almost five hundred people interviewed were the Emperor's chief adviser, the Privy Seal Marquis Koichi Kido, top military leaders, members of Tojo's Cabinet, hundreds of military personnel of every rank, as well as more than fifty survivors of Hiroshima and Nagasaki. He also interviewed numerous Americans, from President Truman and Admiral Nimitz to scores of prisoners of war.

JOHN TOLAND is the author of *Ships in the Sky; Battle: The Story of the Bulge; But Not in Shame;* and *The Last 100 Days.* He lives in Danbury, Connecticut.